HOLLAND

GW00363646

CRUISING THE CORAL COAST

7th EDITION
with 1998 Update Supplement

CRUISING THE CORAL COAST

7th EDITION
with 1998 Update Supplement

ALAN LUCAS

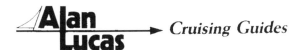

Published by

Alan Lucas Crusing Guides

in association with

Halbooks Publishing
30 Elouera Road
Avalon NSW
Australia 2107

Copyright © Alan Lucas 1994, 1996, 1998, 2000

National Library of Australia Card No.
and ISBN 0 646 27858 4

This edition first published 1994
Reprinted in limp covered edition 1996
Reprinted 1998 with Update Supplement
Reprinted 2000

This work is copyright. Apart from any use as permitted
under the Copyright Act 1968, no part may be reproduced
by any process without the permission of the publisher.

Printed in China by Everbest Printing Co. Ltd

4
00
5

Warning
*This book should be used in conjunction with the latest official charts. Despite a high degree
of confidence that information contained within is correct as of late 1998, neither the author
nor publisher can accept responsibility for omissions and inaccuracies.*

By the same author

Cruising the Coral Coast
Cruising Papua New Guinea
Cruising the Solomons
Cruising New Caledonia and Vanuatu
Red Sea and Indian Ocean Cruising Guide
Sydney to Central Coast Waterways Guide

Just Cruising
How to Build Small Boats
How to Sail
The Schooner

Complete Illustrated Encyclopaedia
The Tools and Materials of Boatbuilding
The Cruising Boat
Fitting Out Below Decks
Fitting Out Above Decks
Fitting Out Mechanically
Cruising Companion

Cruising in Tropical Waters and Coral
Barrier Reef Rendezvous
Cruising to Europe

Cruising Australians

Illustration, photography, design and assembly by the author.

1998 UPDATE SUPPLEMENT

This supplement updates the content of this book to early 1998.

Unless otherwise stated, reference throughout this supplement is directed towards a relevant chart, not the written description. If the written description differs from the statements made in this supplement, disregard the written description in favour of this more contemporary information.

For ease of use and for immediate reference, only page numbers are used in the supplement as the relevant chart is obvious when working through the book navigationally.

Page 39

Tidal flow at the entrance to the Gold Coast Seaway continues to flow for approximately one hour after turn. This over-run should be considered when entering during poor conditions, at which time a rising tide should be used.

Page 39–40

The sand bypass jetty and a complementary structure on the north side of the Gold Coast Seaway entrance carry yellow lights at night.

Page 41

The Main Beach Slipway has been closed and the Southport Marina (owned by the Southport Yacht Club) has been converted from fixed to floating berths.

Minor Nav aid changes have taken place but basic information remains the same when navigating the South Channel.

Page 43

Channels remain the same with only minor nav aid changes.

Page 45

Anchoring is no longer possible at Couran, on South Stradbroke Island, the canal development has been completed. It is known as Couran Cove Resort. Those wishing to visit should seek local information.

A lit South Cardinal beacon replaces the green beacon off the south tip of Never Fail Islands. Opposite, along the southeast bank of Tipplers Passage, a drying sand bank borders the channel.

Shoaling appears to have occurred at the northern end of Tipplers Passage with minor nav aids changed to suit. Deep keelers need a rising tide here. The shallowest part appears to be in the vicinity of the two green buoys shown on the chart on page 45.

Page 47

Nav aids have been changed and improved according to need throughout the entire area of this chart, although channels remain essentially the same. The activities of dredging and silting constantly change the dynamics of some channels, suggesting that local knowledge be gained before taking a deep draft vessel through the southern approaches to Main Channel.

Canaipa Passage had changed little as of Mid-1997, although silting has occurred in the two crossovers towards Cobby Cobby Island.

The sand-spit projecting north from Tulleen Island, at the bottom of the chart, is now indicated by a lit North Cardinal beacon.

Page 49

Channels remain similar to those shown, however silting has been reported in the short link channel near the word "Main" . Minor nav aid changes have occurred.

Page 51

Minor buoy and beacon changes have taken place, notably, the special buoy and red beacon east of Clarkes Point are now lit and the unlit green beacon on the southern edge of Pelican Bank has been removed.

The conspicuous sand blow on North Stradbroke Island, opposite Canaipa, has lost its dominance under a thin layer of grass.

Page 53

Raby Bay Marina is now up and running offering fuel and other services to the public. It is not shown on this chart, but is described on page 56 under the heading ' Cleveland Bay'. It is approximately in the centre of page 53 in the bay formed by Cleveland Point.

Page 57

Beware of shoaling in Manly Boat Harbour, some patches being less than a metre. Without local knowledge, move within the harbour during a rising tide, although approach and entry need not be so critical.

Fuel is available at Moreton Bay Trailer Boat Club's marina near its office on the fourth arm out from the land. As of 1997, it was no longer available at East Coast Marina.

The Port Office is manned for only a few hours per week, out-of-hours bookings for the pile berths require a phone call. Payment may be made at the MBTBC office.

Page 59

The upper reaches of the Brisbane River, and the Botanic Gardens berths in particular, are troubled by the wake of fastcat ferries which now run regular services along much of the river.

Page 60

The privately owned marina, Scarborough Marina, is up and running with all services available to the boating public.

Page 61

The green beacons off Bongaree are now lit.

Page 63

When rounding up for the entrance to Mooloolaba Harbour, be aware that breaking water can carry past the eastern breakwater across the channel. To avoid this, move west of the recommended approach and make a more easterly approach into the entrance.

Anchorage in the Mooloolah River is possible upstream from Minyama Island, although it tends to be crowded most of the time. Late arrivals, unable to book a marina berth, may drop anchor immediately west of the yacht club marina, but strictly as an overnight measure. This advice is not authorised. The use of this anchorage would be a favour, not a right.

The shoal south of The Wharf Marina is now marked by a special mark beacon.

Page 66

Dredging of the inner parts of Noosa Bar is planned for environmental reasons. The bar itself may or may not deepen as a result.

Page 70

As anticipated in the paragraph ' Future Note', the green buoy off Hook Point has long gone and the Inskip Point leads have been reinstated and are lit. Please note that the Wide Bay Bar is always best crossed on a rising tide.

When entering at night, beware the way in which the green beacon marking the entrance to Tin Can Inlet can stand proud and deceive the newcomer into believing it is a turning mark when steering towards the Inskip Point Leads.

Page 72

The outer red beacon in Teebar Creek has been replaced with a lit special mark.

Page 73

The north arm of the marina in Snapper Creek has been extended to the northwest, out of the harbour.

Referring to the Tin Can Inlet chart, at the bottom of page 73, please note that the overhead cable shown at 16 metres has been lowered to 10.6 metres.

Page 75

A number of readers have urged me to warn of sand flies in Garry's Anchorage. This is certainly justified but the same conditions are true of the entire area, certain parts being worse than others . Much depends on weather, time of day and personal susceptibility.

Page 76

Anchorage outside North Head can no longer be suggested owing to mooring congestion.

The sandbank off Separation Point is soft enough in many places to make it unsuitable for walking on and possibly dangerous for children.

Page 77

Buoy numbers along the Mary River have been reduced, with two instead of three green buoys off Buttenshaw Bank and most red buoys removed upstream of Lower Rock Point. Leslie Rocks are marked with a green buoy, and a red beacon adjacent to Crab Island has replaced the green buoy there. All are lit.

The marina at Maryborough now has a fully stocked chandlery and its moorings are of the swing, not fore-and-aft type. Barrie White's Welding Works, in the old Walker Engineering sheds, can sometimes offer alongside berths, as can the Mary River Slipway. These facilities are immediately upstream of the Marina.

Page 79

The red buoys in Devils Elbow have been removed.

Page 80

A West Cardinal beacon has been established just north of Urangan Harbour entrance and a long-running promise to keep the harbour dredged may become a reality during 1998. As of late 1997, the entrance had silted to 0.9 metres LWS.

The marina, now fully operational, did not follow its original plan (as shown on the chart). Some arms run towards the southeast.

Page 86

The shoals in Millaquin Reach have changed radically, forming a dogleg which is indicated by an extra red buoy. Deep keelers are best taken upstream on a rising tide at least three hours after turn.

Page 87

The outer channel beacons of the main entrance channel (off this chart to the east) are now red and green in conformity with all others. All lateral marks now have their lights synchronised.

A fishing boat marina and base has been established in a dredged area on the south bank of the Burnett River immediately north of the words 'Port Bundaberg'.

Page 90

Green beacons north of Monument Point in Round Hill Creek have been replaced with buoys and reduced in number and the red beacon off the caravan park has been removed.

Contrary to the promise of ' good-holding sand' under the heading, ' Anchorage' on page 91, patches can be poor. Dig your anchor in properly and test before leaving the vessel. Generally, depths upstream of the caravan park have reduced from those shown.

Page 92

The two red beacons north of the leads in Pancake Creek have been replaced by buoys.

Page 96

Fitzroy Reef lagoon entrance is marked by three port and two starboard unlit beacons.

Page 101

There are fishing boat berths and facilities along the western side of the Gladstone Boat Harbour with a slipway and dry storage yard where the word 'Fish' is noted. Gladstone Marina berths are identified by the letters E to L from east to west when booking in by radio.

There is a white light on Division Point at the northern end of The Narrows (see Gladstone to Pacific Creek section of chart).

Page 106

Egg and Mud Islands, at the entrance to the Fitzroy River, have broken up into four separate bodies and shoaling has taken place against the south bank of South Channel near the word 'South'.

Rocky Point, at the western end of South Channel , demanded early 1998, that the leads be opened south with the south bank hugged for the best depth. Be aware that this information can change. Gain local knowledge or use a rising tide at least three hours old.

Page 107

The narrow neck of Pirate Point, towards the centre bottom of the Fitzroy River chart has broken through, producing a deep water short-cut which eliminates Winding Reach. Depths in Winding Reach have decreased dramatically in places and the downstream marks noted on the chart as 'Sheer Board' and 'Humbug Mark' have been removed. When passing through the break, favour the east bank, although depths are generally good right across.

The Fitzroy Motor Boat Club allows dinghy landing on its pontoon for a reasonable weekly fee which includes access to club facilities. Do not tie off along the front of the pontoon.

Pages 110

The best approach into Yellow Patch (bottom chart on this page) is approximately as indicated (1997). Within the creek however, depths have changed dramatically. There is now a shallow sandbank filling the bay in which the number '5' is shown , with the best water down to less than two metres LWS towards the large, yellow sand dune. The best channel to this anchorage, once the outside shoals have been negotiated, is straight across from the number '2' off the inner headland towards the Yellow Patch dune.

Page 111

In the bay immediately north of the word 'Svendsen's' on the northern end of Great Keppel Island, there is a detached coral reef. In the bay to its northeast, under the lee of the northern tip, there is a permanently moored reef-viewing craft.

The soundings immediately south of Middle Island Pass, should be moved west, the shoal water off the western tip of Great Keppel Island extends further west than indicated on the chart. The red lit beacon in the middle Island pass has been reinstated and sits on the reef with the notation, 'Rock dries'.

Page 113

North Keppel Island's tourist resort is now occupied by the Environmental Education Centre and may be visited by appointment only. The national park walks are available to all.

Page 114

The Keppel Bay Marina, in Rosslyn Bay Harbour, is fully functional offering most services. The proposed berth plan, shown on page 114, was dumped in favour of arms extending from the southern shore of the harbour.

Page 117

The shoals (each shown as 2.7 metres LWS) between Round Island and Entrance Island readily break in heavy onshore weather. Likewise, the spit extending north from Inner Head can break towards its outer end. In such conditions it is advisable to enter on a flood tide.

Page 122

The drying mud bank along the southern shore of this anchorage in Island Head Creek is wider than shown and is more in the form of a secondary bank with a spit at its northeast tip.

Page 124

A drying rock is located west of Cape Townshend on the shoal marked 1.5 m. This has been marked on the chart printed in this(1998) reprint. It is not shown on previous printings of the 7th Edition. To determine which printing you have, check the imprint information on the back of the title page.

Page 127

To the west of Plum Tree, in the vicinity of the words 'White beach', there are isolated patches shallower than the 3 and 4 metres indicated. Never enter or navigate any part of Thirsty Sound without local knowledge or a rising tide.

Page 131

The lease of Middle Percy Island to long-term resident, Andrew Martin, has been extended another ten years as from early 1998. All the services noted in the description sub-headed 'West Bay' on page 133 will continue. All sailors are welcome.

Page 140

Work on the expansion of Mackay Outer Harbour was commenced early 1998. Its marina will probably be dedicated to recreational craft as suggested by the map on page 141.

Page 147

A marina resort has been suggested for Keswick Island. Details are unknown.

Page 157

The resort in Happy Bay on Long Island is now known as 'Club Crocodile'.

Page 158

Leading beacons now indicate the best approach into Shute Harbour from the northeast. Buoys have been added within the harbour to define mooring areas.

Page 169

A careening jetty within the dinghy harbour of the Whitsunday Sailing Club is available to non-members on application and payment of a fee. Water and power are available.

Dinghies should no longer be taken to the creek at Airlie. This creek may be developed in the future as a tourist boat terminal..

Land reclamation has taken place to the south of the Abel Point Marina and the future might see a breakwater constructed to protect moored craft outside the Marina.

A marina is planned for Muddy Bay where the word 'careen' is shown.

Page 172

On the large scale chart, AUS 253, of Gloucester Passage, it would appear that latitude and longitude are out by as much as four cables.

Page 173

A lit North Cardinal beacon has been established on North Rock off Cape Edgecumbe.

Page 175

The large, dredged basin, which is entered via Magazine Creek has had no expressions of interest for the development of a marina as of late 1997. Visitors may use fore and aft buoy moorings along the southeast bank of the harbour, these being managed by the local harbour authority.

The chandlery has closed and the public toilets and showers are opposite the old chandlery building.

Page 179

Anchorage in the southeast corner of Bowling Green Bay is effected by windward-tide, the stream running southeast during flood and northwest during ebb.

Page 185

A low, fixed bridge is planned for the entrance to the Ross River, which will effectively deny the river to all masted craft and many large commercial vessels. In the event, all facilities will be moved outside the river to a dredged basin adjacent to the words ' South Townsville'.

Meanwhile, the Townsville Port Authority office at the river is now manned for only a few hours per week. Visitors should phone ahead or go alongside the public pontoon and use a local phone. This pontoon is next to the police jetty, both of which are situated immediately south of the floating dock. This dock has been removed.

Sailors seeking a peaceful night at the Motor Boat Club Marina, in Ross Creek, might be a little disconcerted by the fact that a night club operates on the opposite bank, seven nights a week until the small hours of the morning.

In the Breakwater Marina harbour, a dedicated charter boat berthing area has been built on the harbour's north shore, out from the casino.

Page 191

The entrance to Dungeness has radically changed, the channel shown is now fully silted over. The green beacon was still standing in late 1997 as was the special mark, but they have become irrelevant. The two red beacons have gone. The best water in late 1997 was found close against the low headland, off which are found the words 'Dungeness Bank', with the approach approximately southwest. Use a tide of at least your draft plus nearly one metre.

A marina is planned in a basin to be dredged in the vicinity of the cleared mangroves.

A sunken trawler, immediately upstream of the words 'Enterprise Channel', is marked with a lit special mark.

Page 192

A palm Island supply barge operates from Lucinda from a concrete ramp close to the old jetty. This jetty is now derelict with no large ships navigating the Hinchinbrook Channel to Lucinda.

Page 195

The missing page number in the paragraph headed 'Lucinda' should read 192.

Page 199

The contentious development known as ' Port Hinchinbrook' at Oyster Point is under construction. It will have a marina and a 1500 bed resort.

Page 201

Non-guests are not welcome at Cape Richards Resort unless by special arrangement.

Page 205

During March 1998, my friend of over thirty years and one of the region's great character's, Bruce Arthur passed away at his home on Dunk Island. At the time of reporting, the future of his artists' gallery was uncertain, but it can be assumed that jeweller, Susan Kirk, will do her utmost to maintain the premises as a unique feature of Dunk Island and one of Australia's most remarkable artistic displays.

Page 209

The Kiosk and fuel outlet in Mourilyan Harbour has closed. Except for pile berths, there are no facilities here for the visiting sailor.

Page 215

Lit port and starboard buoys indicate the limits of the approach to the jetty of Fitzroy Island.

Page 220

The Marlin Marina was destroyed by cyclone Justin. As of late 1997 it remained in a state of disrepair. It is expected to be up and running again soon, after which dinghies may be accepted in its northwest corner. Check with management before leaving a dinghy there.

Page 221

The Cairns Cruising Yacht Club (CCYS) in Smiths Creek, has increased the number of its berths by adding a second finger pontoon complex downstream from the old. Behind this complex, visitors' dinghies may be secured subject to permission being granted by and payment made to, the squadron's office. If your dinghy does not carry a sticker proving payment, it may be impounded.

Page 225

As of late 1997, the western side of Double Island's reef was lined with fisheries experimental rafts. A small resort now operates on the Island.

Page 227

Dredging to a controlled depth of 2.5 metres LWS was carried out late 1997 in the entrance to Port Douglas. This aligned the channel with the leading beacons.

Closehaven Marina no longer welcomes casual visitors.

On the land close to Closehaven Marina, a clubhouse for the Port Douglas Yacht Club is functioning with bar and other facilities. If leaving the dinghy here, make sure it is clear of the club's small concrete ramp.

The slipway between the Duckpond and the Boat Club was derelict early 1998, but there were plans for its revival.

Swing moorings have pushed available anchorage space upstream of the word 'Moorings' at the bottom of the chart. The ground can be indifferent here, with patches of poor holding. Dig in with plenty of scope then shorten-up to limit your swing.

Page 228

As of early 1998, there was a proposal to deny private vessels the right to anchor within 200 metres of the moored tourist boat facilities in Low Islet Lagoon.

Page 229

The southern entrance to the Daintree River has now closed out, leaving the northern entrance as the only choice.

Page 232

It is likely that a small resort will be developed in Bailay Creek, accessible through the national Park.

Page 233

Swing moorings now occupy the prime anchoring area behind Cape Tribulation.

Page 235

The fairway buoy off the Bloomfield River is now a lit special mark.

Page 239

It has been proposed to limit to two, the number of craft anchored at Hope Island (east) at any given time. Check with the Great Barrier Reef Marine Park office in Cairns.

Page 241

The channel into Cooktown Harbour was dredged in 1997 to a control depth of 2.5 metres LWS and was defined by three red and three green lit beacons. Off the public jetty and a little to its north are two lit special mark buoys.

Water is now more freely available from a number of taps in local parks and from the slipway. The latter remains council owned but may be managed by the local Coast Guard, whose base is next to the slipway.

Please note that the word 'Reef' in naming the Endeavour River, should read 'River'.

Page 255

Please note that the word 'Howich' used to indicate the 'Howick Group' should read 'Howick'.

Page 261

The fuel barge has been removed from the Flinders Islands. Its service is now performed by a number of small cargo and trawler-fleet service vessels.

Page 270

According to cruising couple, Lloyd and Lyn Woods of Lota, Queensland, an alternative entrance into the Lockhart River exists in the channel between the mainland and the large mangrove island to its north. This is the unnamed island between the anchor symbols. Their survey shows up to 4 metres in the channel with a bar at its eastern end.

Page 271

A couple of visitors to the Claudie River have reported being stoned by children on the bank.

Page 273

The fuel barge has been removed from Portland Roads with its function being duplicated by passing coasters.

Ross Pope has retired from Portland Roads but his services are now carried out by his son, Geoff Pope. There is no flight booking agency.

It has been claimed that there is a rocky patch on the Pascoe River bar. Enter with caution.

Page 275

In Hunter Inlet there are patches of rock bottom, making anchoring insecure in places.

Page 283

If your copy of Cruising the Coral Coast, 7th edition, was printed during or before 1996 (see page facing 'Contents'), there is a rock in the Escape River which is not shown on the chart. According to a number of reports it lies on GPS co-ordinates 10º 58.70 south and 142º 40.00 east. This places it approximately half a mile due north of the words ' Red patch'. This position should be plotted on the chart, AUS839, then transferred to the chart in this book as the latter's latitude and longitude are misplaced. This correction has been made to the chart in this reprint of the book.

Page 306

In the historical box headed 'Louis Antoine de Bougainville', the word 'Frankland' in the fifth line should read Falkland.

CONTENTS

1998 Update Supplement   v
Introduction   2
About this book   2
Queensland at a Glance   2

General Information   4
Customs Ports   4
Dangers   4
National Parks   5
Marine Park Categories   5
Anchoring in Coral   6
Cyclone Protection   7
Floods   9
Tides   10
Seas   10
Swell   10
Radio 10
Nav Aids   10
Weather   14

Coral Coast Charts   17

The Coast   21 Sectional coast charts
Point Danger to Double Island Point   21
Double Island Point to Rodd Peninsula   22
Rodd Peninsula to Scawfell Island   24
Broad Sound to Cape Upstart   26
Cape Upstart to Cairns   28
Cairns to Princess Charlotte Bay   30
Princess Charlotte Bay to Bushy Islet   32
Bushy Islet to Torres Strait   34

 **Cruising Guides**

Ports and Anchorages   *37* In order south to north

Gold Coast   37
The Broadwater to Moreton Bay   44
Runaway Bay to Tipplers Passage   44
Tipplers Passage to Russell Island   46
Russell Island to Moreton Bay (via Main Channel)   48
Russell Island to Moreton Bay (via Canaipa Passage)   50
Moreton Bay   52
Dunwich   55
Tangalooma Wrecks   56
Cape Moreton   56
Cleveland Point   56
Manly   56
Brisbane   58
Cabbage Tree Creek   58
Scarborough Boat Harbour   60
Bongaree (Bribie Island)   61
Caloundra   62
Mooloolaba   62
Mudjimba Island   64
Noosa Heads   64
Double Island Point   66
Great Sandy Strait   67
Wide Bay Bar   70
Inskip Point (*Pelican Bay*)   70
Teebar Creek   72
Tin Can Bay   72
Kauri Creek   74
Tuan Creek   74
Garry's Anchorage   74
South White Cliffs   74
Susan River   76
Mary River   76
Maryborough   78
Saltwater Creek   79

Urangan Harbour   80
Balarrgan (*Kingfisher Bay*)   80
Big Woody Island   81
Scarness   81
Hervey Bay   82
Burrum Heads   82
Moon Point   83
Platypus Bay   84
Burnett Heads Boat Harbour   86
Bundaberg   89
Round Hill Creek   90
Pancake Creek   92
Lady Elliot Island   93
Lady Musgrave Island   94
Fitzroy Reef   96
Heron Island   96
North West Island   96
Gladstone   97
Quoin Island   100
The Narrows   100
Pacific Creek   104
Fitzroy River   108
Rockhampton   109
Cape Capricorn   110
Great Keppel Island   111
North Keppel Island   113
Rosslyn Bay   113

Corio Bay   114
Freshwater Bay   116
Port Clinton   116
Pearl Bay   120
Island Head Creek   120
Shoalwater Bay and Broad Sound 123
Strong Tide Passage   124
Cape Townshend   124
Cannibal Group   124
Duke Islands   125
Thirsty Sound   125
North Point Islands   128
Aquila Island   128
Poynter Island   128
High Peak Island   130
Percy Isles   131
South Percy Island   132
Middle Percy Island   133
Whites Bay   133
Blunt Bay   133
Pine Peak and Hotspur Islands   134
Digby Island   134
Scawfell Island   136
Penrith Island   136
Curlew Island   137
Knight Island   138
Prudhoe Island   138
Pioneer River   138
Mackay Outer Harbour   140
Cape Hillsborough   142
Port Newry   142
Victor Creek   146
Keswick and St Bees Island   147
Brampton Island   148
Goldsmith Island   150
Tinsmith and Linne Island   150
Thomas Island   150
Repulse Islands   151
Laguna Quays   151
Shaw Island   154
Lindeman Island   154
Cape Conway   154
Genesta Bay   155
Long Island Sound   156
Palm Bay   158

Happy Bay   158
South Molle Island   158
Planton Island   158
Daydream Island   158
Unsafe Passage   159
Shute Harbour   159
Hamilton Island   162
Dent Island   162
Henning Island   162
Gulnare Inlet   162
Cid Harbour   162
Whitehaven Bay   164
Haslewood Island   164
Apostle and Tongue Bays   164
Border Island   165
Macona Inlet   166
Nara Inlet   166
Langford Island   166
Stonehaven Anchorage   166
Hayman Island   166
Butterfly Bay   166
Funnel Bay   168
Airlie Beach   169
Woodwark and Double Bays   170
Grassy Island   170
Armit Islands   170
Eshelby Island   170
Earlando Resort   170
George Point   170
Gloucester Passage   172
Bowen   172
Greys Bay   176
Upstart Bay   176
Nobbies Inlet   176
Bowling Green Bay   178
Cape Bowling Green   178
Cape Cleveland   181
Magnetic Island   182
Townsville   184
Ross River   186
Cape Pallarenda   187
Rowes Bay   187
Halifax Bombing Range   187
Rattlesnake and Herald Islands   187
Acheron Island   188

Havannah Island   188
Palm Isles   188
Curacoa Island   191
Falcon Island   191
Fantome Island   191
Orpheus Island   191
Pelorus Island   191
Hinchinbrook Channel   192
Lucinda   195
Dungeness   195
Bluff Creek   195
Haycock Island   195
Hinchinbrook Island Creeks   196
Anchorage Point Creeks   196
Boat Passage   198
Scraggy Point   198
Cardwell   198
Hecate Point   199
Agnes Island   200
Shepherd Bay   200
Missionary Bay Creeks   200
Zoe Bay   200
Cape Richards   200
Goold Island   201
Brook Island   203
Family Islands   204
Bedarra Island   204
Dunk Island   204
Stephens Island   206
North Barnard Islands   206
Mourilyan Harbour   207
Innisfail   211
Frankland Islands   214
Fitzroy Island   215
Turtle Bay   216
Mission Bay   216
Cairns   218
Green Island   223
Arlington Reef   223
Upolu Reef   223
Oyster Reef   224
Michaelmas Cay   224
Yorkeys Knob   224
Double Island   224
Port Douglas   226

Low Islets   228
Daintree River   228
Snapper Island   230
Cape Kimberley   230
Bailay Creek   232
Cape Tribulation   233
Undine Reef   234
Mackay Reef   234
Bloomfield River   236
Endeavour Reef   236
Cairns Reef   236
Hope Islands   238
Egret Reef   238
Walker Bay   240
Annan River   240
Cooktown   240
Cape Bedford   244
Three Isles   245
Low Wooded Isle   245
Two Isles   245
Cape Flattery   246
Rocky Islets   246
South Direction Island   247
Turtle Group   248
Eagle Islet   249
Pethebridge Islets   250
Nymph Island   250
Lizard Island   250
Crescent Reef   253
Noble Island   253
Howick Group   254
Coquet Island   254
Snake Reef   254
Howick Island   254
Megaera Reef   256
Watson Island   256
Beanley Islets   256
Ninian Bay   256
Pipon Islets   257
Bathurst Bay   258
Saltwater Inlet   258
Flinders Group   260
Corbett Reef   260
Princess Charlotte Bay Rivers   262
Cliff Islets   262

Wharton Reef   264
Eden Reef   264
Grub Reef   264
Hedge Reef   264
Stainer Islet   264
Pelican Islet   264
Burkitt Island   264
Hannah Island   264
Magpie Reef   264
Noddy Reef   264
Wilkie Islet   266
Hay Islet   266
Morris Island   266
Ellis Reef   266
Bow Reef   266
Lowrie Islet   266
Night Island   268
Lloyd Bay   268
Lockhart River   270
Claudie River   271
Lloyd Island   271
Portland Roads   272
Middle Reef   273
Pascoe River   273
Eel Reef   274
Forbes Island   274
Hunter and Glennie Inlets   274
Space Station   275
Piper Reefs   276
Haggerstone Island   276
Cape Grenville   277
Hicks Island   279
Clerke Island   279
Nob Island   279
Shellburne Bay   279
Bird Islets   279
Hannibal Islets   280
Cairncross Islets   280
Bushy Islet   280
Escape River   280
Newcastle Bay   284
Albany Passage   284
Mount Adolphus Island   287
Cape York   288
Possession Island   290

Simpson Bay   290
Bamaga   291
Thursday Island   292
Torres Strait   298
Bramble Cay   300
Murray Islands   300
Darnley Island   300
Daru   300
Saibai   301
Stephens Island   301
Dalrymple Island   302
Rennel Island   302
Warrior Reefs   302
Coconut Island   302
Bet Island   302
Badu Island   302
Booby Island   302

The Coral Sea   304
Queensland Approaches   304
Cruising the Coral Sea   304
Cato Island   306
Wreck Reef   306
Kenn Reef   306
Saumarez Reefs   306
Frederick Reef   306
Bougainville Reef   306
Osprey Reef   306
Willis Islets   306

Gulf of Carpentaria   308
Weipa   308
Karumba   308
Gove   308

Down the Peninsula   310

Marina Roundup   314

Index   317

INTRODUCTION

This seventh edition of Cruising the Coral Coast is by far the most comprehensive to date. We have been able to increase both the size and number of pages. Inclusion of a lot more detail has been possible and previously ignored anchorages have been added.

A feature of this edition is the inclusion of many more reefs. This is not intended to encourage their use as anchorages so much as to assist in navigational identification. The fact is, tourism and its spin-off of bigger, faster and more frequent sightseeing boats has had a dramatic impact on the Coral Coast and its reefs in particular. At the time of going to press there were moves to ban anchoring behind certain reefs and cays and the reader is advised to be aware of this fact.

As always, the reader is warned against implicit faith in my findings, maintaining a healthy navigational scepticism at all times. Meanwhile, the main aim of this book is to assist those who cruise this extraordinary part of the world.

Launched in California in 1957 and sailed around the world a couple of times, *Renee Tighe* was restored by the author and used in the research and survey work for this book.

About This Book

First written in 1964, this book originally embraced the true coral coast, that part between Gladstone and Thursday Is. Since 1973 it has covered the entire east coast from Point Danger to and including the Torres Strait. This is the 7th edition, the survey for which was done in 1991 and 1993. The 1998 update supplement is the result of a further survey carried out in 1997 and early 1998.

Queensland at a Glance

Queensland is Australia's second largest state with an area of 1,727,000 square kilometres (667,000 square miles). It represents 22.5 percent of the nation's total area and is its closest state to a foreign country (Papua New Guinea).

Its coastline extends north from the border with New South Wales then turns south into the Gulf of Carpentaria. About halfway across the gulf's southern coast, it terminates at the border with the Northern Territory. Its length is more than 5,100 kilometres (app 2760 nautical miles) of which more than 1100 nautical miles are protected by the Great Barrier Reef.

The Great Barrier Reef starts at Lady Elliot Island, a coral cay north of Bundaberg, and ends in the Gulf of Papua towards the mouth of the

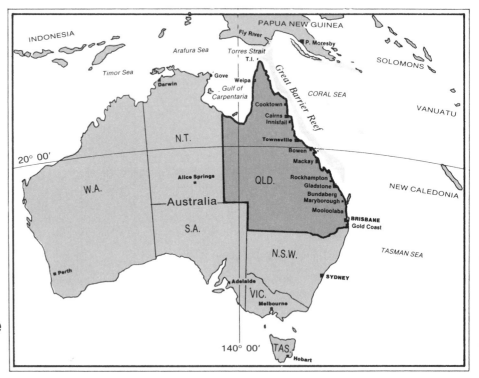

Fly River. The Inner Route, between the reefs and the mainland, is thoroughly charted as are a few passages out to sea. Otherwise, that area between the outer and inner edges of the reefs has been surveyed to standards between sketchy and thorough. Generally, people sailing into this area should treat the exerise as an adventure, not a means of having a relaxing day's sail.

Thanks to the many islands, headlands and reefs, day-sailing is normal practise along the entire Queensland coast. Overnight sailing is perfectly safe anywhere along the inner route, but is rarely necessary.

Until political division in 1859, Queensland was known as 'Moreton

Queensland is shown in detail here including the reefs of the Coral Sea. Logical offshore approaches are indicated by dotted lines the details of which are dealt with at the end of this book. The Coral Sea overlaps the state of New South Wales as far south as latitude 30°S.

Bay', the northern district of the colony of New South Wales. Today it is one of the nation's most vibrant economies, being a major exporter of coal, silica, gold, nickel, grains and frozen meat. Tourism has boomed in the late 1980's and early 1990's and is projected to continue growing, especially in the Japanese market. As a cruising destination it enjoys the status as one of the world's best.

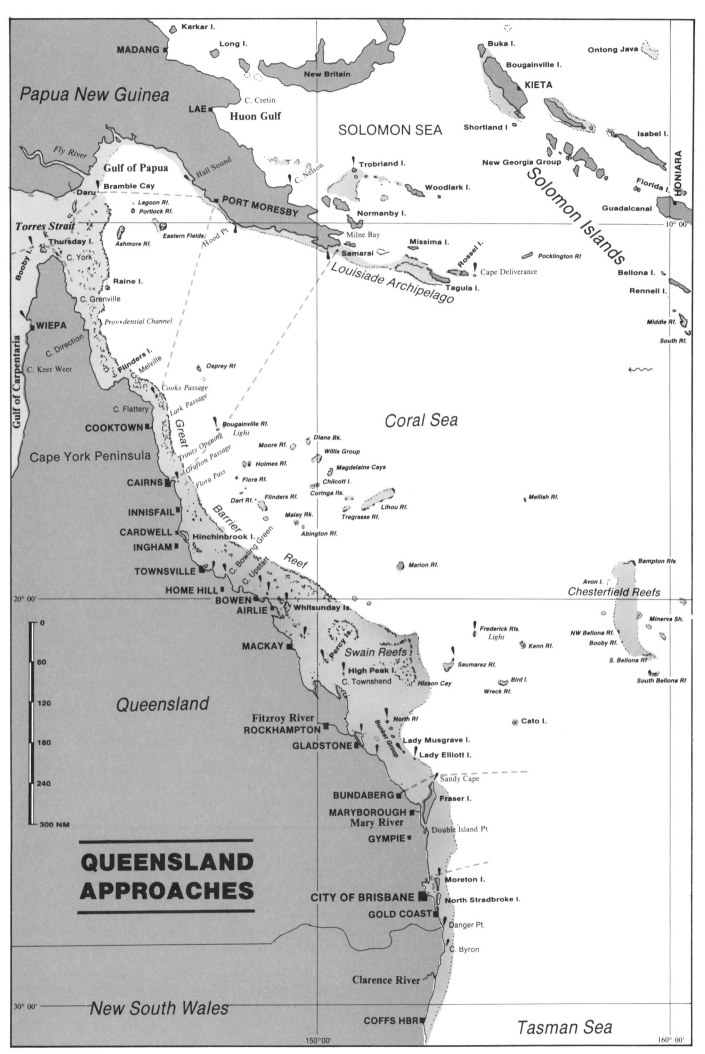

GENERAL INFORMATION

CUSTOMS PORTS. Full inward and outward clearance in all facets of customs, immigration and quarantine is available in the following Queensland ports;

Brisbane
Bundaberg
Gladstone
Port Alma (commercial only)
Hay Point (commercial only)
Mackay
Bowen
Abbot Point (commercial only)
Townsville
Cairns
Thursday Island
Weipa

Australian ports of clearance west of Queensland are *Nhulunbuy* (Gove) on the north-east tip of Arnhem Land and *Darwin*, the capital of Northern Territory.

The nearest foreign port of clearance to Queensland is *Daru* in Papua New Guinea, on the northern side of the Torres Strait. *Port Moresby*, the capital of Papua New Guinea, is the closest major foreign port of clearance.

Australian vessels must be Australian (not State) Registered to clear out. Foreign and returning local vessels must not go alongside or dinghy ashore until fully cleared into Australia. Advance radio notice is preferred.

DANGERS. Australia has more than its fair share of venomous animals, many of which are found in the tropical north. By understanding the problems and taking a few precautions, serious encounters are highly unlikely.

When swimming, choose sand-bottomed lagoons so that sharks may be seen before entering the water. Otherwise, confine your aquatic pleasure to diving. It has been shown beyond reasonable doubt that excess splashing can attract a hungry shark, especially in shoal, mud-bottomed bays and inlets.

During December through March, beware of the sea wasp. Entanglement in its tentacles is almost certain death. If you must swim, wear ladies' pantihose, a skivvy and perhaps some form of head protection, although the latter is unlikely to be necessary. Any onshore wind can wash the sea wasp towards the beaches, but it seems a northerly is the most dangerous wind condition.

When walking through mud, rocks or coral, wear sandshoes or plastic sandals to reduce or deny the effect of standing on stonefish. A full injection from a large stonefish's thirteen spines can be fatal.

Crocodiles have become a menace. Since the ban on hunting they have recovered in extraordinary numbers, none with any memory of man the armed aggressor. Fatalities are increasing. Never swim in any river or in the vicinity of its mouth.

Snakes are rarely seen but must be considered. Many Australians species are so highly poisonous that one bite can deliver enough venom to kill a number of people, let alone a single victim. Beware, especially, the death adder which lies in dust and sand and strikes when trodden on. It is a sluggish reptile and will not necessarily evade your approach.

The taipan is one of the most venomous snakes and lives dominantly on the Cape York Peninsula. It might be encountered anywhere in the bush and its potential for aggression without apparent provocation should be considered despite its rarity.

A golden rule with many snakes is to never sit quietly on or walk along a beach of an evening presuming it to be a sterile environment. Snakes sometimes venture from the scrub line to the sea for reasons uncertain. This seems especially true in the spring season.

Sea snakes are mostly deadly and diving should cease when they are sighted. Considering the potency of their venom it is fortunate that the sea snake has trouble making contact.

Australia's most deadly spiders seem to favour the City of Sydney and environs. They are not a serious problem on the Coral Coast. However, always roll rocks or lift garbage carefully.

Box Jellyfish

Chironex fleckeri, variously known as sea wasp, stinger and box jellyfish, this is one of the most dangerous animals in reef waters. The polyp stage lives in estuaries in winter whilst the medusa (jellyfish) emerges early summer and then remains fairly close to shore. *Chiropsalmus*, a smaller species of box-jellyfish, extend offshore but are not a serious risk.

Registration of Sailing Vessels

Foreign vessels or interstate vessels without registration must obtain Queensland registration after 40 days. Interstate vessels fully registered in their home state must obtain Queensland registration after 90 days. Vessels registered under the Australian Register of Ships are not exempt from the above.

New Pilotage Laws

All ships longer than 70 metres must carry a pilot through Hydrographers Passage off Mackay and along the coast north of Cairns. Amongst other things, it is hoped this will reduce the likelihood of oil spills from tanker collisions and groundings. Nearly 2000 ships traverse the inner channel of the Great Barrier Reef each year, of which 200 are tankers carrying up to 100,000 tonnes of crude oil, diesel and petrol.

Naming the GBR

During his 1801–02 survey of the Australian coastline, Matthew Flinders spent from 22 July to 18 October 1802 along the Coral Coast. He was the first to refer to the reefs collectively as the Great Barrier Reef. Flinders was only 27 years old at the time.

Because of our very special problem with venomous vipers, spiders and sea life, nearly all Queensland hospitals have a good stock of antivenene. It is important to get to hospital within hours and to describe the attacker with fair accuracy. The cruising person struggles to comply with this elementary rule and must therefore be doubly cautious when in the wild.

NATIONAL PARKS. Queensland has more than five million hectares of land dedicated to national park on its mainland and islands. Also, much of its Great Barrier Reef has been placed under the protection of the *Great Barrier Reef Marine Park Authority.*

The different levels of protection are shown below and are indicated on the relevant charts in this book. But because zoning can change, it is recommended that the boat person seeks advice from a National Parks office before pursuing any activity which might contravene the rules. Generally speaking, most basic boating activities are permitted everywhere except in Scientific Research and Preservation Zones.

Because tourism and recreational boating is having a deleterious impact on the coast and reefs in general, there are many suggestions as to how protection might be increased. Amongst these is a ban on anchoring behind certain reefs and cays, limiting the number of boats to any one area and charging a dollar a day per person to raise funds for further research and protective measures.

It goes without saying that it behoves us all to tread softly, leave a clean wake and do nothing that damages our environment.

Detailed information with full colour maps and graphs is available from any Queensland Parks and Wildlife office. The visitor is recommended a visit as early as possible in his or her cruise of the coral coast.

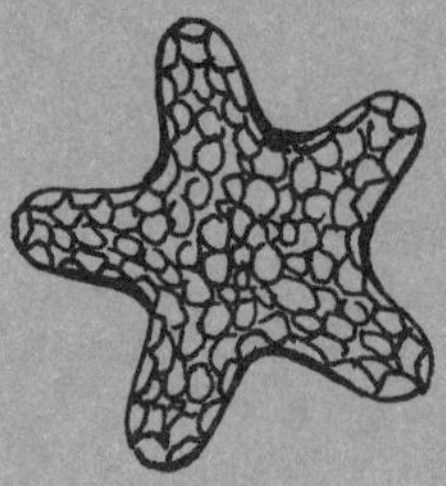

MARINE PARK CATEGORIES	BAIT NETTING AND GATHERING	CAMPING	COLLECTING (RECREATIONAL — NOT CORAL)	COLLECTING (COMMERCIAL)	COMMERCIAL NETTING (SEE ALSO BAIT NETTING)	CRABBING AND OYSTER GATHERING	DIVING, BOATING, PHOTOGRAPHY	LINE FISHING (BOTTOM FISHING, TROLLING ETC)	RESEARCH (NON-MANIPULATIVE)	RESEARCH (MANIPULATIVE)	SPEAR FISHING	TOURIST AND EDUCATION FACILITIES AND PROGRAMS	TRADITIONAL HUNTING, FISHING AND GATHERING	TRAWLING
GENERAL USE 'A'	YES	PERMIT	LIMITED	PERMIT	YES	YES	YES	YES	YES	PERMIT	YES	PERMIT	PERMIT	YES
GENERAL USE 'B'	YES	PERMIT	LIMITED	PERMIT	YES	YES	YES	YES	YES	PERMIT	YES	PERMIT	PERMIT	NO
MARINE NATIONAL PARK 'A'	YES	PERMIT	NO	NO	NO	LIMITED	YES	LIMITED	YES	PERMIT	NO	PERMIT	PERMIT	NO
MARINE NATIONAL PARK 'B'	NO	PERMIT	NO	NO	NO	NO	YES	NO	YES	PERMIT	NO	PERMIT	NO	NO
SCIENTIFIC RESEARCH	NO	NO	NO	NO	NO	NO	NO	NO	PERMIT	PERMIT	NO	NO	NO	NO
PRESERVATION ZONE	NO	NO	NO	NO	NO	NO	NO	NO	PERMIT	PERMIT	NO	NO	NO	NO

5

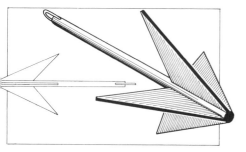

This improved version of a reef pick is made in Townsville or can be home-made using steel plate and round bar. Try to avoid dropping any type of anchor into coral, preferring the sand between or the mud outside the reef patches.

ANCHORING IN CORAL. Happily for the environment, the literal act of anchoring *in* coral is extremely rare, a fact that surprises newcomers to a region like the Coral Coast. In reality, most anchoring is done in mud or sand behind islands and headlands, and sometimes behind main reefs. The dropping of an anchor into or close to pure coral is very much a minority event. But, because it demands a little specialised knowledge to protect both ship and coral, it is reviewed here.

One of the most common times when an anchor must be dropped into coral is when the vessel is taken too close to the reef in the first place. This is very much an act of the sublimely innocent who presume that the closer you get, the safer you get.

Not true. Even when a well developed trade wind is holding the boat well back from the reef, there is danger in being too close. It is unlikely, but has happened, that the wind dies during the night then a flood tidal stream carries the boat over the reef there to strand on the ebb. There *must* be a safe distance off, if only to reduce the likelihood of cable fouling. The answer to this problem is simple. Move back. Anchor in deep water if necessary, but stay away from the reef.

The only time when anchoring on or amongst coral patches is obligatory, is where a lagoon floor extends so far to leeward that to seek its leeward, muddy-bottomed depths, would be to lose the protection of its windward edge. This can happen when seeking protection in full or part lagoons, or where a number of reefs share a common floor yet have a lot of open, deep water between them.

The type of floor involved here is invariably sand, mostly with a scattering of coral heads and patches. These will be seen as brown smudges on the lighter coloured sand and the only confusion likely is their similarity of colour to weed patches. If it is important to differentiate between the two, an echo-sounder run across their tops will decide or, if depths are uncertain, a glass bottomed bucket or goggles will do the same.

Where coral patches are few and far between, the standard anchor and cable can be dropped. Ideally, this will be one of the common mud types, such as Danforth, Plow or Bruce, at the end of all-chain cable. Scope will be at least four times the depth, but on the basis that there can never be enough, lay out as much cable as circumstances dictate and allow.

If there are so many coral patches that cable fouling is possible (to say nothing of coral damage), the cable should be changed for a chain trace on rope. The rope can be protected from chafe by Polyurethane hose.

In those extremely rare cases where the anchor must be dropped into pure coral, without any visible floor in the area, a reef pick is best used, the type illustrated being far more secure than the old rod and pipe type. But try to avoid this type of bottom for the sake of both you and the environment.

With the massive upsurge in tourism during the 1980s, all too often coupled with irresponsible operators, reef damage from charter boat anchors became apparent. This has been addressed in the most threatened regions by the laying of moorings to which all charter boats secure. In some places, aluminium landings have been permanently moored to which vessels secure whilst transferring passengers to smaller boats.

Private boats are next on the list. There is every likelihood that the more popular, and therefore threatened, regions of delicate corals will become banned anchorages, public moorings being established as the only permissible alternative.

Meanwhile, in the interest of all sailors, both now and in the future, reef damage should be minimised or not risked at all. If circumstances allow, avoid anchoring over pure coral, preferring to seek a relatively clear, sandy area.

Beware of coming to anchor behind coral against the sun. If it cannot be avoided, zig-zag across the sun; never move straight into its glare.

Reef types

In categorising reef types, three names are used, these being ribbon reefs, fringing reefs and patch reefs. *Ribbon reefs* occur in the northern part of the Great Barrier Reef where they are relatively narrow walls of coral along the edge of the continental shelf. *Fringing reefs* grow around the shores of continental islands or along parts of the mainland coast. *Patch reefs* are those reefs growing on the continental shelf and are roughly oval or round in shape. All reefs conform to natural limits which denies growth higher than the neap low water level.

CYCLONE PROTECTION. Theoretically, destructive winds can occur at any time of year, anywhere along the Queensland coast. Normally, however, they only occur during the wet season between and including December to March, and seldom move south further than Bundaberg.

Because a cyclone creates a vacuum, the sea level rises within the eye to a height according to pressure gradients and terrain. This can be a whopping 14 metres as occurred during *Mahina*, the great cyclone of March 1899 which wrecked over fifty boats and drowned 300 men in Princess Charlotte Bay, or it may only be a couple of metres. But between the two extremes is the possibility of marina pontoons lifting over their piles and blowing away with hundreds of boats clinging to them.

For this reason, the average Queensland marina is *not* the secure wet season haven one might presume. It is suited only to an average set of conditions which, fortunately, prevail for most of the time. This time might be measured in months or decades, there is no way of being sure. Generally, truly destructive winds strike only once in decades so the odds are in our favour.

The best haven during a cyclone is up a mangrove creek, preferably one not prone to flood run-off. Thus, if you have a choice between a creek penetrating a continental island or the mainland and one situated in a mangrove island, the latter is to be preferred. This reduces the problem of debris sweeping down the stream to foul lines and possibly start an anchor dragging. However, if only flood-prone creeks are available, then they are preferable to bays and inlets.

The wettest and most destructive wind direction is nearly always south-east (the same direction as the prevailing wind). Thus, if only a bay or inlet is available, make sure it gives maximum protection from that direction. If the eye passes close, the wind will swing to the north from which direction it will ease, but not before creating a fearful lee shore to any vessel exposed to the north.

In a creek, wind direction is not as critical because the vessel is completely surrounded by mangroves to which bow and stern lines are secured. If the creek is too wide for this practice, it pays to lie to a pattern of anchors; at least two fanned out from bow and stern.

When seeking protection, try to get upwind of other craft, especially those left to their own devices. Incredibly, it is a common practice for local private and commercial boat owners to run their craft up a creek then go home! Invariably, their vessels cause most trouble, obliging the live-aboarders to care for their own vessels whilst fending off others. The fewer boats you have to windward, the less your inconvenience from absentee owners' vessels.

Having made her fast by whatever means indicate themselves, clear the deck of all soft material including awnings, dodgers, sheets, halyards and sails. This not only protects them, but also protects you in the event of having to work on deck. Flapping material has been known to cause painful eye injury.

With all openings secured, make sure the main hatch can be used with a minimum of fuss for it is almost certain that one or more trips on deck will prove necessary during the blow. Beware also of snakes getting aboard. It is not unusual for reptiles to be swept off the land and around cables and lines on which they then climb to safety aboard your ship. Poisonous black snakes are the most common.

Because the sea level will rise, all warps to trees should be as high as possible to reduce debris snagging, on one hand, and improve accessibility during the blow on the other hand. But allow for leverage on slender trees. If their trunks are not stout enough to take the strain high up, secure down low and stand a double watch for debris.

When the wind has reduced to a tolerable gale, it is entirely possible that other wild life will be found aboard. Typically, birds will huddle under the lee of a deckhouse and be so intimidated by weather conditions that human attention will be ignored. Rats are also possible visitors, but they are more likely to be found in dorade boxes or down below if an unguarded opening provides opportunity.

Throughout the ports and anchorage descriptions in this book, cyclone holes

---

The first cyclone named

As a means of identification, 1964 saw the introduction of women's names to destructive cyclones. The first was *Audrey* which caused damage over the eastern Gulf of Carpentaria 7 to 14 January, 1964. It was followed by *Ada, Althea* and *Wanda* before protests from the women's movement brought in the use of men's names, the first being *Ted*, 19 December 1976.

are periodically noted. Here is a check-list of all useful havens along the east coast of Queensland. Marinas are not included, these being the choice of the reader.

Moreton Bay. In the channels between the Gold Coast's Broadwater and Lower Moreton Bay. Because of flooding, the Brisbane River cannot be recommended.

Great Sandy Strait. At the head of Tin Can Inlet; Garry's Anchorage; to the south of South White Cliffs and in the Mary River upstream of Beaver Rock.

Gladstone region. Graham Creek to the north of Gladstone City in Curtis Island. Any deep creek in Curtis Island north of The Narrows including Badger, Mosquito, Barker, Maria and Pacific. Also, Deception Creek and tributaries are useful as are other creeks to the west forming the Fitzroy River delta.

Capricornia Coast. Head of Port Clinton near the army ramp and the head of Island Head Creek.

Mackay area. Slade, Seaforth and Victor Creeks, all demanding a high tide to enter. Only Victor Creek gives low tide float depths within and also has the best protected entrance (in Port Newry).

Whitsunday Islands. Gulnare Inlet on Whitsunday Island and Woodcutters and Trammel Creeks in Long Island Sound. The latter two subject to high tide to enter, the former requiring some tide depending on draft.

Upstart Bay. In Nobbies Inlet at head of bay. High tide needed to enter, good depths within.

Hinchinbrook Channel. Any of the deep creeks against the island or, preferably, the creeks within the central mangrove forest area.

Mourilyan Harbour. Up the Moresby River as far as possible.

Cairns. Towards the head of Trinity Inlet up any creek with easy access. Best haven is in Garrison Creek into the western side of Admiralty Island.

Port Douglas. As far up Dickson Inlet as depths allow. Also opportunities up the nearby Daintree River, but bar too dangerous to cross if cyclone already developing.

Princess Charlotte Bay. Any of the rivers around this bay subject to high tide to enter.

Lloyd Bay. Up the Lockhart River as far as depths allow. High tide needed to enter but bar well protected from the south-east.

Cape York. Up the Escape River. Well developed cyclones rare in these latitudes.

The best place to be during a cyclone is up a narrow, mangrove-lined creek where lines can be run to stout trees. Use only flood-free creeks such as those near the delta of a river or those that are not a part of a river system.

This marina in the Mary River disappears during heavy floods when heights are such that the wharf deck, top left, goes fully three metres under. During such conditions, all boats are moved downstream to the entrance area.

FLOODS occur in all rivers along the coast, but those most likely to be of concern to the boat owner are, the *Brisbane River* at Brisbane; the *Mary River* at Maryborough; the *Burnett River* at Bundaberg; the *Fitzroy River* at Rockhampton and, to a lesser degree, the *Pioneer River* at Mackay and the *Johnstone River* at Innisfail.

Major floods have occurred in mid winter. But they are unusual. Normally, flooding occurs during the wet season between December and March inclusive. This is when rivers can rise nine metres and more, placing waterfront buildings' eaves under and sending the local fleet scurrying for the river mouth.

And herein lies a problem. With the increasing habit of southern and overseas visitors leaving their vessels in Queensland to fly home for a few months, there is the difficulty of getting a bunch of untended boats down the river to the safety of the delta region. Marina owners and live-aboarders will do their best, but with dozens of boats to move, damage can occur through their being rafted up and towed collectively.

Regardless of how it is done, a boat must be moved downstream ahead of a threatening flood. Flood warnings are usually accurate and days ahead of the event, the upper reaches swelling long before the effect is felt downstream. But, before the river rises to a level where masts will not clear overhead cables, and the stream becomes dangerously swift, the non-flooding delta must be sought. Here, the stream will be strong and continuously ebbing for many days, but at least the water level will remain more or less static.

Most rivers in question have a large, almost unused delta area where there is plenty of space for the town fleet to anchor during a flood. Only the Brisbane River denies this, with its heavy industry around the entrance. In this case, boats would need to scatter to Moreton Bay alternatives such as Manly and Scarborough.

The Burnett River has a similar problem, its sugar loading port being at the entrance. However, upstream of this facility is a reach where only partial flooding is experienced. Alternatively, there is anchorage opportunity in the entrance area, outside the shipping channel, plus the Burnett Heads Boat Harbour which may cram a few more boats in during an emergency.

It has been proven often enough that a flood can be survived in the area affected by a river bursting its banks. In essence, it becomes a matter of running off more anchor cable and accepting the idea that you won't be getting ashore for quite a long time. But it is more than that. There is the worry about debris colliding with the hull and, if large enough, carrying away the anchor. And if the anchor does drag, there is the possibility of hitting overhead cables or being swept ashore in an area that may prove inaccessible by crane and low-loading when the river returns to normal level. In short, it does not pay to remain on station. The most sensible decision is to get down river before the need.

If associated with a cyclone, the rain will be accompanied by potentially destructive winds in which case the advice in the section headed 'Cyclone Pro-

Gympie goes under

Being near the headwaters of the Mary River, which flows down through Maryborough to Hervey Bay, the city of Gympie has more than its fair share of floods. During April, 1989, it went underwater twice and in March 1992, it again went under to record high levels. Then, the water dunked shop awnings.

Rainfall

The driest part of Queensland is in the southwest corner where less than 200 mm falls whilst the wettest parts are on the windward side of a number of mountains along the north Queensland coast. The highest annual mean rainfall is recorded at Babinda, near the coast north of Innisfail at 4561 mm. The lowest annual mean rainfall is recorded at Roseberth, near Birdsville in the state's southwest extreme at 148 mm.

tection' is applicable. However, the one condition both events have in common is the way in which snakes are swept into the stream. Floods are great times for reptiles to seek refuge aboard ship. They need watching. If they get below decks, there could follow days of search and anxiety.

TIDES. Along the entire coast, tides occur normally with approximately six hours duration between high and low water and vice versa. The only differences are in the heights. At the south and north extremes, heights tend to be similar with Brisbane's mean high water springs reading 2.16 metres and Thursday Island's reading 2.5 metres. Roughly midway between the two, at Mackay on the central coast, the mean high spring reaches 5.28 metres. If a graph were drawn from this central height down to the south and north extremes, the slope would be fairly constant.

The highest tides on the coast occur in Broad Sound, 70 miles south-east of Mackay where as much as 40% must be added to Mackay data to arrive at the correct height. The smallest tides are in the Broadwater on the Gold Coast.

The *Queensland Tide Tables* available through Harbours and Marine offices, newsagents and some booksellers, give full details for all ports with secondary stations easily calculated by the tables provided. On this basis it overlaps down the New South Wales coast as far as Coffs Harbour. It also includes a wealth of information regarding weather, radio stations and frequencies, distress procedure, buoys and beacons, marine law, fishing tips and legalities, ramps and fish habitat reserve maps.

SEAS. By rough rule of thumb the height of a Coral Coast wave can be related in feet to the Beaufort wind force. Thus, a wind at Force 4 will produce a wave four feet high on average. In areas where sea height is predicted along with the weather, it is common to be warned of waves to three metres inside the reef and five metres offshore during winds to 30 knots (F7). These warnings often exaggerate wave height, but it must be admitted that such winds will lift a wave beyond the Beaufort figure by a factor of 50%. However, I still maintain that the *average* wave height will relate to the scale's figure. This rule applies to waves inside the barrier reefs only.

SWELL. Depending on the effectiveness of the barrier reefs in reducing or eliminating ocean swell, the inner reef waters will experience moderate to no swell. Typically, maximum swell is felt in the Gladstone to Percy Island section north of which its effect diminishes until north from Cairns to the Torres Strait there is no swell at all, the sea becoming flat as a pancake within hours of a wind dying.

RADIO. The *Queensland Tide Tables* includes a full coverage of all volunteer and government-operated small-ship stations on the coast. Because every boat should have this book aboard as standard equipment, further coverage here would be superfluous. It can be said, however, that as well as such organisations as Air Sea Rescue, Coast Guard and government stations, most marinas monitor VHF channel 16 as do all tourist resort islands and yacht clubs.

Commercial fishermen are well catered for by the various private and government fish depots.

NAVIGATIONAL AIDS. All beacons, buoys and lights within or leading into a harbour are maintained by the harbour in question's own port authority. All buoys, beacons and lights pertaining to coastal navigation between ports are maintained by the Commonwealth Government.

In areas of big tides, and especially in restricted passages, whirlpools and overfalls can occur. These overfalls are in the Whitsunday Group between Whitsunday Island and Hook Island.

A replica of one of Australia's earliest survey ships to chart the Coral Coast, the *Lady Nelson* visits Rockhampton. She is Tasmania's training ship.

Queensland's most famous beach, Airlie is the focus point for tourists and cruising people visiting the Whitsunday Islands. At low tide, swimming becomes impossible here.

The Queensland coast offers a variety of headlands behind which snug, secure anchorage can be found. This is one of her loftiest, Cape Upstart, whose hills have everything from rocky landscape to dense rain forest.

Bottom left: The Wharf Marina is part of a new tourist complex at Mooloolaba.

The Point Danger light stands on the border between New South Wales and Queensland. There are rescue organisations in every port from here north.

Approaching the Gold Coast from the south, the highrise of Surfers Paradise are obvious. The separate group of buildings, extreme right, make good reference for the harbour entrance (Gold Coast Seaway).

Looking out of Cairns Harbour, North Queensland, 'The Pier' shopping complex is seen, left, with the Marlin Marina at its doorstep.

Not dead, just resting! Stranded turtles are a common sight in Port Clinton. The author's yacht, *Renee Tighe* is behind.

Bungee jumping, helicopter flights, joy flights, you name it, there is something for everyone on the Gold Coast. This plane was rolled in a gale not long after this photograph was taken.

Coral and tides

Coral cannot survive out of the water for very long. As a result, it is a fundamental rule of nature that no living coral will be found at a level higher than the neap low tide line. That some dead coral can stand above this level is a result of rubble being pushed up by wave action and not by coral growing to that height.

The tidal contour lines shown here are in metres. The highest tides on the entire east coast of Australia are experienced in Broad Sound, south of Mackay, where up to nine metre highs are possible. The lowest tides are in the Broadwater, Gold Coast, south of Brisbane.

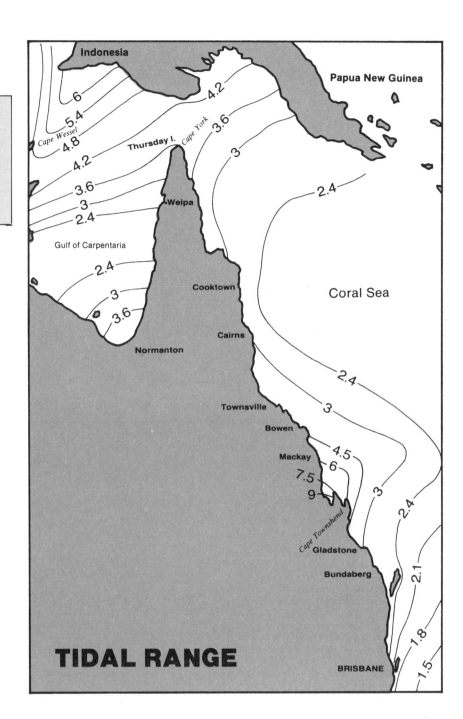

TIDAL RANGE

Thanks to the useful tidal range along much of the Queensland coast, careening is possible in many areas. This is the well known grid on the end of the O'Connell Wharf in Auckland Creek, Gladstone. A similar facility is available in Mackay and makeshift opportunity can be pursued in other ports and anchorages.

11

Cyclone Tracks

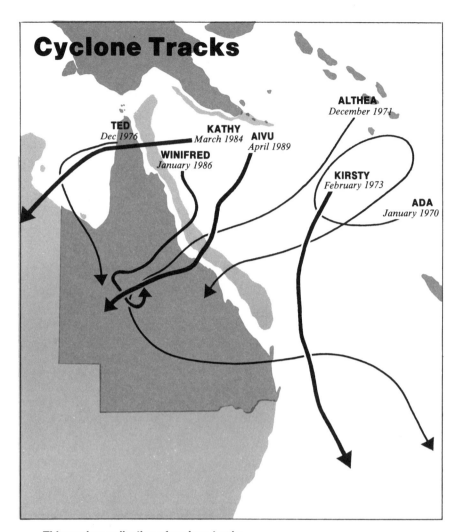

TED
Dec 1976

KATHY
March 1984

AIVU
April 1989

WINIFRED
January 1986

ALTHEA
December 1971

KIRSTY
February 1973

ADA
January 1970

The diagram, right, shows the basic structure of a developed cyclone. Normally developing close to the monsoonal trough over the Coral Sea or Gulf of Carpentaria at around 5° latitude, it is an intense depression around which the wind circulates clockwise. Rapidly rising moist air forms the calm eye which, if it passes over your position, will reverse the wind direction after a period of windless conditions. The whole mass moves as indicated with the strongest winds around the leading semi-circle and diminishing winds around the trailing semi-circle. The direction of the strongest wind on the Coral Coast is nearly always south-east.

This random collection of cyclone tracks shows how destructive winds mostly develop in the Coral Sea, usually out towards the Solomon Islands, then move south-west towards Queensland. After hitting the coast, they often collapse or turn south-east and move out over the Tasman Sea. Of those shown here, *Althea* was the most orderly. It destroyed ten per cent of Townsville during Christmas Eve, 1971, after which it became a rain depression over the land before gathering a little momentum back over the sea.

Cyclone frequency

Of the numerous cyclones that occur in the southern hemisphere, the Bureau of Meteorology track an average of ten per year in the Australian region. Of these, six may be expected to cross the coast. Storm surge heights tend to maximise at around 4 metres although greater heights are entirely possible.

Not to be confused with tidal streams — which can be very strong along parts of the Queensland coast — currents have little effect within the Great Barrier Reef. Even that section of the East Australian Current between Fraser Island and the Gold Coast is often weak or too far offshore to trouble the coastal navigator. The Trade Wind Drift can reach two knots when the south-easterly winds are well developed, especially in the north-west Coral Sea. This must be calculated into any course from North Queensland to Papua New Guinea.

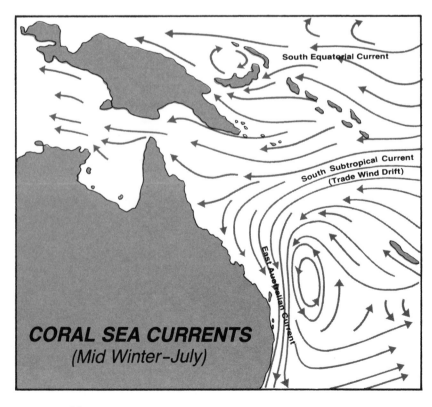

South Equatorial Current

South Subtropical Current
(Trade Wind Drift)

East Australian Current

CORAL SEA CURRENTS
(Mid Winter–July)

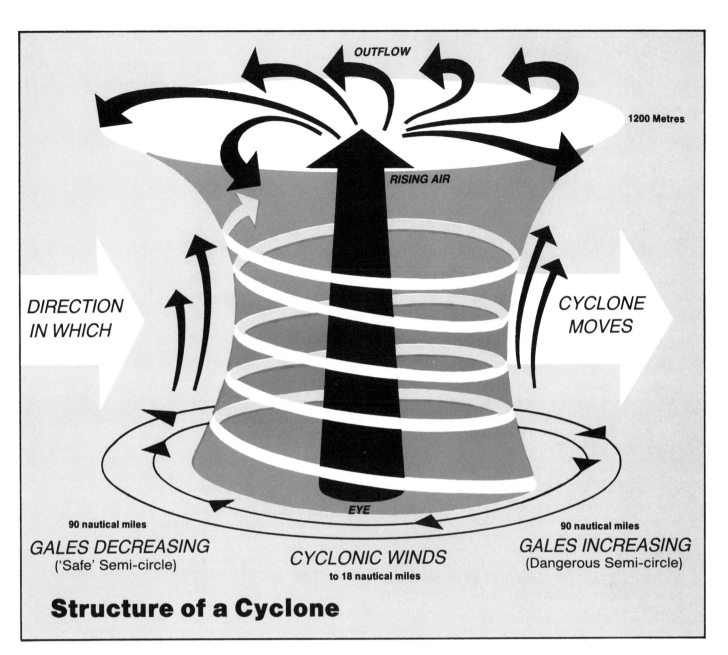

Structure of a Cyclone

OUTFLOW

1200 Metres

RISING AIR

DIRECTION IN WHICH

CYCLONE MOVES

90 nautical miles

GALES DECREASING
('Safe' Semi-circle)

CYCLONIC WINDS
to 18 nautical miles

EYE

90 nautical miles

GALES INCREASING
(Dangerous Semi-circle)

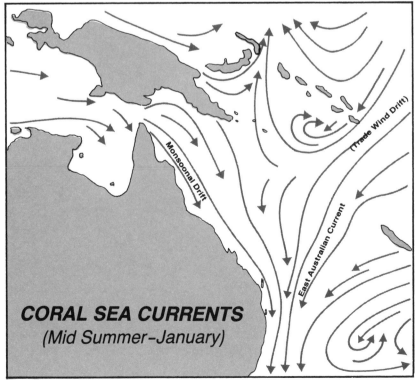

CORAL SEA CURRENTS
(Mid Summer–January)

Monsoonal Drift

East Australian Current

(Trade Wind Drift)

The summer, or wet season, current pattern remains similar to that of winter down the New South Wales coast but reverses in the north-west Coral Sea. This monsoonal drift rarely attains any strength but can become obvious during late January to early March and is often experienced within the Great Barrier Reef. Across the Gulf of Carpentaria it commonly starts in December by which time a distinct southerly set into the gulf can occur.

WEATHER. The entire coast is dominated by the south-east trade wind which is strengthened or weakened according to the gradients of the high-pressure systems which continually sweep across Australia and out into the Tasman Sea.

The strongest and most presistent trade winds blow April through November from Cairns north to the Torres Strait and, depending on the strength of the high, will often blow with similar enthusiasm and strength right down the coast to Brisbane. Otherwise, during this period, a weak influence will continue to blanket the north coast with light to moderate trade winds while the south coast receives calms or cold offshore winds commonly out of the west or southwest. Between the two, roughly from Mackay to Cairns, winds will be variable, sometimes strengthening from the east to north-east towards the afternoon after a calm start to the day.

In the months of October-November, a useful northerly stream blows down the coast from Cairns south and sometimes spreads north as far as Torres Strait. This is interspersed with returns of the south-east trade wind but nevertheless offers a useful force for the southbound sailing craft.

The wet season, December through March, brings north-westerlies to the Torres Strait and sometimes down as far as Princess Charlotte Bay and variables or south-easterlies to the south coast.

Between the two extremes, along the central coast, variables tend to dominate although a low-pressure system offshore in the Coral Sea will most certainly bring strong south-easterlies and tons of rain.

Further weather details will be found strewn throughout the coast descriptions, and the *Tide Tables*, issued by Queensland Transport, now includes a very thorough section on the subject.

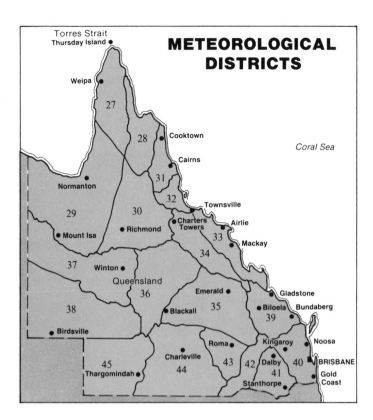

METEOROLOGICAL DISTRICTS

The above map of Queensland's meteorological districts show how the state is broken up into numbered areas. These are not referred to during coastal weather forecasts, typical sections being shown on the map below. Coastal forecasts for the entire coast start at Thursday Island and move south. The most complete forecasts are heard on ABC radio, Official Coast Radio Stations and on evening television on most channels. A few commercial radio stations provide in-depth forecasts for their specific region.

Fog is very rare on the Queensland coast, especially north of Brisbane. This is Rockhampton's road bridge across the Fitzroy River during a mid-winter fog.

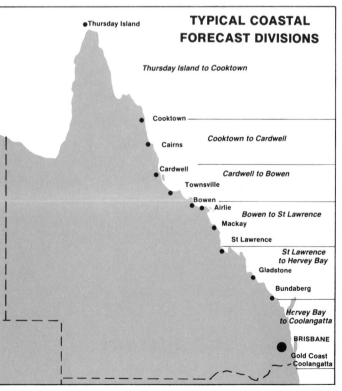

TYPICAL COASTAL FORECAST DIVISIONS

Thursday Island to Cooktown

Cooktown to Cardwell

Cardwell to Bowen

Bowen to St Lawrence

St Lawrence to Hervey Bay

Hervey Bay to Coolangatta

14

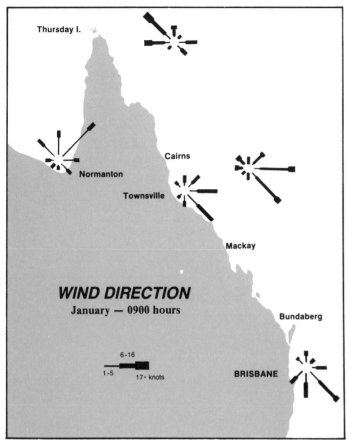

WIND DIRECTION
January — 0900 hours

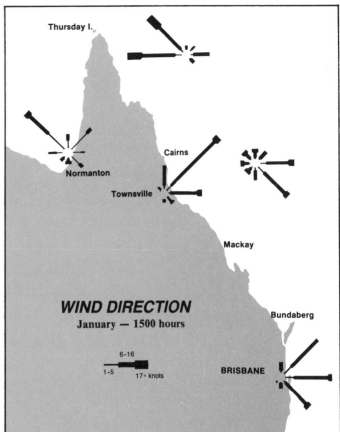

WIND DIRECTION
January — 1500 hours

January is the middle of summer in the south and the wet season in the north. Together with February, it is a month of heightened cyclone activity, especially between Cooktown and Bundaberg.

The afternoon winds of January often favour north-east along much of the coast. The north-westerly flow through the Torres Strait rarely extends south further than Portland Roads.

July is mid-winter in the south and mid-dry season in the north. South-east trade winds predominate, especially in the north. Brisbane often experiences west to south-west winds at this time of year.

Afternoon winds in July vary little, although the south-easterly often moves to the north-east over Townsville. Although it is said that the wind does likewise in the Torres Strait, this is not the experience of the author.

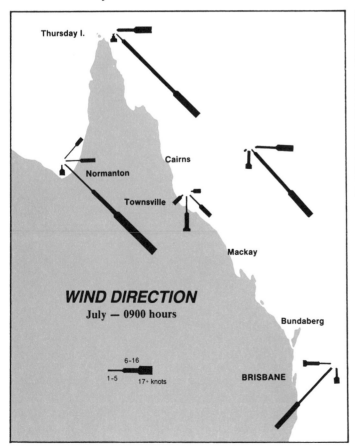

WIND DIRECTION
July — 0900 hours

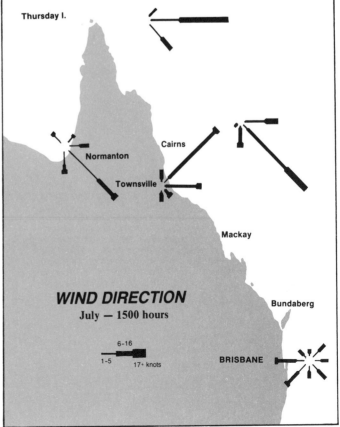

WIND DIRECTION
July — 1500 hours

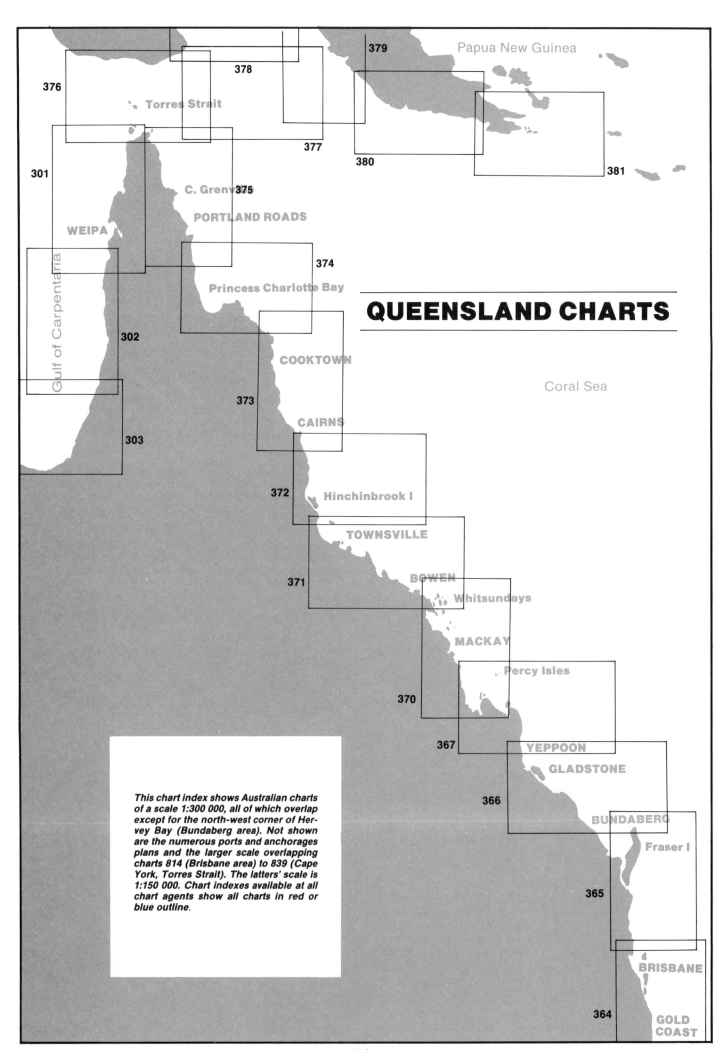

QUEENSLAND CHARTS

376

378

379 Papua New Guinea

Torres Strait

301

C. Grenville 375

PORTLAND ROADS

WEIPA

377

380

381

374

Princess Charlotte Bay

Gulf of Carpentaria

302

Coral Sea

COOKTOWN

373

CAIRNS

303

372

Hinchinbrook I

TOWNSVILLE

371

BOWEN

Whitsundays

MACKAY

Percy Isles

370

367

YEPPOON

GLADSTONE

366

BUNDABERG

Fraser I

365

BRISBANE

364

GOLD COAST

This chart index shows Australian charts of a scale 1:300 000, all of which overlap except for the north-west corner of Hervey Bay (Bundaberg area). Not shown are the numerous ports and anchorages plans and the larger scale overlapping charts 814 (Brisbane area) to 839 (Cape York, Torres Strait). The latters' scale is 1:150 000. Chart indexes available at all chart agents show all charts in red or blue outline.

CORAL COAST CHARTS

Because this book contains a lot of material unavailable in official charts, it is inevitable that the navigator will use it without cross-reference to other publications. Under the circumstances he or she is warned of the possibility of human error on my part, natural changes over many years and sudden changes at the hand of authority. Up-dated charts should be considered the most vital part of the ship's equipment despite the understandable economic resistance to their purchase.

Those the author considers superfluous are marked with an 'S'. Those that might be seen as unnecessary as long as this book and small scale charts are used very cautiously and with common sense are marked with a 'U'. Vital charts are marked with a 'V'.

Charts of the Coral Coast.

AUS 426   Fraser Island to Cumberland Islands. *S*

AUS 427   Cumberland Islands to Cooktown. *S.*

AUS 428   Cooktown to Booby Island and Port Moresby. *S, unless leaving the coast bound for Port Moresby.*

AUS 814   Point Danger to Cape Moreton *(includes plan of Gold Coast Seaway V.).*

AUS 235   Approaches to Moreton Bay. *V.*

AUS 236   Moreton Bay *V*

AUS 365   Cape Moreton to Sandy Cape. *V.*

AUS 817   Hervey Bay. *V.*

AUS 241   Great Sandy Strait *S. This chart is only recommended if Harbours and Marine charts are not carried.*

AUS 243   Port Bundaberg and Burnett River. *U.*

AUS 818   Sandy Cape to Bustard Head. *V.*

AUS 246   Approaches to Port Gladstone. *U.*

AUS 245   Port of Gladstone. *V.*

AUS 244   Plans in Port of Gladstone. *U.*

AUS 819   Bustard Head to North Reef. *V.*

AUS 820   North Reef to Port Clinton. *V.*

AUS 248   Port Clinton. *U.*

AUS 822   Port Clinton to Percy Isles. *V.*

AUS 823   Percy Isles to Mackay. *V.*

AUS 250   Plans of Mackay and Bowen. *U, if the next chart is carried for safety in approaching Mackay.*

AUS 249   Hay Point to Penrith Island. *V.*

AUS 824   Bailey Islet to Whitsunday Island. *V.*

AUS 253   Plans on the East Coast of Australia. *U, if Chart Aus 252 is carried.*

AUS 821   Hydrographers Passage. *U unless transiting through outer reef.*

AUS 252   Cumberland Islands and Whitsunday Passage. *V.*

AUS 254   Stonehaven Anchorage. *U.*

AUS 825   Whitsunday Island to Bowen. *V.*

AUS 826   Bowen to Cape Bowling Green. *V.*

AUS 256   Cleveland Bay. *U.*

AUS 257   Townsville Harbour. *U.*

AUS 827   Cape Bowling Green to Palm Islands. *V.*

AUS 258   Approaches to Hinchinbrook Channel. *U.*

AUS 259   Hinchinbrook Channel. *V.*

AUS 828   Palm Islands to Brook Island and Palm Passage. *V.*

AUS 829   Brook Island to Russell Island. *V.*

AUS 262   Approaches to Cairns. *V.*

AUS 830   Russell Island to Low Islets. *V.*

AUS 831   Low Islets to Cape Flattery. *V.*

AUS 832   Cape Flattery to Barrow Point. *V.*

AUS 833   Barrow Point to Claremont Isles. *V.*

AUS 834   Claremont Isles to Cape Weymouth. *V.*

AUS 836 Cape Weymouth to Olinda Entrance. *U, unless outer barrier reef route taken from Portland roads to Torres Strait. See section this book, 'Cruising the Outer Barrier'.*

AUS 837 Olinda Entrance to Maer Island. *Ditto above.*

AUS 835 Cape Weymouth to Cairncross Islets. *V.*

AUS 839 Cairncross Islets to Arden Island. *V.*

AUS 292 Adolphus Channel to Harvey Rocks. *U.*

AUS 376 Torres Strait. *V, unless terminating at Thursday Island to return back down the Coral Coast.*

AUS 299 Thursday Island Approaches. *U, if the next chart is carried.*

AUS 293 Prince of Wales Channel. *V.*

AUS 840 Arden Island to Bramble Cay. *V. if navigating the North East Channel (Torres Strait).*

AUS 294 Endeavour Strait. *V if transiting the Torres Strait between Cape York and Thursday Island.*

AUS 296 Goods Island to Proudfoot Shoal. *V if heading west from Thursday Island.*

AUS 700 Western Approaches to Torres Strait. *V.*

AUS 701 Vrilya Point to Duyfken Point. *V if proceeding down the west coast of the Cape York Peninsula.*

AUS 301 Booby Island to Archer River. *V if exploring Gulf of Carpentaria.*

AUS 302 Archer River to Nassau River. *As above.*

AUS 303 Nassau River to Wellesley Islands. *As above.*

AUS 4 Approaches to Port of Weipa. *U.*

Queensland Transport — Harbours and Marine Charts.

The following are available from Harbours and Marine offices, most Sunmap shops and Boat Books, whose addresses are shown later. These charts mostly show protected waterways in large scale and should be considered necessary for the areas they cover.

5. Point Danger to Gold Coast Bridge (Southport).
6. Gold Coast Bridge to Jacobs Well. *(The Broadwater).*
7. Jacobs Well to Coochiemudlo Island. *(Lower Moreton Bay).*
8. Coochiemudlo Island to Wellington Point. *(Lower Moreton Bay).*
1.   Southport to Caloundra.
9. Wellington Point to the Blue Hole. *(Moreton Bay).*
4. Pumicestone Passage. *(Bribie Island).*
2. Lower Brisbane River and approaches. *Includes Manly Boat Harbour.*
3. Upper Brisbane River.

Great Sandy Strait. Two sheets as below, 10 and 11.
10. Double Island Point and Tin Can Bay to Boonlye Point *(Southern Sheet).*
11. Boonlye Point to Hervey Bay *(Northern Sheet).*
12. Gladstone Harbour.
13. The Narrows *(Gladstone).*
14. Johnstone River *(Innisfail).*

Chart Agencies.

Boat Books	Boat Books	Boat Books	Boat Books
31 Albany St	109 Albert St	214 St Kilda Rd	9 Axon Street
Crows Nest	Brisbane	St Kilda	Subiaco
2065 NSW	4000 QLD	Vic. 3182	WA 6008
02 439 1133	07 229 6427	03 525 3444	09 382 2122

Historic wrecks

Under the Historic Shipwrecks Act of 1976, the following wrecks are fully protected and must not be disturbed in any way: *Pandora*, lost 28 August 1791 while returning from Tahiti to England with some of the *Bounty* mutineers: *Mermaid*, wrecked on a reef east of Frankland Island, October 1829. Previously used in survey work by Captain P.P. King: *Morning Star*, lost in Temple Bay, 1813–14: *Gothenburg*, three masted, schooner-rigged steamer struck Old Reef, near Cape Upstart 1875 carrying gold bullion from Pine Creek diggings (Northern Territory). Many passengers and dignitaries were drowned because of their heavy money belts: *Quetta*, British India steamer bound for India from Brisbane struck a rock near Mount Adolphus Island February 1890: *Foam*, blackbirding schooner lost on Myrmidon Reef off Townsville, 1877: *Yongala*, passenger steamer sank in cyclone off Cape Bowling Green, 1911.

Queensland is Born

A part of New South Wales since Captain Cook's naming of the country in 1770, Queensland separated to become a colony in its own right on 10 December, 1859. Sir George Bowen was its first Governor.

Queensland rivers are relatively short and those not in commercial use are unsurveyed on official charts. Many such rivers have been surveyed by the author for this book but the reader is warned against implicit faith in the findings. This scene is in the famous Daintree River.

Tasmania's training ship, *Lady Nelson*, is a replica of the tender and escort vessel which accompanied Captain Matthew Flinders during his circumnavigation of Australia aboard *Investigator*. Fitted with a unique 'sliding keel' which allowed *Lady Nelson* to work in shallow water, she joined in Sydney, July 1802, but was forced back when the keel gave trouble in the vicinity of Shoalwater Bay, north of Yeppoon. She is seen here visiting Rockhampton, July 1993.

Travellers along the Queensland coast may use Postal Restante at any post office as a temporary address. Mail is held for one month after which it is returned to sender unless a redirection order is lodged. This costs (1993) $5.00 per month.

Oil Spill Disaster

With so many tankers flying the flag-of-convenience of a nation whose inspectors are poorly trained, whose crew and officer training standards are low and from where falsified papers are sometimes issued regarding ship safety, a serious oil spill on the Great Barrier Reef is only a matter of time. It is argued, however, that such ships are best allowed along the Inner Route where they can easily come to anchor in the event of breakdown or damage rather than crash onto the windward side of the reefs after a similar mishap in the Coral Sea.

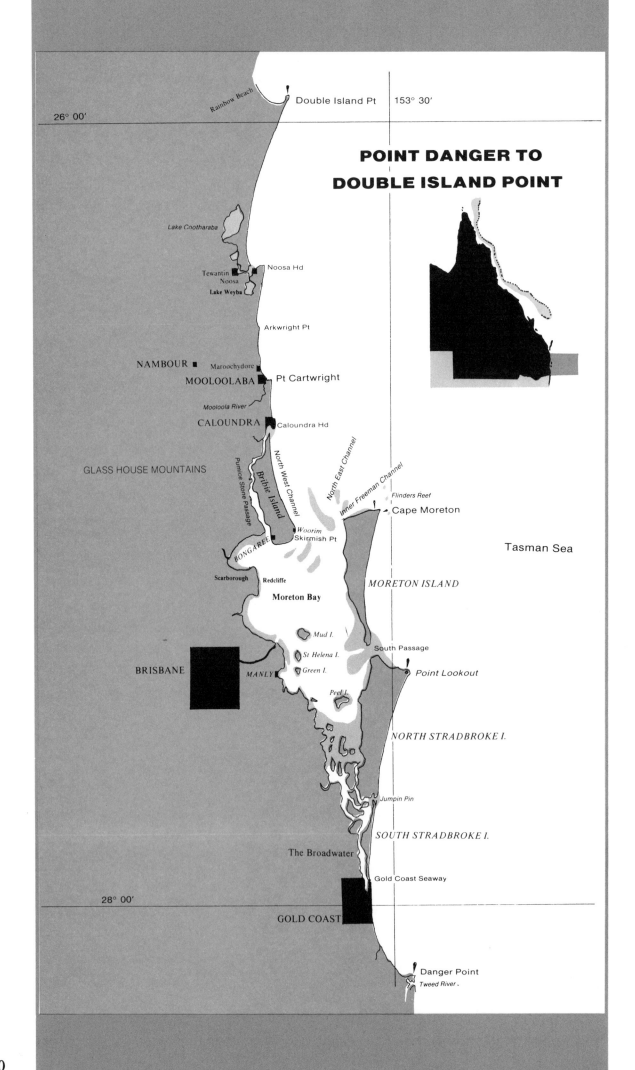

POINT DANGER TO
DOUBLE ISLAND POINT

26° 00'

Rainbow Beach
Double Island Pt   153° 30'

Lake Cootharaba

Noosa Hd
Tewantin
Noosa
Lake Weyba

Arkwright Pt

NAMBOUR ■   Maroochydore
MOOLOOLABA ■   Pt Cartwright

Mooloola River

CALOUNDRA   Caloundra Hd

GLASS HOUSE MOUNTAINS

Pumice Stone Passage

Bribie Island

North West Channel

North East Channel

Inner Freeman Channel

Flinders Reef

Cape Moreton

Woorim
Skirmish Pt

BONGAREE

Tasman Sea

Scarborough   Redcliffe

MORETON ISLAND

Moreton Bay

Mud I.

St Helena I.   South Passage

Green I.   Point Lookout

BRISBANE   *MANLY*

Peel I.

NORTH STRADBROKE I.

Jumpin Pin

SOUTH STRADBROKE I.

The Broadwater

Gold Coast Seaway

28° 00'

GOLD COAST

Danger Point
Tweed River

20

THE COAST

POINT DANGER TO DOUBLE ISLAND POINT. Point Danger boasts a major light supported by flying buttresses and a sign showing New South Wales on one side and Queensland on the other. It is right on the border between these two states where it overlooks New South Wales' most northern river, the Tweed, and Queensland's most developed stretch of coast, the Gold Coast. This development extends up to Paradise Point becoming most intense in the Surfers Paradise area where well over one hundred highrise buildings will be counted.

The Tweed River breakwaters have been blamed for the serious beach erosion experienced by the Gold Coast. Built in the late 1950s early 1960s, it is said that they prevent the migration of sand around Point Danger. That they should *share* the blame, there can be little doubt, but other factors have been conveniently forgotten. These include the acknowledged failure of the Coolangatta region's groynes and the fact that early Gold Coast developers destroyed the sand dunes in their quest to hug the beach. The whole region, as a result, lives in fear of the next cyclone which could remove the entire beach, as has happened in the past.

Beyond the Gold Coast are the relatively uninhabited sand islands of South and North Stradbroke and Moreton Island, the latter protecting Moreton Bay into which runs the Brisbane River after circling through Queensland's capital city of Brisbane.

From Brisbane north — or, more correctly, from Bribie Island north — developmentmania recommences on the stretch known as the 'Sunshine Coast' which includes Caloundra, Mooloolaba and Noosa. These three centres have the rather extraordinary backdrop of the Glasshouse Mountains whose extinct volcanic cores stand as mute testimony to a much larger mountain range in the distant past. Mooloolaba itself is the most developed area with high-rise apartments making a pincushion of the land between Point Cartwright and Maroochydore. From Noosa to Double Island Point nature exerts herself and displays an endless beach backed by coloured dunes capped by well-wooded hills.

Despite the pressures of tourism and urban expansion along this part of the Queensland coast, much natural beauty remains including the sand dunes of the Moreton and Noosa areas, the waterways of the lower Moreton Bay and the wonderful hinterlands behind Surfers Paradise and Southport.

Subject to certain qualifications included in their separate descriptions, Southport and Mooloolaba are available to deep keelers regardless of weather and Brisbane admits ships of all drafts and tonnages. The Broadwater and Moreton Bay offer dozens of marinas, anchorages and expanses of water large enough to navigate without too much anxiety. But groundings are par for the course and constant vigilance is necessary, a fact that can rob a day's sail of some of its pleasure.

Often misunderstood by first-time visitors is the fact that the Great Barrier Reef does *not* start at the border between New South Wales and Queensland. It starts hundreds of miles north off Gladstone, a fact that makes the southern coast of Queensland safe for overnight navigation. Landfalling is free of offshore hazards from the border north to Sandy Cape.

The weather along this stretch of coast is dominantly from the south-east although it can disappear for weeks on end during winter when offshore winds or calms take over. During summer, onshore-offshore breezes occur, the former being just a whisper from the south to west, the latter starting towards midday and increasing towards evening after which they rapidly die. Their direction can be north-east, but is more often east to south-east.

The Brisbane area is famous for its flash storms which bring heavy rain and lightning and sometimes destructive winds that last just an hour or two. They seem most prevalent in the spring and autumn but can occur at any time, advertising themselves by a massive cloud build-up, a fact that is sometimes lost on yachtspeople in the Brisbane River from where city highrise deny a sighting.

Being so heavily populated, the south-east corner of Queensland provides for all the boat persons' needs. It is consequently the logical place to prepare and victual the boat for her cruise north to the true Coral Coast. However, those anxious to move on will find most services duplicated in the north.

Now with an Air Sea Rescue station beneath it, the modernistic Point Danger light tower stands on the New South Wales-Queensland border. From 1971 to 1973 it had an experimental laser light, the first of its type in the world.

Brisbane thunderstorms

Darwin experiences more thunderstorms per year than any other part of Australia. Brisbane, however, has more than her fair share. On 18 January, 1985, a thunderstorm caused wind and hail damage to Brisbane suburbs totalling $180 million and produced the highest wind speed ever recorded in the area. It topped 100 knots at Brisbane Airport.

Sailing in the Great Sandy Strait, Fraser Island background. To fully explore this region, the shoal draft 'Waterwitch' is an ideal craft.

Anchor down off Lady Elliot Island. This tiny cay supports a light and resort and is the first of the Great Barrier Reef chain when sailing north. It is a very poor anchorage.

DOUBLE ISLAND POINT TO RODD PENINSULA. This is a particularly interesting section of the coast because it includes the world's biggest sand island, Fraser Island, and the beginning of the world's longest coral chain, the Great Barrier Reef. The former starts at Wide Bay and ends at Sandy Cape while the latter starts at Lady Elliot Island and continues on up to Papua New Guinea.

A series of low hills hold the coast close up to Double Island Point and then recede inland being replaced by the marginally lower sandhills of Fraser Island which rise to a maximum of about 210 metres. These hills are, in the main, densely wooded and, indeed, still carry some fine stands of hardwoods despite being logged constantly until the early 1990s.

As outlined in its own description later, there are a number of small settlements along the seventy-nautical-mile ocean beach whose lights will be seen at night. During the day, four-wheel drive traffic will often be noted on the beach itself, this form of recreational driving being very popular in the region north from Noosa.

Between Fraser Island and the mainland is the famous Great Sandy Strait offering calm-water passage from Wide Bay to Hervey Bay plus access to the city of Maryborough up the Mary River which enters the strait approximately one third the length of the island from its southern tip. Also of interest to the sailor is the south-tending spur, Tin Can Inlet, which gives access to the popular harbour of Tin Can Bay, also known as Snapper Creek.

Projecting 17 miles north from Sandy Cape is the Breaksea Spit whose composition of sand and dead coral might justify a claim as being the true beginning of the Great Barrier Reef. Certainly the danger is no less and all boats are obliged to go around, not through; although certain fair-weather, local-knowledge passages do exist.

Behind this spit and the northern part of Fraser Island is huge Hervey Bay whose shores all around are low and often featureless. At the bottom are the seaside towns of Pialba, Torquay, Scarness and Urangan — collectively known as the City of Hervey Bay — and at the top on the mainland is the Burnett River which provides easy access to the major city of Bundaberg. Burrum River, between the two, is a useful port of refuge in fair weather and suitable tides.

The land on the western side of Hervey Bay, being delta country to so many rivers and creeks, is low with just a scattering of hills in the background. Not until north of Bundaberg do the hills return to the coast and provide a more interesting backdrop with navigational reference points. Round Hill, at 289 metres, is such a reference point and indicates the area where Round Hill Creek and the town of 1770 will be found.

To the north-west of Round Hill Creek is Pancake Creek behind Bustard Head where deeper water is found and all-tide entry is possible. This is also where the hills better deserve the description of mountains as they circle westward to embrace Gladstone Harbour (Port Curtis).

Navigationally, there are few special dangers on this chart apart from the obvious need to exercise care when amidst coral reefs. Those holding the seaward side of Fraser Island close when working north and hoping to avoid the south-setting East Coast Current are warned that this is not always fruitful and could become subject to areas where, it is said, the current sets on to the beach. This is unproved, but it certainly seems a fact that a reverse current will not always be found against the beach. In fact, it is equally true that the actual East Australian Current is often absent regardless of distance off this coast.

The most predictable currents on this chart are those setting across Breaksea Spit. It is dangerous to underestimate their strength which easily reach 2.5 knots in places and will cause a heavy break against an easterly swell. The current floods westward and ebbs eastward dissipating into and out of Hervey Bay so that very little effect is experienced anywhere within the bay.

Extending north-west from Fraser Island, and overlapping the Curtis region, are the two reef groups, Bunker and Capricorn. Many of these reefs support delightful cays and two form perfect lagoons accessible by displacement craft. These are Lady Musgrave Island, 21 miles north-west of Lady Elliot, and Fitzroy Reef, a similar distance further on in the same direction. Musgrave supports a cay, Fitzroy does not, its only protuberance above water being its reef at low tide.

Tourist resorts are based on both Lady Elliot and Heron Island, the latter also supporting a marine biology research station. Further north on the chart is North Reef whose 19-mile light advertises the south-east side of the Capricorn

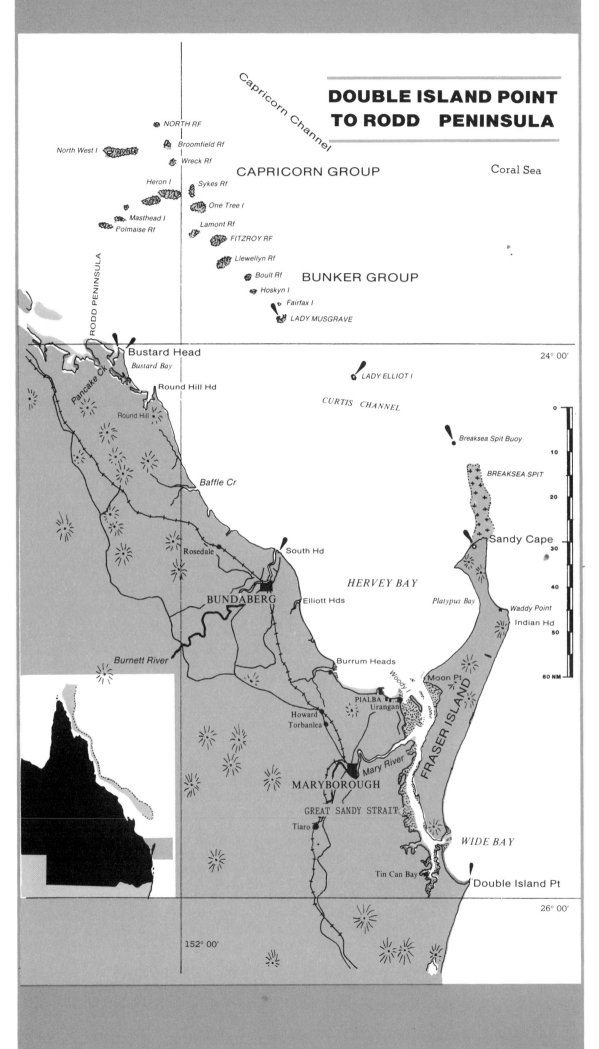

DOUBLE ISLAND POINT TO RODD PENINSULA

Capricorn Channel

NORTH RF

North West I

Broomfield Rf

Wreck Rf

CAPRICORN GROUP

Coral Sea

Heron I

Sykes Rf

One Tree I

Masthead I

Lamont Rf

Polmaise Rf

FITZROY RF

RODD PENINSULA

Llewellyn Rf

Boult Rf

BUNKER GROUP

Hoskyn I

Fairfax I

LADY MUSGRAVE

Bustard Head

24° 00'

Bustard Bay

LADY ELLIOT I

Pancake Ck

Round Hill Hd

CURTIS CHANNEL

Round Hill

Breaksea Spit Buoy

10

Baffle Cr

BREAKSEA SPIT

20

Sandy Cape

30

Rosedale

South Hd

HERVEY BAY

40

BUNDABERG

Elliott Hds

Platypus Bay

Waddy Point

Indian Hd

50

Burnett River

Burrum Heads

Woody I

Moon Pt

60 NM

PIALBA

Urangan

Howard

Torbanlea

Mary River

FRASER ISLAND

MARYBOROUGH

GREAT SANDY STRAIT

Tiaro

WIDE BAY

Tin Can Bay

Double Island Pt

26° 00'

152° 00'

Channel which gives deep-water entry into the inner passage between the Capricorn Group and the Swain reefs. This light is now automatic, but once enjoyed the distinction of being Queensland's only bachelor light, men-only living on the job.

While most coastal anchorages on this section of the coast are tranquil and secure, the reef anchorages are amongst the least secure on the entire coast. None form a good crescent shape to windward and 'to windward' can mean a number of things at different times of year. The prevalent wind is the south-easterly but the westerlies and south-westerlies of the border regions readily affect the coast this far north. As a result, in winds other than developed south-easterlies, one seldom feels secure unless in either of the two lagoons mentioned above and even these can be quite uncomfortable at high tide and, like all reef anchorages, they carry the awesome threat of reef to leeward should the anchor drag.

Those not anxious to see coral in favour of security can day-hop easily enough by anchoring just about anywhere in the Great Sandy Strait, in the Burnett River and in Pancake Creek behind Bustard Head.

RODD PENINSULA TO SCAWFELL ISLAND. The longest navigable
river and the most industrialised town north of Brisbane are located on this section of the coast. They are the Fitzroy River and the Port of Gladstone respectively. Rockhampton, on the Fitzroy River, is famous as a cattle centre while Gladstone has the less enviable reputation of being a producer of pollutants as its huge powerhouse and aluminium smelter pour toxins into the atmosphere around the clock. These, together with coal and other bulk products being shipped out of the port, have given it a healthy economy and an attraction for employment seekers.

In contrast to a muddy river and a muggy atmosphere is Keppel Bay where some of the clearest water on the coast is to be found lapping a very beautiful, beach-fronted coastline. And the mountain chain close behind the beaches enhances the scene while offering some excellent navigational fixes. Of these there is none so useful or conspicuous as Mount Larcom rising some 627 metres a few miles west of Gladstone.

Of the anchorages, Port Clinton and Island Head Creek are unbeatable in both security, isolation and magnificent sandy beaches. Of the two, Island Head Creek is the favourite, its shoreline being less restricted by the Australian Army who regularly play war games on this stretch of coast.

Arguably the prettiest anchorage on the entire coast, Pearl Bay, to the south of Island Head Creek, is a delightful combination of mountains, sand and sea and is well worth visiting.

North and west of this area, the land fragments into two huge bays, Shoalwater Bay and Broad Sound. These are dealt with in detail in this book but cannot be recommended to the less than adventurous, their tides being the highest on the coast with currents amongst the swiftest. A distinct lack of secure anchorages offers further discouragement.

To their north, however, the Percy Isles promise a superior alternative, although it must be admitted, the anchorages do not encourage onboard brain surgery. They do, however, encourage bushwalking, fishing and swimming over superb sand bottom with minimum interference from fringing reefs. Scawfell Island is often used as an ideal interim anchorage en route to the Whitsundays for those preferring to avoid the crowded conditions of Mackay Outer Harbour.

On this chart we see part of the Swain Reefs. These are not thoroughly charted and therefore cannot be recommended to anyone but fishermen with local knowledge or adventurers aware of the dangers. Two more factors go towards discouraging reef exploration here. These are the height of tides which, during springs, allow a formidable sea over the reefs and thus turn otherwise comfortable anchorages into a misery, and their distance offshore denies good navigational fixes when seeking return-course reference.

In contrast to moving amongst reefs, passage along the coast is straightforward enough, the many headlands, islands and rocks displaying well and offering good bearings. Between Island Head Creek and the Percy Isles, cross-currents should be allowed for or, where not known, checked for regularly. This is especially true during spring tides when their extreme range is manifest in their maximum velocity. Tides in the Percy Isles can climb to seven metres while those in Broad Sound reach nine metres. As stated, these are the highest on the entire east coast and second only to the Darwin area for the whole of Australia.

Port Alma pilot station, on Sea Hill Point was disbanded in the early 1960's. The houses are still there as is this dinghy slip and jetty. The delta area of Rockhampton's Fitzroy River is in the distant background.

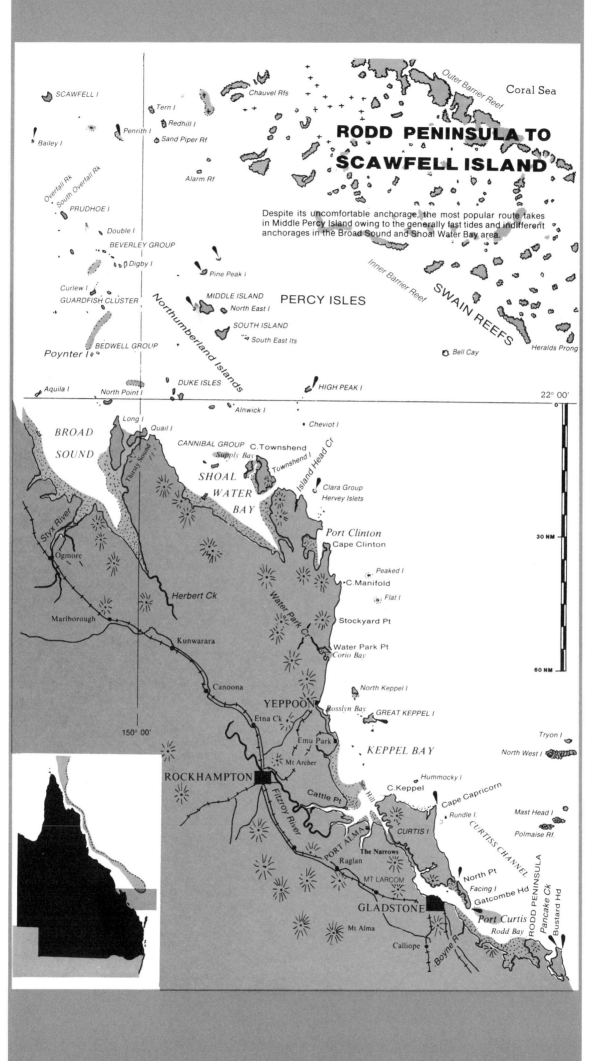

RODD PENINSULA TO SCAWFELL ISLAND

Despite its uncomfortable anchorage, the most popular route takes in Middle Percy Island owing to the generally fast tides and indifferent anchorages in the Broad Sound and Shoal Water Bay area.

Coral Sea

Outer Barrier Reef

SCAWFELL I

Bailey I

Tern I

Penrith I

Redhill I

Sand Piper Rf

Chauvel Rfs

Alarm Rf

Overfall Rk

South Overfall Rk

PRUDHOE I

Double I

BEVERLEY GROUP

Digby I

Curlew I

GUARDFISH CLUSTER

Pine Peak I

MIDDLE ISLAND

North East I

PERCY ISLES

SOUTH ISLAND

South East Its

Inner Barrier Reef

SWAIN REEFS

Bell Cay

Heralds Prong

Poynter I

BEDWELL GROUP

Northumberland Islands

Aquila I

North Point I

DUKE ISLES

HIGH PEAK I

Alnwick I

22° 00'

Long I

Quail I

Cheviot I

BROAD SOUND

Thirsty Sound

CANNIBAL GROUP

Supply Bay

C.Townshend

Townshend

Island Head Cr

SHOAL WATER BAY

Clara Group

Hervey Islets

Port Clinton

Cape Clinton

Styx River

Ogmore

Peaked I

C.Manifold

Flat I

30 NM

Herbert Ck

Water Park Cr

Stockyard Pt

Marlborough

Kunwarara

Water Park Pt

Corio Bay

150° 00'

Canoona

North Keppel I

60 NM

YEPPOON

Etna Ck

Rosslyn Bay

GREAT KEPPEL I

Emu Park

KEPPEL BAY

Tryon I

Mt Archer

North West I

ROCKHAMPTON

Cattle Pt

Hummocky I

C.Keppel

Cape Capricorn

Fitzroy River

Hill

Rundle I.

Mast Head I

Polmaise Rf.

CURTIS I

CURTISS CHANNEL

PORT ALMA

The Narrows

Raglan

MT LARCOM

North Pt

Facing I

Gatcombe Hd

GLADSTONE

Port Curtis

RODD PENINSULA

Pancake Ck

Bustard Hd

Mt Alma

Rodd Bay

Calliope

Boyne R.

25

The Pioneer River, Mackay, almost dries at low tide. It is seen here from the fish wharf, upstream to the road bridge.

The Whitsunday Wrecker

The small, but intense cyclone *Ada* devastated several holiday resorts throughout the Whitsundays during January, 1970. With a central pressure of 962 hPa, it sank several vessels with a loss of 13 lives. Hayman Island guests were taken off by a cargo ship and dropped in Townsville.

BROAD SOUND TO CAPE UPSTART. Scawfell Island, north-east from Mackay, is the overlap reference between this and the previous chart.

The coast is riddled with creeks and small rivers, none of which gives access at low tide and many of which deny float-holes within. The Pioneer River, passing through the City of Mackay, is a fine example, promising, as it does, easy access to the city's doorstep and plenty of space to anchor but denying the exercise by its almost dry state at low tide and two-metre-high banks around its entrance. However, local boat people, with their mud berths or alongside-jetties, make such waterways their permanent base, using high tide to exit and enter. The visitor can sometimes get lucky in this respect, but must never sail in on the assumption that a berth will be available nor that a float-hole will be found for a low-tide stay.

Tides are at their extreme between Broad Sound and Mackay, reaching a potential spring height of 8.5 metres in the former and 6 metres at the latter. They rapidly diminish towards the Whitsunday Islands where heights are as low as 50% Mackay data. But, regardless of the venue on this stretch of the coast, the person unaccustomed to extreme tidal range and strong currents should navigate and anchor with care.

The best-known cruising ground on the entire east coast of Australia is here. This is the Whitsunday Group which is part of the Cumberland Islands. From humble beginnings as pastoral properties, many of the islands developed into tourist resorts from the 1930s onwards. In the later 1980s many resorts ceased their gradual expansion to be torn down and completely rebuilt, some with a view towards the millionaire — if overnight accommodation costing as high as $1500 is any yardstick.

Airlie has always been the mainland base from where tourists reach the islands. Originally by boat, there are now helicopter and jetliner alternatives and most of the pretty, wooden mono-hulled launches have been scrapped in favour of big aluminium catamarans. These operate from the jetties in Shute Harbour with Pioneer Bay (Airlie) proving the most popular stopover for transient yachts and a large sector of the local bare-boat charter fleet.

Reef cruising off this section of the coast cannot be recommended during spring tides and strong winds. The extreme tidal range and its consequent strong currents, plus the excessive depths under the lee of most reefs, make it an unpleasant and sometimes very worrying pastime. Best to wait for neap tides and light weather or, if travelling further north, to save it for the reefs north of Cairns.

The mainland between Sarina and Proserpine is very pretty with hills and valleys and thousands of hectares of sugarcane. Beaches run between most headlands, but a few present difficulties for swimmers at low tide, and during strong onshore weather (especially from the south-east) the water can become unpleasantly murky where mud is stirred at the spring low tide level.

Winds remain dominantly south-east, potentially blowing almost continuously from April through September but often giving their worst during May and again in August with long, pleasant spells of calms and variables between. The westerly influence often reaches this far north giving periods of developed south-west to north-west winds. Much depends on factors such as the El Nino affecting the Pacific's weather as a whole. Consideration should be given to these contrary winds in the absence of a developed south-easterly.

Because a reliable northerly wind blows down the coast during October-November (sometimes November-December), yachts terminating a northern cruise at the Whitsundays should make south no later than November with a willingness to seek anchorage should the south-easterly return for a few days.

Being part of the central coast of Queensland, the Whitsunday area is particularly prone to cyclonic disturbance between December through March suggesting that the area be abandoned or secured by the end of the year. Unfortunately, there are very few suitable cyclone holes except drying creeks and rivers, the very exposed and nearly always crowded breakwater harbour at Mackay or the marinas at Airlie and Hamilton Island. Bowen is undoubtedly the best haven but is also very crowded and likely to turn you away if you do not have an advance booking with the port authority.

The economy minded are advised to fuel and victual at Mackay or Bowen before entering the Whitsundays. There, everything is holiday priced and not necessarily comprehensive or even physically easy to obtain.

Sunset in Port Clinton. Despite its name, this is a non-commercial, isolated area, although with the threat of sand mining hanging over its head, that might change.

The extraordinary Glass House Mountains were named by Captain Cook for the way in which they glinted in the sun. They are between Brisbane and Mooloolaba.

Renee Tighe in Cooktown. This lovely anchorage can pose a few problems during spring tides, strong trades and too many boats.

Townsville is the Coral Coast's largest coastal town outside of Brisbane. Too crowded for anchoring, marinas or public pile berths are mandatory when sailing into here. Her famous landmark, Castle Hill, is behind.

The anchorage off Airlie Beach is often crowded, but there is always room for more.

Bruce Arthur has a tapestry workshop in Dunk Island. Visitors are welcome on open days.

Hinchinbrook Channel is the Coral Coast's finest waterway with its miles of navigable channels, deep creeks and splendid mountain backdrop.

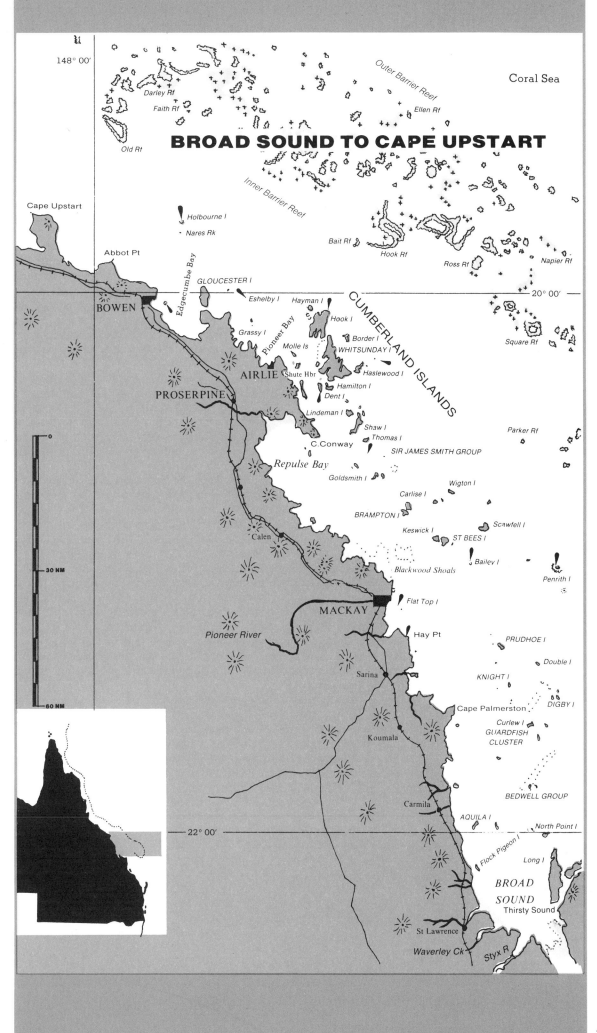

BROAD SOUND TO CAPE UPSTART

Coral Sea

Outer Barrier Reef

Darley Rf

Faith Rf

Ellen Rf

Old Rf

Inner Barrier Reef

Cape Upstart

Holbourne I

Nares Rk

Bait Rf

Hook Rf

Ross Rf

Napier Rf

20° 00'

Abbot Pt

Edgecumbe Bay

GLOUCESTER I

Eshelby I

Hayman I

CUMBERLAND ISLANDS

BOWEN

Grassy I

Pioneer Bay

Hook I

Square Rf

Molle Is

Border I

WHITSUNDAY I

AIRLIE

Shute Hbr

Haslewood I

PROSERPINE

Hamilton I

Dent I

Lindeman I

Parker Rf

C.Conway

Shaw I

Thomas I

SIR JAMES SMITH GROUP

Repulse Bay

Goldsmith I

Wigton I

Carlise I

BRAMPTON I

Keswick I

Scawfell I

ST BEES I

Calen

Bailey I

Blackwood Shoals

Penrith I

Flat Top I

MACKAY

Hay Pt

PRUDHOE I

Pioneer River

Double I

Sarina

KNIGHT I

DIGBY I

Cape Palmerston

Curlew I

GUARDFISH

Koumala

CLUSTER

BEDWELL GROUP

Carmila

AQUILA I

North Point I

22° 00'

Flock Pigeon I

Long I

BROAD

SOUND

Thirsty Sound

St Lawrence

Waverley Ck

Styx R

148° 00'

0

30 NM

60 NM

27

CAPE UPSTART TO CAIRNS.

Leaving the drowned tail of the coastal range behind (the Whitsunday Islands), the mountains trend inland, around the deltas of Bowen's Don River, Home Hill and Ayr's Burdekin River and Townsville's Ross River. They leave substantial reminders of their presence in the form of Mount Abbot (west of Bowen, off this chart) and Upstart (mountain) whose dramatic island-like appearance prompted its naming by Captain Cook.

Upstart Bay provides a collection of anchorages as well as relative protection from onshore weather to the Burdekin River delta whose surrounding land is low and featureless and remains that way all the way to Cape Bowling Green, itself low and featureless and in this sense unique on the coast. Indeed, so low and unstable is Cape Bowling Green that its early lighthouse was moved back in the 1950s to prevent it slipping into the sea. That lighthouse has since been replaced with a rather uninteresting open frame type, the original becoming the subject of controversy as to who should retain it for historical purposes.

The mountains wandering well inland from Townsville rob that bustling city and environs of useful falls of rain leaving it perpetually dry and dusty. But they return with a vengeance in the Hinchinbrook-Cairns coastal stretch creating precipitation of occasionally excessive proportions. Tully, enjoying the effect of the steep, high mountains of Hinchinbrook to windward, has one of Australia's highest annual rainfalls while Cairns, similarly lying to leeward of Mount Bartle Frere, boasts rich, tropical hinterlands. Mount Bartle Frere, incidentally, is Queensland's highest mountain at just over 1600 metres and was proclaimed a national park in 1991.

Reaping the benefit of what is literally windfall rain, the Family Group of islands, immediately north of Hinchinbrook, are the Coral Coast's most tropical, seldom failing to satisfy those who feel other islands fall short in their bid for tropical beauty. Not immediately apparent on approach are their dense rainforest jungles and stunning undergrowth. The reefs off this section of the coast are, as always, coral masses offering numerous anchoring and fishing opportunities.

Townsville has been a major fishing centre since its inception, mackerel boats dominating the fleet until the late 1960s when prawn trawlers moved in to enjoy the grounds offshore and the facilities in town. And while the area offers little of a unique nature in either of these pursuits, it seems true that the best catches of doggy mackerel are to be had in Halifax Bay while the mangrove creeks of Bowling Green Bay and Cleveland yield some of the finest mud crabs.

The weather in this area is dominated by the Tasman high-pressure system whose ridge along the Queensland coast brings prevailing south-east trade winds. However, it is the northern extreme of a good and very useful northerly stream during October through November (sometimes through December and often starting late October). It can also be subject to calms, light offshore-onshore variables and even northerlies when the winter trade wind fails for any reason. Regardless of the potential variations, it can be said that *developed* winds will be from the south-east from May through September, northerlies October through November and south-easterlies again during the December through April transition and wet season.

The wet season is also the cyclone season when destructive winds can strike any part of the Queensland coast. They are most likely to occur from mid December through to mid March but can strike earlier or later. The best places to hide when a cyclone is imminent on this stretch of coast is in one of the creeks at the bottom of Upstart Bay (subject to tide to enter), one of the creeks in Hinchinbrook Channel, the Moresby River in Mourilyan Harbour and Trinity Inlet, Cairns. The Johnstone River at Innisfail would be okay against the piles but swing anchoring is doubtful owing to the poor holding.

This bridge carries the Bruce Highway across the Burdekin River between the sugar towns of Ayr and Home Hill.

Lucinda's bulk sugar jetty projects over five kilometres offshore from the southern entrance to Hinchinbrook Channel. Pelorus Island, the most northerly of the Palm Isles, is distant right.

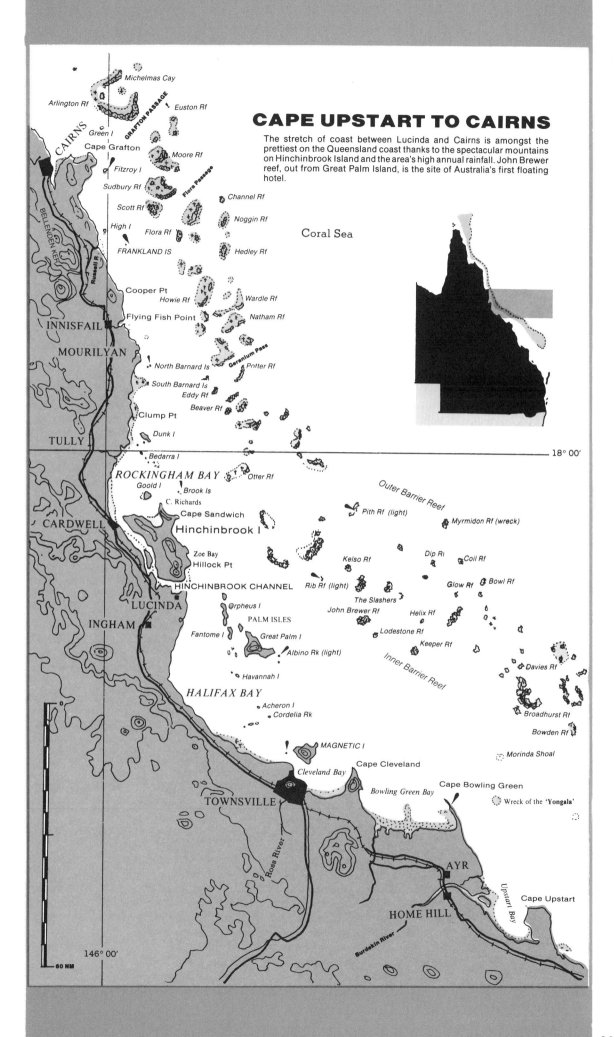

CAPE UPSTART TO CAIRNS

The stretch of coast between Lucinda and Cairns is amongst the prettiest on the Queensland coast thanks to the spectacular mountains on Hinchinbrook Island and the area's high annual rainfall. John Brewer reef, out from Great Palm Island, is the site of Australia's first floating hotel.

Coral Sea

Michelmas Cay
Arlington Rf
Euston Rf
GRAFTON PASSAGE
Green I
CAIRNS
Cape Grafton
Moore Rf
Fitzroy I
Sudbury Rf
Flora Passage
Scott Rf
Channel Rf
High I
Noggin Rf
Flora Rf
FRANKLAND IS
Hedley Rf
BELLENDEN KER
Russell R
INNISFAIL
Cooper Pt
Howie Rf
Wardle Rf
MOURILYAN
Flying Fish Point
Natham Rf
North Barnard Is
Geranium Pass
Potter Rf
South Barnard Is
Eddy Rf
Beaver Rf
TULLY
Clump Pt
Dunk I
Bedarra I
18° 00'
ROCKINGHAM BAY
Otter Rf
Goold I
Brook Is
C. Richards
Outer Barrier Reef
Pith Rf (light)
Myrmidon Rf (wreck)
CARDWELL
Cape Sandwich
Hinchinbrook I
Zoe Bay
Dip Rf
Coil Rf
Hillock Pt
Kelso Rf
HINCHINBROOK CHANNEL
Rib Rf (light)
Glow Rf
Bowl Rf
The Slashers
LUCINDA
Orpheus I
John Brewer Rf
Helix Rf
INGHAM
PALM ISLES
Lodestone Rf
Fantome I
Great Palm I
Keeper Rf
Albino Rk (light)
Inner Barrier Reef
Davies Rf
Havannah I
HALIFAX BAY
Acheron I
Cordelia Rk
Broadhurst Rf
Bowden Rf
Morinda Shoal
MAGNETIC I
Cape Cleveland
Cleveland Bay
Cape Bowling Green
Bowling Green Bay
Wreck of the 'Yongala'
TOWNSVILLE
Ross River
AYR
Upstart Bay
Cape Upstart
HOME HILL
Burdekin River
146° 00'
60 NM

29

Cairns is the last place on the coast heading north offering a full, comprehensive range of boat services. This scene is at the Cairns Cruising Yacht Squadron's marina.

When this beautiful *Endeavour* replica is launched in Fremantle, it may be based on the east coast. The original ship was repaired in Cooktown after hitting Endeavour Reef.

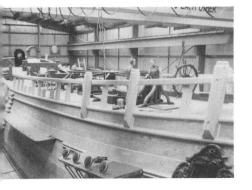

CAIRNS TO PRINCESS CHARLOTTE BAY.

The coast from Cairns to Cooktown — or at least to Weary Bay — rivals some of the world's great tropical beauty spots such as the Marquesas of the Central Pacific and the Grenadines of the West Indies. Here, mountains come right to the sea bringing their rainforests close enough for the sailor to see and to incite such conflict between developers and environmentalists that one is never certain which way the pendulum will swing. Already we see real estate signs advertising 'rainforest blocks' and the ugly scars of roads being pushed through to provide more rapid access. The long-awaited coastal road from Cape Tribulation to Cooktown has been completed with all that that implies.

After its intimate flirtation with the coast, the Great Dividing Range dives inland immediately north of Cooktown where it collapses into a series of hills as it circles the great delta plains of Princess Charlotte Bay. The coast maintains a useful range of conspicuous headlands and hills but what it lacks in lofty grandeur it more than compensates for with a line of sandhills that appear all the way to the tip of Cape York.

These sandhills are first evident out towards Cape Bedford where their colour remains a fairly standard yellow. But from within the bay, stretching to Cape Flattery, the sand whitens to become salt-like in its appearance. This is the famous silica sand zone of Cape York Peninsula where thousands of hectares blind the onlooker and tempt the miner. Indeed, the miner has long since succumbed to the temptation of the Cape Flattery area now in its third decade of active strip-mining.

Unique on the entire east coast of Australia is Cape Melville, the culmination of a string of hills comprised entirely of massive, smooth blocks of stone. There are many theories as to their origin, one being that they are an ice-age hangover, perhaps the rubble left by a glacier whose activity rounded and smoothed the blocks and left them tumbled on top of each other. Black Mountain, near Helensvale south of Cooktown, is a similar mass and why they should be separated by a gap of well over 100 miles is a mystery.

Continental islands all but disappear from here north, giving way to coral cays whose type changes from cays standing isolated on their host reef to sand cays whose identity is all but hidden by mangrove forest extending over the entire reef. Low Islet, off Port Douglas, is the first displaying, as it does, an isolated sand-surrounded cay as well as a large mangrove forest on the same reef, but with the two entities well separated. Further north they become integrated so that the cay's beach is only seen from the west and north, the remainder being hidden by its extensive mangroves. Exactly why this change occurs is uncertain but is probably due to the cay being closer to the mainland's mangrove forests plus the more silted waters offering better breeding grounds.

Contradicting any suggestion of greater silting of these shallower and more confined waters is the wonderfully clear water around Lizard Island, offshore from Lookout Point and 50 miles north of Cooktown. There, not only is anchorage secure and comfortable but the water invites regular swimming and diving.

Navigationally, coral reefs become more threatening because of the greater numbers closer to the mainland. The inner route is inevitably more restricted. Compensating, however, are the more numerous light beacons, radar beacons and, from the small boat's point of view, the fact that there really is plenty of room. Only when a large ship is met in an especially confined channel does one question the last statement; especially at night.

Night-time navigation is by choice, not necessity. However, the choice can become more pressing on the coast north from Princess Charlotte Bay where many folk opt for allnighters instead of rolly anchorages. Meanwhile, on this section of the coast, there are many excellent anchorages, Lizard Island, as stated, being supreme.

It will be noted that the reefs are not only closer to the mainland but they are far more orderly, following each other like a line of obedient caterpillars. The fact that this occurs in the belt of most reliable and persistent trade winds suggests that the winds are in some way responsible. Certainly winds shape coastlines so it is reasonable to presume the reefs would follow suit, especially as they sit squarely on the edge of the continental shelf.

Whatever the cause, the fact is they present a more continuous barrier which acts like a breakwater giving the coast from here to the tip of Cape York an almost swell-free environment. Waves are the product of an existing wind and, as such, collapse very quickly to become flat calm soon after a wind desists.

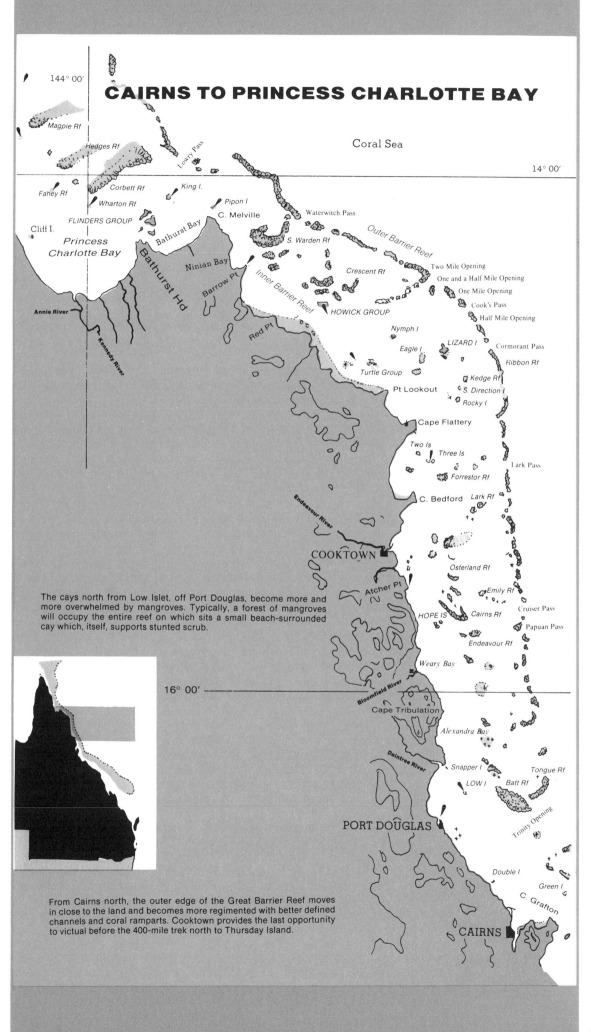

CAIRNS TO PRINCESS CHARLOTTE BAY

144° 00'

Coral Sea

14° 00'

Magpie Rf

Hedges Rf

Lowry Pass

Fahey Rf   *Corbett Rf*   *King I.*

Wharton Rf

Pipon I

FLINDERS GROUP

C. Melville

Waterwitch Pass

Outer Barrier Reef

Cliff I.

Bathurst Bay

S. Warden Rf

**Princess
Charlotte Bay**

Bathurst Hd

Ninian Bay

Crescent Rf

Two Mile Opening

One and a Half Mile Opening

Barrow Pt

Inner Barrier Reef

One Mile Opening

Annie River

Red Pt

HOWICK GROUP

Cook's Pass

Half Mile Opening

Kennedy River

Nymph I

LIZARD I

Cormorant Pass

Eagle I

Hibbon Rf

Turtle Group

Kedge Rf

Pt Lookout

S. Direction I

Rocky I

Cape Flattery

Two Is

Three Is

Lark Pass

Forrestor Rf

C. Bedford

Lark Rf

The cays north from Low Islet, off Port Douglas, become more and more overwhelmed by mangroves. Typically, a forest of mangroves will occupy the entire reef on which sits a small beach-surrounded cay which, itself, supports stunted scrub.

Endeavour River

COOKTOWN

Osterland Rf

Atcher Pt

Emily Rf

Cruiser Pass

HOPE IS

Cairns Rf

Papuan Pass

Endeavour Rf

Weary Bay

16° 00'

Bloomfield River

Cape Tribulation

Alexandra Bay

Daintree River

Snapper I

Tongue Rf

LOW I

Batt Rf

PORT DOUGLAS

Trinity Opening

Double I

Green I

C. Grafton

From Cairns north, the outer edge of the Great Barrier Reef moves in close to the land and becomes more regimented with better defined channels and coral ramparts. Cooktown provides the last opportunity to victual before the 400-mile trek north to Thursday Island.

CAIRNS

'The pearlers lost in the dreadful hurricane on 5th March, 1899' reads the first three lines on this monument on Cape Melville. 50 vessels and over 300 people perished.

Regrettably for those going south at the wrong time of year, the wind rarely desists from 16° south latitude to 5° south latitude from April through October. The south-east trade wind howls continuously, day and night, week after week with respites of only a few days or more. Then it will either fall calm or become variable and be useful only to a motor vessel.

The area between Cairns and Cooktown can be very much one of weather indecision, an unknown quantity at certain times of year. It tends to be the line of demarcation between the October through November northerlies from there south and the south-easterlies that persist from there north. In fact, when the northerlies are well developed they may extend right up to Princess Charlotte Bay but mostly they register as calms and variables with late afternoon north-easterlies up to the Torres Strait. If the northerlies are poorly developed, the area north of Cairns or Cooktown (depending on the exact border of the period) will experience light trade winds and a few more calms than normal.

The most disappointing period is the wet season. So many sailors presume that sailing south will be easy by awaiting the north-westerlies of January-February that are supposed to come with the wet season in the north. In fact, the north-westerlies rarely extend below Princess Charlotte Bay — and mostly stop much further north, the area south experiencing calms or very wet south-easterlies.

Balancing probabilities against uncertainties, it can be said that the south-east trade wind will prevail on this part of the coast for all of winter, much of summer and may or may not give way to northerlies at other times. It will, however, give way to plenty of calms from late October through March. It is also a certainty that the most prevalent time for cyclone disturbance is the wet season between mid December and mid March.

The best cyclone 'holes' on this part of the coast are: well upstream in Cairns Harbour, the upper reaches of Port Douglas's creek, the Daintree River, the Bloomfield River (subject to tide height when entering), Cooktown against the mangroves well upstream from the river entrance and the Kennedy or Annie River in Princess Charlotte Bay. A non-destructive cyclone could be ridden in Owen Channel, the Flinders Group.

PRINCESS CHARLOTTE BAY TO BUSHY ISLET. Princess Charlotte Bay measures 30 miles across and bites into the mainland for a distance of 15 miles. Four rivers drain into its basin across its almost endless beach, the most dominant being the Kennedy River whose tributary, the Annie River, is a port for Marina Plains and was used extensively as a trawler servicing and unloading facility before mother ships and fuel barges operated in the area.

The coast along this entire stretch tends to be unremarkable, the hills being low and mostly featureless. Indeed, the section north from Princess Charlotte Bay to Cape Direction is often referred to as 'the horror stretch'. This epithet refers only to its lack of good anchorages and scenic qualities and does not imply danger. But even in its intended context it is not absolutely fair because there are, in fact, two or three worthwhile anchorages and if one looks at the reef and not at the land then scenic qualities will be found.

North of Margaret Bay we again find an abundance of blinding white silica sandhills and blows which persist to the tip of Cape York, although the silica content appears to reduce dramatically in the far north. They also become interspersed with beautiful red cliffs of bauxite, the colours of which are spectacular in clear conditions. Which raises the question of visibility.

Where there is a trade wind there is haze. This is the result of moisture being gathered from the ocean and then carried along to thicken the air and make it more difficult to visually penetrate. Even on a sunny, cloudless day, visibility might reduce by as much as one third. On this section of the coast, where a well-developed trade wind and a low coastline combine to deny reliable, instant reference, the navigator should maintain regular running checks.

From Cooktown north to Cape York there are very few coastal settlements and those that exist cannot be depended on for services beyond very basic requirements or possible emergency contact. On this chart there is the Aborigine settlement at Lockhart and the small European community at Portland Roads. From the latter, mail can be sent, water collected and some supplies might be purchased if a lift can be arranged into Iron Range. Otherwise, mother ships service the trawler fleet along this part of the coast from which fuel and basic supplies may be sometimes purchased.

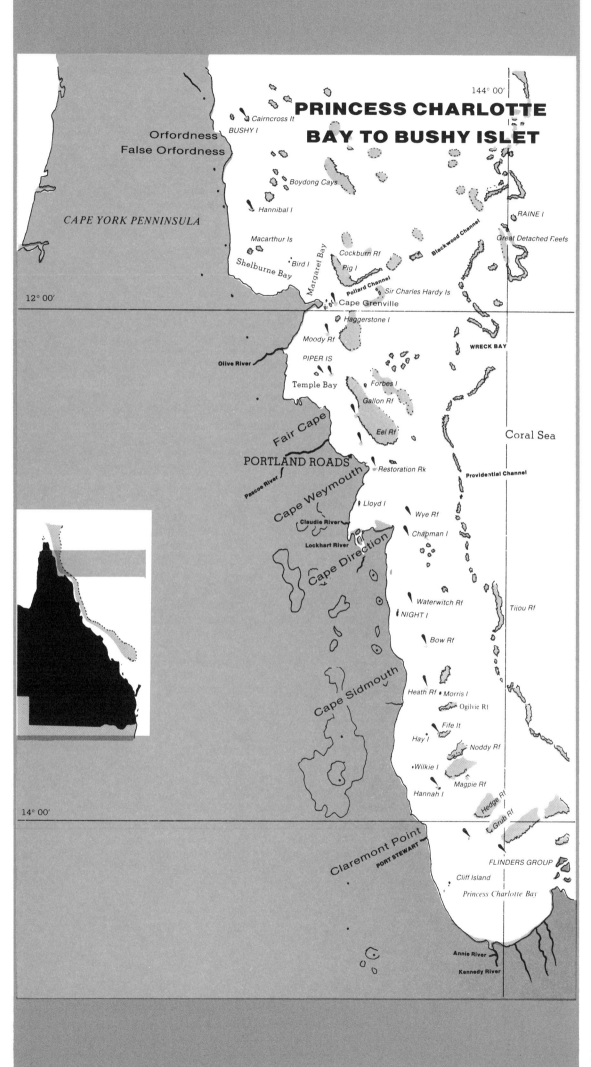

PRINCESS CHARLOTTE BAY TO BUSHY ISLET

144° 00'

Cairncross It
BUSHY I

Orfordness
False Orfordness

Boydong Cays

Hannibal I

RAINE I

CAPE YORK PENNINSULA

Macarthur Is

Margaret Bay

Cockburn Rf

Great Detached Reefs

Blackwood Channel

Bird I

Pig I

Shelburne Bay

Pollard Channel

Sir Charles Hardy Is

12° 00'

Cape Grenville

Haggerstone I

Moody Rf

WRECK BAY

PIPER IS

Olive River

Temple Bay

Forbes I

Gallon Rf

Coral Sea

Eel Rf

Fair Cape

PORTLAND ROADS

Restoration Rk

Providential Channel

Pascoe River

Cape Weymouth

Lloyd I

Wye Rf

Claudie River

Chapman I

Lockhart River

Cape Direction

Waterwitch Rf

Tijou Rf

NIGHT I

Bow Rf

Cape Sidmouth

Heath Rf • *Morris I*

Ogilvie Rf

Fife It

Hay I

Noddy Rf

Wilkie I

Magpie Rf

Hannah I

Hedge Rf

Grub Rf

14° 00'

Claremont Point

PORT STEWART

FLINDERS GROUP

Cliff Island

Princess Charlotte Bay

Annie River

Kennedy River

33

Of the anchorages along this section of the coast, the best are, from south to north; Flinders Group, Morris Island, Night Island, Lockhart River and Cape Grenville. There are numerous others, as the fleet of trawlers noted behind every other islet confirms, but all are uncomfortable to some degree. Trawler crews, remember, are obliged to rest where they can, not where they prefer. The only truly miserable anchorage that the cruising person often finds obligatory is Bushy Islet or Cairncross Islet at the top of this chart. There is nothing else available to those who cannot or will not make the hop from Cape Grenville to Escape River in one day.

The weather on this section of the coast tends to be identical to that previously described. The trade wind dominates in no uncertain way April through October and the dry to wet season transition is often one of calms and variables with only occasional and haphazard northerly winds. These often tend north-north-east in the late afternoon after developing from an easterly or north-easterly. They die soon after dark and are most common from late October to mid December. After Christmas, the wet season should start and continue through to the end of March bringing with it rain, the threat of a cyclone and promise of north-westerlies. These, as stated before, often fail to reach Princess Charlotte Bay and commonly fade in the Cape Grenville area giving way to variables and south-easterlies during any developed rain influence south of there.

Cyclone activity north of 15° latitude tends to be far less active than south of that latitude. However, the months of January, February and March should be watched closely and escape planned if they are cruised. The best cyclone anchorages are in the Kennedy or Annie River (Princess Charlotte Bay), the Lockhart River, or Glennie or Hunter Inlet in Temple Bay. All are subject to tides to enter, the Lockhart River requiring the least tide rise and offering the best general protection while awaiting the tide.

BUSHY ISLET TO TORRES STRAIT.
In fact, this chart extends north to embrace the Fly and Dibiri River delta areas of Papua New Guinea. Torres Strait itself enjoys its own full description at the end of this book.

The east coast of the Cape York Peninsula continues low and uninspiring and the anchorages are mostly poor to middling. However, compensating for the promise of discomfort and lack of scenery is the fact that the Torres Strait is about to open up, freeing the westbound yacht from a lee shore and offering the visitor of all intents a glimpse into a most romantic area. And what the coast lacks from a distance, it more than makes up in close-up.

From south of Bushy Islet to Turtle Head Island, the coast is a wonderful mixture of sand dunes and red cliffs often backed by rising ground littered with bright orange magnetic ant hills. The latter are a product of the bauxite in the area which, one hopes, will never justify mining. The hills in the background are, in the main, densely wooded and hide rainforest whose species are closer to New Guinea strains than Australian.

Offshore, the outer barrier reefs continue their orderly progress along the continental shelf terminating at Bligh Entrance which is the major shipping channel for the eastern approaches to Torres Strait. Interestingly, a number of bold continental islands suddenly impose themselves on an area otherwise confined to reef and low cays. These are the Murray Islands, including the major island of Maer, and, 25 miles to their north-west, Darnley Island. Both major islands are inhabited and almost certainly always have been by Torres Strait Islanders about which more in the section, 'The Torres Strait' at the end of this book.

Between the outer and inner barrier reefs there are hundreds of isolated reefs and cays many of which have not been properly charted. Yet, despite their presence, prawn trawlers work the area at night relying on their radar to prevent wandering from known paths. I, myself, have travelled out there, relieving trawlers of their load, as relief mate on a small mother ship, and never quite became accustomed to steaming through the night in what is, essentially, no man's land. For all that, there are great tracts well charted that might invite the visitor to sail east for the fun of it. I hasten to warn, however, that truly comfortable anchorages simply do not exist until right out under the lee of an outer barrier reef. This practice might be labelled, 'adventure' and as such confined to those prepared to take a few risks to expand their experience.

Anchorages along this part of the coast and into the Torres Strait are poor, as I have said. But there are a few worth noting should comfort become paramount

Torres Strait cyclone

In a region relatively cyclone free, a severe cyclone developed to the east of Cape York in March 1923 and, moving west-southwest, devastated the Torres Strait Islands. During its 12 day life, it crossed the Cape York Peninsula into the Gulf of Carpentaria where it sank the *Douglas Mawson*, a 167 ton steamship en route Burketown to Thursday Island with a loss of 20 lives, 28 March 1923.

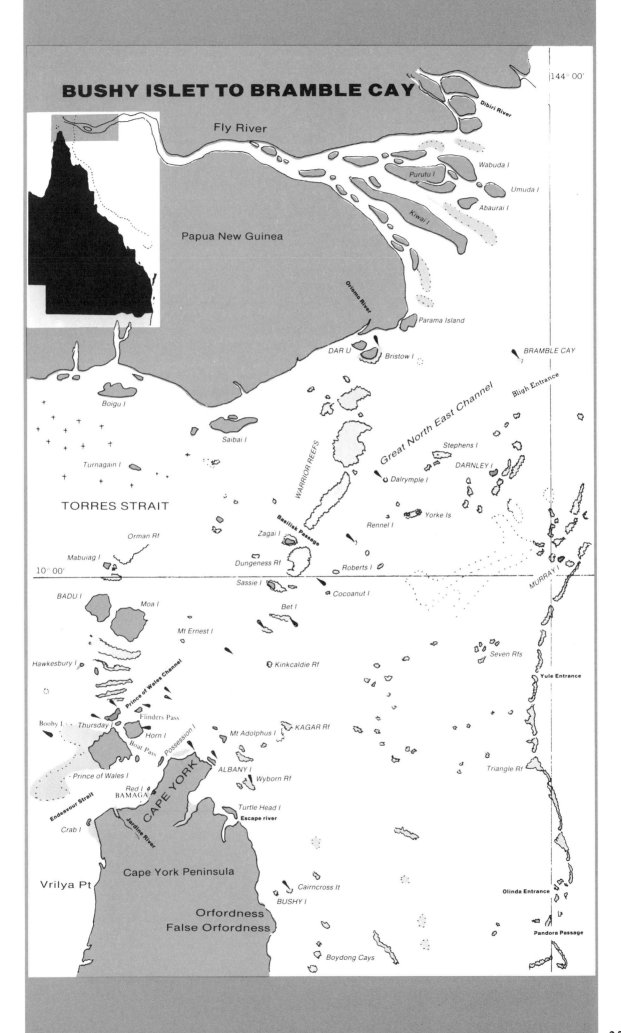

BUSHY ISLET TO BRAMBLE CAY

144° 00'

Fly River

Dibiri River

Wabuda I

Purutu I

Umuda I

Abaurai I

Papua New Guinea

Kiwai I

Oriomo River

Parama Island

DAR U

Bristow I

BRAMBLE CAY

Boigu I

Bligh Entrance

Great North East Channel

Saibai I

WARRIOR REEFS

Stephens I

DARNLEY I

Turnagain I

Dalrymple I

TORRES STRAIT

Yorke Is

Rennel I

Orman Rf

Basilisk Passage

Zagai I

Mabuiag I

Dungeness Rf

Roberts I

10° 00'

Sassie I

Cocoanut I

MURRAY I

BADU I

Moa I

Bet I

Mt Ernest I

Seven Rfs

Hawkesbury I

Kinkcaldie Rf

Prince of Wales Channel

Yule Entrance

Flinders Pass

Booby I. *Thursday I*

Horn I

Mt Adolphus I

KAGAR Rf

Boat Pass

Possession I

ALBANY I

Wyborn Rf

Triangle Rf

Prince of Wales I

Red I

BAMAGA

CAPE YORK

Turtle Head I

Escape river

Endeavour Strait

Crab I

Jardine River

Cape York Peninsula

Vrilya Pt

Cairncross It

Olinda Entrance

BUSHY I

Orfordness
False Orfordness

Pandora Passage

Boydong Cays

35

or, worse, a strong wind threaten a long stay. These are the Escape River, Mount Adolphus and Horn Island (opposite Thursday Island and protecting it to windward). Escape River can be considered a useful cyclone anchorage should one threaten as noted in its own description.

The weather in this section is very much that of the previous section with the subtle difference that the Torres Strait can warp the south-easterly trade wind into an east-south-easterly or even an easterly, the latter usually being a product of lighter than normal winds as might occur late in the season (towards December).

The April through October south-east trade-wind season is a strong and persistent one, often topping 25 knots, rarely dropping below 15 and continuing day and night. Three-day gusty periods can occur every two to three weeks during which time the wind tops 30 and 35 knots. The only good news is that while it is developed from the south-east it will not suddenly move to any other direction and catch you at exposed anchorage. Slants to south-south-east might occur and slants to east-south-east are quite common, but the basic direction remains the same.

November and December can be a period of calms with light afternoon north-easterlies, dying at night when an offshore wind might waft in, but mostly it does not. Thunderstorms are common towards and during December but are very localised and sometimes easily dodged. Depending on the dominating forces at work, a year might produce easier trade winds in general and a lengthier calm period or, conversely, it might produce heavy trade winds which continue to dominate into the so-called 'calm period'. Broadly speaking, it pays to think in terms of south-east winds right through the year, looking to November-December as the best time for transitional calms during which prawn trawling and passages south are easier.

January, February and, sometimes, March, bring the wet season when the winds start blowing from the south-west through north-west. Theoretically, these winds should prevail down the coast as far as Cooktown. In fact, they rarely extend much beyond Princess Charlotte Bay, as earlier stated. This chart shows the area where north-westerlies are most likely to be experienced at this time of year, the north-westerly sometimes blowing almost trade wind-like for six weeks from late January through February.

The wet season can turn this section of the coast and the islands of the Torres Strait from drab dust bowls to flower baskets of riotous colour. Thunder and lightning is commonly associated with heavy rain, but these are small prices to pay for the obvious benefits.

Thursday Island is a full customs, immigration and quarantine clearance port for Australia as is Daru for Papua New Guinea. Those sailing to Papua New Guinea from Thursday Island should wait at Thursday Island until a south-easterly eases before clearing customs outbound. Many folk have prematurely cleared then been obliged to keep seeking extenions as the trade wind pins them down relentlessly, sometimes for weeks. The best time to make the passage is November at which time calms should be anticipated and yet the cyclone season is unlikely to appear. It also allows time to reach a worthwhile destination in Papua New Guinea before its cyclone season (both areas' season is late December through March).

PORTS AND ANCHORAGES

Ports and anchorages descriptions start here at Queensland's most southern port, Gold Coast, from where they run north consecutively to the Torres Strait (Thursday Island).

GOLD COAST. Originally used as a jibe implying that one needed to be rich to visit Brisbane's South Coast, the name 'Gold Coast' grew in respectability until it was officially accepted in the late 1950s. In May 1959, it became the 'City of the Gold Coast.'

The City of the Gold Coast includes a stretch of coast running from the New South Wales-Queensland border to a point approximately 20 nautical miles north within The Broadwater. It includes the well known tourist centre of *Surfers Paradise* and the lesser known commercial centre of *Southport*.

The dominant harbour area of the Gold Coast is in the Southport Boat Harbour at Main Beach. This can be entered from seaward by the *Gold Coast Seaway* which is a man-made entrance through The Spit. In the mid 1980s, it replaced the natural bar which occurred between The Spit and South Stradbroke Island. The Gold Coast Seaway is shown in large scale and is described separately later.

Approach from the south, east or north is clear of offshore dangers except those close aboard the land immediately south-east of *Point Danger*. From all directions, the mass of highrise buildings clustered in the Surfers Paradise area will be seen from at least 20 miles. A second, small cluster of highrise buildings is situated to the north; north-west of the Gold Coast Seaway. They provide valuable reference for the latter.

GOLD COAST APPROACHES

South Stradbroke I.

Hope I.

The Broadwater

Porpoise Pt.

Gold Coast Seaway

Nerang Hd.

SOUTHPORT

MAIN BCH

SURFERS PARADISE
(Highrise)

Nerang River

BROADBEACH

MERMAID BCH

MIAMI

Burleigh Hd.

PALM BCH

Currumbin Rk.

Queensland

Coolangatta Airport

COOLANGATTA

Light

Pt. Danger

Tweed Hds

KIRRA

Cobaki
Broadwater

State Border

New South Wales

Tweed River

Fingal Hd.

Cook I.

Danger Reefs

Outer Rf.

Inner Rf.

Coral Sea

153° 30'

28°00'

0
1
2
3
4
NM 5

The run from Point Danger to the Gold Coast Seaway is hazard-free. In fair weather and with lookout, it is possible to pass between Cook Island and Danger Reefs. The city of Gold Coast runs from Coolangatta to north of Southport.

The author's yacht *Renee Tighe* alongside the visitor's berth, Southport Marina. This is at Main Beach at the southern end of The Broadwater.

Point Danger with Coolangatta high-rise is seen from directly off the Tweed River entrance over which is a single high-rise.

This isolated high-rise is conspicuous in the Burleigh Heads area. The heads themselves are obvious.

These two views of the final approach to the Gold Coast show the concentration of high-rise buildings around the Surfers Paradise area and the separate cluster to their north. The latter group make good reference for the Gold Coast Seaway.

Gold Coast Seaway. Under entrepreneurial pressure to enhance the Gold Coast's maritime development by giving it a safe entrance, this entrance was cut during 1985. Bordered by retaining walls and backed by a wave break island, silting is prevented by a sand bypass pump situated on the beach next to the southern breakwater. In effect, this is a mechanical means of allowing the northern migration of sand to continue without clogging up the new entrance.

Depths and navigational aids are shown on the accompanying plan leaving it only to be emphasised here that the entrance can be dangerous in rough weather. Be prepared to stand off if prudence demands. Generally speaking, a flood tide calms the entrance enough that it can be used in most conditions. Enter against an ebb tide only in light weather.

Having entered the Gold Coast Seaway, dredged channels branch north and south offering minimum depths of around 4.5 metres, low water springs. Turn south for *Main Beach, Surfers Paradise* and *Southport* and north for *Runaway Bay, Paradise Point, Hope Harbour, Sanctuary Cove* and *Brisbane.* In either direction, pass red buoys and beacons to port and green buoys and beacons to starboard.

Tides. Gold Coast Seaway enjoys standard port status in the *Queensland Tide Tables.* For those arriving from New South Wales, Sydney data may be safely used, the times being within ten to twenty minutes of each other either later or earlier. The height at Gold Coast Seaway is slightly lower than Sydney.

Within the Broadwater, tides are later and lower, the exact details of which being covered by the *Tide Tables* in its Secondary Places pages.

Nav Aids. The entrance is covered by two sets of leading beacons, the green light on the end of the northern breakwater doubling as a front beacon for the first set which lead over the bar. On the end of

the southern breakwater there is a red light on an identical white structure.

Within the Broadwater all buoys and beacons are lit for night navigation and all are placed red to port and green to starboard when approaching either Southport Boat Harbour or Brisbane from the entrance. Confusion is not uncommon even in daylight so cautious progress is suggested until orientated.

Anchorage in Southport Boat Harbour (previously called 'Yacht Basin') is not permitted south of the dotted line shown on the chart on page 41. Anchorage elsewhere is permitted subject to channels being kept clear. Considering the restrictions imposed by shoals and local moorings, this can prove difficult.

The best anchorage is the one set aside by the Waterways Authority to the north of Sea World. A six week limit is imposed here, but the anchorage is generally good, although often troubled by wake. During a hyperactive weekend, when skiers, jetskis, helicopters and general traffic blitz the area, noise can be a distraction.

The holding is very good and a dinghy can be landed on the beach next to the Air Sea Rescue base on the corner of Sea World Nara Resort. It is a three kilometre walk down to Main Beach or a bus can be picked up at Sea World Nara Resort or, more regularly, from Sea World itself, one kilometre away.

Moorings. Swing moorings are available for casual rental in the south-east corner of Southport Boat Harbour between Southport Yacht Club Marina and Mariner's Cove Marina. Others are situated further west and towards the Gold Coast Bridge. The managing agent is *Bosuns Locker* near the haul-out yard.

Marinas. There are three marinas in Southport Boat Harbour; these being, in order of berth price; *Southport Marina, Mariner's Cove Marina* and *Marina Mirage.*

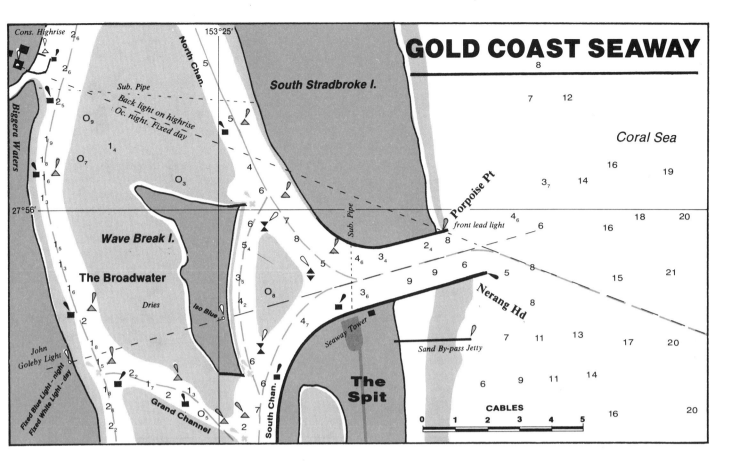

The Gold Coast Seaway is an artificial break in The Spit giving deepwater access to The Broadwater. Turn into South Channel for the Southport Boat Harbour or North Channel for points north. Brisbane can be reached from here in protected waterways.

Southport Marina was privately developed in the mid 1970s and, after fifteen years, was handed over to the Southport Yacht Club in November 1991. Charges immediately went up and living aboard was restricted, however, it remained the best value in the area. For berth allocation, go where indicated on the accompanying chart close to the marina office. Fuel is available in this corner.

Mariner's Cove Marina. Close to and immediately north of Southport Marina, the floating berths here are across the tidal stream making entering and leaving a berth difficult at times. For fuel and berth allocation go to the south-west corner of the marina as shown.

Marina Mirage. Developed by one of Australia's many 1980s high fliers, Christopher Skase, and now owned by a Japanese company, Marina Mirage is a part of the Sheraton Mirage Hotel. Its prices are high, but facilities are good and the berths lie along the tidal stream making manoeuvring very easy.

Marinas north of the Southport Boat Harbour are described next.

Runaway Bay Marina lies against the mainland a little over 4 nautical miles north of Southport Boat Harbour and about 2 miles north of the Gold Coast Seaway. Along its outside face is a private, residents and guests only marina, but inside visitors are welcome on a temporary or permanent basis.

To reach the marina, take the *North Channel* from the Gold Coast Seaway then follow the beacons into the channel between the mainland and *Crab Island*. There is at least 1.8 metres in this channel, but a rising tide is suggested. Off the marina entrance is a red and green buoy, both lit, from where approach is direct towards the (by now) obvious fuel berth.

Being a self-contained, village style development, many shops including chandlery, general store and cafes are in the marina. Serious shoppers will find all they need across the road at a large shopping mall.

Services at the marina include dry and wet storage, all fuels, all boat repairs and a straddle lift. The office is a separate building next to the large launching ramp directly ahead from the fuel berth. Buses connect with Southport and Surfers Paradise.

Sanctuary Cove and Hope Harbour. A little over 4 miles north from the Gold Coast Seaway, within the calm waters of The Broadwater, the South Arm of the *Coomera River* is found. Its entrance is between *Rat Island* and the newly developed *Sovereign Islands*, and is marked by a lit yellow buoy.

Vessels heading for *Hope Harbour* and *Sanctuary Cove* should haul to port, passing the yellow buoy to starboard after which beacons on each side of the river are passed red to port and green to starboard.

En route will be seen the mooring basin of *Paradise Point* with a ramp and boat service on the north-east corner and beyond it is the entrance to *Coombabah Creek*. In fact, there are two entrances to this creek, one on each side of Jabiru Island and both crossed by a common road over two bridges with clearances of 3.4 and 4.7 metres. In no way do they hinder traffic in the main river.

Immediately after Jabiru Island, Hope Harbour is seen to port. Here will be found floating berths, fuel, repair facilities, a 75-tonne straddle lift and shops.

39

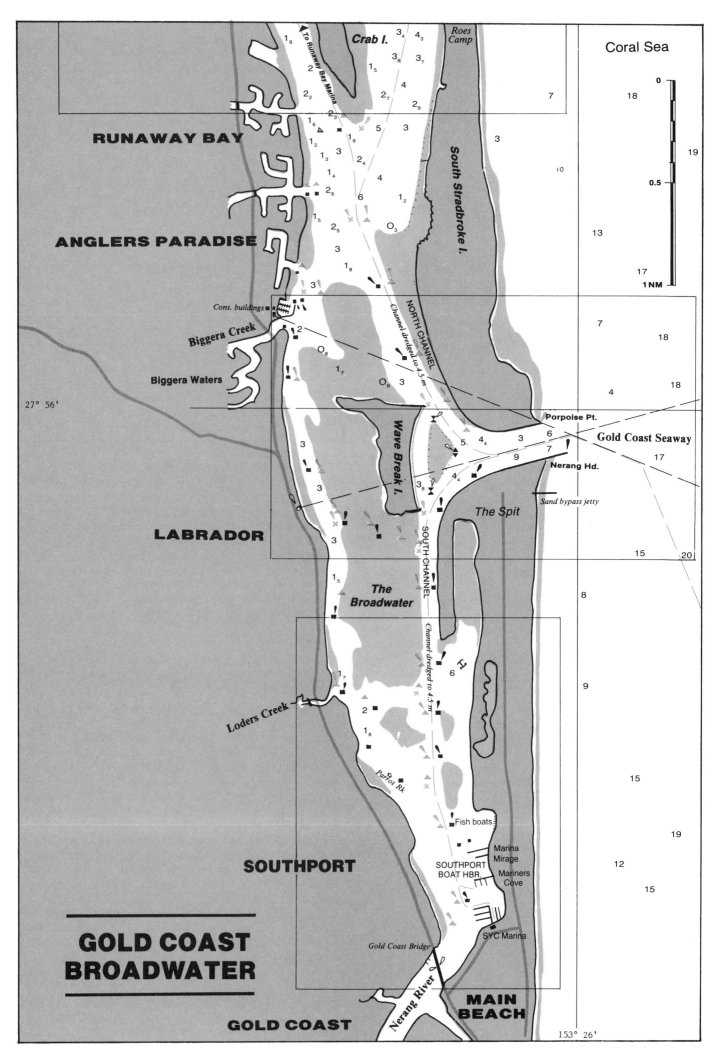

GOLD COAST BROADWATER

RUNAWAY BAY

ANGLERS PARADISE

27° 56'

LABRADOR

SOUTHPORT

GOLD COAST

Coral Sea

Crab I.

Roes Camp

To Runaway Bay Marina

South Stradbroke I.

Cons. buildings

Biggera Creek

Biggera Waters

NORTH CHANNEL

Channel dredged to 4.5 m.

Wave Break I.

Porpoise Pt.

Gold Coast Seaway

Nerang Hd.

Sand bypass jetty

The Spit

SOUTH CHANNEL

The Broadwater

Channel dredged to 4.5 m.

Loders Creek

Parrot Rk.

Fish boats

Marina Mirage

Mariners Cove

SOUTHPORT BOAT HBR.

SYC Marina

Gold Coast Bridge

Nerang River

MAIN BEACH

153° 26'

40

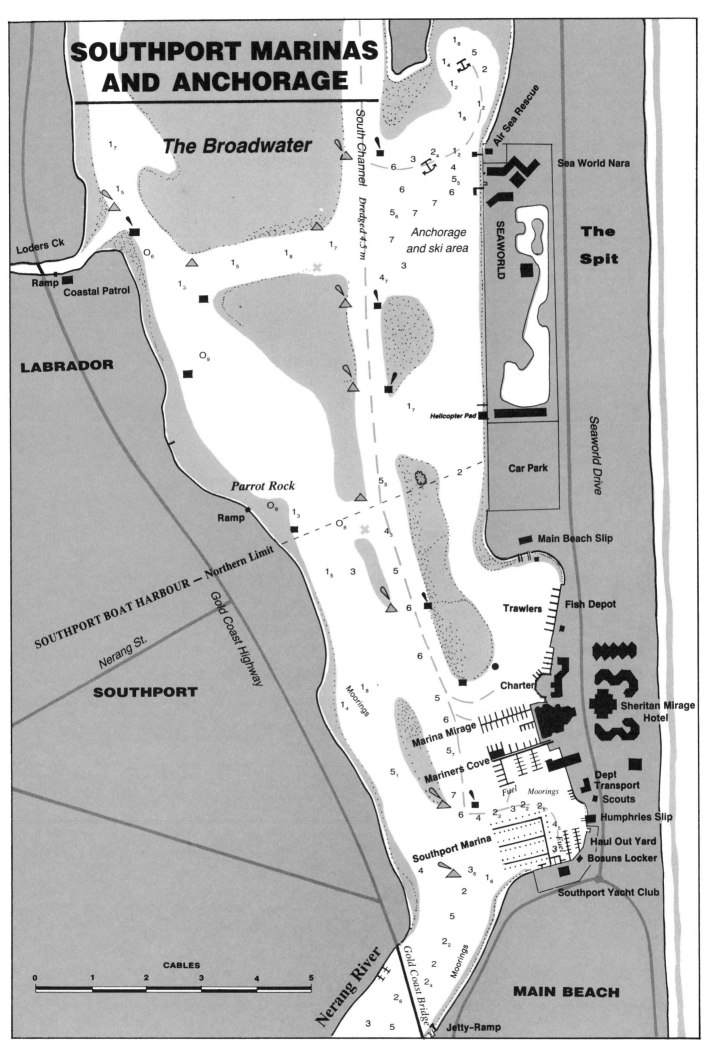

SOUTHPORT MARINAS AND ANCHORAGE

The Broadwater

Loders Ck

Ramp

Coastal Patrol

LABRADOR

SOUTHPORT BOAT HARBOUR — Northern Limit

Nerang St.

Gold Coast Highway

SOUTHPORT

South Channel

Dredged 4.5 m

Anchorage and ski area

Parrot Rock

Ramp

Moorings

Nerang River

Gold Coast Bridge

Air Sea Rescue

Sea World Nara

SEAWORLD

The Spit

Helicopter Pad

Car Park

Seaworld Drive

Main Beach Slip

Trawlers   Fish Depot

Charter

Marina Mirage

Mariners Cove

Fuel   Moorings

Southport Marina

Fuel

Sheritan Mirage Hotel

Dept Transport Scouts

Humphries Slip

Haul Out Yard

Bosuns Locker

Southport Yacht Club

MAIN BEACH

Jetty-Ramp

CABLES

0   1   2   3   4   5

41

Expanding, it will become a self-supporting marine and residential centre.

Continuing up the South Arm, passing a canal development to port, Santuary Cove marina, village and residential area is situated opposite the junction between the south and north arms of the river. Visitors should proceed directly to the visitors' section southeast of the Harbour Master's office which is a conspicuous small building on the outer end of a jetty.

All boat services are available here and the shops carry all that is demanded of a self-contained village. There is even a brewery specialising in Bavarian-style beer.

Runaway Bay Marina is west of the north tip of Crab Island less than 2½ nautical miles north-northwest of the Gold Coast Seaway.

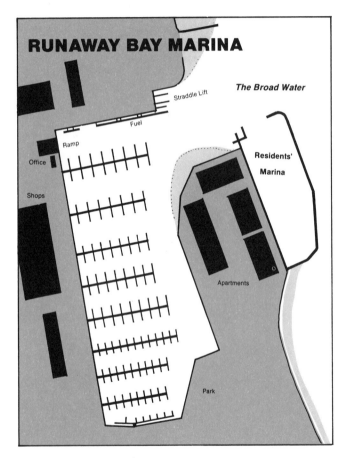

RUNAWAY BAY MARINA

The Broad Water

Straddle Lift

Fuel

Ramp

Office

Shops

Residents' Marina

Apartments

Park

The Southport Bar

Until the mid 1980's, when the Gold Coast Seaway was cut through The Spit to provide reliable access into The Broadwater, the natural opening, known as The Southport Bar, was the only way in. It demanded the respect of any bar, its deepest channel moving according to natural influences. The entrance itself was popularly believed to have moved over two kilometres this century, from the present position of the Southport Boat Harbour to immediately north of the Gold Coast Seaway. In fact, however, a chart dated 1842 shows it as being exactly where it was prior to being sealed in the mid 1980's.

The Gold Coast is a full-on boating area with facilities of every description laid on for the small boat.

Gold Coast Population

In 1991, Gold Coast's population stood at 285,000, but was growing at six times the national average as southerners poured across the border. It is expected to reach 500,000 by the turn of the century. It receives well over 2 million tourists a year.

Looking Back

Taken in the 1960's from the Southport Boat Harbour (then called Yacht Basin), the building, right, is Humphries Slipway whilst the small one, left, is where Main Beach Slip is today. The Spit was virtually undeveloped then with no marinas on the coast anywhere.

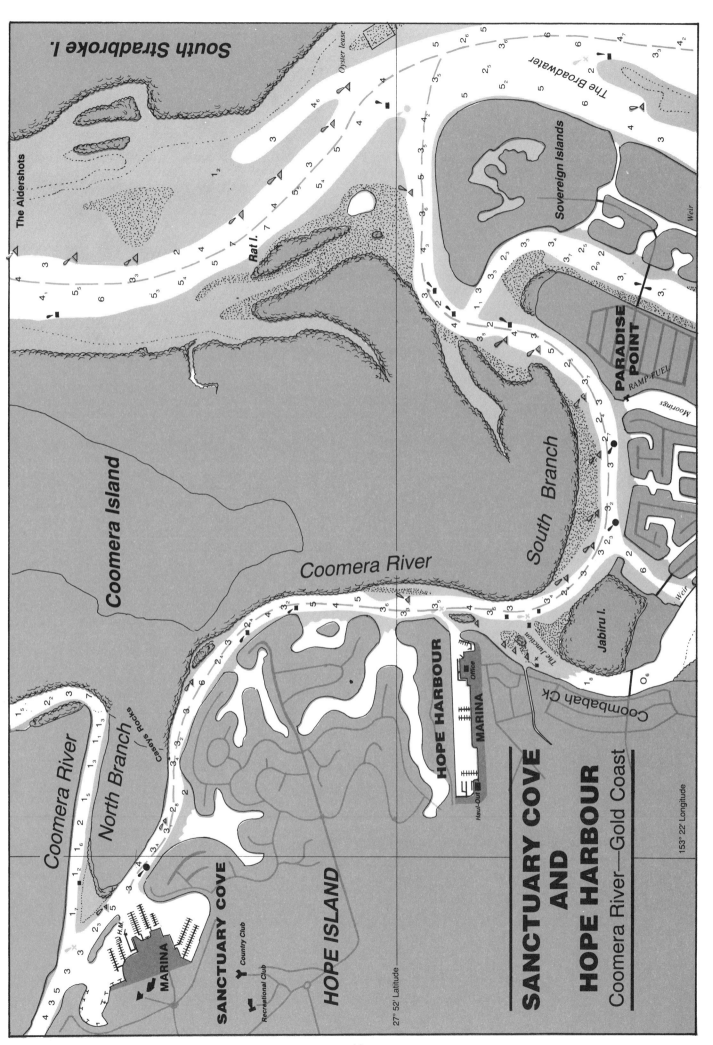

South Stradbroke I.

The Aldershots

Rat I.

Oyster lease

The Broadwater

Sovereign Islands

Weir

PARADISE
POINT

RAMP-FUEL

Moorings

Coomera Island

Coomera River

South Branch

Jabiru I.

The Junction

Weir

Coomera River

North Branch

Casey Rocks

Hope Harbour

Haul-Out

MARINA

office

HOPE ISLAND

Coombabah Ck

SANCTUARY COVE
AND
HOPE HARBOUR

Coomera River—Gold Coast

153° 22' Longitude

27° 52' Latitude

SANCTUARY COVE

Country Club

Recreational Club

MARINA

H.M.

43

THE BROADWATER TO MORETON BAY.

Shown in a series of four charts from here to page 51, an overview is offered here followed by specific navigation notes relating to each chart.

This area is the delta of three main rivers, these being the *Nerang, Coomera* and *Logan*. Their mouths are protected from the Coral Sea by the barrier islands of South and North Stradbroke which in turn provide a complex maze of calm, mostly navigable waterways. The many islands trapped between the mainland and barrier islands create numerous linking channels, but the two main north-south arteries are *Canaipa Passage* and *Main Channel*.

When planning a passage either north or south through these channels it is imperative that deep keelers utilise a flood tide. Depths are generally good regardless of tide height, but beacon confusion, helmsperson distraction and occasional shoal areas should be guarded against. A rising tide is the best protection.

Generally speaking, the least low tide depths of certain places in both channels are around 1.2 metres. But these change both in actual depth and precise positions, tongues of silt growing into and out of the channel. As a broad statement, it is fair to say that *Main Channel* offers the best depths whilst *Canaipa Passage* offers the most scenic route.

The only height restrictions are those of overhead cables across both main channels, the high tide clearance being 23.5 metres across Main Channel at Rocky Point and 23.4 metres across Canaipa Passage at Canaipa Point.

Tides are shown in the official *Queensland Tide Tables* under 'Gold Coast Seaway' for the extreme south part of the Broadwater and under 'Brisbane' for all parts north. Many secondary areas are also covered in the front of the book based mostly on Brisbane.

Tide heights increase going north. Thus, a 1.5 metre high tide in the lower Broadwater might be as much as 50% more in lower Moreton Bay. It also tends to be one hour earlier.

Facilities. Because much of the mainland and many of the islands are inhabited, general facilities such as phone, kiosks, launching ramps, public jetties and even water taxis and ferries will be found in many places. However, in the name of convenience, it pays to start the trip well stocked, especially with fresh water as this can prove troublesome to hose aboard conveniently.

Specific facilities are noted later.

Nav Aids. There are no major leading beacons in this area, all channels being indicated by port and starboard beacons and — where banks are prone to change — buoys. The latter are very much in the minority.

All beacons are passed red to port and green to starboard sailing north to Moreton Bay, ascending any river or entering any secondary harbour. Most are lit in Main Channel, but not so in Canaipa Passage. Night navigation is not recommended in either channel, however, without a good moon, shallow draft or local knowledge.

The relative position of the large scale chart opposite in the Lower Moreton Bay-Broadwater area is shown by the key map.

RUNAWAY BAY TO TIPPLERS PASSAGE.

Runaway Bay Marina, in the south-west corner of the chart opposite, has been described on page 39 under the marina list for the Gold Coast. Another two marinas are located up the Coomera River to the north of Runaway Bay which have also been described (see Hope Harbour and Sanctuary Cove, page 39).

Having sailed north from the Southport Boat Harbour, the main channel is deep and wide and well marked by lit beacons, these being passed red to port and green to starboard heading north. The Coomera River entrance is passed to port beyond which the channel skirts the banks known as *The Aldershots.* Opposite Coomera River entrance, against *Brown Island*, is an enclosed anchorage in two metres, but with an entrance bar of 1.2 metres. The entrance is marked by a red and green beacons both unlit.

Immediately before entering Tipplers Passage, a previously abandoned canal development on South Stradbroke Island has been activated by a local developer, the son of the late Sir Bruce Small. This is to be a resort-residential estate, the resort being at the head of the inner lagoon, residential development intended along the south side. The north arm, just inside the entrance, is available for anchorage, depths being adequate for deep keelers although swinging room is sometimes limited during weekends and holidays. A marina is planned for this basin in the distant future.

Tipplers Passage is an area of hyperactivity throughout the year, numerous tourist boats visiting the facilities daily. Although secure, the anchorage is troubled by wake and noise, distractions which wane by mid afternoon when the place is generally abandoned. The late afternoon is an ideal time to enjoy Tipplers, there being a Parks and Wildlife office, hotel and rescue station ashore. It is a short walk across the island to the surf.

Those trying to avoid the trappings of tourism can take the alternate channel between *Never Fail Islands* and *Woogoompah Island* along which are beacons indicating a measured mile. There is good, out-of-the-way anchorage here in two to three metres against *Tulleen Island* after rounding the green beacon off its western tip. This overlaps onto the next chart.

Bombarded by cruise boats during the day, Tipplers Passage can become a reasonably peaceful anchorage by late afternoon. Ashore there are a number of facilities including a hotel. It is a short walk across South Stradbroke Island to the surf.

The lovely Tasman Seabird, *Joy Too* in Canaipa Passage. This is the prettiest, though shallowest route from the Broadwater to Moreton Bay.

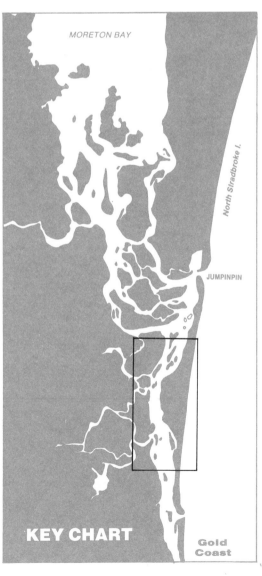

KEY CHART

MORETON BAY

North Stradbroke I.

JUMPINPIN

Gold Coast

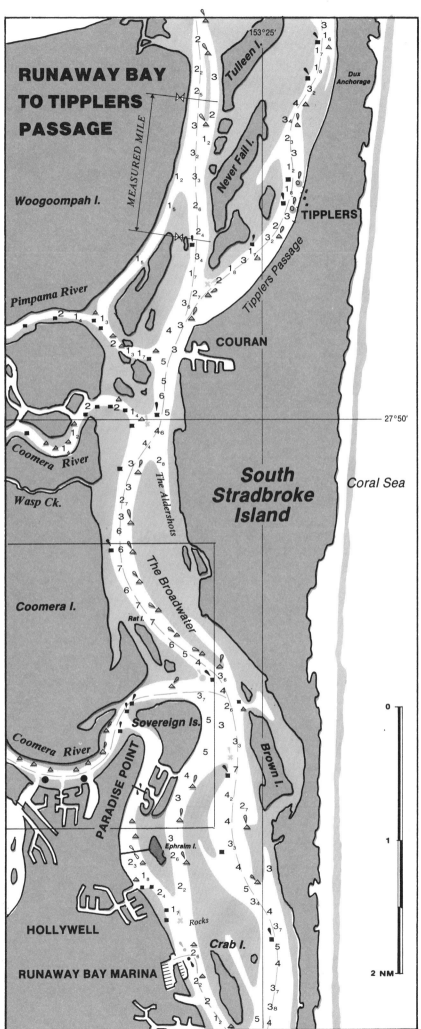

RUNAWAY BAY TO TIPPLERS PASSAGE

Tulleen I.

Dux Anchorage

153°25'

MEASURED MILE

Never Fail I.

Woogoompah I.

TIPPLERS

Pimpama River

Tipplers Passage

COURAN

27°50'

Coomera River

Wasp Ck.

The Aldershots

South Stradbroke Island

Coral Sea

Coomera I.

The Broadwater

Rat I.

Sovereign Is.

Coomera River

PARADISE POINT

Brown I.

Ephraim I.

HOLLYWELL

Rocks

Crab I.

RUNAWAY BAY MARINA

0

1

2 NM

45

Entering Tipplers Passage from the south.

The jetties at Tipplers are for charter and tourist boats only. There is a small public jetty also.

Departing Tipplers to the north, the hills of North Stradbroke are seen ahead.

TIPPLERS PASSAGE TO RUSSELL ISLAND

With the Tipplers area astern, a decision must be made as to the choice of channels north to Moreton Bay. As noted earlier, *Main Channel* has the best overall depths whilst *Canaipa Passage* is the most picturesque. However, both demand the utilisation of a rising tide to clear the shoals and to avoid lengthy groundings. Both are looked at in turn here.

Main Channel. The best way into the south end of Main Channel is via *Whalleys Gutter* which is well beaconed and has a minimum low tide of 1.5 metres. Beyond it, off the south end of Eden Island, another shoal occurs, depths here often reducing to 1.2 metres. Beyond this shoal, nothing less than two metres, low water springs will be encountered all the way to Moreton Bay.

If the settlements of *Jacobs Well* and *Steiglitz* are to be visited, the yellow beacon off Cabbage Tree Point must be rounded to port to enter the channel. From this beacon, dozens of boats will be seen at their moorings leaving grave doubt as to whether there is a channel through them. In fact there is, the clear channel being against the mainland.

At Steiglitz there is the *Horizon Shores Marina* (in canal, off accompanying chart) where vessels of up to 24 metres long can obtain visitor berths and all the facilities expected of a marina. All fuels are available as are repair services, laundry, showers, sailmaker, rigger, chandlery and straddle lift to 30 tonnes.

Jacobs Well is further down channel where, again, moored craft are seen. It offers a boat ramp, fishing club, showers and toilets, petrol, ice and fishing gear.

Returning to our passage north in Main Channel, from Cabbage Tree Point the only overhead cable at 23.5 metres above high water springs is seen, its pylons obvious on each side of the channel. Beyond there, the channel continues between Russell Island and Long Island at which point the next chart overlaps and this description continues on page 48.

Canaipa Passage. Starting again from the Tipplers area, the best way into Canaipa Passage is between *Crusoe Island* and *Jumpinpin*. From either Tipplers Passage

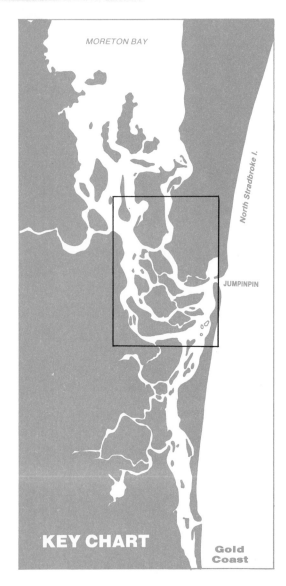

MORETON BAY

North Stradbroke I.

JUMPINPIN

KEY CHART

Gold Coast

The prettiest way north is via Canaipa Passage whilst most facilities are in Main Channel. South of Steiglitz is the beaconed channel into Horizon Shores Marina. Swan Bay is a fish breeding ground. Fishing is strictly prohibited there.

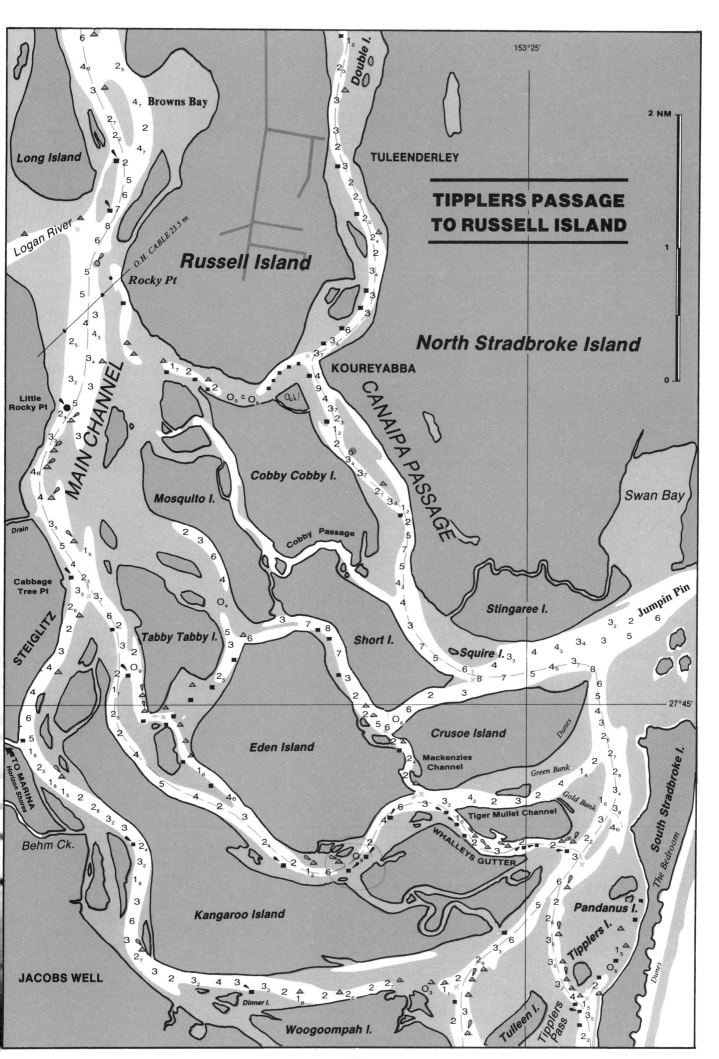

TIPPLERS PASSAGE
TO RUSSELL ISLAND

2 NM

1

0

153°25'

Long Island

Browns Bay

Logan River

O.H. CABLE 23.5 m

Rocky Pt

Russell Island

TULEENDERLEY

KOUREYABBA

North Stradbroke Island

Little
Rocky Pt

MAIN CHANNEL

Cobby Cobby I.

CANAIPA PASSAGE

Swan Bay

Mosquito I.

Cobby   Passage

Drain

Cabbage
Tree Pt

STEIGLITZ

Tabby Tabby I.

Short I.

Stingaree I.

Jumpin Pin

Squire I.

Crusoe Island

Eden Island

Dunes

Mackenzies
Channel

Green Bank

South Stradbroke I.

TO MARINA
Horizon Shores

Gold Bank

Tiger Mullet Channel

Behm Ck.

WHALLEYS GUTTER

Kangaroo Island

Pandanus I.

The Bedroom

Tipplers I.

JACOBS WELL

Dinner I.

Woogoompah I.

Tulleen I.

Tipplers
Pass

Dunes

The eastern tip of Crusoe Island is arrowed. When heading north out of Tipplers Passage into Canaipa Passage, depths between here and Jumpin Pin are good, as shown on previous chart.

The eastern end of Short Island, at the southern entrance to Canaipa Passage, is a very popular fishing spot. The land here is favoured to port (going north) to clear Squire Island. Soon after, the passage is diagonally crossed.

Closer to the eastern end of Short Island, the number of fishing boats is clearly seen as is the erosion along this bank.

or the channel on the western side of Tulleen Island, continue north, past Whalleys Gutter and across towards South Stradbroke Island. If the day is late or a tide must be awaited, a pleasant anchorage exists close to South Stradbroke Island opposite the eastern entrance to Whalleys Gutter after rounding an unlit red beacon. Sound in carefully here as it shoals rapidly.

Jumpinpin is the name given to the barred opening between South and North Stradbroke Island. It happened during a gale early 1895 prior to which there was no North or South Stradbroke; merely Stradbroke Island. The breach was some 300 metres wide and became a favourite alternative entrance to The Broadwater. Another gale and heavy rains in the early 1970s altered its character to such an extent that its use as an avenue to the sea diminished.

Today, Jumpinpin Bar enjoys more stability and ease of identification than it has in decades, however, it should not be used without local knowledge. Nevertheless, this improved stability has made its passing via the inside channels relatively safe. Only in poor weather and a falling tide should the area be avoided.

As can be seen on the accompanying chart (page 47), good depths exist around the eastern corner of Crusoe Island making the approach into Canaipa Passage hazard-free. From this corner, the water remains deep against the port hand shore all the way up Short Island's north-east coast beyond which the course favours North Stradbroke Island.

In the vicinity of Cobby Cobby Island, shoals occur with a least depth of 1.2 metres low water towards the red beacon off Oak Island. Beyond this beacon, good depths again prevail until the shoals in the Willis Island area. This section should be navigated with care and certainly on a rising tide. It will be found on the overlapping chart on page 51. This description continues on page 50.

RUSSELL ISLAND TO MORETON BAY

Via Main Channel. Continuing from where we left off on page 46, Main Channel continues north between Russell Island and Long Island, encountering shoals between Macleay Island and Garden Islands. If the tide is too high to risk grounding, the better route is via the short, narrow channel between Long Island and Garden Islands. This is well beaconed and easy to follow.

Once through this channel, depths across to Pannikin Island are ample and there is a good roadstead for anchoring. Otherwise, continuing north towards Redland Bay; the channel narrows near Snipe Islands before breaking out into lower Moreton Bay with its wider channels. Beware of over relaxing as Moreton Bay has many shoals itself which must be skirted according to route and beacons.

Facilities are good on the islands and the mainland. In *Krummell Passage*, along the top of Russell Island, there is a public jetty, boat ramp, kiosk, cafe, phone, general store and service station. There is also a doctor's surgery.

In *Karragarra Passage*, there is a boat ramp, phone, rubbish bins and jetty. All this area is serviced from the mainland by water taxis and ferries.

In *Weinam Creek*, Redland Bay, there is a council-owned marina where casual berths are sometimes available for a maximum of 48 hours. There is also a 20 minute limit public jetty, four lane ramp, small slipway and Coastguard Station. Depths are good within the harbour, but are limited to around one-metre LWS in the beaconed approach channel. A waterbus and water taxi operate from here and a public phone is nearby. The Bay Village shopping centre is a few kilometres to the north.

The Disappearing Galleon

In the marshes, at the head of Swan Bay, North Stradbroke Island, the taffrail of an ancient galleon has been sighted throughout the Twentieth Century. Vouched for by many responsible people, it disappeared forever towards the late 1950's after a chequered career of comings and goings. Although its existence was never confirmed, speculation ran high that it might have been one of Portuguese navigator, Cristavoa de Mendonca's three caravels that were reputed to have sailed down the east coast 250 years before Captain Cook.

On Canaipa Point, there is an annex of the Royal Queensland Yacht Squadron.

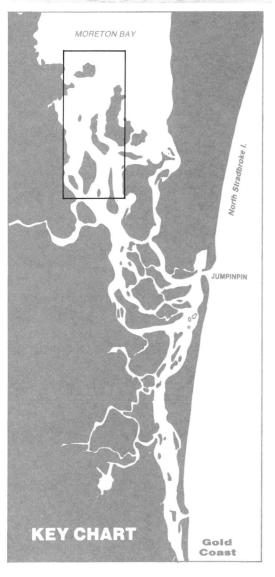

KEY CHART

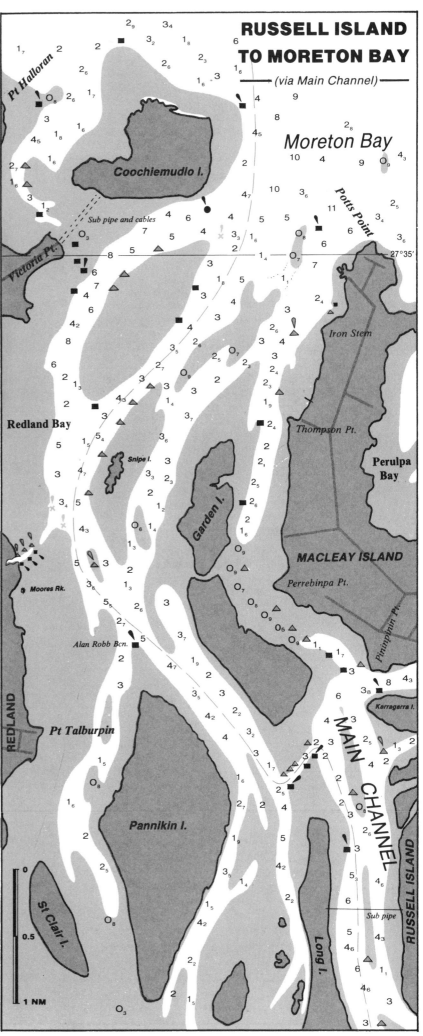

RUSSELL ISLAND TO MORETON BAY

(via Main Channel)

RUSSELL ISLAND TO MORETON BAY

Via Canaipa Passage. Continuing from the description so far on page 48, the Willis Island shoals should be navigated carefully before again finding deep water in the Canaipa Point region.

To starboard, on North Stradbroke Island, a very conspicuous sand blow is seen at the bottom of which is a disused sand mining jetty. Anchoring is good close to the north of this jetty being careful of a drying tongue of mud running south from the green beacon.

Ashore on Canaipa Point will be seen an annexe of the *Royal Queensland Yacht Squadron* across the channel from which are overhead cables at a height of 23.4 metres. Anchorage is possible off the point as long as the narrow channel is not restricted.

Canaipa Passage continues north-west from the sand mining jetty to emerge into Moreton Bay at the *Eric Early Light*. From there, one has the choice of crossing the bay over the top of Macleay Island if bound for Brisbane, or remaining close to North Stradbroke Island if bound for *Dunwich* whose chart and description is found on page 55.

En route, *Price Anchorage* offers fair shelter from sea breezes with the above-mentioned sand mining jetty the best position if a south-easterly is well developed.

The Brig *Amity* replica in Albany, Western Australia.

The Brig Amity

Loaded with troops and convicts, the Colonial Brig *Amity* brought the first white people to Queensland (then New South Wales) on Friday, 10 September 1824, landing them in Moreton Bay. She had previously been used to settle Western Australia as a means of stopping any attempted French settlement. There, she put ashore a detachment of troops and a party of convicts at Albany. A magnificent full-size replica of *Amity* is on display at that, now, major western town.

Anchorages between The Broadwater and Moreton Bay are in well protected channels surrounded by low land. They are all secure but must be clear of channels.

This sand patch in North Stradbroke Island, opposite Canaipa Point, is a feature of the area visible from many miles north, in Moreton Bay. The disused sand jetty is seen at the bottom of the sand patch in both photographs. Opposite, on Canaipa Point, is an annexe of the Royal Queensland Yacht Squadron whose main club is in Manly Harbour.

50

Canaipa Sand Blow

The conspicuous sand blow on North Stradbroke Island, opposite Canaipa Point, is not a natural blow. It was caused by the mining of sand for the manufacture of fibrolite by the Hardie Group of Companies. This activity has ceased.

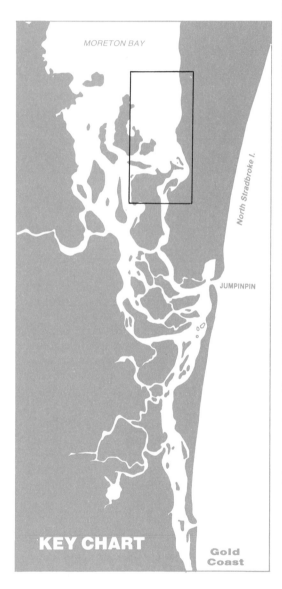

MORETON BAY

North Stradbroke I.

JUMPINPIN

KEY CHART

Gold Coast

During north-west winds, there is very little protection in Moreton Bay from here north. The closest northerly anchorage after leaving Canaipa is Peel Island, off Dunwich.

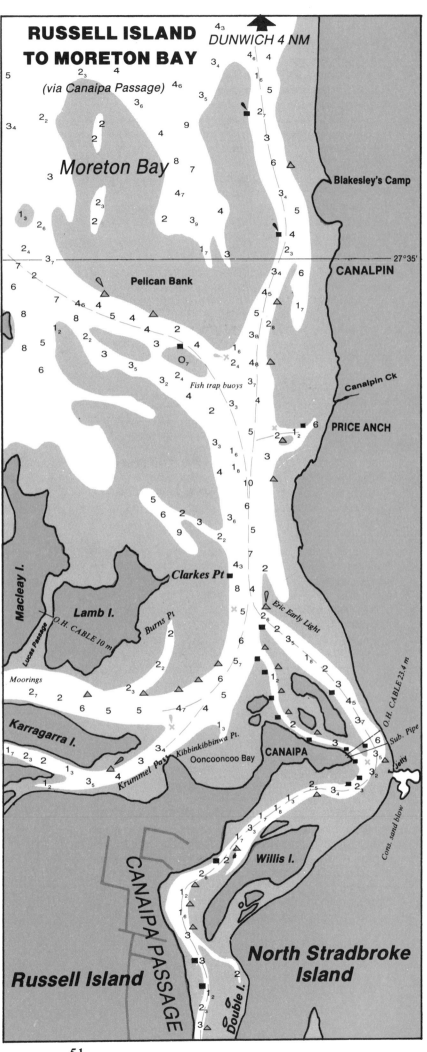

RUSSELL ISLAND TO MORETON BAY
(via Canaipa Passage)

DUNWICH 4 NM

Moreton Bay

Blakesley's Camp

CANALPIN

27°35'

Pelican Bank

Canalpin Ck

PRICE ANCH

Fish trap buoys

Clarkes Pt

Macleay I.

Lamb I.

O.H. CABLE 10 m

Burns Pt

Lucas Passage

Eric Early Light

O.H. CABLE 23.4 m

Moorings

Sub. Pipe

Karragarra I.

Jetty

Kibbinkibbinwa Pt.

Krummel Pass

Ooncooncoo Bay

CANAIPA

Cons. sand blow

Willis I.

CANAIPA PASSAGE

Russell Island

Double I.

North Stradbroke Island

51

MORETON BAY Approximately 15 miles wide and 30 miles long, this sandy bottomed bay is formed by the islands of North Stradbroke and Moreton. It contains numerous bays, inlets, rivers and islands, most of which are within the Brisbane Metropolitan Area. The capital of Queensland, Brisbane, sprawls from each side of the Brisbane River, its centre being about 13 miles upstream. The river empties into the south-west corner of Moreton Bay.

Lower Moreton Bay and the Gold Coast's Broadwater have been described on pages 44 to 51. Following this section are large scale plans and accompanying descriptions of many anchorages within Moreton Bay. Here, the bay is looked at as a whole.

General Notes. Many folk avoid Moreton Bay because of the extra miles it demands without commensurate reward. Typically, north-bound sailors remain at sea to round Cape Moreton and lay direct for Mooloolaba Harbour. South-bound sailors depart Mooloolaba and remain at sea to Coffs Harbour, New South Wales's first non-barred harbour. The alternative is to 'cruise inland' by sailing from the Gold Coast to Bribie Island — or vice versa — within the confines of The Broadwater and Moreton Bay.

To aid in deciding between the two routes, it is emphasised that deep drafted vessels can definitely navigate the channels linking the Gold Coast with Moreton Bay (as described previously), and that anchorage can be enjoyed every night. Most anchorages in the open bay are subject to wind direction, a lee shore in many places being capable of causing distress. As a result, anchorage choice north of the channels between the mainland and North Stradbroke Island is subject to prevailing weather.

Against this is the fact that there are a number of breakwater harbours or canal estates offering marina and/or public berth facilities. There is also the main attraction of Brisbane City where very reasonably priced public berths are available right alongside the Botanical Gardens.

Regardless of your intentions within Moreton Bay, it pays to avoid its eastern side during any threat of winds from the south, through west, to north, there being no protection from same. Even during entrenched onshore winds, anchorages can be uncomfortable under the lee of Moreton Island depending on tide-wind behaviour.

The tide floods from the north, losing itself amongst the islands between the mainland and North Stradbroke Island where it collides with the north-running flood tide entering through Jumpinpin. It ebbs on an almost exact reciprocal course.

Tidal streams run at up to three knots through the northern channels and South Passage, diminishing to around half a knot against the mainland. In all cases it pays to use a flood tide to advantage when entering the bay or any of its rivers. This should be tempered by the fact that a flood tide against a developed south-easterly trade wind creates a very short and unpleasant sea in the northern channels and open parts of the bay.

Being an enclosed waterway, its potential for wave generation is often underestimated by the visitor. Indeed, the first settlement was started at Redcliffe in the belief that open roadstead within the bay would be secure as well as convenient (to sailing vessels needing plenty of space to manoeuvre). Attitudes changed rapidly when the brig *Amity* constantly shipped water over her forecastle during a strong north-easterly wind whilst anchored off Redcliffe.

Depending on wind direction and your position in the bay, waves can reach one and sometimes two metres high and can be dismally uncomfortable if stacked up to windward-tide conditions.

Moreton Bay boasts remarkably clear water over a sandy bottom, this fact diminishing towards the south and increasing towards the north. It can be so clear over the sand banks strewn across and north from the mouth that one tenses waiting for the keel to strike bottom despite the guarantee of ample depth. This fact can be quite unnerving to the newcomer who is advised to adhere strictly to navigation marks until familiarity allows a little more freedom.

Northern Approach. The only entrance used by ships is from the north-west through the *North West Channel*. This starts at Caloundra (at the northern end of Bribie Island, off the accompanying chart) and trends south-east towards Moreton Bay's mouth. Between the southern end of Bribie Island and the north end of Moreton Island, it doglegs towards Moreton Island through *Spitfire Channel* then turns again to lay towards Cowan Cowan on the western side of Moreton Island. From there it runs down the coast of the island in *East Channel* before turning towards Brisbane via *Main Channel*. This is shown by a green line on the chart.

When sailing from the north, the North West Channel is the safest and most logical way to go. However, in fair weather and without excessive draft, it is safe to short-cut across the *North Banks*, steering from a point off Caloundra Head towards Skirmish Point on the south end of Bribie Island. This crosses the North West Channel about one third of the way down its length. If heading for Brisbane, the North West Channel should be entered and held. If heading for Bongaree (Bribie) or Scarborough Harbour, it is best to cross the channel, stand on for Skirmish Point then round up into *Deception Bay*. This latter course is described in the approach to Bongaree on page 61.

North East Approach. Except during north-east gales against an ebb tide, a small vessel may enter Moreton Bay from the north-east through *Inner Freeman Channel*. This passes alongside Moreton Island's north-west tip and cuts off the 30 extra miles demanded of the North West Channel.

The large scale plan on page 54 is best consulted for this entrance where will be seen a bar carrying approximately two metres close north of Comboyuro Point. With a flood tide, this bar can be tame and trouble-free. However, when an ebb tide acts against an onshore wind, it readily breaks in which state it denies accurate identification of the deepest water. Where doubt prevails, it pays to use the Outer Freeman or North East Channel.

Connecting the cities of Gold Coast and Brisbane by protected waterways, Moreton Bay and the Broadwater are cruising grounds in themselves. The safest entrance into Moreton Bay from the north is via North West Channel.

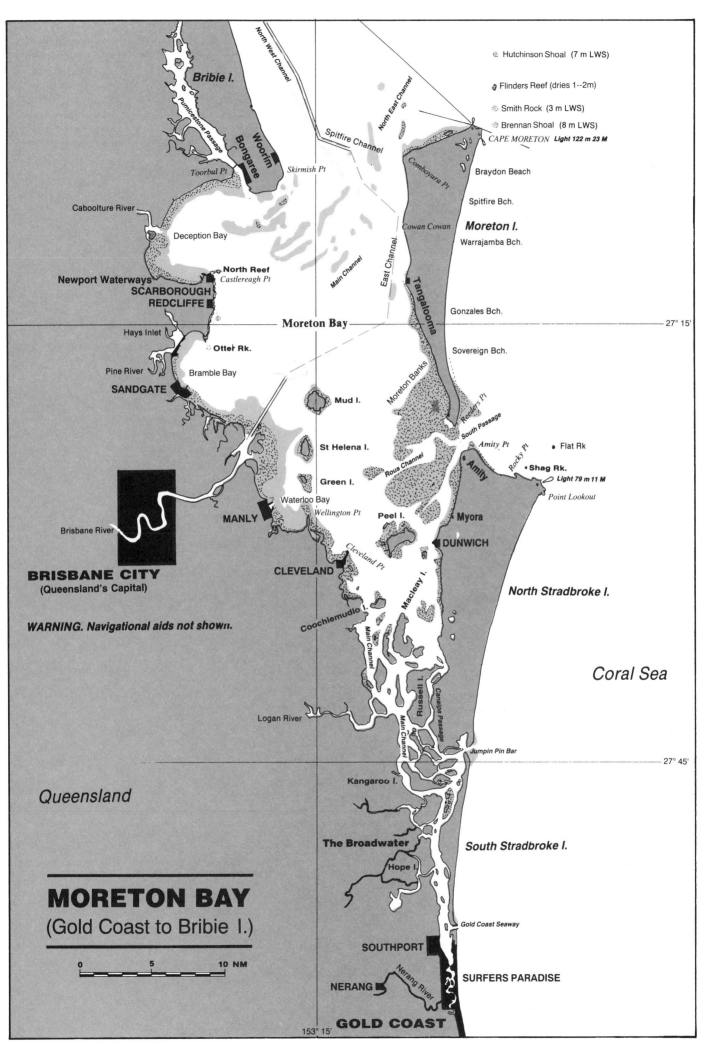

Hutchinson Shoal (7 m LWS)

Flinders Reef (dries 1--2m)

Smith Rock (3 m LWS)

Brennan Shoal (8 m LWS)

CAPE MORETON **Light 122 m 23 M**

Bribie I.

North West Channel

Spitfire Channel

North East Channel

Woorim

Bongaree

Toorbul Pt

Skirmish Pt

Comboyura Pt

Braydon Beach

Spitfire Bch.

Caboolture River

Cowan Cowan

Moreton I.

Deception Bay

Warrajamba Bch.

North Reef

Castlereagh Pt

Main Channel

East Channel

Newport Waterways

Tangalooma

SCARBOROUGH

REDCLIFFE

Gonzales Bch.

Hays Inlet

— Moreton Bay —

27° 15'

Pine River

Otter Rk.

Sovereign Bch.

Bramble Bay

Moreton Banks

SANDGATE

Reeders Pt

Mud I.

Amity Pt

Rocky Pt

Flat Rk

South Passage

St Helena I.

Amity

Shag Rk.

Rous Channel

Light 79 m 11 M

Green I.

Point Lookout

Waterloo Bay

BRISBANE CITY

(Queensland's Capital)

Wellington Pt

Peel I.

Myora

Brisbane River

MANLY

DUNWICH

Cleveland Pt

CLEVELAND

Macleay I.

North Stradbroke I.

WARNING. Navigational aids not shown.

Coochiemudlo I.

Coral Sea

Main Channel

Logan River

Russell I.

Canaipa Passage

Jumpin Pin Bar

27° 45'

Main Channel

Queensland

Kangaroo I.

The Broadwater

South Stradbroke I.

Hope I.

Gold Coast Seaway

MORETON BAY

(Gold Coast to Bribie I.)

SOUTHPORT

0   5   10 NM

SURFERS PARADISE

NERANG

Nerang River

153° 15'

GOLD COAST

Outer Freeman Channel is entered south of the Fairway Buoy, passing close westward of a drying bank separating it from Inner Freeman Channel. The least depth here is 6 metres although 3 metres will be encountered if the vessel drifts westward over Venus Banks.

North East Channel is entered about 5 miles north of Comboyuro Point, passing the Fairway Buoy on either hand then rounding a red buoy to port before steering south into Moreton Bay. This channel is marked by red porthand buoys and merges with North West Channel towards Cowan Cowan.

South Passage. *See general chart page 53* Giving access to Moreton Bay between North Stradbroke Island and Moreton Island, South Passage is a fair weather entrance only. Because its bar changes both in position and depth, it should be approached only during the second half of a flood tide with a minimal swell.

In the embryo days of Brisbane settlement, sailing ships actually favoured this passage because of the 60 miles it saved. In those days the bar carried as much as six metres and could be crossed in less than perfect conditions. So confident were the early administrators that a pilot station was established on nearby Amity Point under the lee of which many vessels transshipped their cargo onto smaller vessels which then proceeded to the Brisbane River.

Today, with many seafaring skills lost or forgotten and a distinct reluctance to send a longboat ahead to take soundings, South Passage should not be anticipated as a reliable way into Moreton Bay. If it is used, however, good, deep water exists in two inside channels; *Rainbow Channel* running south against North Stradbroke Island and *Rous Channel* running south-west into the bay. Both are well beaconed.

Anchorages. These are described and illustrated in detail starting page 55. Here it is noted that Scarborough Harbour provides the best shelter and facilities in the northern section of the bay.

Foreign vessels entering Australia for the first time through Moreton Bay are obliged to clear customs, immigration and quarantine at the entrance to the Brisbane River as described under the heading *Brisbane*. Under no circumstances may anchorage be taken prior to formalities being completed.

Tides in Moreton Bay are based on the Brisbane Bar which lies outside the mouth of the Brisbane River and thus reflects a fair average for the entire bay area. Shown in the official *Queensland Tide Tables* are dozens of secondary places scattered throughout the bay and up its rivers. At the bar, a mean high water springs of 2.16 metres is recorded. Abnormal highs may occur during prolonged, strong north-easterly winds whilst abnormal lows may occur during similar winds from the south.

Nav Aids. Being Queensland's most important and largest commercial port, there is no shortage of buoys and beacons. All are laid red to port and green to starboard when approaching Brisbane regardless of direction. Intermediate harbours within the bay, having their own approach channel are treated as the main port in their final approach.

Leading beacons are employed on most major shipping channels, but because they are always associated with port and starboard marks, the small-boat skipper may safely navigate by the latter only.

History. Moreton Bay was discovered in 1770 by Captain James Cook. He named it after James Douglas, the 14th Earl of Morton, the 'e' being added by mistake

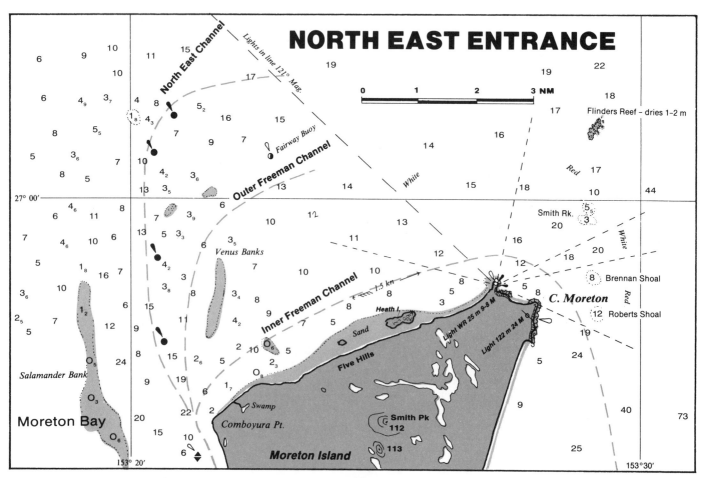

54

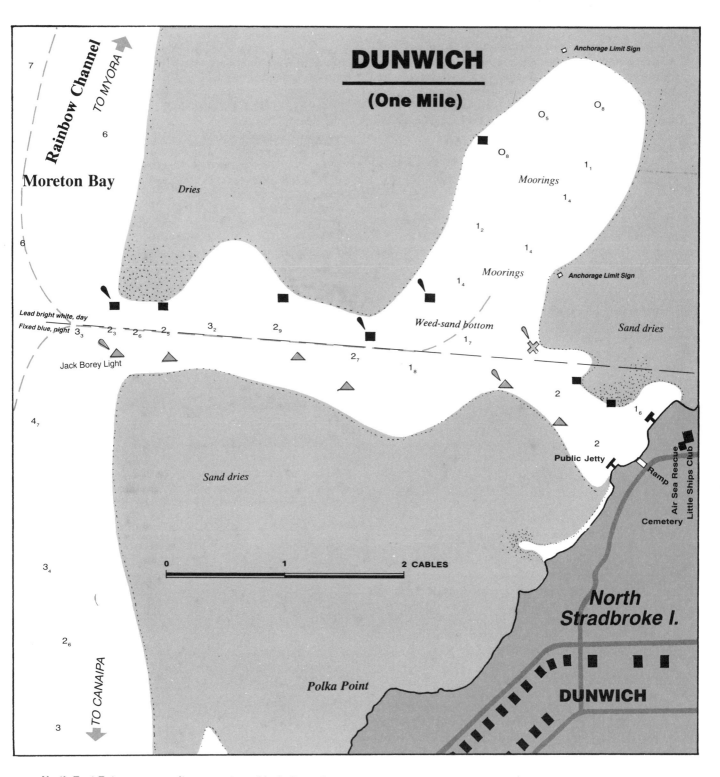

DUNWICH
(One Mile)

Anchorage Limit Sign

Rainbow Channel

TO MYORA

7

6

Moreton Bay

Dries

6

O_5

O_8

O_8

1_1

Moorings

1_4

1_2

1_4

Moorings

Anchorage Limit Sign

1_4

Weed-sand bottom

Sand dries

Lead bright white, day

Fixed blue, night 3_3 2_3 2_6 2_5 3_2 2_9 1_7

Jack Borey Light

2_7

1_8

2

1_6

4_7

2

Public Jetty

Sand dries

Ramp

3_4

2_6

0   1   2 CABLES

North
Stradbroke I.

TO CANAIPA

3

Polka Point

Air Sea Rescue

Little Ships Club

Cemetery

DUNWICH

55

North East Entrance, opposite, presents an ideal alternative entrance into Moreton Bay from the north for small ships. Beware of strong onshore windward-tide. Dunwich, above, is a pleasant though crowded anchorage offering historical interest and services.

in Hawkesworth's edition of Cook's voyages 23 years later. The bay became a penal settlement between 1824 and 1842 after which certain areas remained jails. One was at Dunwich on North Stradbroke Island and another at St Helena Island off the mouth of the Brisbane River. This was Queensland's chief penal establishment for many years being built in 1869 and disbanded in 1923. Excavations by the National Parks and Wildlife uncovered underground cells which have been preserved.

DUNWICH. Situated on the west coast of *North Stradbroke Island* 7 miles south of its northern-most tip (Amity Point), this is a sand mining settlement offering most conveniences to the visitor. It is serviced from the mainland by vehicular barge.

The anchorage is known as *One Mile* and enjoys good all-round protection at low tide when the surrounding sand banks expose. At high tide, during south, through west to north winds, it can be miserable. This is exacerbated by the local moorings denying the laying of enough anchor cable to prevent dragging. Under the circumstances, it should be considered a calm weather anchorage only at which time one must fit in as best as circumstances allow. If the anchorage is packed tight, it is always possible to anchor outside the approach channel.

Ashore, there is the welcoming *Little Ships Club* with its dinghy landing, picnic grounds, bar and bistro and ablution block whilst close by is a public jetty and ramp. In town all fuels can be obtained as can most common foodstuffs. There is also a hardware store, post office, an ANZ bank, dentist, small hospital and *Air Sea Rescue* group.

Between the waterfront and the shops is a cemetery of great historical interest, for Dunwich was one of the first settlements in Queensland (then still New South Wales).

Established as a stores depot and military post in 1827, Dunwich was an important cargo receiving trans-shipment area for materials going into Brisbane and pine logs being floated out of the Brisbane River for shipment to Sydney. Difficult to believe now is the fact that the nearby channel between North Stradbroke Island (then thought to be part of the mainland) and Moreton Island (South Passage) was the only passage used into Moreton Bay. Unpredictable shifts of sand in South Passage later forced the use of Moreton Bay's northern entrance, adding many miles to the voyage to Brisbane, but creating greater security for ship masters.

> ### Flinders Reef wreck
>
> On 11 June, 1939, the ex-minesweeper *Atlantic* was wrecked in Flinders Reef, off Cape Moreton, in heavy seas. One man was drowned but the remaining eight crew members attracted attention by burning clothing and timber in the wheelhouse.

TANGALOOMA WRECKS. Less than a mile north of Tangalooma, off a part of Moreton Island known as *False Patch*, a small boat anchorage has been formed by the scuttling of workboats on Sholl Bank. Comprising fifteen vessels ranging from dredges to dumb barges, a wall 300 metres long paralleling the Moreton coast at a distance of about 180 metres offshore, was commenced in 1963. It was the result of an inability to sell the vessels coupled with the Small Craft Co-ordination Committee's request for the government to provide an emergency harbour on that side of Moreton Island.

Intended to present a lee from westerly winds, the project failed for, while protection is improved, it is not ideal. The anchorage is most uncomfortable during strong winds from south, through west, to north. Depths tend around 5 metres.

CAPE MORETON. The approach and entry into Moreton Bay through *Freeman Channels* and *North East Channel* has been discussed on page 54. The large scale plan is offered to assist in that approach and also to indicate that anchorage can be taken under the lee of the cape when circumstances dictate. Rarely, if ever, free from movement, the anchorage west of *Heath Island* is the best although anywhere along the north-west face of Moreton Island is suitable.

Vessels remaining on the eastern side of Moreton Bay, north from Dunwich, will find Tangaloma Wrecks a useful anchorage providing the wind is in the east. Moreton Island offers good protection almost anywhere under its lee under such conditions.

CLEVELAND POINT is 11 miles south-east of the Brisbane River entrance. One of Queensland's oldest settlements, it has a large shopping centre and canal development known as *Raby Bay Canal Estate*.

Under the lee of the headland is a small boat harbour with ramp and Air Sea Rescue station to the west of which extends the estate. The future promises a large public marina in the south-west corner of this estate which will be approached through its own channel. Meanwhile, entrance to the existing development is towards its eastern end close to the boat harbour. All channels are beaconed. *Not illustrated large scale*

MANLY BOAT HARBOUR is a fully protected haven on the mainland a few miles south of the *Brisbane River entrance*. It is a logical stop for those wanting to victual without visiting the city or who prefer to bus into the city rather than take the boat upriver. The suburb of Manly satisfies all needs and the waterfront services are comprehensive.

The harbour is entered through a channel marked by beacons after which there are a number of berthing alternatives available. These are listed here.

Pile Berths are available through the Port Authority office located on the *W. M. Gunn Jetty*. Proceed to this jetty and secure alongside for allocation.

Royal Queensland Yacht Squadron Marina and general facilities are available to visitors who belong to any boat club outside the Brisbane Metropolitan area. The first night is free after which the standard daily charge is levied. Go direct to the holding area

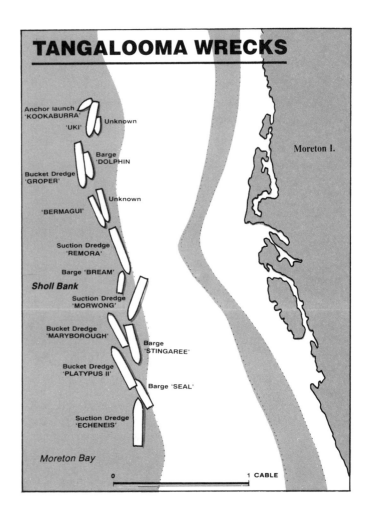

TANGALOOMA WRECKS

Anchor launch 'KOOKABURRA'
'UKI'
Unknown
Barge 'DOLPHIN'
Bucket Dredge 'GROPER'
Unknown
'BERMAGUI'
Suction Dredge 'REMORA'
Barge 'BREAM'
Sholl Bank
Suction Dredge 'MORWONG'
Bucket Dredge 'MARYBOROUGH'
Barge 'STINGAREE'
Bucket Dredge 'PLATYPUS II'
Barge 'SEAL'
Suction Dredge 'ECHENEIS'
Moreton Bay
Moreton I.

0   1 CABLE

Whaling Station

Tangalooma, Moreton Island, was a bay whaling station which opened in 1952, killing its first whale on 6 June of that year. The company's licence allowed 500 whales per season to be killed for five years.

High, steep banks are a feature of the Brisbane River in its upper reaches. Brisbane is described over the page.

Manly Boat Harbour presents an ideal way of visiting Brisbane without ascending the river, public transport being good between here and the city. Boating facilities are excellent here.

MANLY BOAT HARBOUR

0   1   2 CABLES

18' S.C.

BRISBANE

Darling Pt Sailing Sqd
Coast Guard
Ramp
Port Office

Moreton Bay
Trailer Boat Club
W.M. Gunn Jetty

Shops

Pile Berths

Waterloo Bay

Wynnum Manly
Yacht Club

East Coast Marina

Fuel

Fuel

Marina Office

Ramp

Royal Qld Yacht Squadron

---

in front of the marina office next to the obvious straddle-lift.

East Coast Marina is privately owned and welcomes visitors who should go to the fuel dock for allocation.

Wynnum Manly Yacht Club Marina, situated alongside East Coast Marina, is private only with no visitor facilities.

MBTBC Marina. Available only to members of the *Moreton Bay Trailer Boat Club*, this marina extends south from the swimming pool area between the shore and the public marina.

Port Authority Marina, projecting from the W. M. Gunn Jetty, is fully occupied with permanent boats. Berths are rarely, if ever, available for transients.

General Services. Engineering, electronic and electrical repairs, sails and upholstery, fabrication and all hull repairs can be satisfied in or from Manly. Haul-out is by straddle-lift at East Coast Marina and the Royal Queensland Yacht Squadron and chandlery items are well represented in local stores. Fuel can be taken aboard at both the above marinas.

The Future. A canal dredged from the harbour to the town front in the approximate area of the present swimming pool has been suggested. This will place commercial craft closer to the action, but its impact on existing berths is uncertain.

Waterloo Bay extends from *Manly* to *Wellington Point*. To the north of the latter is *King Island* under whose lee fair anchorage can be sought during southerly winds. The water is very shoal demanding a cautious approach. At the bottom of this bay is *Aquatic Paradise Canal Estate* in which is a small marina. This is for residents only.

First Into River

The *Mermaid*, a schooner of 84 tons, was the first known seagoing vessel to enter the Brisbane River. She shipped the first cargo of pine logs (used for masts and spars) out of Brisbane Town.

BRISBANE is Queensland's capital city and is situated about 14 miles up the Brisane River. Much of its industry lines the downstream section of the river whilst its suburbs sprawl north and south along the western shores of Moreton Bay. The city can be visited by boat, there being a mooring area next to the Botanical Gardens.

Brisbane River Approach. Vessels entering *Moreton Bay* from the north can do no better than follow the commercial shipping route down the inside of Moreton Island then diagonally across to the outer end of the main river entrance channel. This starts abeam of *Mud Island* and continues as a straight, dredged line for 3½ miles to the entrance-proper abeam *Bishop Island*. This line is indicated by port and starboard beacons and leading beacons are situated on conspicuous piles towards the centre of Moreton Bay. The average small craft need not adhere to these leads, remaining within the boundaries of port and starboard beacons.

From *Redcliffe Peninsula*, a course can be laid direct for the *Old Bar Cutting* which is the original approach channel to the river entrance. It is still available to small craft and carries adequate depth at low tide for most deep keelers.

From the south, out of the Broadwater or Manly Boat Harbour, St Helena Island should be used as final reference before laying for the main entrance channel which, from this direction, can be safely entered half-way down its length. The *Boat Passage*, lying between Whyte Island and Fisherman Islands is available to shoal-draft motor boats only, the low bridge denying access to any masted vessel.

Up the River. Having entered the mouth between *Luggage Point* and *Fisherman Islands*, the river is ascended by adhering to the obvious leading beacons and port and starboard marks. Small craft can afford to wander considerably, but in the event of disorientation when commercial traffic is heavy, it pays to adhere to the marks as closely as possible at all times giving way to deeper drafted vessels. The Gateway Bridge between Hemmant and Pinkenba carries more than enough height for all masts and commercial ships. It is conspicuous from well outside the river as is an airport control tower to its north.

Pile Berths are situated off the *Botanical Gardens* in the Town Reach between the Story Bridge and the Captain Cook Bridge. There are four rows extending south from the Edward Street passenger ferry and are charged at a very reasonable rate considering their position. The rows are A,B,C and D from the gardens out. The inner row (A) should be used by smaller boats, larger vessels using the outer row. Take an empty berth and report to the office after securing. The office is on the corner of *Ann* and *Wharf Streets* directly uptown. Walk straight up Edward Street and turn right into Ann.

Facilities ashore include dinghy landing, laundry, toilets and showers.

Marina. Accepting casuals is the *Waterfront Place Marina* immediately downstream of the pile berths.

Tides. Brisbane tides are based on predictions at the Bar. Tides change at the Botanical Gardens approximately 1 hour 20 minutes later than the Bar.

Facilities. The City of Brisbane will not be found wanting when it comes to services required by the average sailor. Everything is there somewhere. However, while the city itself could not be handier, such establishments as sailmakers, engineers and so on demand a lengthy walk or use of the excellent public transport system. Considering the distances sometimes involved it pays to phone ahead and to seek knowledge of the correct bus to catch. The environs of Brisbane can be thoroughly confusing to the newcomer.

Customs. Brisbane is a major customs port. Advise ahead by radio and do not land until cleared.

CABBAGE TREE CREEK empties into *Moreton Bay* near the suburb of Shorncliffe between the Brisbane River and Redcliffe. Its dredged, beaconed channel can be negotiated at low tide by keel boats, but a little flood is advisable.

The *Queensland Cruising Yacht Club* has member-owned berths at the marina which are sometimes available to casuals. Off the marina are pile berths where silting can often deny them to keel boats. The town of Shorncliffe and especially Sandgate offer all services. *Not illustrated large scale*

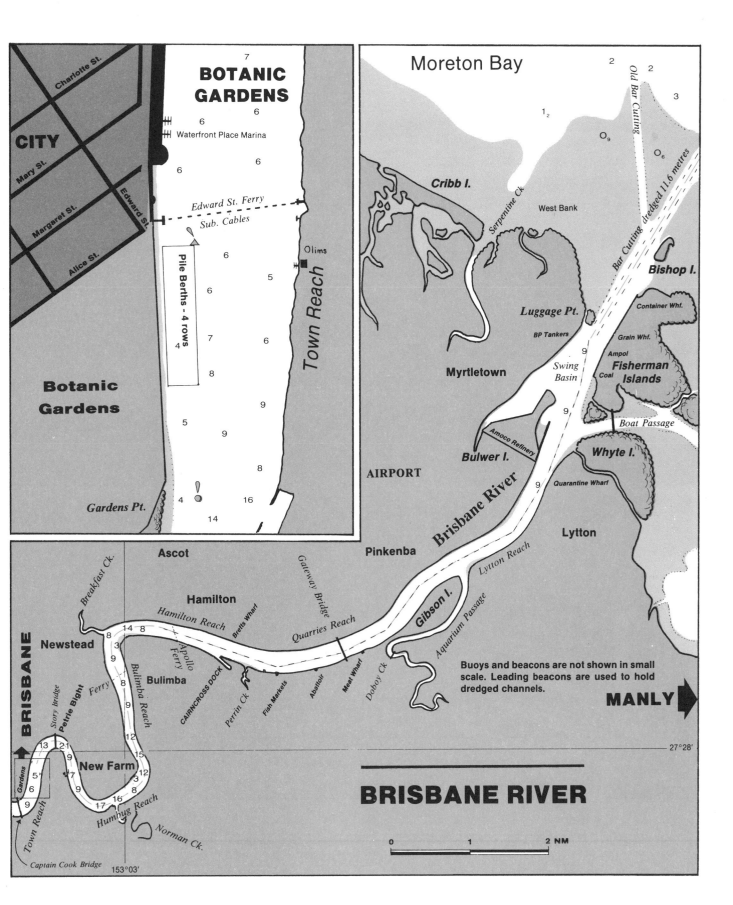

BOTANIC GARDENS

CITY

Charlotte St.

Mary St.

Margaret St.

Alice St.

Edward St.

7

6

6

Waterfront Place Marina

6

6

6

Edward St. Ferry

Sub. Cables

Pile Berths - 4 rows

6

5

6

4

7

8

6

9

9

5

9

8

4

16

14

Botanic Gardens

Gardens Pt.

Town Reach

Olims

Moreton Bay

2

2

2

3

1₂

O₉

O₆

Old Bar Cutting

Bar Cutting dredged 11.6 metres

Cribb I.

Serpentine Ck

West Bank

Bishop I.

Container Whf.

Grain Whf.

Luggage Pt.

BP Tankers

Ampol

Coal

Fisherman Islands

9

9

Swing Basin

Boat Passage

Myrtletown

Amoco Refinery

Bulwer I.

Whyte I.

9

Quarantine Wharf

AIRPORT

Brisbane River

Lytton

Ascot

Breakfast Ck.

Hamilton

Hamilton Reach

Brett's Wharf

Gateway Bridge

Quarries Reach

Pinkenba

Lytton Reach

Gibson I.

Aquarium Passage

27°28'

BRISBANE

Newstead

Story Bridge

Petrie Bight

Ferry

Apollo Ferry

Bulimba

Bulimba Reach

CAIRNCROSS DOCK

Perrin Ck.

Fish Markets

Abattoir

Meat Wharf

Doboy Ck.

8 14 8

3

9

8

12

15

13 21

9

5'

6

9

New Farm

12

8

3

17 16

Humbug Reach

Norman Ck.

Captain Cook Bridge

153°03'

Gardens

Town Reach

Buoys and beacons are not shown in small scale. Leading beacons are used to hold dredged channels.

MANLY ▶

BRISBANE RIVER

0   1   2 NM

The four rows of pile berths paralleling Brisbane's Botanic Gardens provide ideal city-centre security and convenience for the cruising boat. Laundry and ablutions are ashore and dinghy landing is via the ferry pontoon. The berths are shown in the photograph, left, and large scale inset, above.

Floods

The Brisbane River is capable of flooding to such an extent that lower Edward Street is more than two metres underwater. In the 1893 flood, steamers stranded in the Botanic Gardens, close to the area of the present day pile berths.

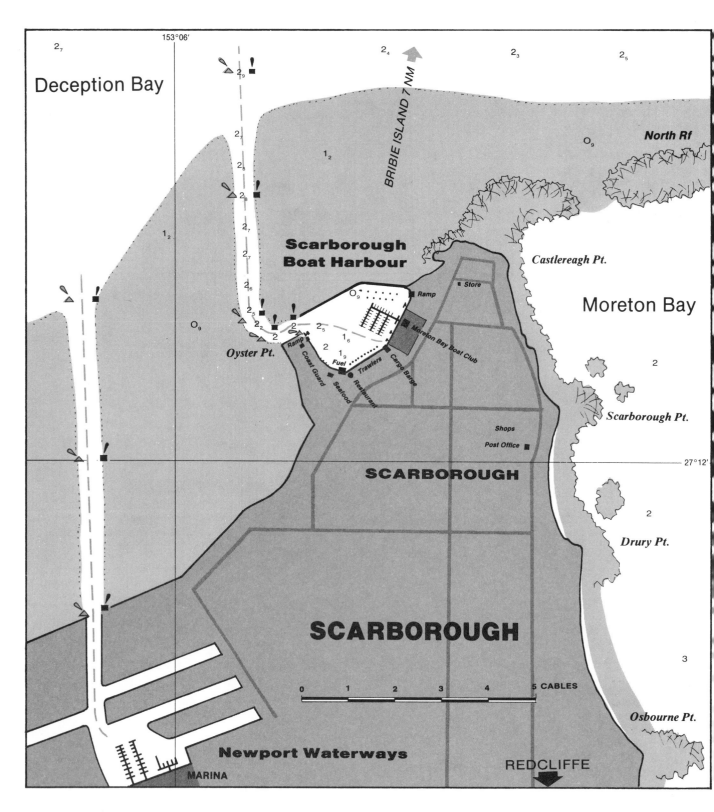

Deception Bay

Scarborough
Boat Harbour

BRIBIE ISLAND 7 NM

Oyster Pt.

Ramp

Store

Coast Guard

Ramp

Fuel

Seafood

Trawlers

Restaurant

Cargo Barge

Moreton Bay Boat Club

Castlereagh Pt.

Moreton Bay

North Rf

Shops

Post Office

SCARBOROUGH

Scarborough Pt.

27°12'

Drury Pt.

SCARBOROUGH

0   1   2   3   4   5 CABLES

Osbourne Pt.

Newport Waterways

REDCLIFFE

MARINA

SCARBOROUGH BOAT HARBOUR. 12 miles north of the Brisbane River mouth and 7 miles south of Bribie Island, this breakwater harbour lies on the western side of *Castlereagh Point*. It is on the southern side of *Deception Bay*.

Approaching from the south, the *Redcliffe Peninsula* is obvious enough for its scattered low cliffs and dense settlement. Its most conspicuous feature is the Redcliffe Hospital chimney which looks like a modern light tower. The remarkable peaks of the Glass House Mountains dominate the distant background during good visibility.

From the north, the chimney again is obvious whilst

Scarborough Boat Harbour is a base for local prawners as well as a Moreton Island cargo and vehicular barge.

the red cliff along Castlereagh Point can be very conspicuous depending on sun angle. From both directions, shoals and reefs are buoyed and beaconed whilst the final approach channel into the harbour is marked by port and starboard light beacons. At night they are unmistakable for their synchronised flashing sequence.

Anchorage. Except in an emergency, it is preferable not to anchor in the boat harbour. Late night visitors should take an empty pile berth or procede straight

60

to a visitor pontoon of the *Morteon Bay Boat Club* near the Moreton Island barge ramp. Check with authorities first thing the next day.

Berths. The Moreton Bay Boat Club's marina opened late 1991, the berths being sold to individuals. Many are empty and are managed by the club. It is always possible that a long-term berth would be available.

Otherwise, the public pile berths, although reduced in numbers to make way for the marina, sometimes have vacancies. Inquiries should be made direct to the local boat harbour supervisor.

Facilities. Fuel is alongside in the southern corner of the harbour with trawler berths to its east and west. A restaurant and seafood outlet is in the vicinity.

Launching ramps are at opposite sides of the harbour with the local *Coast Guard* next to one and a public jetty close to both. Nearby, up the road to the north, is a general store close to which is a bus stop.

Buses run regularly to Redcliffe and beyond to Brisbane City, many passing through Scarborough whose shops are within easy walking distance. For serious victualling, Redcliffe is to be preferred.

The Moreton Bay Boat Club offers its bar, showers and general facilities to visitors for a small fee. With the introduction of poker machines into Queensland late 1991 and the consequent rules regarding lock-up premises, make sure you have a key in the event of the yard being locked and denying access to your boat (if alongside the marina or visitor berths).

BONGAREE is a settlement on the south-west corner of *Bribie Island*, the latter creating a navigable waterway between it and the mainland. Known as *Pumicestone Passage*, it is available only to shallow

draft craft capable of passing under the 4.8 metre high *Toorbul Point Bridge*. Anchorage for deeper, higher craft is to the south of this bridge.

Approach from the north is down the North West Channel although such are the depths between it and Bribie Island's east coast, the full-length beach may be paralleled all the way from near Caloundra to Skirmish Point (south-east tip of Bribie Island).

On rounding Skirmish Point, a red beacon is seen to port on a drying sand bank one mile offshore after which a green beacon is passed to starboard. It marks a shoal with 0.3 metres low water springs. The shallowest part of this channel is immediately south of Skirmish Point with 2.4 metres.

Beyond the green beacon, a yellow beacon is passed to port then the shore along Bongaree is favoured, passing small, green beacons to port as Pumicestone Passage is entered.

From the south, the easiest and least confusing approach is from the vicinity of the Brisbane River approach channel direct to Castlereagh Point, on the Redcliffe Peninsula, passing its green lit beacon to port by a fair margin. From there, steer for a red lit buoy passing it to starboard then round up for the previously mentioned yellow beacon standing off Pumicestone Passage. Again, this is passed to port.

Anchorage can be taken wherever convenient against the Bribie Island shore. The holding can be indifferent depending on location. The best is   upstream , clear of local moorings. Surprisingly, this entire anchorage can be swell-prone even with the wind in the north. The degree of comfort will depend largely on tidal flow.

Tide floods north and ebbs south at a rate capable of creating windward-tide antics in strong winds. The flow continues for some time after predicted turn. Bon-

Newport Waterways

A canal residential development south-west of Scarborough Boat Harbour (see chart opposite), the marina is available to the general public. It sells fuel and boat accessories and has a small shopping complex.

Renee Tighe **alongside a visitors berth in Scarborough Boat Harbour. The Moreton Island barge is left.**

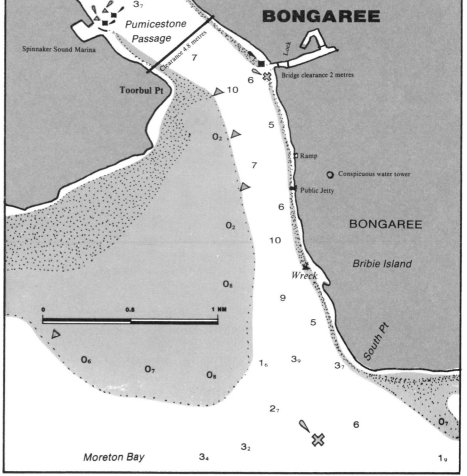

garee will be found in the *Tide Tables* under Pumicestone Passage on Brisbane data.

Facilities. There are no waterfront fixtures here, but Bongaree shops include hardware, general store, post office, ANZ and Westpac Banks and supermarket in the vicinity. More shops and a hotel are situated near the bridge exit at Bellara.

CALOUNDRA *(Not illustrated).* Between the northern end of *Bribie Island* and *Caloundra Head* lies the entrance to Pumicestone Passage, a shallow waterway separating Bribie Island from the mainland. The entrance is barred and extremely dangerous in all but calm weather. It demands a high tide and local knowledge to negotiate.

Against the north bank is good water once over the bar which is indicated by unlit buoys. Along here is a ramp, public jetty and *Australian Volunteer Coast Guard*. The town of Caloundra has all facilities and is the southern-most part of the Sunshine Coast.

MOOLOOLABA is a very popular alternative to the Gold Coast and Brisbane owing to its easier and more instant accessibility from offshore. 27 miles north-west of Cape Moreton and 55 miles south of Wide Bay Bar, its breakwater entrance is safe in all weather subject to the qualifications noted under the heading 'Approach'.

Vessels entering Australia for the first time please note: Mooloolaba is *not* a port of entry, the closest being at the mouth of the Brisbane River to the south, or Bundaberg to the north.

Approach is clear of all offshore hazards except for *Geering Shoal* 5 miles north-east of *Point Cartwright*. This carries 6.7 metres at low water springs and can break in particularly heavy weather. A buoy is positioned off this shoal.

Point Cartwright itself lifts from the horizon at a distance of about 8–10 miles, but its light and control tower, tank and highrise are seen well before this. The highrise buildings on the point are separate from those extending from Mooloolaba and Maroochydore.

The featureless, sand-fronted low land of Bribie Island is seen here with the Glasshouse Mountains behind.

Prawn Trawlers work Deception Bay, between Scarborough and Bribie Island, regularly and should be given a wide berth.

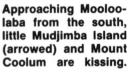

Approaching Mooloolaba from the south, little Mudjimba Island (arrowed) and Mount Coolum are kissing.

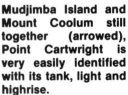

Mudjimba Island and Mount Coolum still together (arrowed), Point Cartwright is very easily identified with its tank, light and highrise.

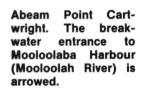

Abeam Point Cartwright. The breakwater entrance to Mooloolaba Harbour (Mooloolah River) is arrowed.

Mooloolaba Harbour entrance is again arrowed. This is taken during an approach from the north.

62

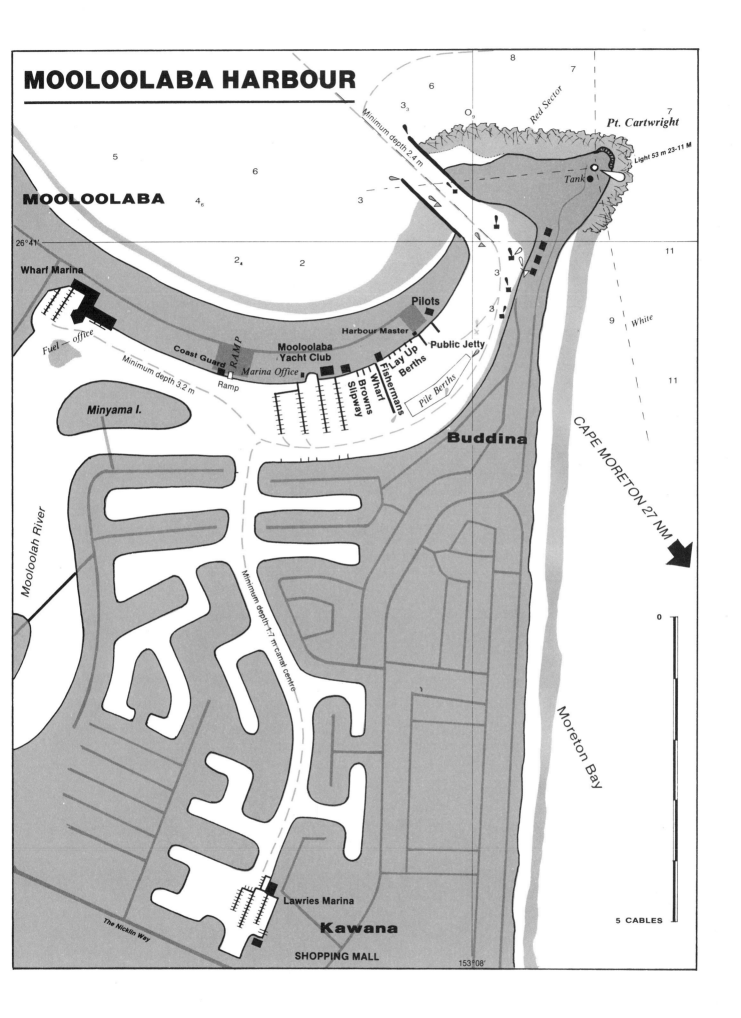

MOOLOOLABA HARBOUR

MOOLOOLABA

26°41'

Pt. Cartwright

Light 53 m 23-11 M

Red Sector

Tank

Minimum depth 2.4 m

Wharf Marina

Fuel — office

Minimum depth 3.2 m

Coast Guard

R.A.M.P

Marina Office

Ramp

Mooloolaba Yacht Club

Pilots

Harbour Master

Public Jetty

Lay Up Berths

Fishermans Wharf

Browns Slipway

Pile Berths

Buddina

Minyama I.

Mooloolah River

White

CAPE MORETON 27 NM

Moreton Bay

Minimum depth 1.7 m canal centre

The Nicklin Way

Lawries Marina

Kawana

SHOPPING MALL

153°08'

0

5 CABLES

63

The breakwater entrance should carry a minimum of 2.4 metres on the leads at low water springs, but periodic silting throws a bar of sand out from the end of the northern breakwater which encroaches seriously on the channel. This is usually cleared by dredge as soon as possible.

Anchorage is not permitted anywhere in the harbour. A berth of some description is obligatory, the details of which follow.

Pile Berths. Dwindling in numbers and destined for extinction, these are nearly always fully occupied. To inquire, go alongside the downstream side of the public jetty close to which is the port office. There is a one hour limit on this jetty.

Mooloolaba Yacht Club Marina can be called ahead on VHF or 27 megs. If arriving after hours, take an empty berth on one of the two upstream fingers (C or D) and report to the nearby office the next day.

The Wharf Marina offers casual berths at competitive rates and can be called on VHF–73 or 27 megs channel 90. When approaching the marina, beware of a drying shoal close off its southern extreme.

Lawries Marina. Although all berths have been sold to individual owners, casual and permanent berths are available from a pool managed at the office. The marina's founder, Keith Lawrie, retains ownership of the hard-stand and haul-out yard which has been improved and expanded.

Nav Aids. All beacons are lit. Beacons line each side of the entrance between the breakwaters where the best water is held by leading lights ahead. Their shapes are unremarkable in daylight and easily missed. However, steering a simple mid course holds deep water. After turning off these leads, green beacons are passed to starboard up to the yacht club after first passing a middle yellow beacon to starboard. This is passed to port when steering for the Public Wharf.

Tides turn approximately 1½ hours earlier than Brisbane data.

Facilities. The town of Mooloolaba is a little over half a mile from the yacht club while a shopping complex is less than that distance from Lawrie's Marina. It offers a better range of commodities making it a favourite place to victual.

Fuel, water and LPG are available alongside at all marinas and water only at the Public Wharf. Trawlers have their own infrastructure to the west of this wharf.

Haul-out by slipway or straddle lift is available at Brown's Yard near the yacht club or by 40 tonne straddle lift at Lawrie's Marina. Chandleries are located at both centres and a sailmaker is established near the yacht club as are various repair shops. Work on every aspect of a boat can be carried out in this area.

MUDJIMBA ISLAND is a tiny speck against the mainland less than 5 miles north of Mooloolaba Harbour. With rocky cliffs to its south-east, it is scrub-covered and surrounded by a rock ledge with a small beach on its north side. The bottom is rocky with a chance of fouling the anchor. It is strictly a calm weather lunch stop.

The island is privately leased with a house ashore built of local stone. At the end of its lease period it may revert to national park.

NOOSA HEADS. 18 miles north of Mooloolaba Harbour and protecting the barred mouth of the *Noosa River*, Noosa Heads is a very popular part of the *Sunshine Coast*. The headland is unremarkable, but the mountain peaks in the background provide good reference. The coast to its north runs up to Double Island Point as a dune and coloured sands-backed beach.

The river entrance is barred and carries no navigation aids. In calm weather at high tide a vessel may enter as long as her draft does not exceed tide height. Imme-

Noosa Heads chart over page.

Point Cartwright Lighthouse stands 53 metres above sea level and is visible for 23 nautical miles. It was established in 1979.

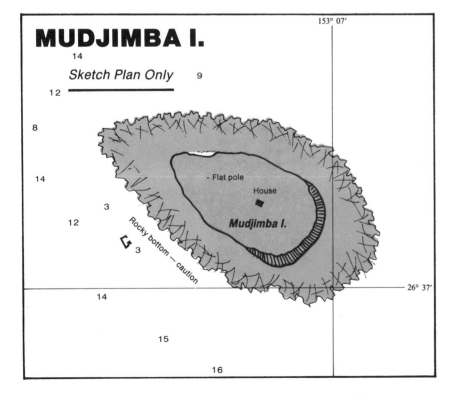

MUDJIMBA I.

Sketch Plan Only

153° 07'

14
12
9
8
14
12
3
3
Rocky bottom — caution
14
15
16

- Flat pole
House
Mudjimba I.

26° 37'

Three views of diminutive Mudjimba Island, 4 miles north of Mooloolaba. In the top photograph, Mount Coolum is to the left of the island with Arkwright Point to its right. Seen again in the centre photograph, Mount Coolum is a distinctive landmark on this part of the coast.

Mount Coolum is abeam with Arkwright Point right.

Arkwright Point abeam. The background in this area is spiked with peaked hills similar to, but not as dramatic as the Glass House Mountains.

Mount Cooroy rises to 424 metres nearly 10 miles west-southwest of Noosa Head.

Mount Cooroy, centre, is to the left of a conspicuous tank and tower on the foreshore hills a few miles south of Noosa Head.

These two photographs show Noosa Head approaching from the south (top) and north (bottom). Laguna Bay, under its lee, is a tolerable anchorage in fair weather. The Noosa River demands local knowledge to navigate.

diately inside the entrance, however, is a confusion of shifting sand banks demanding local knowledge to navigate. The stranger is warned away.

Anchorage under the lee of the headland is tolerable in fair weather although a south-east swell tends to be omnipresent. Getting ashore without being dumped can be a problem. The best place is towards the eastern end of the beach close to the town. All shops are represented here.

The Wharf Marina, Mooloolaba.

65

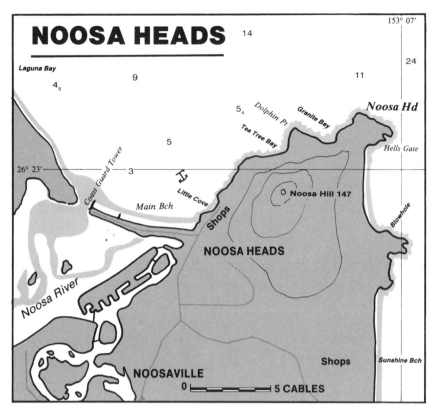

NOOSA HEADS

14

153° 07'

24

Laguna Bay

9

11

4₅

5₄

Dolphin Pt

Granite Bay

Noosa Hd

Tea Tree Bay

5

Hells Gate

26° 23'

3

Coast Guard Tower

Little Cove

Noosa Hill 147

Main Bch

Shops

Blowhole

NOOSA HEADS

Noosa River

Shops

Sunshine Bch

NOOSAVILLE

0 ⊢────────┤ 5 CABLES

Noosa Heads description

previous page.

DOUBLE ISLAND POINT. Giving Wide Bay a semblance of protection from south to easterly winds, anchorage under this headland is one of the most uncomfortable on the coast. It is, nevertheless, obligatory under certain circumstances when awaiting the flood tide over the Wide Bay Bar. It is 45 miles north of Mooloolaba.

Approach. Soon after leaving Mooloolaba, *Noosa Head* with its cluster of houses on the south side will be obvious from where background land extends to the north. This is comprised of steep, grass-covered, coloured sand dunes, patches of which are bare. It extends to Double Island Point which itself rises from the horizon at a distance of around 17 miles. At 10–12 miles it forms into two parts which rapidly become the one, single headland fringed in low, black cliffs to eastward and supporting a lighthouse.

Eleven cables north-north-east of Double Island Point lies *Wolf Rock* which is actually a cluster of

rocks drying 2.5 metres low water springs. Passage between the land and the rocks is perfectly safe, but where doubt prevails sail outside the rock then lay for the inner part of the headland from where shoals are skirted for the anchorage.

Anchorage. Depending on the severity of the prevailing onshore wind, the swell can break along the 2 to 4 metre line making anchorage in close to the beach dangerous. Under these circumstances, the 5 to 6 metre line should be favoured. Otherwise, move in as close as draft and tide allow towards the southern extreme of the bay.

Rainbow Beach is a popular camping and retirement area acting as a base for those vehicles bound for Fraser Island. It has a surf club, shops, service station and communications. As recently as 1965 it did not exist in any form, land release only then being considered by the Gympie Council.

Of Interest. Immediately south of Double Island Point will be noted the rusting, gutted remains of the 1600–tonne ship, *Cherry Venture*, driven ashore by an unseasonal cyclone in July 1973. The then owner of South Molle Tourist Resort, Peter Vagellas, purchased salvage rights and set about dredging a float-pool and channel. His efforts were crippled by heavy onshore winds and the vessel remains. Today she is a favourite attraction for the countless 4WD vehicles driving between Noosa and Rainbow Beach.

DOUBLE ISLAND POINT

Rainbow Beach

Wolf Rock
Dries 2.5 metres

Wide Bay

27

12

10

12

17

24

Double Island Point

10

7

4

10

8

2

21

6

4

1₈

Manned light

7

4

2

24

5

2₄

1₃

4

Cooloola National Park

Poona Lake

Wreck 'CHERRY VENTURE'

Great Sandy Strait is formed by Fraser Island which has become a major destination for 4WD drivers. Vehicular barges operate to the island from Inskip Point, River Heads and Urangan. Most resorts are on the ocean side of the island with one, Kingfisher Bay, located on the strait side opposite Urangan.

The waterways throughout the Great Sandy Strait are lined with mangrove forests in many places, especially against the mainland.

GREAT SANDY STRAIT. Offering a calm-water alternative to the ocean passage outside Fraser Island, Great Sandy Strait runs nearly 40 miles from its southern entrance at Wide Bay Bar to its northern extreme at Hervey Bay. Although dominated by shoal to drying banks, the main navigable passage guarantees freedom of movement to all deep keelers, especially if tides are used to advantage.

Formed by Fraser Island to the east and the mainland to the west, Great Sandy Strait provides access to Snapper Creek and the town of Tin Can Bay, Mary River and the city of Maryborough and the towns of Pialba, Scarness, Torquay and Urangan collectively known as the City of Hervey Bay. Smaller coastal settlements such as Tuan and Maaroom are accessible at high tide.

Fraser Island, the largest sand island in the world, extends a sand bottom across the channel, but the constant movement of tides denies the clarity of water one might expect. This clarity improves and in places becomes brilliant where it fans out into Hervey Bay.

Nav Aids. Although it is not sensible to do so, night navigation is possible owing to all beacons and buoys being lit. All such aids are laid as if Snapper Creek were the main port of approach, red being passed to port and green to starboard sailing south from Hervey Bay to Snapper Creek. When ascending the Mary River, Maryborough becomes the port of approach.

Approach. This has been dealt with under the later headings, *Wide Bay Bar*, *Hervey Bay* and *Urangan*. The Mary River and Tin Can Bay also have their own approach information.

Anchorages. These are shown in large scale after this description of the Great Sandy Straits and will be identified by noting the boxed sections on the overall chart on page 69. Here, anchorage in general is examined.

As a first night anchorage from the south, it is hard to beat *Pelican Bay* or its mouth (see page 71). Sim-

ilarly, from the north, *Urangan Harbour* or the *Susan River* provide the best all-round shelter. These will be found on pages 80 and 76 respectively.

During winds from the east to south-east, anchorage in the northern region can be enjoyed anywhere along Fraser Island, especially in the *Balarrgan* area. With the wind north-east to north, fair haven can be found in a gutter hard against the south-west tip of *Big Woody Island*.

In calm weather, anchorage can be taken anywhere in the Strait with draft and tide allowing.

Creeks. There are numerous tidal creeks penetrating both the island and the mainland allowing keelers into float-holes in certain areas. More commonly, they are available only to shoal-draft vessels which may be obliged to take the bottom at low tide in some creeks. Creek navigation is best left to those whose shallow-draft craft permit the practice.

Tides. The tide floods from both ends meeting in the region of Boonlye Point (Fraser Island) from where it ebbs away north and south. In the *Tide Tables*, Bundaberg is the main port, secondary prediction stations being at *Point Vernon, Urangan, Mary River entrance, Ungowa, Boonlye Point, Snout Point, Elbow Point, Inskip Point* and *Tin Can Bay*.

Tides tend to be lower in the south than the north and a typical average high water springs is around 2.5 and 3.5 south and north respectively. Currents vary but tend to maximise at 3 knots springs in the most restricted channel.

Customs. Late 1987 Maryborough Customs closed its door for the last time, meaning that clearance is no longer possible anywhere in the Great Sandy Strait. The closest clearance port is Bundaberg.

The small scale chart of Great Sandy Strait and Hervey Bay is over the page after which large scale anchorage charts follow.

North White Cliffs, Fraser Island. Superb south-east anchorage can be found here.

Near Balarrgan, this new jetty marks the position of the residential-resort development on Fraser Island.

One of the few reefs in Great Sandy Strait, Boon Boon Rocks are south of Little Woody Island against Fraser Island. They are marked with a yellow beacon.

Moon Point is a low headland on the western side of Fraser Island where anchorage can be found.

Marinas. There are marinas at Snapper Creek, Maryborough, and Urangan.

Haul Out and Repairs at Snapper Creek, Maryborough and Urangan.

Victuals at all the above centres with Maryborough the best in price and services.

Warning. The First Edition of charts produced by the Department of Harbours and Marine gives the wrong numbers for all red marks on the southern sheet. These marks are correct in Tin Can Inlet only. Numbers are correct on the northern sheet and, as a result, confusion arises when moving from one sheet to the other and finding the numbers do not tally. The red beacons on the southern chart should all read 2 figures higher than that shown. Thus, S34 becomes S36 and so on.

Navigation. Theoretically, a vessel drawing as much as one metre could successfully pass through the shallowest part of the Strait at low water springs. However, without local knowledge of the gutters within gutters, it is almost certain that a visitor will hit, probably to the south of Turkey Island. It definitely pays to use the tide to advantage. It also pays to get right through the shallowest section before the tide turns, the habit of riding the flood current to Boonlye Point and the ebb current out threatening a stranding.

Despite the excellence of the navigational aids, it also pays to use binoculars to locate the next buoy or beacon well ahead of time. Many strandings occur because of a last-minute inability to find a beacon that was assumed to be obvious. Sometimes they blend into the background, become confused with other boats or are short-circuited by aiming for one beyond the next in logical progression.

From the south, after crossing Wide Bay Bar, the water is deep right across the channel and Fraser Island can be favoured to starboard to Elbow Point from where the first red beacon is sighted.

Passing the first red beacon to starboard (sailing north), a set of leading beacons are sighted towards the north-east which are held until close to the front beacon. The bank to starboard is then paralleled until back-leads are brought together for the run north towards Garry's Anchorage. En route will be found green buoys which are passed to port.

These buoys introduce a simple system of keeping green marks to port and red to starboard all the way through the straits. The shallowest area is between *Moonboom Island* and *Turkey Island* where a rising tide is essential if a keel boat is to clear. This section is best navigated after the second or third hour depending on draft.

Once past Turkey Island, the channels are very deep and easily held with a set of leading beacons helping with the exit from *Ungowa* (where will be seen a jetty, ramp and house).

From the north, navigation into the Great Sandy Straits is easier in that navigation marks are passed red to port and green to starboard as is one's instinct. However, initial entry into the channels from the open space of Hervey Bay can prove confusing to newcomers and this subject is dealt with on page 82.

Individual parts of the Great Sandy Strait are described in the following pages.

Great Sandy Strait and Hervey Bay constitute a worthwhile cruising ground in themselves. The boxed areas indicate the large scale charts following this small scale chart.

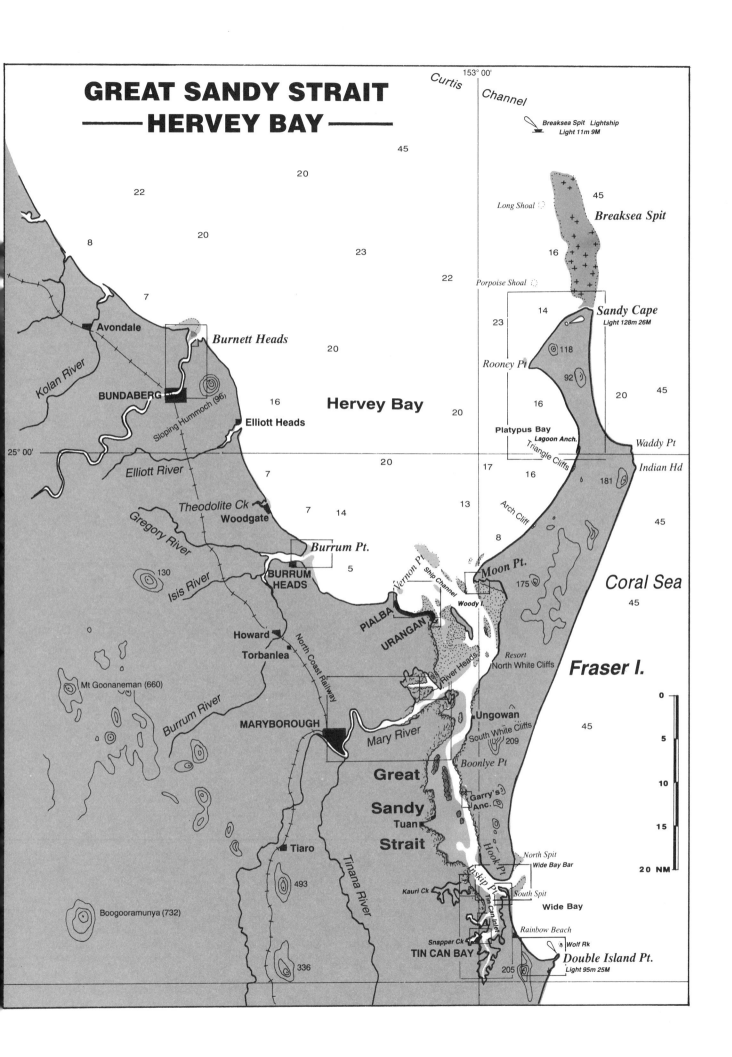

GREAT SANDY STRAIT
— HERVEY BAY —

Curtis Channel

153° 00'

Breaksea Spit Lightship
Light 11m 9M

45

20

22

Long Shoal

45

Breaksea Spit

8

20

16

23

Porpoise Shoal

22

7

Avondale

Burnett Heads

23

14

Sandy Cape
Light 128m 26M

20

118

BUNDABERG

Rooney Pt

92

Kolan River

Sloping Hummoch (96)

16

Hervey Bay

20

16

20

45

Elliott Heads

Platypus Bay
Lagoon Anch.

Waddy Pt

25° 00'

Elliott River

20

Triangle Cliffs

Indian Hd

7

17

16

Theodolite Ck

13

Arch Cliff

181

Woodgate

7

14

8

45

Gregory River

Burrum Pt.

5

Vernon Pt.

Ship Channel

Moon Pt.

Coral Sea

130

BURRUM HEADS

175

Isis River

Woody I.

45

Howard

PIALBA

URANGAN

Fraser I.

Torbanlea

North Coast Railway

River Heads

Resort
North White Cliffs

Mt Goonaneman (660)

Burrum River

MARYBOROUGH

Mary River

Ungowan

South White Cliffs

209

45

0

Great

Boonlye Pt

5

Sandy

Garry's
Anc.

10

Tuan

Strait

15

Tiaro

North Spit
Wide Bay Bar

Tinana River

493

Hook Pt

South Spit

20 NM

Boogooramunya (732)

Kauri Ck

Inskip Pt

Wide Bay

Tin Can Inlet

Rainbow Beach

Snapper Ck

Wolf Rk

336

TIN CAN BAY

205

Double Island Pt.
Light 95m 25M

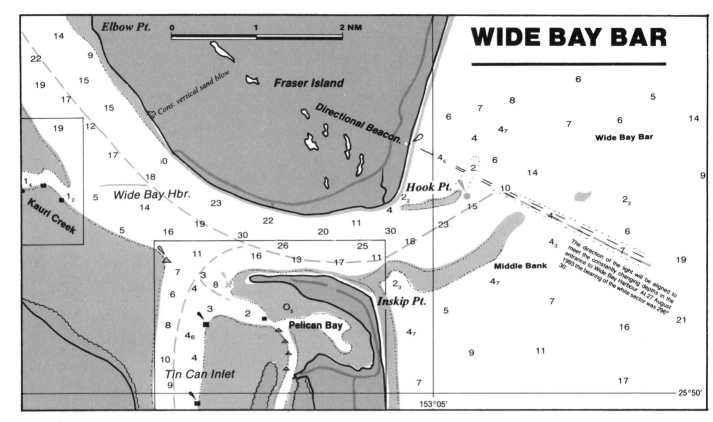

WIDE BAY BAR

WIDE BAY BAR. Extending north-east from *Inskip Point* for some 3 miles is a shoal sandbank protecting the southern entrance of the *Great Sandy Strait*. Known as Wide Bay Bar, it lies 8½ miles north-north-west of Double Island Point and demands some care in its crossing.

The Bar usually carries a minimum of 4 metres low water springs, but ridging can occur to reduce this figure. *Middle Bank* constantly breaks and an isolated bank to its north occasionally breaks. The best course is between the two as indicated by a directional beacon situated on the south end of Fraser Island on Hook Point.

The intense white sector of the directional beacon bears 296° 30′ True which should be established whilst still in deep water outside the bar. This bearing will be altered according to bar changes.

Having crossed the bar on the above beacon, ~~a green buoy off Hook Point is then passed to starboard from where deep water is found right across the entrance between Hook and Inskip points. This green buoy may~~ be scrapped in favour of a beacon. 232°M

Inskip Point is a low, vegetated sand peninsula. The name refers to both its western and eastern extremes. Towards its western end, tourist barges operate.

Tin Can Bay Air Sea Rescue can give a bar update, otherwise let commonsense and observations be your guide, avoiding breaking water and making sure to turn towards the green buoy well ahead of the shoals it advertises yet not before the Middle Bank shoals have been cleared.

On those rare occasions when Wide Bay Harbour is entered against a strong westerly wind, beware the troubled windward-tide seas between Hook and Inskip Point.

Future note. Leading beacons or a directional beacon on Inskip Point will replace the green buoy in future.

INSKIP POINT describes the vegetated sand spit which runs west from the sea on the southern side of Wide Bay Bar. It is an ideal place of refuge for those arriving into the Great Sandy Straits late in the day and anxious to get the anchor down.

The most popular and convenient anchorage is in the vicinity of the yellow beacon and its closest neighbour, the first red beacon in Tin Can Inlet. During heavy weather, when the swell carries in this far, it pays to move south-east towards the unlit red beacon north of Pannikan Island. Because it is a popular spot with working trawlers and local recreational craft, crowding can occur in which case the channel must be kept open by moving right into the creek south of Pelican Bay or into the bay itself. Alternatively, stay in Tin Can Inlet and move south towards the second red beacon.

The creek between the mainland and Pannikan Island guarantees total shelter from all winds and is often totally empty. To enter, pass the yellow beacon to port then the red beacon close to port after which four green beacons are passed to starboard. Continue past the old wooden jetty and launching ramp to drop anchor wherever convenient. Use a rising tide.

Future marina

Probable developments in the Tin Can Bay region include a marina in Pelican Bay, south of Inskip Point, and a bridge across Tin Can Inlet linking the towns of Tin Can Bay and Rainbow Beach. This will affect masted craft ascending the inlet to its head but will not hinder those whose destination is Snapper Creek.

Wide Bay Bar is the southern entrance to Great Sandy Strait. It is best crossed with a flood tide.

Pelican Bay is referred to in the description as 'Inskip Point', that being its most common area name.

Tin Can Bay Marina, described over the page, offers berths and support services to the casual sailor. It is in Snapper Creek towards the southern end of Tin Can Inlet.

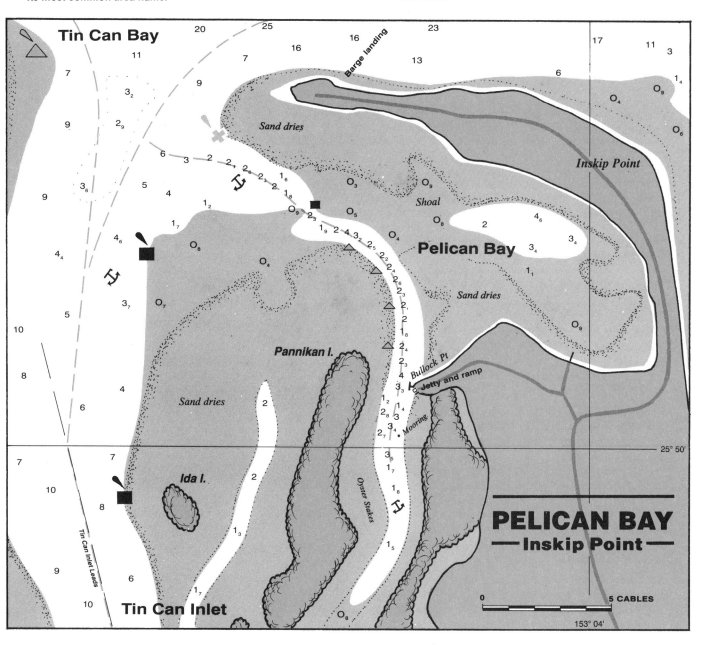

PELICAN BAY
— Inskip Point —

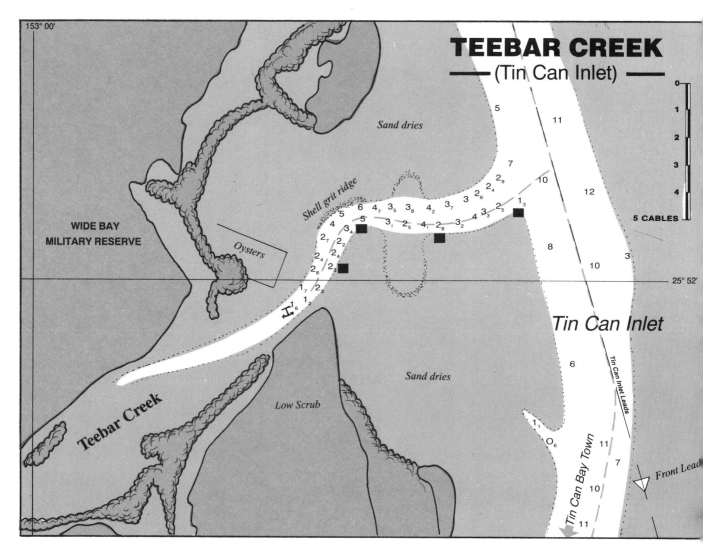

TEEBAR CREEK
—— (Tin Can Inlet) ——

TEEBAR CREEK penetrates into the *Wide Bay Military Reserve* close to the north of Tin Can Bay township. It has a deep, well beaconed entrance and very secure anchorage, especially if your draft allows you to tuck up behind the headland. Beware fish trap buoys which are often set in the area and especially along the side of the channel.

TIN CAN BAY. Very few places along the Queensland coast have the identity crisis of this area for the terms 'Tin Can Bay', 'Tin Can Inlet' and 'Snapper Creek' can all refer to the same place. In fact, *Tin Can Bay* is the open water west of Inskip Point, *Tin Can Inlet* is the inlet striking south from Inskip Point and *Snapper Creek* is the small boat harbour for the town of Tin Can Bay.

Approach to Snapper Creek is by *Tin Can Inlet* which is beaconed as illustrated on page 73. From its entrance, the leading beacons are difficult to see but will be found through binoculars.

Eyeball navigation is easy at mid to low tide when the surrounding sandbanks are visible, but towards high tide the best water can be difficult to find in overcast weather. It pays to use the beacons in the absence of local knowledge.

Final approach into Snapper Creek is through a well-beaconed channel under *Eudlo Point*.

Anchorage is definitely not permitted in Snapper Creek from its entrance to the marina entrance. Shallow-draft boats may proceed further upstream and anchor, though even they may take the bottom at low tide.

Owners of deep-drafted vessels unwilling to rent a berth have the alternative of anchoring outside the creek. Best out-of-the-way positions are shown on the plan and the best landing is at *Norman Point*. At low tide, a fair walk across flats is necessary but these are all fine, firm sand with some mud at low water springs and a sprinkling of oyster rocks between there and low water neaps.

Berths. Fore and aft moorings are available in Snapper Creek. Long term rent is very reasonable, daily rent is more than half marina charges. Apply at the Public Wharf.

Marinas. Trawlers have stern-to facilities immediately upstream from Tin Can Slipways while private boats may enter the dredged basin upstream of the trawlers and enjoy alongside floating finger berths. Call ahead on VHF or go alongside the end of the dock immediately inside the marina entrance.

Facilities in Tin Can Bay are low key but useful. All fuels are on the waterfront or at the service station and foods both fast and slow in town. There are phones and a post office as well as the inevitable pub. The slipway and marina each offer haul-out and repair services. There is a restaurant at the marina.

Cyclone Hole. The isolationist or the person obliged to seek the best shelter against an impending cyclone will find good security at the head of Tin Can Inlet, upstream from Snapper Creek. Using a young flood tide, move upstream to the head of navigation and drop anchor close to a headland to port.

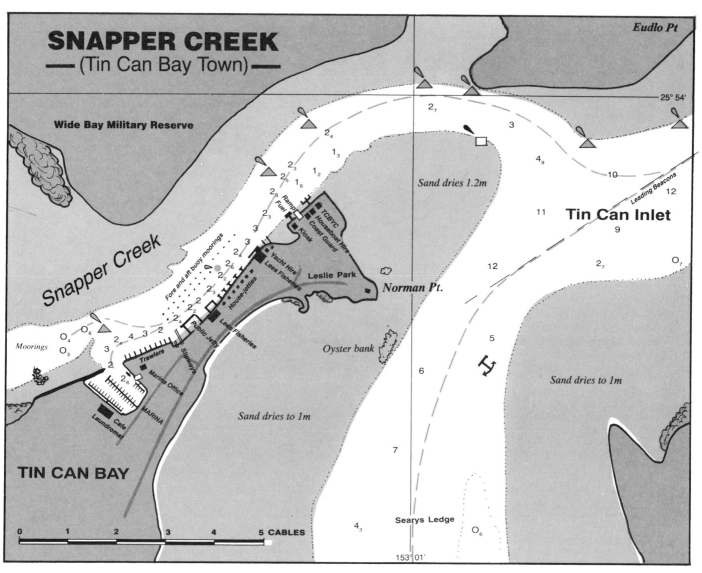

SNAPPER CREEK
── (Tin Can Bay Town) ──

Wide Bay Military Reserve

Snapper Creek

Moorings

Fore and aft buoy moorings

TCBYC
Houseboat Hire
Coast Guard
Ramp
Fuel
Kiosk

Yacht Hire
Lees Fisheries
House Jetties
Leslie Park
Public Jetty
Lees Fisheries
Slipways
Trawlers
Marina Office
MARINA
Cafe
Laundromat

TIN CAN BAY

Norman Pt.

Oyster bank

Sand dries to 1m

Sand dries 1.2m

Tin Can Inlet

Leading Beacons

Sand dries to 1m

Searys Ledge

Eudlo Pt

25° 54'

153° 01'

0   1   2   3   4   5 CABLES

Teebar Creek, opposite, is about halfway down Tin Can Inlet between Inskip Point and Snapper Creek. The marina in Snapper Creek, above, offers most services or casual anchorage can be taken outside the creek where suggested.

Anchorage in Snapper Creek beyond the marina is suitable only for shoal draft vessels.

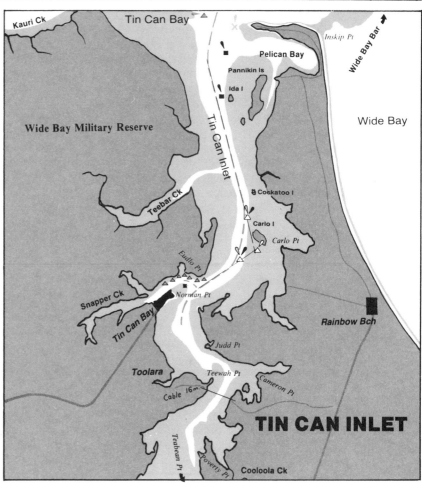

Kauri Ck
Tin Can Bay
Inskip Pt
Wide Bay Bar
Pelican Bay
Pannikin Is
Ida I
Wide Bay Military Reserve
Tin Can Inlet
Wide Bay
Teebar Ck
Cockatoo I
Carlo I
Carlo Pt
Eudlo Pt
Snapper Ck
Norman Pt
Rainbow Bch
Tin Can Bay
Judd Pt
Toolara
Teewah Pt
Cameron Pt
Cable 16m
Teebean Pt
(Poverty) Pt
Cooloola Ck
TIN CAN INLET

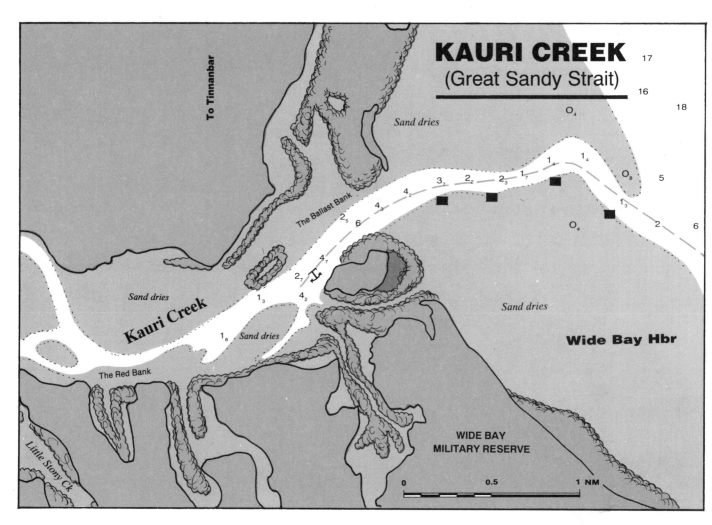

KAURI CREEK
(Great Sandy Strait)

Kauri Creek should be entered with a flood tide only.

KAURI CREEK. Seen as a break in the mangroves and low lying land 4 miles west of Inskip Point, Kauri Creek was the area's first timber cutting site. It provides safe haven in good depths which are obtainable via a shallow channel marked by red beacons which are passed to port. Being in the Wide Bay Military Reserve, there are restrictions regarding going ashore.

TUAN CREEK. *Not shown large scale.* Against the mainland to the south-west of Stewart Island, this creek is entered via a snaking channel which almost dries in places at low water springs. The channel is well beaconed and a vessel using her draft in high water should experience no difficulty.

The creek has deep water at low tide but is obstructed by an overhead cable of around 10 metres and is restricted by local moored craft. There is a launching ramp into the creek and nearby is a hire boat business. At nearby Boonooroo is a Coast Guard station.

GARRY'S ANCHORAGE is in a channel formed between Stewart Island and Fraser Island approximately 14 miles up the Great Sandy Strait from Wide Bay Bar. It gives total protection from all winds suffering only windward-tide annoyance under some circumstances. There is a minimum depth of one metre and a maximum of 6 metres low water springs. Anchorage is possible anywhere according to wind.

SOUTH WHITE CLIFFS. *See small scale chart page* 77 . A part of Fraser Island directly east of Turkey Island and well beyond the shallows of that area, very deep water runs along these beautiful sand cliffs. There is a yellow beacon and a steel jetty, a hangover from the sand mining days. To the north is a more recent hangover; the house and jetty of Ungowa Forestry station where there is also a public picnic area.

In all winds but a strong northerly, the best anchorage is about 1.5 miles south of the yellow beacon where the water shoals to around 3 metres. The holding is good and protection improves at low tide when a semi-lagoon is formed by drying sandbanks.

Slave Trade

Maryborough has the dubious distinction of being the first area to call for indentured labour from the Pacific Islands. The first labour ship arrived on 9 November, 1867 with 84 Kanakas aboard. She was the schooner *Mary Smith* and would be the first of many 'blackbirding' ships as the slave trade spread rapidly to other ports in Queensland.

Ashore at Garry's Anchorage are picnic, camping and toilet facilities.

74

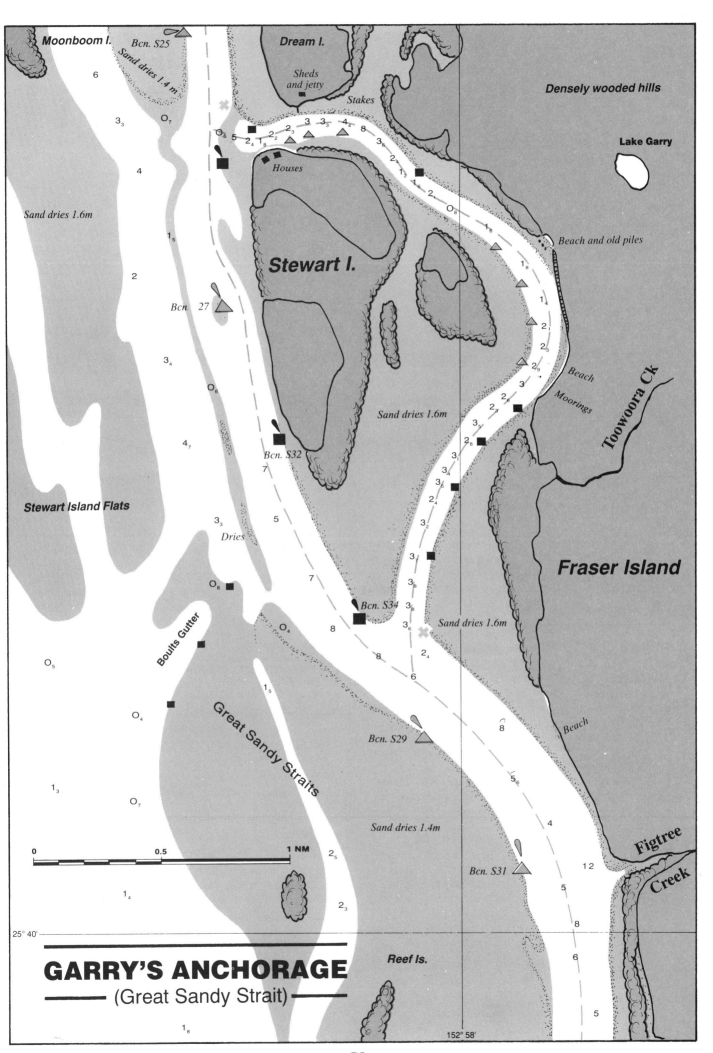

Moonboom I.

Bcn. S25

Sand dries 1.4 m

Dream I.

Sheds
and jetty

Stakes

Densely wooded hills

Lake Garry

6

3₃

O₇

4

Sand dries 1.6m

1₅

2

Bcn. 27

3₄

O₆

4₇

Houses

Stewart I.

3 3₃ 4₄ 8

2₂ 2₃

O₆ 5 2₄ 1₈

3₆

2₇

2₁

O₈

1₆

1₈

Beach and old piles

1₈

2₁

1₄

2₃

2₉

3

O₈

Sand dries 1.6m

2₆

2₃

3₅

2₈

3₁

3₁

3₆

2₄

3₂

3₁

Beach
Moorings

Toowoora Ck

Fraser Island

Stewart Island Flats

Dries

3₃

5

7

7

Bcn. S32

O₈

Boults Gutter

O₅

O₄

1₃

O₇

Great Sandy Straits

1₅

O₄

Bcn. S34

3₈

3₆

8

8

2₄

6

Sand dries 1.6m

Bcn. S29

8

5₆

4

Beach

Figtree

12

Creek

5

8

0   0.5   1 NM

1₄

2₅

2₃

Sand dries 1.4m

Bcn. S31

5

25° 40'

1₈

Reef Is.

152° 58'

6

5

GARRY'S ANCHORAGE
(Great Sandy Strait)

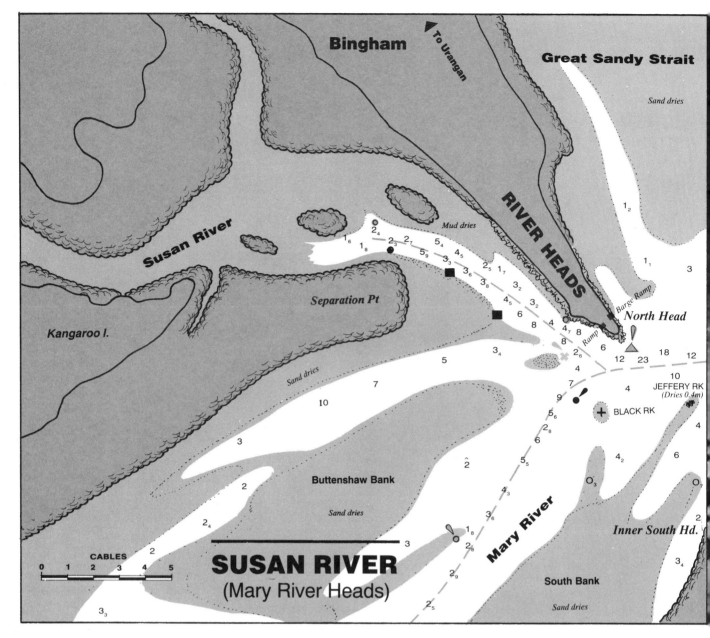

SUSAN RIVER
(Mary River Heads)

CABLES

0 1 2 3 4 5

SUSAN RIVER. This river shares the same mouth as the Mary River under River Heads on which is a blossoming settlement. It provides perfect anchorage in all but fresh south-west to south-east winds. Then a considerable and often untenable chop works in especially during an ebb tide. According to local boatman, Ted Baker, better anchorage in such winds is found outside River Heads in a basin where will be seen a vehicular barge at her mooring.

The Susan River may be ascended beyond the anchor shown on the accompanying plan where anchorage can be had in all-round security regardless of wind direction or strength. Use a flood tide and sound for low-tide floating well in advance of the change.

At the suggested anchorage, the holding is excellent and a sandbank exposing close to its west presents a good place for children to play at low tide. Getting ashore at River Heads can be a problem unless the dinghy is outboarded down to the ramp. Otherwise, go straight ashore at high tide from where a road can be followed to the top of the hill where there is a small mixed business selling food and fuel.

Tide information is the same as for the Mary River mouth based on Bundaberg data. The ebb past River

The Susan River, above, branches off the Mary River immediately inside the latter's north headland. The City of Maryborough can be reached by deep keeler up the Mary River.

Heads, between its rocky foreshore and the nearby sand bank, can be exceptionally strong during springs, often denying a vessel of average power any headway.

MARY RIVER. Rising in the foothills around Gympie, over 40 miles south of its entrance, the Mary River empties into the Great Sandy Strait 8 miles south of Urangan. The City of Maryborough lies on the banks of the river 19 miles upstream and is described separately after this account.

Approach from the Great Sandy Strait is in good deep water passing a yellow beacon to port followed by a red beacon to port after which the mouth is entered passing a green beacon to starboard.

Buoys and Beacons. Except for the Beaver Rock Leads, all leading beacons in the Mary River have been abandoned in favour of port and starboard buoys and beacons passed red to port, green to starboard ascending the river. They are all lit.

76

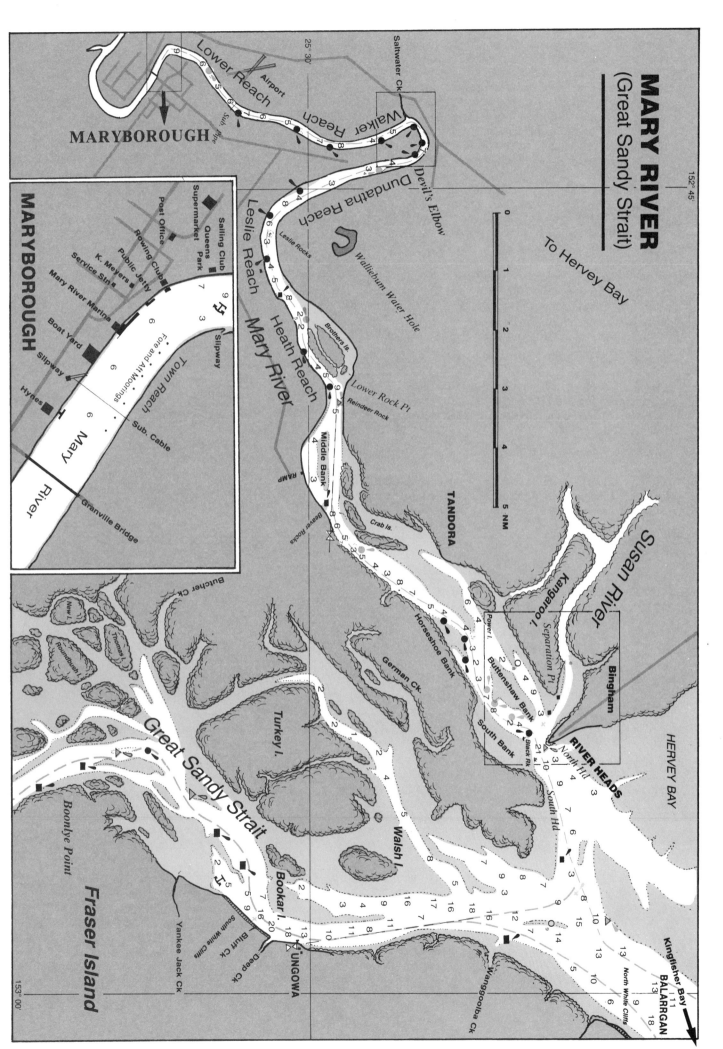

MARY RIVER
(Great Sandy Strait)

To Hervey Bay

152° 45'

Saltwater Ck

Walker Reach

Devil's Elbow

Dundatha Reach

Walliebum Water Hole

Lower Reach

Airport

25° 30'

MARYBOROUGH

Leslie Reach

Leslie Rocks

Heath Reach

Mary River

Brothers Is.

Lower Rock Pt

Reindeer Rock

Middle Bank

Beaver Rocks

Crab Is.

TANDORA

Kangaroo I.

Power I.

Separation Pt

Buttenshaw Bank

South Bank

Bingham

RIVER HEADS

North Hd

South Hd

Black Rk

Susan River

HERVEY BAY

Horseshoe Bank

German Ck.

Walsh I.

Turkey I.

Bookar I.

Great Sandy Strait

Boonlye Point

New I.

Roundbush I.

Thomas I.

Butcher Ck.

RAMP

Fraser Island

South White Cliffs

Bluff Ck

Deep Ck

Yankee Jack Ck

UNGOWA

Wanggoolba Ck

North White Cliffs

Kingfisher Bay
BALARRGAN

153° 00'

0   1   2   3   4   5 NM

MARYBOROUGH

Supermarket
Post Office
Queens Park
Rowing Club
Sailling Club
Public Jetty
K. Meyers
Service Stn
Mary River Marina
Boat Yard
Slipway
Hynes
Fore and Aft Moorings
Town Reach
Sub. Cable
Mary River
Slipway
Granville Bridge

77

Navigation. By passing all buoys and beacons appropriately and avoiding the habit of cutting corners, Maryborough will be reached without distress. The shallowest spot is where a spur of sand encroaches on the channel which, at that point, is indicated by the Beaver Rock Leads. A dogleg, as shown on the accompanying chart, may be necessary when the southern point of Crab Island comes abeam. The navigator is warned, however, that these instructions are loose. He or she is best advised to utilise a height of tide that eliminates the risk of grounding. It is suggested that the river be entered early in the second half of a flood tide. This minimises the chance of grounding and promises immediate refloating as well. The favourable current will also carry you right up to Maryborough.

Another area of potential concern is Leslie Rocks just before turning into Dundatha Reach. These rocks will not be seen and the extent to which they extend across the river should not be underestimated. Hold the south bank close to avoid them if minimum tide height is being worked.

Limits. Working spring tide, a draft of 3 metres could easily ascend to Maryborough. Heightwise, the only restriction is the Maryborough-Granville Bridge at around 4 metres above high water. This is upstream of the city anchorage.

Anchorage. The river being, in the main, deep, presents no difficulties in finding an anchorage en route upstream should this be necessary. Mostly the holding is good in mud or sand but there are areas of difficult penetration and some care is needed where windward tide is strong. Keep out of the channel and display an anchor light in the event of river fishing boats moving at night.

Tides and Currents. Mary River tidal predictions are based on Bundaberg and are stated for the mouth (Bingham) and the city of Maryborough. They tend to be 40% greater than Bundaberg and later by a constant of approximately one hour at Bingham and 2 and 3 hours later at Maryborough for high and low water respectively. A typical spring range is 3 metres although this is often greater at Maryborough since the building of an irrigation barrage across the river upstream of the city. Spring tidal flow runs at about 3 knots at the city and 4 at Bingham and turns later than tidal predictions.

Of Interest. In 1847, C.J. Burnett explored down the river that would soon bear his name, the Burnett, as well as the (then) Wide Bay River whose name would soon after be changed to the Mary River in honour of Governor Fitzroy's wife, Lady Mary. Months after having this honour bestowed on her, Lady Mary was killed when thrown from a horse in Parramatta Park, Sydney.

In fact, Burnett was not the first to explore the Mary River, being beaten to it by Andrew Petrie and a party of explorers a few months before. Regardless, the city of Maryborough quickly developed and became a port of entry in 1859, the same year that Queensland separated from New South Wales to enjoy its own identity. Regular trading vessels including the 124-ton paddlewheeler, *William Miskin* plied the river carrying wool, timber, tallow and hides from town. Aborigines were sometimes picked up at the entrance to be used as river pilots.

Maryborough's economy consolidated around sugar, timber and engineering, Walkers Engineering having produced many small ships and locomotives over the years.

MARYBOROUGH.
19 miles up the Mary River and a little more by road from Hervey Bay, Maryborough offers good security and facilities for the boat person. Being a city famous for its engineering companies and foundries, there is little that cannot be achieved in mechanical repairs, casting and fabrication. The city also enjoys a worker's economy despite its aspiration towards tourism and, as a result, it is certainly the most reasonably priced area for all repairs and victualling, a fact that can make the long run up the river worthwhile.

Approach is by the Mary River as described. The last mile and a half to the Granville Bridge is unbeaconed after a green buoy is passed to starboard.

Granville Bridge has a maximum headway at low tide of about 7 metres. A new bridge has been proposed further downstream in the vicinity of the sailing club to better serve Granville during floods.

Anchorage can be taken where convenient. Owing to a line of moorings and the clear space demanded for marina approach, the closest anchorage tends to be off the sailing club. During busy periods, it may be necessary to drop anchor well downstream of this position. At all times maintain a clear channel against the west bank.

Getting Ashore remains a problem in Maryborough despite the convenience of the new public jetty. This is the only public place available, but it has the problem of all-tide access. If the dinghy is left for any length of time, care must be exercised against it hanging up or drowning.

Mary River Marina is comprised of a fixed and floating section, the latter being mostly occupied by permanents. The visitor is usually obliged to use the fixed section where rafting is often necessary. Fuel is available here as are showers, toilets and a small stock of yacht hardware.

Hyne's Jetty is upstream of the marina and is occasionally available to private craft. Inquire ahead.

Moorings opposite the marina are fore and aft type and their use allows dinghy access through the marina and makes available showers and toilets.

Floods. The level of the Mary River can rise enough that waterfront buildings go underwater, making it an insecure place for absentee mooring, especially during summer.

Facilities are adequate for most demands in Maryborough, although certain specialised services in the electronic field are unavailable. Haul-out by slipways or rubber tyred cradle can be organised through the marina, the Motor Boat Club or through two slipways.

Diesel fuel and water are available alongside with petrol from a nearby service station. All shops are represented in the city whose close proximity makes victualling easy. There are also a number of excellent

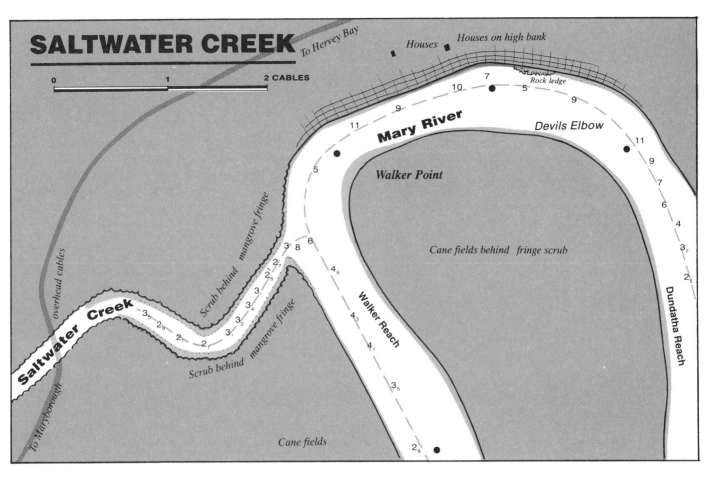

SALTWATER CREEK

To Hervey Bay

0   1   2 CABLES

Houses   Houses on high bank

Mary River

Rock ledge

Devils Elbow

Walker Point

Cane fields behind fringe scrub

Scrub behind mangrove fringe

Scrub behind mangrove fringe

Dundatha Reach

Walker Reach

overhead cables

To Maryborough

Saltwater Creek

Scrub behind mangrove fringe

Cane fields

engineering shops from diesel repair to foundry. And for the steam buff, the local live steam club runs its model trains in Queens Park regularly.

Transport. Maryborough is connected to points north and south by road, rail and air. A bus connects it with Hervey Bay as does a branch rail.

SALTWATER CREEK. Entering the *Mary River* opposite Walker Point, this creek has good depths most of the way up to the Maryborough-Hervey Bay road bridge. Although offering very good shelter in a cyclone, the fact that the whole river floods as high as 6 metres and more, cancels out its advantage. The creek is useful only as an isolated and probably mosquito-plagued anchorage or as a fishing venue.

Devils Elbow has some of the deepest water in the Mary River plus the useful offshoot, Saltwater Creek. Hervey Bay Road passes close to the houses on the high bank on the outside of Devils Elbow.

As yet unspoilt by excessive development, Maryborough is a charming old town on the banks of the Mary River about 20 miles upstream from its mouth. Below is the town hall whilst bottom left shows a model C38 raising steam for an exhibition in Queens Park. Engineering skills are a feature of Maryborough.

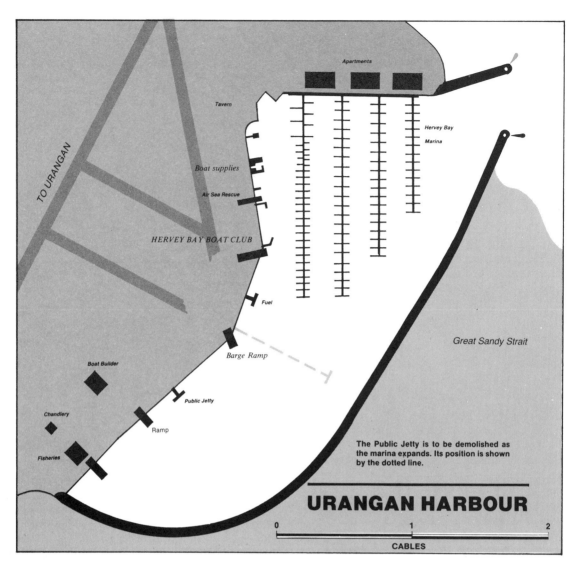

URANGAN HARBOUR

0   1   2
CABLES

The Public Jetty is to be demolished as the marina expands. Its position is shown by the dotted line.

URANGAN BOAT HARBOUR. 8 miles north of the Mary River for shoal-draft boats working a high tide and 17 miles around Big Woody Island for all other boats, Urangan Boat Harbour offers all essential facilities and is secure in all winds.

Approach from the Great Sandy Strait is by the recommended and well-beaconed channel passing to the east of Big Woody Island, close around its northern tip then direct for the harbour entrance. From *Duck* and *Picnic Islands* the distance can be reduced marginally by passing between the southern tip of Big Woody Island and a drying bank one cable to its east then holding the island all the way to the beacon (S3) standing 5 cables north of *Datum Point*. This beacon is rounded to port after which red beacon EU2 is similarly rounded then yellow beacon EU1 is passed to starboard from where the harbour mouth is easily identified and laid for direct.

From Hervey Bay, the Fairway Buoy must be located for orientation before entering the main Great Sandy Strait approach channel from where course is steered to pass the next buoy to either side and the following two to port. On this course the lowland of the Urangan area (*Dayman Point*) will become identifiable and features such as the old sugar loading wharf will eventually be seen. The head of this wharf carries a green light at night and is just one mile north of the Boat Harbour.

When approaching from Hervey Bay at night, beware the tendency to presume the Fairway Buoy carries a dominant light. It does not.

Anchorage is not possible within the harbour. In calm or westerly weather, there is plenty of room outside the harbour taking care not to obstruct the entrance in any way.

Marina. Built in 1992, the *Great Sandy Strait Marina* occupies the harbour almost in its entirety, replacing the public pile berths and jetty. Casual berths are available with a fuel dock against the land to the west of the marina. Villa apartments and shops are a part of the complex.

Facilities include the marina services, slipway and two public launching ramps plus the *Hervey Bay Boat Club* where visitors are welcome. The nearest shopping centre is at the town of Urangan which entails a long walk or a short bus ride. The town is near the root of the old sugar jetty. A marine supply shop is next to the Air Sea Rescue base at the harbour.

BALARRGAN. *See main chart page 77* Also known as *McKenzies Jetty* and *North White Cliffs*, anchorage here is in Tyroom Roads under the lee of Fraser Island. Subject to windward-tide antics and strong gusts during a well-developed south-easterly wind, the anchorage is secure and basically comfortable and the opportunity to walk long distances ashore considerable. A road leads from here inland and a tourist-bus operator is based here, the vehicles often being seen in from the old jetty.

North from the old jetty will be seen a new jetty behind which is a resort-residential development. Known as *Kingfisher Bay*, it offers a few services including a general store.

Regardless of exactly where you anchor in the Balarrgan area, it makes a fine place to rest before heading off into Hervey Bay or whilst awaiting a suitable tide for the ascension of the Mary River whose entrance is obvious to the west.

BIG WOODY ISLAND. *See main chart page 69* . Big Woody is nearly 5 miles long and less than 3 cables wide in places. It stands offshore from Urangan where it separates the Great Sandy Strait into two parts; that to the east having good navigable water and that to the west being comprised mostly of drying sand banks.

Close off its eastern side is a thin ribbon of sand outside of which the main channel trends. Buoys and beacons mark this ribbon. By way of a change, it is possible to venture between it and Big Woody, the only restriction being a 3-metre gutter at the south tip where the island and the shoal almost join. Visual navigation is easy enough regarding the extent of this shoal but, when entering from the south, hold the island very close.

There are small beacons on the eastern side marking a measured nautical mile and a disused lighthouse stands close to the centre.

Anchorages during developed winds are not brilliant around Big Woody although an excellent northerly anchorage exists in a gutter west and north from South Point where there is 4 metres low water springs. Display a light at night as this channel is often used by a Fraser Island barge.

SCARNESS. One of four shopping centres forming the *City of Hervey Bay*, Scarness offers anchorage close to the shelving shore and facilities enough for the passing boat.

Approach from the Great Sandy Strait is best passing the yellow buoy, *S4*, to port then steering for Point Vernon. This passes over shoals of less than 1.2 metres low water springs so it depends on state of tide and draft. Deeper drafts must dogleg north around the north-western tail of Dayman Point spit before rounding up for Scarness which, from the spit, can be identified for its small tidal jetty. There is a boat hire business immediately east of this jetty.

From the north, the Fairway Buoy should be located, passed to either side then course laid for the second buoy (*S2*), from where a right-dogleg course can be laid for Scarness. At all times allow for the lateral effect of currents which, during spring tides, can be strong.

Anchorage is in good-holding, grey sandy mud and is well protected from all winds west through south to south-east. It can be uncomfortable when the latter is strong and especially against the tide, but is secure enough for sorties ashore and an overnight stay. The best dinghy landing is near the boat hire. When outboarding, beware of a scattering of rocks below low tide near the beach.

Facilities at Scarness are limited but shopping centres to its east (Torquay) and west (Pialba) have everything the average shopper will want. A bus services this coastal strip and there is a service to Maryborough.

Following the description of Hervey Bay, over the page, anchorages around the bay are described after which Bundaberg follows.

A problem harbour since its inception in the early 1970's, Urangan Harbour has now been stripped of many public facilities to be replaced by a marina. Most services are offered here and a bus connects it with shopping centres to the west.

Protected from the south-east trade winds, this anchorage offers a relatively convenient way to go shopping if the Urangan marina is missed.

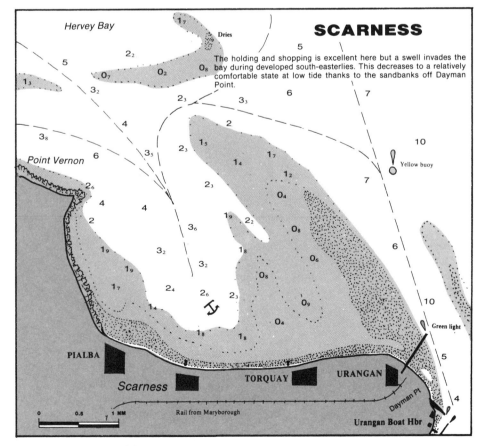

SCARNESS

The holding and shopping is excellent here but a swell invades the bay during developed south-easterlies. This decreases to a relatively comfortable state at low tide thanks to the sandbanks off Dayman Point.

HERVEY BAY. Acting as a funnel above the spout of the Great Sandy Strait, Hervey Bay is formed by the northern section of Fraser Island and the mainland between Pialba and Bundaberg. 47 miles east to west and 33 north to south, its depths range from the drying banks towards the Great Sandy Strait to a 36-metre hole in the centre. Generally, they range around 18 metres.

Although a lee from the prevalent south-easterly wind is created by Fraser Island, the fact is seas readily build up to 2 and 3 metres during strong winds and are as short and steep as anywhere within the reef further north. The only protection available is close under Fraser Island or in the Burrum or Burnett River, the latter being the only river or creek in the area offering all-tide entry.

The bay can be entered from the north quadrant in clear water free of obstructions while the south is entered through the already described Great Sandy Strait. Also described (see page 22) is the eastern approach which is to the north of Breaksea Spit, a sand and coral shoal extending 17 miles north from Sandy Cape.

From any point in the bay, the surrounding land is uninspiring being generally low with just a few hills from which a position can occasionally be fixed. Mostly, however, the navigator depends entirely on course and speed to arrive at the correct destination, one of the most common failings being in finding the fairway buoy into the Great Sandy Strait when sailing south. Tide, which can run diagonally across the course at rates of up to 1½ knots, or an unknown deviation, can place a vessel too far east and beyond the buoy amongst the rapidly shoaling ground in that area. It pays to favour, if anything, the deeper water to the buoy's west so that a miss brings up Point Vernon's two radio towers well ahead of any danger.

The weather is as described on page 22 with the localised difference being that the bay can generate its own patterns when developed systems are not affecting Queensland's weather or are non existent. Surprisingly, it can be extraordinarily cold for a sub-tropical region, demanding the need to seek warmth during a midsummer's night. And this phenomenon is not restricted to the logic of offshore winds, a northerly often failing to warm the night under certain circum-

stances. But offshore winds are the most common culprit and these readily generate off the lowland of the mainland, especially out of river and creek entrances. Like most variable conditions, the offshore wind dies early to be replaced by a calm or light onshore wind by midday. Under these circumstances, the sailing can be slow but pleasant with a light wind on each beam during the course of a day and night.

Being a very popular runabout area with a big amateur fishing population, the bay is well covered by the volunteer Air Sea Rescue groups, a permanent station being established at Urangan in the south and Burnett Heads in the north. With a repeater situated on Fraser Island, VHF reception is strong and clear in any part of the bay should assistance of any kind be required.

Hervey Bay was named by Captain Cook in 1770 after Captain Augustus John Hervey, 3rd Earl of Bristol. It was first examined hydrographically by Captain Matthew Flinders aboard the *Norfolk*.

Whale watching has become a major industry in Hervey Bay with at least nineteen boats licensed to carry tourists to the grounds from Urangan. The best region for sightings appears to be the central bay area or towards Platypus Bay.

The whales are en route back to their feeding grounds in the Antarctic icepacks after mating and calving in the warm waters of the Great Barrier Reef. During their northern migration, they rarely feed and are thus under considerable stress on their return. It has been suggested that chase boats — be they ever so benign in intent — add to this stress. It is also pointed out that the whales keep returning to be pursued by thousands of sightseers during a season that commences early August every year.

BURRUM HEADS is a small settlement on the south head of the Burrum River mouth. It lies less than 12 miles west-north-west from Point Vernon.

Approach. The land in the area being low and essentially featureless, approach is best by holding the land as near as possible without running foul of the extensive shoals until Burrum Point or Head is identified. From seaward, *Burrum Point* rises first, soon after which *Burrum Heads* lifts with its indistinct scattering of houses.

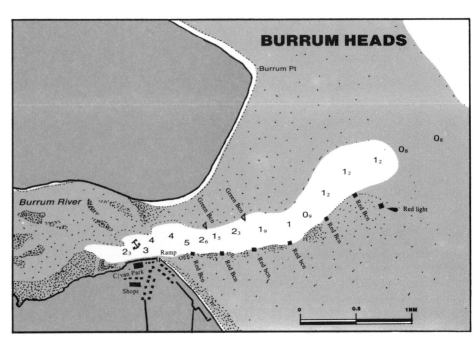

Opposite Page. When departing Moon Point to the north, beware of confusion amongst the sand banks.

Working a tide, it is possible to take a shoal draft boat many miles up the Burrum River.

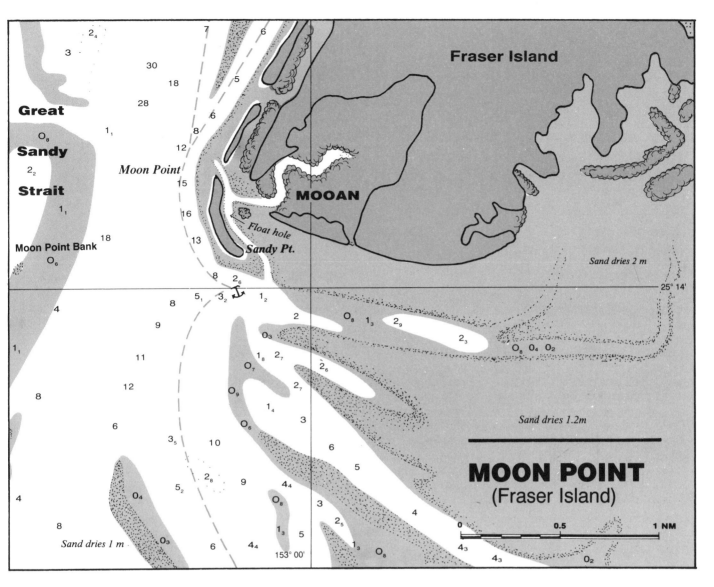

Under no circumstances approach the river entrance without adequate tide to clear the bar plus a little for wave drop. There is rarely a swell of any consequence here but onshore winds can make entry hazardous unless ample tide height related to draft is available. Marginal clearance should only be tried during calm to light weather. The shallowest water is not in the vicinity of the outer beacon but further offshore. The beacon will be seen before these shoals are encountered.

On a straight approach, miss the outer beacon (the only one lit) by at least 100 metres to port then continue a course that passes the next red beacons about 50 metres off. Two green beacons stand further inshore in the vicinity of the last three reds. These delineate the starboard banks which are not as high as those to port.

From the last red beacon continue upstream at the same distance off to enter the anchorage where will be seen a number of local boats at moorings. Generally there remains ample space for visitor anchoring.

Anchorage. Considering that Burrum Heads should be saved for light weather it is safe to predict that the anchorage will be very comfortable. However, during strong onshore winds from south-east through to north-east, windward-tide conditions can be rather trying during ebb flow and especially at the start of the run when the outer banks are covered. The bottom is good holding, however, and with enough scope paid out the anchorage is basically secure.

Ashore there is a public ramp, caravan park, hotel and a small shopping complex capable of satisfying most transient needs. There is a post office and STD phones as well as a very pleasant restaurant. Petrol and LPG are available and, in an emergency, a lift to the nearest large town might be arranged. Otherwise there is no transport out of Burrum Heads.

MOON POINT. The last headland on Fraser Island before Sandy Strait opens up into Hervey Bay, Moon Point is on a low wooded islet almost connected to Fraser Island by creek mangroves. It lies 3½ miles north-east of Big Woody Island.

Approach from Sandy Strait or Hervey Bay from the main strait channel is best from the vicinity of green beacon S5 from which a nearly straight line to Moon Point maintains the best water. Beware of the effect of current which sets north-west during ebb tide and south-east during flood. This can press a vessel on to the drying banks to each side of this course. When covered, these banks are nearly always visible as light-green water.

From Platypus Bay (Hervey Bay) the coast immediately north of Moon Point can be hugged to pass inside a parallel drying bank. Where this nearly joins Moon Point there is a minimum of 3 metres low water neaps.

Arch Cliff is scrub-covered sand cliff on Fraser Island easily identified from a good distance off.

From the north, Arch Cliff, right, is obvious. The smaller 'arch cliff', left, is unnamed.

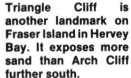

Triangle Cliff is another landmark on Fraser Island in Hervey Bay. It exposes more sand than Arch Cliff further south.

Triangle Cliff from the north.

Anchorage is where shown on the plan for wind south-east to north-east. It is not very comfortable when the south-easterly is at strength with the surrounding banks covered. It is excellent during easterlies to north-easterlies. The nearest northerly anchorage is the Mary River mouth or into the Strait near Turkey Island. Urangan is suitable, but a berth is obligatory.

Of Interest. Ashore on the western edge of the islet there are basic camping facilities including a trash can. The beach in that vicinity is used by the Urangan vehicular barge to land 4WDs on Fraser Island. Traffic here can be remarkably heavy during the height of the tourist season which has extended from a winter pursuit to most of the year. Although uninhabited, the area here is known as Mooan.

PLATYPUS BAY is the indentation against Fraser Island between Moon Point and Rooney Point. In effect, it is the eastern part of Hervey Bay. Anchorage can be enjoyed anywhere along its southern half (not shown opposite) during south-east winds, but the most interesting one is known as *Lagoon Anchorage* as described later.

The Hervey Bay chart on page 69 shows the bay in its entirety where will be seen *Arch* and *Triangle Cliffs*. These are the best landmarks in the bay when sailing north from Moon Point. Arch Cliff is more obviously an arch when seen from the north from which direction it can appear like the Sydney Harbour Bridge complete with pylons.

Another landmark is *Station Hill* which lifts as an 'islet' from about 16 miles. Fraser Island is otherwise lacking in easily identified features. Its hills are well wooded but unremarkable whilst the beach in Platypus Bay is continuous with a few rock ledges scattered along

its length, especially north of Arch Cliff. The beach is backed by endless dunes and sand blows.

During south-east winds, the 20 miles between Moon Point and Lagoon Anchorage is one of the coast's best sails. Fraser Island creates relatively few gusts and lulls and the bay remains essentially calm, allowing a vessel to reach along in absolute comfort. It is untenable during northerlies in terms of anchorages except under Rooney Point as noted later.

The trickiest part of Platypus Bay is in departing or arriving at Moon Point anchorage. *Outer Banks*, to its immediate north, can be difficult to accurately identify under some conditions. There are two alternatives (without standing off wide for Ship Channel), these being to hug Fraser Island extremely close to pass through the gutter between Moon Point and Outer Bank, or to stand off and pass through a wider channel through the middle of the banks.

The following anchorages in Platypus Bay are shown on the accompanying chart.

Lagoon Anchorage. Also known as Wathumba Creek (sometimes pronounced 'Watoomba'), the lagoon here mostly dries at low water springs. It is no place for deep, single keelers whilst offering all-weather haven to runabouts or any vessel able to take the bottom. There is a float hole available to most deep keelers during neap tides, but this can be worrying if the wind shifts south-west to west.

To enter the lagoon, select a tide matching your draft plus at least 0.6 metres and pass the small, often headless, red beacons to port. During strong trade winds, a slight swell can run along this part of the coast demanding greater care regarding tide-draft matching.

Anchorage outside the lagoon can be taken anywhere, sounding into the most suitable depth. Ashore, on both headlands, will often be seen weed so dense and piled up that it can be mistaken for a rock ledge. This impression continues underwater with the numer-

84

Rooney Point Wreck

Off Rooney Point, on the edge of Ferguson Spit, the American barque *Panama* was wrecked during a cyclone in 1864. To the site's north-east, at Bool Creek, Matthew Flinders landed in 1802, and although he spent several days in the area, failed to prove that Fraser was an island.

Although fog is a rare occurrence along the Coral Coast, Hervey Bay can generate its own weather conditions in the absence of dominant patterns. This is Platypus Bay late winter.

Despite the beach in Platypus Bay being a proclaimed 'No Vehicle' zone, it is quite common to see 4WDs along here. The anchorage under Rooney Point is delightful in northerly winds.

PLATYPUS BAY

(Fraser Island)

0 1 2 3 4 5 NM

Breaksea Spit

Hervey Bay

Fraser Island

Bool Ck.

Wocco Lagoon

Boola Lagoon

Bare Hill

Lake Wanhar

Goochee Lagoon

Station Hill

Lake Minker

Ferguson Spit

Rooney Pt.

Teahwan Rks.

Blowah Rks.

National Park

Platypus Bay

Light 128 m 26 M

Sandy Cape

Manann Beach

Orchid Beach

Wathumba Ck.

Yeerall Ck.

24°45'

25°00'

153°15'

LAGOON ANCHORAGE

Wathumba Ck

Many weed patches

Dries 0.6 m

Yeerall Ck

Fraser Island

LAGOON ANCH.

ous weed banks showing like coral in places.

On the north headland is a National Park campsite with all facilities including tables and seats, toilets, shower, trash cans and barbeque.

Rooney Point is a delightful anchorage in north-east to north winds where depths reduce to around 5 metres close to the beach. The holding is good in sand. From here the looms of Maryborough, Bundaberg and the Sandy Cape Light are all easily seen.

Sandy Cape is only suitable as an anchorage during calms or light to moderate trade winds. Even then, a swell invades the coast, keeping a vessel rolling depending on tidal flow. This ebbs north-east and floods south-west along the coast at rates up to 2 knots during springs.

The light can be approached up a steep, sandy track from the anchorage, much of which is consolidated by timber sleepers. The steep approach up the sand hill was one of the major problems in the construction of this light which first operated on May, 1870. It

eventually boasted a school for the education of the lightkeepers' children and was hailed as a major navigational aid at a time when Breaksea Spit was considered the worst hazard on the east coast of Australia.

Breaksea Spit. Extending north from Sandy Cape for nearly 17 miles, this vast area of shoal water is marked at its northern extreme by a lightship anchored 5 miles beyond the spit. Comprised largely of rather poor coral scattered over sand, the spit has a width of nearly 4 miles in one place and has a number of channels between the coral patches. With local knowledge and fair weather, short cuts can be taken across the spit.

The visitor is warned against taking short cuts regardless of state of tide or weather. A swell nearly always invades the entire spit and tidal streams can reach three knots during springs. They flood west and ebb east and must be considered when sailing up either side of the spit. Always allow for tide-induced leeway.

Breaksea Spit is shown in its entirety — albeit at a smaller scale — on the Hervey Bay chart on page 69

85

The Burnett Bar

Prior to its first dredging, the depth over the Burnett River bar was 1.5 metres. This was deepened to 1.8 metres in 1883 at which time vessels drawing as much as 4.2 metres could enter and ascend to Bundaberg on a high tide. Today, the bar admits drafts of up to 9 metres at low tide.

Burnett Heads Boat Harbour has a small marina and public fore and aft buoy moorings. Space is at a premium here.

The two charts here show the Burnett River from its mouth (opposite page) to the Town Reach where road and rail bridges prevent further navigation by masted vessels. Burnett Heads Boat Harbour is seen in the large scale inset and is described below. The river above this harbour to and including Bundaberg is described over the page.

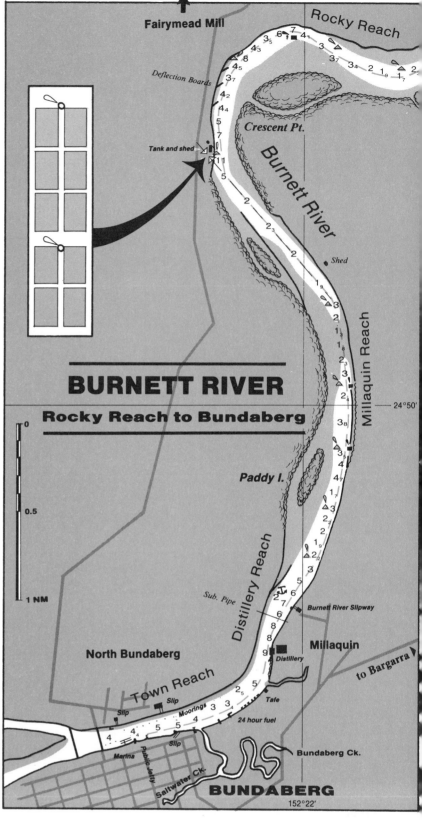

BURNETT RIVER

Rocky Reach to Bundaberg

BURNETT HEADS BOAT HARBOUR.

Situated under the lee of the Burnett River's *South Head*, 10 miles from Bundaberg, this small facility presents an alternative to ascending the river in pursuit of services.

Approach from the south and east out of Hervey Bay presents few difficulties and no offshore hazards. The land being low, however, can demand greater attention to detail.

Sloping Hummock, south of Bundaberg and said to be an extinct volcanic core, is the most conspicuous landmark in the area and will be seen in good conditions from 20 miles even to the details of its two similar radio towers. Working up the coast, when Sloping Hummock is sighted, *Point Vernon* and a vague outline of Fraser Island will also be discernable astern. The water tower on *Elliot Heads* is a good en-route landmark as is a similar tower at Bargara Beach which can be seen 15 miles away through the binoculars. When seeking landmarks on this coast always allow for cane-fire haze that can cut visibility down to less than half.

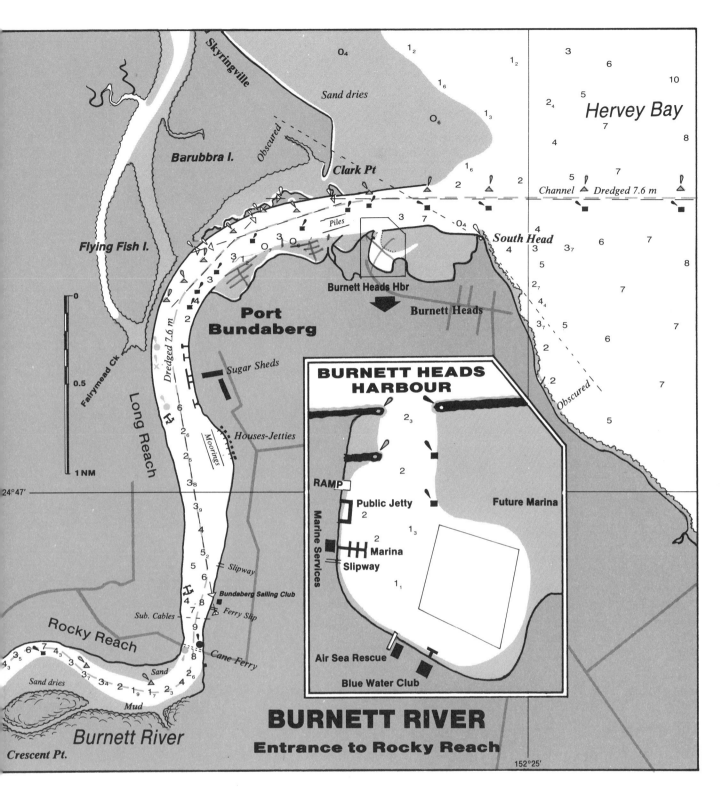

BURNETT RIVER
Entrance to Rocky Reach

This is experienced from July through December. A standby Breaksea Lightship is sometimes anchored outside of the river.

From the north-west, commonly with Round Hill Creek the last anchorage, Double Sloping Hummock (mountain) is unremarkable but identifiable as the most conspicuous mass ashore. It remains in sight all the way and provides a single bearing if required.

A water tower on the coast in the region of Moore Park is the first unnatural object sighted as the Burnett River is approached after which Sloping Hummock pops up followed closely by the sugar sheds and a water tower close to the South Head Light which, itself, rises soon after. A second column to its south-east will also be seen.

Final approach from the south can short-cut into the approach channel. From the north take care to box well out around the shoals stretching east and north from *Barubbra Island* (north head to the Burnett River). At night one or more lights might be seen in the vicinity of the small settlement on Barubbra Island known as *Skyringville*.

Harbour Entry is through a break in the wall with red and green beacons to port and starboard respectively.

Nav Aids. Burnett Heads form Port Bundaberg which is a major sugar loading facility receiving large overseas ships regularly. As a result, all aids are substantial, well-maintained and lit for night-time entry. The outer fairway piles are red to port and white (light) to starboard whereas all thereafter are red to port and green to starboard.

Tides. Bundaberg is a standard port in the *Tide Tables*. It experiences a typical spring range of 2.2. metres. Currents are strong during springs in the entrance channel and immediately inside the river. These currents flow across the mouth of the Burnett Heads Boat Harbour.

Anchorage within the harbour is restricted by moorings, marina and shoals. Officially it is prohibited. Temporary anchorage is possible outside the harbour.

Marina. Extending from and operated by *Burnett Heads Marine*, there are 12 berths for vessels up to 45 feet with power, water and showers. Call on VHF 81 or go to fuel dock on the outer end.

Air Sea Rescue is located in the harbour operating seven days a week between 0700 and 2100 hours. It is very helpful in matters of advance information regarding berths, customs clearance and weather.

Public Moorings are sometimes available in the boat harbour, although most are permanently leased. Check by phone.

Facilities. The public jetty is used by the catamaran *Lady Musgrave* morning and evening most days during the year but may be relocated to the main harbour. There is a one hour limit here.

Burnett Heads Marine has or can arrange all repair service and offers a slipway to 50 tonnes and hardstand to 20 tonnes. Water is at the public jetty and all fuel is at the marina. The *Blue Water Club* opens every afternoon and evening and welcomes visitors. The small shopping centre nearby has basics and is connected to Bundaberg by bus.

Midtown Marina, up the Burnett River, is on the south bank handy to the City of Bundaberg. Private and public fore and aft moorings are also available in the vicinity.

A typical beacon in the Burnett River. The tidal flow is obvious.

These sheds and a tank (out of sight) are landmarks on the Burnett River between Rocky Reach and Millaquin Reach. The leading beacons, showing the best water between these two reaches are arrowed.

Town Reach, Burnett River. The bridge is ahead with the public jetty and marina, left and fore-and-aft public moorings, right. Bundaberg City is on the left bank.

BUNDABERG. Claimed by promoters to be 'where the Barrier Reef begins', Bundaberg is, in fact, 10 miles up the Burnett River whose entrance is 42 miles south of the nearest reef at Lady Elliot Island. However, it is close enough and has proven a very popular clearance port for overseas boats intending to start their Coral Coast cruise where the coral starts.

Approach has been noted for the Burnett River upstream as far as the above-noted Burnett Heads Boat Harbour.

Anchorage is possible anywhere in the Burnett River except the designated Port of Bundaberg (except off-channel between markers 12 and 14); in any navigable channel; and in the Town Reach (Bundaberg). The best places are opposite the sailing club downstream of the cane ferry, and opposite Burnett River Slipway, downstream from the distillery. Set an anchor light at night.

Pile Berths are located outside and immediately upstream of the Burnett Heads Boat Harbour and towards the east bank of the river upstream of the sugar loading facility. The latter are usually fully occupied by local craft and shore access is difficult anyway.

The group of pile berths near the river entrance experience swell and were, in any case, unavailable up to 1994 for public use being at the time a means of testing various timber treatments. Beware at night as they are poorly lit.

Ascending the River. Having entered the mouth (see Burnett Heads Boat Harbour description), the ascent to Bundaberg City will be looked at.

From Burnett Heads the river sweeps south, the dredged harbour area being well defined with port and starboard piles and leading beacons. These can be rather confusing at night if strict adherence is the aim. Otherwise, forget the leading beacons and just remain between the channel limit piles.

When the last jetty has passed to port, pick up the *Long Reach Leads* which are visible ahead as blue lights by night and bright white by day. Hold these until obliged to move off to starboard where good water can be found right across the river. The *Bundaberg Sailing Club*, a ramp and a broad sandy beach are situated between these leads.

Immediately after the sailing club is the cable cane ferry which operates almost continuously, around the clock, during the July to December cane crushing season. It gives way to river traffic and acknowledges your right of way by dousing its flashing light.

Beyond the ferry, the river swings hard right into *Rocky Reach* where the channel is shown by port and starboard beacons which take traffic across to the starboard bank in the vicinity of Fairymead Sugar Mill which is obvious a little way inland and ahead from this Reach.

The old ex-pumping station is passed, then, as a wharf and tank fall astern, backleads line up to show the best water up to *Millaquin Reach*. A green buoy indicates the end of this leading beacon run and introduces the shallowest part of the river which lies between this buoy and the next green buoy and red beacon (the latter being on the end of a training wall).

The water deepens alongside the training wall and progress continues past another red beacon and three green buoys from where a course favouring the port bank is steered up to the city.

Bundy Rum

A by-product of sugar refining, rum has been distilled on the banks of the Burnett River, downstream from Bundaberg, for many decades. The main product, Bundaberg Rum, is an Australian icon, one of the many that have become foreign owned. In the early 1990's Bundaberg's distillery was bought out by an English company.

Nav Aids. All buoys, beacons and leading beacons are lit. Pass red to port, green to starboard ascending the river.

Fore and aft moorings between buoys along the north side of *Town Reach* are public and reasonably priced. Phone the Port Authority on 59 4233 after securing to a mooring. Privately leased moorings of a similar type extend from the marina towards the bridge.

Marinas. The most accessible on a casual basis is Midtown Marina where many services are available including fuel and chandlery. Berths may also be available on John Lenthall's jetty, diagonally opposite.

Customs. Clearance is available at Burnett Heads. Do not ascend the river.

Facilities. The City of Bundaberg lacks nothing in the way of shops and services and most nautical demands can be satisfied. There are a number of slipways, fuel docks and repair facilities.

Of Interest. Within easy striking distance of the city is the Hinkler House Memorial Museum which is the house in which Bert Hinkler lived while in Southampton, England. It was dismantled and shipped to Bundaberg in 1983, there to stand as a fitting reminder that one of Australia's greatest aviators was born and bred in Bundaberg. From a beach (Mon Repos) just outside of the city he flew to a height of thirty feet in his home-made glider at the age of nineteen. Anxious to increase his knowledge and prowess as a flier, he joined a wandering show before moving on to England where he joined the Royal Naval Air Service and was later awarded the DSM after service in France as an Observer Gunner during World War I.

In February 1928 he flew from England to Australia in 15½ days in an Avro Avian alone then tried to repeat the effort in 1933. Sadly, he crashed into the Italian Alps and was buried with full Military Honours in Florence.

The site of Bundaberg was settled in 1866 by timbergetter John Stuart and his brother after searching the area for ash and white cedar to be used in cask construction. Recognising the potential of the rich volcanic soil they established the sugar industry which would become Bundaberg's major income earner.

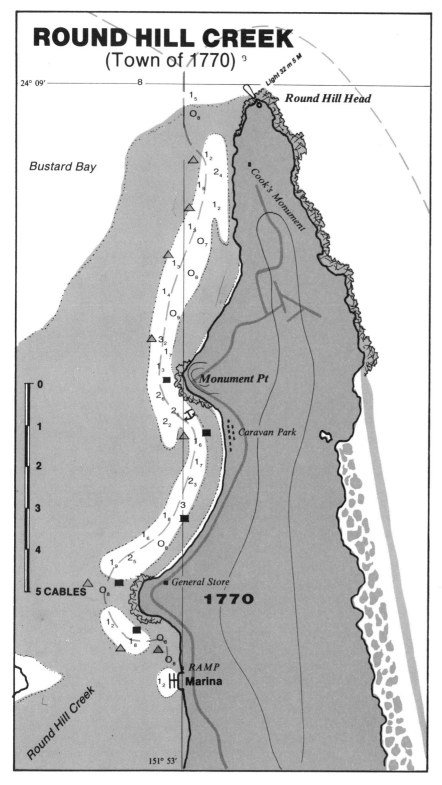

ROUND HILL CREEK
(Town of 1770)

Bustard Bay

Round Hill Head

Light 32 m 5 M

24° 09′ — 8 —

Cook's Monument

Monument Pt

Caravan Park

0
1
2
3
4
5 CABLES

General Store

1770

RAMP
Marina

Round Hill Creek

151° 53′

ROUND HILL CREEK. Penetrating south into the mainland at the bottom of Bustard Bay, Round Hill Creek is 46 miles north-west from the Burnett River entrance and 12 miles south-east from Pancake Creek. It is the site of Captain Cook's first landing on what would one day become Queensland. It now boasts a delightful little retirement and holiday centre known as *1770*.

Approach. The coast is clean in both directions with no offshore dangers. The headland is not seen until about 12 miles off at which time it lifts as an 'islet' off a larger 'island', the latter being its body running south to high ground. Round Hill, a separate hill 6 miles south of the headland, can be seen nearly 30 miles away in good conditions.

The Bar. The sandbank protecting the western side of the northern part of Round Hill Creek is a mixture of high drying banks and very shoal water at low water springs. The deepest water over these shoals becomes the entrance and because these depths change from one position to another, so the best entrance changes.

Late 1992, the best course over the bar was approximately 170° magnetic keeping the first and third green beacons slightly open to starboard. This, over my three decades of experience with this creek, is close to the most common situation. However, caution is advised. If in doubt, call Air Sea rescue for the latest information.

90

Round Hill Head is, literally, round or domed as seen in this approach from the south-east.

Looking into Round Hill Creek. Rocky Point is down the coast, left. This is the view when approaching the bar when its deepest water is off the point.

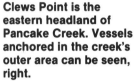

Table Hill is a feature of the land west of Pancake Creek.

Clews Point is the eastern headland of Pancake Creek. Vessels anchored in the creek's outer area can be seen, right.

The inner anchorage in Pancake Creek is very snug and secure. It is reached by adhering to a set of leading beacons within the creek.

Captain Cook in Bustard Bay

Having passed around Break Sea Spit, which Captain Cook named soon after naming Sandy Cape (20 Sunday, 1770), *Endeavour* sailed west across Hervey Bay which he deduced as being a bay from the flights of boobies, presumably heading for freshwater at the head of the bay. He also named Hervey Bay. On Wednesday 23, the ship anchored in Bustard Bay and a party went ashore to examine Round Hill Creek. According to Cook's journal, *this channel I proceeded to examine, and found three fathom water till I got about a mile up it, where I finally met with a shoal, upon which there was little more than one fathom, but having passed over it, I had three fathoms again.*

Of the country in this area he was not very flattering, saying; *The country here is manifestly worse than Botany Bay: the soil is dry and sandy, but the sides of the hills are covered with trees, which grow separately, without underwood.* He named Bustard Bay after dining on a large bustard and it proved to be the first place in Queensland where Captain Cook landed.

Anchorage within the creek is secure over good-holding sand although sometimes restricted where windward-tide conditions are extreme coupled with an excess of boats. During neap tides and light to moderate winds, conditions are superb except where a sea has developed from the north. Then high tide can be uncomfortable.

The best anchorage will depend on draft, the deepest water being in the vicinity of Monument Point where maximum swinging room is enjoyed. A deep gutter also runs between the camping ground and the general store but shoals rapidly to its west. Reasonable swinging room, however, will be found towards the general store.

Nav Aids. A white light displaying 5 miles is situated on the north tip of Round Hill Head, and, within the creek, are unlit green and red starboard and port beacons showing the best water.

Tides. Round Hill Creek does not enjoy secondary port status in the *Tide Tables*. However, details supplied for nearby Pancake Creek apply almost exactly although there appears to be slightly less range. Pancake Creek experiences 77% of Gladstone's range while Round Hill Creek is closer to 73%. The times are similar at 35 minutes earlier.

During spring tides, a current capable of causing some inconvenience against a strong wind occurs causing a vessel to sheer around her anchor. Owing to the restricted channel, the ebb should be watched. Most water evacuates during the first half of an ebb cycle.

Facilities. The marina is full and not available to casuals, but offers diesel fuel, repair services and intends installing a slipway. Ashore there is a general store, public phones, bank agency, liquor store and fast foods.

PANCAKE CREEK

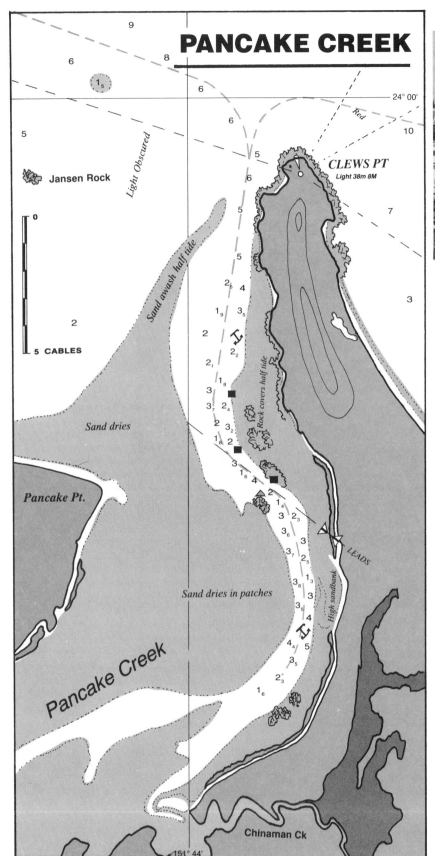

Jansen Rock

0

2

5 CABLES

CLEWS PT
Light 38m 8M

Light Obscured

Sand awash half tide

Rock covers half tide

Sand dries

Pancake Pt.

Sand dries in patches

High sandbank

LEADS

Pancake Creek

Chinaman Ck

Red

24° 00'

151° 44'

The marina in Gladstone Boat Harbour is an obligatory facility for those sailing to that city. A new bridge connects it to the city across Auckland Creek. Gladstone is described on page 97.

Pancake Creek is one of the mainland's best anchorages as long as the inner part can be reached. Minimum depth on the leads at low water springs is 1.4 metres.

Below left. The careening grid in Gladstone is a great way of cutting haul-out costs. It is across the end of the O'Connell Jetty. Note the new opening bridge across Auckland Creek in the background.

PANCAKE CREEK. With its deep entrance and good shelter, Pancake Creek is well recommended. It lies under the lee of the Bustard Head-Clews Point headland 12 miles north-west of Round Hill Creek and 30 miles east-south-east of Gladstone.

Approach from the seaward is clear of dangers until a line of rocks stretching north from Bustard Head is encountered. Known as *Inner, Middle* and *Outer Rocks*, all expose up to one metre above high water springs except for one tidal patch which dries over two metres low water springs.

During daylight hours in fair weather it is safe to pass between these rocks standing a good lookout. Beware of holding Inner Rock too close when rounding its north owing to a shoal extending in that direction from the rock. Do not pass between it and the mainland.

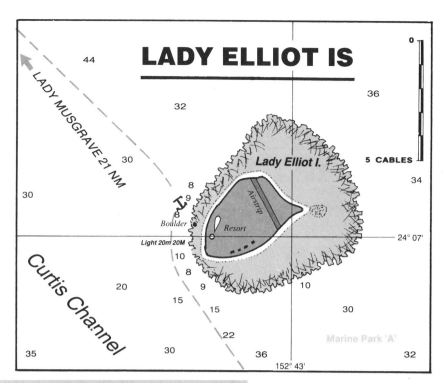

LADY ELLIOT IS

From Pancake Creek, the mainland is temporarily abandoned in favour of the offshore reefs and cays north to North West Island. Gladstone Harbour is the next mainland anchorage after Pancake Creek. Its description will be found immediately after North West Island.

The three photographs show Lady Elliot Island being approached from the south and its anchorage entered around its western side. The airstrip clearing in the trees is obvious in the centre pic as is the light on the island's left hand side. The best anchorage, bottom, is comfortable only in calm weather.

A line of sand dunes stretches between Round Hill Creek and Bustard Head and to the immediate south of Bustard Head are large sand blows which can be seen from seaward and from the west. When approaching from the latter direction, out of Gladstone, beware of *Jansen Rock* one mile west of Clews Point.

Anchorage. During calm or trade wind weather, the outer anchorage, to the north of the red beacons, makes an ideal overnight stop despite a modicum of swell finding its way in. For total security and comfort, the inner anchorage is ideal and is approached after rounding the red beacons then using the lead beacons which show the best water between rocky outcrops.

LADY ELLIOT ISLAND lies 42 miles east of north from the mouth of the Burnett River, Bundaberg, and 46 miles west of north from Sandy Cape, Fraser Island. It is a coral cay supporting a lighthouse and tourist resort and is the first of the chain of reefs, islands and cays comprising Queensland's Great Barrier Reef. Sadly, it is also the last resting place of the Sydney racing yacht, *Apollo*, whose crew became confused by the lights of the catamaran *Bagatelle* which hit Lady Elliot Reef ahead. She got off while *Apollo* remained despite every effort by her owner, Jack Rooklyn and crew. The accident reminds us all that disaster can overtake the best of us.

The cay is sighted from a distance of about 10 miles, appearing from the south as a low, upturned saucer. It has no remarkable features although the airstrip clearing becomes apparent closer in. The light stands proud enough to be identified from well off.

Anchorage off its north-west corner is very swell-prone and heavy rolling can be expected during developed trade winds. Only during calm to light winds, when the vessel rides bow to tidal stream, can some comfort be anticipated.

It is possible to drop anchor in about 7 metres at which depth the bottom can be seen clearly enough that coral can be avoided and the anchor lobbed onto sand. The cable may well foul coral if great care is not exercised.

Lady Elliot Island is where Australia's beche-de-mer industry began, it being a spin-off from Matthew Flinders' loss of the *Porpoise* on which he was returning

93

to England to present the results of his Australian surveys. In 1803 both *Porpoise* and a second vessel in the small fleet, *Cato*, hit Wreck Reef 170 miles north-east of Lady Elliot. A third vessel, the *Bridgewater*, failed to render assistance, standing off to sea and abandoning Flinders who organised the survivors on the sand cay then sailed a ship's cutter to Sydney with a picked crew. Later, one of *Porpoise's* survivors told pioneer trader James Aickin that he had seen many sea-slugs (beche-de-mer) on Wreck Reef. Following up, Aickin did not find the numbers economical but did at Lady Elliot thus starting an industry that swept north along the whole coast.

LADY MUSGRAVE ISLAND.

Lying 50 miles north of Bundaberg's Burnett River mouth, Lady Musgrave is part of the *Bunker Group* which parallels the Curtis coast. The nearest land is Bustard Head, 35 miles west.

Because it is a near perfect example of a navigable coral lagoon, and is often the first coral experience of the southern visitor, it is all too often the venue of distress for reasons discussed later.

Approach is clear of hazards from west through south to north-east except for Lady Elliot Island lying 20 miles to its south-east. From the north-west, the chain of reefs and cays of the Bunker Group must be negotiated in daylight only.

If approaching from offshore, beware the extent of Musgrave's reef to the south-east, especially in late afternoon when the sun is ahead, denying useful visibility.

Regardless of direction, the actual cay of Lady Musgrave will be seen from a distance of about 9 miles. Its beach lifts when about 3 miles off. Yacht masts in the lagoon are usually a feature and these will be seen from around 5 miles away.

There is a trellis light on the western tip visible at night for 14 miles. Marking the lagoon entrance and dangers within are port, starboard and isolated danger beacons.

Entering the lagoon. The position of the lagoon entrance is easily identified from about 4 miles off by sighting the red and green beacons through binoculars. There are one red and two green beacons, all unlit.

Being aware that a strong tidal flow can run through the entrance during spring tides, hold a mid channel course until inside the lagoon at which time turn towards the island passing an isolated danger beacon to port. A second isolated danger beacon will be seen towards the island and this, too, is best passed to port.

When seeking anchorage, move cautiously amongst the coral heads assuming, but not implicitly believing, that all dark brown coloured patches carry at least 3 metres low water springs whilst those of a yellow colouring are very shoal and possibly expose at low tide.

Anchorage outside the reef, off the island, is swell prone but easy to escape should condition become intolerable. Anchorage within the lagoon can be taken wherever suitable, the most popular position being as close to the island as possible. The bottom is excellent holding sand.

As suggested earlier, the lagoon anchorage can cause a lot of distress to the small boat sailor who, if new to reef country, tends to presume that an enclosed lagoon promises all-weather comfort. This is far from the truth.

During a developed trade wind at high tide when the reef is fully covered, waves can run across the lagoon high enough to cause such violent hobby-horsing that the foredeck might dip underwater on a regular basis. Even at low tide, the motion can become intolerable,

Left. An isolated danger beacon in Lady Musgrave Lagoon. *Right.* Lady Musgrave Island is a classic coral cay of which there are hundreds along the Coral Coast.

Lady Musgrave Island as seen just after the lagoon has been entered.

Lady Musgrave Island from the favourite anchorage area. Note the tourist punts, right.

LADY MUSGRAVE IS
(Bunker Group)

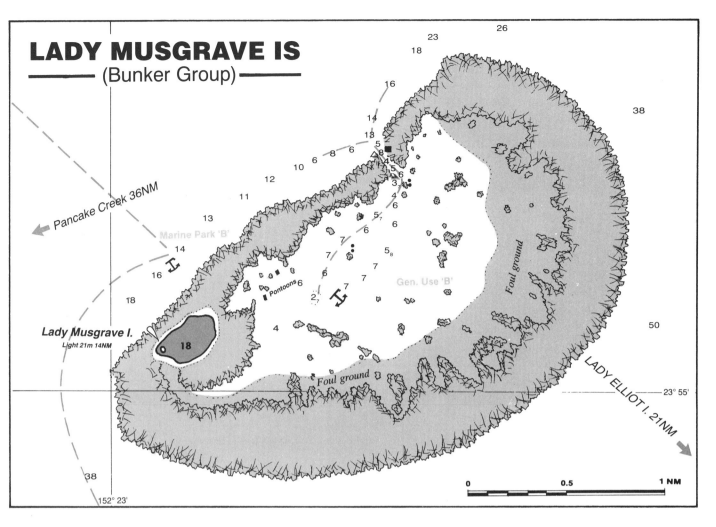

Perhaps the Coral Coast's most famous reef anchorage, lagoons of this type with a navigable entrance are, in fact, extremely rare anywhere in the Great Barrier Reef.

leading to plans of urgent escape.

Escape through the narrow entrance is possible regardless of the weather, but there is an element of risk. This, with the certain knowledge that sea conditions outside will also be miserable, with the nearest shelter to leeward being Gladstone some 60 miles across a rough sea, encourage one to remain in the lagoon. The result can be a thoroughly miserable few days — or even weeks if the strong wind prevails — during which time many folk have exhausted their food and water to become literally desperate in their need to reach civilisation.

When the above is mixed with the ongoing anxiety of knowing that if the anchor drags at night a jagged coral reef waits to claim your ship, it can be appreciated that Lady Musgrave is not the perfect place presumed by so many.

Of Interest. Lady Musgrave is a *Maritime National Park 'B' Zone* which denies it to trawling, spear fishing and coral and shell collecting. Ashore there are picnic facilities whilst close to the island's eastern tip, moorings and a pontoon are permanently established to service tourists visiting from Bundaberg aboard the catamaran, *Lady Musgrave*.

Between November and January, loggerhead and green turtles nest here with their hatchlings emerging as late as March. During the same period, mutton birds

nest ashore by burrowing in the sand. Be careful of their nests when walking ashore.

It is popularly believed that the lagoon entrance was blasted out to admit vessels calling to collect guano. Goats were certainly introduced to help shipwrecked sailors, their numbers rapidly increasing and the island slowly being stripped of vegetation. They were eliminated during the early 1970s. The light was established in 1974.

NOTE. Wreck and One Tree islands, in the Capricorn Group, are Preservation and Research Zones. Boating of any description is not allowed within their vicinities.

The Reefs off Gladstone

The two groups of reefs and coral cays paralleling the coast off the Gladstone area are collected together under the names *Bunker Group* and *Capricorn Group*. Except for the lagoons of Lady Musgrave Island and Fitzroy Reef, there are no reefs of a shape offering comfortable anchorage. Depths under their lees also tend to be excessive. The groups are best cruised in fair weather. The best trade wind anchorage, in terms of easy escape if necessary, is North West Island.

95

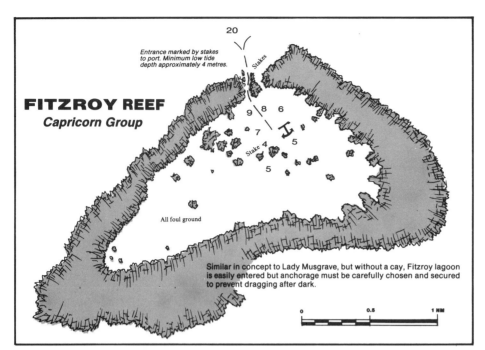

FITZROY REEF
Capricorn Group

20

Entrance marked by stakes to port. Minimum low tide depth approximately 4 metres.

Stakes

9 8 6

7

Stake 4 5

5

All foul ground

Similar in concept to Lady Musgrave, but without a cay, Fitzroy lagoon is easily entered but anchorage must be carefully chosen and secured to prevent dragging after dark.

0   0.5   1 NM

Fitzroy Reef is zoned *General Use 'B'* meaning that boating, fishing, and crabbing is allowed.

The main entrance into Gladstone Harbour (Port Curtis) is via South Channel thence Golding Cutting. The small vessel may cheat a little but not at the expense of fetching Jenny Lind Bank or East Bank. Most visitors from the north use the tidal waterway. The Narrows, as described on page 100.

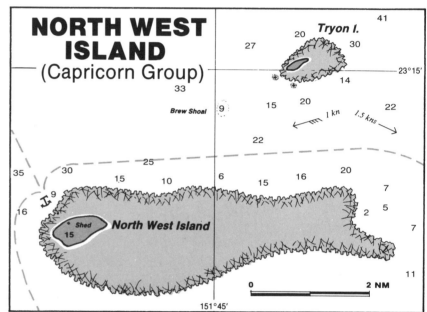

NORTH WEST ISLAND
(Capricorn Group)

North West Island is zoned *General Use 'B'* but with a vertical band of *Marine National Park 'A'* projecting north and south of the eastern half of the island.

41

20   *Tryon I.*

27   30

33   23°15'

14

Brew Shoal   9   15   20   22

1 kn   1.5 kns

22

35   30   25   20

1.5   10   6   15   16   7

9

16   5

2

Shed   *North West Island*   7

15

11

0   2 NM

151°45'

Nearly a Resort

Reminding us that there is nothing sacrosanct about a national park where money is involved; just two years after North West Island was declared a national park in 1980, the Queensland Government attempted to sell development rights to Japanese businessman, Yohachiro Iwasaki or P & O. The plan was dumped after public outcry.

FITZROY REEF is 20 miles north-west of Lady Musgrave Island and offers similar anchorage in a large lagoon which has a narrow entrance near its northern extreme. There is ample water in the channel for low-tide entry and plenty of depth and space between coral heads inside for secure anchoring although indifferent holding in certain areas must be considered. Because movement after dark is impossible, the anchor must be well dug in before dusk.

Within the entrance channel are steel stakes to port. These may be covered at high tide or missing, throwing most dependence on eyeball navigation. Low-tide slack water is the best time to enter for its better definition of the channel sides and coral heads within the lagoon. Anchorage is best immediately south-east of the entrance.

HERON ISLAND. *Not illustrated large scale* A coral cay supporting a tourist resort and biological research station, non-guests are not welcome here. It has a small harbour on the western tip which is always congested.

The only useful trade wind anchorage is under the lee of neighbouring *Wistari Reef* whose steep-to depths demand a lot of cable.

NORTH WEST ISLAND is a coral cay situated on the western edge of its east-west reef. It lies nearly 15 miles north-west of Heron Island. National Park facilities are ashore as are the remnants of the island's past as a turtle cannery. Anchorage will be according to the prevailing wind, the best being against a south-easterly towards a marker on the edge of the reef which will be roughly in line with a hut ashore. It is good holding on a sandy ledge at around 9 metres.

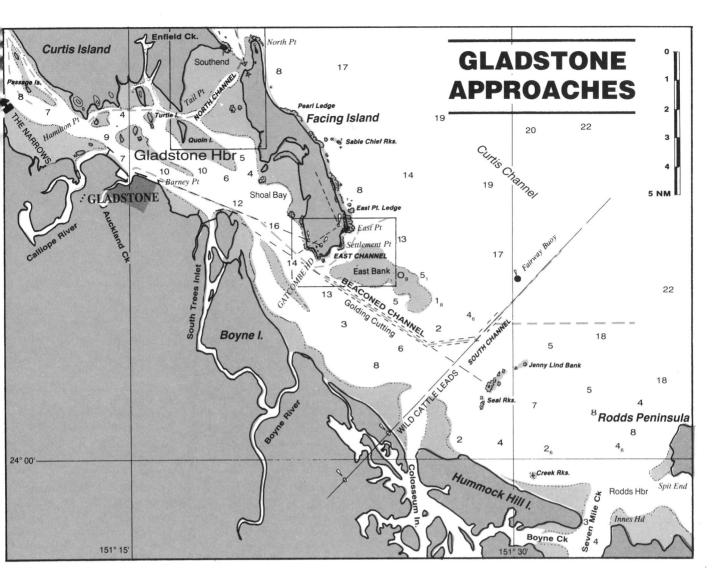

GLADSTONE
APPROACHES

GLADSTONE. The coast's most industrialised city north of Brisbane, Gladstone is situated on the shores of Port Curtis (also Port Gladstone). It was first surveyed by the author's great grandfather, Francis Peter MacCabe in 1863–5, a memorial to which stands in the Port Curtis Historical Village near the Calliope River bridge.

Anchorages are generally poor throughout the harbour, shoals restricting penetration into the many enticing bays. Casual visitors needing services should go direct to the *Gladstone Boat Harbour* in which is a marina. Call ahead on VHF or 27 megs or go alongside to enquire. Pets are not allowed here and access to the City of Gladstone is easy via an opening bridge across Auckland Creek. This was completed in 1993.

Facilities include all shops, slipways, yacht club, repair services of all descriptions plus a careening grid on the north end of O'Connell Wharf.

Gladstone Approaches. There are four ways into Gladstone Harbour, these being; from the north via *The Narrows*; from the north-east via *North Channel*; from the east via *East Channel*; and from the south via the *South Channel*. The first three are shown in large scale and are described separately later. Here the main approach channel, obligatory to all commercial shipping and sensible for all boats coasting up from the south is looked at in detail. It is known as *South Channel*.

Ships are obliged to arrive off South Channel at the fairway buoy from where Wild Cattle Leads are held into the first part of the dredged channel. This channel is lined with red and green lit port and starboard beacons all the way from the buoy to Gatcombe Head.

Small boats may safely short-cut from the Rodds Peninsula area to off Jenny Lind Bank thence direct into the channel wherever convenient. Beware the outer limit of *Seal Rocks* which cover at high tide and can be difficult to see in calm, reflective conditions. The main body of the rocks expose one metre high water springs. A loose back-lead for this course is Bustard Head open of Rodds Peninsula.

With local knowledge it is possible to continue this short-cut straight across the dredged channel, crossing the corner of East Banks then entering the Golding Cutting towards Gatcombe Head. Strangers to the port should maintain orientation by remaining in the cutting once it is entered.

After dark, all channels should be held from the fairway buoy into port to avoid confusion, the lighted beacons making no sense to the stranger out of context. Regardless of the time of approach, a flood tide will cut hours off the trip and, during developed trade winds, calm the outer harbour seas.

East Channel is an all-weather entrance to Gladstone Harbour between Facing Island and East Banks. Foul ground extends off Facing Island north from East Point

97

Gatecombe Head, under the highest land, is on the southern end of Facing Island. East Point is extreme right.

Gatecombe Head is left with Settlement Point, right. The channel separation beacon for East Channel is seen, right.

and should be given a wide berth on approach from seaward. Tides run at up to three knots off Gatcombe Head and are best used to advantage. The small boat harbour under Rocky Point is for runabouts only.

In winds east to north-east, good overnight anchorage can be taken where shown near Observation Point. In developed winds from other directions it pays to press on for Gladstone or creeks within The Narrows area.

North Entrance. One of four entrances into Gladstone Harbour, North Entrance is about six miles north-east of Gladstone City between the islands of Facing and Curtis. There are good depths up to and immediately within the entrance, allowing it to be entered in foul weather, but shallows within demand a flood tide and caution.

The least depth is 0.9 metres between rock patches immediately after turning off the entrance leads onto the *Farmers Reef Leads*. A tide complimentary to your draft is necessary to clear this bar.

If bound for the settlement of Southend, turn to starboard off these leads and anchor in the limited swing basin to the west of the jetty. Leave plenty of

room for the Gladstone-Southend ferry to manoeuvre. This is a troubled anchorage during strong winds and care must be exercised against falling back over shallow ground when the tide ebbs.

If bound for Gladstone, turn to port off the Farmers Reef Leads, passing a yellow beacon to starboard after which a series of red and green beacons are passed to port and starboard respectively. The next shallow spot is near the first red beacon after passing Quoin Island, but this should be no problem if the first shoal is cleared successfully. Beyond this shallow spot, the channel continues along the southern shore of Curtis Island before breaking out into the main harbour area (see chart on page 97 for orientation).

If your destination is somewhere down the western shore of Facing Island, turn south-east soon after passing the last red beacon before Quoin Island. Depending on general visibility and water quality at the time, the

East Channel, below, and North Channel, right, are alternative entrances to Gladstone Harbour (Port Curtis). East Channel has good water throughout whilst North Channel demands a rising tide. Its bar is in protected waters.

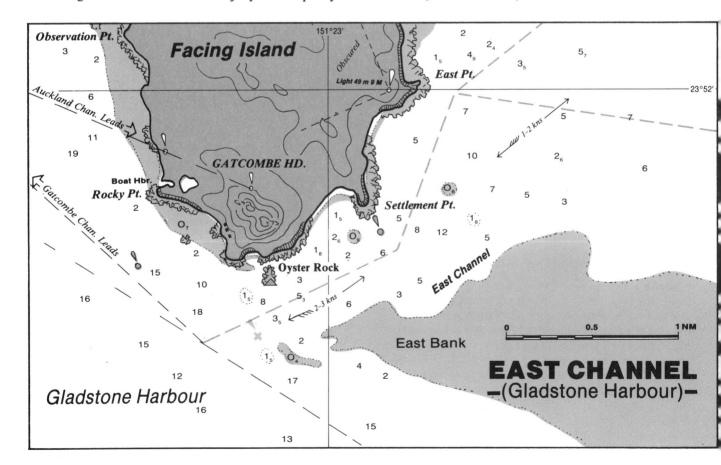

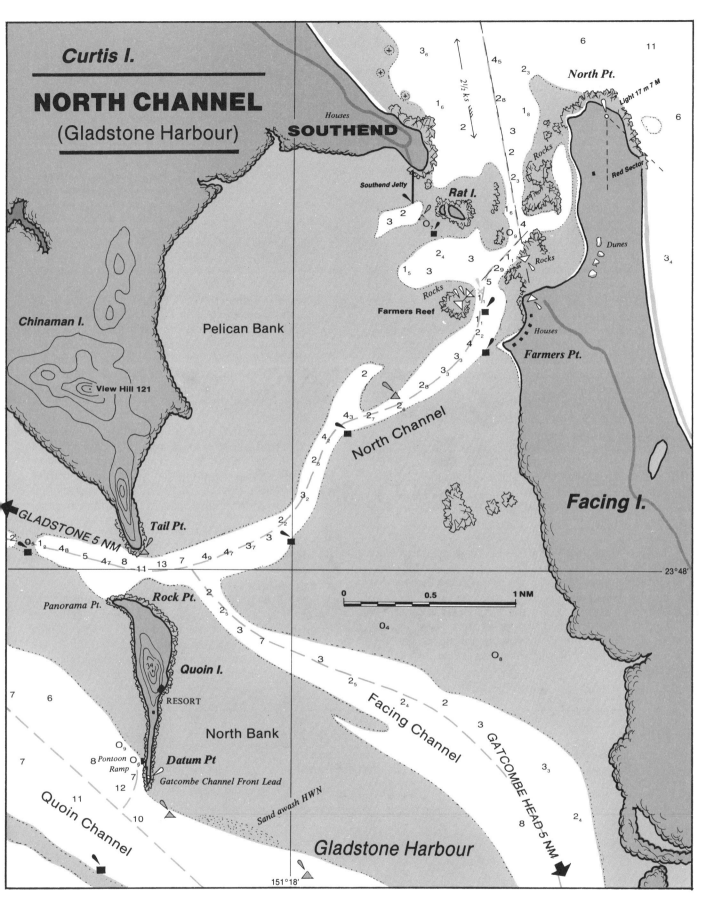

Curtis I.

NORTH CHANNEL
(Gladstone Harbour)

SOUTHEND

Houses

North Pt.

Light 17 m 7 M

Red Sector

Rocks

Southend Jetty

Rat I.

Dunes

Rocks

Rocks

Farmers Reef

Houses

Farmers Pt.

Facing I.

Chinaman I.

Pelican Bank

View Hill 121

North Channel

Tail Pt.

GLADSTONE 5 NM

23°48'

0   0.5   1 NM

Panorama Pt.

Rock Pt.

Quoin I.

RESORT

North Bank

Facing Channel

GATCOMBE HEAD 5 NM

Pontoon Ramp

Datum Pt

Gatcombe Channel Front Lead

Quoin Channel

Sand awash HWN

Gladstone Harbour

151°18'

edge of the shoals are not always easy to identify. Proceed with caution.

Tides turn a little earlier than Gladstone with the flow moving in a contrary direction for some time after turn. In the Quoin Island region, the flow can be unpredictable, influenced, as it is, by water moving in and out through both North Entrance and South Channel at opposite ends of Facing Island.

Persons proceeding north outside Curtis Island should turn to the next anchorage along that coast, Cape Capricorn. Persons travelling through The Narrows read on.

Tides are rapid in Gladstone Harbour suggesting that a favourable stream be used whenever possible.

The Clinton Coal Wharf is outside and to the north-west of the marina which is off Auckland Creek.

QUOIN ISLAND. Boasting kangaroos and wallabies and supporting a small tourist resort, Quoin Island lies within Gladstone Harbour about two miles north-east of the city. On Datum Point is the front lead for Gatcombe Channel leads, the transit of which can be held almost up to the island when approaching from the south-east.

Serving the resort from Gladstone is a small launch which berths at a pontoon jetty on the western side of Datum Point.

During strong south-easterlies the anchorage can be dismal, especially when plagued by windward-tide. Beware of fetching the edge of the vast shoals extending west from the island.

The modern resort has a bar, swimming pool and restaurant.

THE NARROWS. This is a calm waterway between the mainland and Curtis Island linking *Gladstone Harbour* with *Keppel Bay*. Although deep for most of its length, the central area, known as the *Cattle Crossing*, dries at low water springs to heights of 2 metres. This demands that your draft plus 2 metres be used in tide height before attempting the passage. This can be fine-tuned as noted later under the heading 'Tides'.

Because it is imperative that the Cattle Crossing be negotiated close to the top of the tide, Gladstone or Sea Hill Point must be departed at a time which takes this into consideration. The distance from Gladstone to the first drying banks is 12 miles whilst the distance from Sea Hill to the first drying banks is 9 miles. To this must be added the distance to the approximate central part of the drying area which is nearly 3 miles in each case.

As can be deduced from the above, the area of drying sand banks is about 6 miles long. The drying height of these banks is very difficult to establish exactly owing to the variations in finding datum. My recent survey suggests that it may be a little less than 2 metres, but have indicated that figure (east of the Cattle Crossing) for safety's sake.

Tides flood from each end, meeting and mingling in the vicinity of *Boat Creek*. Thus, regardless of which way you are travelling, your exit speed will be reduced by an opposing flood stream.

Tide times in The Narrows vary from one end to the other by as much as 35 minutes, being later than Gladstone data by 20 to 55 minutes. To the person about to take a keel boat through, this difference can be reduced to a safe half an hour later than data. Thus,

The pontoon at Quoin Island. The resort is on the other side of the island to the north.

Approaching Quoin Island from the south. A channel beacon is seen, right.

100

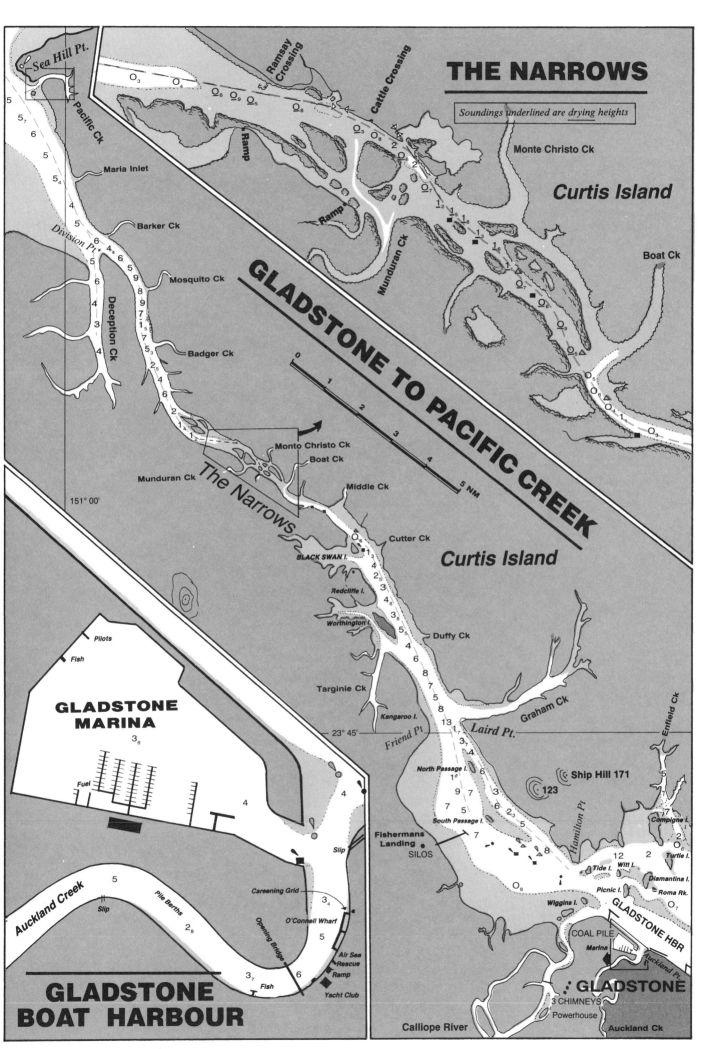

THE NARROWS

Soundings underlined are drying heights

GLADSTONE TO PACIFIC CREEK

Sea Hill Pt.

Pacific Ck

Ramsay Crossing

Cattle Crossing

Monte Christo Ck

Curtis Island

Maria Inlet

Ramp

Ramp

Munduran Ck

Boat Ck

Barker Ck

Division Pt.

Mosquito Ck

Deception Ck

Badger Ck

Monto Christo Ck

Boat Ck

Munduran Ck

The Narrows

Middle Ck

Cutter Ck

Curtis Island

BLACK SWAN I.

Redcliffe I.

Worthington I.

Duffy Ck

Targinie Ck

Graham Ck

Entield Ck

Kangaroo I.

Friend Pt.

Laird Pt.

23° 45'

North Passage I.

Ship Hill 171

123

South Passage I.

Hamilton Pt.

Compigne I.

Fishermans Landing

SILOS

Turtle I.

Tide I. Witt I.

Diamantina I.

Picnic I.

Roma Rk.

Wiggins I.

GLADSTONE HBR

COAL PILE

Marina

GLADSTONE

3 CHIMNEYS

Powerhouse

Calliope River

Auckland Ck

151° 00'

0 1 2 3 4 5 NM

GLADSTONE MARINA

Pilots

Fish

Fuel

Slip

Auckland Creek

Pile Berths

Slip

Careening Grid

O'Connell Wharf

Opening Bridge

Air Sea Rescue

Ramp

Fish

Yacht Club

GLADSTONE BOAT HARBOUR

Mount Larcom, left, is a conspicuous landmark in the Gladstone region. It is seen here from The Narrows.

Steaming south, out of the Cattle Crossing area, the leads are arrowed astern. This is the shallowest part where sandbanks dry as much as 2 metres LWS.

The leading beacons south of the Cattle Crossing are seen here.

From the splintered deck of the barge wreck, the entrance to Pacific Creek is seen here. The shed and tank are conspicuous when entering.

The Narrows' famous Cattle Crossing where cattle are walked across the shallows at low tide between the mainland and Curtis Island.

The lovely motor sailer, *Accolade* exiting The Narrows.

if it is high tide in Gladstone at 0700 hours, think 0730 for The Narrows. Better still, work on Gladstone time so that the late factor in The Narrows becomes a bonus.

Another confusing factor when nutting out the best time to navigate The Narrows is the variation in actual tide height. At both ends of the shoal area, it is higher than Gladstone, but it is higher at the western end than it is at the eastern end. This can be as great as nearly 33%. Looking at this by simple example; if Gladstone data is 4 metres, the western end of The Narrows at Ramsay Crossing will be 5.3 metres whilst the eastern end near Boat Creek will be 4.5 metres (in round figures). Between the two — where banks dry the highest — the height would be somewhere between the two. Probably around 4.9 metres.

It can be appreciated that, when working out water levels above drying banks in The Narrows, Gladstone data can be increased by nearly 25%. In the name of safety and to avoid embarrassing groundings, it is better to think 15%.

Regardless of how it is worked out, never navigate the region without at least one more spring tide of greater height predicted for the following day and remember that any deduction is only as good as your ability to steer the right course.

Nav Aids are plentiful through The Narrows in the form of unlit beacons which are passed red to port and green to starboard heading north. At each end of the Cattle Crossing are leading beacons which show well enough. Beware, however, of early morning when steering east into the sun at which time the Ramsay Crossing beacons can be difficult to sight.

Anchorages. Whilst there is always plenty of time to depart Gladstone or Sea Hill Point to be in The Narrows ahead of high water turn, circumstances or preferences can make a preliminary anchorage very sensible. Such anchorages exist in abundance and are looked at here.

On the Gladstone side there is absolute haven in *Graham Creek* where depths range around 3 and 4 metres, the best entry depths being against the south head (Laird Point). This is so secure that it rates well as a cyclone hole.

Still on the Gladstone side, and much closer to the action, it is possible to anchor in good low tide depths between *Black Swan* and *Redcliffe Islands*. This places you as close as it is sensible to get to the drying area.

On the Sea Hill side, *Badger Creek* has good clear low tide depths. When approaching from the north, stand off to the western side of the main channel to skirt a shoal bank.

A sensible alternative to Badger Creek is to remain out in the main channel where there is more swinging room and less mosquito attack. A strong wind can annoy with windward-tide antics, but usually after dark the wind lifts leaving the vessel serenely tide-rode.

History. Colin Archer, the designer whose name is almost synonymous with the so-called 'double-ender' yacht, was one of the earliest persons to navigate The Narrows. As noted in the Rockhampton description later, the Archer brothers had moved their grazing interests from the Wide Bay district to the upper Fitzroy River. Colin Archer sailed stores north aboard the *Elida* and backloaded wool to Gladstone for transhipment to Sydney. Later he chartered the 85 ton *Albion* and sailed her north through The Narrows.

First beaconed in 1867 as the passage became a regular route between Gladstone and Rockhampton, attempts to dredge the drying banks commenced in 1890 and again in 1896, on both occasions the contractors involved having to abandon the project. In desperation, hand labour was tried to reduce the height of drying banks so that the regular Gladstone-Rockhampton steamer, *Premier* could maintain communication. At that time, The Narrows had 10 light beacons and a lightkeeper's residence on Monte Christo Island.

Entering Pacific Creek, the low headland on which a tank and shed are seen, left, with the higher hills of Curtis Island behind.

Faint in the centre is omnipresent Mount Larcom seen between Curtis Island and Pilot Island whilst entering Pacific Creek.

The author's yacht *Renee Tighe* spends a day aground whilst surveying Pacific Creek entrance for this book.

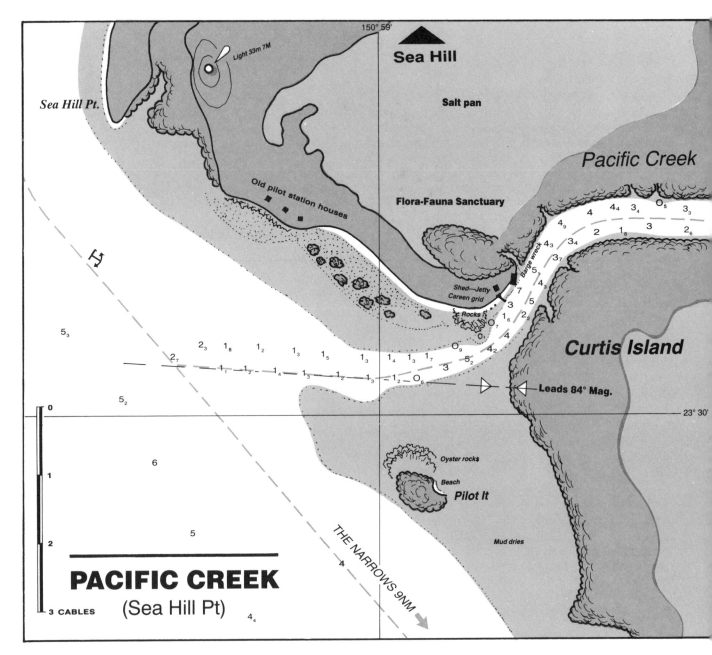

Light 33m 7M

Sea Hill Pt.

Sea Hill

Salt pan

Pacific Creek

Old pilot station houses

Flora-Fauna Sanctuary

Shed—Jetty
Careen grid

Barge wreck

Rocks

Curtis Island

Leads 84° Mag.

Oyster rocks

Beach

Pilot It

Mud dries

THE NARROWS 9NM

PACIFIC CREEK
(Sea Hill Pt)

3 CABLES

PACIFIC CREEK lies under *Sea Hill Point* on the north-west tip of Curtis Island. It provides total security and even cyclone protection with only windward-tide and mosquitoes to consider. The latter can be surprisingly subdued considering the mangroves on each side.

A logical first anchorage after passing through The Narrows from Gladstone, there can arise the problem of reaching it on the same tide used to get through The Narrows. Often the tide is falling on arrival off the creek, a state not recommended when entering. It is better to anchor off the entrance and await the next tide than to risk a grounding on an ebb tide.

The Bar is untroubled by swell of any kind, leaving only depths and state of tide to be considered. With local knowledge, and by wandering off the leading beacons in certain places, it is possible to find nearly one metre of water over the bar at spring low tide. Realistically speaking, it is best to think in terms of half a metre or less when balancing draft against tide range. Enter only on a flood tide and hold the small, leading beacons in line. Do not run in too close to the front lead before abandoning their transit for it

sits well back from the edge of a very soft mud bank.

Having abandoned the leads, favour the starboard bank without hugging it to clear around the rock ledge which continues underwater towards centre channel. This carries 0.1 metres low water springs.

Anchorage within the creek is possible anywhere along its length or into its major offshoot towards its head. The most popular anchorage is as close to the old jetty, shed and barge wreck as possible, but if cramming for position, allow plenty of swinging room for windward-tide antics.

Tides are based on Gladstone data and are similar in height. They turn five minutes earlier, but the flow does not change direction for as long as half an hour after turn.

Of Interest. The tiny oyster-bound mangrove islet off Pacific Creek's entrance is unnamed. I have called it 'Pilot Islet' on the accompanying plan to remind us that Sea Hill was, until the 1960s, the pilot station for Port Alma and the Fitzroy River.

The original pilot station, intended to serve ships ascending the Fitzroy River to Rockhampton, was built

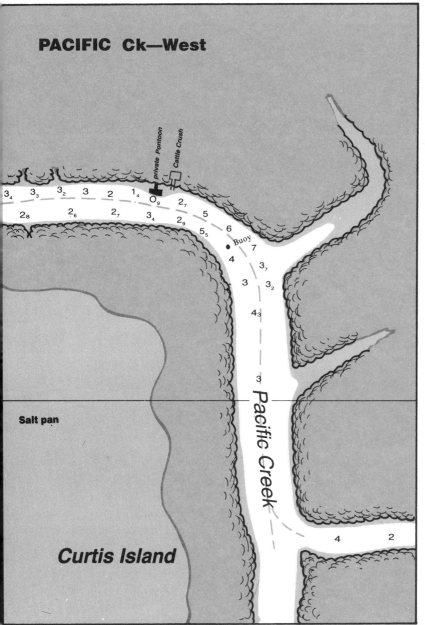

PACIFIC Ck—West

3_4 3_3 3_2 3 2 1_4 O$_9$ 2_7

private Pontoon   Cattle Crush

2_8 2_6 2_7 3_4 2_9 5

5_5 6

Buoy 7

4 3_7

3 3_2

4_3

3

Salt pan

Pacific Creek

Curtis Island

4 2

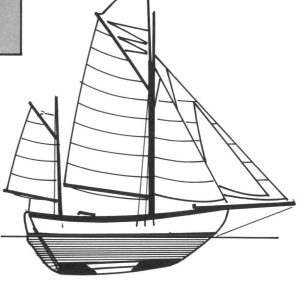

The Fitzroy River entrance is split by Mud Island (centre) and Egg Island to its immediate left. The main channel is to their south. Casuarina Creek, bottom of picture, is a deep, navigable waterway offering secure, isolated anchorage.

The Redningskoite pilot cutter of about 11 metres was one of Colin Archer's earliest successes. The son of a Norwegian mother and Scottish father, he lived and worked in Tolderodden, Norway, except for the few years he spent in Australia. Then, the Rockhampton-Narrows area was his backyard.

between Sea Hill and Cape Capricorn close to Cape Keppel in 1864 from which time vessels were boarded near offlying Keppel Rocks. It is interesting that one of the original pilots was Charles Haynes who, in 1856, served aboard the full-rigged ship *Morayshire* when she removed the descendants of the *Bounty* mutiny from Pitcairn Island to Norfolk Island.

Because of problems in boarding vessels in all weather off Keppel Rocks, that station was transferred to Sea Hill Point in 1919. It was then referred to as 'Little Sea Hill'. Pacific Creek gave good shelter to the boats and it was closer to Port Alma, a deep water port rapidly proving its suitability as Rockhampton's ocean outlet.

Rockhampton itself closed to commercial shipping in 1965 at which time the Sea Hill Point Station was closed and its activities were then based in Port Alma.

The old pilot station houses remain at Sea Hill Point as does the jetty and boatshed near the mouth of Pacific Creek. These are now privately owned.

To the west of Pacific Creek, the Fitzroy River empties into the southern corner of Keppel Bay. Two charts covering its entrance to Rockhampton are shown over the page followed by a full description.

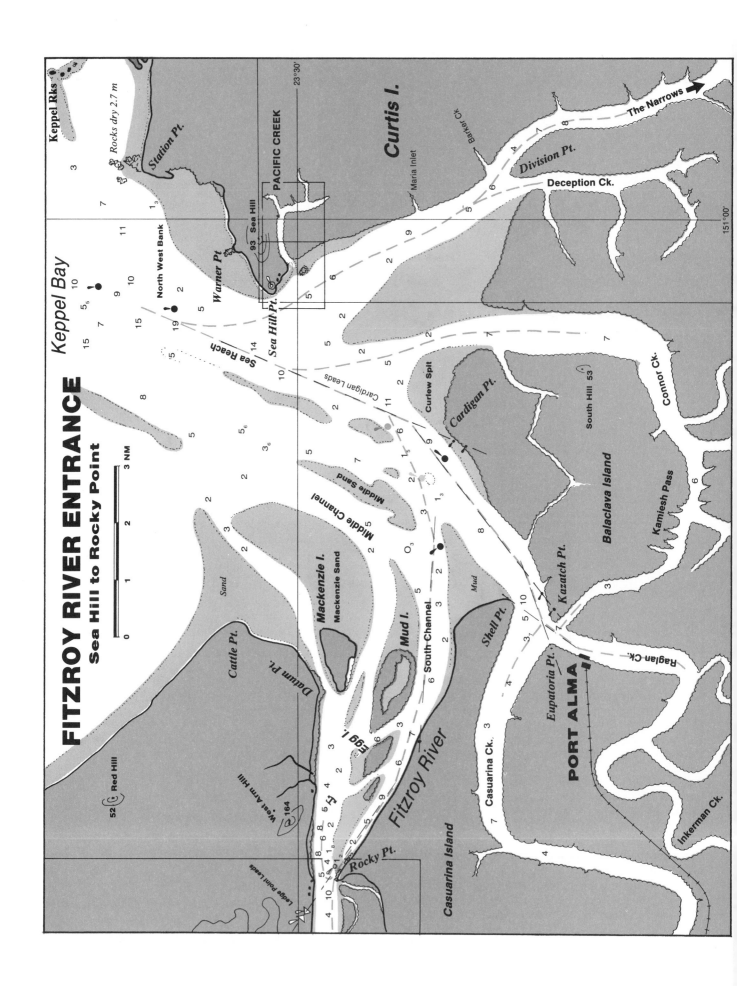

FITZROY RIVER ENTRANCE
Sea Hill to Rocky Point

Keppel Bay

Keppel Rks

Rocks dry 2.7 m

Station Pt.

PACIFIC CREEK

Sea Hill

North West Bank

Warner Pt

Sea Hill Pt.

Curtis I.

Maria Inlet

Barker Ck

Division Pt.

Deception Ck.

The Narrows

Sea Reach

Cardigan Leads

Curlew Spit

Cardigan Pt.

South Hill 53

Connor Ck.

Red Hill 52

Middle Channel

Middle Sand

Mackenzie I.
Mackenzie Sand

Balaclava Island

Kamiesh Pass

Cattle Pt.

Sand

Datum Pt.

Mud I.

South Channel

Mud

Shell Pt.

Kazatch Pt.

Raglan Ck.

West Arm Hill
164

Egg I.

Fitzroy River

Casuarina Ck.

Eupatoria Pt.

PORT ALMA

Inkerman Ck.

Ledge Point Leads

Rocky Pt.

Casuarina Island

3 NM

0   1   2   3

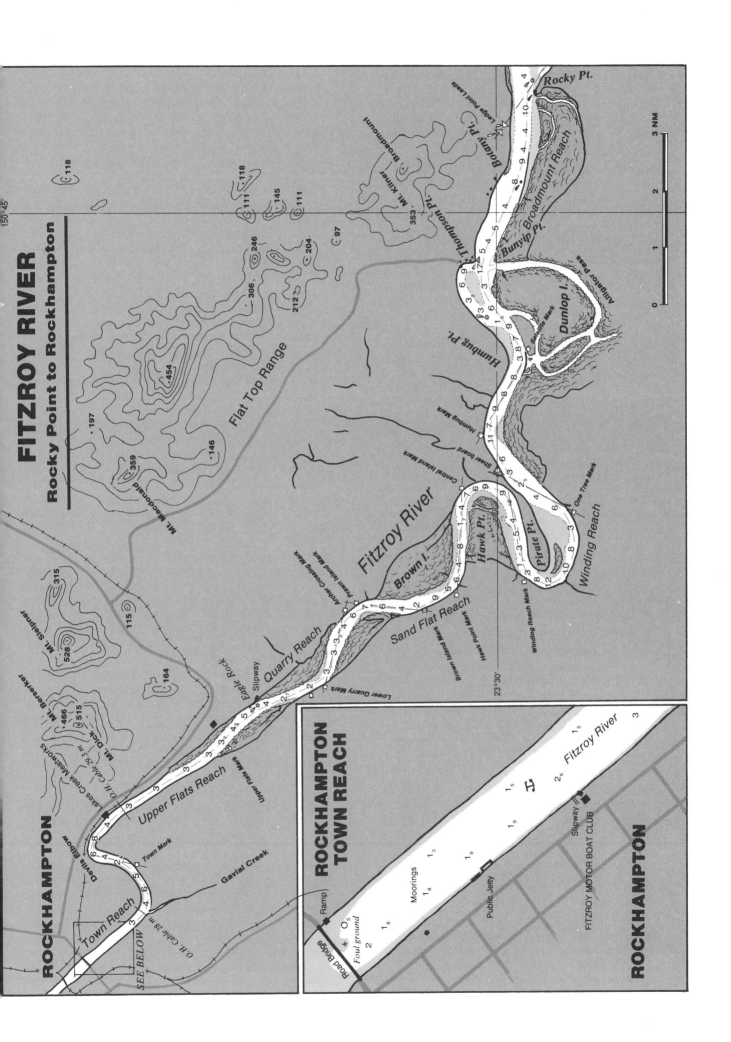

FITZROY RIVER
Rocky Point to Rockhampton

Flat Top Range

Mt Macdonald

Mt. Kilner

Mt. Stelpner

Mt. Dick

Mt. Berserker

Lakes Creek Meatworks

Fitzroy River

ROCKHAMPTON

Town Reach

Devils Elbow

Gavial Creek

Town Mark

Upper Flats Reach

Upper Flats Mark

O.H. Cable 28 m

O. H. Cable 22.3 m

SEE BELOW

Eagle Rock

Slipway

Quarry Reach

Lower Quarry Mark

Archer Crossing Mark

Prawn Island Mark

Sand Flat Reach

Brown I.

Brown Island Mark

Hawk Pt.

Hawk Point Mark

Pirate Pt.

Winding Reach

Winding Reach Mark

One Tree Mark

Central Island Mark

Sheer board

Humbug Mark

Humbug Pt.

Satellite Mark

Dunlop I.

Alligator Pass

Bunyip Pt.

Broadmount Reach

Broadmount Pt.

Thompson Pt.

Botany Pt.

Ledge Point Leads

Rocky Pt.

23°30'

150°45'

ROCKHAMPTON TOWN REACH

Road Bridge

Ramp

Foul ground

Moorings

Public Jetty

Slipway

FITZROY MOTOR BOAT CLUB

Fitzroy River

ROCKHAMPTON

3 NM

0 1 2

107

FITZROY RIVER. This is the longest navigable river on the Coral Coast, giving access to the major city of *Rockhampton* over 30 miles upstream from its mouth at the bottom of Keppel Bay. Rockhampton itself enjoys its own description; here we will look at the river and its navigation.

General Description. Rising in the hills and mountains to the north-west of Rockhampton, the Fitzroy river trends mainly south-east to empty into the vast wetlands of its delta under the lee of Curtis Island. A barrage immediately upstream of Rockhampton holds back the fresh water for irrigation while below the barrage the water is salt regardless of the state of tide.

Ascending the river, the delta wetlands give way to solid ground on which cattle are grazed. There are scattered hills at varying distances from the river. Near the mouth, the hills come straight down to the river whereas upriver they recede into the background.

There is a small settlement at *Thompson's Point*, about 10 miles upstream then nothing but nature until the Lakes Creek Meatworks just before Rockhampton and at the end of a string of houses, pontoons and private moorings. Around the 'S' bend known as Devil's Elbow, immediately upstream from the meatworks, the City of Rockhampton is found beyond which navigation is impossible owing to a bridge and the previously noted barrage (weir).

Limitations. Given tide, time and determination there is no reason why a vessel drawing more than 4 metres could not reach Rockhampton. But a more realistic maximum would be 3 metres with the typical depth of cruising yachts being child's play with sensible planning.

Overhead, the only limitations are power cables immediately downstream from Rockhampton City with a high tide height of 28 metres. A second cable near Derwent Rock has 29.3 metres H.W.S.

Nav Aids. Navigational aids upstream from Satellite Island (2 miles upstream from Thompson's Point settlement) are unlit except for Eagle Rock green buoy off Nerimbera Slipway.

Most aids are in the form of simple steering marks, the old leading beacon system being abandoned except for those showing the best water over the shoals at the entrance and again through the narrow channel off Rocky Point.

Tides are based on Gladstone data in the *Tide Tables* and are of similar height. Tide turns at the entrance close to the same time as Gladstone and two hours later at Rockhampton although there the actual flow might turn as much as two hours later again. The range can be as great as 4 metres during springs.

Currents can run at about 3 knots during springs and will gain speed quickly after a slack-water period of about one hour.

Navigation. Always using a flood tide, the river should be entered as soon as you can clear the entrance bar to the north-west of Balaclava Island which carries 1.5 metres low water springs. This usually leaves the bulk of the flood tide to enjoy all the way to Rockhampton or at least a substantial distance upstream depending on time of day and speed of vessel.

When entering the river from the Sea Hill area, *Cardigan Leads* on Balaclava Island should be held then abandoned as a green buoy comes abeam from where a yellow buoy will be just visible. Pass the green to starboard then the yellow buoy close to port after which a red buoy is also passed to port.

From the red buoy, the river proper is entered and a white tower is used as a steering mark to pass *Mud Island* fairly close to starboard from where the port bank is brought close aboard before turning along that shoreline.

A second mark, immediately after the last, known as *Garden Hill Steering Mark* is noted soon after which the *Ledge Point Leading Beacons* will be seen low down on the high land on the other side of the river. These show the best water past *Rocky Point*.

Depths increase dramatically as Rocky Point is cleared and course is laid for the next red buoy which is passed to port. Beware of wandering too far to port in this stretch as a training wall parallels the course and covers at high tide.

From the last red buoy, steer towards *Thompson's Point* where by now will be seen a number of corrugated iron shacks and a lit green beacon.

With Thompson's Point abeam to starboard, where by now an old jetty and wreck will be seen, steer to pass a green buoy wide to starboard then close towards the land where a steering mark will be seen on *Satellite Island*.

From Satellite Island, lay course direct for *Humbug Mark* then, when the land to starboard is close, sheer away and hold a parallel course until a second mark is abeam at which time turn for *One Tree Mark*.

From One Tree Mark, the river winds around *Pirate Point* during which time the port bank should be held reasonably close until *Winding Reach Mark* is abeam from where the starboard shore is closed. This is one of the shallower parts of the river, a fact only critical if anchorage has been taken overnight and the early flood tide is being used.

On the narrow neck of land forming Pirate Point there should be a steering mark known as *Central Island Lower Mark*. Hold the land fairly close to starboard as it turns to port until *Central Island Mark* is abeam to starboard then lay for *Hawke Point Mark* and hold its shoreline close to port until *Brown's Crossing Mark* is abeam to port. From there steer for *Prawn Island Mark* (which can be obscured by trees), hold its shore close to starboard until *Archer's Crossing Mark* is abeam then steer for *Lower Quarry Reach Mark*.

The river straightens out here and the vessel is held close to the port bank until *Quarry Reach Mark* is abeam to port then she is pointed towards the green buoy of *Eagle Rock* and Nerimbera Slipway.

After passing the green buoy to starboard, steam midstream up past the houses, pontoons, moored craft and the meatwork's remarkable wharf, entering *Devil's Elbow* on the outside of its curve. A steering mark on the outside of this curve may or may not be standing but, either way, turn quickly so as to bring the port bank close which is then followed around to Gavial Creek immediately upstream from which are the power cables at 28 metres above high water springs. From here, Rockhampton is well in view and the anchorage can be approached on a mid-stream course as the moored and anchored craft are encountered.

Anchorage. Whether or not a stop is made en route up to Rockhampton will depend very much on the time of day that entry is made and the speed of the vessel. Most of us are obliged to stop en route.

Good, secure anchorage can be found in most stretches of the river being certain only to avoid the channel in the event of a river fishing boat moving after dark and, where close to a bank, to allow for windward-tide movement.

Anchorage at Rockhampton is described separately next.

ROCKHAMPTON.
Well known for the main northern railway running through its centre along one of the city streets, Rockhampton has many historic, stone buildings. To those who enjoy river travel and down-to-earth places, the diversion is well worthwhile.

The city provides well for the average shopper, although boat parts can be hard to find. The *Fitzroy Motor Boat Club* caters for local interest and the *Town Reach* has plenty of anchoring space as long as the visitor is prepared to remain downstream of the main body of boats. Alongside fuel and water is available with a little organising. Haul-out can be arranged downriver at *Nerimbera Slipway*.

The photographs below relate to Cape Capricorn and its approaches described on the next page. All features shown are along the north coast of Curtis Island which protects the mouth of the Fitzroy River from the sea.

Rockhampton has the Coral Coast's richest hoard of old stone buildings, most of which are situated along the Town Reach.

From the suggested anchorage under Cape Capricorn, this sand blow is a feature. The lighthouse and houses are seen left of centre.

Looking into Yellow Patch from outside its barred entrance, the huge coloured sand blow is obvious, centre.

Cape Keppel is a relatively dominant headland on the northern tip of Curtis Island.

Keppel Rocks lie off Cape Keppel and have a shoal patch extending from their west.

Sea Hill at 93 metres high is conspicuous when approaching the Fitzroy River delta. Sea Hill Point is less dominant, right.

109

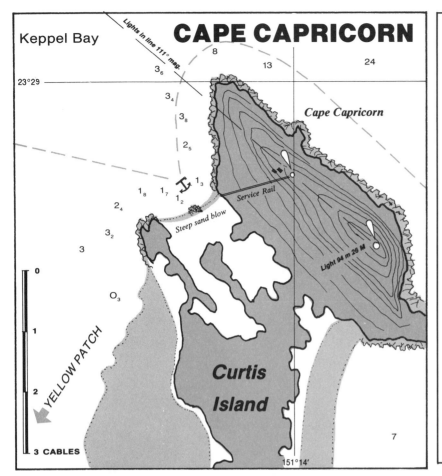

CAPE CAPRICORN

Keppel Bay

Lights in line 111° mag.

23°29

Cape Capricorn

Service Rail

Steep sand blow

Light 94 m 26 M

YELLOW PATCH

Curtis Island

3 CABLES

151°14'

YELLOW PATCH. This superb anchorage close to the remarkable yellow sand blow on Curtis Island extracts a price from those seeking its protection. A long sand bar with only about 0.5 metres low water springs must be negotiated. This, in itself is easy enough with a suitable tide, but when strong trade winds are blowing, a beam swell works across the bar threatening to heavily bounce any vessel wandering off track. This is exacerbated by the fact that the best 'track' is almost impossible to visually identify under such circumstances.

All things considered, those without fresh local knowledge should save Yellow Patch for calm weather. The bar position shown here is the most constant, but it can move dramatically at times.

The deepest anchorage is near the headland at the northern end of the sand blow, the water shoaling immediately south, off the sand. The anchor shown on the accompanying chart, close west of Cape Capricorn, is suggested only as a place to hold awaiting a tide for the bar.

CAPE CAPRICORN. So named because it lies almost exactly on the Tropic of Capricorn (23° 30'), this lofty headland is the northern extremity of Curtis Island. It supports a major lighthouse with a second light down the hill to its north-west. The two lights in transit indicate an approximate border between the shoals of Keppel Bay and the deeper water beyond. It can be used at night to maintain the best course between Cape Keppel and Hummocky Island.

Approach from the south is along the coast of Curtis Island beyond which Mount Larcom remains dominant and easily seen in fair visibility. *Rundle Islet* presents the only hazard but is easily sighted from a distance of 10 miles whilst the Cape itself is seen from about 18 miles. The light displays for 26 miles and covers Rundle Islet with a red sector.

The cape is a grass capped, rock-bound headland with large sand blows under its lee. These blows are

Navigators using charts whose corrections predate 1987 are warned that the light on Rundle Islet, close to Cape Capricorn, has been removed.

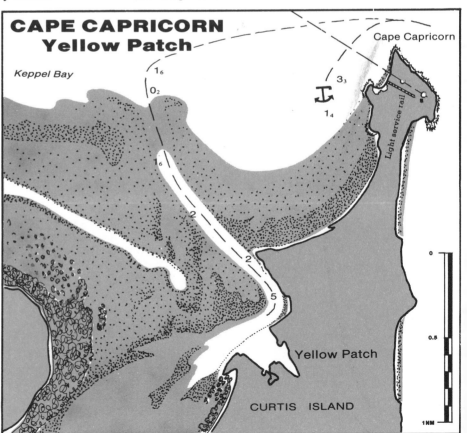

CAPE CAPRICORN
Yellow Patch

Keppel Bay

Cape Capricorn

Light service rail

Yellow Patch

CURTIS ISLAND

1 NM

110

seen from a considerable distance when approaching from the north.

Anchorage off the sand blow in the vicinity of the service rail is remarkably free from swell even in the most boisterous south easterly winds. Holding is good in sand and surge is experienced.

Of Interest. The lighthouse on Cape Capricorn was erected in 1875. A tramway with a gradient of 1–7 is used to haul supplies and equipment up from the beach. The station is served by a small high speed catamaran and is now automatic after well over a century of being fully manned. The keepers' houses remain.

Tropic of Capricorn

The Tropic of Capricorn is the sun's southern limit of declination at 23° 30′. It passes through the Cape Capricorn headland almost exactly one mile south of the actual cape.

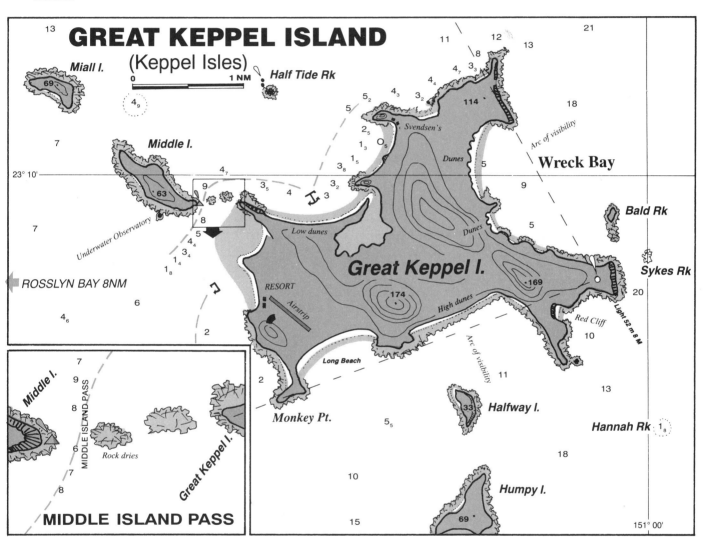

GREAT KEPPEL ISLAND (Keppel Isles)

GREAT KEPPEL ISLAND has a tourist resort whose latest extensions climb the hill towards the south-west corner and are conspicuous from the mainland. There is a wonderful collection of swimming beaches, most of which are free from fringing reefs. The resort beach shelves a long way offshore denying close anchoring by other than moderate draft during neap tides.

Approach. Great Keppel is a dominant, although unremarkable feature of Keppel Bay easily seen from Cape Capricorn and Sea Hill Point. Rocks, islets and islands encountered en route are easily seen and avoided.

Anchorage is most popular off the resort despite the above-noted disadvantages. It is comfortable in very light weather only. The best northerly anchorage is

off *Long Beach* whilst the best trade wind anchorage is in the large bay west of Svenden's house. The bottom is sand and the bay is swell affected.

Remote and rugged, with rocky headlands and high sand dunes, the land around *Wreck Bay* makes it a delightful stop in calm to offshore weather.

The passage between Middle Island and Great Keppel Island is deep and clear. Hold Middle Island close on the tip of which is a green, lit beacon. A red beacon should be on the reef opposite but was completely missing in 1993.

Facilities. The resort offers its guests every convenience from spas to restaurants whilst its day guest facility to its north, known as *Wapparaburra* sells a fair cross-section of goods suitable for topping off the pantry.

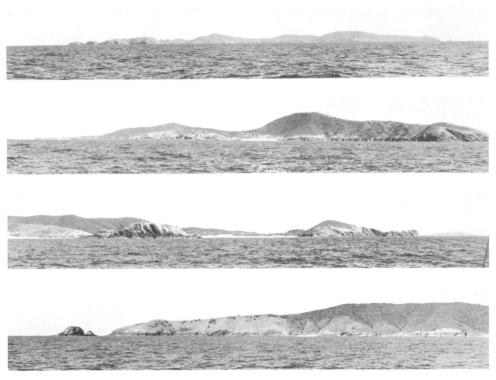

Great Keppel Island bears approximately north-west with Humpy Island transiting its south-west corner, left.

Great Keppel's south-east capes support a light and display remarkable red cliffs.

The north-east cape of Great Keppel is seen right with Bald Rock left. Wreck Bay, between the two, is a lovely calm weather anchorage.

Looking south at Bald Rock kissing Great Keppel's south-east head.

The north-east tip of Great Keppel Island is rock-faced with bare hills behind.

Looking into Svendsen's Beach, north Great Keppel Island. The best trade wind anchorages are in this vicinity.

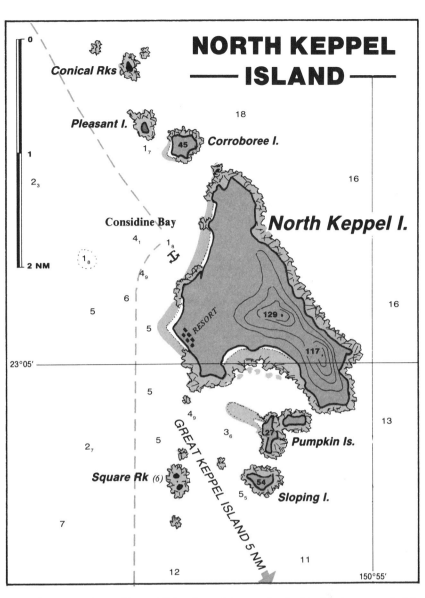

NORTH KEPPEL
— ISLAND —

Conical Rks

Pleasant I.

Corroboree I.

18

16

Considine Bay

North Keppel I.

RESORT

16

13

Pumpkin Is.

Square Rk (6)

Sloping I.

GREAT KEPPEL ISLAND 5 NM

23°05′

150°55′

North Keppel Island is a National Park whilst both North and Great Keppel islands are classified *General Use 'B' Zones*. A section of both islands' western coasts are zoned *Marine National Park 'A'* whilst Middle Island is zoned *Marine National Park 'B'*.

PEAK ISLAND, in Keppel Bay, is a National Park with its surrounding waters zoned *Preservation Zone*. Boating of any description is not allowed in its vicinity.

At enormous public and private expense, Rosslyn Bay Boat Harbour was fully enclosed during the late 1980's in preparation for a marina. The development company became a recession victim and the project, to be called 'Keppel Gateway Harbour', was abandoned. Eventual development, however, is inevitable.

NORTH KEPPEL ISLAND. A National Park with picnic and ablution facilities provided, this island has a small tourist resort on its south-west corner. It does not offer comfortable anchorage during a developed wind and is best saved for light weather and picnic stops.

ROSSLYN BAY. Developed as a harbour starting in the early 1970s, Rosslyn Bay is the gateway to the Keppel Islands and is unmistakable for its remarkable volcanic core. The harbour entrance is narrow demanding some caution against collision, but its interior is secure against all winds.

Along the eastern side are ferry jetties, public jetty, 24 hour fuel jetty, fisheries and fish base, the welcoming Capricornian Cruising Yacht Club and a Coast Guard Station next to the public ramp. In the opposite side of the harbour, a marina complex is to be built.

Approaching Rosslyn Bay from Great Keppel, Bluff Point is left with Double Head right. Rosslyn Bay Harbour is behind Double Head.

Double Head is a conspicuous landmark on this part of the coast. The harbour breakwater can be seen extending from its right.

Double Head's two peaks are volcanic cores 70 million years old as are nearby Bluff Point and Pinnacle Rock.

113

The three photographs here show the northern approach to Rosslyn Bay. From a good distance off (top), Double Head provides good reference even though its breakwater extension cannot be easily seen. As the bottom photograph shows, the entrance is narrow demanding care in its negotiation.

Pile berths are sometimes available by applying at the harbour office near the public jetty and anchoring is possible until the marina fully occupies the remaining space. This is not expected to happen until 1995.

Ashore, there is a general store and service station, laundrette, tiny chandlery, bar, bistro and coffee lounge and a bus connecting Rosslyn Bay with Emu Park, Yeppoon and Rockhampton.

Yeppoon shopping centre is the most comprehensive in the region and offers the last opportunity to victual before Mackay (going north). Its creek dries at low tide and is suitable only to local craft whose mud berths line the banks.

CORIO BAY. Also known as *Waterpark Creek*, this delightful spot is 13 miles north of Rosslyn Bay and 28 miles south of Port Clinton. Despite a shallow bar of 1.5 metres low water springs demanding a high tide to enter, it is worth the hassle unless heavy onshore weather prevails in which case the entrance should be considered dangerous.

When shaping up for the entrance, a useful backlead exists that puts a vessel right on course. This is Outer Rock against the northern half of Barren Island, both easily sighted and identified from this distance. Alternatively, bring the south tip of the north headland to bear 300° magnetic and proceed towards the northwest intending to bring the headland close aboard to starboard.

Anchorage is best as far up the inside of the headland as possible taking care to allow for windward-tide antics that can move a boat over shoaling water before the tide fully runs out. In light weather a vessel will obediently lie to current only in which case she will hold the best depths of the narrow channel.

MOORINGS NOTE. Much of the future marina area in Rosslyn Bay has been taken up with moorings which command a daily charge. The marina shown on the chart, below left, is unlikely to be built before 1995.

The panorama shows Cape Manifold (the island) from the north. Passage between the island and the mainland is deep and clear.

ROSSLYN BAY

0 1 2 CABLES

MARINA

Fishing Boat Berths
Public Jetty
Pile Berths
Double Hd
Fuel
Harbour Office
Fish Co-op
Fuel
Keppel Island Terminal
Fisheries
Capricornia Cruising Club
Coast Guard
RAMP
Laundrette etc

23° 09′ 36″

150° 47′ 18″

Shoal draft vessels may continue upstream beyond the line of soundings shown here exercising caution and using a flood tide until the best anchorage is found.

The map here shows the areas destined to be strip-mined for such minerals as zircon, rutile, ilmenite and monasite if the Byfield Residents Action Group and other concerned environmental groups fail in their fight to save it. At the time of going to press, an inquiry was being held but with little promise of nature winning over commercial interests. With green promises being broken by both the State and Federal Governments, compromise is the best that can be expected.

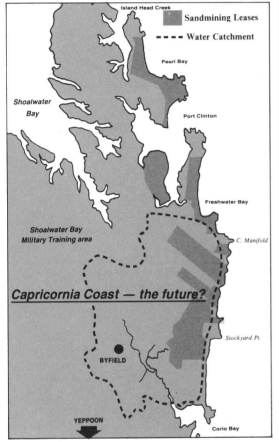

Island Head Creek

Sandmining Leases
- - - Water Catchment

Pearl Bay

Shoalwater Bay

Port Clinton

Freshwater Bay

Shoalwater Bay Military Training area

C. Manifold

Capricornia Coast — the future?

Stockyard Pt.

● BYFIELD

YEPPOON

Corio Bay

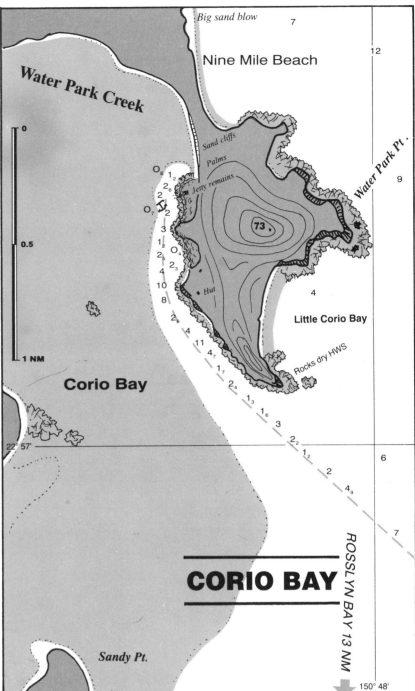

Big sand blow

Nine Mile Beach

Water Park Creek

Sand cliffs

Palms

Jetty remains

Water Park Pt.

Little Corio Bay

Hut

Rocks dry HWS

Corio Bay

22° 57'

CORIO BAY

ROSSLYN BAY 13 NM

Sandy Pt.

150° 48'

Sailing north from Rosslyn Bay, the unnamed island off Cape Manifold is an obvious landmark.

Cape Manifold and its unnamed island are abeam. To the right is Cliff Point which protects Freshwater Bay.

115

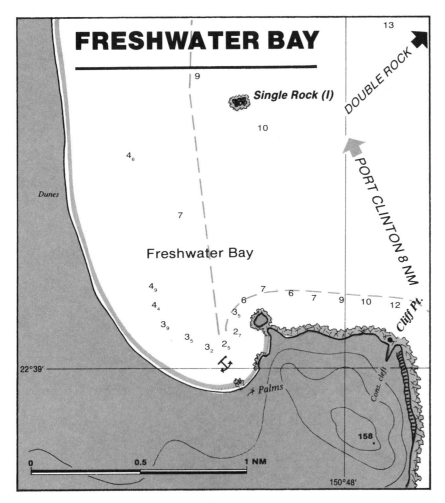

FRESHWATER BAY

Single Rock (I)

DOUBLE ROCK

13

9

10

4₆

Dunes

7

Freshwater Bay

4₉

4₄

3₉

3₅

3₂

2₇

2₅

3₅

6

7

6

7

9

10

12

PORT CLINTON 8 NM

Cliff Pt.

Cons. cleft

22°39'

Palms

158

0   0.5   1 NM

150°48'

FRESHWATER BAY is 8 miles south of Port Clinton and 3 miles north-west of Cape Manifold. Its approach is included in that for Port Clinton following this.

Formed by *Cliff Point* on whose corner will be seen a distinct cleft, it is sand bottomed with a delightful beach. Army exercises are often carried out in the area.

The anchorage is very swell-prone but useful and pleasant for a short stop.

Cliff Point is rounded for Freshwater Bay anchorage.

This islet and remarkable rock are a feature of Cliff Point headland. This is from the anchorage.

PORT CLINTON is an uninhabited mainland harbour 42 miles north of Rosslyn Bay Boat Harbour. It provides shelter from all winds, but is included in the Australian Army's Shoalwater Bay training area. Owing to the danger inherent in the presence of unexploded ammunition and aerial bombs, access ashore beyond the high tide mark is prohibited. It is also possible that the area will be sealed off altogether, in which case notice will be given in *Notice to Mariners*.

Approach. The coast north to Port Clinton is clear of dangers, the few islands and rocks being easily seen. *Flat Island*, 18 miles south-east of Port Clinton and lying well offshore, is sighted at a distance of nearly 15 miles. The much higher *Peaked Island*, 5 miles to its north, is seen at a much greater distance.

Stockyard Point is a treeless grass-covered headland

with an obvious dirt road creasing its skull, and the two pyramid mountains always conspicuous on this section of the coast are known as *The Peaks*. South of Stockyard Point is an obvious yellow sand patch and north is a run of grass-covered dunes with occasional sand blows.

Cape Manifold is a dominant headland and its island immediately offshore is seen after the headland itself is identified. Passage can be made between this island and the land, but outside is less hazardous, especially in developed onshore winds. The tidal disturbance off this island can be considerable.

North from Cape Manifold, *Quoin Islet* slopes like a sphynx towards the west while *Entrance, Delcomyn* and *Dome* Islands tend to merge, Dome being most obvious for its high dome shape.

From the north, Dome Island again makes good

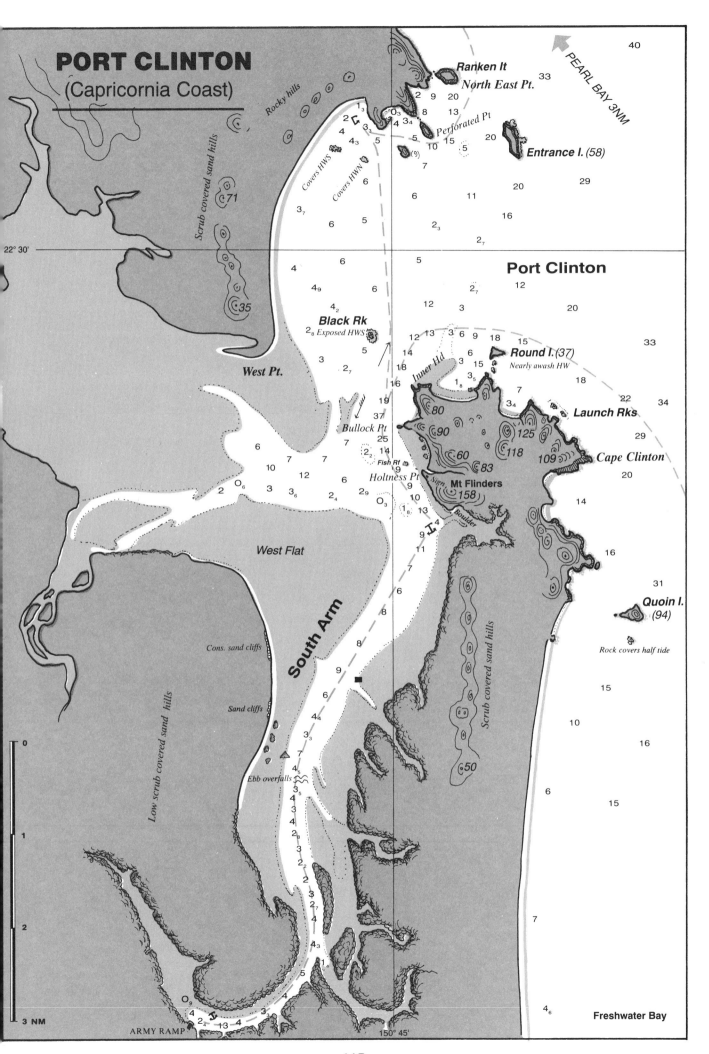

PORT CLINTON
(Capricornia Coast)

Rocky hills

Scrub covered sand hills

71

35

Ranken It

North East Pt.

Perforated Pt

Entrance I. (58)

PEARL BAY 3NM

40

33

Covers HWS

Covers HWN

22° 30'

Port Clinton

Black Rk
Exposed HWS

West Pt.

Inner Hd

Round I. (37)
Nearly awash HW

Launch Rks

Cape Clinton

Bullock Pt

Fish Rf

Holtness Pt

Mt Flinders
158

Sign.

Boulder

West Flat

South Arm

Cons. sand cliffs

Sand cliffs

Low scrub covered sand hills

Scrub covered sand hills

Quoin I.
(94)

Rock covers half tide

Ebb overfalls

50

0

1

2

3 NM

ARMY RAMP

150° 45'

Freshwater Bay

117

Cape Clinton is the southern headland to Port Clinton. The northern headland is distant right with Entrance Island offshore.

Port Clinton's inner north head is seen here with Launch Rock and Round Island right.

Approaching the anchorage to the south of Mount Flinders in Port Clinton.

One of the many lovely corners in Port Clinton is Flinder's watering place in the northern corner.

The land fronting Port Clinton's western shore is low with endless sand dunes.

Ascending South Arm, Port Clinton, peaked Mount Solitude is an easily seen feature.

A typical offshoot creek of Port Clinton. A few offer shoal draft exploration potential.

Towards the head of South Arm, Port Clinton, the army ramp is seen (arrowed).

The army ramp in close-up. South arm shoals rapidly beyond this ramp.

118

reference and passage between the mainland and Delcomyn Island is deep and safe as is the water immediately west of Entrance Island.

Final approach into Port Clinton is best made using the natural transit of *Black Rock* in line with *West Point*. In fact, this takes you over a patch slightly shallower than the surrounding depths, but is of little consequence. Alternative entry over equally deep water can be made by rounding *Round Island* fairly close then standing on for Black Rock until the shallow sand bar is crossed and deeper water is found.

Either way, as soon as the bar is crossed, haul to the south and favour the land until at anchor. Beware of *Fish Rocks* which remain covered at low water springs and are very difficult to see.

Tides, are based on Mackay data in the *Tide Tables*, changing 1 hour 20 minutes earlier and with a range of 85%. Tidal flow in the port can be very strong during springs causing inevitable windward-tide discomfort when a strong wind prevails.

Anchorage in shoaling water is difficult to find, the best place being towards the mouth of the creek to the south of *Mount Flinders*. During strong winds, a swell invades this area but this can be reduced and eventually killed by moving upstream.

When moving upstream, use a flood tide to avoid the distress of running aground. Even in conditions of good visibility it can be difficult to clearly define the channel when the banks are fully covered. There should be two beacons en route, a red and a green, but they are poorly maintained — if at all — and should not be relied upon.

Anchorage upstream is secure anywhere, but is best in the vicinity of the army launching ramp which is unmistakable for the way its embankment protrudes from the mangroves. A cyclone could be ridden here.

At low tide it is possible that large turtles will be seen stranded on the sandbanks. Whether this is an error or a function of nature is not certain, but it seems that they survive okay and need to be left alone.

At the northern end of Port Clinton are a number of small bays where northerlies can be ridden in comfort. The best in a north-easterly is the most westerly, tucked up into the corner formed by beach and headland. Otherwise all are suitable in true north to northwesterly winds. This is by far the prettiest part of Port Clinton but is quite untenable during trade wind conditions.

A brush with commercialism

Port Clinton (once known as Port Bowen) was used commercially in 1887 when cattle from a neighbouring station were shipped south. The *Delcomyn*, a steamer of 1,184 tons, entered the port on three occasions to load about 355 head of cattle from a wharf built by the station owner. The steamer had a draft of 5 metres.

This headland protects a delightful bay in the north-west corner of Port Clinton during northerly winds.

Perforated Point, right, has conspicuous pine trees on its peak. It is one of the northern headlands in Port Clinton.

Approaching Pearl Bay from the south, holding the land close in fair weather, Delcomyn Island is seen, right, with Dome Island dead ahead. Pearls Bay's headland is left. The small beach, left of the headland, is a pleasant calm weather anchorage.

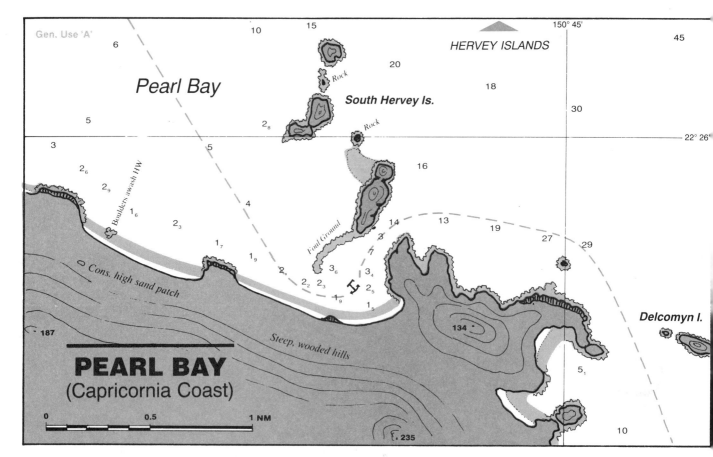

Pearl Bay

HERVEY ISLANDS

South Hervey Is.

Boulders awash HW

Cons. high sand patch

Steep, wooded hills

PEARL BAY
(Capricornia Coast)

0   0.5   1 NM

Fowl Ground

Delcomyn I.

PEARL BAY. One of the coast's prettiest anchorages, being surrounded by high, steep, densely wooded hills and fringed with a superb hard-sand beach which extends into the water to give clear inviting conditions, Pearl Bay lies between *Port Clinton* and *Island Head Creek*.

Approach from Port Clinton can be made inside *Entrance* and *Delcomyn Islands*, rounding the mainland fairly close to pass between the island immediately north-west of Pearl Bay's headland and the headland. A minimum of 3 metres low water springs will be found in this passage, most of which is much deeper. Although there is minimal fringing reef in this passage, favour the middle.

From Island Head Creek, steer direct for the bay intending to pass well west of the islets within. The southernmost of these islets has an extensive reef from its west which must be rounded by holding the mainland close.

Anchorage is best where shown. The bottom is sand, the holding is good but conditions are not always comfortable during onshore winds. It does, however, promise security when the south-easterly blows and is ideal in south to south-west winds. Although acceptable during light northerlies, it is best to make for Island Head Creek or Port Clinton if they strengthen.

Tides. Use the same data as for *Port Clinton*.

Note. Pearl Bay is part of the Army's Shoalwater Bay training area as noted in the description of Port Clinton.

ISLAND HEAD CREEK. More compact and secure than Port Clinton, Island Head Creek offers delightful anchorages and pretty surroundings. It is a part of the Shoalwater Bay Army training area as mentioned in the Port Clinton description.

Approach. From the south, the *Clara Group*, immediately offshore from Island Head Creek, provides good reference and *Brown Rock* shows well. The southern headland hills of the creek are covered mostly in grass with scattered clumps of pine trees, the latter starting to become common in this area. The headland foreshore has a series of low cliffs at the base of its hills while south head is conspicuous for its remarkable rock strata.

From the north, Island Head appears as two hills, the northern-most one having the highest cliffs and the southern one displaying much more grassland over its rounded peak. The south headland of the creek is heavily wooded with bare patches of grass while the background hills are all heavily wooded. The two headlands to the immediate north of Pinetrees Point show a pink tinge to their foreshore rocks.

Final approach into the creek is best made approximately midway between Island Head and the southern headland's projecting rock from where the course lays for the obvious rocks ahead and to starboard. These rocks must be passed very close after which turn towards the beach which is then favoured into the creek proper.

An alternative entrance exists more directly from the mouth, past the land close to port thence curving

The passage between the mainland and South Hervey Islands is narrow but deep. It is arrowed here.

Pearl Bay is surrounded by an amphitheatre of hills.

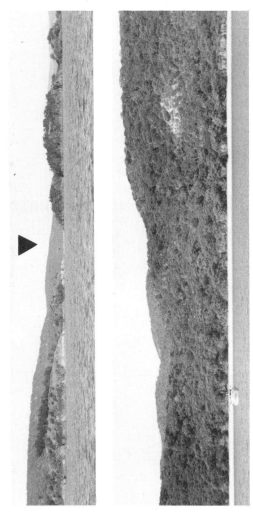

During developed south-east trade winds, Island Head creek is the last comfortable anchorage until the Cumberland Islands are reached. There are, however, a few creeks where comfort can be enjoyed in the Shoalwater Bay area.

A large scale plan of the head of Island Head Creek is over the page.

Pearl Bay from the north. The islands have been called 'South Hervey Islands' in this book but are, in fact, officially unnamed.

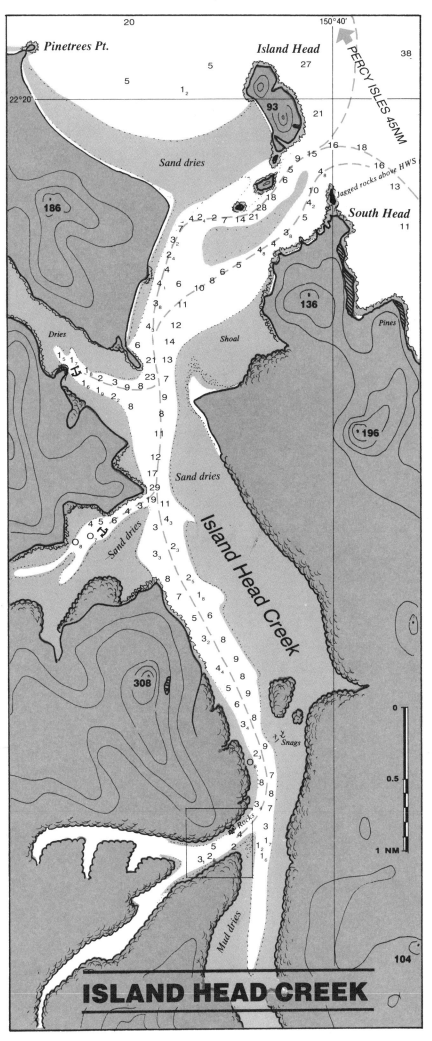

ISLAND HEAD CREEK

ISLAND HEAD CREEK

Rock covers HWS

Mud dries

Island Head Creek

The head of Island Head Creek provides a secure haven in which a cyclone could be weathered.

Bottom. Looking up Island Head Creek soon after entering. Anchorage off the beach, right, is ideal during northerly or calm weather.

slowly into the main body as shown on the accompanying chart. This tends to have better depths, but is not as easy to define. With a flood tide, neither course should cause any concern, especially if the tide is a couple of hours old.

Anchorage in fair weather is best off the first beach to starboard after entering, preferably towards its southern end. This area is very active during south-easterlies at which time it pays to move as far upstream

as proves necessary. By far the best anchorage is near the head of the creek shown in the separate large scale plan. This is an excellent cyclone anchorage.

Alternative anchorages exist in the first and second offshoot arms; the first having far more swinging room than the second. Both demand care when seeking anchorage to ensure floatation at low tide.

Tides can be based on Mackay-Port Clinton. The flow can be one hour later upstream.

Approaching Island Head Creek out of Pearl Bay, Brown Rock can be seen separated from the mainland, right.

Closer to Island Head Creek from the south-east, Brown Rock is more obvious offshore and the actual Island Head can be seen between it and the mainland.

The south head of Island Head Creek has diagonal strata rock with pine trees along the ridge.

122

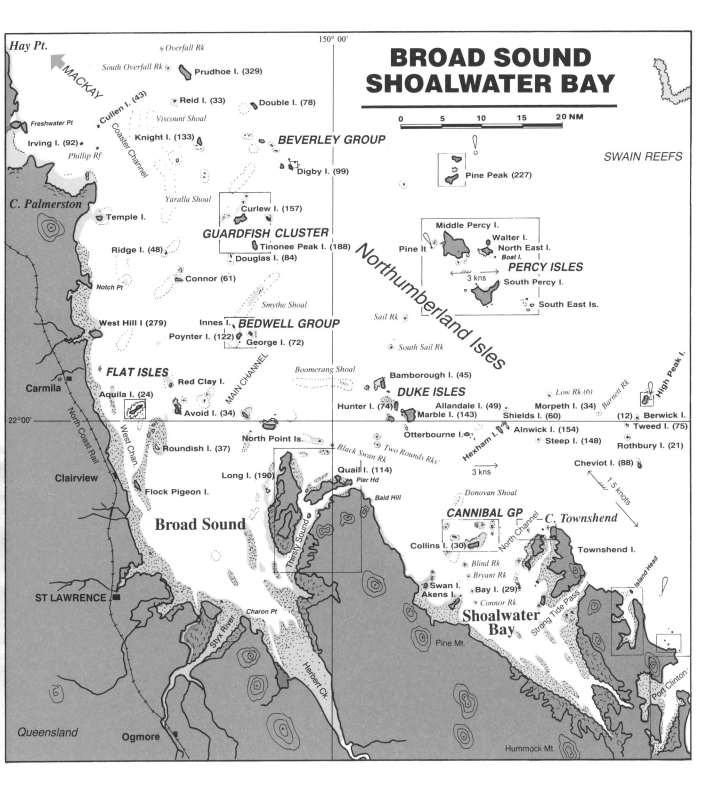

BROAD SOUND SHOALWATER BAY

Hay Pt.

MACKAY

Overfall Rk

South Overfall Rk

Prudhoe I. (329)

Reid I. (33)

Double I. (78)

Cullen I. (43)

Coaster Channel

Viscount Shoal

Freshwater Pt

Knight I. (133)

BEVERLEY GROUP

Irving I. (92)

Phillip Rf

Digby I. (99)

150° 00′

0 5 10 15 20 NM

Pine Peak (227)

SWAIN REEFS

C. Palmerston

Temple I.

Yaralla Shoal

Curlew I. (157)

GUARDFISH CLUSTER

Ridge I. (48)

Tinonee Peak I. (188)

Douglas I. (84)

Middle Percy I.

Walter I.

North East I.

Pine It

Boat I.

PERCY ISLES

3 kns

South Percy I.

South East Is.

Notch Pt

Connor (61)

Smythe Shoal

West Hill I (279)

Innes I.

BEDWELL GROUP

Poynter I. (122)

George I. (72)

Sail Rk

South Sail Rk

FLAT ISLES

Red Clay I.

Boomerang Shoal

Bamborough I. (45)

DUKE ISLES

Low Rk (6)

Barnett Rk

High Peak I.

Carmila

Aquila I. (24)

MAIN CHANNEL

Avoid I. (34)

Hunter I. (74)

Allandale I. (49)

Morpeth I. (34)

Marble I. (143)

Shields I. (60)

Berwick I.

(12)

22°00′

North Coast Rail

West Chan.

Roundish I. (37)

North Point Is.

Otterbourne I.

Alnwick I. (154)

Tweed I. (75)

Hexham I.

Steep I. (148)

Rothbury I. (21)

Clairview

Long I. (190)

Black Swan Rk

Two Rounds Rks

3 kns

Cheviot I. (88)

Flock Pigeon I.

Quail I. (114)

Pier Hd

1.5 knots

Bald Hill

Donovan Shoal

Broad Sound

CANNIBAL GP

C. Townshend

North Channel

Collins I. (30)

Townshend I.

Island Head

ST LAWRENCE

Charon Pt

Blind Rk

Bryant Rk

Swan I.

Bay I. (29)

Akens I.

Connor Rk

Strong Tide Pass

Styx River

Shoalwater Bay

Herbert Ck.

Pine Mt.

Port Clinton

Queensland

Ogmore

Hummock Mt.

Northumberland Isles

SHOALWATER BAY AND BROAD SOUND.

These two large bays lie to the west of Cape Townshend which itself is on Townshend Island which is separated from the mainland by Strong Tide Passage. This name somehow sets the scene for what can be expected in this area as a whole. Beset by the biggest tides on Australia's east coast and short of good anchorages, it is not a place to relax except in calm weather during neaps. And even then, in certain passages, the tides can run remarkably fast due, no doubt, to the imbalance of heights between the two bays. This difference can amount to as much as one and a half metres, a fact that is registered in and around Thirsty Sound.

Tides are based on Mackay data, itself an area of extreme range. Against the mainland, in Broad Sound, the range is greater by 40% while against the east coast

of Shoalwater Bay it is greater by only 14%. Remembering that Mackay can experience spring highs of around 6 metres, it can be appreciated that the height in Broad Sound can reach 8.5 metres while in Shoalwater Bay it attains around 7 metres. This mass of water running into and out of the bays and their numerous creeks and channels creates currents of up to 6 knots and possibly more in certain very restricted spaces.

Because a strong current will carry a swell beyond expected limits, very few anchorages are calm at any time and when a wind of any strength is blowing, windward-tide performances can be breathtaking. Against this is the fact that a very strong current will hold a vessel stern up to the strongest wind and thus negate the antics an hour or so after turn. But even

123

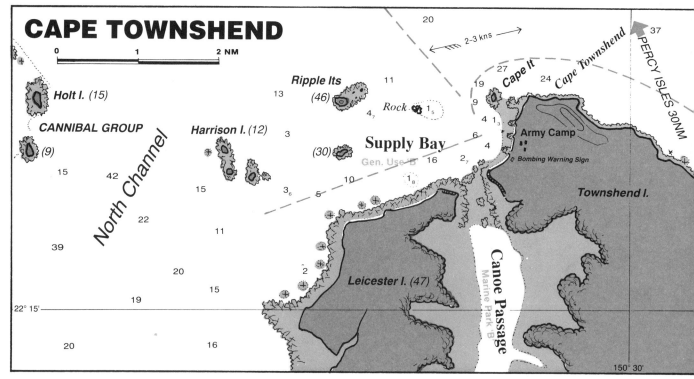

CAPE TOWNSHEND

0   1   2 NM

Holt I. (15)

CANNIBAL GROUP

(9)

15

42

22

39

20

19

20

North Channel

Ripple Its
(46)

13

Harrison I. (12)

(30)

15

3₆

11

15

2

20

3

Rock

4₇

1₅

11

5

10

Supply Bay

Gen. Use

16

1₈

Cape It

19

27

9

24

Cape Townshend

9

4 1₃

6

4

2₇

Army Camp

Bombing Warning Sign

37

PERCY ISLES 30NM

20

2-3 kns

Townshend I.

Leicester I. (47)

Canoe Passage
Marine Park 'B'

22° 15'

16

150° 30'

Cape Townshend is an ideal anchorage from which to launch off to the Percy Isles or west into the Shoalwater Bay and Broad Sound region. The latter is by far the least popular route.

then it can be unpleasant for the simple reason that wind against 6 knots of tide stacks up sizeable chop that makes rowing ashore miserable and life aboard anxious.

For all that, there is a sense of adventure in exploring this area. It scarcely need be said that isolation is almost guaranteed, other vessels rarely being seen. There is also the potential of good fishing and crabbing.

The anchorages, inlets and passages described in detail next are only representative and not necessarily the best, but they do include those along a most logical path. The stranger to this area will do his own thing but is advised against ascending the mainland creeks in Broad Sound. Snags, bores and embarrassing groundings are all too possible, and regardless of where you venture, never lose sight of the fact that tides fall rapidly, far too fast at times to float the boat immediately after a grounding. Try to move only on a flood tide or time your runs to be in deep water during ebbs.

At all times when using the following information, bear in mind that much of the Shoalwater Bay area is army reserve and, as such, is off limits to shore parties.

STRONG TIDE PASSAGE is a six-mile-long

channel between the mainland north of Island Head Creek and Townshend Island. Spring tides bring currents of up to 6 knots which flood south-west and ebb north-east. Entering from seaward, *Reef Point* is beach fronted with its rocks offshore standing well above high water and easily seen on approach. The northern headland is low scrub-capped cliffs with broken rock at their base. All beacons sighted in this area relate to bomb aiming and not to general navigation.

Using a flood tide and bearing in mind the speed at which it will carry you through, pass *Reef Point Rocks* at a safe distance rounding up close to the

southern tip of the northern headland. If in doubt about underwater obstructions in the vicinity, the centre of *Crane Islet* placed over the tip of the second headland provides a good transit. Crane Islet at 6 metres high is easily seen from outside the channel and is conspicuous for its small peak.

Beyond Crane Islet, steer across to favour Triangular Islets before entering Shoalwater Bay. At all times watch for rock patches. *Not illustrated large scale*

CAPE TOWNSHEND provides good shelter from

all winds save those from the west to north quadrant. It is the site of army encampment when training is in progress and signs warn of bombing practice.

Cape Townshend itself is a combination of bald grass slopes and well wooded hills terminating in sloping, rocky cliffs. It is visible as an 'island' when approaching from the west with the main body of Townshend Island being sighted from Thirsty Sound.

Anchorage is in shoaling water over sand towards the beach which is divided by a number of rocky outcrops. If absolute freedom from swell is preferred, a dinghy survey of the nearby north entrance to *Canoe Pass* will establish the right time and tide to take the mother ship in. There is ample low water depth within the pass, but be careful of rocky outcrops and isolated patches which are not shown on the accompanying plan. Canoe Pass may be exited, or entered, from its south-west end at any state of tide, there being increasingly deep water towards that end.

CANNIBAL GROUP. Lying six miles west of

Cape Townshend and spreading a further seven miles in that direction, the Cannibal Group of islands shares a rather messy seabed rise with depths ranging from 10 to 2 metres with many shoals, ledges and heads. Bringing up anchorage anywhere is subject to good visual approach and a willingness to accept the fact that comfort is unobtainable during a developed onshore wind.

124

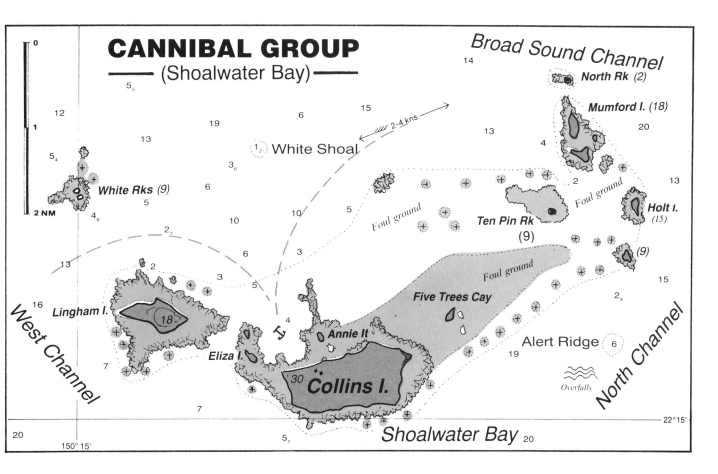

CANNIBAL GROUP
—— (Shoalwater Bay) ——

The Cannibal Group is entirely under oyster lease, the lessees living on Collins Island. Private oyster gathering is not allowed.

During a south-easterly, anchor towards a conspicuous house approximately three-quarters the island's length to the west. Beware of ledges and isolated rocks on final approach and do not expect to escape a current of up to 3 knots springs.

In the interest of identification for those passing across to the north of the Cannibal Group, the following is offered. *Mumford, Holt* and the satellite islets in their vicinity are a mixture of pockmarked cliff-faces capped in scrub and wooded cays while *Ten Pin Rock* is well-named for its vertical dominance and easy identification from a considerable distance. *North Rock*, at 3 metres above high water provides excellent reference in conjunction with *Mumford Island* and *Cape Townshend* for the best water between *White* and *Donovan Shoal*. The northern tip of Cape Townshend, kept midway between North Rock and Mumford Island, is an easily seen and safe transit.

Collins Island is the largest of the group and has a house on the north face behind a full-length beach. It displays low, red cliffs on the east end and the highest ground at 30 metres is at the west end. No coconut palms are in evidence from offshore and the vegetation is generally stunted.

Lingham Island rises a maximum of 18 metres with its peak on the east end and a conspicuous group of trees on its west end. A beach runs full length along its north side and a natural vertical seam, or similar mark, behind this beach can be mistaken for a beacon from a distance.

White Rocks, the most westerly of the Cannibal Group, is an isolated group of two rocks close together rising 9 metres and presenting an easily identified bearing. Other good bearings in the general area of Shoalwater Bay are *Pine Mountain* rising 373 metres and a second group to its south-east which is part of the *Normanby Range*. Both are on the mainland and show well as do the rugged mountains around Island Head Creek which are part of the *Peninsula Range*.

DUKE ISLANDS *not illustrated large scale* Lying off the mouth of Shoalwater Bay, north-west of the Cannibal Group, these islands are part of a cattle station. The homestead is on Marble Island, the largest of the group.

An enjoyable area in light weather, the islands lack good shape for comfort during a trade wind. However, surprisingly good is *Hunter Island* whose south-west headland provides remarkable shelter. Here will be seen horses, cattle and possibly deer on the beach.

THIRSTY SOUND is 25 miles magnetic-west of Cape Townshend where it separates the mainland from *Quail* and *Long Island* and gives a second channel between those islands. The tide runs very swiftly regardless of neaps or springs, south-west during flood and north-east during ebb. There is a cattle station on both Quail and Long Island with a settlement (Plum Tree) under the lee of Arthur Point where very basic amenities will be found. There are also numerous houses on the headland displaying seawards.

Approach from all directions must be with a flood tide preferably in its second or third hour to allow time for floating off in the event of a grounding and then to find anchorage well before it turns.

From Broad Sound the land is low and swampy with a dominance of mangrove forests on both sides. *Island Bluff*, rising sheer to 22 metres is good reference when making for the entrance as are the low red cliffs 3 miles to its north. The mangrove islands fragmented around the south end of *Long Island* are not easily separated visually until in very close, however the southern tip is identified in time to relate it to the low red cliffs when orientating for the entrance.

Having made the entrance after taking due care to avoid the sandbanks offshore, hold the mangrove islands close for the best water and proceed cautiously.

When a conspicuous, higher-than average, scrub-covered islet is seen to the north-north-east within the Sound, steer for its eastern side in a very slight curve to the east to avoid fouling the shoals to its south-south-west. This curve should not be too extreme lest a rock covered at low water springs is found (although that is unlikely with a flood tide at the rate it rises in this area).

Beyond the scrub islet, the channel between Long and Quail Island will become obvious as will a large sandbank off the starboard bow that only just covers on high water neaps and is one of the very few banks easily seen from a distance when covered. When dry it stands very high and can appear as a complete barrier across the sound.

The best water around this sandbank is against the south-west tip of Quail Island from where the course should move over and favour the mainland to avoid a group of rocks which never dry and are always difficult to see. When the second creek to starboard in this reach is abeam, steer north to gain centre channel then hold that position until clear to sea between Pier Head and Arthur Point.

From Shoalwater Bay — the most common approach — *Arthur Point* is low and steep-sided with a well wooded, pyramid-like hill immediately inland which shows many miles to sea. Cliffs to the south of Arthur Point are mostly light coloured with a conspicuous grey cliff further south where a rounded grassy hill terminating in its own cliff will be seen.

Pier Head, opposite Arthur Point and forming the north gatepost to Thirsty Sound's eastern entrance, is covered mostly in coarse grass with tufts of scrub. The background land is well wooded and is mostly of low undulating hills. Houses are seen south of Arthur Point which display well from seaward.

According to *Australian Chart 822*, a minimum of 1.8 metres covers a bar across the entrance. My soundings did not find this but the navigator is warned just in case. However, even at this minimal depth, a flooding tide will not only present ample depth but will also flatten any swell working against the coast. Generally speaking, this entrance is safe in all weather dependent on a commonsense approach.

Steering a middle course between Arthur Point and Pier Head, pass into the Sound and move towards Quail Island to insure clearing a shoal curving off inner Arthur Point. This is exaggerated on the chart.

Favouring Quail Island, continue into the narrow neck where to starboard will be seen the cattle station buildings and to port is a white beach. From here do a reciprocal course to that previously described.

From the north, between *Long* and *Quail Island*, the sea and swell diminish considerably by the time the narrow entrance is encountered. This is advantageous because by then some anxiety will be felt about the exact location of *Narrows Rock*. This is impossible to see except, perhaps, at low water springs. When working a flood tide it is always covered by troubled, dirty water. Missing it is by guesswork alone and this is best achieved by holding Tide Island as close as possible without hitting its rock reef.

Approaching the area from the north, hold *North Point* close and steer a compass course towards south-east to hold the best water outside a drying bank off Long Island between Southport Hill and North Point. Do not be fooled by what appears to be the *Middle Pass* opening up ahead of time. The best evidence of Middle Pass opening up is the sighting of two houses within the channel on Long Island.

Tide Island, opposite Narrows Rock is very difficult to identify against Quail Island, but eventually shows as poor scrub above a low stone and earth embankment with mangroves fringing its southern end.

With this islet astern, steer a middle course between Long Island and a mangrove-fringed scrub-covered island to port standing off the south-west end of Quail Island. When its southern end is abeam, steer to pass Quail's south end fairly close from where navigation can follow that described for the previous two approaches.

Anchorage anywhere in Thirsty Sound is subject to windward-tide but can be guaranteed calm otherwise. The shallowest areas are seen in the accompanying plan leaving it only to be said that wherever you drop anchor be absolutely certain the vessel will not ground on the ebb. It is very easy to underestimate the true height of tide in this region even during neaps.

Of Interest. Captain Cook anchored the *Endeavour*

Channel Islet is the north-easternmost island of the North Point Isles north of Long Island.

With Channel Islet. left foreground, Wild Duck Island is seen in the distance.

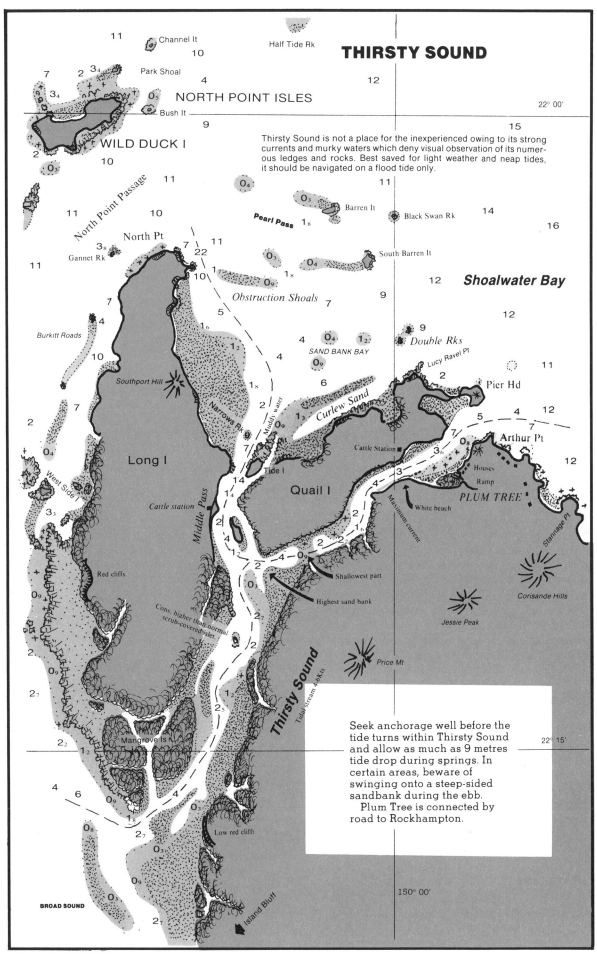

THIRSTY SOUND

NORTH POINT ISLES

22° 00'

Channel It

Half Tide Rk

Park Shoal

Bush It

WILD DUCK I

Thirsty Sound is not a place for the inexperienced owing to its strong currents and murky waters which deny visual observation of its numerous ledges and rocks. Best saved for light weather and neap tides, it should be navigated on a flood tide only.

North Point Passage

Pearl Pass

Barren It

Black Swan Rk

North Pt

Gannet Rk

South Barren It

Shoalwater Bay

Obstruction Shoals

Burkitt Roads

Southport Hill

SAND BANK BAY

Double Rks

Lucy Ravel Pt

Pier Hd

Narrows Rk

Muddy water

Curlew Sand

Arthur Pt

West Side I

Long I

Tide I

Cattle Station

Houses

Ramp

PLUM TREE

Cattle station

Middle Pass

Quail I

White beach

Maximum current

Stannage Pt

Red cliffs

Shallowest part

Corisande Hills

Highest sand bank

Cons. higher than normal scrub-covered islet.

Jessie Peak

Thirsty Sound

Price Mt

Mangrove Is

Tidal Stream 4.6Kts

Seek anchorage well before the tide turns within Thirsty Sound and allow as much as 9 metres tide drop during springs. In certain areas, beware of swinging onto a steep-sided sandbank during the ebb.

Plum Tree is connected by road to Rockhampton.

22° 15'

Low red cliffs

150° 00'

BROAD SOUND

Island Bluff

Gen. Use 'B'

127

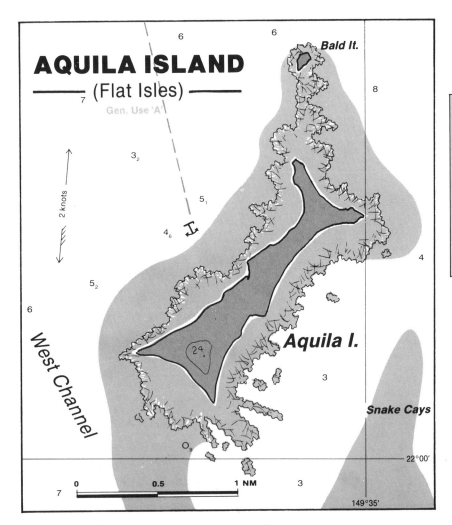

AQUILA ISLAND
—ᵧ (Flat Isles) ——
Gen. Use 'A'

Bald It.

Aquila I.

West Channel

Snake Cays

22°00'

149°35'

0   0.5   1 NM

St Lawrence

About 20 miles south of Aquila Island, in Broad Sound, is the small settlement of St Lawrence. Heard daily in small ships' weather forecasts as a division between central and south coast weather, St Lawrence was once the site of a boiling down works and pastoral outlet. A wharf was built and St Lawrence Creek was buoyed around 1863–4. The port became quite busy when it served as an outlet for the Peak Downs copper mines. Trade died towards the end of the century.

'about a league within the entrance of the inlet' on 29 May 1770. He believed it to be the entrance to a river and hoped to careen here and find fresh water. Investigating with Solander and Banks, they failed to find water. Thus its name, Thirsty Sound. They also chose not to careen but did see the remarkable mud skipper for the first time in Australia. Climbing a 'considerable hill', Cook observed his position but found his azimuth compass deviated by a whopping 30 degrees. This hill he named Pier Head and later it proved to be the only part of the coast shared by both Cook and Flinders as an observation point. There is a monument to this effect.

NORTH POINT ISLANDS are comprised of one major, one minor and numerous satellite islands 3 miles off Long Island. The largest, *Wild Duck Island*, has a conspicuous wedge shape towards its west extreme while *Turn Island* is unremarkable with an undulating hill. Both are beach fronted with a fringe of tidal rocks wrapping right around. Anchorage cannot be recommended here except in calm to light weather. *Not illustrated large scale*

AQUILA ISLAND. Situated in the north-west corner of *Broad Sound* and just 3 miles off the mainland, Aquila is the largest and most useful island of the group known as *Flat Isles*. With the highest land just 24 metres high towards its south-east corner, yellow beaches and rather poor vegetation, it falls short of a tropical paradise. However, it is easily the best trade wind anchorage in the area, having good holding

towards the jagged, rocky fringing reef and suffering acceptable swell invasion. The latter varies according to strength and direction of tidal stream.

Approach from the north is relatively clear whilst from the south it is very messy, there being numerous islets, reefs and shoals fanning from south through south-east to north-east. From offshore, the shortest approach is to the south of *Avoid Island* taking great care to identify and clear north of *Escape Cay*. If arrival can be timed for low tide, the dangers will be easily identified and the snuggest anchorage found at an ideal time.

POYNTER ISLAND is the largest of the four main islands comprising the *Bedwell Group* and the only one where anchorage in other than calm weather might be considered. It lies 14 miles north-north-west from Long Island (Thirsty Sound) and is north from Broad Sound.

Approach from the south-east is clear of danger after North Point Isles, although heavy seas against the current at low tide will break over the 2-metre patch of *Boomerang Shoal* and, to a lesser extent, over the 4-metre patch on *Lake Shoals*. Those sailing direct out of Shoalwater Bay should beware of *Half Tide Rock*, 4½ miles east-north-east of Wild Duck Island. Depending on wind and tide conditions, it can pay to lay for *Channel Islet* (off Wild Duck Island) and use it as a departure point.

From the east, *South Sail Rock* standing 2 metres above high water springs is a good departure point from where clear water is enjoyed right to the Bedwell Group.

128

Poynter Island is the last anchorage described under the collective heading of 'Shoalwater Bay and Broad Water'.

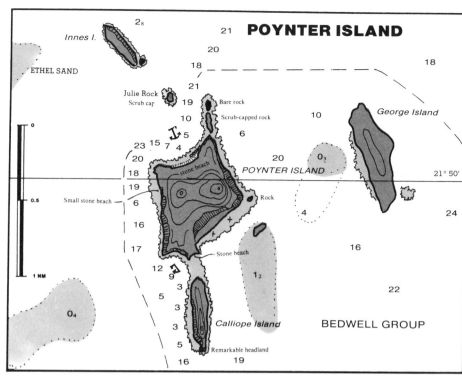

The Bedwell Group islands are unproclaimed, but their surrounding waters are zoned Marine National Park 'B'.

From the north, *Smythe Shoals* and *Emily Patches* may cause concern depending on wind, tide and draft. None of these sand-bottomed shoals need concern the average small craft during any tide higher than neap low.

From all directions, the 122-metre peak on Poynter is dominant and will be seen well ahead of any departure point losing its reference value.

On final approach from the south, *George Island* should be passed to the east or *Calliope* to the west as indicated. From the north, *Julie Rock* kissing Poynter leads through the best water immediately west of *Emily Patches*. This rock can be difficult to identify

until opened from Poynter.

Tides are big in this area, being similar in range and time to Mackay data. During springs the current sets at up to 3 knots through the Bedwell Group, while neaps can produce no current at all although 1 knot should be anticipated. The tide floods south-west and ebbs north-east and should be allowed for in any approach navigation.

Anchorage in winds south to east is best in the north bay of Poynter Island where will be seen a stone beach. At neap low tide, sand exposes here below a half-tide rock ledge. The rocky isthmus projecting north from

Approaching Poynter Island from the south, Calliope Island is seen in front of Poynter with George Island right.

Looking north along Poynter Island's west coast. Innes Island is left.

Looking into Poynter Island's anchorage from the north.

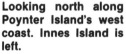

These rocks off the north tip of Poynter Island are not shown on official charts.

the island supports two distinct high and dry masses, the outer one being of bare rock, the inner having a scrub cap. These are not shown on *Australian chart 822 Port Clinton to Percy Islands*.

In winds east to north and especially when strong from the north-east, the bay formed between Poynter Island and Calliope Island gives excellent shelter. The reef connecting them is easily sighted and depths along its edge tend to be around 3 metres. The bottom at both anchorages is sand with the possibility of rock or coral patches.

During a well-developed northerly, or a wind west of south or north, suitable shelter cannot be found in the Bedwell Group. The nearest anchorage is Middle Percy Island 26 miles to the east-north-east, or Thirsty Sound to the south. In winds with a westerly component, anchorage can be taken under the lee of Hunter Island in the *Duke Islands* 21 miles south-east.

Swain Reefs

Lying east of the Percy Isles, the Swain Reefs are a collection of hundreds of individual coral reefs strewn over an area in excess of 2500 square miles. They represent the southern end of the main Great Barrier Reef chain and are only partially surveyed. Venturing into the area demands a constant lookout and a secure anchorage found well before dusk. Many reefs offer fair anchorage, a few with partial lagoons and others with small cays. Baron Reef and an unnamed reef south of Recreation Cay are Preservation Zones with anchoring banned altogether whilst the remaining area is divided into General Use 'B' Zone or Marine National Park 'B' Zone.

Gen. Use 'A'

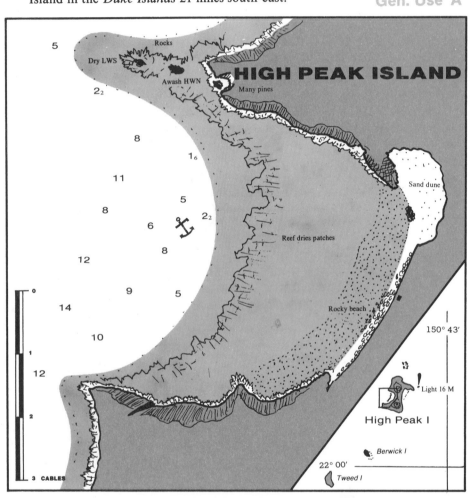

High Peak Island is safe during trade wind weather but thoroughly uncomfortable. It is best saved for calm conditions.

HIGH PEAK ISLAND. Lying 23 miles north from Island Head Creek and demanding a dogleg in the popular course to Percy Isles, High Peak provides isolation at the expense of a thoroughly uncomfortable anchorage when the trade winds blow. A major unmanned light is situated on a small satellite to its east.

Approach. From Island Head Creek, High Peak Island is visible as a small dominant peak with its low land showing to its right. *Cheviot Island*, en route, is heavily wooded with high, sloping, bare rock faces along its south side. *Berwick Island* which lifts at a distance of about 10 miles has a flat top, while *Barnett Rock*, visible for 13 miles, has a round top. The satellite islet on which the High Peak Light is situated becomes visible at a distance of approximately 15 miles. *Tweed Island* has a steep bare side with a grass dome ridged in pine trees. *Rothbury Islet* is a bare rock with small satellites.

Anchorage is best where shown in the plan despite its depth. To find shallower water is to encounter coral heads too close to the surface for comfort. The risk of fouling the anchor and cable also increases. A big swell invades this bay during the prevailing south-east season and it should be considered a calm-weather anchorage only.

Tides. High Peak Island enjoys secondary place status in the *Tide Tables*. It is based on Mackay.

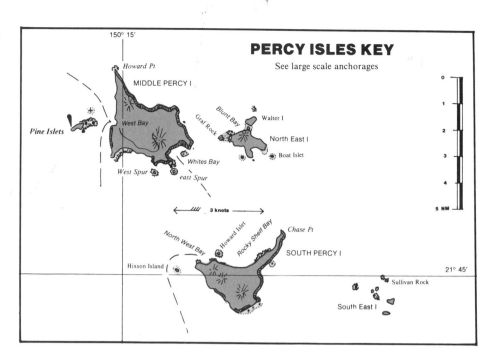

PERCY ISLES KEY

See large scale anchorages

The Percy Isles are very popular with northbound traffic between Island Head Creek and Mackay or the Whitsundays despite uncomfortable anchorages. Anchorages shown in large scale are South Percy Island, below, and Whites Bay and North East Island over the page.

PERCY ISLES are part of the *Northumberland Islands* and lie 40 miles north-north-west of Island Head Creek and 24 miles north-west of High Peak Island. They present a logical and very popular stepping-stone en route to Mackay and the Whitsundays despite uncomfortable anchorages.

Approach. From the south-east, South Percy Island rises as two major dots with minor dots immediately east. Soon after, South East Islets lift as do North East Island and Middle Percy Island depending on the exact approach course. A direct course from High Peak Island is clear of dangers while a course from Island Head Creek encounters *Steep Island* which can be seen from Island Head Creek and offers a good reference mark. On either route, allow for the lateral effect of tides: West on the flood and east on the ebb.

From the north-west, Middle Percy is seen from at least 30 miles and a conspicuous sand blow immediately south of *West Bay* can lift as early as 18 miles.

Tides are based on Mackay, turning 20 minutes earlier with a 10% greater range. Currents run at up to 3 knots between the islands.

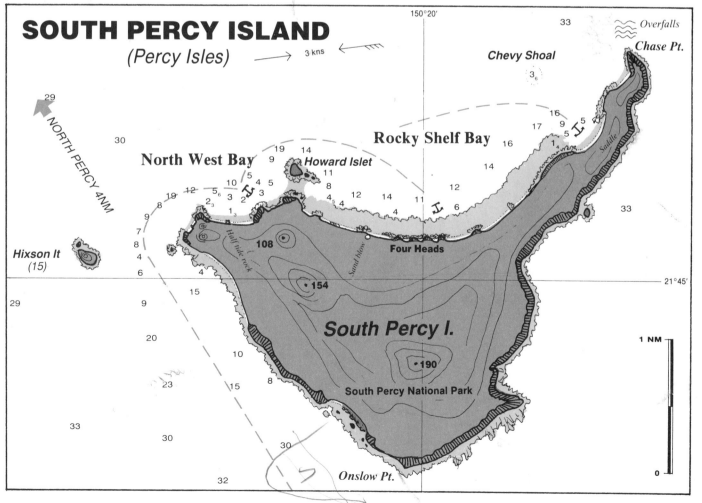

SOUTH PERCY ISLAND
(Percy Isles)

SOUTH PERCY ISLAND is a large continental island whose vegetation is a mixture of grass and scrub with areas of pine trees. Its south coast has mottled cliffs and small, grey pebble beaches with a conspicuous red scar out towards *Chase Point*.

The west coast is inhospitable with a rocky ledge, pebble beaches and some sand mostly hidden behind mangrove fringes. Unless prepared to anchor well off, it does not invite the pursuit for shelter against a north-easterly.

Generally speaking, the island is only suitable for calm or trade wind anchoring, the best sites being along the north shore in North West Bay or Rocky Shelf Bay as noted here.

North West Bay experiences a continual north-easterly swell during any prevailing wind. Because an ebb tide carries a vessel stern up to a light wind, comfort is actually improved when the wind is strong enough to overcome the tidal stream. The bottom is easily seen being hard sand which is good holding. The beach ashore is superb and the creek behind it is salt.

Rocky Shelf Bay enjoys less tidal stream effect but has a difficult to define fringing reef of rock and coral which can prove hard to see except at low tide. It is all too easy to over run it when coming to anchor.

Depending on the exact direction of a trade wind and its strength, the best of the anchorages tends to be those indicated by anchors. The eastern one, near Chase Point, allows the closest approach to the beach whilst the middle one is the handiest. Both demand careful approach if the shallowest water is being sought.

Such is the nature of the fringing reef that there are places where it is possible to cross it at high tide and enjoy a float hole between it and the beach at low tide. This is subject to personal survey and is not recommended to the overnighter who must waste time awaiting tides. It also demands that a reef lies astern, adding an element of tension to the visit.

Although rock-fringed in many places, the beaches along Rocky Shelf Bay are magnificent, inviting long walks and quick dips. Bushwalking is also relatively easy on an island that has been partially denuded by wild goats.

South Percy Island is three miles off, approaching from the south.

Onslow Point, South Percy Island's southern tip, is abeam.

South Percy Island's western head is seen here around which North West Bay is found. Hixson Islet, out of picture to the left, can be passed to port on this approach.

Entering North West Bay from the west. Howard Islet ahead.

Rocky Shelf Bay occupies most of South Percy's north shore which is a series of small headlands and beaches. The fringing reef must be approached cautiously.

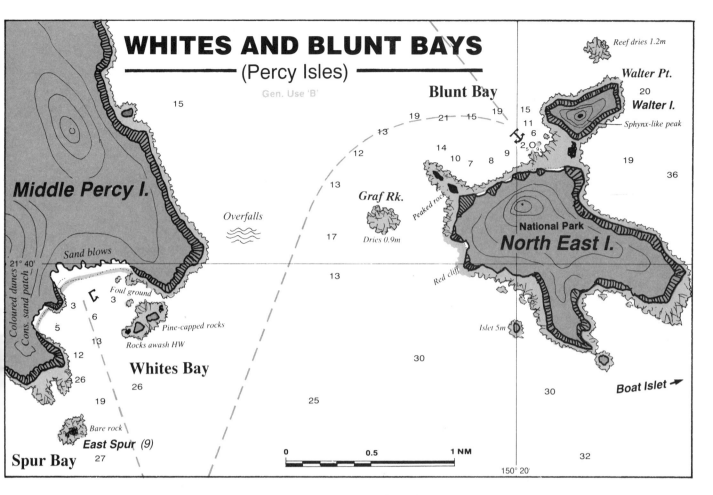

WHITES AND BLUNT BAYS
(Percy Isles)

Gen. Use 'B'

Middle Percy I.

15

Overfalls

Sand blows

Coloured dunes
Cons. sand patch

21° 40'

Foul ground

3   3

5   6

13

12   13

Pine-capped rocks

Rocks awash HW

Whites Bay

26

26

19

Bare rock

East Spur (9)

Spur Bay   27

13

17

13

13

19   21   15   19

Blunt Bay

Reef dries 1.2m

Walter Pt.

20

Walter I.

Sphynx-like peak

12

14

10   7   8   9

15

11

6

2   5   9

19

36

Graf Rk.

Dries 0.9m

Peaked rock

Red cliff

National Park
North East I.

Islet 5m

30

30

Boat Islet →

32

25

0   0.5   1 NM

150° 20'

MIDDLE PERCY ISLAND is the largest of the *Percy Isles* but the one offering the least protection during trade winds. *West Bay* is the only haven during sea breezes whilst *Whites Bay* is good during northerlies. Both of these bays are described separately later.

Middle Percy Island has been grazed by sheep for many decades and is the only one inhabited, Andrew Martin holding the lease since the early 1960s. Latterly, other inhabitants have put down roots here.

Close to the west of Middle Percy is *Pine Islet* on which is established a light visible 16 miles. Established in 1885, and always a difficult light to supply and maintain, it was manned until the late 1980s. It is now automatic. Anchorage off the islet is only marginally less comfortable than West Bay, but the bottom is generally foul.

West Bay. The rolling is abominable during any developed wind in this bay, but such is its beauty and fame that it is seen as an obligatory stop by many. The holding is good in sand and at times it can be quite crowded.

Ashore, care of Andrew, are showers and barbeque facilities as well as a communal building where local wares can be bought. These include goat skins and honey.

The tidal boat harbour is a unique feature of West Bay that can be entered at high tide. A vessel will dry out at low tide on sand. Arrangements must be made before entering and it pays to do a low tide survey.

This panorama shows South Percy Island from the north. South East Islets are just visible, left.

Owned by fisherwoman, Margaret Beaumont since the 1970's, the *Islander* (below) was built on Middle Percy Island by the White family. It was prefabricated at the house then re-assembled on the waterfront.

WHITES BAY. Named after the White family, Claude, Harold and Mary, who lived on Middle Percy Island for over forty years up until the early 1960s, this is an excellent northerly anchorage. *Rescue Bay*, off the chart to its west, is deceiving in that it looks good but is definitely inferior.

BLUNT BAY is formed by the islands of *Walter* and *North East* almost touching each other across a common reef. During developed trade winds, it is the most comfortable anchorage in the Percy Isles, suffering more from heavy surge than rolling swell. The bottom is rough with coral patches unless deeper than 9 metres. When approaching from south or east beware of *Graf Rock* and an isolated reef off *Walter Point*.

Never having been cleared for sheep grazing, North East Island is well wooded and isolated with pebble beaches along its north face and splendid rock formations around its perimeter. Walter Island is a rugged, sheer-sided appendage with a sphinx-like peak.

133

North East Island seen from the eastern end of South Percy Island. Little Boat Islet is right.

Looking into the anchorage in Blunt Bay which is formed by the reefs between North East Island (right) and Walter Island (left).

Penrith Island is a continental type with a large fringing reef. Anchorage is poor except in calm weather.

PINE PEAK AND HOTSPUR ISLANDS

lie close to each other six miles north of Middle Percy Island. Neither offer good shelter and should be considered fair-weather stops only.

Well named for the forest of pine trees on its highest peak, Pine Peak Island offers the best anchorage in *Battle Bay* if a light southerly is blowing and especially if a trade wind is anticipated overnight. The reef edge is fragmented in many places and should be approached with care. Lead triangles painted on the rocks to the north-east of the light are for light maintenance use.

DIGBY ISLAND

is the largest and most southerly of the *Beverley Group* lying about 20 miles north-west of Middle Percy Island. The lagoon-like anchorage looks much better than it is. However, it provides fair haven en route to Mackay.

Approach. From Middle Percy, Digby Island with a couple of its neighbours, is visible after clearing Pine Islet. The group is a mixed bag of wooded and barren islands with many rock outcrops, Digby itself being mostly bald from the south-east. The group forms up from five small peaks at 18 miles, a sixth lump to the right being Prudhoe Island.

As the group is brought up close, little *Penn Islet* can be difficult to identify until it separates from the background islands and *Keelan* is identified by its vertical strata cliff face along the full length of its east coast. *Still Islet* is a rugged, cliff-faced vegetated rock nearly flat on top displaying a few conspicuous white patches on the rocks.

Final approach to the anchorage can be mid channel between *Keelan Island* and *Henderson Island* where 21 metres rapidly reduces to the 4 to 6 metres of the sand-bottomed lagoon.

From the west, approach can be made between *Noel* and *Hull Islands* then finally between Henderson and Digby taking care to skirt around a fringing finger of reef encroaching into the channel from the northern extreme of Digby.

Anchorage is in good-holding sand speckled with a few small coral rocks. Towards the gap between Digby and Keelan Islands the ground is foul and the passage should not be attempted without personal survey.

The anchorage is secure against winds around the

Hotspur Island, right, has an unnamed neighbour, left.

Hotspur Island, right, and its unnamed neighbour in close-up. Calm weather anchorage can be found under their lees.

Snare Peak Island, right, and Snare Rocks, left, lie about 5 miles south-south-east of Penrith Island.

134

The Sydney yacht *Fruition* sailing off Penrith Island.

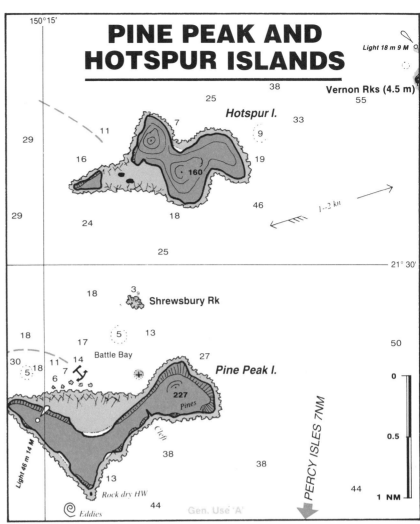

PINE PEAK AND HOTSPUR ISLANDS

150°15'

Light 18 m 9 M

Vernon Rks (4.5 m)

38   55
25   33
11   7   Hotspur I.
29   9
16   19
160
29   24   18   46   1–2 kn
25

21° 30'

18   3₉ Shrewsbury Rk
18   17   5   13
30   11 14 Battle Bay   27   Pine Peak I.
5 18   50
6   227
Pines
Cleft
38
38   PERCY ISLES 7NM
13
Rock dry HW   44   44
Eddies   Gen. Use 'A'

Light 46 m 14 M

0
0.5
1 NM

clock but is uncomfortable in any developed wind associated with a swell. It should be considered as a fair-weather anchorage unless anxious to get the anchor down despite the promise of some heavy rolling.

Ashore there are basic National Park camping facilities, and Digby's dominantly grass hills make for relatively easy walking. The beach is sand at one end and stone at the other, both with half-tide fringing rock ledges. A break in this ledge presents the best dinghy landing.

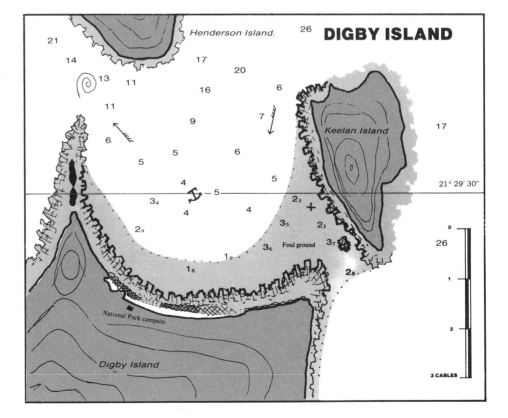

Digby Island and all members of the Beverley group are national parks in a *General Use 'A' Zone*.

DIGBY ISLAND

21   Henderson Island.   26
14   17
13 11   20
11   16   6
9   Keelan Island   17
6   7
6
5   6
5   5
4   21° 29' 30"
5
3₄   4   2₃
4   4
2₉   3₅   2₃
3₆ Foul ground 3₇
1₉   1₉   2₈
1₈
National Park campsite   2₈

Digby Island

0
26
1
2
3 CABLES

135

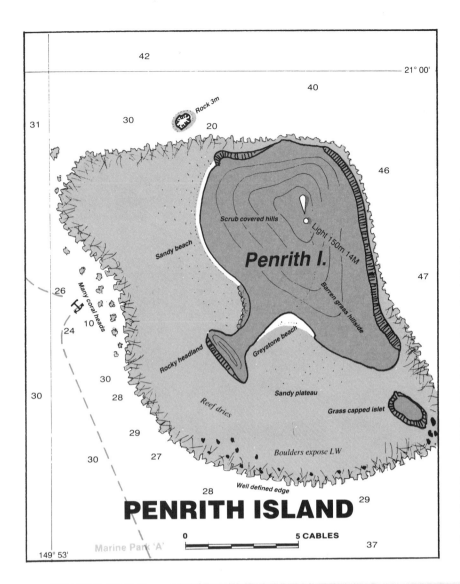

On the map:
42
40
21° 00'
31
30
20
Rock 3m
46
Scrub covered hills
Light 150m 14M
Penrith I.
Sandy beach
47
26
Many coral heads
Barren grass hillside
24
10
30
Rocky headland
Greystone beach
30
28
Sandy plateau
Reef dries
Grass capped islet
29
30
27
Boulders expose LW
28
Well defined edge
29
PENRITH ISLAND
0   5 CABLES
37
149° 53'
Marine Park 'A'

Scawfell Island is zoned *Marine National Park 'B'* around its east and south coasts. Refuge Bay is *General Use 'B'*.

Below right : Curlew Island and those of the group east and north are national parks within a *General Use 'B' Zone*.

PENRITH ISLAND lies a little over 40 miles north-west of Middle Percy Island. Threatened with tourist development during the entrepreneurial expansion of the late 1980s, it remains uninhabited with the only man-made object being its welcome light.

When approaching from the Percy Isles, both *Snare Peak Island* and Penrith Island lift as single, small dots from over 25 miles away. Penrith Island later produces a smaller dot to the left which eventually resolves into a single island. The south-eastern side is mostly barren grassland whilst the remainder is mostly scrub covered. The light is near the centre of the island on the highest peak.

The only shoaling water is amongst scattered coral heads close to the western side of the reef. Otherwise, the better anchorage, off the north-west tip, is very deep. There is no relief from swell when any wind is developed.

Penrith Island is a national park whose waters are zoned *Marine National Park 'A'*.

SCAWFELL ISLAND. Approximately 60 miles north-west of Middle Percy Island, Scawfell is an ideal alternative to Mackay for those bound from the Percy Isles to the Whitsundays.

Approach from the Percy Isles is peppered with enough islands and islets to provide good en route reference. Scawfell itself rises from the horizon at a distance of about 35 miles as a single wide pimple after which a second then a third pimple appears to its west eventually uniting into a single mass. A few miles beyond the first sighting of Scawfell, St Bees Island appears to its left at which time Middle Percy Island starts to break up astern.

Because most people do the Percy-Scawfell trip in a single hop, night arrival is common. Under such circumstances, if Penrith Island cannot be passed before dark and no moon is promised, it can pay to sail outside Penrith where distance judging off its light is less critical. This also places you on a safer final approach to Scawfell outside *Derwent Island* and *Three Rocks*.

Bailey Islet light will be seen under most conditions beyond its ten mile range. This allows a bearing to be taken from outside Three Rocks. There is also the loom of Mackay which often gives enough background light to sight Three Rocks on the darkest night. But nothing is certain and a wide berth is always the safest course.

On final approach, beware the south-setting flood tide which can push a vessel too close to Scawfell's northern and western headlands.

Anchorage during winds from south-west through south to north-east is best in *Refuge Bay*. A developed trade wind sends a surge into the bay which causes little discomfort depending on a vessel's displacement. A developed north-easterly makes life miserable in the bay, but is tenable for a limited period. Scawfell does not offer good northerly anchorage, its southern shore providing very little worthwhile shelter which, anyway, is steep-too and deep.

Holding is good in Refuge Bay. Beware isolated coral heads along the edge of the fringing reef if seeking close anchorage to either beach.

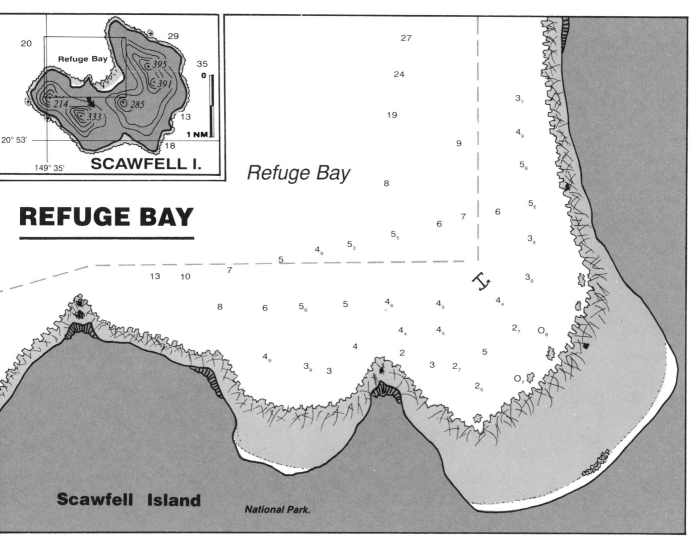

20

Refuge Bay

29

395

391

35

214

333

285

13

18

20° 53'

149° 35'

0

1 NM

Refuge Bay

27

24

19

9

8

7

6

5₅

4₉

5₃

5

5₆

6

7

3₇

4₉

5₈

5₆

3₉

3₉

3₉

REFUGE BAY

13 10 7

8 6 5₆ 5 4₆ 4₅ 4₄

4₄ 4₅ 5 2₇ O₈

4₉ 3₉ 3 4 2 3 2₇ 5 O₇

2₅

Scawfell Island

National Park.

CURLEW ISLAND is the largest of the *Guardfish Cluster* lying 8 miles south-west of Digby Island. Although close off the mouth of Broad Sound, tidal streams are comparatively mild at about 2 knots springs and sometimes zero during neaps.

Dominant features of the island are a knob hill on the north face at the western end of the beach and a sand dune visible 9 miles behind this beach. Of the other islands in the group none are so conspicuous as *Bluff Island* whose north-west end is an overhanging cliff. At its south-east end is a pillar of rock noticeable when the island is abeam.

Anchorage from south-east winds is in good-holding sand off the beach in shoaling water. When entering from the west, the channel between the two rocks off the north-west corner of Curlew Island and *Tinonee Bank* is narrow but deep and the bank can be seen as a light-green patch during the highest tide. From the south-east it is safe enough to pass between Curlew and *Treble Islet*, but wiser to pass outside the latter in heavy winds.

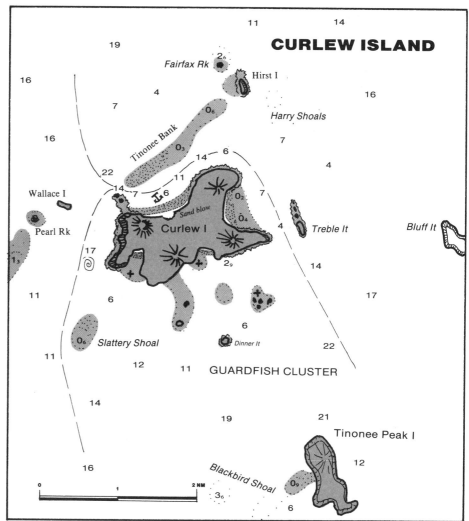

CURLEW ISLAND

11 14

19

16

16

Fairfax Rk 2₆

Hirst I

7

4

O₆

Harry Shoals

16

O₃

Tinonee Bank

7

14 6

7

22

14 11

Wallace I

14 7 O₂ 7

Sand blow O₄

Pearl Rk

17

Curlew I

4 2₉

Treble It

14

Bluff It

1₃

11

6

17

O₆

Slattery Shoal

6

Dinner It

22

11

12

11

GUARDFISH CLUSTER

14

19

21

Tinonee Peak I

12

16

Blackbird Shoal

O₉

3₆

6

0 1 2 NM

137

KNIGHT ISLAND *See chart page 123*. West-north-west of *Digby Island* by about 11 miles, Knight Island offers calm weather anchoring only. A rocky, scrub-covered mass with a distinctive rock outcrop on its peak, there is a shed and aerial on its highest hill. The coast is very rugged with broken rock along its east coast with rock-bound rubble beaches along its west coast. When approaching the latter, be aware of an isolated rocky islet.

PRUDHOE ISLAND is the most dominant land mass in the region having a high, southern peak and a lower northern peak with a deep saddle between the two. 7 miles north of *Knight Island* and useful only in calm weather, it has good fringing coral towards the saddle which is easy to over-run at high tide. Off this reef, Prudhoe Shoal runs south offering the only fair depths around the island. *See chart page 123.*

PIONEER RIVER. Emptying into the sea 3 miles south of *Mackay Outer Harbour*, the Pioneer River has high drying sand banks across its mouth and scarcely enough water inside to float a canoe at low tide. However, the tides of the area promising as much as 6 metres springs and 4 metres neaps means most deep keelers can enter and remain off the City of Mackay long enough to secure supplies if the Outer Harbour is packed out. Calm weather is necessary for the following.

Approach is from the south-east on an approximate line drawn from the Hay Point coal pile towards the red beacon opposite *East Point*. This was true for late 1993 but the navigator is warned that the banks change periodically. Local knowledge is best sought or, in calm weather, the vessel may be brought to anchor off the entrance at low tide so that proper observations can be made. With East Point close abeam to starboard,

Approaching Scawfell Island from the south-east, Derwent Island is foreground left with Three Rocks under the left-hand side of Scawfell.

Scawfell Island as it appears approaching from the west. Here it bears about 85°. Refuge Bay is under the arrow.

Treble Islet lies off the eastern head of Curlew Island. Passage between the two is okay.

The south-east head of Curlew is unmistakable from a fair distance.

Bluff Island, with its vertical rock on its south end and overhanging cliff on the north end is a good landmark. It is part of the Guardfish Cluster.

A feature of the Pioneer River is its riverbank mud berths where local vessels dry out at low tide supported on each side by bush poles. Except in the mildest of neaps, keel yachts cannot float in this river at low tide. The City of Mackay is on its south bank.

138

Knight Island bears south-east. Waratah Island is right with Curlew Island behind.

Knight Island is easily recognised by its knob peak.

Prudhoe Island is a dominant mass on the Percy-Mackay passage. To the extreme left is Overfall Rock.

Reid Islet lies about three miles south of Prudhoe Island.

hold this shore until obliged to cross for the south bank as indicated by the green dotted line on the chart

The entrance banks dry 1.9 metres meaning that a tide height of your draft plus 1.9 metres, plus a little for error, should be used. If any sea is running, add another half metre.

Anchorage in deep, low tide holes is sometimes possible close to the training wall near the fish wharves, but they cannot be relied upon and demand local knowl-

edge to find. As a rule, it is best to presume the river will have a maximum of a couple of feet at low water and act accordingly. If a wharf can be arranged to lean against it is possible to remain, otherwise, enter ahead of high tide and get the shopping done in ample time to escape on the same tide.

Facilities. Mackay is capable of providing most needs including fuel, water and all foodstuffs.

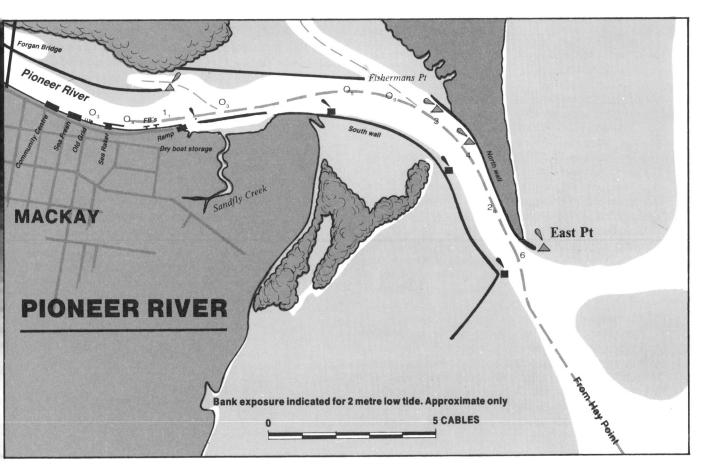

MACKAY

PIONEER RIVER

Bank exposure indicated for 2 metre low tide. Approximate only

0   5 CABLES

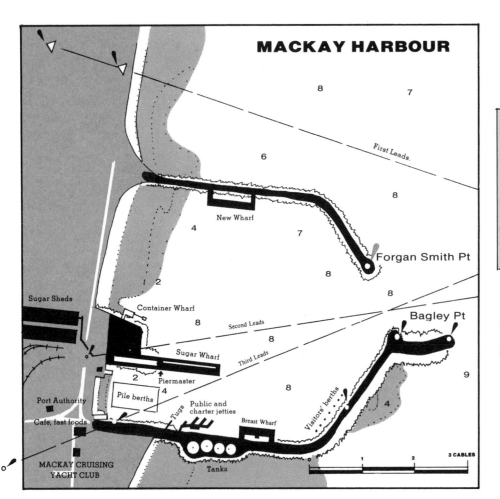

MACKAY HARBOUR

First Leads.

8   7

6

8

New Wharf

4   7

Forgan Smith Pt

8

1 2

8

Sugar Sheds

Container Wharf

8   Second Leads

8

Sugar Wharf   Third Leads

Bagley Pt

8

2   Piermaster

4

Pile berths

Port Authority

Cafe, fast foods

Tugs   Public and charter jetties

Visitors' berths   9

Breast Wharf

4

MACKAY CRUISING YACHT CLUB

Tanks

3 CABLES

0   1   2   3

A Port for Mackay

Early this century, when it became plain that the Pioneer River would never be suitable as a port, ideas were submitted for a port off its entrance. Amongst them was a plan to build finger piers from under the lee of Flat Top Island which, itself, would be connected to the mainland with an iron viaduct some 2000 metres long.

The two photographs on the opposite page show the sulphuric acid tanks behind the pile berths and yacht club, left, and the existing visitor pile berths with the molasses tanks behind, right. These pile berths will go when the harbour is extended, as illustrated bottom right.

MACKAY OUTER HARBOUR is a man-made breakwater harbour projecting out from the beach 2½ miles south of Slade Point. While continuing to satisfy the demands of commercial shipping, it has battled to keep up with the private boating boom and is often best avoided despite the very best efforts of its Piermaster.

Approach from the south-east is the most common, most boats coming from Percy or Digby Island. *Round Top Island* is the first landmark in the immediate vicinity of the harbour to rise from the horizon with *Flat Top* lifting soon after. Of the man-made objects, the tank farm on the southern breakwater and the sugar storage sheds rise at around 10–12 miles and *Mount Bassett* becomes recognisable to their left. The stone for the breakwater construction came from this mountain, the quarried face becoming obvious as it closes. To the north of the harbour a line of sand blows is seen soon after the tanks and sheds.

On final approach the first leading beacons are best adhered to despite ample water to each side of their transit. These are then abandoned for a second, then third, set of leads which are of little consequence to the small boat. However, if freelancing the entrance, beware of cross current of up to 2 knots setting south on the flood and north on the ebb.

From the north, *Slade Island* can be rounded to its east, a course assisted by a buoy off its eastern tail; or between Slade Island and the mainland, orientating the final approach on a red port-hand buoy lying 1¼ miles north of the harbour mouth. From there, leading marks can be used up to, but not into, the harbour. These marks stand on the breakwaters, the

front lead being the *Forgan Smith Point* light and the backlead being a special light near the visitor pile berths.

Anchorage. Except under extraordinary circumstances and with the permission of the Piermaster, anchoring is forbidden in Mackay Harbour.

Berths. For information, call the Piermaster on VHF who will do his best to accommodate you one way or another. Ideally, you will be directed to one of the visitor pile berths but could be allotted another berth temporarily abandoned by its permanent owner. During moderate onshore weather, a surge works into the harbour and makes life aboard at the pile berths a little noisy and occasionally bothersome. It also makes dinghy landing on the breakwater hazardous. The best landing in all weather is on the beach.

Fuel and Water is available from the Tourist Jetties. Petrol must be carted from town or at least a service station between town and the harbour.

Repairs are no trouble but the slipway is geared more for big boats than small yachts. A careening grid near the slipway is a suitable compromise for those needing to effect simple repairs or paint the bottom. Chandlery items are available locally and Mackay hardware stores are well stocked with many boat-orientated items of equipment and material.

In from the harbour's south-west corner is a haul-out yard to where boats are taken from the launching ramp via a special, ingenious trailer. The service is provided at a fair rate and the yard is an ideal venue for bottom work or dry storage.

By 1996, it is hoped that Mackay Outer Harbour will contain a separate small craft area by breaking through the existing south-east corner and continuing the wall south-west then west as seen here. The proposed public marina will hold 150 vessels whilst tourist vessels will be expanded or diverted to new facilities as shown.

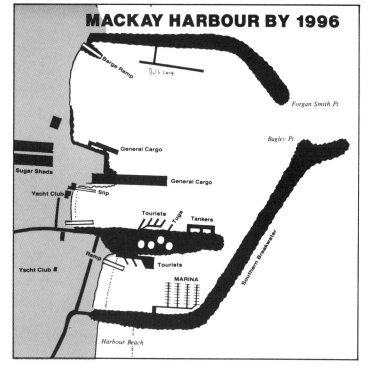

MACKAY HARBOUR BY 1996

Forgan Smith Pt

Bagley Pt

Barge Ramp

Bulk carg

General Cargo

Sugar Sheds

General Cargo

Yacht Club

Slip

Tourists

Tugs

Tankers

Yacht Club

Ramp

Tourists

Southern Breakwater

MARINA

Harbour Beach

Victuals are easy to find in Mackay City but a taxi is the only way to get them back to the ship.

Fast Foods, confectionery and meals are available at the Harbour Lights cafe at the harbour where will also be found a public STD phone.

The Cruising Yacht Club of Mackay is one of the best clubs on the coast and offers very reasonably priced evening meals.

Transport. There are no buses to, or passing near, the outer harbour. The visitor is obliged to walk, hitchhike or call a cab. It is 5 kilometres into town.

The Future. Recognising the need to ease congestion in Mackay Outer Harbour, plans are in hand for a marina to the north at Slade Point. Alternatively, a marina may be built in the existing harbour. Neither project had started as of 1993.

Looking Back

Pre-pile berths

Taken in 1963 by the author from his yacht at anchor, this view now is clogged with crowded pile berth moorings. The vessel is the pilot boat, *Effie*, a 45 foot launch built by Crowley of Brisbane. She was stationed here soon after her launching when Mackay Outer Harbour opened for business on 26 August, 1939.

In 1963 there were only two local boats and two visiting boats in the entire harbour when this photograph was shot.

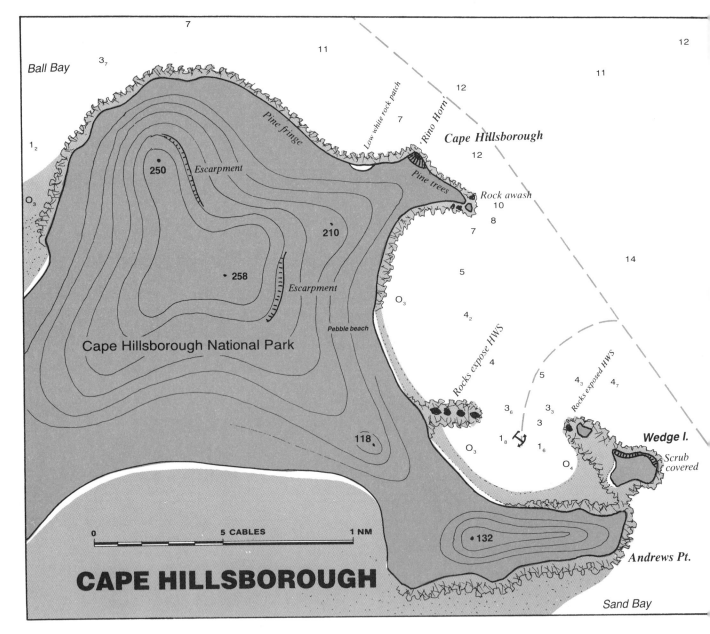

Ball Bay

Pine fringe

Escarpment

•250

210

•258

Escarpment

Pebble beach

Cape Hillsborough National Park

118•

0   5 CABLES   1 NM

CAPE HILLSBOROUGH

Low white rock patch

Rino Horn

Cape Hillsborough

Pine trees

Rock awash

Rocks expose HWS

Rocks exposed HWS

Wedge I.

Scrub covered

•132

Andrews Pt.

Sand Bay

CAPE HILLSBOROUGH is a rugged promontory between Mackay and Port Newry opposite Brampton Island. Scrub covered, with escarpments and pine forests, it is an unmistakable landmark whose identity is further highlighted by a 'rino's horn' at the actual cape. Well named, *Pinnacle Rock* is a nearby conspicuous feature which remains so for over 20 miles distant.

Ball Bay, under Cape Hillsborough's lee, is a suitable calm weather anchorage for those wanting to stop overnight. Shoal sand extends a long way offshore. There is a settlement towards the western end of the bay.

Wedge Island is a literal wedge with its peak to seaward. It gives a modicum of protection to the bay between it and Cape Hillsborough but does little to prevent a swell surging in. Anchorage is suggested in light weather only.

PORT NEWRY. Formed by a group of islands against the mainland 23 miles north-west of Mackay Outer Harbour, Port Newry is non-commercial, having only a small tourist resort in an area zoned National Park. Although a popular anchorage for trawlers, it is often missed by cruising people in favour of offshore Brampton Island and the Whitsundays in general.

Approach along the coast is by a simple process of elimination, lofty *Cape Hillsborough*, 7 miles south of the port, being an unmistakable landmark. The only danger from the south is *Blackwood Shoals*, a sandy bottom area carrying low tide depths of as little as 2.4 metres. To avoid a reported patch of just 0.6 metres north of Green Island, it pays to steer direct from Slade Point to Green Island thence Cape Hillsborough, stand-

The 'rhino's' horn of Cape Hillsborough is a conspicuous feature from a considerable distance up or down the coast.

142

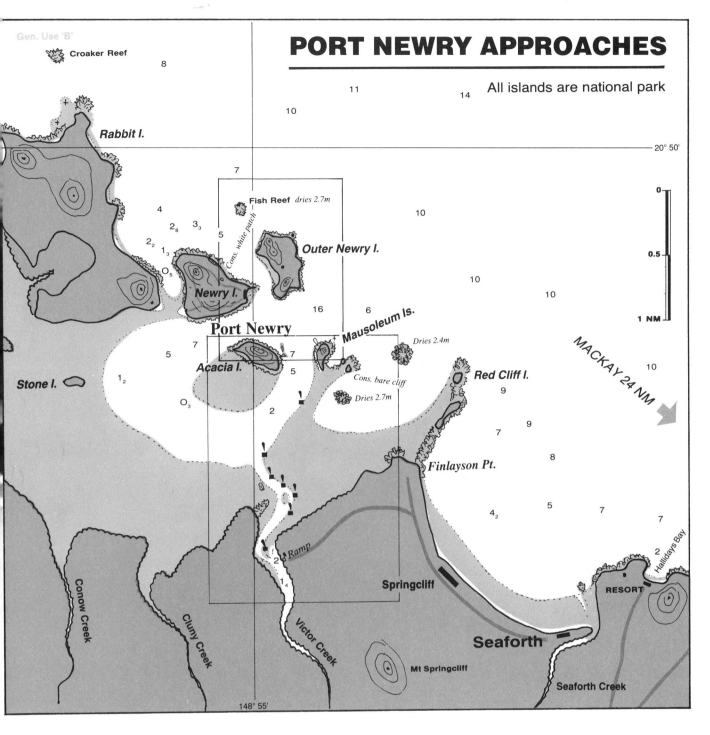

PORT NEWRY APPROACHES

All islands are national park

Gen. Use 'B'

Croaker Reef

8
11
14
10

20° 50'

Rabbit I.

7

Fish Reef *dries 2.7m*

4

2 8   3 3

5

Cons. white patch

Outer Newry I.

10

2 2   1 3

O 5

Newry I.

10

16

6

10

Port Newry

Mausoleum Is.

Dries 2.4m

7

Acacia I.

5

5

Cons. bare cliff

Red Cliff I.

9

Stone I.

1 2

5

O 3

Dries 2.7m

MACKAY 24 NM

10

2

9

7

9

Finlayson Pt.

8

7

5

7

7

Ramp

2 1

Victor Creek

4 2

5

2

Hallidays Bay

Springcliff

RESORT

Conow Creek

Cluny Creek

1 4

Seaforth

Mt Springcliff

Seaforth Creek

148° 55'

0
0.5
1 NM

---

ing off each by about one mile.

Approach from Brampton Island, the course can be direct allowing only for tidal streams which can behave illogically in this area.

Approach from the north, Cape Hillsborough continues to dominate with *Pinnacle Rock* leaving little doubt as to its identity, being very literally a spire of rock. *Mount Jukes* is obvious in that its height seems greater than its base width. In pinpointing the exact location of Port Newry, there is a conspicuous white 'dot' half way up Newry Island's highest hill which is otherwise scrub-covered.

Final approach is in deep water between Mausoleum Island and Outer Newry Island or between Outer Newry and Newry Islands taking care to avoid *Fish Reef.*

Anchorage during south-easterlies is best where shown under the lee of Outer Newry Island. This remains suitable in all winds except developed north-westerlies when a move to the lee of Newry Island is suggested. Surprisingly, a north-west swell works its way into this area, but can be nullified by moving as far west as shoaling water allows. The limit tends to be when the gap between Rabbit Island and Newry Island is fully open.

An alternative southerly anchorage exists under the lee of Mausoleum's south-tending sand spit. This is best at low tide.

Of Interest. During the frantic search for a means of taming the Pioneer River to create a useful commercial port for Mackay (long before its present breakwater harbour was considered), Port Newry was seriously proposed as the logical, natural harbour for the region. A wharf of 'ferro-cement' was considered projecting from Acacia Island's north-west tip which would be connected to the mainland by a two mile embankment

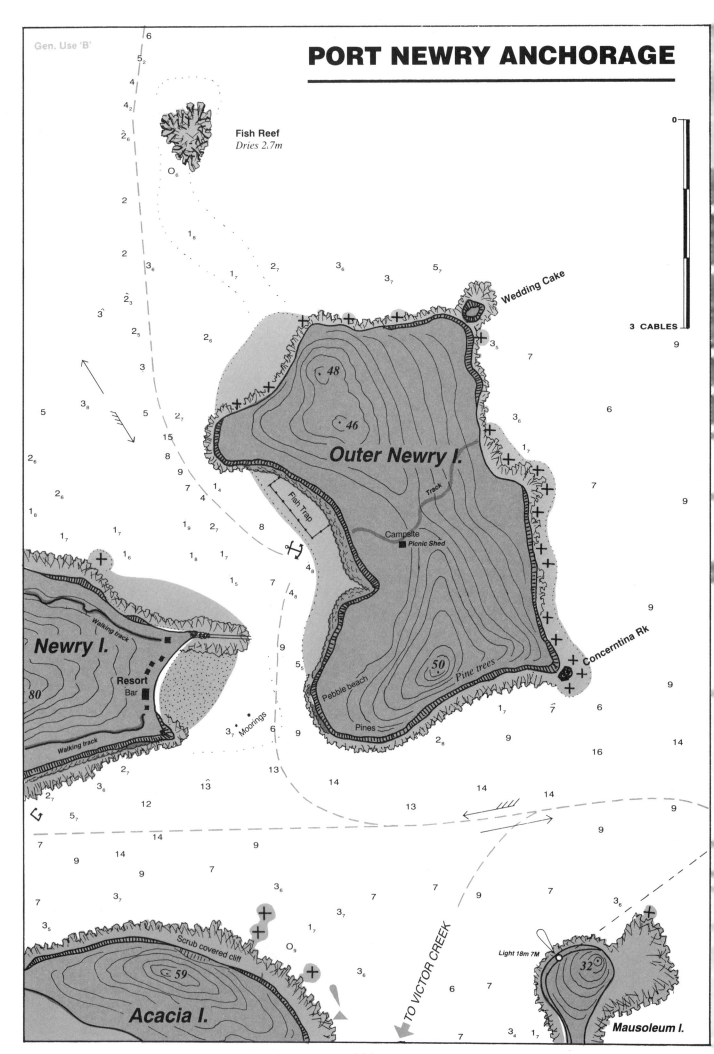

PORT NEWRY ANCHORAGE

Gen. Use 'B'

Fish Reef
Dries 2.7m

Wedding Cake

Outer Newry I.

Track

Fish Trap

Campsite
■ Picnic Shed

Newry I.

Walking track

Resort
Bar

Walking track

Moorings

Pebble beach

Pine trees

Pines

Concertina Rk

3 CABLES

Acacia I.

Scrub covered cliff

TO VICTOR CREEK

Light 18m 7M

Mausoleum I.

144

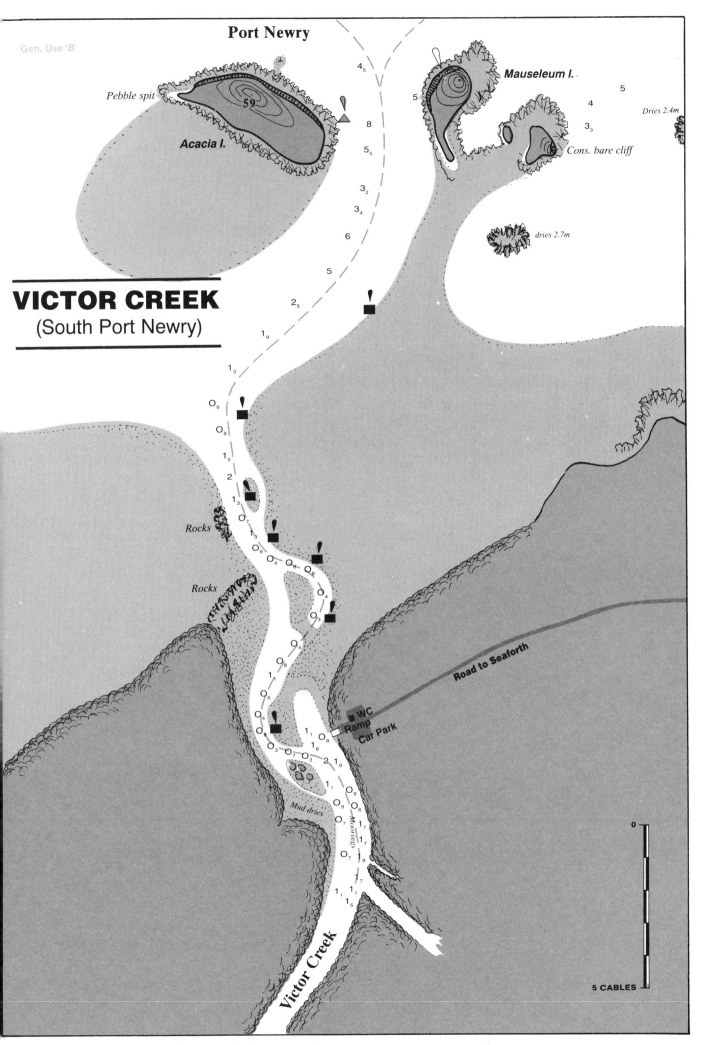

Port Newry

Pebble spit

Acacia I.

59

4₅

5

Mauseleum I.

5

4

5

Dries 2.4m

8

5₅

3₃

Cons. bare cliff

3₂

3₄

6

dries 2.7m

VICTOR CREEK
(South Port Newry)

5

2₅

1₉

1₃

O₉

O₉

1₅

2

1₃

Rocks

O₇

1₃

O₉

O₄ O₆ O₂

O₄

O₃

O₄

Rocks

O₈

1

O₆

Road to Seaforth

O₄

O₉

1₁ O₈

WC

O₃ O₃ 1₈

Ramp

Car Park

2 1₉

1₁

O₉

O₉ O₆

Mud dries

O₉

1₇

O₇

Moorings

1₇

1₉

O₇

1₇

1₁ 1₁
1₅

Victor Creek

0

5 CABLES

145

Approaching Port Newry from the south-east. The arrow indicates the southern entrance.

Closer to Port Newry, the entrance is obvious. Red Cliff Island is left and Outer Newry Island is under the boom.

A yacht enters Port Newry. Mausoleum Island is dominant, right.

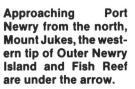

Concertina Rock is a conspicuous feature of the south-east tip of Outer Newry Island.

Approaching Port Newry from the north, Mount Jukes, the western tip of Outer Newry Island and Fish Reef are under the arrow.

With the north tip of Rabbit Island protruding into the picture, left, The Brothers Islands are seen bearing north-west.

Port Newry is a popular anchorage with working prawn trawlers. The small resort on Newry Island is in the background.

and a ten mile rail link with Mackay.

That this never came about is a blessing, for Port Newry remains as one of the Whitsunday area's better secrets, offering security and pleasant surroundings to the visiting sailor. The resort on Newry Island reminds one of the embryo, do-it-yourself holiday places common to the Whitsunday area before high rise and high fliers sent it all up-market.

National Park camping facilities are established on Outer Newry, Newry and Rabbit Islands.

VICTOR CREEK. Approached from *Port Newry*, between Acacia Island and Mausoleum Island using a tide height at least equal to your draft, Victor Creek has low tide depths adequate for anchoring. Its channel, though tortuous, is well beaconed with the shallowest part being immediately after the second last beacon. All are lit for night use.

It pays to enter as soon as you have enough tide to move. This promises good delineation of the channel, the banks to each side of which being high sand and possibly still exposed, if not just submerged.

At the mouth of the creek proper is a large concrete launching ramp, toilet, car park, trash cans and very poor tap water. The road connects with Seaforth where supplies may be purchased.

Anchorage is secure although occasionally tight with moored craft.

KESWICK-ST BEES ISLANDS

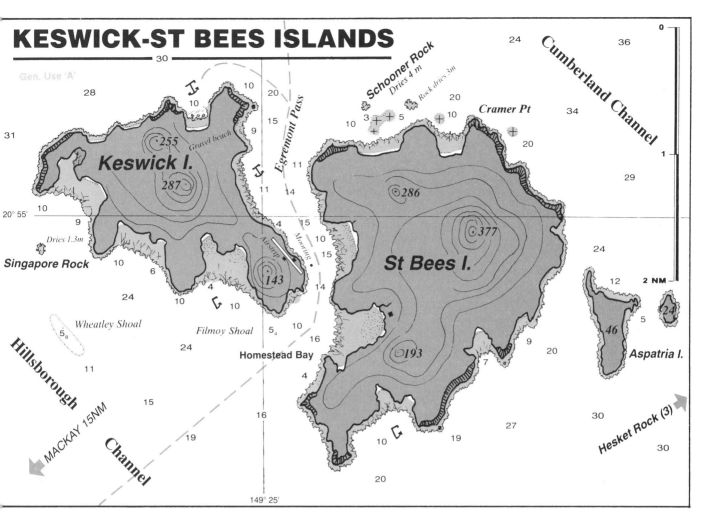

KESWICK-ST BEES ISLANDS, 15 miles north-east of Mackay Outer Harbour are the first of what are commonly referred to as 'The Whitsundays'. In fact, these two islands are part of the Cumberland Islands, the Whitsunday Group being 45 miles further north.

The channel between the two islands, *Egremont Pass*, lulls one into presuming it to be ideal anchorage. Sadly, the water in this pass is deep and fast reaching 4 knots at springs which, when against the wind, raises a steep little chop and makes boatwork unpleasant. The only way to find water of an acceptable depth for anchoring is to move in close to the fringing reefs of St Bees,

during onshore winds, and Keswick during offshore wind. Against this practice is the obligation to hold the reef too close for comfort and to drop anchor on foul ground. One thus has the double worry of fetching the reef or, conversely, not recovering the anchor. Under the circumstances, Egremont Pass is best saved for neap tides and light weather.

The best south-east anchorage is against Keswick about opposite the north-west tip of St Bees. The water shoals a little here and the current eases, but one does have reef and land dead astern.

The easiest and safest anchorage during strong trade winds is in the bay on the north side of Keswick. By moving up to the fragmented fringing reef here as close as possible, 11 metres can be found. Rolling can be heavy.

St Bees Island was settled as a sheep property by the Busuttin family who later moved to Brampton to raise remounts for the Indian Army. The next lessee of St Bees was killed in a plane crash off Mackay in the late 1950s after which the island remained in limbo for a number of years. It is now owned by an American whose intent was to start a tourist resort.

Keswick Island is also inhabited, the house being near the airstrip towards the south-east corner in Egremont Pass. An Air Sea Rescue base is operated here, all the usual channels being monitored.

The anchorage at Port Newry.

Cape Hillsborough is distant left with the highest peak of Rabbit Island, right. Outer Newry Island is centre in this panorama from the north.

BRAMPTON ISLAND is the southernmost of the Whitsunday tourist resorts, lying 20 miles north of Mackay Outer Harbour. There is a reef-filled, non-navigable channel between it and Carlisle Island which is a Marine Park B Zone. Casual visitors may avail themselves of the showers, fast food outlet and bar subject to permission being gained from management. Resident guest facilities are out of bounds.

Approach. The near perfect wedge shape of Carlisle Island is unmistakable from a good distance, especially when approaching from Scawfell Island, as is common. Except in the various bays and between the islands, fringing reef is minimal allowing fairly close rounding of all headlands. Beware of isolated rocks (*Helvellyn* and *Devereux*) to the south-east of both islands. To the north-west, a string of rocky islets are easily seen and identified.

Anchorage during the prevailing south-easterly is best towards the shoaling ground connecting Brampton Island with *Pelican Island* in the bay once known as McLean Bay. Some swell works in and windward-tide can be annoying, but generally conditions are good. Dinghy landing can be a problem over rocks on either side of the deep water jetty nearby.

Alternative, isolated anchorage is possible in Maryport Bay against Carlisle Island, where indicated.

During north-easterly winds, excellent shelter is enjoyed in *Western Bay* as close to the fringing reef as necessary. In northerly winds, a move into *Dinghy Bay* is recommended.

If reasonable access to the resort is required during northerly winds, anchorage is okay in *Turtle Bay* towards Carlisle Island. But beware a southerly change here. Not only is embayment more complete, but Helvellyn and Devereux Rocks can be a serious hazard when groping your way out at night.

Of Interest. Brampton Island was originally used as a coconut plantation, most of the Coral Coast's coconut palms being transplants from here. It was settled by the Busuttin family who, after experimenting with chinchilla rabbits, raised cavalry horses primarily for the Indian Army. With mechanisation, came the demise of this endeavour so they started a small resort in 1933. They sold out in 1959 after which it changed hands twice before being bought by Roylen Enterprises in 1962.

Started by Tom McClean, Roylen Enterprises operated a fleet of ex-wartime 112 foot Fairmiles out of Mackay on five day cruises. The purchase of Brampton broadened the operation and Tom's son, Fitz, moved from the boats to the island which he managed for many years. During his time, the tramway was built from the jetty to the resort copying the successful use of this type of transport then in operation on Hayman Island. The latter's tram has long gone; Brampton's continues to provide a unique service.

Roylen Enterprises are still in evidence with their modern fleet of catamarans, although the island was sold in 1985 to a subsidiary of Australian Airlines.

Skiddaw Peak, right, is a conspicuous feature of Carlisle Island. Brampton's southern headland, left.

Cockermouth Island, east of Brampton Island, provides calm weather anchorage.

Skiddaw Peak, on Carlisle Island, bears about west. Edgell Rock is close to its right.

The anchorage off the resort jetty is the best available during trade winds.

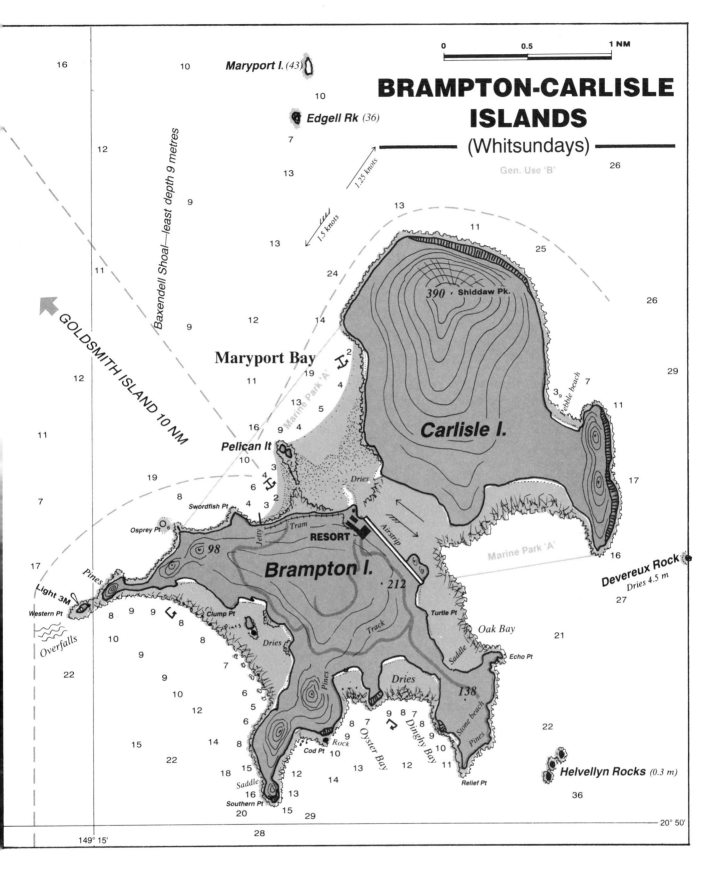

BRAMPTON-CARLISLE ISLANDS
(Whitsundays)

Gen. Use 'B'

0   0.5   1 NM

16
10
Maryport I. (43)
10
Edgell Rk (36)
7
13
26
12
9
1.25 knots
1.5 knots
13
13
24
11
25
26
Baxendell Shoal—least depth 9 metres
11
9
12
14
390 · Shiddaw Pk.
29
12
Maryport Bay
11
19
13
2
4
24
Pebble beach
7
3 9
11
GOLDSMITH ISLAND 10 NM
16
9 4
Marine Park 'A'
6
5
Carlisle I.
11
Pelican It
10
4 3
Dries
17
19
4
6
2
8
Swordfish Pt
4 3
7
Osprey Pt 6
RESORT
Tram
Airstrip
Marine Park 'A'
16
17
Pines
Jetty
98
Brampton I.
· **212**
Devereux Rock
Dries 4.5 m
Light 3M
Western Pt
8   9   9
8
Clump Pt
Pines
Turtle Pt
Oak Bay
21
27
Overfalls
10
8
Dries
Track
Saddle
Echo Pt
22
9
7
Pines
138
9
6
Pines
Dries
22
10
6
Stone beach
12
7
8 7
Pines
Helvellyn Rocks (0.3 m)
15
14
8
Cod Pt
Rock
10
Oyster Bay
9 8
8
Dinghy Bay
10
11
22
22
13
12
36
18
15
14
Saddle
16
13
Relief Pt
Southern Pt
20
15
29
28
20° 50'

149° 15'

Brampton resort is under the arrow in this view from
Maryport Bay. Carlisle Island, left.

149

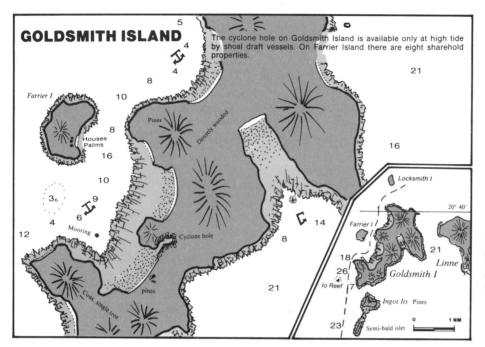

GOLDSMITH ISLAND

The cyclone hole on Goldsmith Island is available only at high tide by shoal draft vessels. On Farrier Island there are eight sharehold properties.

Brampton coconuts

Also a part of the Cumberland Islands, Brampton Island was first used as a government plantation, growing coconut palms from seeds imported from Indonesia. Most coconuts along the Queensland coast originated from this source, there being no indigenous coconut palms.

Goldsmith and Thomas Islands are part of the Cumberland Islands the northern end of which is comprised of the famous Whitsunday Group.

GOLDSMITH ISLAND is 10 miles north-west from Brampton and is uninhabited, although Farrier Island, close to its north-west face has a number of cabins on its south-east shore. These are privately owned and are not all occupied at once.

Anchorage is in good holding in the bay immediately south of Farrier Island. If crowded, try the bay to Farrier's north-east at the cost of a little swell during developed south-easterly winds.

In light northerlies, Goldsmith anchorage remains comfortable, but with any strength it is necessary to shift to the south side. The bay under Goldsmith's south-easternmost headland is excellent.

TINSMITH AND LINNE ISLANDS. *Not illustrated* Lying close east of Goldsmith Island with good depths between, these islands are suitable for settled, calm weather only. There is no comfortable anchorages during a developed wind although the western side of Linne Island is okay in north-easterlies.

THOMAS ISLAND. Less than 9 miles north of Goldsmith Island, Thomas Island is densely wooded with many pines and a few superb beaches. In the bay on the north face, these beaches nearly reach spring low-tide level before a very narrow fringing reef extends beyond. The small islet within the bay has a long rock reef extending south-west, drying at low tide. Approach from the south between *Dead Dog Islet* and *Fairlight Rock* is safe enough, but tidal overfalls are experienced in the region and a watch must be kept for a drying rock to the immediate south of Fairlight Rock. On final approach around the northern headland, beware of a drying rock to its north.

Anchorage during south to east winds is good although a south-east swell attacks the bay from the north-east with a developed wind from the south-east. This holds a boat beam up to the swell and conditions can become trying. Overall, however, it is a delightful anchorage.

Protection from northerly winds can be enjoyed in the bay immediately west of Dead Dog Island favouring Thomas Island on approach to avoid a shoal extending west from the islet.

Thomas Island is a national park in a *General Use 'B' Zone*. Most activities are allowed here.

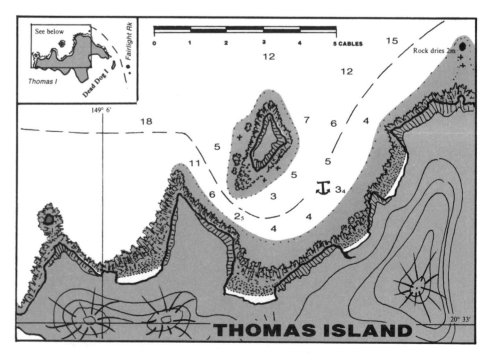

THOMAS ISLAND

From Cook's Log

Having passed and named Cape Hillsborough, *Endeavour* paralleled the coast towards Repulse Bay. By sunset of Saturday 2, 1770, she came to anchor, Captain Cook unsure as to whether a passage existed straight ahead (into the bay) or not. Under way the next morning, the low land of the head of the bay was sighted and the ship stood offshore to pass outside Cape Conway. Of Repulse Bay he wrote; *In all parts there was safe anchorage* (for vessels of that era), *and I believe that, upon proper examination, some good harbours would be found in it.*

REPULSE ISLANDS

North Repulse I.
Scrub covered

CAPE CONWAY 4.5NM

15

Repulse Bay

East Repulse I.
Mostly barren

20° 36'

The Repulse Islands are suggested as an anchorage only during fair weather. To their west is the new marina of Laguna Quays Resort.

Cons. white scar

Dries

Palm tree cons.

Dries 1.8m

Below. Julian Henry and first mate aboard the ferro-cement Hartley *Skansen* in Port Newry.

South Repulse I.
Scrub and grass

All islands are national park

Gen. Use 'A'

148° 52'

REPULSE ISLANDS are three continental islands at the entrance to Repulse Bay about 4 miles south-west of *Cape Conway*, the gateway to the Whitsundays. They are all grass and scrub covered with the northern one being densely wooded and relatively lush. The western side of all islands offers the best anchorage, but none reduce the swell to a useful degree. The area is best for picnic stops or light weather only.

Repulse Bay was named by Captain James Cook when, coasting along on *Endeavour* hoping that the bay would prove to be a passage, he had to reach off to clear around Cape Conway when the head of the bay was sighted. By good lookout and common sense he avoided that greatest of the early navigator's nightmares; embayment.

LAGUNA QUAYS RESORT is a development well under way in the early 1990s on the mainland at Midge Point, Repulse Bay. Centred around golf, it has a marina which is available to the public. A sketch map is over the page.

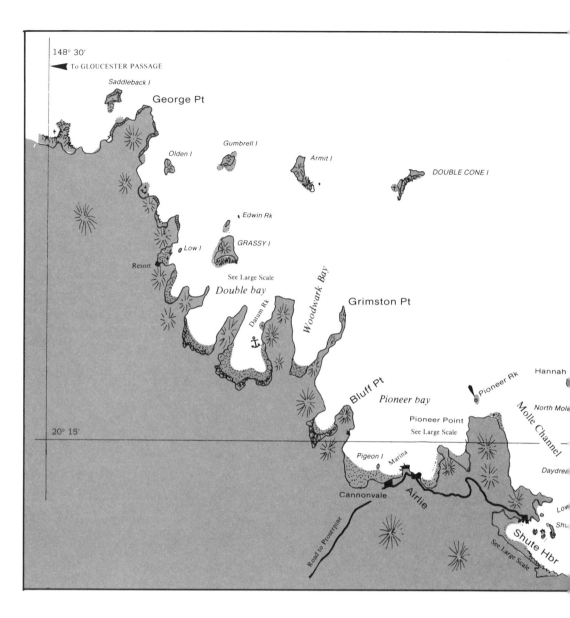

The Whitsunday area's mainland centre, Airlie Beach, lies west from North Molle Island and Pioneer Point.

Laguna Quays Resort marina is north of Midge Point, Repulse Bay.

The Whitsundays

Between Mackay and Bowen is Queensland's greatest concentration of islands. These are the Cumberland Islands, often collectively called 'The Whitsundays'. In fact, the Whitsunday Group is the northernmost of the Cumberland islands comprising the islands of Whitsunday, Hook and their smaller close neighbours.

All islands except Hayman, Dent and Hamilton are national park, although tourist resorts exist in their midst, these being on South Molle, Lindeman and Long Island. The main commercial harbour is Shute Harbour and the main centre and recreational harbour is at Airlie Beach. All services are expensive in the area suggesting that cruising vessels passing through victual well at either extreme (Mackay or Bowen).

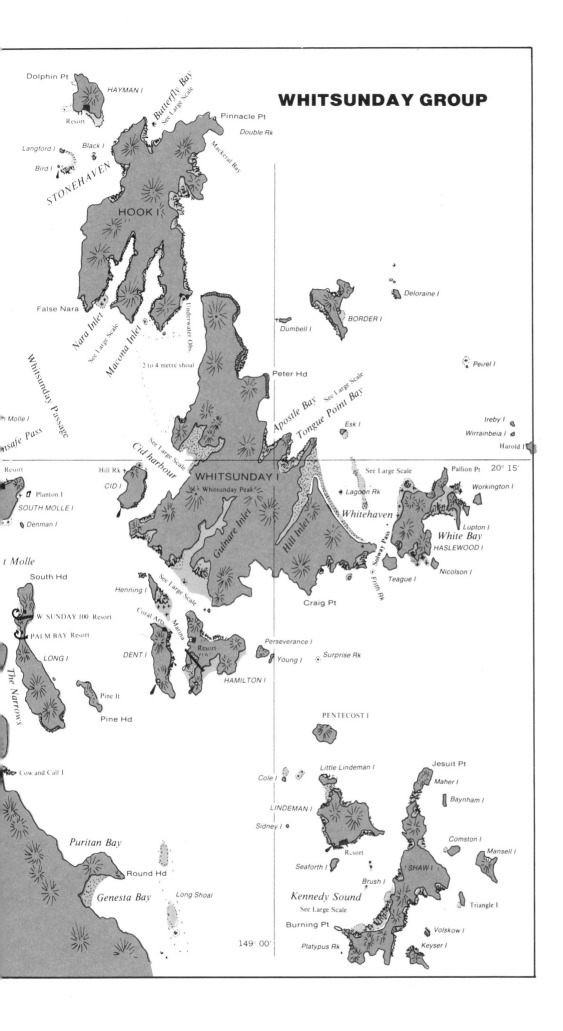

WHITSUNDAY GROUP

Dolphin Pt
HAYMAN I
Butterfly Bay
See Large Scale
Pinnacle Pt
Double Rk
Resort
Langford I
Black I
Mackerel Bay
Bird I
STONEHAVEN
HOOK I
False Nara
Nara Inlet
See Large Scale
Underwater Obs.
Macona Inlet
2 to 4 metre shoal
Whitsunday Passage
Peter Hd
insafe Pass
Deloraine I
BORDER I
Dumbell I
Petrel I
n Molle I
Apostle Bay
See Large Scale
Tongue Point Bay
Esk I
Ireby I
Wirrainbeia I
Harold I
See Large Scale
Cid harbour
See Large Scale
Pallion Pt
20° 15'
Resort
Hill Rk
WHITSUNDAY I
See Large Scale
Workington I
Planton I
CID I
Whitsunday Peak
Lagoon Rk
Whitehaven
Lupton I
SOUTH MOLLE I
Gulnare Inlet
White Bay
Denman I
Hill Inlet
HASLEWOOD I
t Molle
Nicolson I
South Hd
See Large Scale
Solway Pass
Teague I
Henning I
Frith Rk
Coral Arts
Craig Pt
W. SUNDAY 100 Resort
Marina
Perseverance I
PALM BAY Resort
Resort
LONG I
DENT I
Young I
Surprise Rk
The Narrows
HAMILTON I
Pine It
Pine Hd
PENTECOST I
Cow and Calf I
Jesuit Pt
Little Lindeman I
Maher I
Cole I
Baynham I
LINDEMAN I
Sidney I
Comston I
Mansell I
Puritan Bay
Resort
Round Hd
Seaforth I
SHAW I
Genesta Bay
Long Shoal
Brush I
Triangle I
Kennedy Sound
See Large Scale
Burning Pt
Volskow I
149° 00'
Platypus Rk
Keyser I

153

SHAW ISLAND is unique for its contrast between hills and valleys, two valleys being so low as to almost sever the island in profile view. Both, strangely enough, boast a single, tall coconut palm which is conspicuous from either side. One of these valleys is the narrow neck of *Neck Bay*.

Anchorage can be taken during a trade wind anywhere under the lee of Shaw Island in Kennedy Sound. Strong currents and swell can be annoying in extreme weather but overall conditions are comfortable. Neck Bay is a most popular anchorage, but superior comfort in heavy weather will be found in the south-east corner of Kennedy Sound in shallower water.

Northerly winds are best handled in the bay on the southern end of Shaw Island or under the lee of Lindeman Island.

LINDEMAN ISLAND.

The centre of dispute when the, then, Premier Sir Joh Bjelke Petersen backed a scheme that would sell off national parkland on Lindeman Island as freehold building blocks, the tourist resort on Lindeman Island is now operated by Club Med. Visitors must book into the resort. Anchorage is in very good holding mud south of the resort outside the fringing reef. The best south-east anchorage is in the bay on the north-west corner from where walks into the national park are easy.

CAPE CONWAY.

The south-east extreme of the Conway National Park and, in a sense, the true gateway to the Whitsunday Islands, Cape Conway is the eastern sentinel of *Repulse Bay*. It does not offer any anchorage, but is described here for the offshore dangers it advertises.

Close to its south-west is *Cape Rock* which dries 2.7 metres low water springs. Because tidal disturbances can be extreme here, it is not easily sighted when underwater.

Close to the north east of Cape Conway are *Ripple Rocks* which stand 5.5 metres above high water springs and can be seen from a distance of about 4 miles. They comprise two bodies, the south-eastern body being lower than the other. To their east-south-east is a rock which dries 1.2 metres low water springs and can prove even more difficult to sight than Cape Rock when covered.

Less than 2 miles north east of Cape Conway is the southern tip of 4 mile long *Long Shoal*, a sand bar that dries in parts. There are ample depths between it and the mainland.

Because of the hazards of rocks and shoals, plus the tidal disturbances of the area, Cape Conway is best given a very wide berth, vessels from the south

Lindeman Island is Australia's first Club Med resort and, as such, is off limits to the casual visitor.

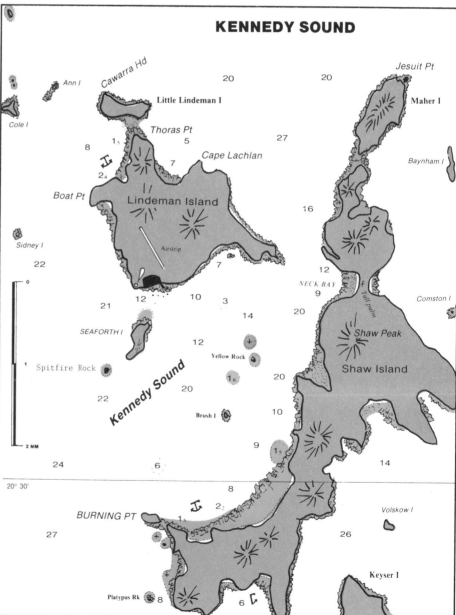

KENNEDY SOUND

154

Bare boat chartering in Australia started in the Whitsundays in the 1970's. This base is in Shute Harbour.

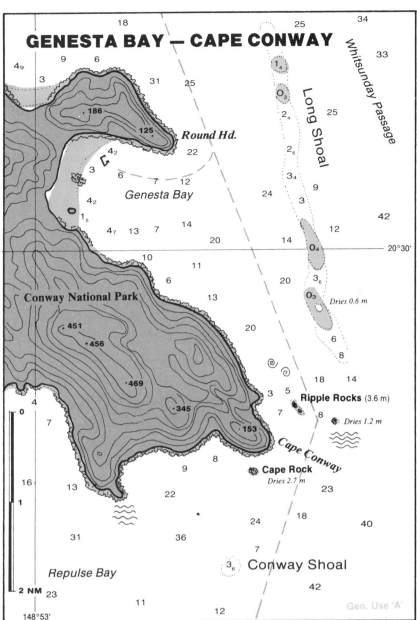

GENESTA BAY — CAPE CONWAY

Round Hd.

Genesta Bay

Conway National Park

· 451
· 456
· 469
· 345
153

Long Shoal

Whitsunday Passage

20°30'

Ripple Rocks (3.6 m)

Dries 1.2 m

Cape Conway

Cape Rock
Dries 2.7 m

Dries 0.6 m

Repulse Bay

3·6 Conway Shoal

Gen. Use 'A'

148°53'

staying well out on the official chart's recommended track. However, in fair conditions and when determined to round the cape close, it pays to navigate on visuals; that is, use *Ripple Rocks* as the known factor and hug them close. They can be passed on either side, but with extreme caution if being approached on a bearing that might over-run the drying rock to their south-east. Low tide is the logical best time for the above exercise.

GENESTA BAY lies against the mainland 3.5 miles north of *Cape Conway*. Surrounded by jungle covered hills and etched by beaches around its head, good holding in shoaling water can be found west from *Round Head*. It is suitable only in calm or northerly conditions when the wind favours north-west.

Cape Conway, right, bears a little east of north with Repulse Bay to its left. Distance off is 4½ miles.

From 2 miles off, Ripple Rocks (arrowed) can be seen off Cape Conway.

Ripple Rocks are now plainly in view. Tidal rocks, 4 cables east of Ripple Rocks, are not easily seen even when exposed at low tide. Care is needed when rounding Cape Conway this close.

155

LONG ISLAND SOUND is formed by five miles long *Long Island* against the mainland to the south of Shute Harbour. A very pretty passage with lofty, densely wooded hills on both sides, it experiences very strong tidal streams which set south on the flood and north on the ebb.

Entrance from the south is encumbered by *Three Fathom Patch* which has a minimum depth of around 5 metres whilst the northern entrance has shoals of similar depth against the mainland. Otherwise, depths throughout are well into double digits. The area of greatest tidal disturbance is *The Narrows* where eddies can take control from a lax helmsman.

Near the south-west corner of Long Island, *Paradise Bay Resort* is obvious by its buildings, but anchorage here is untenable during any developed wind. Moorings are available to visitors making the facilities ashore accessible.

There are two other resorts on Long Island, these being *Palm Bay* and *The Island* as described later under their own headings.

Against the mainland are two creeks offering cyclone protection. These are; *Woodcutter Bay* and *Trammel Bay*, both having drying entrances demanding a high tide to enter.

Round Head is 5½ miles south of Long Island Sound. It is Genesta Bay's northern headland.

Approaching Long Island Sound from the south, Long Island is dominant, centre. Pine Island is seen, right.

Within Long Island Sound, the mainland's Spit Point is left and Fire Point is right.

Looking into Palm Bay resort with its dredged basin in which visitors may lie stern-to the beach for a price.

'The Island' resort, in Happy Bay, Long Island, has a jetty on Humpy Point connected to the resort with a boardwalk over the rocks.

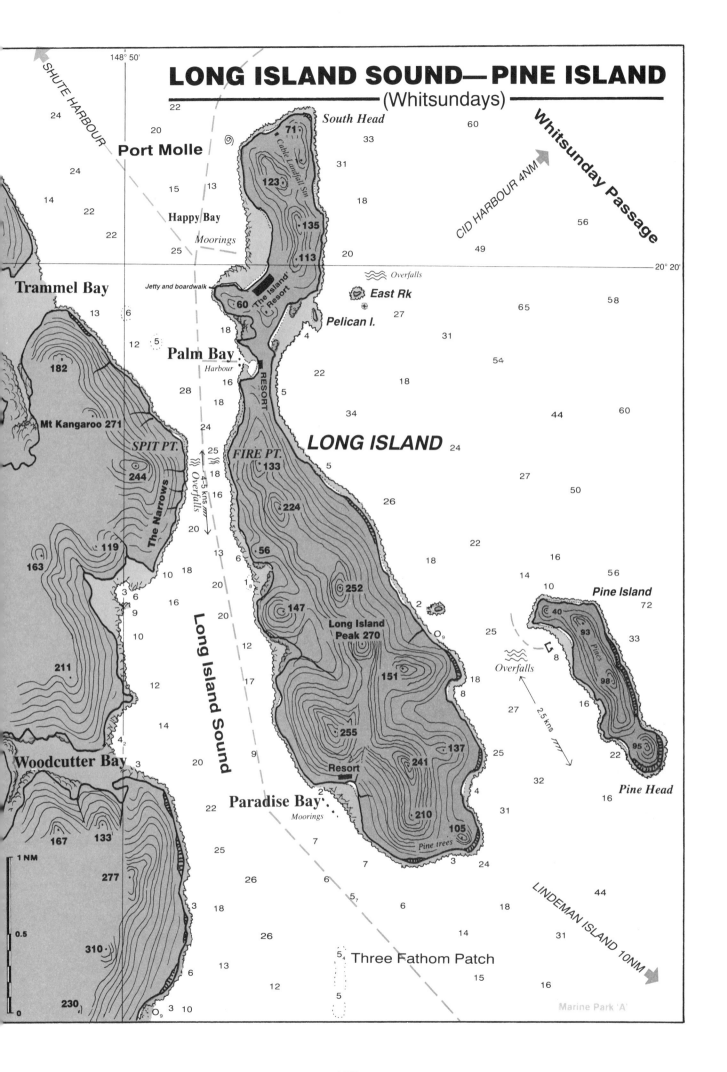

LONG ISLAND SOUND—PINE ISLAND
(Whitsundays)

SHUTE HARBOUR

148° 50'

24

20

24

14

22

22

25

Port Molle

22

15   13

Happy Bay

Moorings

Trammel Bay

13   6

12   5

Palm Bay

Harbour

28

16

18

24

25

18

16

SPIT PT.

The Narrows

244

Overfalls
4-5 kns

20

13   6

18

20   8

20

12

17

9

Jetty and boardwalk

60 The Island Resort

71

Cable Landfall Stn

123

135

113

South Head

33

31

18

20

60

Whitsunday Passage

CID HARBOUR 4NM

56

49

Overfalls

East Rk

Pelican I.

27

4

22

5

34

LONG ISLAND   24

65

58

31

54

18

60

44

27

50

FIRE PT.
133

224

56

5

26

22

252

147

**Long Island
Peak 270**

2

O 9

25

18

8

27

16

14

56

10

Pine Island

40

93

Pines

72

33

16

Mt Kangaroo 271

182

119

163

211

3   6

9

10

12

14

4 2

10

18

16

12

Long Island Sound

Woodcutter Bay

167   133

277

310

230

O 9

22

25

26

18

26

13

12

3

20

9

Paradise Bay

Moorings

7

7

6

5 7

6

5

255

Resort

2

137

241

210

105

Pine trees

151

8

Overfalls
2.5 kns

95

Pine Head

22

32

4

31

3   24

16

18

44

31

16

LINDEMAN ISLAND 10NM

Three Fathom Patch

5 4

15

14

1 NM

0.5

0

Marine Park 'A'

PALM BAY. Offering no anchorage, but now with a lagoon dredged to 2.5 metres in the fringing reef, Palm Bay has a small, informal resort behind the beach. Moorings, with stern to beach, are available inside the lagoon whilst swing moorings are outside.

HAPPY BAY (The Island) is just 4 miles southeast of Shute Harbour where, under the lee of *Long Island*, it provides excellent shelter from the trade wind. Moorings now occupy the best part of the bay, but anchoring is possible outside the moorings. Without hindering other vessels, try to get as far into the bay as possible to avoid the strong tidal streams working through Long Island Sound.

The resort was originally known as Happy Bay, later Whitsunday 100 and is now called 'The Island'. Use of its moorings can be arranged by radio and this is mandatory if the facilities of the resort are to be used. The resort jetty off Humpy Point, which is connected by a headland boardwalk, is not available to recreational boats.

SOUTH MOLLE ISLAND is a national park with good walking tracks and a resort in *Bauer Bay* (also called *Moonlight Bay*). Visitor moorings are laid off the resort, the rental of which allows access to the facilities of the resort. When going ashore, use the jetty, not the beach. Moorings can be arranged by radio.

Anchorage is possible outside the moorings, but shore access is not necessarily granted. Do not anchor east of the jetty nor obstruct its approach. During trade winds, Bauer Bay suffers heavy wind bullets and beam swell.

PLANTON ISLAND lies against *South Molle's* east coast, forming a small bay in which northerly winds can be weathered. Tidal disturbance can be quite dramatic here suggesting neaps as the best period.

DAYDREAM ISLAND is noted as *West Molle* on the official charts. Its original tourist resort complex on the south end has been given over to day-guest facilities, anchorage off which is best off the western

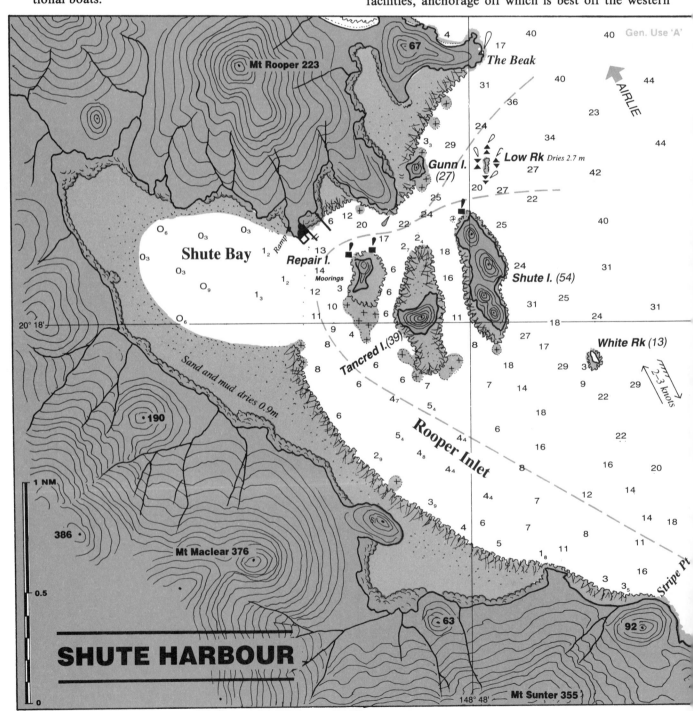

SHUTE HARBOUR

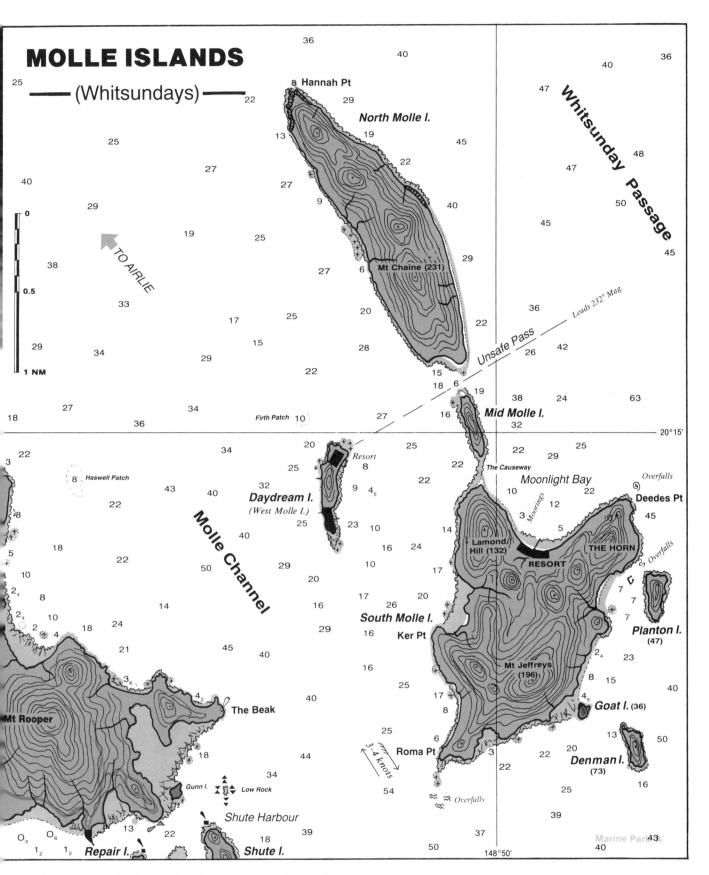

MOLLE ISLANDS

—— (Whitsundays) ——

Whitsunday Passage

North Molle I.

Hannah Pt

Mt Chaine (231)

Unsafe Pass

Leads 232° Mag.

Molle Channel

Haswell Patch

TO AIRLIE

Firth Patch

Mid Molle I.

The Causeway

Moonlight Bay

Overfalls

Deedes Pt

Moorings

Daydream I.
(West Molle I.)

Resort

Lamond Hill (132)

RESORT

THE HORN

Overfalls

Planton I.
(47)

South Molle I.

Ker Pt

Mt Jeffreys
(196)

Goat I. (36)

Mt Rooper

The Beak

Roma Pt

Denman I.
(73)

Gunn I.   Low Rock

Shute Harbour

Overfalls

Repair I.   Shute I.

Marine Park

20°15'

148°50'

side north of the jetty. This is a calm weather-only anchorage, there being no shelter nor shallow enough ground for protection against any developed wind.

The new resort is on the northern end of the island which is serviced by its own small marina on the eastern side. This is not available to visitors.

UNSAFE PASSAGE is a navigable channel between *North Molle* and *Mid Molle Islands*. Allowing for tidal stream, hold leading beacons in line about 232 magnetic. These beacons are on Daydream Island.

SHUTE HARBOUR is a great place to stay away from, it being the main port for the Whitsunday tourist resorts. Private boats are much better having their pick-ups, victuals and fuel arranged in Airlie where anchorage is always possible even on busy days. However, for those who need to know, the following is relevant.

At the head of Rooper Inlet, under the lee of a group of islands, Shute Harbour can be entered from the north-east or south-east as indicated on the accompanying chart. Channels and hazards are buoyed and beaconed and depths are good.

159

Moorings fill most available space but anchorage is sometimes available to their west against the shoaling water of *Shute Bay*. Shoal draft vessels able to take the bottom can move into this bay to gain more isolation.

Berths are unavailable between 0800 and 0900 and again between 1600 and 1700 during peak hour charter operations. Otherwise, either the Lloyd Roberts Jetty or the more recent Number 2 jetty can be used for pick-up and fuel (Lloyds Roberts Jetty the latter) after payment of a berthing fee. The third jetty is bare boat charter only.

South Molle as it appears when emerging from the northern end of Long Island Sound.

South Molle Island from the south. Much of it was cleared for grazing early this century.

Daydream Island's buildings are seen to the left of Unsafe Pass where a sail can be seen. North Molle is background left with South Molle entering picture, right. Mid Molle is off-centre right.

Looking into Moonlight Bay where South Molle resort is situated. Planton Island is left.

Unsafe Pass, between Mid Molle Island, left, and North Molle Island, right, as it appears on the Daydream Island leads (under arrow).

Unsafe Pass is opening up from the north, outside North Molle Island, right. South Molle's resort is behind the beach, left.

Sailing south into the Whitsunday Passage, North Molle Island is left with Pioneer Point, right.

Looking south at North Molle Island, right, and South Molle Island, with its conspicuous peak, left.

160

Very much an area of leisure,
Whitsunday Passage is also used by
commercial shipping.

From the Lions Lookout, Shute
Harbour's Coral Point is left with
Shute Island, right. This is the
harbour's main entrance. Despite a
new car parking station, vehicle
space is tight and often congested in
this hub of Whitsunday wandering.

One of Shute Harbour's two tourist jetties,
this is adjacent to the original wharf built
in the early 1960's. A floating bare boat
charter base is seen above.

Airlie Beach is around the headland from
Shute Harbour where there is greater
opportunity to anchor and more facilities
for the transient sailor.

A fair northerly anchorage exists in the bay
formed by Planton Island, left, and South
Molle Island, centre. Deedes Point
dominates.

For Airlie Beach, turn to page 169.

161

DENT ISLAND forms the south-east gatepost to the Whitsunday Passage and supports a major light on its western side. Once fully manned, it is now automatic. It was built in 1879 to a design similar to the light on Lady Elliott Island.

On the north-east corner is Coral Arts, a business started in 1954 by Bill and Leen Wallace after moving across from Hamilton Island. Bill, an ex-World War 11 pilot, and Leen had previously cruised the reef aboard the yacht *C'est La Vie*.

With a golf course on the north end of the island owned by Hamilton Island resort, a name change to 'Hamilton West' is being encouraged.

Anchorage is generally very poor anywhere around the island regardless of its apparent suitability for a given wind. To visit Coral Arts, it is possible to anchor over the reef moving in cautiously on a flood tide and getting out well ahead of grounding. Anchoring on reef may become illegal.

HAMILTON ISLAND 8 miles north-west from Lindeman Island and immediately south of Whitsunday Island, Hamilton Island was developed as a tourist resort in late 1970s-early 80s.

The marina situated in the bay on the west face was the first of its kind on the Coral Coast and was also the first real attempt to provide for, rather than reject, the passing boat person. Unfortunately it is very expensive at three to four times mainland rates on a daily basis. Without a big crew to spread the cost, it is unaffordable to the average cruising family. However, where employment is gained, there may be a reduction on staff berths.

Apart from the usual resort facilities at Hamilton, there are shops, a straddle-lift and hard-stand yard, fuel dock and chandlery.

To enter the marina, bring the leading beacons in line and proceed slowly. Inner and outer port and starboard buoys are automatically passed correctly on these leads after which direct course can be laid for the receiving dock. Usually boats are directed, attention to newcomers being very good. When berths are unavailable, it is sometimes an option to anchor in the south-west corner of the marina at a price.

When approaching Hamilton Island from the south, up Dent Passage, favour Dent Island to port to stand well clear of the end of Hamilton's air strip. Being capable of handling domestic jets, strict laws relating to masted vessels off the end of the strip apply.

HENNING ISLAND. Once boasting a prolific goat population, Henning Island is too small and steep-to to offer good protection. It is best used in light weather at which time its beaches offer good swimming. Tidal flow is strong here.

GULNARE INLET cuts north-east into *Whitsunday Island* opposite Henning Island. Totally protected with good holding mud, the anchorage is popular and often cramped around the best low-tide depths. Use a flood tide to enter to insure against stranding on the semi-barred entrance.

CID HARBOUR is formed by a bight in Whitsunday Island and by Cid Island partially enclosing it. Cid Island is 7 miles east-north-east of Shute Harbour on the eastern side of the Whitsunday Passage. Its harbour is extremely popular with all boating folk who take advantage of the national park facilities including toilets, tables, showers and barbecue pits. Anchorage is secure and mostly comfortable in the most severe trade wind and is only untenable in developed northerlies, especially if they favour north-west.

Whales are a common sight in the Whitsundays during their northern winter migration.

Gulnare Inlet bears ENE. A rising tide is necessary to safely negotiate the entrance by deep keelers.

Henning Island's northern anchorage is suitable only in light weather.

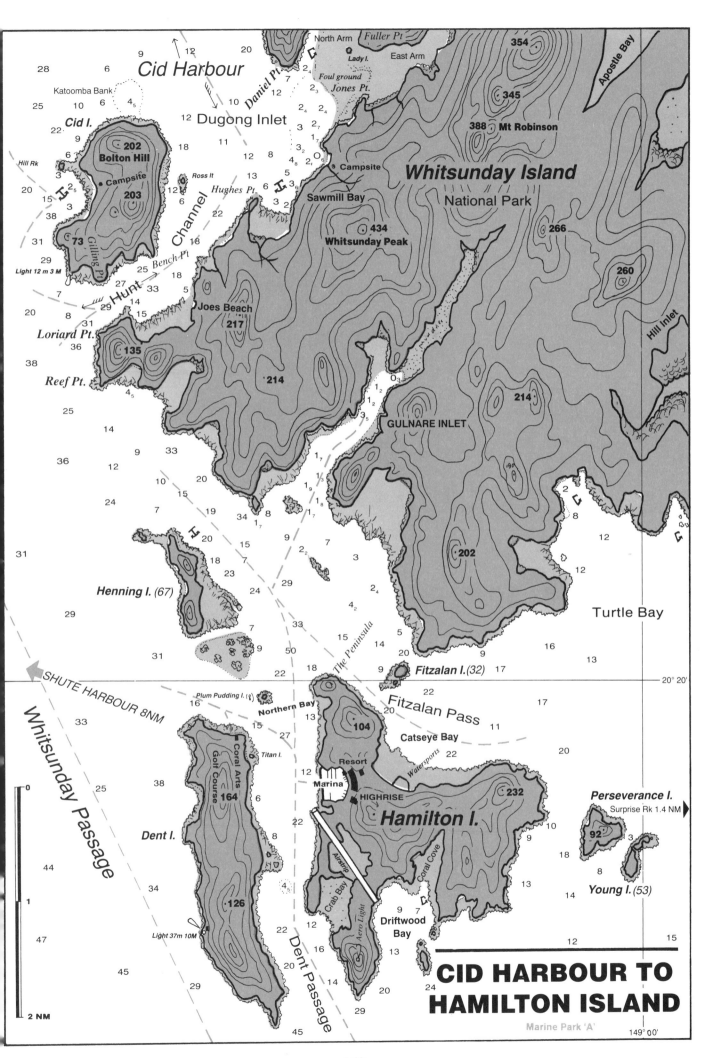

CID HARBOUR TO HAMILTON ISLAND

Cid Harbour

28   6   9   12   20

Katoomba Bank   6   10   4₅   10

25   10   6   12   **Dugong Inlet**

Cid I.   12   11

22   9   18   12   8   5

Hill Rk   6   ⚓   13

20   2₅   *Ross It*   6

15   3   ⚓ 202   *Campsite*   22   Hughes Pt.

38   3   **Bolton Hill**   12   18

31   **203**   25   Bench Pt   18

29   **73**   27   33   5

Light 12 m 3 M   *Hunt*   14   15

7   29   *Joes Beach*

20   8   31   **217**

36   *Loriard Pt.*

38   **135**   **214**

Reef Pt.   4₅

25   14   **GULNARE INLET**

36   12   9   33

24   15   20

31   10   7   19   34   8

Henning I. (67)   20   18   9   7

23   24   29

29   7   33   15

31   50   18   *The Peninsula*   **202**

22   16   *Fitzalan I.(32)*   17

SHUTE HARBOUR 8NM   *Fitzalan Pass*

33   *Plum Pudding I.*   **Northern Bay**   13   20   **Catseye Bay**   11

25   15   27   *Titan I.*   **104**   22

38   *Coral Arts Golf Course*   12   **Resort**   *Watersports*   22

164   6   **Marina**   **HIGHRISE**   **232**

Dent I.   8   22   **Hamilton I.**   10

34   **126**   *Airstrip*   9

44   4₅   *Crab Bay*   13

Light 37m 10M   16   *Driftwood Bay*   14

47   22   12   9   7

45   20   13

29   14

Whitsunday Passage   *Dent Passage*   24   45

North Arm   *Fuller Pt*   **354**   *Apostle Bay*

Lady I.   *East Arm*   **345**

Foul ground   **388 Mt Robinson**

Jones Pt.

Campsite   **Whitsunday Island**

Sawmill Bay   **National Park**   **266**

434   **260**

Whitsunday Peak   *Hill Inlet*

214

Turtle Bay

2   8   12   12   16   13   17   20

Perseverance I.   Surprise Rk 1.4 NM

92   3

18   8   *Young I. (53)*

12   15

Marine Park 'A'   149° 00'

20° 20'

WHITEHAVEN BAY is formed by *Whitsunday Island* to the west and *Haslewood Island* to the east. It can be entered through the deep but tide-troubled *Solway Pass* or from the north down the coast of Whitsunday or around Haslewood. Within the bay is a long sandbank extending south from *Esk Island* which dries in places and in particular at its southern end. Navigation to either side of this bank is safe with the exception of *Lagoon Rock* which is just exposed at high water springs. It lies on the west side of the bank and has navigable water to each side.

Whitehaven Beach, along Whitsunday Island, is world famous for its incredibly fine, salt-like sand. Backed by dunes, national park facilities are at its southern end and at its northern end *Hill Inlet* cuts south and offers high-tide access and a few low-tide float holes to shallow-draft craft.

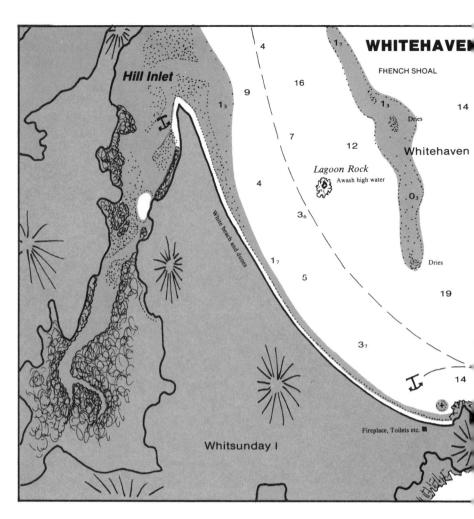

Anchorage in Whitehaven Bay is uncomfortable during a developed south-east to north-east wind. During light conditions, the most popular corner is that off the national park facilities.

HASLEWOOD ISLAND stands outside Whitsunday Island forming glorious Whitehaven Bay. The best south-east anchorage is in the shallow bay south-west of *Pallion Point* while the best northerly anchorage is in *White Bay* taking due care to avoid a few coral heads isolated from the main, vast fringing reef half-filling this bay.

APOSTLE AND TONGUE BAY. Offering good holding in pretty surroundings, these two bays are on the eastern face of Whitsunday Island where they experience considerable swell in fresh south-east winds despite the modicum of protection offered by Haslewood Island to windward. Except for a small beach which uncovers at low tide at the base of a smooth, black rock face in Apostle Bay, going ashore obliges a landing on rock. Enthusiast bushwalkers and rock climbers will enjoy this area and those wanting relative isolation might happily accept the slight discomfort of a beam swell.

Hayman Ownership

Hayman Island is owned by Ansett Transport Industries which is part of Sir Peter Abeles' multinational TNT transport group. During the late 1980's, about $300 million was spent in upgrading it as one of the world's top four resorts.

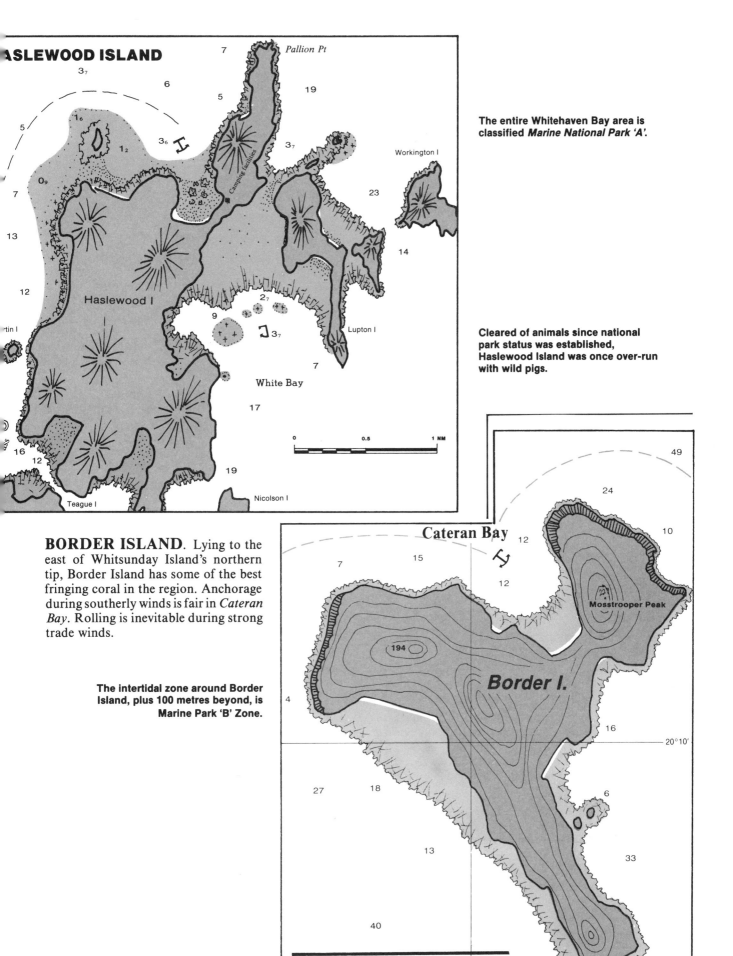

HASLEWOOD ISLAND

7
Pallion Pt
3₇
6
5
19
1₆
5
3₆
1₂
3₇
Workington I
0₉
23
7
13
14
12
Haslewood I
Camping facilities
rtin I
9
2₇
3₇
Lupton I
7
White Bay
17
16
12
19
Teague I
Nicolson I

The entire Whitehaven Bay area is classified *Marine National Park 'A'*.

Cleared of animals since national park status was established, Haslewood Island was once over-run with wild pigs.

0   0.5   1 NM

BORDER ISLAND. Lying to the east of Whitsunday Island's northern tip, Border Island has some of the best fringing coral in the region. Anchorage during southerly winds is fair in *Cateran Bay*. Rolling is inevitable during strong trade winds.

The intertidal zone around Border Island, plus 100 metres beyond, is Marine Park 'B' Zone.

Cateran Bay
49
24
10
12
15
7
12
Mosstrooper Peak
194
4
Border I.
16
20°10'
27
18
6
13
33
40
14
29
22

BORDER ISLAND

0   5 CABLES

29
22
25
Marine Park 'B'
149°02'

MACONA INLET. Surrounded by densely wooded, rugged hills studded with pine trees, and offering a scattering of beaches unavailable in neighbouring *Nara Inlet*, Macona is the least comfortable anchorage of the two. This is a marginal factor based on its slightly wider expanse of water which tilts a little more towards the prevailing south-easterly wind.

Approach. There is a yellow buoy off the eastern headland which must be passed to the south. In the entrance to Macona Inlet there is a small coral head that is just awash at low tide and difficult to see at other tides. To avoid it, hold the western headland close. It is possible to enter favouring the opposite headland but detached reefs from its fringing reef make accurate directions impossible.

Anchorage can be taken anywhere. Bare boats and other vessels often crowd the inlet, but such is its commodious nature that everyone fits and it remains possible to enjoy relative isolation if second-best is accepted. The bottom throughout is fine grey mud and excellent holding.

Tides are based on Mackay with Hook Island shown as a secondary port experiencing 52% of its height turning 25 minutes earlier. This is close enough but the ratio in both Macona and Nara is probably closer to 60%.

Windward-tide conditions can prevail, a deep keeler being held beam up to 10 knots of wind.

Of Interest. Until the late 1960s, this inlet was known as *Moana Inlet* on all charts. It is unclear whether the change to Macona was a misprint or a correction.

NARA INLET. A prettier and more popular anchorage than Macona, Nara penetrates Hook Island a little deeper and is narrower giving it more of a fiord feeling. It is nothing to find dozens of boats at anchor in Nara, most favouring the head of the inlet.

Approach. A green beacon is situated on the eastern headland and displays a flashing green light. This headland should be held close to avoid an area of reef lying from mid channel and almost reaching the opposite shore.

Anchorage is secure but can be choppy during strong trade winds. With so many boats using it, there is little in the way of choice obliging a visitor to grab what space is available. Try to get upstream of Refuge Bay to reduce the effect of wind waves. The holding is very good.

Tides are similar to Macona Inlet. There could be a marginal increase in windward-tide effect depending on the exact anchorage.

LANGFORD ISLAND lies close to Hayman Island and shares its reef with *Bird Island*. Often crowded with bare boats and Hayman guests, it can offer fair anchorage depending on weather and popularity of the moment.

STONEHAVEN ANCHORAGE. Once a mooring area for the early Hayman Island flying boats, Stonehaven Anchorage lies under the lee of Hook Island and is protected from the north by Hayman Island.

Approach along the west coast of Hook Island is by logical progression. The land can be held fairly close owing to the minimal fringe of reef along here. These reefs broaden, however, in Stonehaven.

Approaching via *The Narrows*, between Hayman and Hook Islands, presents no difficulties, although those under sail may find there is a complete loss or reversal of wind during a fresh south-easterly wind. A strong current must also be allowed for and the swell will prevail until abeam of *Stanley Point*.

From the west, the reef on which stand *Langford* and *Bird Islands* can be passed either end allowing for the southerly bulge if passed to the south.

Anchorage is not swell-free during moderate to strong trade winds but is comfortable enough and there is little windward-tide nuisance. The bottom is sand and coral patches; noisy but secure. Watch out for isolated gonkers in the bay between *Ian* and *Anchor Points*. This bay offers the best anchorage while all positions in Stonehaven experience tremendous wind bullets off steep-faced, 450-metre-high Hook Peak.

Of Interest. The roots of Hayman Island's existence as a resort are in Stonehaven Anchorage. Partners of the 1930s, Joe Ellis and Bert Hallam started the resort here, moving over to Hayman soon after. They sold out to Ansett Industries in 1948 and Bert moved to Cooktown where he bought the old Sovereign Hotel.

HAYMAN ISLAND is the most northerly resort island of the Whitsunday Group and is one of the originals. A massive rebuilding program in the 1980s saw the demolition of the jetty and Hayman Rockit (tram) and their replacement by a 25 berth marina excavated from the fringing reef. Having gone up-market, overnight berths are only available to those willing to take a room at night. Casual visitors are welcome, daylight only, subject to fair dress sense and departure before 1700 hours. Call the marina office on VHF, HF or 27 megs.

Blue Pearl Bay is the only worthwhile anchorage at Hayman, being on the west coast under the lee from the trade wind. The island is not a national park, but limited areas ashore are available to visitors. These are indicated on a large sign near the beach.

BUTTERFLY BAY is one of the Whitsunday Islands' prettiest places being surrounded by the well-wooded, steep mountains of Hook Island. Now rather crowded, the best anchorage right at the head of the bay is often occupied obliging a visitor to drop anchor in one of the other two indentations which grow progressively less comfortable the further out you go.

During south-east winds a roll invades Butterfly Bay but the holding is good in sand and scattered coral heads. Be aware of fringing and isolated reefs towards the head of the bay.

In keeping with protective policies aimed at minimising reef damage in the Whitsundays, Butterfly Bay may be the first to have public moorings. Anchoring may well be outlawed here.

Hook and Whitsunday Islands are national parks; Hayman is not. The marine zones are indicated in grey. ▷

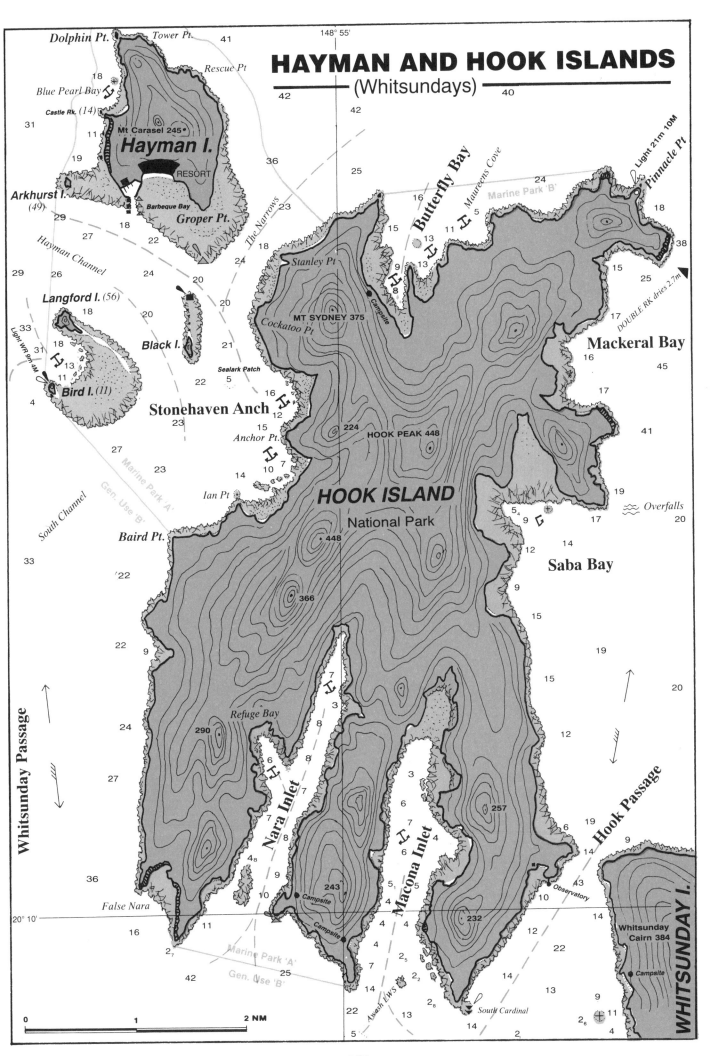

HAYMAN AND HOOK ISLANDS
(Whitsundays)

148° 55'

Dolphin Pt. Tower Pt. 41
Rescue Pt
42
18 40
Blue Pearl Bay 42
Castle Rk. *(14)* 31
11 **Mt Carasel 245**
19 **Hayman I.**
Arkhurst I. RESORT
(49) 29
27 18
22 **Groper Pt.**
Barbeque Bay

36

Hayman Channel 29 26 24
The Narrows 23
25 16 Butterfly Bay
Maureens Cove 24
Marine Park 'B'
18 15 11 5
Stanley Pt 13
20 9 13
Langford I. *(56)* 18 8
33 18 20 Cockatoo Pt 8
31 20 **MT SYDNEY 375** Campsite
11 **Black I.** 21 Light 21m 10M
Bird I. *(11)* 22 Pinnacle Pt
4 Sealark Patch 5 18
Stonehaven Anch 16 15
23 12 38
27 15
23 Anchor Pt. 224 **HOOK PEAK 448** Mackeral Bay
14 10 16
Ian Pt 17
Baird Pt. **HOOK ISLAND** 41
'22 National Park 448 19
33 Overfalls 20
5₄ 9
366 12 14 Saba Bay
22 9 257 15
24 290 9
7 15 19
Refuge Bay 3 20
8 12
Whitsunday Passage 24 8
6 3 **Hook Passage**
27 8 6 257 19 9
Nara Inlet 6 14
8 4 Observatory 43
4₈ 9 243 **Macona Inlet** 6 10
36 10 Campsite 5₁ 5 **WHITSUNDAY I.**
False Nara 4 14
20° 10' Campsite 4 **Whitsunday**
16 11 4 4 12 **Cairn 384**
2₇ 7 22 Campsite
42 Marine Park 'A' 2₅
Gen. Use 'B' 25 14 13 9
22 Awash LWS 14 2₂ 2₈ 11 2₆
13 South Cardinal 4
5 2 4

South Channel
Marine Park 'A'
Gen. Use 'B'

Light WR 9m 4M
DOUBLE RK dries 2.7m
25
17
45
17
41
19
17

0 1 2 NM

167

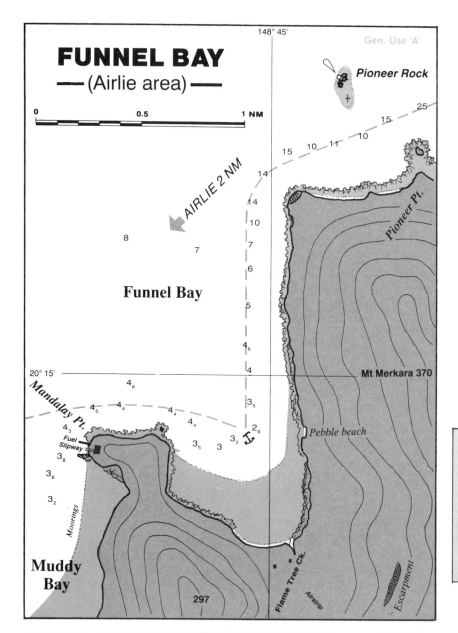

FUNNEL BAY
— (Airlie area) —

0   0.5   1 NM

148° 45'

Gen. Use 'A'

Pioneer Rock

AIRLIE 2 NM

25
15
15 10 11 10
14
14
10
7
6
5
8
7
4₆
4
3₅
2₉
4₆
4₄
4₅ 4₄ 4₄
4₃
3₅ 3
3₈
3₆
3₂

20° 15'

Funnel Bay

Pioneer Pt.

Mt Merkara 370

Pebble beach

Mandalay Pt.

Fuel
Slipway

Moorings

**Muddy
Bay**

297

Flame Tree Ck.

Airstrip

Escarpment

FUNNEL BAY. Within clear sight of Airlie, the hub of the Whitsundays, Funnel Bay offers secure, pleasant anchorage during all but northerly winds. Inland, from the head of the bay, there is a caravan park and Whitsunday Airfield. Otherwise, the lofty, wooded hills give an air of isolation. They also generate bullets of wind which can increase the true wind speed by at least fifty per cent. The holding is excellent.

Around *Mandalay Point* there is a fuel dock, slipway, dive centre, bare boat charter company and resort. Moorings extend south from the slipway but anchorage is possible beyond their line or to their immediate south-west.

Flame Tree Creek, at the head of Funnel Bay, can be used as a cyclone hole, having low tide float depths inside the entrance. The bar dries, demanding your draft plus a small reserve in tide height to enter.

Port of Airlie

In the western corner of Muddy Bay, where beach careening has been a nautical tradition for many decades, there is to be a marina and residential-resort development known as 'Port of Airlie'. A project of FAI Insurance, property department, it is a fifteen year plan due to start when council approval is given. As of late 1993, no start had been made.

Pioneer Rock light stands 6 cables north of Pioneer Point. Passage between the two is safe but unnecessary.

Looking Back

Cannonvale Wharf

Damaged by a 1950's cyclone and under increasing tourist boat pressure, the Cannonvale Wharf was abandoned in the early 1960's in favour of Shute Harbour. The Abel Point Marina now occupies this site.

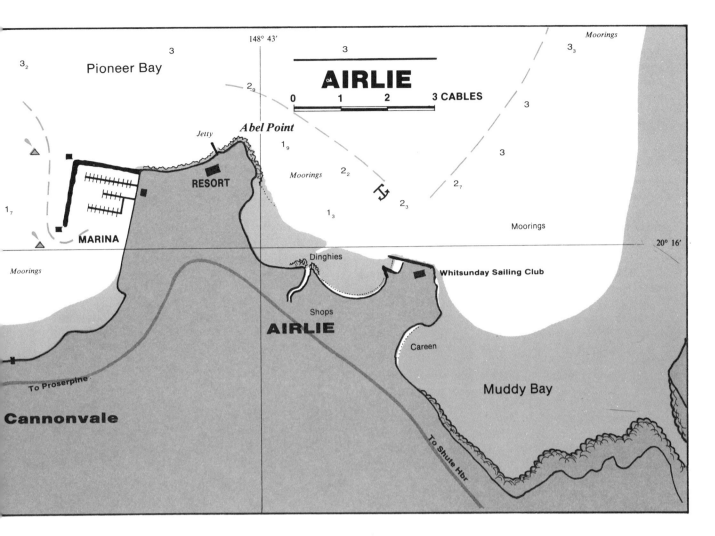

AIRLIE

AIRLIE BEACH is the nerve centre of the Whitsunday tourist trade. Its main street is almost wall-to-wall booking offices and certain commodity prices are so high that one might lose sight of the fact that it is not an isolated area. Generally, however, sanity prevails and the shopping is affordable for those wanting just a few items to keep going. Certainly, Airlie should not be considered for serious bulk victualling, Bowen, to the north, being far superior in choice of goods and much cheaper.

Approach from Molle Channel is in good water straight across the bay after rounding *Pioneer Rocks.* Deep water exists between these rocks and *Pioneer Point* but beware of standing out too close to the rock. Under sail, to a spanking south-easterly, be prepared for lulls and bullets once under the lee of Pioneer Point.

From the north, the bay is equally clear for direct approach and *Bluff Point* provides good reference until the buildings of Airlie are sighted.

Anchorage outside the moored craft off Airlie Beach is in good holding mud. Although often very crowded, such is the expanse of the bay that there is always room beyond the outer line of boats. Trailer-sailers and small multi-hulls are able to anchor stern up to the beach at high tide where they dry at low tide. The beach is quite unattractive at low tide and cannot be reached by dinghy.

Dinghy access is via a special channel which has silted badly but continues to admit rowing boats at low water neaps. The new breakwater off the *Whitsunday Sailing Club* has created a more convenient dinghy area, although crowding and damage can occur.

Marina. Sheltered from the east and north by an 'L' shaped breakwater, Abel Point Marina caters for casual visitors alongside its floating berths. Call ahead by radio or enter the harbour and go alongside the fuel berth for allocation.

Facilities. Fuel and water are available alongside at *Mandalay Slipping Service* on Mandalay Point and in the marina at Abel Point. Most shops are represented in Airlie with transport to Shute Harbour or Proserpine available. The local chandlery is well stocked and the Whitsunday Sailing Club welcomes visitors. Sailmaking and general repairs are no problem in the area and multi hulls can careen on a grid in Muddy Bay. Mandalay Slipway can take vessels up to about 85 tonnes.

Of Interest. About where the marina's breakwater starts is the site of the old timber jetty that once served all the charter boats in the Whitsundays. Despite cyclone damage, it continued to serve into the early 1960s before being replaced by the Lloyd Roberts Jetty in Shute Harbour.

Ex National Park

Up until the 1960's, Hayman Island enjoyed national park status. During that period, the government gave the late Sir Reg Ansett perpetual and special lease title over the whole island for resort development.

169

WOODWARK AND DOUBLE BAYS.
Under the lee of *Grimston Point*, which is Pioneer Bay's western sentinel, comfortable anchorage in good-holding mud is enjoyed in any of these three bays. A mere 6 miles from Airlie, they provide isolated alternatives, although this will end if a development comprising two large marinas, hotels and 360 private homes goes ahead.

During strong trade winds, a swell works into all three bays but is rarely severe. The best escape from it is towards the south-east corner of the middle bay taking due care of the shoals here. The nearest northerly anchorage is under the lee of Grassy Island, as noted next.

GRASSY ISLAND
GRASSY ISLAND lies immediately north of the westernmost bay of Double Bay where it provides a modicum of northerly defence to that bay. Closer under its south side, good northerly anchorage is available. During trade winds, the north-west face is acceptable, but far from comfortable. Ashore the land is poor with sparsely wooded grasslands, the only dense scrub being a patch down the hill on the south side. The beaches along the north face are rock fringed and sometimes difficult to land while a good sandy beach wraps around the south-west corner.

Grassy Island was once leased by Boyd Lee who commercially fished the area in the 1930s, was involved in early resort development and is well-mentioned in Norman Caldwell's remarkable book, *Fangs of the Sea*. The foundations of his old house are still in evidence on the southern side of the island.

ARMIT ISLANDS
ARMIT ISLANDS are a group of four continental islands 3 miles north-east of Grassy Island. They boast good beaches on their south sides and are mostly scrub covered to leeward. The larger island provides tolerable north-east anchorage in the reef-fringed bight on its south-west corner. Generally these islands should be saved for calm weather or quick lunch and swim stops.

ESHELBY ISLANDS
ESHELBY ISLANDS lie a little over 4 miles north of Armit, the larger of the two supporting a light showing 9 miles. Being a nesting place for the threatened bridled terns, it is a *Marine Park Preservation Zone* with anchoring prohibited.

EARLANDO RESORT
EARLANDO RESORT is on the south shore of a mainland bay directly opposite the south tip of *Grassy Island*. Offering its facilities to visiting sailors, it has a bar, walks and all the usual trappings. Of special interest is the creek whose interior offers a good cyclone hole but whose entrance demands a high tide to negotiate.

GEORGE POINT
GEORGE POINT is the last major headland before entering Gloucester Passage, the bay formed between the two offering a number of anchoring opportunities during calm or south-east weather.

The passage between George Point and Saddleback Island is safe for navigation, and the first bay under the lee of George Point is remarkably comfortable even if the wind is in the east. Beware of the fringing reef which almost fills this bay; it can prove difficult to sight at high tide.

The Beach Plaza, Airlie Beach, typifies the town's modern, tourist appeal.

Armit Islands share a common reef. Here they bear north-east.

Gumbrell Island bears north. Eshelby Island is right, distance.

Olden Island is abeam with the mainland behind. The 388 metre peak, left, is a conspicuous feature of the area.

George Point and Cape Gloucester are almost in line. Cape Gloucester is the north tip of Gloucester Island.

Entering Lady Musgrave lagoon. This is one of the few navigable lagoons in the Great Barrier Reef chain and as such is a magnet to those seeking their first coral experience. Some get more than they bargain for.

The visitor piles off Brisbane's Botanical Gardens make the city very accessible and affordable. Ashore, there are toilets, showers and laundry with dinghy access to the back of the ferry pontoon. That's the suburb of Kangaroo Point in the background.

Gladstone public marina. This is linked to the city by an opening bridge over Auckland Creek.

Outrigger canoe events have become very popular along the Queensland coast with this meet on the Gold Coast.

Island Head Creek, between the Keppel and Percy Isles, is a favourite anchorage for its security in all winds and scenic beauty.

This sand blow is under the lee of Cape Capricorn on the northern tip of Curtis Island, Keppel Bay. A more spectacular sand blow, known as 'Yellow Patch' is inside a creek to its south-west. Using the right tide, the creek can be entered for absolute security.

The centre of Australia's most precious rainforest region, the Daintree River penetrates the coast a few miles north of Port Douglas.

Below: Sailing close to headlands along the Coral Coast is not a recommended practice where fringing reef is involved. Always give them a wide berth unless certain of their steep-to nature.
Right: The advent of GPS has already started the reduction of lighthouse numbers along other parts of the Australian coast, but not, as yet, along the Coral Coast. This is the Sea Hill light on Curtis Island.

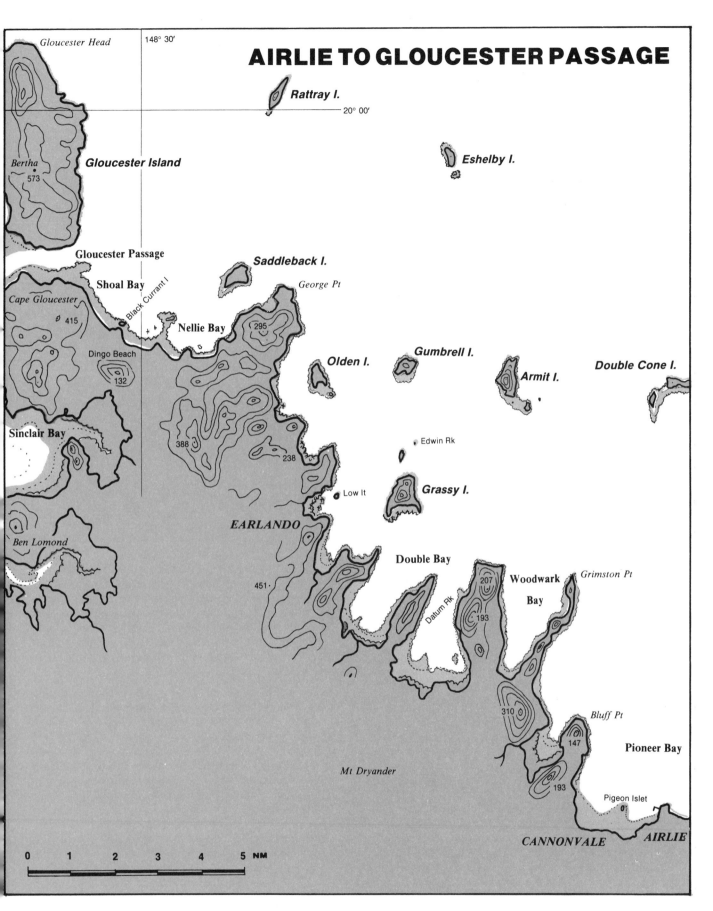

AIRLIE TO GLOUCESTER PASSAGE

Gloucester Head

148° 30'

Rattray I.

20° 00'

Eshelby I.

Gloucester Island

Bertha
573

Gloucester Passage

Saddleback I.

Shoal Bay

George Pt

Black Currant I

Cape Gloucester

415

Nellie Bay

295

Olden I.

Gumbrell I.

Double Cone I.

Dingo Beach

132

Armit I.

388

238

Edwin Rk

Sinclair Bay

Low It

Grassy I.

Ben Lomond

EARLANDO

Double Bay

207

Woodwark

Grimston Pt

451

Datum Rk

Bay

193

310

Bluff Pt

147

Pioneer Bay

Mt Dryander

193

Pigeon Islet

0'

CANNONVALE   *AIRLIE*

| 0 | 1 | 2 | 3 | 4 | 5 NM |

Grassy Island.

171

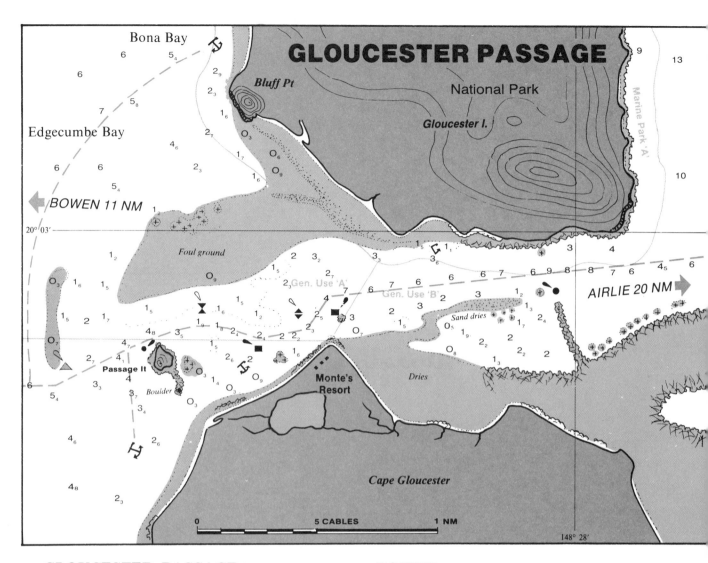

GLOUCESTER PASSAGE

Bona Bay

Edgecumbe Bay

BOWEN 11 NM

Bluff Pt

National Park

Gloucester I.

Foul ground

Gen. Use 'A'

Gen. Use 'B'

Sand dries

AIRLIE 20 NM

Passage It

Boulder

Monte's Resort

Dries

Cape Gloucester

Marine Park 'A'

20° 03'

148° 28'

0   5 CABLES   1 NM

GLOUCESTER PASSAGE is an easily navigated, well-beaconed channel between Cape Gloucester and Gloucester Island, 21 miles from Airlie and 12 miles east of Bowen. In fact, the cape and island help form Edgecumbe Bay, the western corner of which is Bowen Harbour.

All beacons and buoys are lit with red to port sailing west. The tide floods east and ebbs west and can reach 3 knots during springs. A flood tide is advisable when working very deep draft, but the average keeler will clear at low tide as long as the channel is held.

Anchorage in south-east winds can be taken under Gloucester Island or the Cape as shown on the plan. Gusts can be severe under the island owing to its abrupt mountain chain generating considerable bullets. It is not as bad under the cape. Totally calm anchorage with fewer bullets can be enjoyed right down in Sinclair Bay with the mountain, Ben Lomond, bearing south.

Northerly winds can be avoided under the lee of Gloucester Island in the channel where shown by a half anchor. Depending on the exact slant of the wind, it can fail entirely to reach this spot even when the wind tops 20 knots.

Monte's Resort, on the tip of Cape Gloucester, is available to sailors. It has a bar and small shop.

Looking east through Gloucester Passage. Passage Island, right.

BOWEN. Offering a return to suburban sanity and economies after the excesses of the Whitsunday-Airlie Beach area, Bowen is well-recommended to those needing security surrounded by low-key, but more than adequate, facilities. The fully enclosed boat harbour lies in the north-west corner of Edgecumbe Bay some 35 miles from Airlie Beach and 12 miles from Gloucester Passage.

Approach from Gloucester Passage is the most common, and the leg across Edgecumbe Bay can be one of the area's great sails being under the lee of the land across the bay. As Bowen is approached, *Flagstaff Hill* appears as a plain bald, low hill with the old disused lighthouse on *North Head* obvious at around 5 to 7 miles. *Stone Island* appears as an equally bald hill with cliffs along its northern point. *Sinclair Head* (on Stone Island) is seen, but not as conspicuously as the disused light on North Head. *Edgecumbe Heights*, out near Cape Edgecumbe, appears as a separate entity and is rugged, with houses dotted on the hillside to its south.

Bowen's water storage tanks become obvious crossing Edgecumbe Bay at around the same time as the main harbour leads are seen on the land to port. These are of no consequence to the small boat whose course must seek the outer green buoy which is passed to starboard to avoid the foul ground extending south from Stone Island. From there, the next buoys are

172

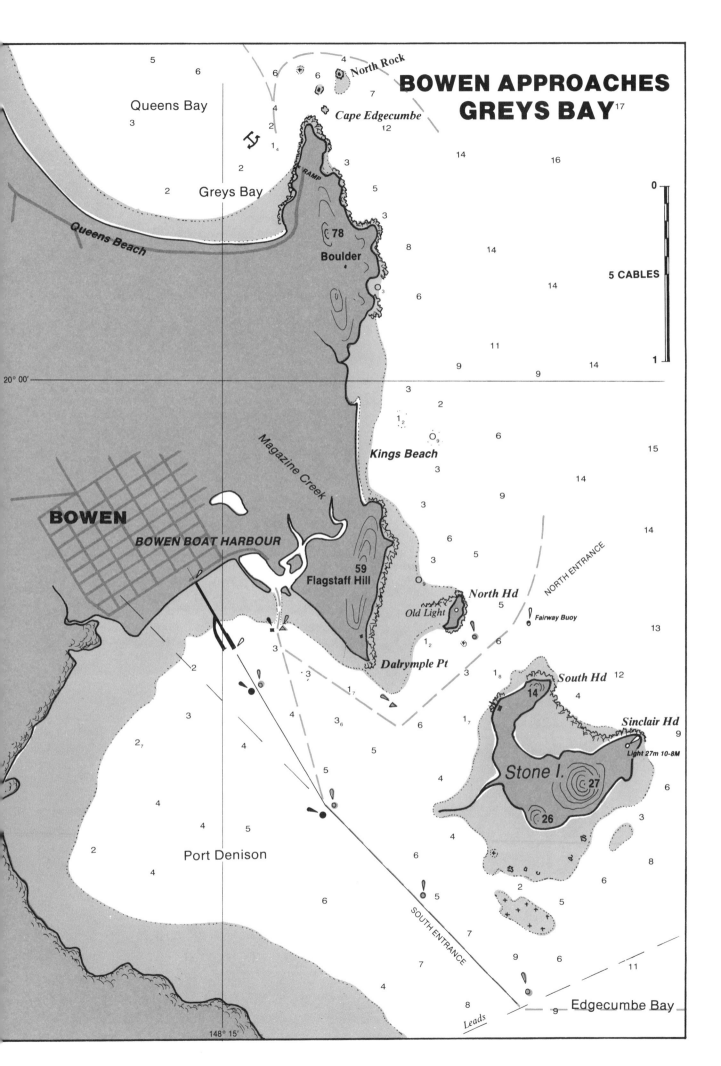

BOWEN APPROACHES
GREYS BAY ¹⁷

Queens Bay

North Rock

Cape Edgecumbe

Greys Bay

Queens Beach

78
Boulder

Kings Beach

Magazine Creek

BOWEN

BOWEN BOAT HARBOUR

59
Flagstaff Hill

North Hd

Old Light

Fairway Buoy

NORTH ENTRANCE

Dalrymple Pt

South Hd

Sinclair Hd

Stone I.

Light 27m 10-8M

14

27

26

Port Denison

SOUTH ENTRANCE

Edgecumbe Bay

Leads

20° 00'

148° 15'

0

5 CABLES

1

173

As of late 1993, Magazine Creek, Bowen, had been dredged and stripped of mangroves awaiting expressions of interest for the private development of a marina. Meanwhile, it makes an attractive anchorage. It is entered through the Bowen Boat Harbour channel. Right, is the fuel dock of Bowen Ice and Seafoods.

Mother-town of Queensland

Known as the mother-town of Queensland last century, Bowen's darkest hour came in the late fifties. At a time when bulk sugar loading facilities were being planned for Queensland ports, it seemed inevitable that Bowen would become the outlet for both Proserpine to the south and Home Hill-Ayr to the north. Instead, bulk loaders went to Mackay and Townsville respectively. Added to this were two destructive cyclones in 1958 and 1959. Despite these setbacks, Bowen had one of the fastest growing populations in North Queensland between 1954 and 1961.

Previously a major outlet for Collinsville coal, Bowen lost to Abbot Point's deep water bulk loader a few miles to the north.

This small marina in Bowen Boat Harbour belongs to the North Queensland Cruising Club. It is adjacent to the public pontoon. Pile berths are in the background with trawlers ranged along the opposite bank.

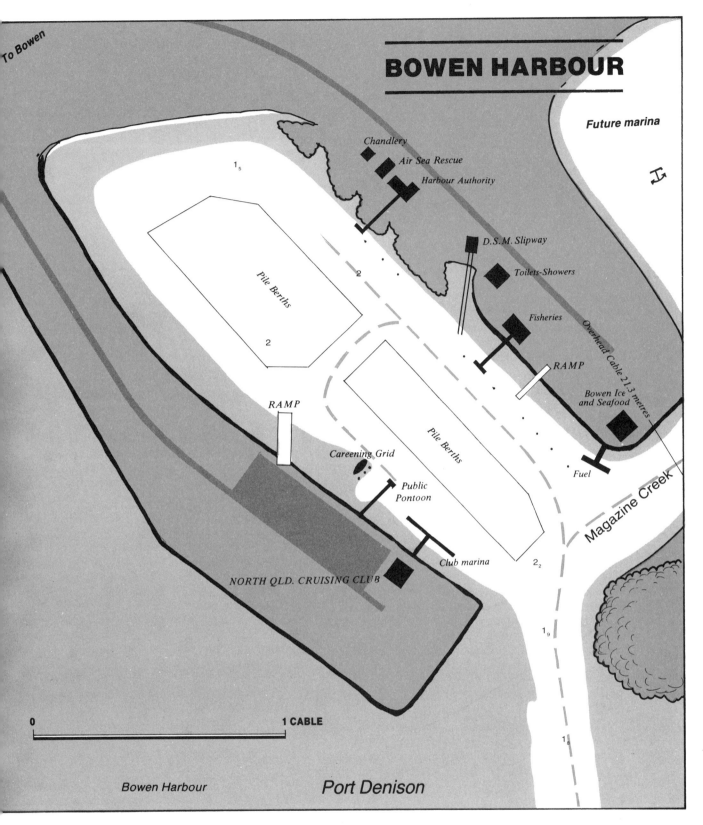

BOWEN HARBOUR

To Bowen

Future marina

Chandlery
Air Sea Rescue
Harbour Authority

1_5

Pile Berths

2

2

D.S.M. Slipway

Toilets-Showers

Fisheries

Overhead Cable 21.3 metres

RAMP

Bowen Ice and Seafood

RAMP

Careening Grid

Public Pontoon

Pile Berths

Fuel

Magazine Creek

Club marina

2_2

NORTH QLD. CRUISING CLUB

1_9

1_8

0   1 CABLE

Bowen Harbour   **Port Denison**

---

easily sighted and followed, although a direct course can now be laid for Bowen Boat Harbour's entrance, the general whereabouts of which can be identified from here.

From the north, *Cape Edgecumbe* is seen as an island when abeam of *Abbot Point* after which it quickly joins up with the mainland which rises soon after. Beware only of the shoals extending from the *Don River* delta and the rocks in close to Cape Edgecumbe. On final approach, *North Entrance* between Stone Island and the mainland provides a minimum of 3 metres low water springs and is indicated by a fairway buoy and two inner green marks all of which are lit.

Final approach to the boat harbour is through a narrow dredged channel marked by port and starboard piles.

Nav Aids. All harbour buoys and beacons are lit for night-time navigation.

Tides are based on Townsville data in the *Tide Tables* and turn 50 minutes later. Their range is similar.

Anchorage is possible in the main harbour subject to remaining clear of commercial activity. It makes little sense, however, the harbour being open to the south-east trades and drying banks demanding a long row ashore. Until the marina is started in Magazine Creek, next to the existing boat harbour, anchorage is possible in the dredged basin. Check with harbour control.

Pile Berths within the boat harbour are applied for by going alongside the public pontoon. A supervisor will allocate a berth.

Facilities. Bowen shopping centre has a few supermarkets and all the usual shops; enough to fully victual any vessel. Fuel and water are on the waterfront and a chandlery is close by. The *North Queensland Cruising Club* welcomes visitors and the slipway can handle any craft capable of entering the harbour. It has most repair services. The club's marina sometimes has casual berths available.

Of Interest. With its natural harbour — albeit, facing to windward — and rapid growth after first settlement in 1861, Bowen seemed destined to be a major force in Queensland. For one reason or another, it always lost to other centres even if those other centres demanded an expensive man-made breakwater to provide harbourage. It did, however, become the logical outlet for the coal fields of Collinsville, 88 kilometres inland. Initially shipping through Bowen Harbour (Port Denison), a bulk loading facility at Abbot Point, north of Bowen, now handles the lot.

A local abattoir kills as many as 90 000 head of cattle annually and a solar salt evaporation plant produces some 15 000 tonnes of salt a year. But for all that, Bowen is best known for its small crop farming, producing extraordinary quantities of tomatoes, mangoes, rockmelons, capsicums, chillies and watermelon. The Bowen Mango, incidentally, is probably the best in the world having little fibre and lots of beautiful meat.

At one stage, Bowen went awfully close to hosting an alumina refinery, low metal prices saving it just in time. The elation over its loss is not, of course, shared by many locals who need the employment industry offers. But visitors and immigrants to Bowen are attracted by its *lack* of heavy industry and their presence alone probably creates as much employment. Physically, Bowen is not an especially attractive place, but it has a heart and soul unique on a coast rapidly yielding to whatever promises the fastest buck. While other places become computerised machines, Bowen remains human and this is its real attraction.

GREYS BAY lies in the south-east corner of *Queens Bay* under the lee of *Cape Edgecumbe*. Although swell-prone, anchorage is secure here and useful to those wanting to stop in the Bowen area without entering its harbour.

UPSTART BAY lies approximately 40 miles north-west of Bowen and is formed by the lofty rise of Upstart and Station Hills and the low delta area of numerous creeks and rivers, notable amongst them being the Burdekin River. Excellent shelter is available in all but strong northerlies.

Approach from Bowen is by logical progression along the coast, Gloucester Island behind and Upstart ahead remaining in view depending on haze. Abbot Point coal loading facility is obvious as a detached tower from a distance and a long jetty close in.

From the north, Upstart is easily seen after rounding Cape Bowling Green. The land comprising Upstart headland is steep and rugged with many rock outcrops bursting through native scrub. Off the tip of the Cape itself is a small, white rock 7 metres high known locally as *The Bun*.

Anchorage can be taken anywhere along the west face of the cape taking care only to remain a sensible distance off the beach which has numerous half-tide rocks between and, in places, in front of the beaches. Quick overnight anchorage can be found immediately after rounding The Bun. Houses by the dozens dot the entire west coast and are, in the main, owned by people from the Home Hill-Ayr area. An anchor light is indicated owing to fairly regular runabout traffic.

A long, low swell rounds the headland and moves down the bay causing a slight roll at anchor. Those wishing to remain in the area with greater comfort can move down to the south-east corner towards the entrance of *Nobbies Inlet*.

If the wind shifts east, or even north-east, anchorage as close as possible to the southernmost beach of the headland is remarkably comfortable. Beware of a drying spit of sand projecting from this area. The holding is excellent.

Navigation Aids. There is a flashing white light on a rock close to the headland 3 miles south of the cape. Another, with a limited arc of visibility, stands on the south headland of the Burdekin delta while a third light shows the entrance to Molongle Creek. According to official information this is flashing red. It was noted to be flashing white with a second fixed green in the vicinity.

Of Interest. Upstart Bay played a role in the coastal development of Queensland by providing easily entered and exited anchorage to early survey and supply ships spreading north from Sydney and, later, Brisbane. The two towns, Ayr and Home Hill directly inland from the bay are joined by a long bridge over the Burdekin River and are both sugar producing centres, Inkerman, Pioneer and Kalamia Mills going into production between 1883 and 1914. Ayr was named after the birthplace in Scotland of a Premier of Queensland, Sir Thomas McIlwraith, and was first surveyed in 1881. Home Hill, on the south side of the river, developed after the Inkerman Mill started production in 1914. The area has diversified into tobacco, cotton and vegetables.

Cape Upstart itself was named by Captain Cook for its dominance amidst alluvial land.

NOBBIES INLET. Penetrating the lowland in the south-west corner of *Upstart Bay*, this creek has useful depths at low tide for secure anchorage in all weather. Its subsidiary, *Cape Creek* is a handy cyclone hole.

Against it is the fact that the entrance is barred right across and its best channel is impossible to locate by lookout, the water being too muddy. The best approach tends to be with *Nobbies Lookout* on a bearing of about 125° magnetic. Beware of confusing a similar set of three hills on the inlet's north headland. I have called these 'False Nobbies Lookout' on the accompanying chart.

Depending on draft, use a flood tide at least three hours old and enter cautiously, favouring the south bank once over the entrance shoals. With increasing depths come better identification of the banks at which

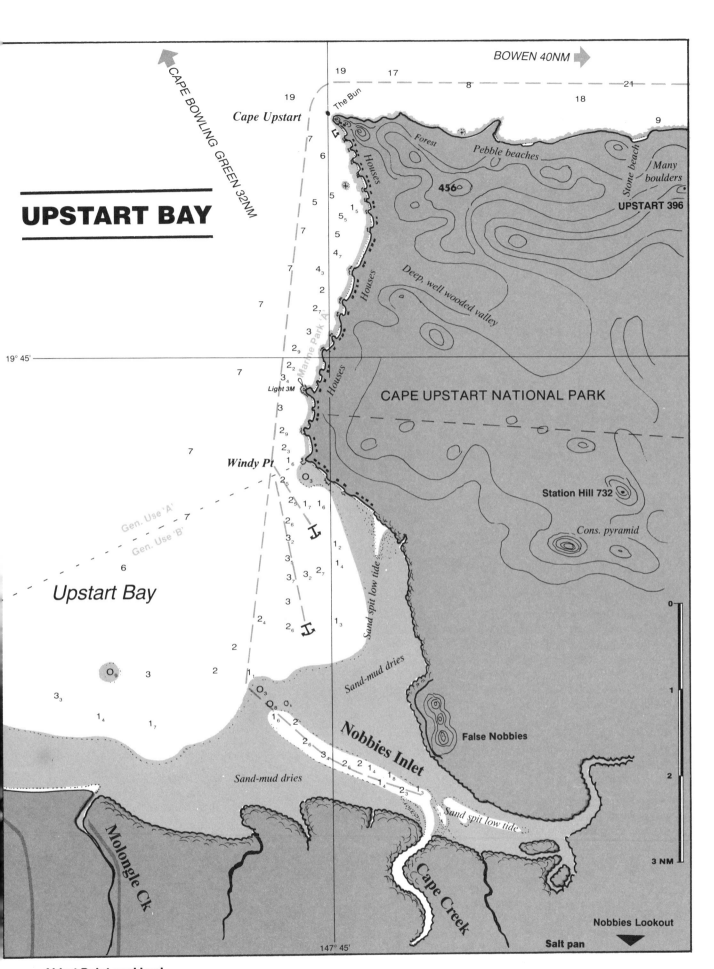

UPSTART BAY

CAPE BOWLING GREEN 32NM

CAPE BOWLING GREEN

BOWEN 40NM

19   17   8   21

19   18   9

Cape Upstart

The Bun

7

6

Forest

Pebble beaches

Stone beach

Many boulders

456

UPSTART 396

Houses

5   5   5

1₅

5₅

5

4₇

7

4₃

2

2₇

Houses

Deep, well wooded valley

2₉

19° 45'

2₂

7   3₄

Light 3M   3

2₉   Houses

CAPE UPSTART NATIONAL PARK

2₃

Windy Pt   1₆

7   2₅   O₃

2₅   1₇   1₆

Gen. Use 'A'   7   2₆

Gen. Use 'B'   3₂   1₂

Station Hill 732

3₅   1₄

Cons. pyramid

6   3₇   3₂   2₇

3

Upstart Bay   2₄   2₆   1₃

2

O₉   3   2   1₁

3₃

O₃   Sand spit low tide

1₄   1₇   O₈   O₄

1₆   2

2₆

Sand-mud dries

3₄

2₆   2   1₄

False Nobbies

Nobbies Inlet

Sand-mud dries   1₄   1₈   2₃   1₃

Sand spit low tide

0

1

2

3 NM

Molongle Ck

Cape Creek

Nobbies Lookout

Salt pan

Abbot Point coal loading facility is seen from a good distance off between Bowen and Cape Upstart. Mount Luce is behind the wharf-head with Mount Roundback, left.

177

After rounding the headland, Cape Upstart is seen in the distance to the west.

The Bun and Cape Upstart. There is fair anchorage in the first bay south of the cape.

In the mouth of Nobbies Inlet, False Nobbies Lookout is abeam with Station Hill (Cape Upstart headland), right.

As the mass of land comprising Cape Upstart headland flattens out, Nobbies Lookout, distant left, and False Nobbies Lookout, closer right, are seen. They are indicators for Nobbies Inlet.

time eyeball navigation is possible. Immediately before Cape Creek, a drying sand bank bars the inlet leaving a shoal area across Cape Creek's entrance. Further ascension of Nobbies Inlet is only possible by awaiting a near full tide to clear the bank's northern tip. It is better to anchor downstream of the bank where good swinging room and depths are available.

CAPE BOWLING GREEN. The lowest cape on the coast, Cape Bowling Green offers good anchorage between Upstart Bay and Townsville or Magnetic Island.

Approach from the south is clear of dangers and the coast from Upstart to Bowling Green is low-wooded with a continuous beach and dunes. There are no good marks ashore unless in close enough to identify creek entrances and the settlement at Lynch's Beach. The mountain range is well in the background and often indistinct under cloud or haze. Cape Upstart, however, usually stands proud regardless of haze.

At a distance of approximately 10 miles, Cape Bowling Green rises as a series of scattered dashes with a single palm tree dominating. Thereafter, a treeline takes shape outside this palm until the end of the Cape can be identified. Its open framework light tower is conspicuous.

From the north, the Cape is sighted again at about 10 miles distance at which time Cape Cleveland and Magnetic Island continue to offer good back reference. Bowling Green Bay is surrounded by low marshy land and offers no identifiable landmarks.

Anchorage is in good-holding mud in shoaling water. The degree of comfort will be dependent on state of tide and strength of wind. A windward-tide condition prevails here when the south-east setting flood current holds a vessel beam up to the south-east wind.

By tucking in as close as possible to the north-west-seeking sand spit, north-easterly wind can be well tolerated. Any further into the north and the anchorage becomes untenable. The closest northerly wind shelter to the south is Bowen and to the north, Townsville-Magnetic Island.

If long-term comfort is wanted during strong trade winds, the south-east corner of the bay can be entered after rounding drying banks extending west from Russell Island. Because of the potential for disorientation and lack of good marks, work on course and distance to clear these banks, after which, steer a course for the bottom of the bay, anchoring just before the shoals. The water is muddy in this bay confusing and often denying visual observation.

Of Interest. Offshore from Cape Bowling Green will be seen on all updated charts the notation 'Historic Wreck'. This is the *Yongala*, a 3500 ton steamer that disappeared with all hands during a cyclone in 1911. Her position and fate remained a mystery until soon

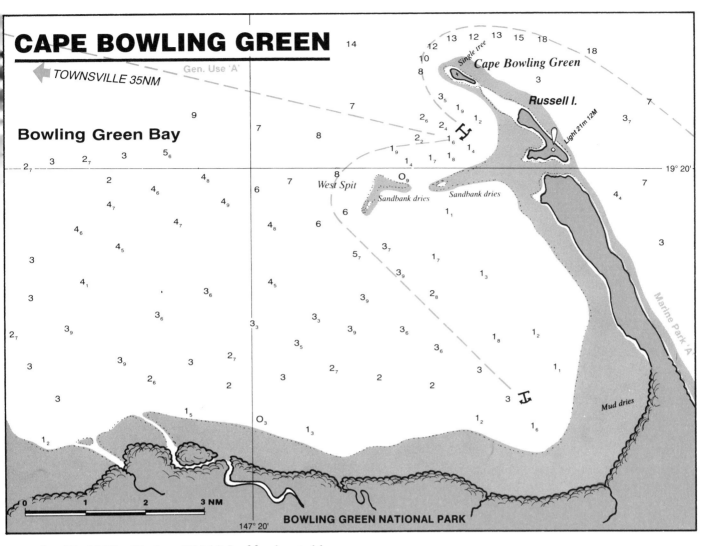

CAPE BOWLING GREEN

← TOWNSVILLE 35NM

Gen. Use 'A'

Bowling Green Bay

14

Single tree

Cape Bowling Green

Russell I.

Light 21m 12M

Marine Park 'A'

West Spit

Sandbank dries   *Sandbank dries*

19° 20'

Mud dries

0   1   2   3 NM

147° 20'

BOWLING GREEN NATIONAL PARK

after World War II when *HMAS Lachlan* located her by echo sounder. Divers found her anchor cable streamed aft suggesting it had run when being prepared for dropping anchor under the shelter of Cape Bowling Green and perhaps tripped her into the foaming sea. The, then, lighthouse keepers did mention seeing a light which, in retrospect, is confirmed as being the ill-fated ship as she was making for anchorage.

Townsville diver and businessman, Doug Tarca obtained the salvage rights but chose to have her proclaimed a National Park. As a result, she remains in surprisingly good condition within sight from the surface on a flat calm day and makes a good snorkel to those enthusiasts who can await the right weather.

Cape Bowling Green light was erected in 1874 at a time when Queensland had twenty-three lights, leaving this low, dangerous cape unmarked. Recognising its importance, a full station was constructed including keepers, houses and a 300 metre-long catwalk between the light and the settlement. This guaranteed access regardless of tide height.

Originally built too close to the sea and from then on plagued by shifting and disappearing sand, a gale in May 1908 undermined its foundations so greatly that it had to be supported with stays until it could be bodily moved back. In fact, it was dismantled and re-erected next to the houses where it has remained ever since. The houses have long since gone after automation.

Described on page 184, Townsville is a day's sail west from Cape Bowling Green. It is best known for its landmark, Castle Hill.

179

Cape Cleveland approaching from the east.

Cape Cleveland from the north. Twenty Foot Rock is to the left of the land.

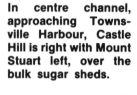

In centre channel, approaching Townsville Harbour, Castle Hill is right with Mount Stuart left, over the bulk sugar sheds.

Further up-channel, Townsville Harbour is about to be entered. The casino is arrowed and the sugar sheds, left, are obvious.

The City of Townsville is built along the western bank of Ross Creek. Built in the early 1970's, the 'pepper pot', centre, is a conspicuous landmark but is slowly disappearing behind other highrise.

180

The Townsville entertainment centre is situated on the western breakwater near the casino.

Townsville has many lovely old buildings including Customs House extreme right. This building is occupied by Television North Queensland Channel 7 (TQN7).

Landmark Under Threat

Castle Hill, the 285 metre high granite plug dominating Townsville's landscape, is to have a hotel, restaurant, office block and residential development all serviced by a cable car if its provisional heritage listing is ignored.

The development is to be known as 'Panorama' and will be built by the Hong Kong-based company, AIS Investments. Townsville Council, which approved the project in June 1991, opposes heritage listing despite strong and enduring community attachment for Castle Hill exactly as it is.

CAPE CLEVELAND

Cape Cleveland Light WR 64 m 26–21 M

Salamander Reef

Red Sector

Four Foot Rk.

Twenty Foot Rk.

Red Rock Bay
Red Rock Pt

Gen. Use 'A'

Long Beach

White Rock Bay

Paradise Bay

Bray It.

Bare It.
C. Woora

Launs Beach

557
Mt Cleveland

TICKLEBELLY

Bald It.
Cape Ferguson

Scientific Research
Chunda Bay

MAGNETIC I. 8 NM

0   0.5   1 NM

Townsville's first hotel, built in 1865, is still in business, now orientated towards discotheque.

CAPE CLEVELAND. Being just 11 miles out of Townsville and an easy sail from Cape Bowling Green, most folk stand on for port rather than stop here en route. However, if late arrival in Townsville doesn't appeal, then Cape Cleveland provides anchorage suitable for a night's sleep before pressing on.

In developed trade winds, a swell persists around the cape, attacking an anchored vessel beam-on. This is exacerbated by the need to remain well offshore in deep water. However, by moving in as close as draft allows, fair comfort can be found.

The major light on Cape Cleveland was erected in 1879, along with its associated dwellings. All were prefabricated in Brisbane. It was a manned station until 1988 when, like so many such stations, the light was automated.

When approaching the cape from the east, beware the offshore rocks, all except Salamander Reef being fully exposed at high water springs. *Salamander Reef* dries 0.6 metres and usually breaks even during mild conditions. It is fanned by a red sector of Cape Cleveland light.

Ticklebelly Harbour is a small breakwater enclosure under *Cape Ferguson* 6 miles south-east of Cape Cleveland. It is not public and may not be entered by private craft. Operated by AIMS (Australian Institute of Marine Science,) it is a research facility to improve our knowledge of sealife, mangrove growth and corals. Its activities extend as far as the Fly River in Papua New Guinea.

Cape Cleveland is the eastern headland to Cleveland Bay and the gateway to Townsville from the south. Magnetic Island and Townsville follow over the page.

MAGNETIC ISLAND. Shown opposite, Magnetic Island lies off the City of Townsville and forms the western side of Cleveland Bay. 5,184 hectares in area — of which more than half is National Park — it is a suburb of Townsville as much as it is a tourist island. With a population of around 2000, it receives well over 100,000 visitors a year who are catered for in a number of hotels and resorts. Two ferry companies service the island along with a vehicular ferry and water taxis.

Separating Magnetic Island from the mainland at Cape Pallarenda is *West Channel*, a navigable strait for small boats approaching Townsville from the north. Off the eastern side of the island is the entrance to *Sea Channel*, a dredged and beaconed alleyway to Townsville Harbour for ships of excessive draft. These approaches are dealt with in the separate Townsville description following this.

The various bays are described separately here. It need only be emphasised that very few promise comfort in any developed wind and only Nelly Bay Marina promises all-weather security.

Picnic Bay is Magnetic Island's main ferry destination and, as such, is very busy. The anchorage is tight with moorings and is further limited by the ferrys' swing basin. If space permits, the best position is to the west of the jetty towards the swimming enclosure (which is removed in winter).

Picnic Bay is no place to be during developed winds from east to south-east and in general should be considered a temporary anchorage only.

Ashore there are shops, hotel, golf course and buses connecting other destinations on the island.

Nelly Bay is being developed as a marina and commercial boat harbour. Owing to a shortage of funds, it lay dormant in a less than half finished state in 1993. It was to be called *Magnetic Quays*, but this may change with new ownership should its development be restarted. When completed it will offer the only such haven on the island.

Nelly Bay, meanwhile, has shops and a resort hotel.

Florence Bay. Strictly for calm weather only, this bay has a delightful beach making for a pleasant place to swim. There is no development here, the bay being designated a Marine National Park.

Horseshoe Bay is the island's best refuge during developed trade winds. Despite constant swell invasion, it is tolerably comfortable depending on how far the south-east corner can be penetrated. Shark nets and moored craft occupy much of the area.

Close to the launching ramp is a boat hire, a few tourist orientated shops, a public phone and post box. The nearest post office is at Arcadia, near Alma Bay. A bus stop is nearby.

In the south-east corner of Horseshoe Bay is a yellow buoy marking the wreck of the *Argonaut*, a three masted schooner later used as a floating restaurant. She burnt and sank here, most of her remains being salvaged by authorities in the late 1970s.

Five Beaches Bay is a part of the national park and, as such, promises seclusion. However, it is only suitable to calm weather, an easterly swell moving along this part of the island with considerable weight at times. If tucking into *Maud Bay* against a light trade wind, beware the isolated coral heads along the fringing reef.

Young Bay is one of two bays close to *West Point*. Shoaling ground demands a fair offing when dropping anchor but, surprisingly, this does not matter much during northerly winds. A useful wind shadow continues a considerable distance offshore. It is untenable in winds north-west through south to south-east, although not much of a sea accompanies winds off the mainland.

The marina on Magnetic Island at Nelly Bay is to be known as Magnetic Quays. At the time of going to press (late 1993) development remained stalled. Horseshoe Bay is the best anchorage during developed south easterly winds.

Bay Rock

One of the coast's earliest light stations, Bay Rock was originally manned by one keeper. In 1902 when lightkeeper, Gordon, disappeared without trace, his widow and children carried out his duties for months until a replacement keeper arrived. According to an aboriginal friend of the author's, Bay Rock was a favourite stopping place for dugout canoes en route to Townsville from Palm Island.

West Point, Magnetic Island, as it appears when Bay Rock is abeam to starboard, approaching West Channel from the north.

Bay Rock supports a light indicating the fairway into West Channel, between Magnetic Island and the mainland from the north.

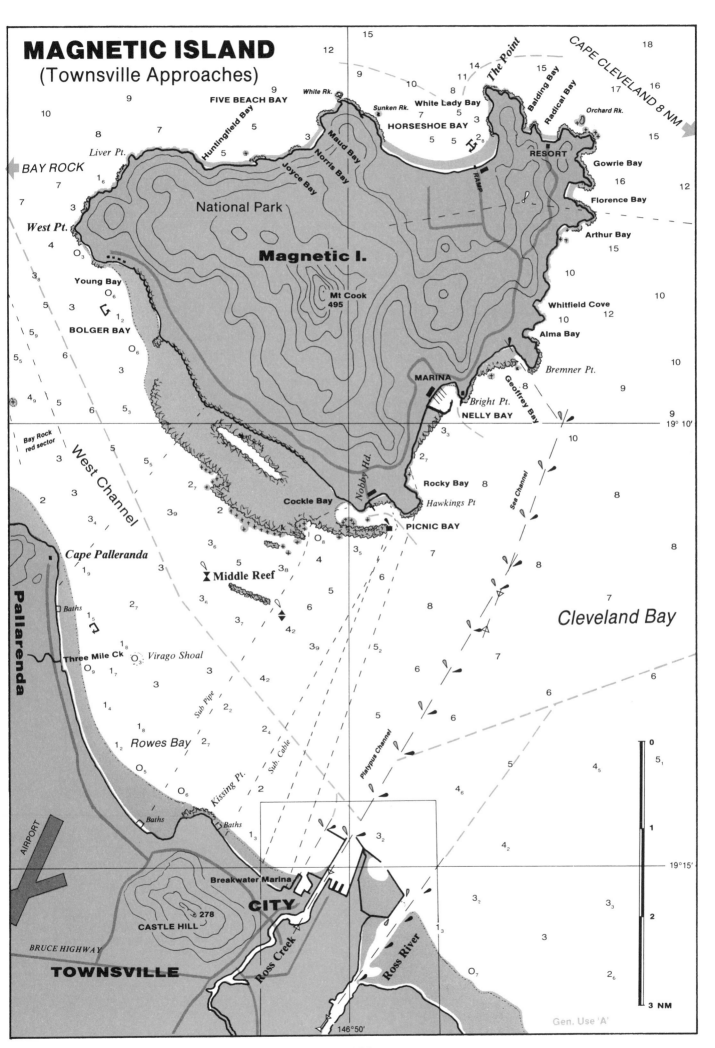

MAGNETIC ISLAND
(Townsville Approaches)

CAPE CLEVELAND 8 NM

The Point

Balding Bay

Radical Bay

White Lady Bay

HORSESHOE BAY

RESORT

Orchard Rk.

Gowrie Bay

Florence Bay

Arthur Bay

Whitfield Cove

Alma Bay

FIVE BEACH BAY

White Rk.

Sunken Rk.

Huntingfield Bay

Maud Bay

Norris Bay

Joyce Bay

Liver Pt.

BAY ROCK

National Park

Magnetic I.

Mt Cook
495

West Pt.

Young Bay

BOLGER BAY

Bay Rock
red sector

West Channel

Cape Palleranda

Baths

Three Mile Ck

Virago Shoal

Sub. Pipe

Rowes Bay

Pallarenda

Middle Reef

Cockle Bay

Nobby Hd.

Hawkings Pt

PICNIC BAY

Rocky Bay

MARINA

Bright Pt.

NELLY BAY

Geoffrey Bay

Bremner Pt.

Sea Channel

Cleveland Bay

Platypus Channel

Sub. Cable

Kissing Pt.

Baths

Baths

AIRPORT

CASTLE HILL

278

BRUCE HIGHWAY

TOWNSVILLE

Breakwater Marina

CITY

Ross Creek

Ross River

19° 10'

19°15'

146°50'

Gen. Use 'A'

0

1

2

3 NM

183

TOWNSVILLE. Lying a little over half-way between Brisbane and Thursday Island and offering every conceivable facility to the boat person, Townsville is Australia's largest tropical city. It is in the south-west corner of Cleveland Bay, easily within sight of Magnetic Island. The city is on the north bank of Ross Creek whilst the southern suburbs are between Ross Creek and Ross River. There is no way of remaining in Townsville without paying either marina or public mooring fees as noted later.

Approach. From the south and east, *Cape Cleveland* is dominant and can be taken close aboard subject to its off-lying rocks as noted previously under the heading 'Cape Cleveland'. Once around the cape, the position of Townsville is marked by *Castle Hill* and the roof of the sugar shed to its left. *Cape Pallarenda* appears to the right as an 'island' kissing *Magnetic Island.*

Unless anxious to orientate oneself properly after dark, the average small craft can safely cut straight across Cleveland Bay direct from Cape Cleveland to Townsville using Castle Hill as a steering mark. This course enters the main harbour approach channel (Platypus Channel) well down towards the harbour mouth where minimum surrounding depths of 3 metres low water springs will be encountered. The channel itself is dredged to 10.7 metres.

From the north, presumably from Great Palm or Hinchinbrook Channel, a direct course for *West Channel* (between Cape Pallarenda and Magnetic Island) may be steered with due regard to the islands en route. *Rattlesnake Island* makes a good mark from a distance of up to 20 miles and when held under *Mount Stuart* provides a good transit to ensure safe passage past *Pandora Reef.*

Because this direct route passes through the *Halifax Bay bombing exercise area*, the navigator should check with Townsville Radio as to whether it is activated or not. For further details see 'Halifax Bay'.

When the area is activated and all craft are obliged to hold east of the range, Castle Hill proves a good mark which, when held over West Point (Magnetic Island) holds you outside the danger area. From the north, Castle Hill is twin peaked.

West Channel can be safely entered after dark allowing for confusion when certain navigation lights merge with each other and background city lights. In particular, *Middle Reef* lights can prove difficult to separate from Platypus Channel lights but they do become obvious in time to avoid disorientation and once separated prove useful reference should anchorage until dawn be chosen instead of a night-time entry into Townsville.

Night or day, vessels bound for Breakwater Marina should use the conspicuous Sheraton Hotel-Casino building as a reference mark.

Anchorage. With marinas or pile berths occupying every available space in both Ross Creek (city centre) and Ross River (southern suburbs), anchorage is impossible in any long term sense. The only place where the anchor may be dropped prior to choosing a berth is under the lee of the breakwater outside Breakwater Marina. This is quite snug, but is in shoaling water which limits draft. Under no circumstances should the vessel be allowed to encroach on the marina approach channel. Access ashore from this anchorage is thoroughly inconvenient and sometimes impossible, making it a temporary measure only.

The following lists the commercial options in Townsville.

Port Authority Berths in the form of fore and aft piles are available to casuals in Ross River. They are rarely available in Ross Creek, these being fully occupied by permanents. To use a berth in the river, secure to an empty berth and report ashore to the office on the trawler wharf immediately north of Ross Haven Marine. Showers and toilets are located here and a dinghy access pontoon is in the south corner of the trawler wharf.

Breakwater Marina is under the lee of a reclamation area on which is established the Sheraton Hotel Casino. It is approached outside the western side of the main harbour, entering its channel between port and starboard beacons. Leading beacons assist, these being fixed white light by day and blue by night.

A berth may be booked ahead by VHF or by going alongside the fuel berth or where otherwise directed immediately after entering the harbour.

All berths are pontoon type with lock-up access to common ground around the main building. There is a straddle-lift to 30 tonnes, brokerage, fuel, ablution block, repairs, chandlery, laundry, power and water to each berth and it is a short walk into the city. The floating piers are A through to E from north to south.

Townsville Motor Boat Club. Situated in Ross Creek in the heart of the city, this club has a floating marina with casual berths. Generally speaking, casual berths are on the outside towards the western extreme, but any berth may be allocated. Book ahead on VHF or go direct to the fuel berth for information. Be prepared for some very tight manoeuvering into and out of the fuel berth.

All facilities of the club are granted a visitor whilst boat support industries are ranged close by. These include chandlery, chart agent and repairs.

Further berthing information is noted under the heading *Ross River* on page 186.

Townsville Facilities are typical of a city, offering all services. Apart from city and suburban shopping malls, these include chandleries, repairs in all materials, electronics, mechanical engineering and fabrication and rigging. Straddle lifts of 30 and 60 tonnes are at Breakwater Marina and Ross Haven Marine respectively and alongside fuel is available in all centres. Public landings are scattered throughout, all with a 30 minute limit.

Customs. Townsville is a full customs clearance port. Incoming foreign vessels should radio at least 3 hours ahead.

Of Interest. Townsville was named after Robert Towns

> **Townsville offers three main venues to the small boat: These are *Breakwater Marina*, *Ross Creek* and *Ross River*. The only place where public pile berths are easily available is in Ross River from where it is a two kilometre walk into the city.**

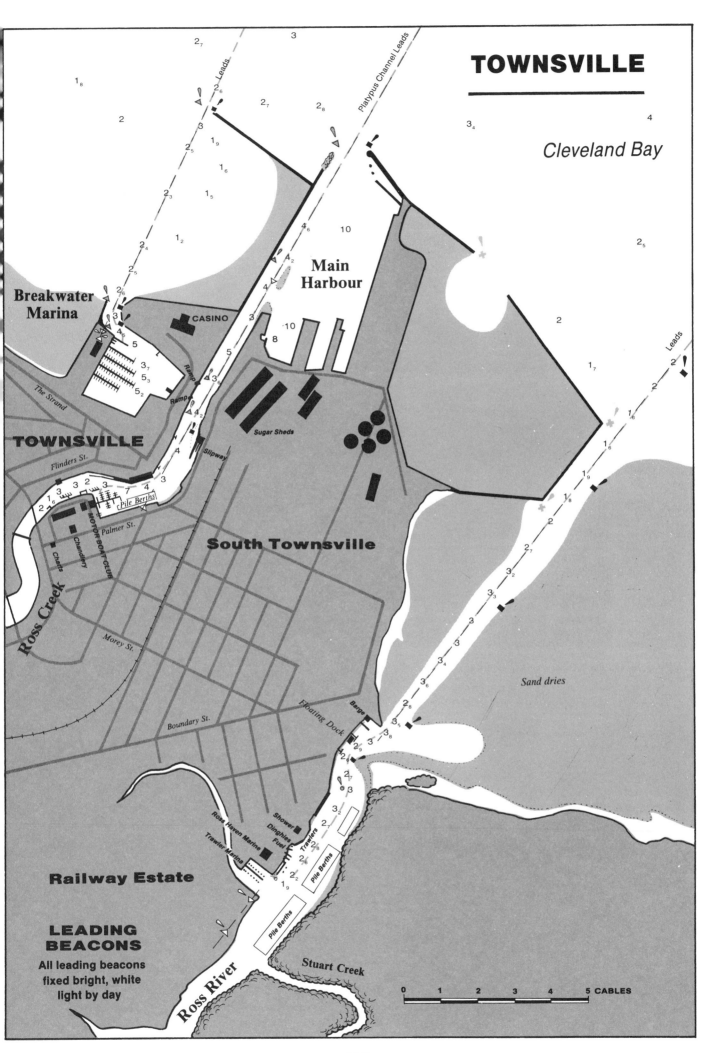

TOWNSVILLE

Cleveland Bay

Main Harbour

Breakwater Marina

CASINO

TOWNSVILLE

The Strand

Flinders St.

Sugar Sheds

Pile Berths

MOTOR BOAT CLUB

Chandlery

Charts

Palmer St.

South Townsville

Ross Creek

Morey St.

Boundary St.

Ramp

Ramp

Slipway

Floating Dock

Barge

Sand dries

Leads

Platypus Channel Leads

Leads

Shower

Dinghies

Fuel

Ross Haven Marine

Trawler Marina

Trawlers

Pile Berths

Railway Estate

LEADING BEACONS

All leading beacons fixed bright, white light by day

Pile Berths

Pile Berths

Stuart Creek

Ross River

who reluctantly approved of the area as a site for his cattle boiling-down works in the mid 1800s. Situated on the banks of the Ross River, nearby Ross Creek blossomed as a place of settlement and expansion until it became Queensland's largest northern city and once the intended capital for a new state that never eventuated.

From the mouth of Ross Creek, a breakwater harbour was built capable of handling the largest merchant ship of the period. Regular dredging and expansion has kept it in line with ship development. Ross Creek itself became choked with private craft, charter boats and fishing vessels, the former being relegated to pile berths, the latter enjoying alongside facilities where today will be found Great Barrier Reef Wonderworld. Now the creek caters only to private and charter vessels, all fishing boats being relocated to Ross River.

Townsville is the main outlet for inland Mount Isa Mines and Greenvale Nickel to the north, and since the 1950s has been a major bulk sugar exporter. Now it has added a number of attractions aimed at increasing tourism. These include the living corals of Reef Wonderland and the casino.

The outer entrance to Breakwater Marina is between a wall-end and a beacon. The casino is arrowed.

This is the last port-hand beacon when entering Ross River. Facilities are along the starboard bank with pile-berths to port. Mount Stuart is in the background.

Down like dominoes

During the height of cyclone Althea which hit Townsville Christmas Eve, 1971, the Harbour Board dredge broke adrift and was swept up Ross Creek taking many boats with it. The first hit was the then VIP-tug, *Joyce Hiley* which fetched ashore in the corner of the yacht basin next to the Motor Boat Club. The dredge, meanwhile, smashed through the fleet of fishing and recreational craft on pile berths (no marina then) sinking two yachts and badly damaging another. Although low tide at the time, the storm surge plus flood rains, had surrounding shores under a metre of water carrying smaller boats onto parks. One dory ended up on the verandah of a nearby hotel. Many boats managing to remain secure to the pile berths smashed their transoms or counters on the top of the just-exposed piles.

The author's yacht, *Renee Tighe* alongside at Ross Haven Marine, Ross River, Townsville.

ROSS RIVER. Located immediately east of Townsville's main harbour, Ross River caters for private craft and the fishing industry.

Approach is via a long, straight channel dredged to 2.4 metres low water springs. Its entrance and fairway beacon is found just outside the line of the main harbour eastern extension. Four port-hand red beacons (lit) indicate the channel and leading beacons displaying a steady white light during the day and fixed red at night further assist. These can be difficult to find until committed to the channel.

Upon entering the river mouth proper, an inner red beacon is passed to port then a green buoy is passed to starboard after making a course alteration to port around the red beacon.

Anchoring is not allowed in the developed part of the Ross River, the only possibility being upstream of the pile berths. This is subject to draft and need for facility access.

Pile Berths are available to casuals and can be applied for by taking an empty berth then reporting to the officer on the trawler wharf.

Marinas. Trawlers are well catered for in this respect, there being the above-noted trawler wharf, a marina at a creek entrance and, between the two, the floating pontoon of Ross Haven Marine. The latter is available to private craft if not packed with trawlers, the latter enjoying preference.

Facilities in Ross River include a floating dock, straddle lift, chandlery, general store and hotel nearby, and an easy walk into the city. For pile berth patrons there is a dinghy pontoon (always crowded), showers and toilets.

186

Sand cays on the edge of a coral reef can make delightful swimming venues. This one is off the Cairns region.

Mary River Marina, Maryborough. Most river cities offer good facilities at prices lower than those on the coast.

Looking back, this is a scene from the film *Age of Consent* on the wharf at Dunk Island, 1968. The late James Mason is wearing a hat.

One of *Endeavour*'s cannons being swung aboard after their salvage in 1969. Captain Cook dumped six cannons along with a lot of ballast to escape his grounding on Endeavour Reef, south of Cooktown.

Following the reinstated cane tram tracks between Mossman and Port Douglas is the 'Bally Hooley', seen here departing Marina Mirage, Port Douglas. It is a great hit with tourists.

Riding the thermals off the coast between Cairns and Port Douglas.

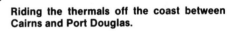

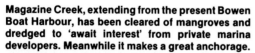

Because of its shallow and often uncertain bar, the Daintree River is seldom visited by cruising boats. Beyond the vehicular ferry, its depths are such that multi-hulls come into their own.

Since the tourism boom of the 1980's, the Great Barrier Reef has been bombarded with visitors, many of them taking advantage of the high speed cats operating out of Port Douglas.

Magazine Creek, extending from the present Bowen Boat Harbour, has been cleared of mangroves and dredged to 'await interest' from private marina developers. Meanwhile it makes a great anchorage.

Gladstone is a favourite place to careen, its grid on the end of the O'Connell Wharf and ample tide range proving ideal for the operation.

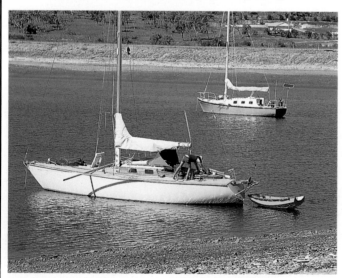

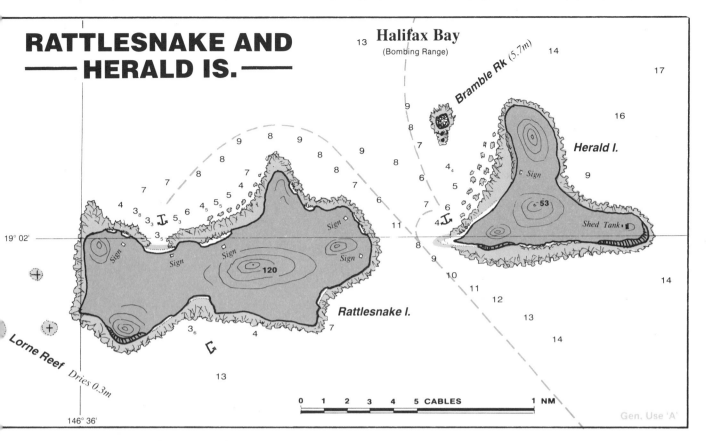

CAPE PALLARENDA is an up-market suburb of Townsville with a general store, public phone, post box and garage with petrol close to the baths. More serious shopping is best to the south at Rowes Bay.

Anchorage is excellent in grey mud but is only suitable in calm conditions or light offshore winds. On the cape is a radar station on which is a fixed light whilst around the headland showing to the north is a conspicuous boulder high on the hill.

ROWES BAY. For last minute shopping, or in trying to avoid stopping in Townsville itself, Rowes Bay is an option there being a very complete shopping centre close to the water near the baths. The shoals are more extensive here and, although tolerable in moderate winds, there is little peace of mind. It is best used in suitable weather and at all times beware of the submarine cables and pipe in the vicinity.

As a matter of interest, I was tug skipper on the pipeline job in 1970, helping to lay it from Rowes Bay to Picnic Bay. About a year later, cyclone *Althea* so completely destroyed the line that to this day, 13,000 feet have never been accounted for. It was a lesson in the sub-surface power of a destructive wind.

HALIFAX BAY BOMBING RANGE. This area is clearly defined on chart *Aus. 827 Cape Bowling Green to Palm Isles*. It triangulates around *Rattlesnake* and *Herald Islands* and includes *Acheron Island* and *Cordelia Rocks*. Under no circumstances may it be encroached upon during air force practice owing to the use of live missiles and bombs. The game gets

serious as witnessed by the fatal crash of a fighter-bomber into Great Palm late 1987.

Activation of the range can be discovered through *Notice to Mariners* or, more easily, by calling Townsville Radio on VHF 16 when close to the area. If activated, sail around the restricted zone and do not be tempted to watch the planes through binoculars as their laser aiming devices can cause eye damage.

When sailing outside the restricted area and anxious not to lose too much ground, there are two natural transits that can prove useful. These are; *West Point* (Magnetic Island) under *Castle Hill* to clear the east extreme, and the highest hill on the south end of *Orpheus Island* slightly closed over the south-west headland of *Great Palm Island* to clear the north-east corner of the range.

RATTLESNAKE AND HERALD ISLAND. A favourite with working trawlers as a daylight anchorage, these two islands lie 17 miles north-west of Townsville. They are almost in the exact centre of the *Halifax Bay Bombing Exercise Area*.

A mixture of grass and scrub, the highest island, Rattlesnake, is the dominant mass on approach whilst Herald is seen as two mounds of similar size with a low saddle between.

The sand spit off the western tip of Herald Island gives good shore access and it can be anchored off either side according to wind direction. It is a light weather anchorage only, however.

During trade winds, the anchorage under the lee of Rattlesnake Island is snug but swell-prone whilst the bottom demands some care when setting the anchor.

Approaching Rattlesnake (left) and Herald (right). They bear about north-west, distance three miles. The two peaks of Havannah Island can be seen, distant right.

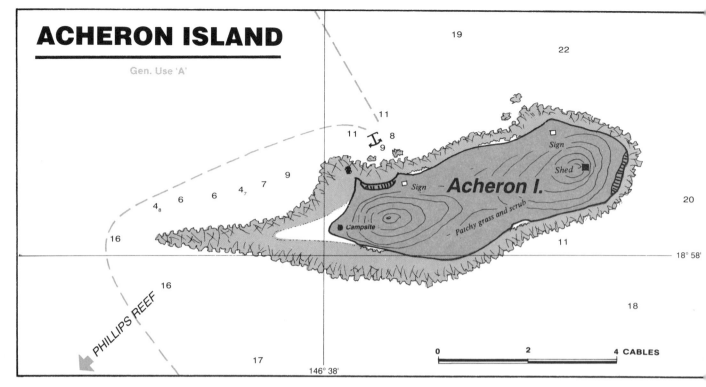

ACHERON ISLAND

Gen. Use 'A'

PHILLIPS REEF

Acheron I.

Patchy grass and scrub

Sign

Shed

Sign

Campsite

0   2   4 CABLES

ACHERON ISLAND. 12 miles north-west of Magnetic Island and giving only light weather anchorage, Acheron Island is within the *Halifax Bay Bombing Range* as described above. From a distance it appears as a long, fairly low island having equal height hills at each end and a low saddle between. There is a shed on the eastern hill top and warning signs around the foreshore. The sand spit is a delightful landing, and anchorage is in deep water over sand and scattered coral.

HAVANNAH ISLAND. Part of the *Palm Isles*, Havannah is 30 miles north-west of Townsville. Its two pyramid peaks are a dominant landmark of the area, showing well when approaching from up or down the coast. Anchorage is suitable only in calm conditions and is best off the delightful sand spit projecting from its north-west tip.

PALM ISLES. Lying off the coast at the northern end of Halifax Bay and including some six major and eight minor islands, Palm Isles provide interesting cruising. Because many are controlled by the *Aboriginal Council* on Great Palm Island, permission should be sought before going ashore on Great Palm and its immediate neighbours.

The best trade wind anchorages within the group are in *Casement Bay* (Great Palm) and *Little Pioneer Bay* (Orpheus). The islands are described individually here with many anchorages shown in large scale on the accompanying charts.

Great Palm Island is inhabited by an aboriginal community in Casement Bay. Regrettably, crime has become rampant here and it cannot be recommended to the visitor. However, if services are required, a supermarket, liquor store, post office and fuel store are publicly available.

Casement Bay gives good shelter during onshore winds, the best place being tucked up against the reef in its southeast corner. Regular Townsville flights can prove noisy, but not to the extent of distraction.

Towards the north of this bay, an all-tide, dredged channel gives access to the jetty through the fringing reef. This is not available to visitors without permission.

Coolgaree Bay is comfortable with the wind in the east. The creek here is useful as a cyclone hole, but demands a high tide to clear the extensive banks and fringing reef. Beware of offlying gonkers along the fringing reef.

North East Bay. Despite the inevitable swell running into this bay in all but the calmest weather, anchorage here is recommended to those wanting a reef-free swim

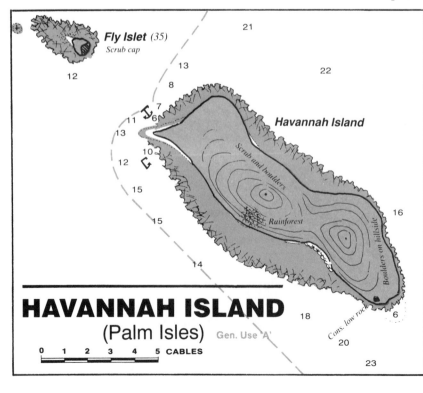

Fly Islet (35)
Scrub cap

Havannah Island

Scrub and boulders

Rainforest

Boulders on hillside

Cons. low rock

HAVANNAH ISLAND

(Palm Isles) Gen. Use 'A'

0   1   2   3   4   5 CABLES

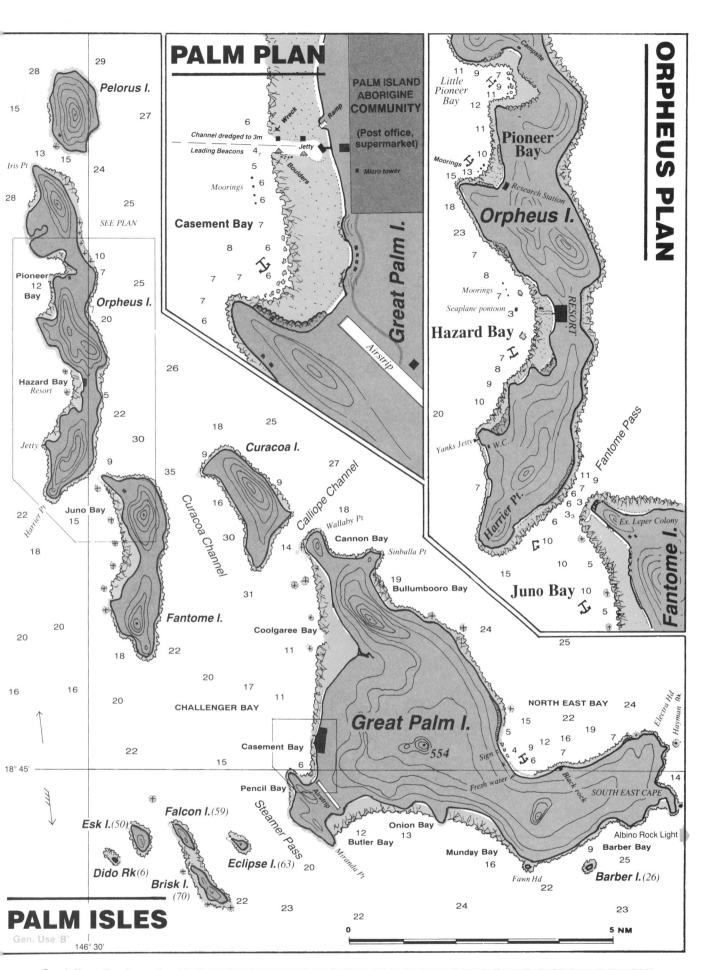

PALM PLAN

28   29

Pelorus I.

15   27

13   24

15   15

Iris Pt

28   25

SEE PLAN

Pioneer
12   Bay
7   25

Orpheus I.

20   7

Hazard Bay
Resort   5   22

Jetty   30

9   35

22   15   *Juno Bay*

18

PALM ISLAND
ABORIGINE
COMMUNITY
(Post office,
supermarket)

■ *Micro tower*

Wreck   Ramp
Channel dredged to 3m   6   Jetty
Leading Beacons   4 7
Moorings   5
6
6
6

Casement Bay   7

8   6

7   7   6

7

6

26

18   25

9   *Curacoa I.*   27

9   9

16   18
Wallaby Pt

30   14   Cannon Bay
Sinballa Pt

31   19   Bullumbooro Bay

Fantome I.   Coolgaree Bay

18   22

20

17
11
CHALLENGER BAY

Casement Bay

6
Pencil Bay
Airstrip

11   *Juno Bay*   *Fantome I.*

11
9   Little
7 9   Pioneer
11   Bay
12

11   *Pioneer
Bay*

10   *Orpheus I.*

Moorings   13
15

18

23   7

8
Moorings

Seaplane pontoon   3   RESORT

Hazard Bay

7
8
9

10

20

Yanks Jetty W.C.

7   *Harrier Pt.*

15

11   9   *Fantome Pass*
6 3
6 3 3
6   *Ex. Leper Colony*
10
5
10
Juno Bay   10
25   5

Great Palm I.

Great Palm I.   554

NORTH EAST BAY   24

15   22   19
12   16   *Electra Hd*
4   7   7   *Hayman Pt*
6

Fresh water   *Black rock*   SOUTH EAST CAPE

18° 45'   15   6   14

Albino Rock Light
12   Onion Bay   13
Butler Bay   9   Barber Bay
Eclipse I.(63) 20   Munday Bay   25
16   *Barber I.(26)*
Fawn Hd   22

Falcon I.(59)

Esk I.(50)   Steamer Pass

Dido Rk(6)   *Miranda Pt*

Brisk I.
(70)   22   23   22   24   23

16   16

20   20

20

22

PALM ISLES
Gen. Use 'B'
146° 30'

0   5 NM

Cordelia Rocks, 3
miles south-east of
Acheron Island, are
encountered en route
to the Palm Isles from
Townsville.

189

Havannah Island from the south. Its twin peaks are landmarks in the Halifax Bay region.

The sandspit off the north-west tip of Havannah Island makes a good fair weather landing. Fly Islet is left.

Looking north along the west coast of Great Palm Island. The smoke is from the Aboriginal settlement.

The settlement at Great Palm Island is in Casement Bay. Its jetty, centre, has a dredged approach channel.

Looking north-east at Fantome Channel with Orpheus Island left and Fantome Island, right.

Looking along the west coast of Orpheus Island.

Orpheus Island resort in Hazard Bay.

Looking Back

Cyclone Althea

During Christmas Eve, 1971, cyclone *Althea* hit the Palm Isles on its way to Townsville. The cargo vessel, *Cannon Bay*, unable to escape the (then) tidal wharf after unloading, was driven ashore by wind and tidal surge. Of all the island's vessels, she was the only one salvaged but was soon after retired in favour of private charter. The author was skipper at the time.

ashore. Conditions are ideal with a shelving beach in the south-west corner and a freshwater creek nearby. According to one reader, an isolated coral head exists in the vicinity of the black rock.

Northerly anchorages are along the south side of Great Palm in depths of around 12 metres.

CURACOA ISLAND

CURACOA ISLAND has a small sand spit on its north-west corner where a pleasant picnic stop is possible, otherwise depths and exposure are too great for comfort during any developed wind.

FALCON ISLAND

FALCON ISLAND and its neighbours off the south-west tip of Great Palm Island offer a great diversity of anchorages, but none should be considered during moderate to strong winds. A good north-east anchorage can be found midway along the western side of the common reef of *Brisk* and *Falcon Islands*.

FANTOME ISLAND

FANTOME ISLAND once supported a leper colony, the author being involved in its transfer to Great Palm Island Hospital in the early 1970s. Remains of the settlement will be found on the island's north-west tip, to the south of which is the best anchorage in *Juno Bay*.

One of the area's best northerly anchorages is against Orpheus Island in Juno Bay.

Fantome Channel. Good low tide depths prevail throughout this reef-bottomed passage, but the possible existence of a shallower than charted coral patch recommends it to rising tide and calm weather use only.

ORPHEUS ISLAND

ORPHEUS ISLAND is a national park with picnic facilities and pontoon landing a mile north of Harrier Point. This landing is known as *Yanks Jetty* and is on the site of a ship degaussing station built during World War II. Although public, it is also used by a local tourist vessel.

Hazard Bay provides good anchorage where shown in large scale taking care to stand outside offlying coral patches beyond the main fringing reef. Do not anchor near the resort's moorings and especially its float plane pontoon. The resort is strictly out of bounds to non-guests.

Threatened with extinction after the illegal fishing activities of Asian fishermen, the giant clam was farmed at Orpheus Island in an attempt to boost its numbers. So successful was the experiment that the Australian Navy was called in to help move the shells to other locations.

Pioneer Bay is occupied by a number of moorings relating to the *James Cook University Research Station.* Anchorage outside them is secure and comfortable, but is in deep water. The research station is on an old fishing lease owned by Roger and Fran Dyasson who fished from Orpheus for seventeen years.

Little Pioneer Bay. When lack of demand allows first choice of position, this anchorage can be one of the best in the Palm Isles. Tuck in as far as fragmented fringing reef allows.

Ashore are national park facilities, and up the hill are the ruins of past attempts to settle this bay. One relic is of a house built of coral rock by an oyster lessee who abandoned it after suffering infectious cuts; the other of a sheep station homestead. Heavy stock losses sent it into rapid decline.

PELORUS ISLAND

PELORUS ISLAND. Owing to the great depths and steep-to nature of this reef fringed island, anchorage around Pelorus is difficult. It should be saved for fair weather and an inclination to go snorkelling. There is a private house on the south-west corner.

Dungeness is a small settlement near the mouth of the Herbert River. There are good depths inside but a shallow bar must be negotiated when entering. It is described on page 195.

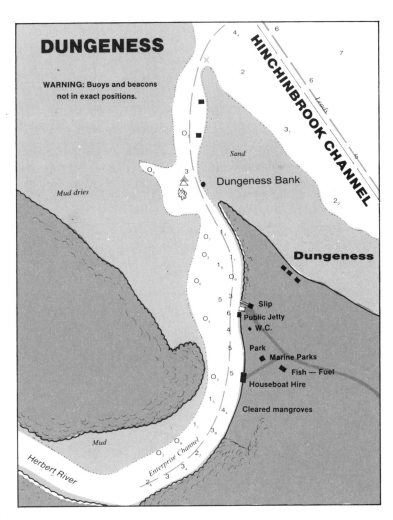

The imposing mountains of Hinchinbrook Island make a splendid backdrop to the many anchorages in Hinchinbrook Channel, the description of which starts over the page.

HINCHINBROOK CHANNEL is the most scenic, calm waterway on the east coast of Australia having the spectacular peaks of Hinchinbrook Island to the east and the rugged Cardwell Range to the west. There are vast areas of wetlands which create a maze of secondary channels and creeks as well as dry land where shore access is possible. The island is a national park with the only inhabited section being the tip of *Cape Richards* where a small tourist resort operates (see separate description later).

The sugar-port town of *Lucinda* is situated on the mainland at the channel's southern entrance while the town of *Cardwell* is at the north extreme, the distance between the two, by water, being close to 26 miles. Calm, secure anchorages are guaranteed if the visitor is willing to risk mosquito attack and anchor in one of the creeks. Otherwise, the channel itself is free of swell but prone to windward-tide chop depending on exact position of the chosen anchorage, rate of tide and strength and direction of wind.

Depths. Molasses tankers drawing as much as 6 metres navigate the length of the channel from the north to load molasses at Lucinda's inner wharf. They cannot cross the barred southern entrance which carries less than 2 metres at low water springs. They can, however, use the northern entrance with sufficient tide. In other words, there is ample depth for the average keeler which, unlike its commercial sisters, can enter Hinchinbrook Channel from the south.

Southern approach. From a distance of 11 miles the sugar sheds of Lucinda and the tower on the end of the bulk sugar conveyor wharf projecting 3 miles east from Lucinda can be seen. The tower is an ideal ref-

erence point for its proximity to the final approach to the shoals across the southern entrance. Six cables north of the tower is the fairway buoy and immediately beyond it the leading beacons come into line. Regrettably, these beacons cannot be seen from this distance, even through binoculars if the weather is inclement, obliging one to steer for the southern end of the sugar sheds until the leads are found.

In fact, with a flood tide building depth over the shoals, there is no need to fuss too much about the entrance leads because they actually take a boat over a shallow tongue with less depth than that available to its south. It can thus pay to open the leads south and this is achieved by rounding the fairway buoy close to port and steering for the sheds as stated.

The leads, when sighted, are as illustrated, the front lead being painted on the conveyor wharf, the back lead on a tower on Lucinda Point. When the front lead is brought up close, the conveyor wharf is paralleled towards the end of the molasses wharf. The first buoy encountered before this wharf is *red* and is passed to *starboard*. This sets the pattern for the entire passage through the channel, all reds being passed to starboard and greens to port.

Northern approach is typically from the Family Islands, Dunk Island in particular, which lies 18 miles north of the channel.

The north entrance of Hinchinbrook Channel can be identified from Dunk Island by the high land of Hinchinbrook Island obviously overlapping background mainland mountains. Where they 'V' down is a fair initial reference point. In fact, as the distance shortens, the true entrance to the channel is to the

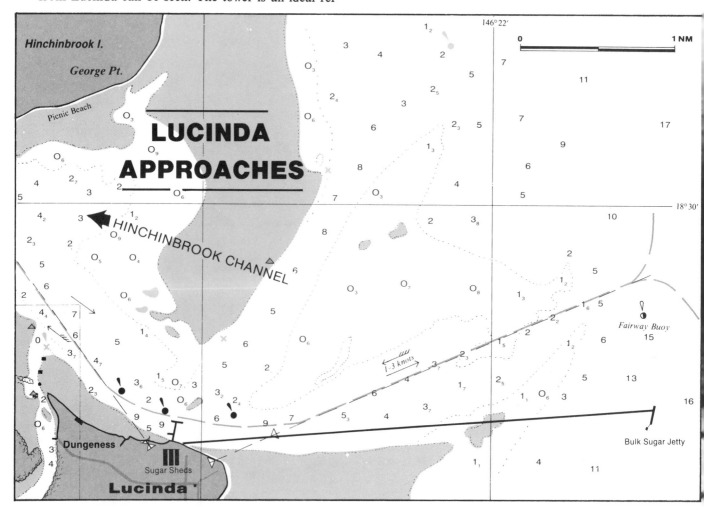

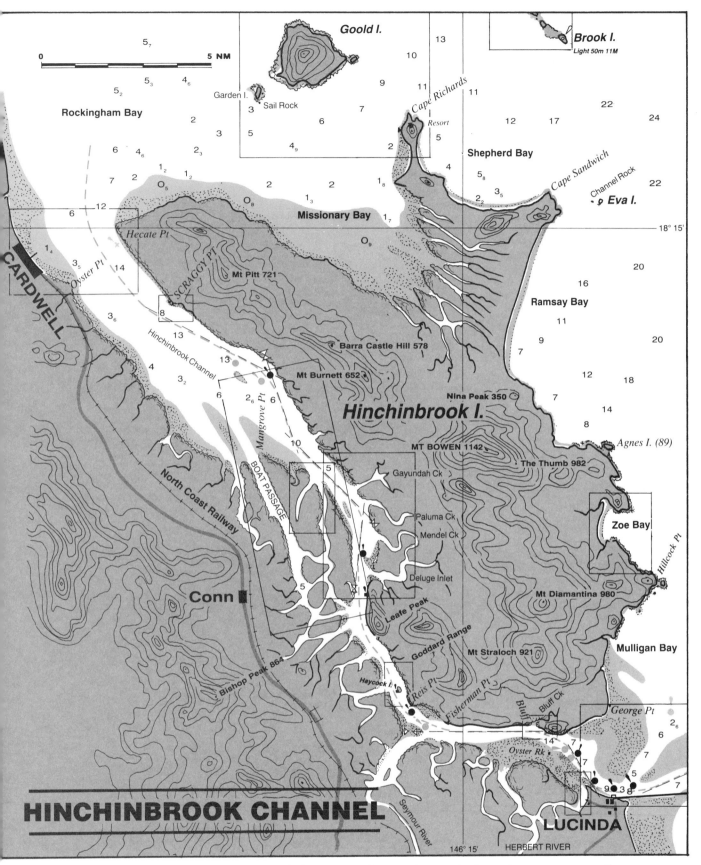

HINCHINBROOK CHANNEL

west of this reference, the low projecting land of *Hecate Point* rising progressively, starting at a distance of 12 miles and fully lifting at a distance of 7 miles when the true point can be identified. Although the water is of adequate depth into the northern entrance, a flood tide adds a little speed even though it can stack up a shorter sea if a south-easterly is well developed.

Navigating the channel from either end is easy enough, there being good depths regardless of tide throughout.

Inattentiveness is the only enemy, groundings sometimes occurring when the helmsman becomes distracted for too long.

Tides. At the north entrance, *Goold Island* is a secondary observation point based on Townsville data in the *Tide Tables*, while at the south, *Lucinda* is a standard port. Heights are slightly higher in the south than the north and typical high water springs is 2.2 metres.

During spring tides, streams within the channel can

193

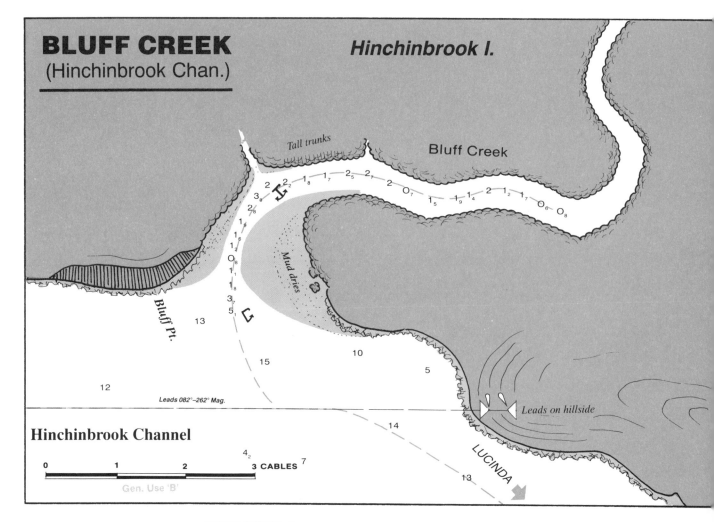

BLUFF CREEK
(Hinchinbrook Chan.)

Hinchinbrook I.

Tall trunks

Bluff Creek

Mud dries

Bluff Pt.

13

15

12

Leads 082°–262° Mag.

10

5

14

Leads on hillside

LUCINDA

13

Hinchinbrook Channel

0   1   2   3 CABLES   7

4_2

Gen. Use 'B'

The entrance to Bluff Creek is east of Bluff Point behind which is seen Hinchinbrook Island's Mount Straloch.

Diminutive Haycock Islet provides an ideal first night's anchorage in the Hinchinbrook Channel going north. The best position is between it and Hinchinbrook Island.

Lucinda Leads

LUCINDA ENTRANCE

Front lead painted on sugar conveyor. Back lead on trestle on Lucinda Point.

Both black centre on orange background.

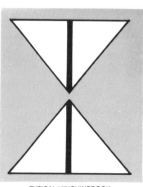

TYPICAL HINCHINBROOK

CHANNEL LEADING BEACONS

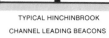

194

attain 3 knots, especially close to the entrances. They flood from both ends meeting in the vicinity of Mendel Creek from where they ebb in the opposite direction.

LUCINDA

LUCINDA. The entrance to Lucinda is the southern entrance to Hinchinbrook Channel as just described.

The settlement is based on the bulk sugar loading facility and comprises a general store and post office. Anchorage off is uncomfortable but suitable for a quick shopping sortie. The most convenient place is to the west of the wharf where shown on the chart, page 000. The best dinghy landing is close to the front lead of the up-channel beacons where slabs of concrete offer a rough ramp-landing.

DUNGENESS

DUNGENESS is a small settlement west of Lucinda and close to the *Herbert River* entrance. The river (known here as *Enterprise Channel*) is deep enough for all-tide anchoring but its entrance nearly dries at low tide springs. To enter, use a tide of at least your draft and beware of a flood tide carrying you too far west when rounding up for the beaconed entrance.

At the anchorage there is a launching ramp, jetty and slipway capable of handling large trawlers. By road, it is about two kilometres to Lucinda shops.

BLUFF CREEK

BLUFF CREEK. Penetrating the fringing mangrove forest under the imposing backdrop of Mount Straloch, Bluff Creek is 3 miles north-west of *Lucinda*. It is an ideal first anchorage after entering the Hinchinbrook Channel from the south. There are, however, conditions to this proposal.

The entrance is barred with soft, sticky mud which carries only 0.8 metres at low water springs. Depending

on your keel shape and power available, it may be possible to plow through and improve that figure. But, regardless, some tide is needed by most craft. This demands a flood tide which can be the same one used to cross the bar into Lucinda.

During strong south-east weather, powerful gusts churn the water in the vicinity of Bluff Creek and a semblance of swell can also arrive off its mouth. Under these circumstances it pays to carry on for Haycock Island anchorage unless absolutely confident of tide height related to your draft.

The deepest water in the creek is inside the entrance where shown. Swinging room is severely limited, but such is the holding that minimum scope is acceptable. Otherwise, move up the creek where wind gusts are reduced but mosquito attack increases. It may be necessary to lay a stern anchor to prevent swinging into the trees.

HAYCOCK ISLAND

HAYCOCK ISLAND. Less than 8 miles up the Hinchinbrook Channel from Lucinda, this diminutive speck marks the ideal spot for a first night anchorage after entering the channel from the south. *Reis Point* gives good protection from the prevailing wind and the tidal stream is reduced enough that windward-tide is less of a nuisance than elsewhere. The bottom is mud.

Pub With No Beer

Inland from Lucinda, the town of Ingham had the original pub with no beer which inspired the famous song of 1957 by Slim Dusty. The pub stood on the site of the present day Lees Hotel and was drunk dry by United States servicemen in 1943.

The mouth of the Herbert River — known simply as 'Dungeness', is illustrated on page 191 and described above. Close to Lucinda, it is a very secure anchorage.

Gayundah Creek

It is uncertain, but Gayundah Creek may have been named after the gunboat *Gayundah*, one of two 360 ton, two-gun ships commissioned by the Queensland Government in 1884. Gayundah is also the name of one of Queensland's oldest towns. It is situated on the Burnett River.

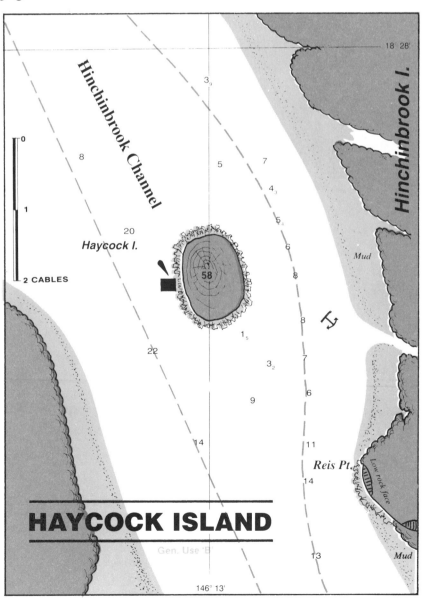

HAYCOCK ISLAND

195

HINCHINBROOK ISLAND CREEKS. These creeks will all be found about halfway along the Hinchinbrook Channel. They all penetrate the island's mangrove fringe and emanate from a mountain stream. Their source can often be traced by dinghy.

In terms of easy entrance and absence of in-creek shoals, *Gayundah Creek* is the best and therefore the most popular. However, *Paluma Creek* provides easily accessed anchorage within its mouth whilst *Mendel Creek* and *Deluge Inlet* allow considerable inland penetration. Deluge Inlet has a 0.9 metre bar across its inner entrance demanding a flood tide.

Although the bottom is mostly mud, shoals and drying banks tend to be hard sand allowing them to be seen when underwater despite the lack of water clarity. However, in the name of common sense and safe navigation, a flood tide is best used wherever in doubt about their navigation.

All creeks provide splendid shelter from destructive winds, however, all experience a strong run-off current during the associated heavy rains. As a result, debris can cause some distress to an anchored vessel. It is better to shelter in a mangrove forest unattached to any land mass. The best such shelter in this region is either of the Anchorage Point creeks next described.

ANCHORAGE POINT CREEKS. Nearly 11 miles south-east of *Cardwell* and opposite *Gayundah Creek*, these two creeks penetrate south into Hinchinbrook Channel's central mangrove forests. Both are easily entered and both have good depths and excellent, good holding mud bottoms.

Rather uninspiring compared to the island creeks, they are a better choice when seeking shelter from a cyclone owing to their non-flooding nature.

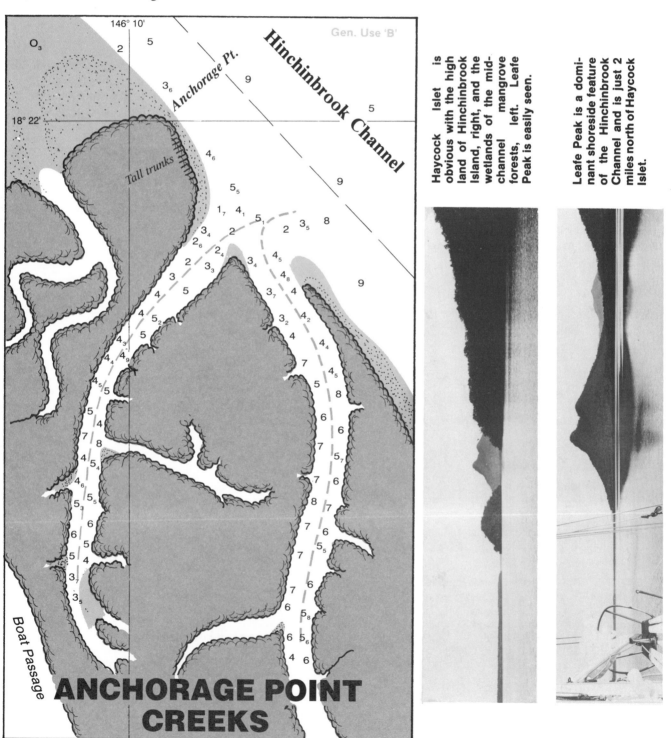

Haycock Islet is obvious with the high land of Hinchinbrook Island, right, and the wetlands of the mid-channel mangrove forests, left. Leafe Peak is easily seen.

Leafe Peak is a dominant shoreside feature of the Hinchinbrook Channel and is just 2 miles north of Haycock Islet.

ANCHORAGE POINT CREEKS

HINCHINBROOK CREEKS

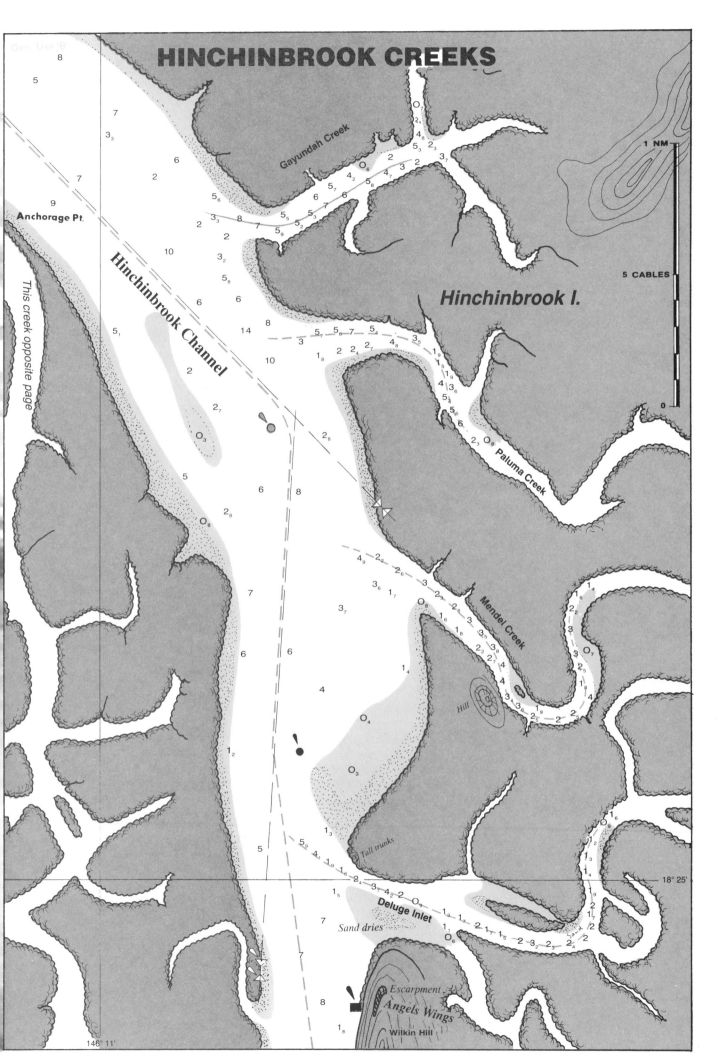

Gen. Use 'B'

8

5

7

3₃

6

7

2

7

9

Anchorage Pt.

Gayundah Creek

O₇
2₁
4₈
5₃

2
8
3₇

O₆
4₂
5₈
4₇
2
3
2

5₇
6

6
5₆

6
5₅
5₃

2
3₃
7
5₅
5₂
5₉

2
3₂

5₈

6
6

14
8

10

5₁

This creek opposite page

Hinchinbrook Channel

2

2₇

O₃

O₈

5

2₈

O₈

7

6
6

6

4

O₄

1₂

O₃

5

1₃

5₉
4₁
1₉
1₆

2₄
3₁
4₂

1₅

7

Hinchinbrook I.

5₇
5₇
7
5₄
3₅

3

5₇
1₉
1₅

2
2₄
4₈
1₉
4
4₉
5₇

1₈

O₈
2₃

Paluma Creek

4₉
2₂
2₆
3

3₆
1₇
3₂
2₆

3₇
O₈
1₆
2₆
1₈
3
3₈
2₂
4
2₅
1₈
4

Mendel Creek

1₄
2₂
3
2₆
2₅

O₇
3₃
3₆
1₉
2₅
2

Hill

1₄

O₉
1₆
1₂
1₃
1₄

8

1₈

7

Deluge Inlet
O₃
1₃
1₇
2₁
1₅
2
3₂
2₃
2₄
2

2₄
3₄
4₂

1₉
1₇
1₂
2

Sand dries
O₆

Tall trunks

Escarpment
Angels Wings
Wilkin Hill

146 11'

18° 25'

1 NM

5 CABLES

0

197

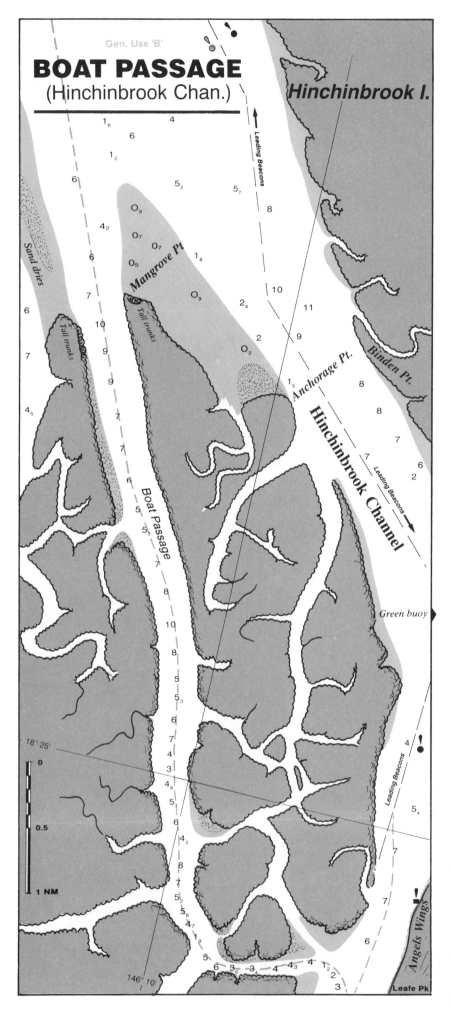

BOAT PASSAGE
(Hinchinbrook Chan.)

Gen. Use 'B'

Hinchinbrook I.

Leading Beacons

Sand dries

Mangrove Pt.

Tall trunks

Tall trunks

Boat Passage

Anchorage Pt.

Binden Pt.

Hinchinbrook Channel

Leading Beacons

Green buoy

Leading Beacons

Angels Wings

18° 25'

146° 10'

Leafe Pk

0

0.5

1 NM

BOAT PASSAGE. A little used thoroughfare in Hinchinbrook Channel, Boat Passage runs down the western side of the channel's central mangrove forests. It is entered from the north directly from Scraggy Point and from the south opposite Leafe Peak.

The northern entrance is deep and wide, but care is nevertheless needed to keep away from the sandbanks on each side. Under some conditions, visual identification of the channel edge can be difficult.

The southern entrance is narrow and shallower, having only 1.2 metres over its sand bar. A flood tide is suggested and visibility of the banks on each side of the entrance is generally good.

SCRAGGY POINT is an attractive area of beach and freshwater creek with Aboriginal rock fish traps on the intertidal zone. It lies 3 miles south-east of *Hecate Point* and boasts national park facilities. Sadly, it is often badly abused by those who refuse to take their garbage with them.

Anchorage off is troubled by windward-tide during south-east winds, but usually calms off after dusk when the wind lifts. Holding is excellent in mud and shore access reasonable except at low tide.

CARDWELL lies at the base of a mountain range on the mainland opposite Hinchinbrook Island's north-west tip (Hecate Point). It is easily the largest shopping centre in the district offering post office, hardware, hotel, supermarkets, bank (NAB and Westpac), service station, cafes and so on. Water can be hosed aboard at the jetty and fuel can be arranged through a local charter company.

Anchorage off Cardwell is wide open to all but offshore winds, but the holding is brilliant in soft mud and a good sized dinghy will make it ashore properly handled. Go to the concrete jetty at low tide and the beach at high tide.

The beach is a relatively narrow strip of sand separating land from mud flats and cannot be reached by dinghy on tides less than one metre high. The end of the jetty has about half a metre of water at spring low tide.

Marina. Excavated and carrying about 2 metres of water at low tide, is a marina site at *Oyster Point* south of Cardwell which started in the late 1980s but died during the recession of the early 1990s. As of late 1993 it was being used as an anchorage, but completion is expected in the future.

198

HECATE POINT has been thoroughly described in the Hinchinbrook approach, page 192. Here it is reviewed as an anchorage; logically one chosen in the late evening after sailing down from Dunk Island.

Unless a developed wind fails to lift after dusk, Hecate Point is comfortable enough for a night's rest before pressing on into the Hinchinbrook Channel. Its yellow light is very weak but will be seen through binoculars from about 4 miles. The best anchorage is in the light's vicinity as close to the land as possible. This tends to be at the 5 metre line where good holding mud is encountered. Windward-tide can be a nuisance until the wind dies and the tidal flow changes approximately 20 minutes later than predicted high and low times.

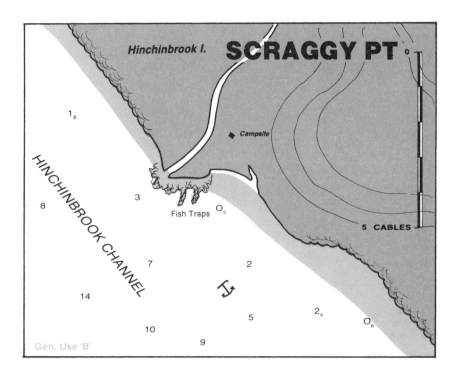

Looking into Gayundah Creek. With an unbarred entrance and general good depths within, this tends to be Hinchinbrook Channel's favourite haven.

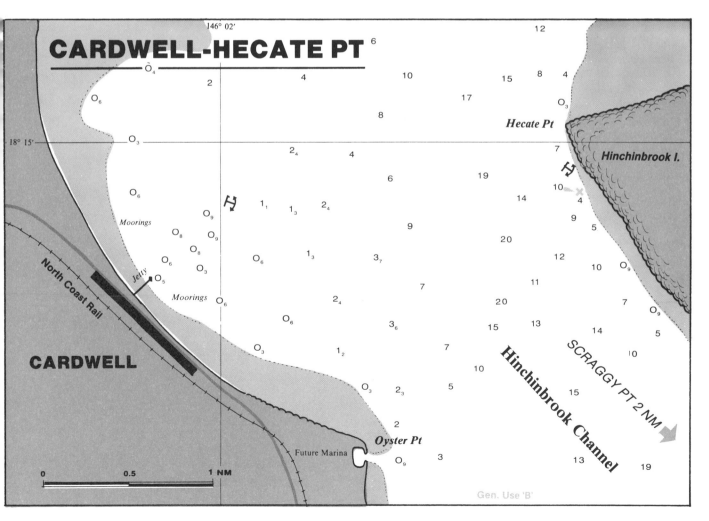

199

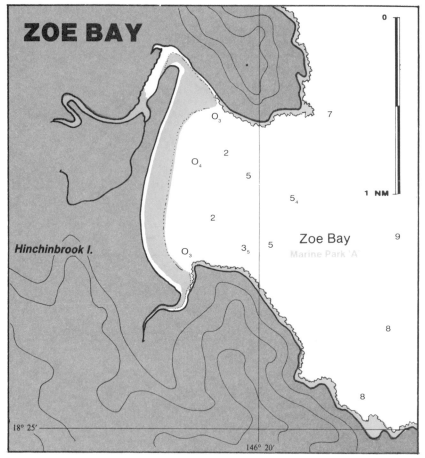

ZOE BAY

Hinchinbrook I.

Zoe Bay
Marine Park 'A

18° 25'

146° 20'

Above: Cardwell Jetty with Hinchinbrook Island behind.
Below: One of the many splendid anchorages in Hinchinbrook Channel.

ZOE BAY. Being wide open to seaward, this lovely bay on the east coast of *Hinchinbrook Island* is for calm weather only. Its south creek is very rocky with only shallow pools within at low tide. The north creek has good depths within where a keeler could lie snug and secure subject to a tide of no less than her draft to enter, complemented with perfect weather.

From the south corner of Zoe Bay, a short walk finds a delightful waterfall and splash pool together with a splendid deep, freshwater creek.

AGNES ISLAND. A popular anchorage for resting trawlers, the bay west of Agnes Island into Hinchinbrook Island is a useful stopover for vessels remaining at sea instead of passing through the channel.

SHEPHERD BAY is the large indentation between Cape Sandwich and Cape Richards on Hinchinbrook's north-east corner. It has good holding and marvellous beaches, but is useful only in light weather.

MISSIONARY BAY CREEKS are interesting to explore especially if cyclone security is needed. Most creeks carry good low tide depths, but all have bars which demand high tide to cross. Use only a flood tide to compensate for confusion.

CAPE RICHARDS. Hinchinbrook Island's most northerly point, Cape Richards separates Shepherd Bay from Missionary Bay and supports a tourist resort known as *Hinchinbrook Island Resort*.

Casual visitors to the resort should seek permission from management before availing themselves of the resort's facilities.

Anchorage off the resort is in mud with only a slight surge and occasional windward-tide behaviour. To clear resort access for workboats, anchor to the south of the pontoon. If a more isolated and marginally more comfortable anchorage is preferred, move south, off the accompanying chart, to the next head where national park facilities are established ashore.

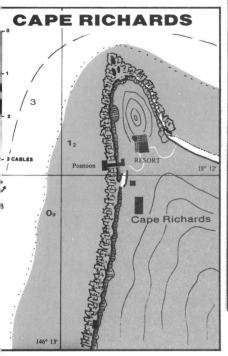

CAPE RICHARDS

Pontoon
RESORT
Cape Richards

18° 12'

3 CABLES

146° 13'

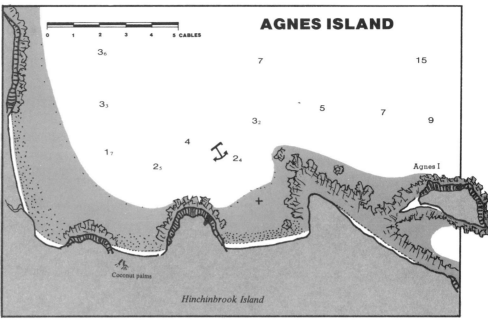

AGNES ISLAND

0 1 2 3 4 5 CABLES

Agnes I

Coconut palms

Hinchinbrook Island

GOOLD ISLAND. Densely wooded with a delightful sand spit off its south-western tip, Goold Island offers indifferent anchorage during any developed wind. Despite the calming effect one might expect from having Hinchinbrook Island to windward, a considerable swell works around the island during a developed south-easterly. At that time, the best anchorage is where shown towards the north side of the shoal water extending out from the sand spit.

The northerly anchorage is little better in terms of comfort, a confused wave pattern often attacking the south side of the island. It is endurable, however, and very handy to the beach. When approaching this anchorage, beware the poor visibility when seeking the fringing reef.

Another northerly anchorage exists under the lee of Garden Island tucked in towards its sand spit as close as rapidly shoaling water allows.

Ashore on Goold Island there are national park picnic facilities including toilet, tables and walking tracks. The dunes along the south side of the spit are suffering from erosion and this is being combated by the placement of access 'ladders'.

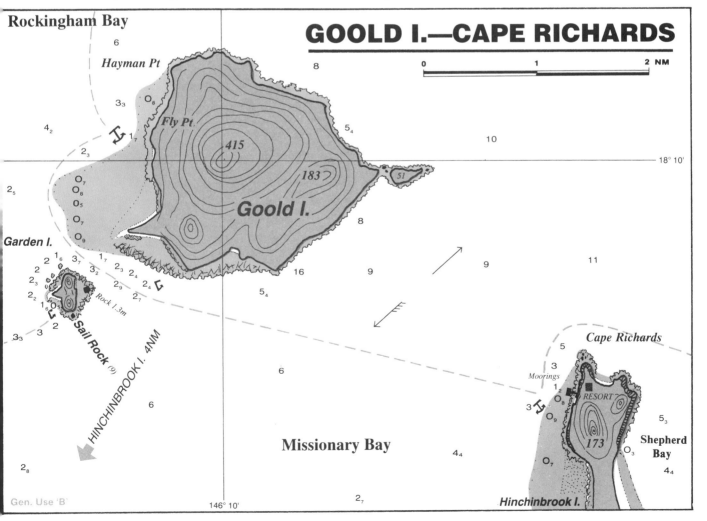

GOOLD I.—CAPE RICHARDS

Rockingham Bay

Hayman Pt

Fly Pt

415

183

51

Goold I.

Garden I.

Rock 1.3m

Sail Rock

HINCHINBROOK I. 4NM

Gen. Use 'B'

146° 10'

Missionary Bay

18° 10'

Moorings

Cape Richards

RESORT

173

Shepherd Bay

Hinchinbrook I.

Hecate Point, on the north-west tip of Hinchinbrook Island, is a mangrove forest.

The Cardwell jetty is tidal, deep keelers needing about half tide to approach. Otherwise, the anchorage off is secure though rough at times.

Looking south at Garden Island. Hinchinbrook Island behind and Goold Island, left.

Goold Island and Garden Island are in line. There is a pleasant fair weather anchorage off Garden Island's western side.

Hudson Island, right, bears north. Bowden Island is left with Dunk Island in the distance.

Smith Island bears south-east, left, with Bowden Island, right.

Dunk Island bears NNW. Kumboola Island, left, shares the same fringing reef.

Dunk Island, north. Woln Garin Islet off its south-east tip is right.

Kumboola Island with its tiny satellite is seen, left, with Dunk Island, right. Vessels at anchor close to its spit during northerly weather are obvious between the two.

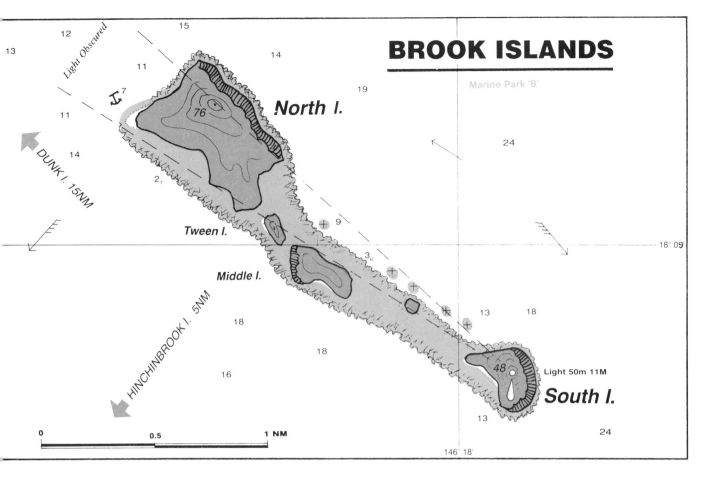

BROOK ISLANDS

North I.

Marine Park 'B'

Tween I.

Middle I.

South I.

Light 50m 11M

Light Obscured

DUNK I. 15NM

HINCHINBROOK I. 5NM

| 0 | 0.5 | 1 NM |

BROOK ISLANDS. Sharing a common reef 2 miles long, Brook Islands are useful only as a lunch stop unless the weather is calm to light. The best anchorage is close to the sand spit on the north-western tip of *North Island*.

The group lies a little over 4 miles north from Hinchinbrook Island and supports an automatic light on the southern end. A small obscured arc fans the islands.

203

The Dunk Island anchorage becomes untenable during brisk northerlies, although tourist boats continue to use the jetty (below). Purdaboi — also known as 'Mound' — Island is obvious, left. The best anchorage during northerlies at Dunk Island is along its southern shore. Otherwise, along its western shore is tolerable whilst being more convenient to facilities. The pic, right, shows the author's yacht off the edge of the fringing reef on the southern side.

FAMILY ISLANDS. Owing to zoning anomalies early this century, much of Dunk Island is freehold and all of Timana and Bedarra are freehold. All other islands in the group are *Marine Park General Use 'B'* which means that only trawling is banned with most other pursuits, including camping, available by permit.

Dunk and Bedarra Islands are looked at separately later, they offer the only reasonable all-weather anchorages in the group. The following looks at the remaining islands with a view to light weather stopovers.

Hudson Island is the south-eastern most of the group with a smooth, sloping rock face and boulders on its southern end and a small beach with coconut palms halfway along its western side. More palms are seen behind the sand spit off its north-western tip. Anchorage in 8 metres off this sand spit is the best available in terms of depth and shore access.

Bowden and Smith Islands lie close north of Hudson Island and provide tolerable anchorage between the two behind a linking fringing reef. Both have dominant sand spits off their western tip and both are densely wooded and rock-bound. Off Bowden's south west tip is a sandy shoal which may have a coral head. Caution is necessary when coasting along its western shore.

Coombe and Wheeler Islands both offer useful depths if able to anchor in close. Like their neighbours, they are well wooded and rock-bound with a scattering of rubble beaches. Shore access is not as attractive as the others.

BEDARRA ISLAND (Richards Island) is all freehold, most of which has been taken up by Australian Airlines who have developed this beauiful island into two resorts each catering for 32 guests. *Bedarra Hideaway* lies on the eastern corner where will be seen a jetty projecting over the fringing reef and *Bedarra Bay* is situated on the south-eastern corner where the holiday home of a wealthy individual once stood. Both resorts are exclusive.

On the north-east corner, artist Noel Wood's property has recently been subdivided into seven blocks and sold off. Noel is Queensland's oldest island dweller, having lived on Bedarra since 1936. *Not illustrated large scale.*

DUNK ISLAND is the largest and most northerly of the *Family Group* of islands, all of which lie in Rockingham Bay whose southerly extreme becomes the Hinchinbrook Channel. Lying 13 miles north of Goold Island, Dunk supports one of the coast's more tasteful resorts and a couple of privately owned houses.

Approach from the south is by logical progression through the islands of Rockingham Bay, Dunk being dominantly visible as soon as Hinchinbrook Island is cleared. From the north, the *North* and *South Barnard Islands* should be cleared to seaward with particular attention given to *King Reef*, 2 miles south of *Stephens Island*, if beating to windward and tacking close to shore. On final approach, *Purdaboi Islet* may be passed either side.

Anchorage is in *Brammo Bay* to the north of the vegetated sandspit on which will be seen day-guest facilities. Because it is often very crowded it may be necessary to anchor well out or as close to the fringing reef as possible. Beware of this practice as the edge of the reef can be difficult to define at high tide. Regardless of where the anchor is dropped, leave clear access to the jetty which is used regularly by the Dunk Island supply barge and numerous charter boats. The holding is excellent in mud and a low, north-east swell persists during trade-wind weather.

During northerly winds, anchorage can be found in 8 metres about midway along the south coast, east of *Kumboola Islet*. More popular but at the cost of a considerable swell is the south side of the sandspit on which is situated the day guest facilities. Security and degree of comfort will be dictated here by draft. Shoal draft can tuck well under the lee whilst deep keelers are obliged to remain offshore.

Facilities. The actual resort is out of bounds to casual visitors although flights into and out of the island can be arranged at the office. Day guests — as boating people are classified — have their own facilities near the jetty. These comprise a bar, dive hire shop, fast foods and similar outlets. Camping is allowed with a permit to the east of the day-guest area and parasailing is operated from the end of the sand spit. Boats may also be hired. The jetty is semi-public and may be used to embark and disembark crew. It is taken over by the dozens of game fishing boats that gather in the area for the annual sailfish contest held in September.

Bruce Arthur Tapestries. Towards the south-west extreme of Dunk Island, and a little way inland, will be found the home and studio of Bruce Arthur. Bruce has lived an isolated, artistic life since giving up professional wrestling in the mid 1960s.

As a wrestler, Bruce rose to become Australia's middleweight champion, competing in both the Olympic and Commonwealth Games before turning professional, a facet of the game that is more theatrical than serious. Interested in art, he migrated north to nearby Timana Island where the chance meeting with Scottish master-weaver, Jock Loutitt, set him on the course he has steered ever since. Now Bruce enjoys tremendous respect and demand from the art-buying public who may visit his studio on Tuesday and Friday mornings for a small entrance fee.

Of Interest. In 1896, Townsville journalist E.J. Banfield took out a lease on Dunk Island and later gained an agricultural homestead block on which he and his family lived until his death twenty years later. Writing four books while on the island, his most famous became *Confessions of a Beachcomber*.

The ownership of the island passed to Spencer Hopkins then Hugo Brassey who started to develop it for tourism. He started the airstrip that runs across the peninsula near the anchorage. After a number of owners after Brassey, Eric McIllree, the founder of Avis Australia car rentals, bought the island in 1963 and set about updating the resort. After his death in 1973, the island again changed hands to Australian Airlines, previously known as Trans Australia Airlines. Dunk was the venue for the 1968 James Mason-Helen Mirren film, *Age of Consent*.

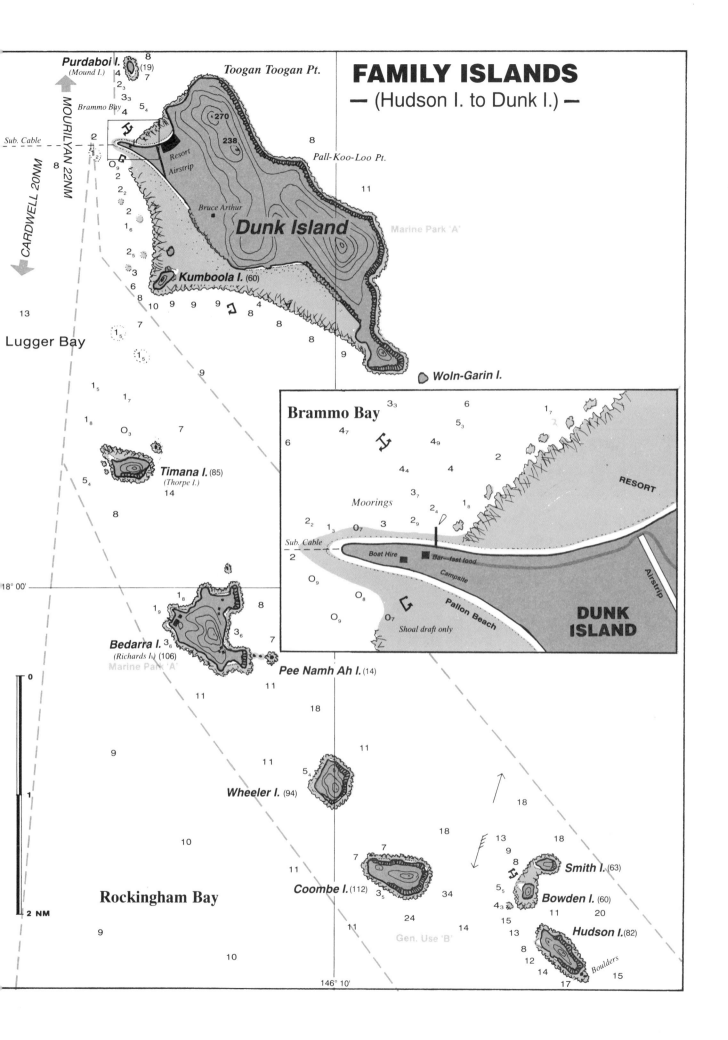

FAMILY ISLANDS
— (Hudson I. to Dunk I.) —

Purdaboi I. (19)
(Mound I.)

Toogan Toogan Pt.

CARDWELL 20NM

MOURILYAN 22NM

Sub. Cable

Brammo Bay

Resort
Airstrip

270

238

Pall-Koo-Loo Pt.

Bruce Arthur

Dunk Island

Marine Park 'A'

13

Lugger Bay

Kumboola I. (60)

Woln-Garin I.

Brammo Bay

Moorings

Sub. Cable

Boat Hire

Bar—fast food

Campsite

RESORT

Pallon Beach

DUNK ISLAND

Airstrip

Shoal draft only

O₃

Timana I. (85)
(Thorpe I.)

18° 00'

Bedarra I.
(Richards I.) (106)

Marine Park 'A'

Pee Namh Ah I. (14)

0

1

2 NM

9

10

11

9

10

Rockingham Bay

Wheeler I. (94)

Coombe I. (112)

Gen. Use 'B'

Smith I. (63)

Bowden I. (60)

Hudson I. (82)

Boulders

146° 10'

205

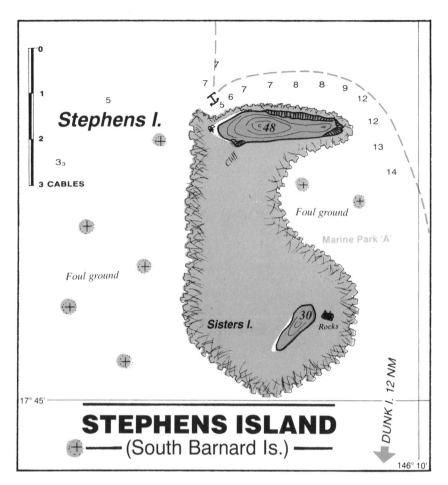

Stephens I.

Foul ground

Marine Park 'A'

Foul ground

Sisters I. Rocks

17° 45'

STEPHENS ISLAND
—— (South Barnard Is.) ——

DUNK I. 12 NM

146° 10'

STEPHENS ISLAND. The largest of two islands comprising the *South Barnard Islands*, Stephens Island is a continental type 11 miles north of Dunk Island. It was once settled by Steve Illidge who, last century, built a house for he and his Aboriginal wife and worked beche de mer commercially. At one time he owned a fleet of six boats and sent his children south for their education. He was wiped out by a cyclone in 1890.

Approach from the south is obstructed by *King Reef* which extends nearly 3 miles off Murdering Point. The edge of the reef is easily identified in fair weather. By keeping Hutchison Island, in the North Barnard Islands, wide open of Stephens, King Reef will be avoided. At low to mid tide, the outer edge of the reef shows as a mass of exposed rocks.

The anchorage is troubled by southeast swell, but is tenable and is best off the beach which wraps around the western tip of Stephens Island.

Stephens Island (right) and Sisters Island (left) share a common reef. They comprise the South Barnard Islands.

NORTH BARNARD ISLANDS. Extending to over 5 miles south-east of Mourilyan Harbour, this small group offers a delightfully scenic anchorage in fair weather. It cannot be recommended during a developed wind.

The best anchorage is under the lee of *Kent Island* towards its close neighbour, Jessie Island. The sandspit here makes an ideal landing spot and the island has some wonderful rain forest.

The light on Kent Island was first exhibited on 21 December 1897 and was intended as an automatic type. Because it tended to blacken its glass, a keeper became necessary. It has long since reverted to automation.

Innisfail, a few miles north of Mourilyan, is a charming, peaceful town well recommended to the visitor.

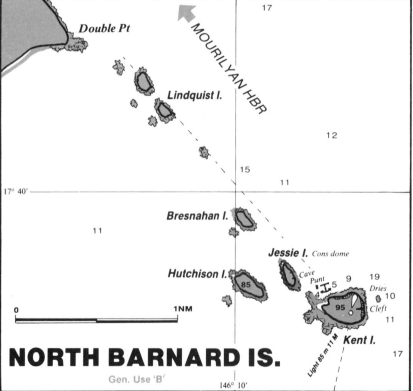

Double Pt

MOURILYAN HBR

Lindquist I.

17° 40'

Bresnahan I.

Jessie I. *Cons dome*

Cave Punt

Hutchison I.

Kent I.

Light 85 m 11 M

NORTH BARNARD IS.

Gen. Use 'B'

146° 10'

The North Barnard Islands. Double Point is left with Kent Island, right.

Ascending the Moresby River, Mourilyan. It provides good cyclone protection.

The navigable extent of the Moresby River is shown here. The actual harbour of Mourilyan, at the mouth of the river, is shown in large scale over the page. The upper limits of the river provides a good cyclone hole.

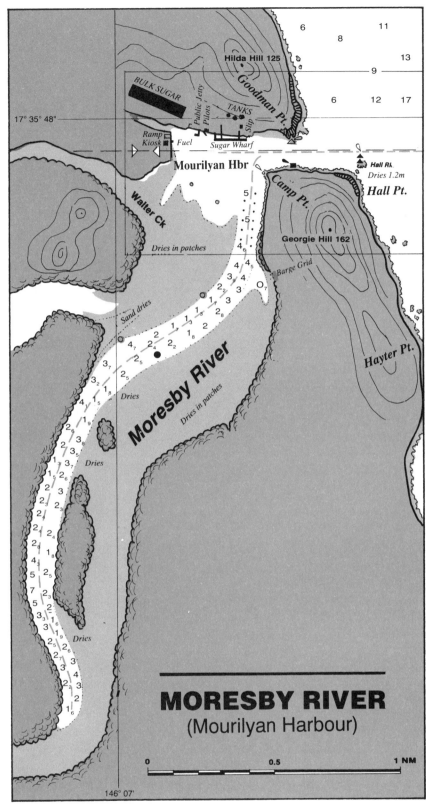

MORESBY RIVER
(Mourilyan Harbour)

0   0.5   1 NM

MOURILYAN HARBOUR is 20 miles north of Dunk Island and is formed by the mouth of the *Moresby River* which empties into the sea between two high, heavily timbered hills known as Georgie and Hilda, south and north respectively. All-round protection is enjoyed here by vessels of all sizes.

Approach from the south is best outside the North Barnard Islands from where course is laid direct for the entrance. From that distance the true entrance is unidentifiable, appearing as a mountain overlap. As the entrance opens, two tanks first appear followed by smaller buildings of the sugar loading complex then the conveyor wharf itself. Beacons at the entrance will be seen.

From the north, *Meaburn Rock* is the only offshore danger but is marked with an east cardinal black and yellow buoy and has 3.35 metres over it at low water springs. Otherwise, a course close to the land can be steered there being no other offshore dangers.

Because a current of up to 5 knots can run through the entrance, a capable engine is necessary if the port is entered during a spring ebb tide. Otherwise await slack water or flood and, in any event, find the leading

Mourilyan Harbour's entrance is unique for the steep headlands on each side. Here they are kissing approaching from the south.

The headlands open up to reveal the bulk sugar loading infrastructure including sheds, tanks and gantry.

In this photograph, the loading facility is fully evident. That this harbour was missed by early navigators is easy to understand.

The leading beacons into Mourilyan Harbour are in line (under arrow). The sugar wharf is right with small-boat pile berths around headland to the left.

To the west of the sugar wharf is this complex of fuel jetty, launching ramp and kiosk in Mourilyan Harbour.

beacons well outside the entrance then hold them in fair transit until within the harbour. The entrance is 190 metres wide but the channel is 91 metres wide with a dredged depth of 8.5 metres low water springs. Light beacons define Hall Rock and Point, the two headlands at their closest points and the swing basin within. The leading beacons are all-red triangular boards each with a vertical white stripe. They are lit by fixed red neon lights during the night and by fixed white lights during the day, the latter only being displayed when a ship enters port.

Anchorage and Berths. As the entrance is cleared, two rows of steel-pile berths will be seen to the south close to the steep land. A vacant berth may be taken after which the caretaker on the Sugar Wharf should be paid.

Alternatively, anchorage may be found anywhere as long as it properly clears the swing basin which is outlined by yellow buoys. Good depth will be located to the west of a shoal immediately to the west of the pile berths, otherwise, move upstream of the pile berths and seek anchorage wherever suitable being careful not to obstruct the channel up Moresby River.

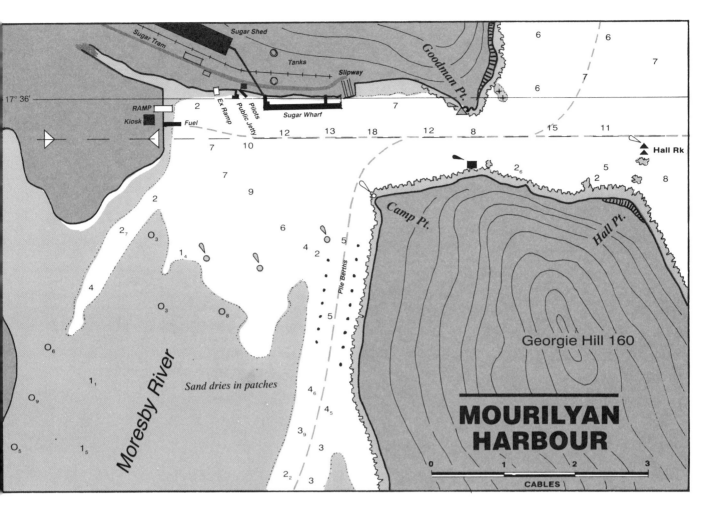

Moresby River provides good depths for a considerable distance upstream, as shown on the accompanying chart. A cyclone could be ridden here whilst under the more general circumstances of recreational anchoring, isolation will be enjoyed at the cost of convenience to Mourilyan Harbour.

Facilities. Mourilyan is a no-frills commercial port specialising in the dispatch of bulk sugar and molasses. There is no transport to the town of Mourilyan, 10 kilometres inland, but taxis can be summoned or a hitch anticipated.

There is a public jetty, launching ramp and STD phone on the north bank near the sugar and pilot jetties and a Coast Guard station near the western end of the sugar wharf. It monitors all the usual channels and frequencies.

Near the north-west corner is a fuel jetty and kiosk, the latter having only basic supplies.

Tides. The *Official Tide Tables* include Mourilyan as a standard port. It experiences an average maximum range of 2 metres.

Of Interest. Mourilyan was converted from a bag-sugar loading centre to a bulk facility in the late 1950s at which time the natural entrance was widened and deepened. Being a rock ledge, drilling and blasting was necessary. The terminal started operations in June 1960, and is capable of loading a ship at the rate of 1400 tonnes per hour. The associated sugar storage shed is the longest of its type in the world.

Understandable to anyone who has passed Mourilyan harbour without ever realising it was there, it took an accident to bring about its discovery.

The brig *Maria* set sail from Sydney for New Guinea loaded with gold prospectors high on the promise of new fields in 1872. A cyclone forced her to run for the Queensland coast on which course she struck a reef off the Hinchinbrook area. The skipper and six of his best oarsmen immediately fled the scene in the best boat leaving the hapless prospectors to fend for themselves.

Before *Maria* slipped to her grave, rafts were fashioned and most of the passengers managed to escape, landing on the coast around Cardwell. With awareness of the disaster came the need to search the coast for other survivors who might have fallen into native hands, some of whom were thought to be hostile. Captain Moresby, aboard the 1000-ton paddlesteamer, *Basilisk*, recently returned from Port Moresby and stopping over in Cardwell, raised steam and got under way.

Contradicting the hostile-native assumption, he found a few survivors on the beach to the north who had been cared for by the indigenes who openly wept when relieved of their charges. Proceeding north, Moresby was surprised to see two hills open up to disclose a beautiful, snug harbour fed by a south-tending river. The harbour he named after his lieutenant, Mourilyan, and the river after himself.

Mourilyan tragedy

With a natural depth of only 1.3 metres over solid rock, Mourilyan Harbour's entrance would prove a difficult one to dredge. By placing explosives in rock crevices, it was first deepened to 4.2 metres in 1884. During later deepening, in 1959, the vessel *Mourilyan*, equipped with a Priestman grab, sank with a loss of three lives. During the night of September 1, she filled through her anchor roller fairleads which were set in openings through the hull below the main work deck.

209

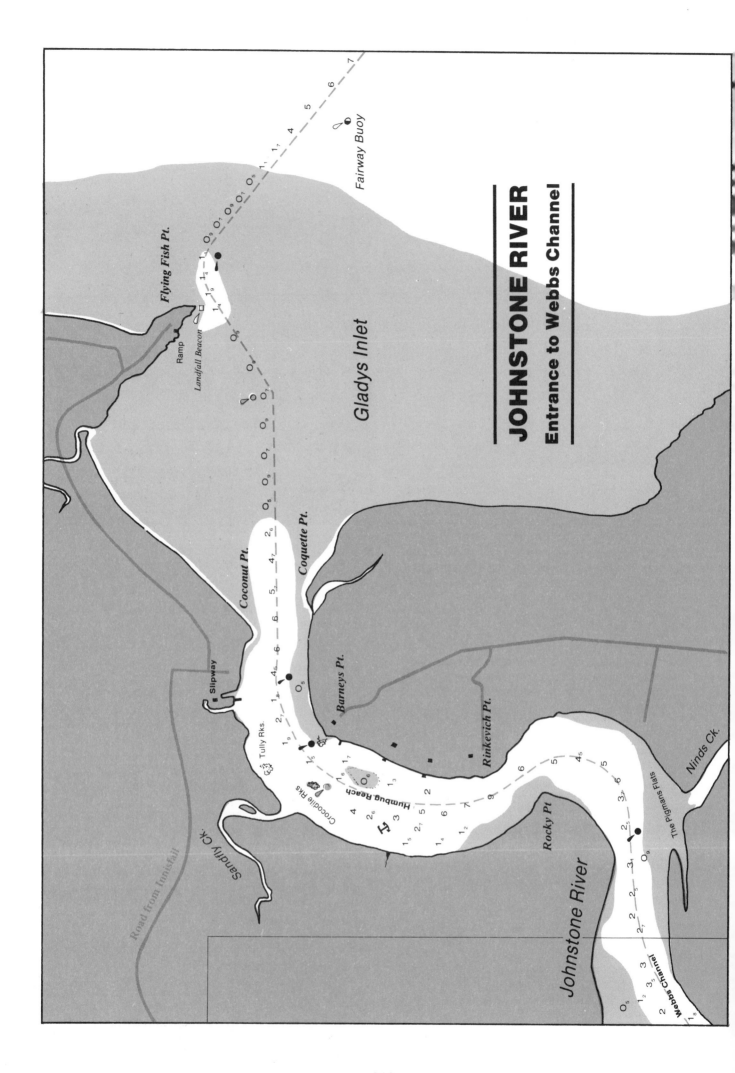

JOHNSTONE RIVER
Entrance to Webbs Channel

Fairway Buoy

Flying Fish Pt.

Ramp
Landfall Beacon

Gladys Inlet

Coconut Pt.

Coquette Pt.

Slipway

Tully Rks.

Barneys Pt.

Rinkevich Pt.

Humbug Reach

Crocodile Rks.

Road from Innisfail

Sandfly Ck.

Johnstone River

Rocky Pt

Ninds Ck.

The Pigmans Flats

Webbs Channel

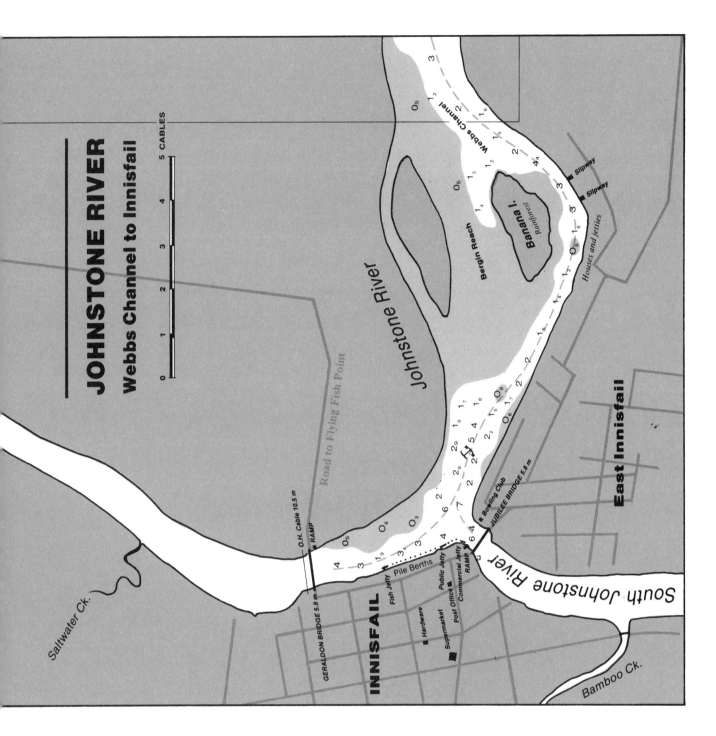

INNISFAIL is a delightful coastal town on the Johnstone River whose mouth is situated between *Flying Fish Point* and *Thompson Point*, 6½ miles north of Mourilyan Harbour. The town is approximately 3 miles upstream from the inner mouth which lies between *Coconut Point* and *Coquette Point*.

Approach. Mourilyan Harbour offers an ideal place in which to await conditions suitable for the Johnstone River bar which carries only 0.6 metres low water springs. Rough rule of thumb says that a vessel drawing 1.8 metres will easily clear on a 1.6-metre tide, Mourilyan Harbour data. In moderate to rough onshore weather, half a metre should be added to allow for wave lift and fall.

From the south, Flying Fish Point is obvious from abeam of Mourilyan by a few houses on the ridge of the low headland. There is a peaked and a domed hill in the background more or less to the left and right of Flying Fish Point respectively depending on exact angle of approach. Above *Etty Bay*, in a dip in the Moresby Range running from Coquette Point to Mourilyan Harbour, conspicuous houses will be seen. Well before the shallow water of the bar is encountered, houses along the beach front outside Flying Fish Point become obvious.

From the north, the houses along the ridge of Flying Fish Point's headland identify the point well enough and at about the time that the beach houses are seen, tall radio masts inside the river are sighted (dependent on haze or cloud).

On final approach, hold deep water until the Fairway Buoy is sighted then pass it to port aiming for Flying Fish Point and a little to its east. A red buoy off the point soon becomes apparent and this is passed close to port, hauling around quickly to pass the landfall beacon on Flying Fish Point to starboard. From here continue across to the green buoy, passing it to starboard then aim for the centre of the now-conspicuous inner entrance to the river.

Approaching the Johnstone River from the north, Mount Maria, right, is abeam. The river mouth is arrowed.

Mount Maria is seen again further north with Flying Fish Point arrowed.

Cooper Point about north-west (right). The small pyramid hill to the extreme left of picture is a feature of the coast.

Cooper Point is abeam. It is 6½ miles north of the Johnstone River entrance (Innisfail).

Flying Fish Point as it is passed entering the Johnstone River. Its landfall beacon is right.

This lovely house and grounds is on inner Coquette Point, Johnstone River entrance.

The shallowest water is on the bar between the Fairway Buoy and the red buoy then again in the vicinity of the green buoy. As long as the bar is cleared, the second shoal area will also be cleared, especially as a flood tide should be used when entering the Johnstone.

Ascending the Johnstone. Before Coquette and Coconut Points are abeam, the river deepens to more than seven metres and remains deep to *Webb's Channel* between the mainland and *Banana Island*. In that area the shoals are deeper than the bar depth meaning they are easily cleared once having entered the river.

Having entered the river, two red buoys will be seen and passed to port after which *Crocodile Rocks* green buoy is passed to starboard. These rocks dry high at low tide.

From Crocodile Rocks maintain a mid-river position favouring *Rinkevich Point* by the time it is abeam from where the west-tending bend can be taken again in mid-channel passing a red buoy to port after completing

the turn. From this red buoy steer for the port bank which is then held close aboard past *Banana Island*. On this stretch the port bank is lined with houses, pontoons and boats.

Beyond Banana Island, the City of Innisfail is easily sighted on the left bank of the river immediately beyond the best anchorage area. This lies upstream from approximately half-way between Banana Island and the city.

Anchorage can be taken wherever space permits downstream of the Bowling Club allowing for the effects of windward tide during gusty winds. The holding is not brilliant and demands plenty of scope if any security is to be enjoyed.

Alternative anchorage upstream of the Bowling Club is available favouring the west bank. A daily charge is levied here.

Berths alongside the steel piles driven beside the park on the city side of the river are available through the Shire Council, their distance apart being such that a

212

vessel must lay *alongside*, as against between, them. Four fore and aft pile berths exist between the Public Jetty and the Commercial Jetty. These are mostly occupied.

Tide is based on Mourilyan Harbour with Flying Fish Point as the secondary port. Tides can turn as much as 1½ hours later at Innisfail and currents can attain a speed of 2 knots during springs.

Fuel and Water. There are no bowsers on the waterfront, however diesel can be delivered to the Public Jetty from a local agent. Water is tapped on both the Public and Commercial Jetties. Petrol and LPG must be carted from town.

Repairs. There are no chandlers in Innisfail although a few stores have boat parts, and paint is easily purchased in a hardware store. Power (240 volts, 50 cycles) can be taken from power points on the Public Wharf and in the park when lying alongside the pile berths. A long extension cable is necessary and arrangements must be made with the authorities.

Haul Out. There are three slipways in Innisfail, one near Coconut Point at the river mouth and two in Webb's Channel. All repairs can be carried out by very well-respected boatbuilders.

Ablutions Block. In the park close to the Public Jetty is a toilet and shower block offering a large tub in which to handwash clothes. The hot water has been disconnected leaving cold showers only available.

Victuals. Innisfail is a very compact, complete shopping centre whose stocks should satisfy the average shopper. Like all Queensland towns, the place tends to shut down on Sunday but even then hot bread is available, the laundromat is open and all newsagents open in the morning. A couple of small fast food outlets and at least one small general store also open for business on Sunday.

History. While searching for survivors of the brig *Maria*, Captain Moresby in the paddle-steamer *Basilisk* discovered the Johnstone River, then named the Gladys River. Furthering the search for survivors of that famous wreck, *HMS Governor Blackall* was dispatched from Sydney with Lieutenant Gowland, and Sub-Inspector Johnstone aboard who combed the coast from Mourilyan to Cooper Point.

Dalrymple, who figured largely in the establishment of Cardwell, found the Johnstone River from inland and praised it as 'all fitted for tropical agriculture of which fully 300 000 acres are suitable for sugar'. Later, George Elphinstone, while searching for a coastal outlet for the Palmer River goldfields (Cooktown was eventually chosen), named the river after Johnstone and the two points in Gladys Inlet, Coquette and Flying Fish, after his two survey vessels.

The first white settler in the area was Henry Fitzgerald who surveyed and settled Mackay. With eleven Europeans and twenty Kanakas he cleared land and planted cane at Flying Fish Point in 1880 and built a mill in 1882 which precipitated a rush to the area. The township, up river from his plantation, was later named Geraldton in his honour but was later changed to Innisfail after the ancient poetical name for Ireland.

When the Palmer River goldfields died for want of easily mined ore, many Chinese drifted into Innisfail, opening general stores and growing bananas. Junks and sampans on the Johnstone River, ferrying bananas down to ships waiting off the entrance, were a common sight.

With the final abolition of slave labour, Japanese were tried, but soon immigrant Italians flooded in and took over the field labour. Not content to remain labourers all their lives, they purchased their own holdings and asserted their rights as Australians. Instead of becoming transient cane cutters like so many Australians of the period, they settled and eventually became a major political and commercial force in and around Innisfail. This led to considerable friction, giving rise to a branch of the Mafia in the area known as the Black Hand. There are stories of blackmail and extortion and there was even a shoot-out in the main street when a man who had had both ears severed for informing, shot down his aggressor.

Riverbank pile berths in Innisfail are close together obliging a vessel to lie alongside. A few are available to casuals at a fair rent. In the pic above, the Jubilee Bridge across the South Johnstone River is seen with the Commercial Jetty, right.

Flying Fish Point is centre picture approaching from seaward. The fairway buoy has just been passed.

213

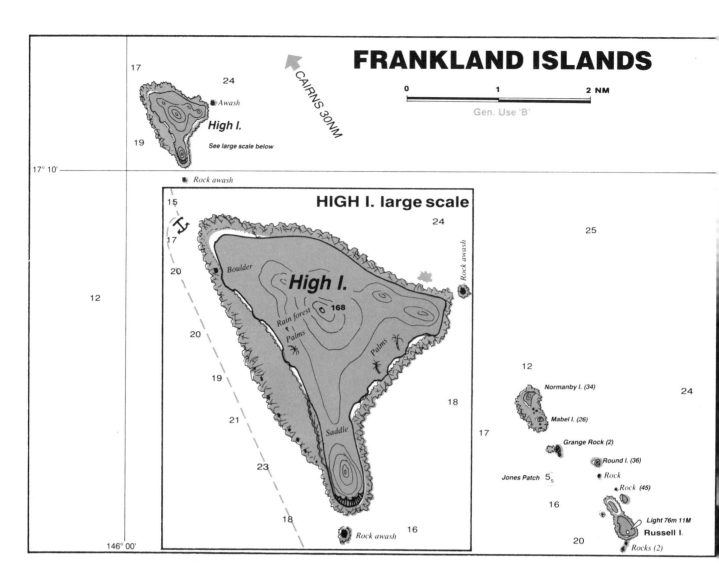

FRANKLAND ISLANDS

0   1   2 NM

Gen. Use 'B'

HIGH I. large scale

High I.

168

Boulder

Rain forest
Palms

Palms

Saddle

Rock awash

Rock awash

CAIRNS 30NM

Awash

High I.

See large scale below

17° 10'

146° 00'

Rock awash

Normanby I. (34)

Mabel I. (26)

Grange Rock (2)

Round I. (36)

Jones Patch 5₅   *Rock*

Rock (45)

Light 76m 11M

Russell I.

Rocks (2)

FRANKLAND ISLANDS. 17 miles north of Innisfail (*Flying Fish Point*) and scattered along 7 miles, the Frankland Islands do not offer good shelter but do provide delightful calm weather stopovers. If a developed onshore wind must be weathered, *High Island* is the best. This is shown in large scale on the chart.

The islands are described independently here.

Russell Island is the southernmost of the group and supports an automatic light on its south side which is high and rock-bound. Extending from its northern end is a remarkable vegetated spit with a narrow fringing reef. Although in deep water, anchorage is best along this spit's western side. On the other side of the spit, sharing Russell Island's fringing reef, is a scrub-capped rocky islet.

Round Island. One of the more conspicuous lumps when seen from a distance, this island is almost surrounded by steep, rocky cliffs. *Grange Rock*, to its immediate west, exposes 2 metres above high water springs and appears as two distinct rocks.

Normanby Island has high ground on its eastern extreme with the remainder comprising a low, vegetated spit fully surrounded by a sandy beach. At low tide, this sand exposes and joins up with the sand spit on the north end of *Mabel Island* which shares the same reef. Anchorage off the east or north of Normanby enjoys good shore access.

High Island the most northerly of the *Frankland Islands*, is separated from Normanby Island by 4 miles. High Island is close to the mainland opposite Palmer Point which is 3 miles north of the Mulgrave River entrance. It provides a logical place to await a tide suitable for entering the river.

A beautiful, uninhabited island, with rainforest cloaking its leeward side, the best trade wind anchorage is off the sand spit on the north-west tip. The swell can be heavy and the ground is deep, but it is the best available in the area.

214

Caught up in the glitz of the tourist dollar, this memorial in Innisfail is a sobering reminder that sugar has been and may be again, North Queensland's biggest earner.

FITZROY ISLAND

0   5 CABLES

14

25   17   15

19

CAIRNS 15NM

30

Bird Rock
Rocks dry HWS

Lighthouse Walk

Light WRG 145m 22–16M

Welcome Bay

25

• 269

17

13

9

8

Boulder Walk

Moorings

16° 56'

13

7   *Moorings*

Resort

Fitzroy I.

10

6   *Piled boulders*

7

12

Nudey Beach

19

24

Secret Garden Walk

34

146° 00'

FITZROY ISLAND is a little over 2 miles off the mainland in the region of *Cape Grafton* which is, itself, 8 miles east of Cairns. A continental type rising to 269 metres it is densely wooded and supports a resort and major light.

Approach is direct from any direction. The island rises from the sea 25 miles away and is the outermost of the 'islands' of Cape Grafton and Grant Hill.

Anchorage is on sand and scattered coral patches in delightful water as close to the steep coral rubble beach as the fringing reef and moorings allow. Between the deep water and the reef is a strip of sand bottom at around 5 metres deep or, further out, depths of around 9 to 15 are found. Swell can be a nuisance.

Ashore there is a resort that caters mainly for day guests, backpackers being attracted to the island's facilities and camping grounds. In from the jetty is an excellent complex of fast foods, bar, cafe, boutique and dive hire, set around a swimming pool. There are showers and toilets.

The light can be visited by walking track from the resort. Erected temporarily in 1943 it became a permanent structure in 1959 primarily as an aid for the Grafton Passage. It is constructed of stainless steel and ceramics.

The jetty at Fitzroy Island is busy with ferry traffic from Cairns. It is a popular resort with back-packers with good day guest facilities.

Fitzroy Island provides fair anchorage under its lee during trade wind weather. Often crowded, it is sometimes necessary to move as far south of the jetty as possible.

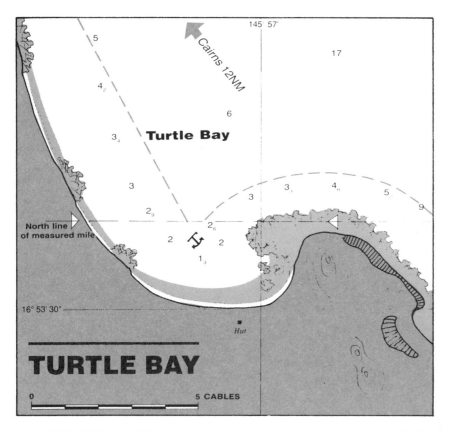

Turtle Bay

145° 57'

17

Cairns 12NM

5

4₂

6

3₄   **Turtle Bay**

3

North line
of measured mile

3   3₁   4₆   5   9

2₉

2₆

2   1₃   2

■ Hut

TURTLE BAY

0   5 CABLES

16° 53' 30"

TURTLE BAY. On the mainland just south of *Cape Grafton*, this lovely bay offers picturesque anchorage if not one free from swell. It invites a long stay in good weather and a picnic stop and swim otherwise. The beaches and background hills are magnificent.

Transiting across the bay are beacons which represent the northern end of a measured mile, the southern transit being at the northern end of King Beach. The beacons are not well maintained and might be missing or, at best, hard to see. They are of no consequence to the recreational sailor.

MISSION BAY. The most secure and comfortable open anchorage between Dunk Island and Cairns, Mission Bay suffers only from very severe wind bullets and a little swell during strong trade winds. The bottom

A rival for Cairns

A popular publican from the Hodgkinson gold-fields, 'Old Bill' Smith, was the first to succeed in finding a track down to Trinity Inlet (Cairns) in 1876. This was followed by a rush of speculators, but 'Old Bill' moved a little further north to the flood-plains of the Barron River where he started a rival town called Smithfield. The untimely shooting death of Smith, a destructive cyclone and heavy floods combined to spell disaster for the town and to give Cairns a competitive edge it has never lost.

is very good holding mud and anchorage should be sounded to snug into the bay as far as tide and draft allow.

In the south-west corner of the bay is the *Yarrabah* Aborigine settlement. Landing is by permission only.

Looking south into Turtle Bay. Fitzroy Island is distant left.

Rounding Cape Grafton, left, Rocky Island in Mission Bay is obvious in distance, right. There is good anchorage in this commodious bay. Beware of strong trade wind bullets.

MISSION BAY

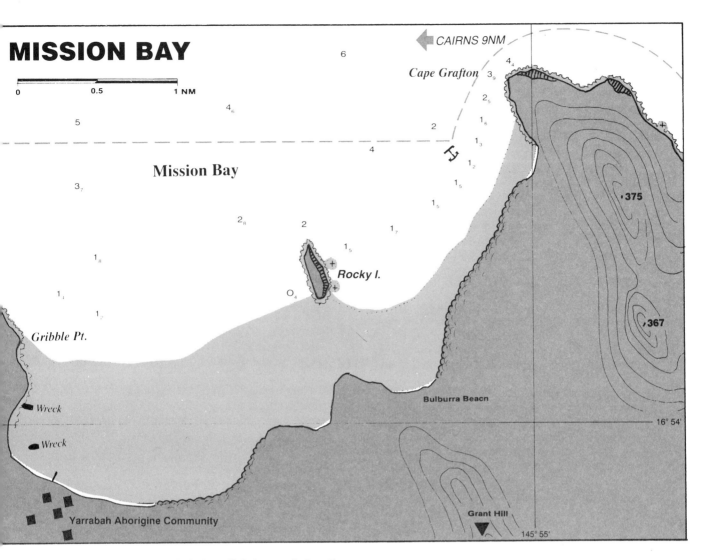

0 0.5 1 NM

Mission Bay

Cape Grafton

CAIRNS 9NM

Rocky I.

Gribble Pt.

Wreck

Wreck

Bulburra Beacn

Grant Hill

Yarrabah Aborigine Community

16° 54'

145° 55'

·375

·367

Dawn on the Daintree. This beautiful river, a day's sail north of Mission Bay, is a popular but seldom realised target. Its shallow, shifting bar denies entry during inclement weather. It is fully described on page 228.

217

CAIRNS. With its international airport receiving at least one JAL 747 every day, many hotels, two tourist islands and numerous other tourist developments and operations owned by Japanese companies, Cairns has become more and more foreign to its inhabitants. The latest developmental threat is a twin-city project on the east side of Trinity Inlet which will be connected by a road and bridge across Admiralty Island. This is also Japanese funded and appears to be inevitable despite very strong local resistance.

From the sailor's point of view, a spin-off is the number of waterfront facilities now available and the opportunity to perform any service or repair to the ship. Being the closest port to the well defined and beaconed Grafton Passage (through the Great Barrier Reef), Cairns tends to be a favourite port of entry for foreign yachts.

Approach through Grafton Passage is between the reefs of the Great Barrier Reef which form a wide, natural opening nearly 15 miles long. *Euston Reef*, the outermost sentinel, is passed to port. It supports a light beacon visible for 10 miles. The reef, incidentally, is a scientific research zone with anchoring and venturing ashore strictly prohibited.

Fitzroy Island is visible from the entrance in daylight and at night its light is visible soon after passing Euston Reef. The white sector is held, the red or green sectors to each side indicating danger.

From the south, Fitzroy Island and Cape Grafton are rounded in good deep water or the passage between the two may be taken in safety.

After rounding Cape Grafton for the run across Mission Bay to Cairns entrance channel, beware the violent gusts during a strong trade wind. To hold upwind, it is safe to pass *False Cape* close and maintain that course into the entrance channel which, under these circumstances, will be entered about half way down its length.

From the north, *Murray Prior Range*, which terminates at False Cape, makes a good steering reference.

The entrance channel is lined on each side by port and starboard beacons and its centre is held by a white light sector on The Pier's roof.

Anchorage. Cairns Harbour (Trinity Inlet) is commodious enough to drop anchor well upstream beyond the junction with Smiths Creek. The distance from town is considerable, however, and most visitors clamour for the town anchorage opposite The Pier and Marlin Marina. This can be very crowded and is constantly bombarded by commercial wake, but it is very handy.

A happy medium is to anchor in the general area opposite the entrance to Smiths Creek where some northerly wind protection is enjoyed and a powered dinghy cuts the distance ashore.

Pile Berths. Extended upstream during the early 1990s these are available through the port authority whose office is in the Trinity Wharf complex opposite.

Marinas. The Marlin Marina is immediately to starboard on entering port. It is part of The Pier shopping complex and is only a short walk from town. Extensions are planned in the future which will be to the north of the existing wall. On this wall, the Cairns Yacht Club is to be established.

Commercial fishing vessels have two marinas in Smiths Creek; one near its entrance, the other towards the upstream end of the waterfront development within.

Cairns Yacht Club. Long established to the north of Trinity Wharf, the proposed move to the above-mentioned marina area will allow expansion. Meanwhile, it welcomes visitors and allows its small rigging beach to be used for dinghy landing. This is subject to non-interference with its own events.

Cairns Cruising Yacht Squadron. Now with a small marina off its expanded premises, this club also welcomes visitors and makes available its dinghy landing

---

Bottom Right. Entering Cairns Harbour. The town anchorage is left with the Marlin Marina in The Pier shopping complex, right. Pile berths are about centre against the mangroves.

The small marina of the Cairns Cruising Yacht Squadron is but one of many facilities for the sailor in this large, natural harbour.

CAIRNS APPROACHES

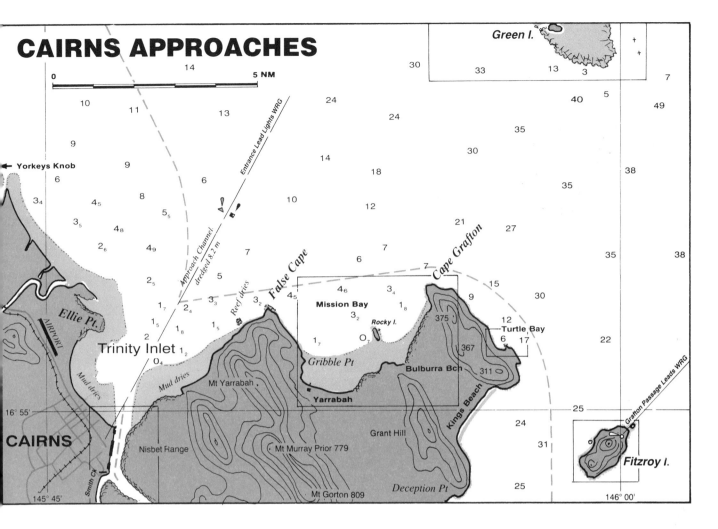

Cairns in small scale is shown above with two large scale plans of the entire Cairns Harbour over the page.

pontoon when possible. Its haul-out yard is commodious with a straddle lift capable of hauling most visiting craft. It is in Smiths Creek.

Customs. Cairns is a full clearance port. Radio ahead and follow instructions. Do not go alongside until cleared.

Tides. Cairns is a standard port in the *Tide Tables* and experiences an average maximum range of 1.8 metres. Maximum springs rarely exceed 2.9 metres.

Haul-out. Most such facilities are concentrated in Smiths Creek where straddle lifts of up to 150 tonnes capacity are available as well as slipways and a dry dock. Coconut Slipway, up Trinity Inlet on its eastern side, has a steel cradle on a concrete pad ideally suited to private craft. Its prices are often the most competitive.

Mail Collection. Because of its popularity with tourists of all types, Cairns Mail Centre has always been a busy place, often seeing queues of people extending out into the street. The new centre, built to alleviate this problem, is almost as bad, especially, it seems, since delivery became computerised.

There is little the customer can do about this; however, those planning on basing themselves in, or near, Smiths Creek, might consider having their mail forwarded to Post Office, Bungalow.

Fuel and Water. Trawlers have a facility on the jetty immediately inside the mouth of Smith's Creek. Private craft may go alongside the Marlin Jetty and order fuel from the nearby service station. Time is strictly limited here and it is best to wait until local charter boats have cleared their guests. Generally, after 10.00 hours and before 15.00 hours is best. LPG is also available here.

Repairs. Every facet of the boating industry is represented in Cairns offering repairs to sails, engines, rigging, spars, electronics, hulls of all materials, aluminium and steel fabrication and so on. Chandleries are well stocked and resins of all types are available.

Victualling. The grab-it-while-it's-going mentality that seems to pervade all tourist areas prevails in Cairns making it the most expensive town in which to bulk-victual on the east coast of Australia (barring those of a more isolated nature). However, compared to Port Moresby, Thursday Island and Darwin it is cheap and should be considered thus if heading in those directions.

There are plenty of supermarkets to choose from plus a few shopping malls out of town. The latter are serviced by commuter bus from the city centre. For

219

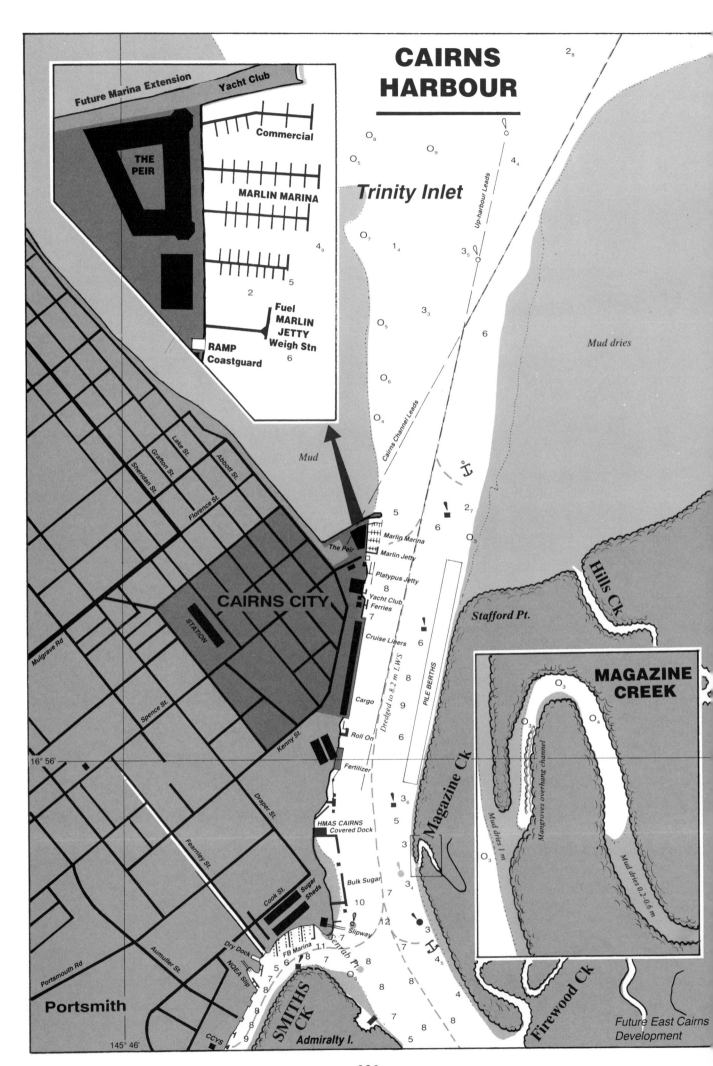

CAIRNS HARBOUR

Future Marina Extension **Yacht Club**

THE PEIR

Commercial

MARLIN MARINA

Fuel
MARLIN
JETTY
Weigh Stn

RAMP
Coastguard

2 8

O 8

O 5   O 9

Trinity Inlet

4 4

O 7   1 4   3 5

Mud dries

3 3

O 5

6

O 6

O 4

Cairns Channel Leads

Up-harbour Leads

Mud

5

Marlin Marina

6   2 7

The Peir   Marlin Jetty

O 3

Platypus Jetty

Yacht Club
Ferries

Cruise Liners   6

Stafford Pt.

Cargo   9

Roll On   6

Fertilizer

Hills Ck

Magazine Ck

MAGAZINE CREEK

O 3

O 3a   O 4

Mangroves overhang channel

Mud dries 1 m

O 3

Mud dries 0.2-0.6 m

Lake St.
Abbott St.
Grafton St.
Sheridan St.
Florence St.

CAIRNS CITY

STATION

Mulgrave Rd

Spence St.

Kenny St.

Draper St.

Fearnley St.

Dredged to 8.2 m LWS

PILE BERTHS

HMAS CAIRNS
Covered Dock   3 6

5

3

Bulk Sugar   3 4

Cook St.   Sugar
Sheds   7

10

Dry Dock   FB Marina   1 2

NQEA Slip   8   8

Portsmouth Rd   Aumuller St.

Portsmith

145° 46'

CCYS

**SMITHS
CK**

Admiralty I.

Serrab Pt.

3

7

8   8

7   8

9

8

4 5
O

8

4

7

8

5

Firewood Ck

*Future East Cairns
Development*

16° 56'

220

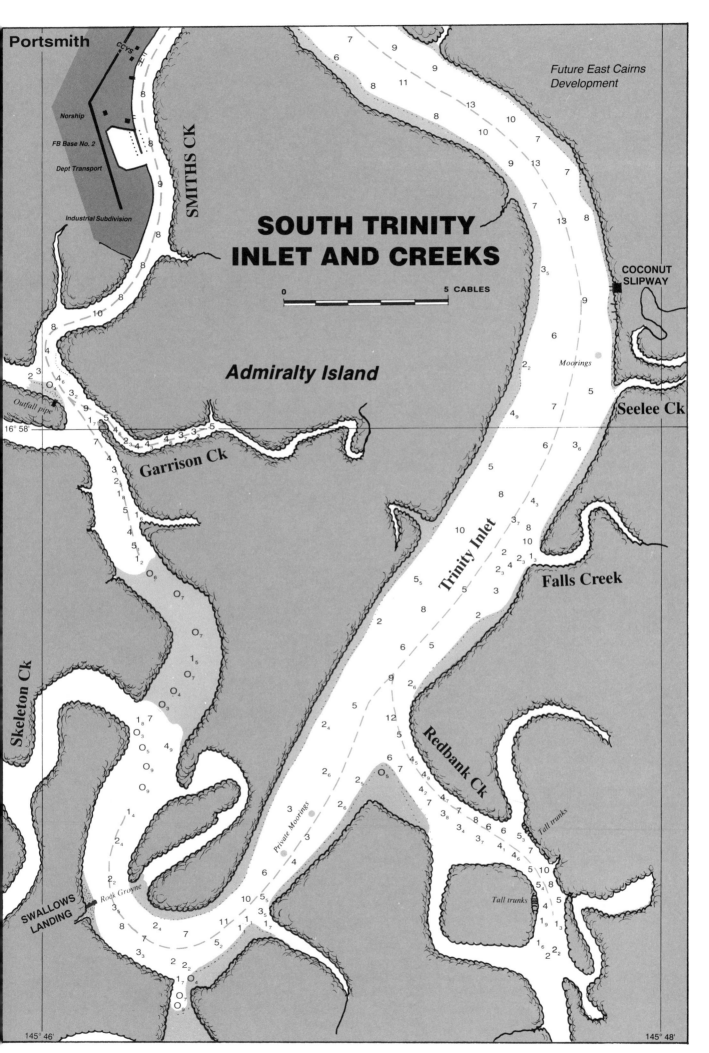

SOUTH TRINITY INLET AND CREEKS

Portsmith

CCYS

Norship

FB Base No. 2

Dept Transport

Industrial Subdivision

SMITHS CK

Admiralty Island

Outfall pipe

16° 58'

Garrison Ck

Skeleton Ck

SWALLOWS LANDING

Rock Groyne

Private Moorings

Trinity Inlet

Redbank Ck

Falls Creek

Moorings

COCONUT SLIPWAY

Seelee Ck

Future East Cairns Development

Tall trunks

Tall trunks

0   5 CABLES

145° 46'

145° 48'

221

Marlin Marina is in front of The Pier shopping complex off the eastern tip of Cairns City.

During the late 1980's, hotels blossomed behind the Cairns waterfront threatening to block the air flow over the town.

fresh fruit and vegetables, *Rusty's Bazaar* gives the best deal and is held every Saturday.

Of Interest. Cairns came into being when the founder of the Palmer Goldfields, James Venture Mulligan, found gold again, this time on the Hodgkinson River, and needed an outlet port other than Cooktown.

In the beginning, ships ascended Trinity Inlet up to Swallows Landing, that being the nearest access to dry ground. As Cairns expanded, wetlands were filled until 'dry ground' existed right to the present harbour foreshores. Nowadays, the only wetlands are the narrower than apparent fringes along the eastern and upper western shores and good mangrove forests on Admiralty Island and at the head of the inlet. Sadly, these are inexorably being pushed back by advancing development and, as noted earlier, will be crossed by road and bridges.

Fascinating for its determination and tragic for its futility is the story of Canadian loner, Bill Moodie. In the early 1960s he settled on the banks of Trinity Inlet amidst the mangroves and a long way from town, there to build an extraordinary boat. Measuring some sixty feet it was of mangrove logs stacked and notched as is the method used in log cabin building. Between these logs tar would be pressed and the finished craft was expected to float complete with corrugated-iron deckhouses and mangrove-tree masts.

A very determined fellow, Moodie cut his logs by hand in the most hostile of environments (mud and mosquitoes) and travelled to town by rowing boat for supplies using the ebb and flood tides. Sadly, he never finished his remarkable boat, dying before launching. Investigation later showed that he left a bank balance of $82 000 in Cairns that to this day has never been claimed by relatives.

Getting ashore in Cairns can be a problem in places. This is the only dedicated landing pontoon in Smith Creek courtesy of the Cairns Cruising Yacht Squadron.

Looking up Trinity Inlet from the anchorage opposite Smith Creek. Arvo and Raili Nokelainen's big trimaran, *Raili III* is in the foreground.

222

GREEN ISLAND. Now owned by a Japanese company, Green Island was threatened with unprecedented development in 1992, many proposals being contentious and therefore not necessarily foregone conclusions. An effort by the company to deny public access at the public wharf was blocked, but so busy is it with tourist boats and ferries that 'public use' is something of a misnomer anyway.

The jetty doglegs out from the western end of the island and is approached through a gap in the reef which enters a semi-lagoon. Much of this lagoon is needed as a swing basin, leaving some room to anchor to the north of the jetty and as close to the island as possible. Caution is necessary as dark patches on the bottom can look like shoal coral patches, and vice versa.

Because it is such a busy place, the visiting sailor is advised to remain outside and drop anchor where shown on the accompanying chart. This is off the north-west tip of the reef where a clear, sandy bottom at around 9 to 12 metres is easily seen. It is not comfortable during a developed sea, but is secure.

Ashore are many tourist attractions including an underwater observatory on the end of the jetty, a hotel and accommodation, theatre, crocodile farm and picnic facilities. The island and reef form a national park.

ARLINGTON REEF runs off the accompanying chart for more than 6 miles to border Cairns' major ocean access channel, Grafton Passage. Being a tight crescent shape, it offers good anchorage inside its south-east corner. The approach between Arlington and Upolu Reefs is safe enough with local knowledge, but has many coral heads scattered across its southern entrance. Use it with care and a good lookout.

UPOLU REEF has a delightful sand cay on its north-west corner close to which secure anchorage can be found during calm to moderate trade wind conditions. With the wind much above 10 knots, it becomes quite sloppy, but endurable for the excellent swimming it offers.

Because of their close proximity to Cairns, these reefs tend to be the busiest on the coast. Green Island was to undergo a multi-million dollar facelift during the mid-1990's.

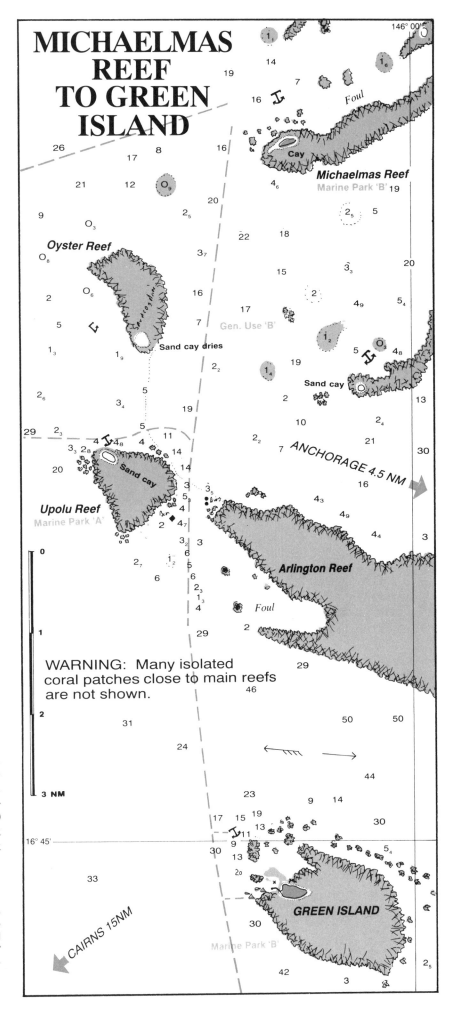

MICHAELMAS REEF TO GREEN ISLAND

WARNING: Many isolated coral patches close to main reefs are not shown.

OYSTER REEF has a tidal sand cay on its southern tip and provides fair haven during north-easterly winds where shown. Like most of the bottom in this entire region, there are countless scattered coral heads on clear sand. Most are below a level of concern for the average keeler, but constant vigilance is nevertheless advised.

MICHAELMAS CAY has always been a favourite with Cairns people, but has latterly been swamped with tourism. It is the destination of an endless stream of runabouts, cruising yachts and charter boats with one hundred boats visiting the cay during any one day not being uncommon. One marvels that its famous tern breeding ground manages to survive the human onslaught.

When coming to anchor, pick your way carefully amongst the many coral heads to anchor in their midst over sand or remain offshore to anchor in clear but deep water at around 16 to 25 metres.

The unnamed reef between Michaelmas Cay and Arlington Reef has fair anchorage but, again, must be approached with great caution, especially when coming to anchor.

YORKEYS KNOB Less than 7 miles north-west of the Cairns Harbour approach channel and 5 miles south-east of Double Island, Yorkeys Knob is the name of a headland and settlement on the mainland. Tucked under its lee is the *Half Moon Bay Marina* where casual berths should be available through a berth pool operated by the Yorkeys Knob Boating Club.

DOUBLE ISLAND lies on the northern end of a reef close to the mainland, 13 miles north-west of Cairns. On the south-east corner of the same reef is the smaller island of *Haycock*. Both are well wooded with barren east faces.

The least swell-troubled anchorage is off the western end where will be seen a large private home, generator shed and beach. A few moorings are in the vicinity.

Easily visible over on the mainland is a large public jetty which serves the settlement of Palm Beach. A TV tower is a conspicuous feature of the mainland there. A marina is planned on the mainland close to Double Island.

The Palm Cove Jetty, easily seen from the anchorage off Double Island, is unprotected from south-east winds and is therefore only suitable for mainland access during fair conditions.

Double Island is close to the mainland north of Cairns near the settlement of Palm Cove. There is a private house ashore.

The *Bally Hooley* is a tourist train operating between Port Douglas and Mossman along the old sugar tram route.

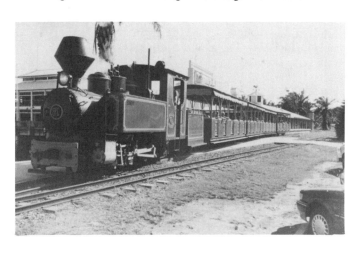

The distant saddleback of Double Island is clear here on seaward approach. Haycock Island, left, shares the same reef.

Double Island from the anchorage. There is a private house ashore here.

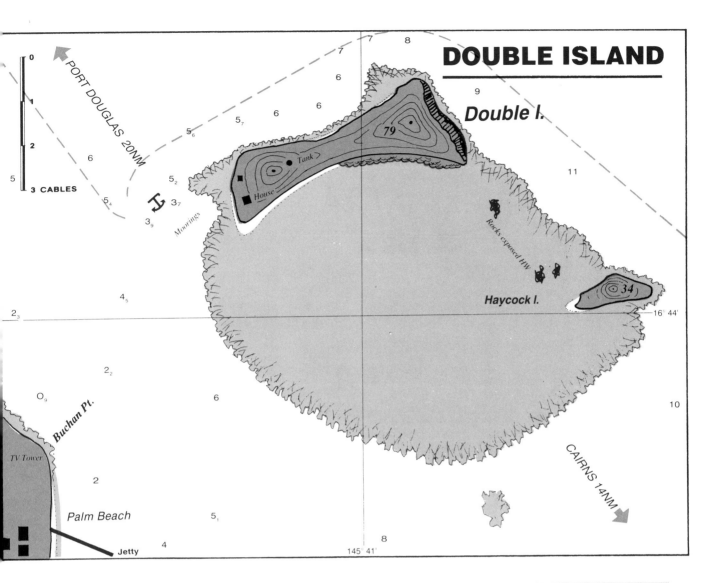

DOUBLE ISLAND

Double I.

PORT DOUGLAS 20NM

3 CABLES

Moorings

Tank

House

Rocks exposed HW

Haycock I.

CAIRNS 14NM

Buchan Pt.

TV Tower

Palm Beach

Jetty

16° 44'

145° 41'

The Brisbane-built, US owned yacht, *The Other Woman*, with a length of 58 metres and a draft of over 3 metres, managed to enter Port Douglas despite its shoal bar.

Marina Mirage, Port Douglas.

225

PORT DOUGLAS. Lying snug under Island Point on the mainland 34 miles north-west from Cairns, Port Douglas offers total security and a choice of berths or anchorage as well as facilities.

Approach. The land in the vicinity of Port Douglas is high and densely wooded providing many opportunities for the hand-bearing compass. From the north, steer direct for Island Point from *Snapper Island* and from the south take care to pass safely outside *Wentworth* and *Egmont Reefs*, the latter having a beacon on its south-east end which becomes visible at around the time that the low-lying land between the mainland and Island Point becomes visible. The reefs themselves can be difficult to identify from any distance, especially at high tide, and more especially because Port Douglas is often approached against the sun. From close to Egmont Beacon *Low Islets* lift above the horizon as two islets and *Double Island*, to the south-east, drops away as two separate dots.

Final approach into the port is on leading beacons with port and starboard buoys defining the channel limits. These buoys are moved when necessary and they often conflict with the leading beacon's transit. In this case, believe the buoys only.

Anchorage is prohibited between the two marinas where expansion is planned. Continue upstream beyond the last pile berths and, remaining clear of any swing moorings, drop anchor in the stream favouring one side or the other to leave a clear channel. The bottom is good holding mud and access back to town is easy by outboard dinghy.

Pile Berths are available to visitors. Check in at the public landing where a phone number is displayed or call ahead on VHF Channel 91.

Marinas. A few berths are available in *The Duckpond* (check with the nearby chandlery) whilst the two marinas, *Mirage* and *Closehaven*, at opposite ends of the dredged harbour, have casual berths. Both can be called ahead by radio.

Nav Aids. All buoys and beacons are lit for night use. The major light on Island Point has a red sector fanning the offshore reefs to the south-east.

Tides. Port Douglas enjoys Standard Port treatment in the *Tide Tables*. Times and heights are similar to Cairns.

Fuel is available from the fish wharf and Mirage Marina. The latter demands some tight manoeuvring, being deep within the complex as indicated on the chart.

Water is piped to all marina berths or can be taken aboard at the public landing.

The Boat Club has been absorbed into the *Combined Clubs*. Visitors continue to be welcome.

Victualling. The town of Port Douglas will satisfy most demands and coffee freaks will enjoy the expensive but high quality cafes in the Marina Mirage complex. There are hotels, a small supermarket and an excess of restaurants. General boat repairs, slipping and servicing can be carried out and a fair range of parts will be found.

Approaching Port Douglas from the north, Island Point is dominant left with peaked Black Mountain at 1055 metres high in the background.

Entering Port Douglas (Dickson Inlet). The leads must sometimes be abandoned in favour of port and starboard buoys.

Looking up Dickson Inlet, the old bagged sugar loading wharf (now a museum) is left with marinas and pile berths ahead.

The old wharf is a nautical museum owned by well known diver, Ben Cropp. It is the first building passed when entering Port Douglas.

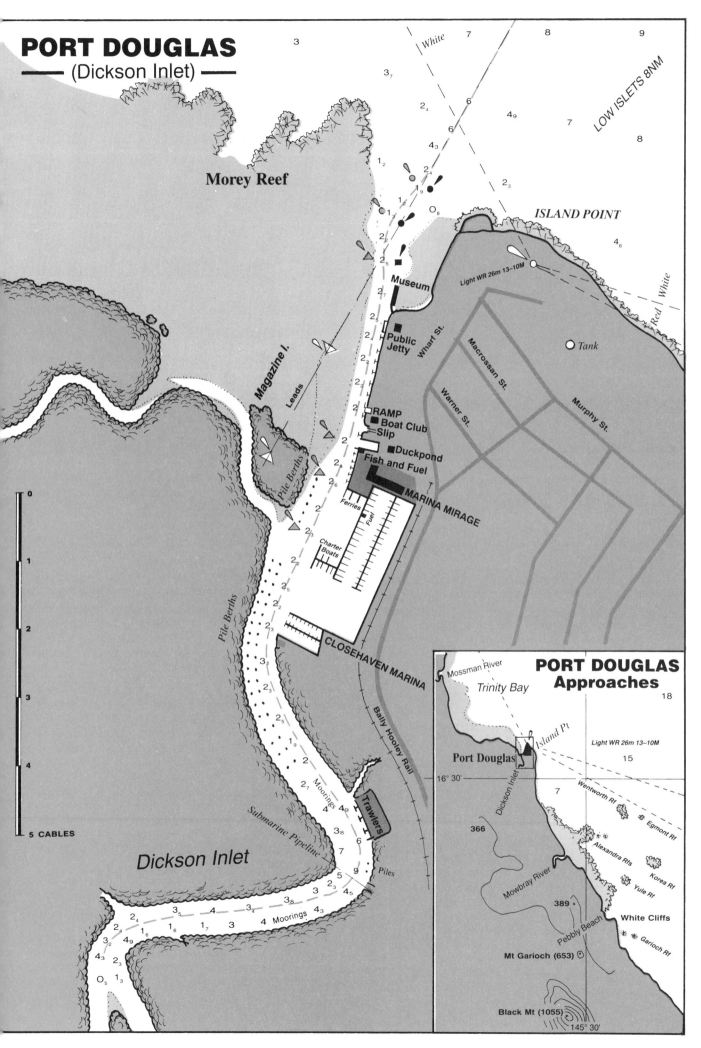

PORT DOUGLAS
— (Dickson Inlet) —

Morey Reef

White

LOW ISLETS 8NM

ISLAND POINT

Museum

Light WR 26m 13–10M

Red | White

Magazine I.

Leads

Public
Jetty

Wharf St.

Macrossan St.

Tank

Murphy St.

Warner St.

Pile Berths

RAMP
Boat Club
Slip

Duckpond

Fish and Fuel

MARINA MIRAGE

Ferries

Fuel

Charter
Boats

Pile Berths

CLOSEHAVEN MARINA

Bally Hooley Rail

0

1

2

3

4

5 CABLES

Moorings

Trawlers

Submarine Pipeline

Dickson Inlet

Piles

Moorings

PORT DOUGLAS
Approaches

Mossman River

Trinity Bay

18

Port Douglas

Island Pt

Light WR 26m 13–10M

15

16° 30'

Dickson Inlet

7

Wentworth Rf

366

Egmont Rf

Alexandra Rfs

Mowbray River

Korea Rf

Yule Rf

389

White Cliffs

Pebbly Beach

Garioch Rf

Mt Garioch (653)

Black Mt (1055)

145° 30'

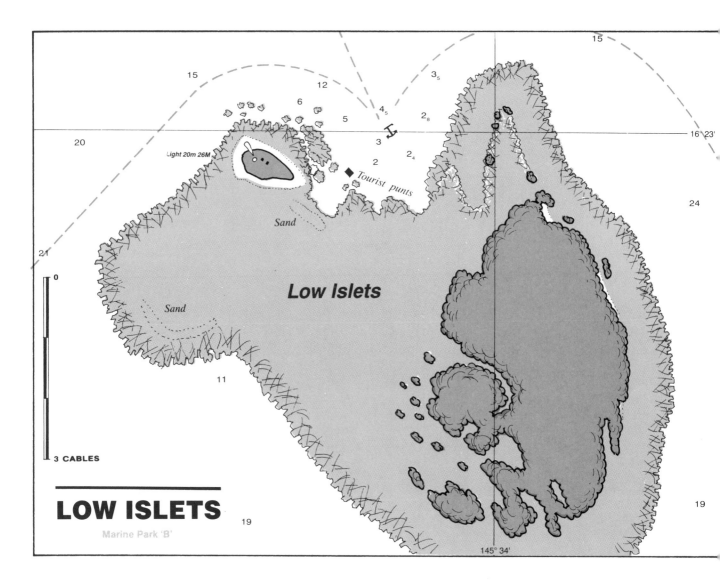

LOW ISLETS

Marine Park 'B'

LOW ISLETS. Situated 7½ miles north-east of Port Douglas and a popular destination for tourists emanating from that port, Low Islets provide delightful surroundings and good anchorage over sand and scattered coral. The two islets comprise a mangrove forest on the south-east edge of the reef and a palm studded cay towards the north-west. The latter supports a lighthouse.

The small cay is sighted from a distance of about 9 miles from where the lighthouse dominates. The mangrove cay being lower is sighted at a distance of about 8 miles.

Anchorage is in the half lagoon on the northern side and is secure against the strongest trade wind. It is untenable during northerlies at which time the closest haven is in Port Douglas or under the lee of Cape Kimberley.

Of Interest. The lighthouse on Low Islet was established in November 1878 with cottages for the light keepers. A cyclone in 1911 completely denuded the islet of foliage exposing the lighthouse and all buildings. In 1928, the Great Barrier Reef Research Expedition, comprised of British scientists, was established on Low Islets. Their findings were considerable and represented some of the earliest serious study of coral reefs and associated marine life.

The light was automated in 1990.

DAINTREE RIVER. Emptying into the northern corner of *Trinity Bay*, 10 miles north of Port Douglas, the Daintree River is navigable by deep drafted vessels working a flood tide for approximately eight miles. Shown opposite and described here is the most useful part of the river from its entrance to the vehicular ferry, a distance of around five miles.

Approach from any direction enjoys good reference in *Cape Kimberley* and *Snapper Island*. The actual river mouth is seen as a break in the beach at *Halls Point*, but can only be reached after skirting south-tending sand banks and finding the deepest water over the bar.

The Bar This moves according to the way in which silt is distributed around the entrance. The channel through it tends to be most stable and permanent where shown opposite by leading beacons. This channel had closed as of late 1993 with the relevant beacons in a state of disrepair.

The new channel is to the north and is indicated by a fairway buoy immediately outside and a green buoy immediately inside the entrance.

Considering the transitional state of the Daintree bar, the navigator working maximum draft should seek local knowledge from Port Douglas and calm weather only should be used. The possibility of the channel reverting back to its original position should also be borne in mind. If this happens, it can be presumed

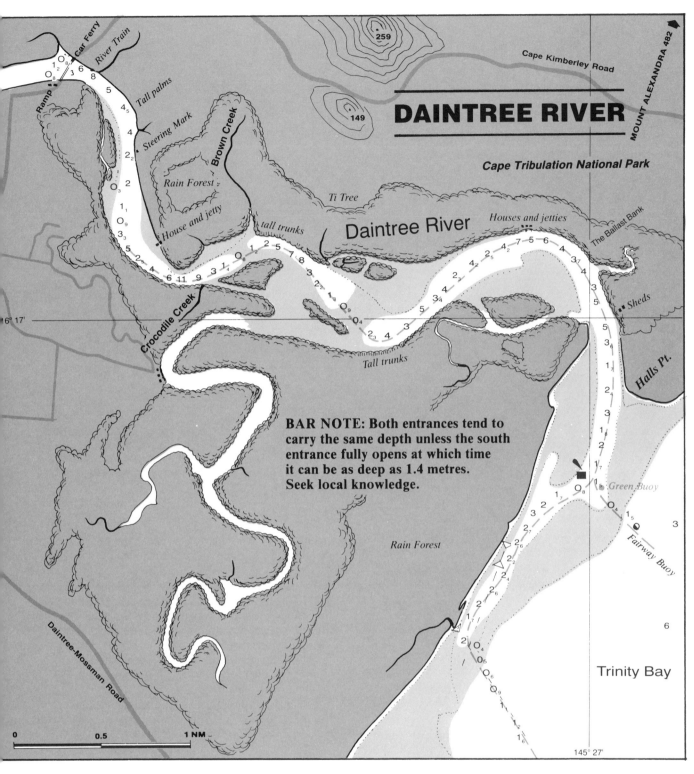

DAINTREE RIVER

Cape Tribulation National Park

Daintree River

BAR NOTE: Both entrances tend to carry the same depth unless the south entrance fully opens at which time it can be as deep as 1.4 metres. Seek local knowledge.

Trinity Bay

Car Ferry
River Train
Tall palms
Steering Mark
Brown Creek
Rain Forest
House and jetty
tall trunks
Ti Tree
Houses and jetties
The Ballast Bank
Sheds
Halls Pt.
Green Buoy
Fairway Buoy
Ramp
Crocodile Creek
Tall trunks
Rain Forest
Daintree-Mossman Road
Cape Kimberley Road
MOUNT ALEXANDRA 482

0   0.5   1 NM

6° 17'

145° 27'

The deepest channel across the Daintree River bar as of late 1993 was indicated by a fairway buoy outside the bar and a green buoy immediately inside. The old beaconed channel is shown in detail above on the basis that the bar may revert back to its original form in the future.

that the leading beacons will not be reinstated in favour of the continued use of buoys.

Ascending the Daintree. Having passed inside Halls Point, houses will be seen on the opposite bank towards the north-west. They provide good reference when steering in such a way that holds the best water between the sand banks extending north from the western headland and the ballast banks which lie submerged along the mangroves to starboard. These are the result of early trading vessel dumping their ballast before loading produce from the Daintree in the days before road connections.

With the houses abeam, the course turns south-west and lays towards the southern bank where tall man-

Into calm water in the Daintree River, a house on the far bank provides a fair steering mark.

Although wide and mostly navigable, the best water must be adhered to in the Daintree. Thornton Range runs along the north side of the river.

Entering the final bend before steering north towards the vehicular ferry which is just around the bend after this one.

Looking up the final reach before the ferry. Thornton Peak dominates the background.

grove trunks will be seen. Beyond them, the course again turns north-west soon after which the first shoal is encountered. This carries a depth of 0.9 metres LWS and will be cleared easily if the bar has just been cleared on the same tide.

Beyond this shoal the river deepens dramatically before again shoaling beyond Brown Creek by which time the port bank should be favoured. After again attaining good depths, it shoals again immediately after the corner near Crocodile Creek is rounded demanding that the port bank be hugged until crossing the river diagonally to maintain the best depths up to the vehicular ferry.

Tides. Maximum range tends to be around three metres, but is more commonly around two. Nearby Port Douglas is the best reference, it being a standard port in the *Official Tide Tables*.

Beacons. These comprise the already mentioned beacons between the bar and Halls Point outside the river entrance. They may be moved, decreased or added to according to circumstances. Within the river there are no official beacons, but steering marks are sometimes maintained by local boat people. They should not be depended on nor presumed to be easily seen.

Warning. Crocodiles inhabit the Daintree River. Swimming is extremely hazardous.

Anchorage. During a developed wind from any direction, windward-tide will occur. However, the bottom is good holding and well chosen swinging room is more than adequate for a secure comfortable stay anywhere

along the river's length. Because it is a popular recreational boating venue, an anchor light is advised.

SNAPPER ISLAND. Lying a couple of miles east of the Daintree River, Snapper Island offers calm weather anchorage only, which is in deep water off its western tip. Behind the beach here will be seen picnic facilities, the island being a national park.

Northerly anchorage is fair under the lee of *Cape Kimberley* over a sand bottom. Beware of foul ground in the corner.

The graves on Snapper Island are those of passengers shipping out of Port Douglas who, after suffering shortages ashore, overindulged the ship's fare, dying from its richness. Because bodies would not keep in the tropics, they were buried on the island which became known as the Garden of Death and the Graveyard of Queensland.

More recently, the Queen of England, during her 1970 Bicentennial Cook Celebrations visit, picnicked here and left behind a box of silverware. It has since graced the mantelpiece of a local fisherman.

CAPE KIMBERLEY fingers its way to the east-south-east trying to reach Snapper Island across Penguin Channel. It provides good shelter under its lee during true north to west winds in shoaling water towards a beach which runs from the Cape down to the Daintree River mouth. Beware of underwater patches when closing the beach.

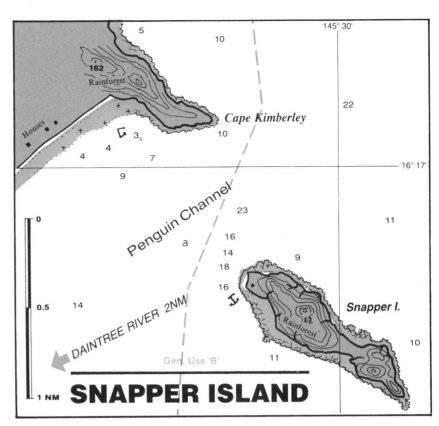

SNAPPER ISLAND

Daintree Ferry

Capable of carrying the largest articulated vehicle, the Daintree Ferry operates continuously between the hours of 0600 and midnight.

No Power

In a bid to curb development in the rainforest region north of the Daintree River, Premier Wayne Goss announced in July 1993 that the electricity grid would not cross the river. Instead, alternative power sources would be encouraged.

Snapper Island is a fair weather anchorage only. The sand spit on the north-west corner provides good landing at high tide.

Snapper Island bears about north-east. A poor anchorage, the best spot is near the beach, left.

Bailay Point, centre, and Cape Kimberley, left, from the north. Snapper Island is extreme left.

Snapper Island, left, and Cape Kimberley, right, form Penguin Channel between

Looking north from near Penguin Channel. Cape Kimberley is close left with Cape Tribulation distant right.

Black Rock lies close to the land 2 miles north of Cape Kimberley.

Approaching Bailay Creek. The entrance is under the twin peaks near centre pic. The creek's bar dries at low water springs.

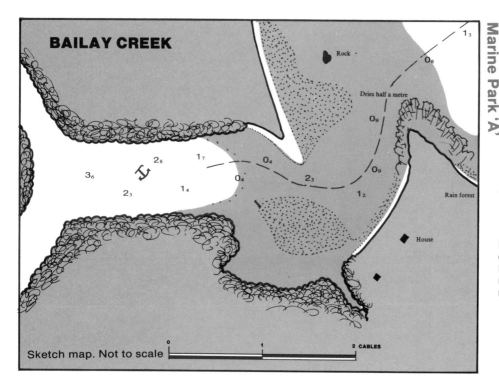

BAILAY CREEK

Rock

Dries half a metre

House

Rain forest

Marine Park 'A'

Sketch map. Not to scale

0   1   2 CABLES

Bailay Creek is a high-tide, calm weather-only haven. Development as a resort-marina remains a persistent rumour.

BAILAY CREEK flows into the south-west corner of *Alexandra Bay* 9 miles around the Cape Kimberley Headland from the mouth of the Daintree River. It is strictly a calm-weather, shoal-draft anchorage and one that can only be entered at a tide equal to the vessel's draft plus 0.5 metres.

Approach. On entering Alexandra Bay, the creek entrance will be found at the south end of the bay-long beach. The low headland formed by this beach and native scrub should bear approximately south-west, favouring the eastern headland which is high, rocky and well wooded.

As soon as a south-tending creek is nearly abeam to port, haul sharp around to favour the steep sand headland to starboard beyond which the water deepens into an all-tide anchorage.

Anchorage is confined between mangrove-lined banks and the best water is towards the 'Y' junction where it separates into two tributaries.

CAPTAIN COOK. Historically, this section of the Coral Coast has more significance then any other part of Australia for it was here where *Endeavour* came close to disaster. Had she been lost with all hands during her encounter with the reef, it is entirely probable that we would be all speaking French now, the British Crown being reluctant to act on recommendations based on Cook's voyage at a time when France was actively expanding her Pacific interest.

However, as we all know, *Endeavour* did survive to sail back to England leaving us only to conject on Captain Cook's extraordinary decision to sail offshore during the night when he should have come to anchor. This happened immediately north of Cape Tribulation and leaves us in no doubt that neither he nor any of his officers had any notion of the extent of the barrier reef. Even in this day and age of accurate charts, excellent navigational aids and electronic wizardry aboard ship, one does not sail amongst coral reefs after dark.

Captain Cook's decision to sail offshore was based on his desire to get around a danger sighted ahead before dusk. This was the Hope Islets and his actions are well documented in his journal.

'*At this time* (when close to the mainland) *we shortened sail and hauled off east north east and north east by east close upon the wind for it was my design to stretch off all night as well as avoid the danger we saw ahead*' (Hope Islets).

Deepening their water, they were alarmed when it suddenly shoaled (probably passing over the tail of Pickersgill Reef), but it deepened again as the following confirms.

'*But meeting at the next cast of the lead with deep water again we concluded that we had gone over the tail of the shoals which had been seen at sunset and that all danger was past; before ten we had twenty and one and twenty fathoms and this depth continuing the gentlemen left the deck in great tranquillity and went to bed*'.

Soon after, *Endeavour* struck the reef that would bear her name.

232

CAPE TRIBULATION. Until recently the lonely, isolated domain of a few timber-getters, Cape Tribulation has been overrun with tourism. 4WDs and tourist buses pour in daily and the contentious Cooktown coast road slashes the rainforest mountains. As noted under the heading, 'Captain Cook', it was named for the part it played in the *Endeavour's* near loss.

A low but very conspicuous headland from north to south, the cape offers only a semblance of protection from a trade wind and is best saved for light weather. The beach shoals well out denying the luxury of tucking in behind the headland except with shoal draft and neap tides. When approaching from the north, hugging the coast, beware the way in which the fringing reef projects further out than expected.

Below left: One of *Endeavour's* cannons being hoisted aboard the (then) Torres Strait lighthouse service vessel, *Wallach*. She participated in their recovery from Endeavour Reef in the late 1960's.

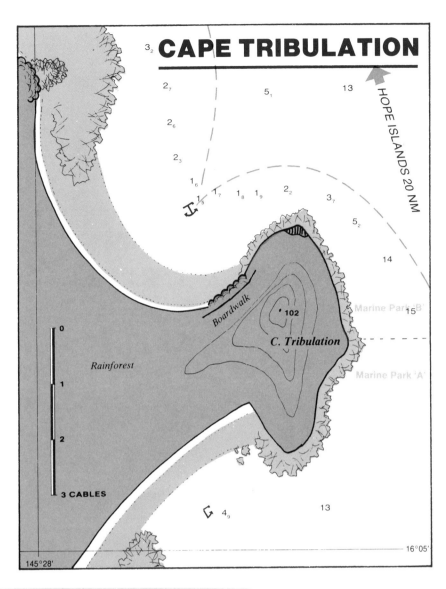

Cape Tribulation from the south. It offers fair weather anchorage only.

These two photographs show Cape Tribulation from the north. Its headland is distinctive and easily recognised from north or south from a good distance. It has become a big tourist destination.

233

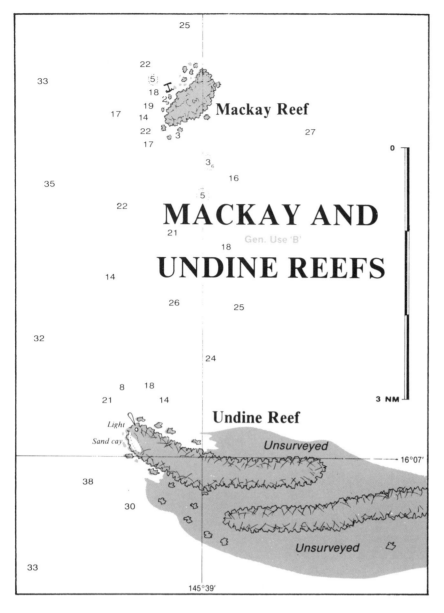

25

33

22
5
18
19
14
22
17

17

3

16

Mackay Reef

27

0

35

22
5
21
18

MACKAY AND
UNDINE REEFS

Gen. Use 'B'

26

25

32

24

8   18
21   14

Light

Sand cay

Undine Reef

Unsurveyed

16°07'

38

30

Unsurveyed

33

145°39'

3 NM

Mackay Reef is a popular fishing spot. Its anchorage must be approached with caution.

is an all-white, lit beacon on the tip of the reef with an old beacon pile nearby. There is a sand cay to the south-east of the beacon.

MACKAY REEF is 3.6 miles north of *Undine Reef* and is less than one mile long. A sand cay, fully exposed at high water springs is a feature about half way along its north-west face and shallow anchorage over a sand floor amidst numerous coral gonkers is possible under its lee. There are many isolated coral heads off its south-west tip and extending north from its north-east tip. Navigate the area with extreme caution and a good lookout. It is very troubled in developed weather.

PICKERSGILL REEF holds the false promise of a beautiful, quiescent lagoon. Regrettably, it is not available to displacement craft which are obliged to remain outside in deep water. Lying 10 miles off the mainland, adjacent to the *Bloomfield River*, it is a fishing stop only. Beware the many coral heads around its perimeter. There is a tidal sand cay on its north end and a sprinkling of boulders are seen at low tide along its edge.

UNDINE REEF lies nearly 10 miles off *Cape Tribulation* and does not offer good protection from south-easterlies. Much of its north coast is unsurveyed leaving only its western tip a known factor. Suitable only as a fishing stop, anchorage is in a variety of depths, 9 metres being about as shallow as one should seek. There

The Bloomfield River entrance is between high ground on its south and lowland on its north. The drying channel 'S' bends to its north. Here, the entrance is centre.

Taken just outside the drying offshore bar, a beacon can be seen to the right. Use only a flood tide of a height at least equal to your draft plus half a metre.

PICKERSGILL REEF

Gen. Use 'B'

0 1 NM

Pickersgill Reef

Bloomfield Survey

The mouth of the Bloomfield was first surveyed by George Elphinstone Dalrymple who led an expedition from Cardwell in 1873 to examine the mouths of other rivers including the Moresby (Mourilyan), Johnstone, Mulgrave and Daintree. He used the cutters *Flying Fish* and *Coquette*.

Pickersgill Reef lies 12 miles east-north-east of the Bloomfield River. It is classified General Use 'B' Zone.

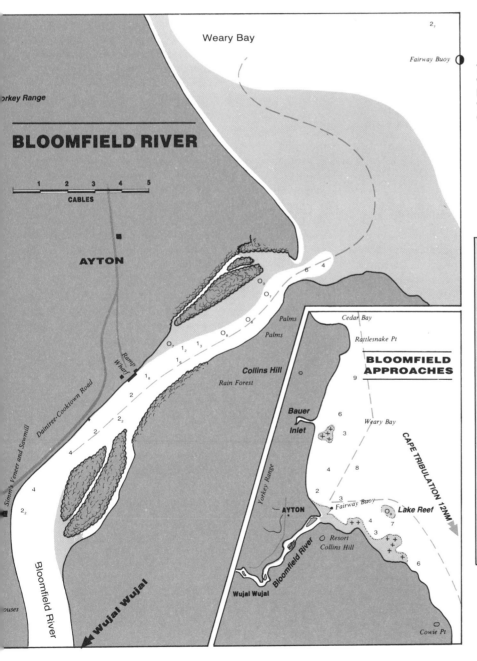

BLOOMFIELD RIVER

Weary Bay

Fairway Buoy

The Bloomfield River offers ample water inside, but less than none on its bar at low water springs. It is a calm weather exercise, details of which are over the page.

Cedar Bay Incident

On August 29, 1976, police and customs agents, wearing paramilitary gear, swooped on an isolated hippie commune in thick scrub at Cedar Bay. The raid cost more than $50,000 and involved a helicopter, light aircraft and a naval vessel. 12 young people were arrested on what was basically trumped up charges of drug possession.

The police were later accused of taking part in any orgy of wanton destruction which led to 25 charges including arson being laid against four police officers.

The event highlighted the xenophobia of the National Party then led by (some say dictated by) Premier Sir Joh Bjelke-Petersen. It thrust him into a slinging match with the State Opposition, civil libertarians, church groups and even his own police commissioner, Ray Whitrod who resigned over the issue.

It has since been suggested that the real purpose was to track down an escaped criminal whose successful evasion of police frustrated them into taking it out on the innocents of Cedar Bay.

BLOOMFIELD RIVER. 30 miles south of Cooktown and less than that north of the Daintree River, the Bloomfield empties into the south-west corner of *Weary Bay*. Its drying bar at low water springs demands a tide half a metre deeper than your draft plus a little for misjudgement. The entrance is safe only in calm weather.

Approach from the south is close to the land, standing off far enough to clear *Lake Reef* which lies 1 mile offshore to the east of the river entrance and carries 0.9 metres water low water springs. It is very difficult to sight in calm weather and care must be taken. A good transit to establish its position is *Donovan* and *Cowie Points* in line.

From outside Lake Reef, the fairway (safewater) buoy can be seen lying off the river mouth to its north-east. Its position is latitutde S15° 55′, longitude E145° 22.8′. It carries a flashing light. The river should not be entered at night, however.

From the north, the land can be held close, and the transit of *Obree Point* and *Rattlesnake Point* used to clear outside the foul ground off *Bauer Inlet*. This inlet is visible from seaward only as a depression in the beach which runs from Rattlesnake Point to the river mouth. The fairway buoy is easily sighted from the north.

The old 'S' shaped channel is shown by a dotted course-line on the chart (previous page) which was indicated by port and starboard beacons. These beacons will be removed in 1994 and are not shown here. In fact, the channel had disappeared altogether as of late 1993 with surrounding banks drying to a height of at least half a metre. This figure must be added to your draft when choosing a tide of suitable height and calm weather is essential.

It is possible that the original channel may open up which, in the 1960's, tended directly north from the river mouth.

Nav Aids As noted above, there is a fairway buoy north-east of the river entrance which carries a flashing light. The old red and green beacons indicating the now silted channel will be removed in 1994.

Anchorage outside the river, awaiting sufficient tide height, is in very messy, good-holding mud. Anchorage inside is cleaner and can be subject to windward-tide, but is otherwise calm and comfortable. The best anchorage is immediately upstream or downstream of the earth-fill wharf making sure to be clear of any vessel entering to load logs.

Facilities. The general store at Ayton caters for a broad cross-section of travellers. Basic necessities will be found there. A restaurant between the wharf and Ayton caters to the passing motorist.

Of Interest. Weary Bay was named by Captain James Cook as his men wearily hauled *Endeavour* north from the reef that nearly claimed her to Cooktown where she was temporarily repaired. The river was visited the next century when cedar-getters ranged North Queensland after cutting out the Northern Rivers area of New South Wales. Tin scratchers and goldminers also worked the Bloomfield and latterly it has become a favourite alternative-lifestyle settlement.

The Cairns-Cooktown road passes the Bloomfield, cutting along the north bank where will be seen power lines and the occasional dust of a passing vehicle in the dense jungle.

ENDEAVOUR REEF is a two-part reef running east-west for nearly 5 miles. It is where Captain Cook came to grief in 1770 and where his cannons, much of the ballast and a kedge anchor were found by the Academy of Natural Sciences of Philadelphia, U.S.A. Using a simple magnometer, they established the exact position of the jettisoned objects, ending decades of speculation that Captain Cook was wrong. Many professional divers had previously swum the reef from one end to the other, announcing that there was nothing to be found.

In January, 1969, the (then) Torres Strait lightship, *Wallach*, under the command of Len Foxcroft, was used to transport the objects to Cairns from where they went to laboratories for preservation prior to museum display. The dive and recovery vessel was owned by Vince Vlassof, best known for starting the Green Island underwater observatory.

Endeavour Reef offers suitable anchorage in fair conditions, but can be miserable during developed winds. Beware of the isolated gonkers around much of its perimeter and don't expect clear anchorage in depths much under 16 metres.

CAIRNS REEF is one of the larger inner barrier reefs at nearly 9 miles long. It hooks around to windward to create a vast area of semi-enclosed water at the head of which good protection from the swell is enjoyed. Regrettably, because it is nearly 8 miles from the leeward corners to the anchorage, there is little incentive to stop here.

Large, conspicuous boulders are a feature of Cairns Reef and around the inside edge of the lagoon are numerous isolated coral heads. When coming to anchor, these heads are on a sand floor with useful depths between. Approach with caution and anchor where sensible.

Bee Reef, close to the west of Cairns Reef's western tip, has an easily seen headless beacon near its centre. There is good water between the two reefs.

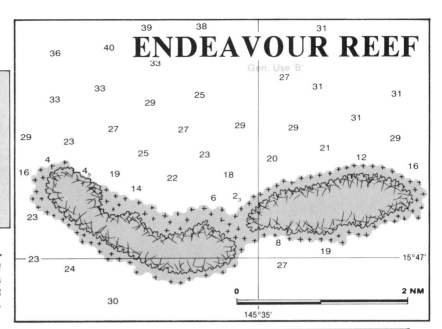

ENDEAVOUR REEF

Mission Impossible

The first mission dedicated to the care and religious conversion of Aborigines on the Cape York Peninsula was established in 1886 on the property of unsuccessful sugar planter, L.G. Bauer, on the Bloomfield River. The same poor soil that defeated Bauer doomed the mission to failure, especially as it was subject to flooding and the Aborigines were lured away to the tin-mining camps and beche-de-mer fisheries. It closed at the turn of the century.

Captain Cook's ship, *Endeavour* struck the weather side of this reef in 1770. Luckily, the weather was calm at a time when south-east gales commonly blow.

Looking Back

The One That Got Away

The Dutch ship *Straat Chatham* lies on the windward edge of Gubbins Reef, 2½ miles off the mainland northwest of Hope Islands. She went aground despite leading beacons which indicate the best water between the reef and the mainland. It is believed her skipper had a momentary lapse, calling for the wrong rudder adjustment. The accident occurred late 1972 immediately after which she was relieved of 1600 tonnes of cargo to lighten her. The coaster, *Tobiclipper* is alongside for that purpose. She spent three weeks on the reef before backing off in relatively sound condition.

Cairns Reef demands a long slog to windward to reach its protected corner during trade wind weather. Hope Islands are shown in large scale over the page.

Ballast from the *Endeavour* comes aboard the lighthouse service vessel, *Wallach* in 1969 during the recovery of jettisoned items.

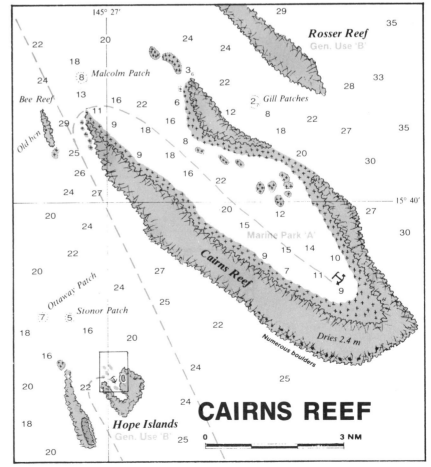

CAIRNS REEF

237

Hope Islands are comprised of two cays, each on its own reef.
The best anchorage is in the semi-lagoon towards the cay on
the easternmost reef as seen here. Take care in rounding up
for the anchorage as there are numerous coral patches.

HOPE ISLANDS. 12 miles north-north-east of the Bloomfield and 20 miles south-east of Cooktown, the Hope Islands are comprised of two separate cays on two separate reefs, there being a deep navigable channel between them. The westernmost of the cays is predominantly mangroves while the eastern cay is prettily beach fringed with national park picnic facilities ashore. The best anchorage is to the west of this cay in a semi-lagoon formed by a fragmented reef.

Approach. An overall view is gained on the Cairns Reef chart, page 237. The best approach to the eastern cay anchorage is via the channel between the two islands. This is especially so in the afternoon at which time the sun is behind you when seeking anchorage. Beware calm conditions with the sun too low for visual reef identification. Proceed with extreme caution up to and within the lagoon.

Anchorage is best where shown, close to the western side of the eastern cay within the lagoon. The bottom tends to be very foul, but generally an anchor recovers with a minimum of fuss. If worried, use an anchor buoy.

The only other anchorage during trade wind conditions is off the north-west tip of the western reef. This does not escape the swell and is best used as a fishing or lunch stop only.

The closest all-weather havens to Hope Islands are the *Bloomfield River* to their south and *Cooktown* to their north.

EGRET REEF lies 9 miles east of *Cooktown Harbour* and supports a light on its western side. It is possible to anchor on sand close to this light in about 8 metres amongst scattered gonkers. Alternative anchorage can be sought anywhere across its north-west face, but great care must be taken of the many coral heads and patches. Navigation between them is mostly possible, but only in conditions of good visibility.

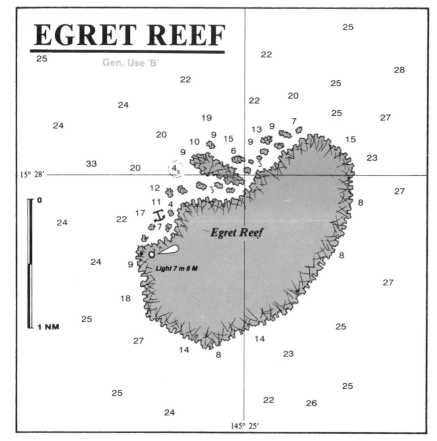

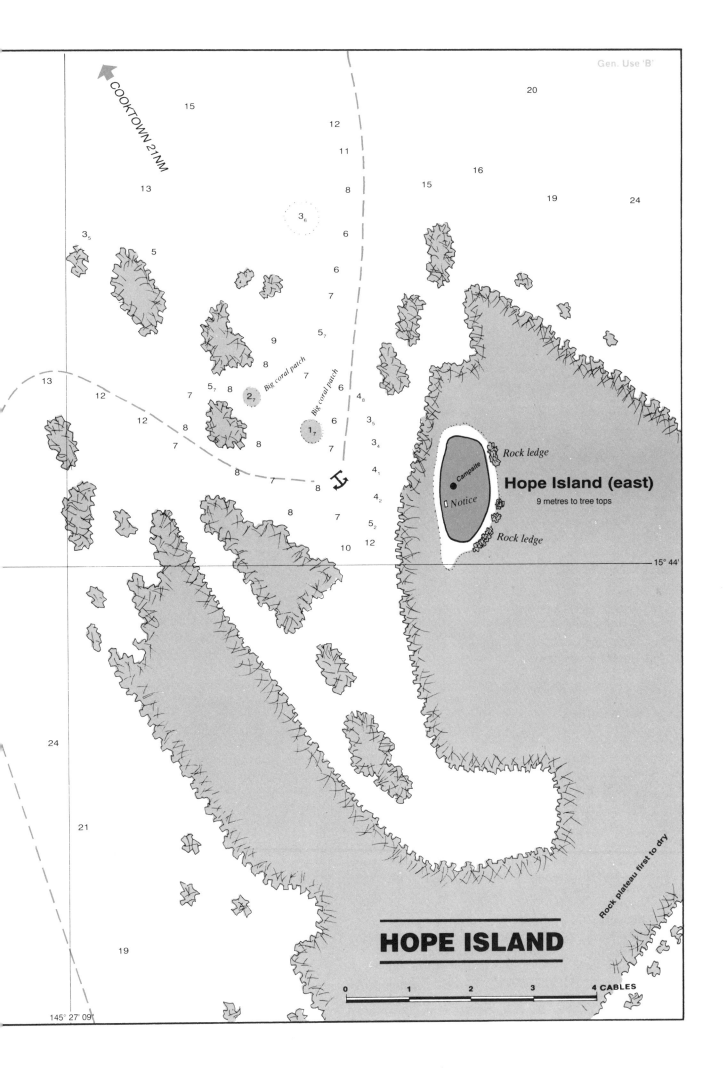

COOKTOWN 21NM

20

15

12

11

13

16

8

15

19

24

3₆

6

3₅

5

6

6

7

9

5₇

8

Big coral patch

7

5₇

8

2₇

Big coral patch

6

4₈

13

7

6

3₅

12

12

6

3₄

8

7

7

4₁

13

8

4₂

8

7

5₂

8

7

12

10

Campsite

Hope Island (east)

Rock ledge

□ Notice

9 metres to tree tops

Rock ledge

15° 44'

24

21

Rock plateau first to dry

19

HOPE ISLAND

0   1   2   3   4 **CABLES**

145° 27' 09"

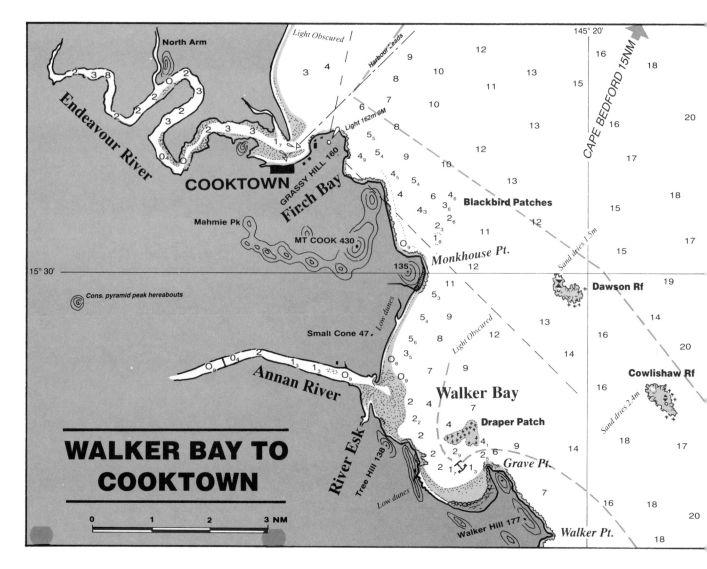

The small scale chart above shows Walker Bay, the Annan River and general southerly approaches to Cooktown. The best approach with a boisterous trade wind astern is by the dotted line as indicated although passage inside the reefs is safe enough.

WALKER BAY. An anchorage much used up until the mid 1960s by Torres Strait Islanders working the trochus shell beds from their luggers, Walker Bay is secure but thoroughly uncomfortable during a developed trade wind.

Grave Point is a mangrove covered rocky projection and there is depth enough to pass between it and *Draper Patch*. The latter does not expose at low tide nor does it show well to the naked eye. Care is needed.

If neap tides allow you to snug up close to the headland, comfort will be improved. Otherwise, anchor according to the dictates of tide and draft. The bottom is good holding sand.

ANNAN RIVER. This is for runabouts only, although a displacement craft could be taken in during calm conditions after a careful low tide survey.

The bar nearly dries at low tide and its best depths tend towards the south-east, although breakouts can occur in any direction. A conspicuous pyramid shaped hill upstream provides good reference and there are all-tide float holes upstream.

COOKTOWN. Lying on the south bank of the Endeavour River, nearly 70 miles north of Port Douglas, Cooktown is the last town on the coast before the top of Australia is reached at Cape York and Thursday Island.

Approach from the south-east can be made either inside or outside *Cowlishaw* and *Dawson Reefs*, the latter course promising more predictable clearance around *Blackbird Patches* which carry only 1.8 metres low water springs. The dominant landmark from any direction is *Mount Cook* 2 miles south-east of the town and, closer in, *Grassy Hill* is conspicuous, more from the east than north-east. Both Cowlishaw and Dawson reefs are beaconed as illustrated and, of interest, Cowlishaw claimed the Sydney flier, *Solo*, then owned by the late Vic Myers. Circumnavigating Australia in the early 1960s she fetched the reef and held for a week in heavy south-east trades yet was eventually hauled off with remarkably little damage.

From the north, Mount Cook can be seen after Cape Bedford is rounded and then used as a steering mark. When beating down against the trade winds, beware of an onshore current that can run at half a knot. *Indian Head* provides good interim reference. When entering the harbour, keep the leading beacons up to three boards open to the north for the best water over the bar.

Anchorage. Cooktown Harbour is the mouth of the *Endeavour River* which, during neap tides and light

240

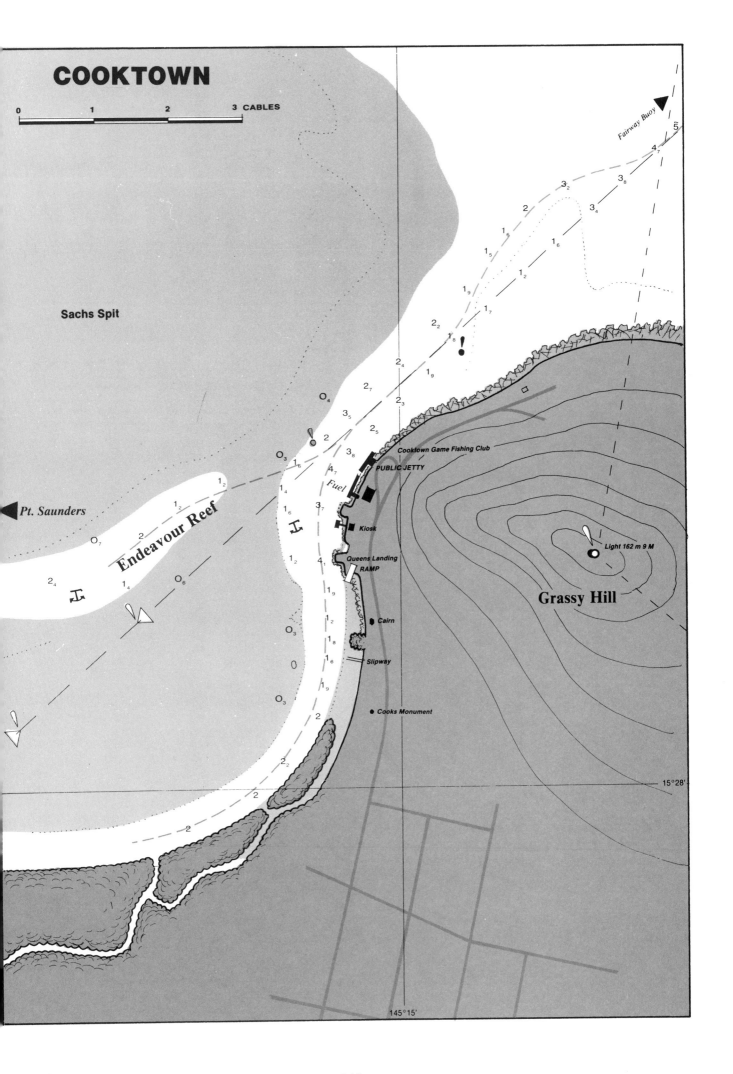

COOKTOWN

0   1   2   3 CABLES

Sachs Spit

Fairway Buoy

5₁

4₇

3₂   3₈

2   3₄   3₆

1₆   1₆

1₅   1₂

1₉   1₇

2₂   1₇

1₈

2₄   1₉

2₇

O₄   2₃   2₅

3₅

2   3₈

O₃   1₆   4₇   Fuel   Cooktown Game Fishing Club

1₄   3₇   PUBLIC JETTY

◄ Pt. Saunders   1₆   Kiosk

1₂   4₁   Queens Landing

RAMP

1₂   Endeavour Reef   1₉

O₇   1₂   1₂

2   O₃   1₈   ● Cairn

2₄   1₄   O₆   1₆   Slipway

O₃   1₉

2   ● Cooks Monument

2₂

2

2

Grassy Hill

Light 162 m 9 M

15°28'

145°15'

241

Approaching Cooktown from the east, Mount Cook at 430 metres high dominates to the left with Mount Saunders at 287 metres high dominating right. Grassy Hill, with the Endeavour River mouth to its right, is near centre.

Closer in, Mount Cook continues to dominate, left of centre with high Monkhouse Point extreme left. Grassy Hill and the river entrance is right.

Grassy Hill in close. There is a light at its peak. Mount Saunders, right.

The Cook Family Tragedies

Despite being away for years on end, Captain Cook managed to father six children, three of which died in infancy. The eldest, James, rose to command H.M. *Spitfire* but died in mysterious circumstances aged 31 when being taken out to his command at anchor in Poole Harbour. Nathaniel, the second, was lost at the age of 16 on H.M.S. *Thunderer*, which foundered in a cyclone in the West Indies, 1780. Hugh, the youngest, died in 1793, when only 17, possibly of plague, at Cambridge where he was studying for the church. Mrs Cook survived the entire family to die at Clapham on 13 May, 1835, aged 93.

Cooktown's defence against Russian invasion in the 19th century is in the foreground with Captain Cook's monument behind. Cooktown has a very special place in Australian history, being where white man first settled — albeit, unwillingly — on Australia's east coast.

With Grassy Hill close aboard, the public jetty in Cooktown appears and the dunes on Point Saunders, right of centre, are obvious.

On the leading beacons, the public jetty is clearly in view with the anchorage immediately beyond.

The anchorage in Cooktown is pleasant during neap tides but can be a worry during spring tides if it is crowded.

to moderate winds, can fool the visitor into believing it is excellent in both security and capacity. But, when heavy trades are associated with spring tides and their resultant 2 to 3 knot run, an anchored craft will sail around her anchor, heel to gusts, jerk upright to lulls and at all times be a danger to herself and other boats when conditions are crowded. And, unfortunately, conditions are very often crowded nowadays.

The greatest single problem is in finding swinging room within the restrictions of the low tide area. Often there is no room at all and a visitor is obliged to sail straight out. However, those prepared to rig and set a stern anchor may find space upstream close against the mangroves. The holding is good, the gust effect nullified and the fear of collision with other boats negated. Mosquitoes can be troublesome, but these come and go according to weather.

The holding in the swing area is good in sand, but demands plenty of scope in strong winds, a luxury often unaffordable when crowded. An alternative swing area is towards *Point Saunders*, but a shoal bar must be negotiated to enter.

Tides are based on Cairns and are almost identical in time and height.

Nav Aids. The main light on Grassy Hill is visible from a distance of 9 miles with an arc limited to between south-east and north-north-east.

The bar leading beacons are white 'V's' displaying flashing white lights.

Fuel and Water. Diesel fuel is available from two pontoons and water from the same pontoons as well as the Public Jetty. At the latter, the council must be notified and a fee paid. Water may also cost at the pontoons depending on the amount of fuel taken. Petrol must be carted from a service station in town. Gas is similarly available.

Victualling. Nothing is cheap in Cooktown, but those who need to top off before Thursday Island must do so. The shops include small supermarkets, hardware stores, boutiques, banks, post office, fast foods, coffee lounges, hotels, motels, caravan parks, laundromat and so on. Yacht hardware is not available. The newsagent, on the other hand, has a fair collection of charts and associated items.

History. Having freed his ship from Endeavour Reef, Captain Cook and his men struggled into the Endeavour River, there to spend 48 days in repair and refit as well as to rest the sick and refill the larder. While stranded there, they established a number of historical firsts, it being the first recorded place in Australia where Englishmen spent more than a few days ashore; where the kangaroo was first sighted and named and where the first true contact with the Australian Aborigine occurred, the indigenes slowly but surely trusting in the visitors' sign of peaceful intent.

One hundred years later, Cooktown became main port for the inland Palmer River goldfields boasting a population of over 30 000, with 163 brothels and

Top. Renee Tighe in Cooktown. Grassy Hill is behind.
Bottom. Main Street, Cooktown. The lovely old Westpac
building is a reminder of a past steeped in gold.

94 licensed purveyors of booze. The harbour was similarly impressive with a continuous flow of ships loading and unloading the promises of a rosy future. This, sadly, came crashing down with the expiration of gold in commercial quantities and Cooktown degenerated into a ghost town of just 300 folk towards the middle of this century.

A few things held on. The old Cooktown-Laura railway continued running until the late 1950s after which its rails were torn up and sold as scrap or for sugarcane tramways in the Mourilyan district and the Public Wharf remained twice its present length until the early 1970s when much rotted away and was never replaced. Sadly, the old powder magazine on the foreshore, north of the Public Jetty, has been allowed to deteriorate to a ruin. In its original state, this little building was unique for its absence of metal fastenings to prevent accidental ignition of powder stored within.

CAPE BEDFORD. Unique on the entire coast for its escarpment wrapping around a conspicuous plateau, Cape Bedford projects north to defend a large bay from the trade wind.

Approach is clear of danger in close and the headland will be seen for at least 25 miles in average conditions. From the south, down near Gubbins Reef, it is sighted as a series of three 'islands'; two of similar size and an eastern one much smaller. These 'islands' quickly join up but do not connect to the mainland until about 15 miles distant. The land between the mainland and the cape is all sand with many fine dunes.

Anchorage is in shoaling water with very good holding in mud. During moderate to strong trade-wind conditions a beam swell works across the bay but its severity will depend on exact location. During neaps, when a vessel can move well into the bay towards the saddle between the headland's two main mountains, conditions are comfortable. During springs, when anchorage must be taken well offshore, rolling must be accepted.

Of Interest. With no evidence of any habitation around the bay, one or more lights ashore at night might confuse. These are usually related in some way to the Hope Vale Aboriginal settlement not far inland, fishing camps sometimes being established for a few days. The original mission station was situated in the south-west corner of the bay and was run for sixty years by Pastor Swartz. He took over at the age of nineteen after his predecessor was eaten. Communications with the outside world consisted of flashing morse by mirror to the (then) manned lighthouse on Grassy Hill, Cooktown.

Cape Bedford remained Captain Cook's most dominant view of the mainland during problems he encountered when trying to reach open water immediately after departing Cooktown. Some fifteen miles east of Cape Bedford,

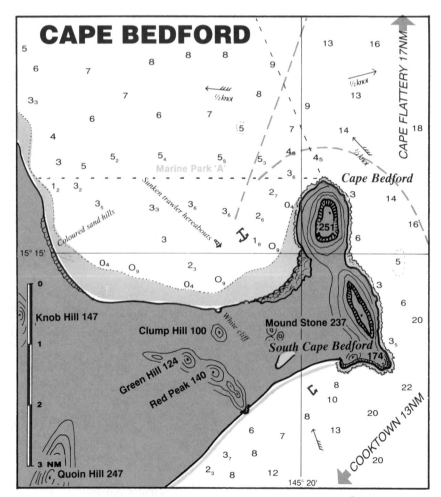

244

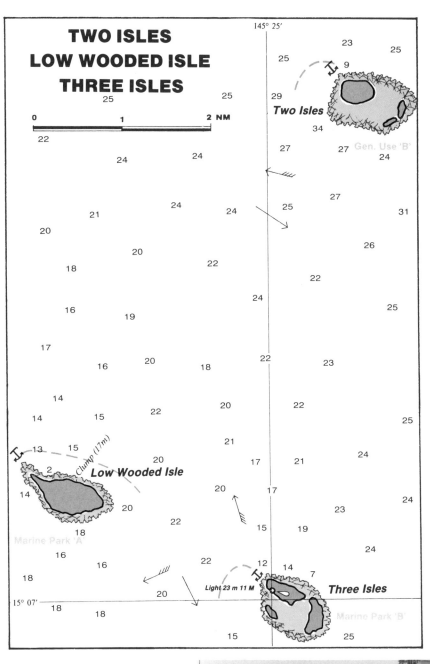

**TWO ISLES
LOW WOODED ISLE
THREE ISLES**

probably amongst the reefs to the north of Lark Reef, he brought *Endeavour* to anchor rather than risk further progress through the shoals. The next morning, Monday 6 August 1770, he and his crew awoke to a strong gale from the southeast which obliged them to 'veer away more cable, and strike our top-gallant yards'.

With time to study the area from aloft, Captain Cook became convinced that there was no passage to the east and that a continued course to the north was inevitable. Of interest, they felt so desperate that, 'It was the master's opinion, that we should beat back the way we came but this would have been an endless labour, as the wind blew strongly from that quarter, almost without intermission'.

Conditions off Cape Bedford deteriorated to the extent of more cable being veered, another anchor dropped and more tophamper brought down until *Endeavour* stopped dragging. She did not continue her journey until the 10th at which time she closed the land towards Cape Flattery.

THREE ISLES is halfway between *Cape Bedford* and *Cape Flattery*, on the outside of the recommended shipping route. Supporting three low, scrubby cays, the common reef has a light on its western side. Anchorage is poor and only suited to light weather or as a lunch stop.

LOW WOODED ISLE is another scrubby cay on the other side of the shipping channel to Three Isles. With less depth along its northern side, anchoring is easier here although, again, it is suggested in calm weather only.

An American Liberator crashed in Low Wooded Isle during World War II, its remains were still visible up until the 1970's.

TWO ISLES is 5 miles north of *Three Isles* and is similar in every respect. Both the flood and ebb tide can run at up to half a knot towards Cape Flattery. It has nothing to recommend it as an anchorage, although a delightful spot for a quick swim and walk.

Up until the mid 1980's, all silicone sand loading from the Cape Flattery strip mine was done by barge out to ships at anchor. Now direct loading is done at the wharf on the southeast corner of the headland.

245

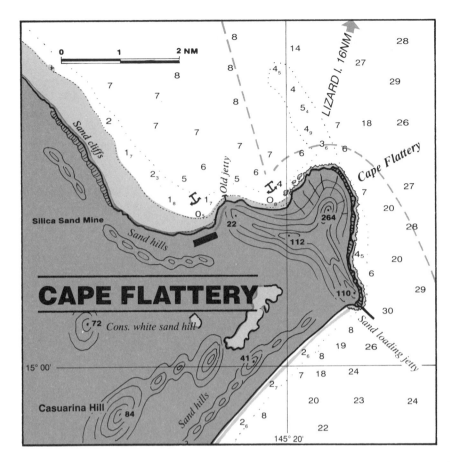

CAPE FLATTERY

Silica Sand Mine

Sand cliffs

Sand hills

.72 *Cons. white sand hill*

Casuarina Hill 84

Sand hills

Old jetty

Cape Flattery

Sand loading jetty

15° 00'

145° 20'

LIZARD I. 16NM

is seldom enough to cause discomfort and is more or less depending on state of tide.

Ashore. The accommodation, canteen and general facilities ashore are part of the Japanese-owned silica sand strip-mining operation. Its first shipment of 7,210 tons of silica sand was exported on 20 February, 1968. Since then, annual shipments have regularly topped half a million tonnes. Until the late 1980s, ships lay to anchor in the bay and were loaded by special barges from a jetty on the inner headland. Nowadays, ships load direct from a deepwater jetty on the south-east tip of Cape Flattery. There is an airstrip and STD phone ashore in the event of emergencies.

Cape Flattery bears north-west. Anchorage is good under its lee during strong trade winds.

CAPE FLATTERY provides excellent anchorage from the south-east trade wind under the lee of either of its two dominant headlands. It is 35 miles north of Cooktown and 18 miles south of Lizard Island making it an ideal stop en route between the two. It does not provide any shelter from a northerly, the nearest anchorage for such winds being to the south of Cape Bedford or in Lizard Island lagoon.

Approach. Cape Flattery appears as two distinct hills from a distance of 25 miles north or south, the western one being more peaked and slightly lower than the other which rises to 264 metres. When about 15 miles away the low land between them becomes obvious.

From Lizard Island, a direct course can safely be steered for the outer peak then the anchorage itself laid when abeam Martin Reef. *From the south*, Low Wooded Island can be passed to either side and the cape then held fairly close. On the south of the headland a wharf will be seen about which more will be said later.

On final approach from the south, a shoal spit must be crossed as Cape Flattery is rounded and the anchorage laid. This carries at least 2.4 metres low water springs 3 cables off which deepens to at least 3.5 metres 5 cables off.

Anchorage is in shoaling water in the first or second bay according to preference. The second bay, some claim, is calmer by a slim margin, both experiencing a low easterly swell during trade-wind conditions. This

History. After the problems encountered off Cape Bedford, where *Endeavour* got under way after dragging anchors and having her tophamper struck to hold station, Captain Cook continued north, passing Cape Flattery and hoping for a passage out of the reefs and shoals to the north. He named it Cape Flattery because at the time, when it bore approximately south-west, it seemed *Endeavour* might be free of threatening shoals. Unfortunately she was only being 'flattered' into such presumption on the part of her officers. Captain Cook's positioning of the cape was remarkably accurate considering the period. He was just one minute of latitude and not quite three minutes of longitude in error.

ROCKY ISLETS. A rather uninspiring wooded island devoid of coconut palms, but well endowed with beaches, Rocky Islet has two satellites, the south-eastern one being wooded, the south-western one being bare rocks and standing on its own separate reef.

Approach from the north is in good water all the way. From the south a number of reefs and their satellites must be avoided. Steer as if remaining in the main shipping channel past Cape Flattery and turn when Rocky Islets' south-eastern islet transits with *South Direction Island's* southern tip. This course clears shoals that would bother the average deep-keeled sailing vessel. It also promises a good strike on the trailing line as shoals of safe depth are crossed.

246

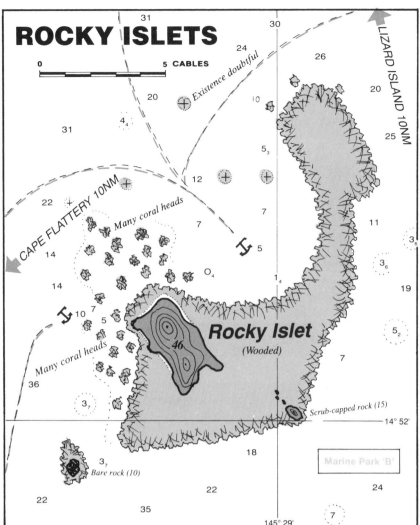

ROCKY ISLETS

0   **5 CABLES**

Existence doubtful

Rocky Islet
(Wooded)

Many coral heads

Many coral heads

Scrub-capped rock (15)

Bare rock (10)

Marine Park 'B'

145° 29'

14° 52'

LIZARD ISLAND 10NM

CAPE FLATTERY 10NM

On final approach the south-western islet can be taken close, but from it to the main island, and off the latter's north-west tip, stand a good watch for isolated gonkers. There are dozens of them in the area with a typical depth of 4 to 12 metres between.

Anchorage off the western face of the main island can be found amongst the coral gonkers during daylight and fair weather, or outside them otherwise. The transit of *High Rock* kissing *South Direction Island* indicates the clearest water close to the island, but under no circumstances relax your lookout up to anchorage.

The best anchorage is in the half-moon lagoon formed by a coral reef extending east and north from the main island. As near as can be ascertained, the anchorage area indicated on the plan is clear of coral heads offering a bottom of good-holding sand. However, the detached reefs off the main island's western-most tip continue north for a considerable distance and spread into the lagoon. Final approach into this lagoon, therefore, must be by lookout and care and the anchor should be tested against dragging to prevent concern after dark.

The coral head shown by the chart and my plan to exist off the western tip of the main reef could not be found by the author but should be presumed to be there and treated accordingly.

SOUTH DIRECTION ISLAND.

A splendid island for its steep, peaked mountain, isolation is almost guaranteed here owing to an element of danger both in entering and remaining at the anchorage. There is no beach here and therefore no easy landing.

Approach from the south is best by standing out from Cape Flattery and passing under or over Rocky Islets. A good natural transit exists which clears north of these islets; this is *High Rock* just showing behind *South Direction's* north tip.

From the north, stand well west to miss Kedge Reef and the shoals extending one mile north of the island.

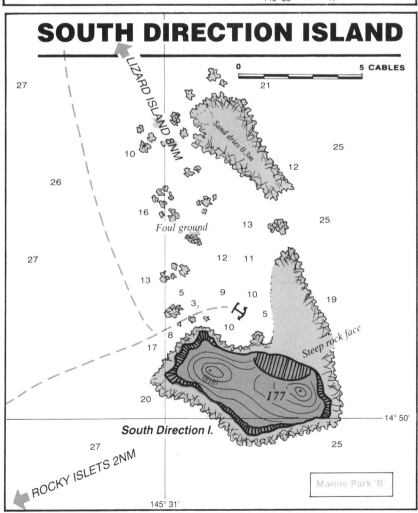

SOUTH DIRECTION ISLAND

0   **5 CABLES**

Sand dries 0.3m

Foul ground

Steep rock face

South Direction I.

LIZARD ISLAND 8NM

ROCKY ISLETS 2NM

Marine Park 'B'

14° 50'

145° 31'

247

Final approach into the anchorage must be by eyeball navigation. There are dozens of coral heads surrounding the clear anchorage area some of which pose a threat to high-tide navigation while others are deep enough for low-tide navigation. Trust none, proceed slowly with the sun behind and try to use a flood tide. The approach indicated on the plan is not necessarily the deepest.

Anchorage is in the lagoon formed by the island and its north-seeking reef. The bottom is good-holding sand at 9 metres or shoaling depths towards the reef where more coral heads may be encountered. It is a fair-weather anchorage only unless absolutely certain the anchor will hold overnight and some heavy rolling at high tide is acceptable.

Of Interest. South Direction and North Direction Islands provide good reference value when negotiating *One and a Half Mile Opening*, a passage through the outer barrier reefs 13 miles north of Lizard Island. Older charts advertised this reference, later ones do not. The transit was loose, based on a guesstimate of distance between the two islands' peaks which are held open.

North Direction, a similar land mass to South Direction but with a fine beach and sand spit on its north-west tip, offers no anchorage whatsoever.

TURTLE GROUP. Comprising nine reefs within an area 2 miles long and 3 miles wide, the Turtle Group lies nearly 6 miles north of *Lookout Point*. Of the nine reefs, six support rather poor, vegetated cays which are visible at a distance of 7 miles, and one has a tidal sand cay. Others also have tidal sand extensions to their cays.

Off-lying the group, immediately south and west, are coral patches with less than 1.8 metres covering them at low water springs. Depths in, and close around, the group vary greatly but 7 metres can be found when seeking anchorage.

Anchorage is suggested only in calm weather or in moderate weather where nothing else is available at the end of a day's run. Good northerly anchorage will be found towards the gap between the two southern-most reefs (which have the largest cays).

Of Interest. The 1845–6 overland expedition of Ludwig Leichhardt's from the south-east corner of Queensland ended at Port Essington, Northern territory. From there, passage back to Sydney was taken aboard the *Heroine*, owned and skippered by Captain Martin McKenzie. En route, they stopped at the Turtle Group to drop off a trepanging party of fifteen. On his return — by rescue vessel after losing his own ship further

South Direction Island bears east.

No beaches and steep, rocky foreshores are a feature of South Direction Island. Anchorage here is for calm weather only.

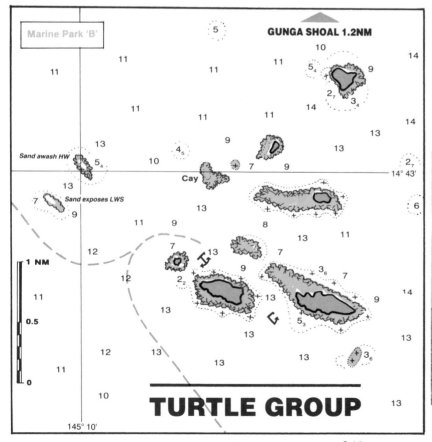

248

EAGLE ISLAND

Marine Park 'A'

```
        23
    20        25              29
16      15  12
    12    3₃        18    LIZARD ISLAND 3NM
16          27
16    16
    11    7
16              Eagle I.
    6   3₂  3₅
9    2₇              20
14          13
    15    1₉    Eyrie
13          Reef    4₅
15          Dries 1.5m    22
    1₈        3₆
15    2₂        5    14°43'
    7          22   Boulders
    7        4
9          5    24
14        4
15    22        24   24
    22
145°23'
```

0   0.5   1 NM

Future suburbia?

The coastal strip north of Cape Flattery to Cape Melville, a total of more than 200,000 hectares, was on the international market for $26½M as of late 1993. Representing 7% of the Cape York Peninsula's east coast, it is a wilderness area of extraordinary diversity which includes wetlands, rain forest and delicate sand dunes. Along its shore is Australia's biggest remaining area of sea grass on which an estimated 2000 dugongs graze. Owned by Cairns real estate agent, George Quaid, it is being promoted as a future game park, eco tourist resort or residential area. Government intervention on environmental grounds is a remote possibility.

Eagle Islet is an uninspiring cay on the large and attractive Eyrie Reef. Be careful of the fragmented coral patches when coming to anchor.

south — Captain McKenzie found the camp abandoned. The trepanging party was later found on the mainland further north where stories of hardship and native attack were told.

The Turtle Group was a favourite turtle and dugong hunting ground for mainland aborigines who often camped for many weeks catching, killing and curing these animals.

EAGLE ISLET. A cay without any tropical foliage and a remarkably straight half-tide rock ledge along its south-eastern edge, Eagle Islet sits on the north-west corner of *Eyrie Reef* less than 5 miles from Lizard Island. Despite the poor scrub and grass it supports, the bird life is prolific with eagles being a common sight.

Approach. From the south there is good water between *Martin* and *Eyrie Reef* with the dozens of boulders on the south-east corner of Eyrie providing excellent reference. Also, towards the south-west point, along the inner edge of this reef, a string of tidal sandbanks assists identification.

From the north, the scattered underwater heads must be cleared visually during a cautious approach using the islet as reference. To its north-east is a long tidal sandbank and on the north-east edge of the reef are a few small boulders, two being dominant.

Final approach should be made with Palfrey Island and Eagle Islet open south to clear off-lying submerged dangers. As the anchorage is brought up, watch for a scattering of coral heads along the inner edge of the reef which, in places, is actually a sand floor with scattered heads rather than a well-defined edge.

Anchorage can be taken anywhere within the reef's inner crescent depending on exact direction of onshore wind. A strong south-easterly suggests the inner south-east corner while during east to north-east winds, the islet itself can be held closer and its opportunity for convenient landing enjoyed more fully. Anchorage will be found in good-holding sand with some floor coral patches at around the 10-metre level. Shallower waters tend to carry more heads that threaten navigation.

During winds from north around to south-west, the best nearest anchorage is the Lizard Island lagoon.

Eagle Islet with Lizard Island behind. Fair anchorage is found under its lee thanks to its vast reef formation.

249

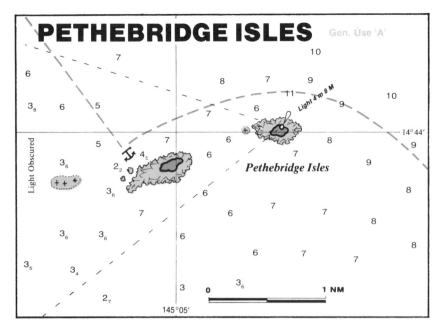

PETHEBRIDGE ISLES

Gen. Use 'A'

Pethebridge Isles

0 ___ 1 NM

The hills around Watsons Bay, Lizard Island, make a great backdrop to an even greater anchorage.

PETHEBRIDGE ISLETS. Less than 4 miles west of the *Turtle Group*, these two low, scrubby cays are in shallow water close to the mainland. The outer cay carries a light whilst the inner cay provides the best anchorage. By no means comfortable in a developed wind, protection is better than expected. Beware clouded water on final approach, there being a few coral heads off the main reef.

NYMPH ISLAND *Not illustrated* Seven miles north-west of *Eagle Island*, Nymph Island is as wide as it is long and occupies most of its host reef. The native scrub is dry without any palm trees and surrounds a shallow lagoon in the southern half which is unavailable to boats. The highest trees are concentrated towards the north-east corner where they rise to a maximum of 10–12 metres above high water. The island is visible at about 8 miles.

Surrounding much of the island is a rock ledge which is just awash at high water springs, and off the northwest corner are a group of detached coral patches. On the fringing reef edge in this corner, the reef dries higher than normal and displays numerous boulders with one being especially dominant. Coral sand runs around parts of the island, especially across the north face.

Anchorage in calm weather can be found in shoaling depths off the north-west corner, but with due regard to the scattered off-lying coral patches.

LIZARD ISLAND. Offering the best anchorage on the north coast, Lizard is a rather dry island lying 50 miles north of Cooktown and 15 miles from *Point Lookout*, the nearest part of the Australian mainland. Ten to 13 miles east to north of the island are seven well-defined outer barrier reef openings available to those departing for, or arriving from, Papua New Guinea.

Anchorage during the April to November south-east trade wind season is best in *Watson's Bay*. The holding is excellent in sand and the water is clear enough for the bottom to be easily seen at all times. Except when the wash from numerous game fishing boats enters the bay, conditions are movement free. This does not take into account the gust and lull behaviour during moderate to strong trades.

Watson's Bay is better than fifty per cent clear of reef, the bulk of which lies to the south in the form of a large isolated patch and a fringing patch that touches on the southern headland and projects into the resort bay next door. A fringing ledge runs along the north headland and a small isolated head lies towards the beach in the north-east corner. The resort has buoyed this coral head as well as the northern edge of the large isolated patch with small white buoys. These must not be relied upon nor should their position be presumed definitive.

The Lagoon provides perfect haven during northerlies

Lizard Island supports a tourist resort and scientific research station. It also has one of the best trade wind anchorages on the coast.

Watson's Bay anchorage, behind Lizard Island, suffers from severe trade wind bullets, but is otherwise delightful on all fronts. Watsons Bay and North West Bay are not official titles, the names being first used by the author to identify them properly in the second edition of this book (1974).

250

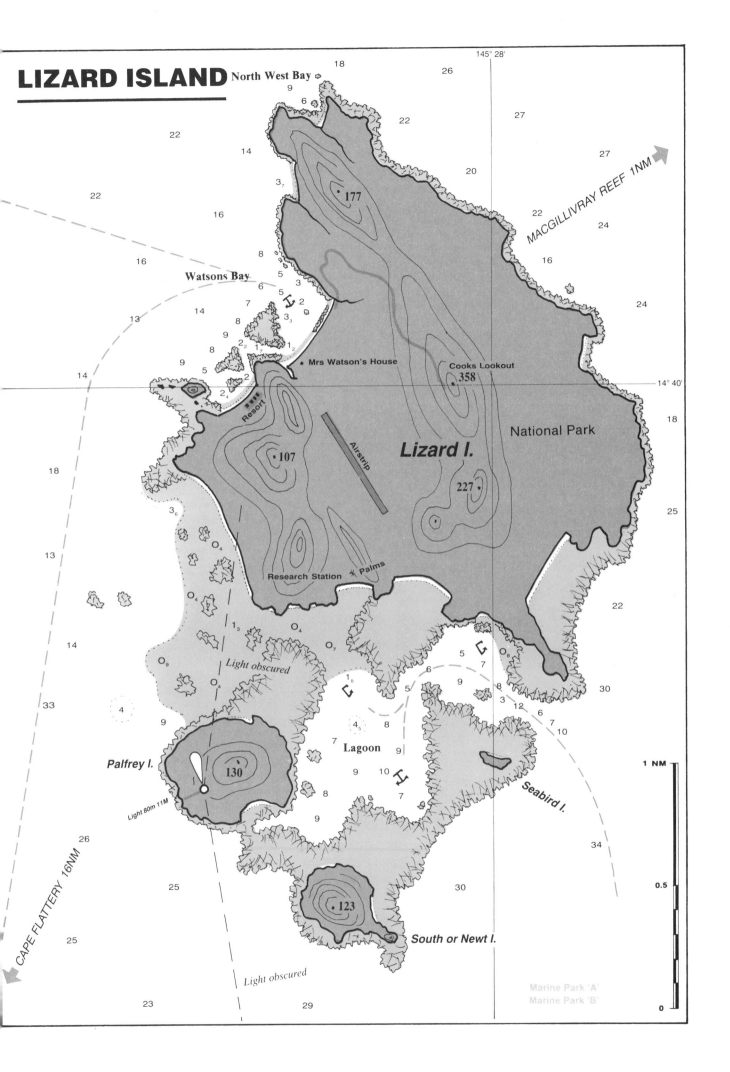

LIZARD ISLAND

North West Bay

18
9
6
26
22
27
145° 28'
22
22
27
14
20
27
MACGILLIVRAY REEF 1NM
3₇
177
16
22
24
8
16
Watsons Bay
5
3
24
6
5₅
2
7
14
3₃
8
9
Mrs Watson's House
Cooks Lookout
16
8
2₂
1₇
1₂
358
14
9
5
14° 40'
Resort
2₄
18
Lizard I.
National Park
107
Airstrip
18
227
25
3₆
O₄
National Park
13
O₄
1₇
22
14
1₃
O₄
O₇
5
O₈
30
O₉
Light obscured
6
7
3
12
33
O₄
1₈
5
9
8
6
10
4
9
7
10
4₅
8
Lagoon
7
9
Palfrey I.
130
9
10
34
Light 80m 11M
8
7
26
9
25
30
123
25
South or Newt I.
25
23
29

CAPE FLATTERY 16NM

Light obscured

Seabird I.

Research Station

Palms

1 NM

0.5

0

Marine Park 'A'
Marine Park 'B'

and, in fact, winds from all directions. Although deep and commodious with a safe entrance, the visitor is warned against entering during strong trades at which time the entrance can break right across. There is also the risk of dragging anchor with reef to leeward during the night, a prospect that must always be considered in any lagoon. The holding, however, is excellent and with ample scope, dragging is unlikely.

Approach. Lizard Island is easily seen 30 miles away and more. During typical wind haze, this distance might be reduced by half. It is easily approached day or night, thanks to its clear water directly south and west-north-west plus a major light on its satellite, *Palfrey Island*, which stands on the western slope of Palfrey, 80 metres above sea level and is seen at a distance of 11 miles.

From the outer barrier entrances, approach is clear in a direct line from all reef openings with the exception of those to the east. From that direction *MacGillivray Reef* with its tiny tidal sand cay on its north-west tip must be avoided.

On closer approach, Lizard and its two satellites, *South Island* and *Palfrey Island*, appear drab, dry and bald in patches with many rock outcrops and faces. All belie the real beauty of this group which is its combination of reef, water and sand.

Tides. Lizard Island tides are based on Cairns data being 10 minutes later and 12% lower. An average spring range tends to be around 1.6 metres.

Research Station. Lizard Island Research Station is situated near the south-west corner and is available for public tours at 09.30 hours Mondays and Fridays only.

Fresh Water. A sign indicates the way from the national park campsite in the north-east corner of Watson's Bay.

Cook's Lookout. Starting from the National Park signs and facilities at the northern end of the beach in Watson's Bay is a cleared track leading north-west then south-east up the hill to Lizard's highest mountain of 358 metres. At the place where Captain Cook so eagerly sought escape from the shoals of the coast waters, a rock cairn has been erected close to which will be seen a brass pointer to places local and overseas as well as a VHF duplex booster with its own batteries and solar cells. This is for the game fishing boats and must not be touched. At the base of the cairn will be found a visitors' book in a plastic box. Visitors are encouraged to enter their name and address and comments that come to mind.

To the north of the cairn, back down the slope a few hundred metres, will be found rock formations built by Aborigines for ceremonial purposes. Possibly hundreds of years old, this ground was not discovered until 1972 when a film group, led by Peter Marjason, stumbled on it and sent the information to southern museum authorities for confirmation. The fact that Lizard Island was obviously used for ceremonial purposes may explain why Mrs Watson was so savagely attacked, as detailed later.

Despite the ground being somewhat inconsequential in appearance, its historical value should be respected and damage avoided. It is possible to walk between the rows of rocks without disturbing then in any way.

History. Lizard Island was named by Captain James Cook when he used the island as a vantage point from which to seek escape for *Endeavour* when he became convinced that further passage north might risk embayment. He did not, as is so often presumed, anchor *Endeavour* here. She remained off Lookout Point from where Cook had sighted Lizard before venturing offshore in the pinnace with Mr Banks the botanist. On reaching Lizard he immediately ascended the hill, 'with a mixture of hope and fear proportioned to the importance of our business and the uncertainty of the event'. He noted the outer barrier reef passages. Descending to the beach, he camped overnight and returned to the hill the following morning only to find that haze had reduced visibility. Fortunately he had sent the pinnace out to survey the channels and their combined observations decided Cook to sail *Endeavour* east and off soundings.

One hundred and ten years later, when North Queensland was being populated by a hardy race of folk anxious to exploit her natural wealth both on the land and offshore, Mary Phillips became Mary Watson by marriage to one of two partners who worked beche-de-mer (sea slug) from their base on Lizard Island. Mr Watson, with his partner, Fuller, sailed

Near the lookout on Lizard Island is this group of rocks whose religious significance to Aborigines may have caused the attack on Mary Watson.

north to fish the slug near Night Island, leaving Mary — now with baby — alone with her two Chinese servants.

An uneventful month passed, then one of the servants went to the garden and was never seen again. His pigtail, however, was found on the mainland many months later. Aborigines then kept Mrs Watson and her remaining servant under surveillance until they eventually ambushed the servant, spearing him twice before he escaped back into the house under the cover of Mrs Watson's gun.

Badly wounded, the servant helped launch a beche-de-mer boiling tub in which the three of them made their escape from the island. Offshore they became a plaything of the trade wind which carried them to Watson Island after a worrying stranding and escape from a reef en route where more Aborigines were encountered.

On Watson Island, the three perished from thirst, their bodies being found a few months later by the Aboriginal member of a passing trading schooner. They were interred in Cooktown where a memorial was erected and stands to this day, and the diary kept by Mrs Watson during her last few days, and the tub, were sent to the Brisbane Museum where they can still be seen.

CRESCENT REEF is close north-east of the *Howick Group*, its northern tip poking into uncharted waters. It should be rounded to the west only, an easterly approach being very hazardous.

Because of the proximity of other reefs to windward and seaward, protection here is good, although the ground is foul. Use it only in conditions of good visibility and the anchor can be visually placed in a preferred area.

Top Right. **Mrs Watson's house from where she and her Chinese servant fled from Aborigine attack only to perish from thirst on Watson Island in the Howick Group.**

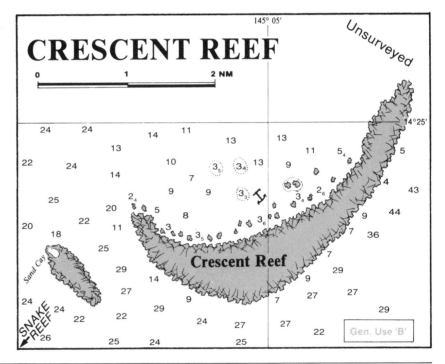

NOBLE ISLAND *Not illustrated* Lying just 2½ miles north of the mainland at *Red Point* and 10 miles west of *Howick Island*, Noble Island has a remarkable, unmistakable peak that is possibly a long-extinct volcanic core. Extending west from the base of this core is a low, flat area of mangroves. It is suggested as an anchorage only during light conditions when a shore party may enjoy the challenge of bushwalking and rock climbing. Details here pertain more to navigating the area than to Noble Island itself.

Noble can be seen as far away as 23 miles when, from the east and south-east, it rises as one, two, then three peaks while from the north as a single remarkably steep-sided peak. When north of *Ninian Bay* it can be confused as being a tiny islet off Barrow Point.

From the north, *Brown's Peak*, on the mainland, 8 miles south-south-east of Noble, rises when abeam the northern headland of Ninian Bay. When placed directly behind Noble Island, a very useful transit is created to ensure safe passage inside *Unison Reef* which, early in the morning, can be difficult to see.

Of Interest. According to one of Ion Idriess's wonderful books on mining in this area, early surveyors accidentally dug up a gold nugget on Noble Island worth £30,000 leading to the opening of a gold mine on the mountain.

HOWICK GROUP. This collection of wooded cays and reefs sprawl across the inner route between Lizard Island and Cape Melville being a similar distance from both. Shown in large scale on *Australian Chart 832*, commercial shipping can pass through the group or around it, depending on draft. Deeper draft passes through assisted by a number of lights from the north tip of Howick Island to the north tip of Watson Island.

Tides are 90% of, and a few minutes later than, Cairns data and there is no stream worthy of special note.

The islands and reefs in the group are described separately here.

COQUET ISLAND is the southern-most of the Howick Group and supports one of the many navigation lights for this section of the coast. The light is mounted on a conspicuous red trellis on the western tip.

The island is 16 metres to the tops of the trees which are mangroves to the east and native scrub to the west, the latter being in the minority. A break in the reef along the northern side allows relatively easy dinghy landing and a small lagoon in the eastern end admits shallow-draft vessels at high tide.

Anchorage in general cannot be recommended except in light weather in 13 metres on the north side.

SNAKE REEF. Disputing its name, Snake Reef is almost as wide as it is long and lies 2 miles east-north-east of *Howick Island*. It is not a good shape for anchoring nor are there shoals encouraging the practice around its perimeter. However, to aid recognition, it sports a tidal sand cay on the north-west end, easily seen at half tide, plus clusters of boulders along its south-east and western edges which also display well at half tide.

When navigating this area at night it is worth noting that *Megaera Reef Light* and *Watson Island Light*, when kept in line, ensure good clearance of Snake Reef. The green sector of Megaera Reef also covers the reef's southern edge. This sector must be actively avoided.

HOWICK ISLAND. A logical anchorage for day-hoppers going to or from Lizard Island, Howick is unique for its continental island and huge mangrove swamp occupying an entire reef. A second area of dry ground on the north-west tip provides beach landing for persons visiting here.

Approach. The island rises as two, then three small land masses, the central one being dominant, from a distance of around 10 to 12 miles. At 6 miles the surrounding mangrove trees lift above the horizon. Because of its continental high ground, confusion is minimised, all other islands of the Howick Group being mangrove forests on their own reefs, with just a fringe of the latter extending from the treeline.

The channels between the islands and reefs of this area are deep and well defined with light beacons, this being a major commercial shipping route. Deeper-draft vessels take the channel to the north of Howick while shallower-draft vessels short-cut to its south below Coquet Islet. As a result, some wake is experienced at the recommended anchorage.

Anchorage behind Howick is best towards the dry land on the north-west tip where 9 metres can be found in good-holding mud and patches weed towards fragmented reef. Be careful on final approach as the water can be murky here, hiding coral heads at high tide. A well-developed south-east trade wind sends a beam swell along the north of Howick which can make conditions uncomfortable.

Anchorage against northerlies can be found on the other side of the island in 15 metres. Owing to the likelihood of returning south-easterlies, be certain to have room to manoeuvre should it be necessary during the night. Generally, if the northerly continues brisk into the evening it will not change during the night except to a calm.

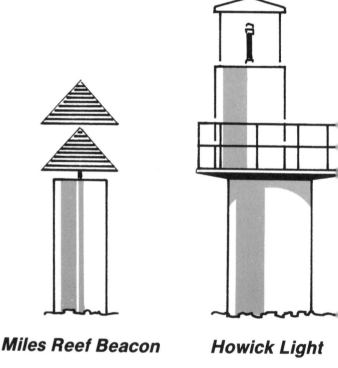

Miles Reef Beacon   **Howick Light**

Watson Island and its light situated on the end of its reef.

The Beanley Islets are situated along the south-west edge of their host reef.

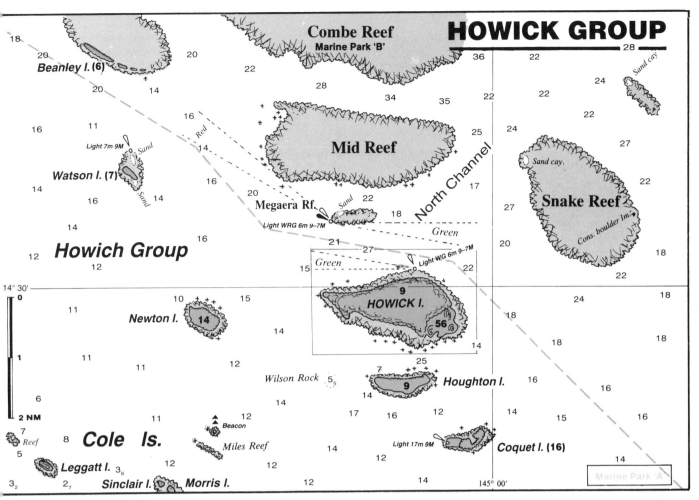

HOWICK GROUP

Combe Reef
Marine Park 'B'

Beanley I. (6)

Mid Reef

North Channel

Watson I. (7)
Light 7m 9M

Howich Group

Megaera Rf.
Light WRG 6m 9–7M

Sand cay

Snake Reef
Cons. boulder 1m

Green

Light WG 6m 9–7M

Green

HOWICK I.

Newton I.

Wilson Rock

Houghton I.

Beacon

Miles Reef

Light 17m 9M

Coquet I. (16)

Cole Is.

Reef

Leggatt I.

Sinclair I.   Morris I.

Marine Park 'A'

14° 30'

0

1

2 NM

145° 00'

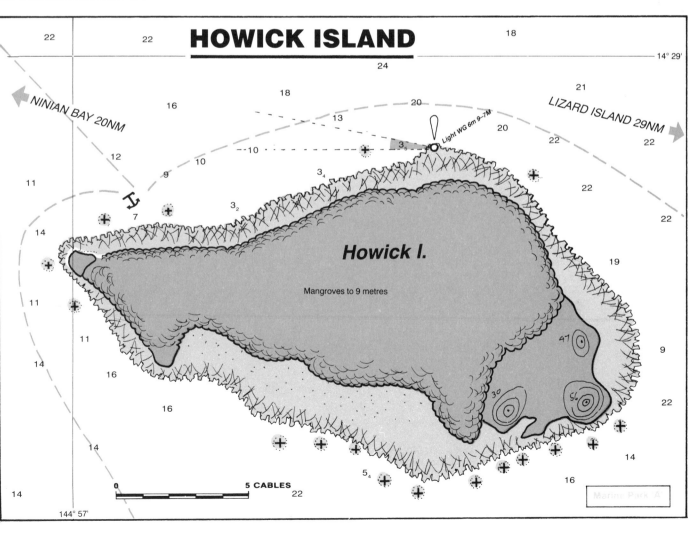

HOWICK ISLAND

14° 29'

NINIAN BAY 20NM

LIZARD ISLAND 29NM

Light WG 6m 9–7M

Howick I.

Mangroves to 9 metres

0   5 CABLES

144° 57'

Marine Park 'A'

255

Howick Island from the anchorage. During trade winds, the best place is near the north-west tip where will be seen a beach.

The nearest secure northerly anchorage to Howick is 33 miles to the south-east in Lizard Island lagoon, or 52 miles north-west in the Flinders Group. Otherwise there is a 5 metre patch under the southern corner of *Munro Reef* where some protection against a returning south-easterly is offered by *Switzer Reef* to its close south. Beware here, however, of swinging back on to the reef as the shoal patch is only a narrow ledge.

Of Interest. Immediately above the high water mark behind the rock fringed beach at the recommended south-east anchorage, there is a simple grave marked with a wooden cross and covered in shells. To the east, in from the beach where it continues behind the mangrove fringe, there is evidence of a permanent camp or temporary dwelling.

MEGAERA REEF is immediately north of *Howick Island* where it supports a light showing the other side of the restricted channel between the two. This light has the already-noted green sector covering the south end of Snake Reef plus a red sector covering the south-west edge of *Mid Reef* plus *Beanley Islets*.

Megaera Reef fully exposes at low water neaps and supports a small tidal sand cay on its north-west tip as well as low boulders in the same general area. It is fully covered at high water springs.

The light structure is a white column, offset towards the top exactly the same as the Howick and Watson lights.

WATSON ISLAND. So named because it was here that Mrs Watson died after escaping Aborigine attack on Lizard Island, this island is dominantly mangroves standing 7 metres above sea level and only partially occupying its host reef. On the southern and northern extreme of this reef, and not connected with the island, are large sand cays standing above high water. At low tide, a few boulders display in the vicinity of the light which is of the type on Howick and Megaera Reef.

Anchorage can be taken on the north-west tip of Watson Island in 12 metres, but is recommended for calm weather only.

BEANLEY ISLETS are a string of mangrove cays along the south-western edge of their host reef. Only the separately named *Ingram Island* (on the same reef) has a wraparound beach as does the islet on the western tip of neighbouring *Combe Reef*. The latter is easily seen at the same time as the Beanley Islets and can be confused as one of them. There is no anchorage in this area worth suggesting, although the adventurous will find shoaling water over sand amidst many isolated coral patches in the bay in Combe Reef's northern face. There is also shoal water directly off Combe Island, but this is less comfortable than the bay during developed trade winds.

NINIAN BAY. Slashing the mainland west of *Bar-*

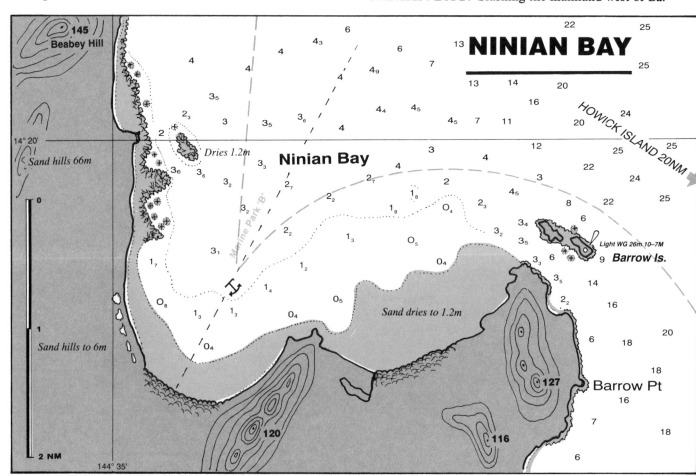

PIPON ISLETS

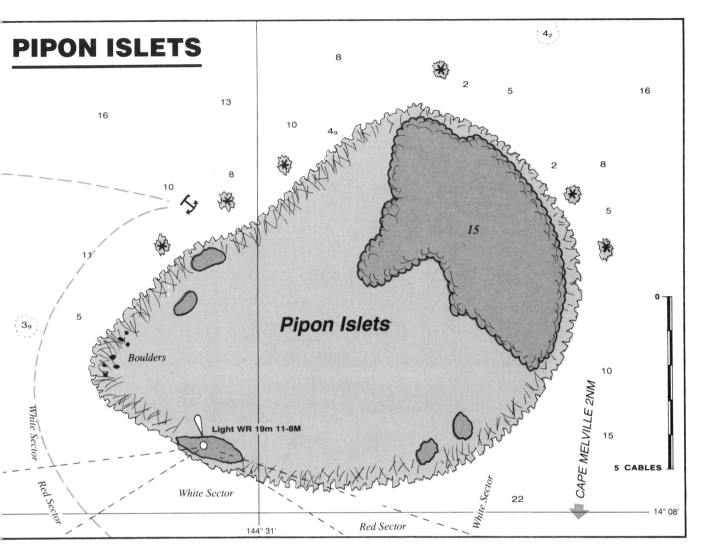

8

4_2

2

5

16

16

13

10

4_9

2

8

10

8

2

5

11

15

5

Boulders

Pipon Islets

3_9

5

10

Light WR 19m 11-8M

15

White Sector

5 CABLES

CAPE MELVILLE 2NM

White Sector

White Sector

22

Red Sector

14° 08'

144° 31'

Red Sector

0

row Point and *Islands*, Ninian Bay lies 22 miles west-north-west from Howick Island and provides tolerable anchorage in south-east trade winds. It is unacceptable when the wind goes north of east and is better or worse depending on tide state. A neap tide that permits deep penetration into the bay promises some comfort, while a spring tide, demanding that the boat lies well offshore, is a guarantee of some heavy rolling in trade-winds of more than 15 knots.

Approach. From the south-east, *Barrow Point* and its offshore island carrying the white, square-based light is easily identified at 11 miles from which distance it can be seen underlapping the background hills. From the north, the bay is found by logical progression down the coast from *Cape Melville*, standing offshore enough to avoid the inshore shoals and islets. On final approach, a fringe of mangroves will be seen to extend along the foreshore from between the western end of Barrow Point and the headland further west. That headland provides fair reference regarding the best anchorage area. About half-way down the bay will also be seen a patch of bare sand dunes.

Anchorage towards the inner headland is in good-holding sandy mud although the density of the seagrass of this entire area can dictate security.

PIPON ISLETS, lying a little over 2 miles north of *Cape Melville*, comprise a number of low cays on a single reef, the largest being a mangrove forest on the eastern side. Anchorage is lively but secure along the north-west face during heavy trade-winds and is best in about 10 metres. Beware a few isolated coral heads along the fringe.

After the loss of the Channel Lightship in cyclone Mahina (see notes in next section *Bathurst Bay*), it was decided to build a permanent light structure on the western edge of Pipon Reef. It was an iron tower standing 20 metres high and was complemented with two lightkeepers' cottages on the nearby reef. Whilst it streamlined the operation and covered Channel Rock with a red sector, it demanded an extraordinary communication system between light and dwellings. A punt was used attached to a guest warp and pulled across. At low tide the keepers trudged across exposed coral.

257

1

1. **Barrow Point**, extreme right, bears west.

2

2. North Bay Point, left, is Ninian bay's northern headland. Here it is left, bearing south.

BATHURST BAY

BATHURST BAY. Twelve miles wide and formed by an indentation in the mainland between *Cape Melville* and the *Flinders Group* of islands, this bay lies 15 miles north from Ninian Bay and directly east of huge Princess Charlotte Bay. Cape Melville and the hills to its south are comprised of massive, smooth boulders piled on top of each other.

Approach from the south is best at a minimum distance of 1½ miles offshore and an absolute maximum of 3 miles. The first clears the coastal shoals, the second provides ample clearance from *South Warden Reef* lying just 4 miles offshore.

In the restricted area between *North Bay Point* and South Warden Reef, do not expect large ships to alter course on your behalf and beware of their habit of coming out wide then steering diagonally across the track towards *Barrow Island* when southbound.

The land in this region is, as stated, comprised of piled up boulders amongst which some foliage struggles and at the base of which some large sand blows will be seen between *Rocky Point Islet* and *Cape Melville*.

On final approach from the south it is perfectly safe to pass between *Cape Rock* and *Boulder Rock* taking due care to keep the best water which is a maximum of 7 and a minimum of 2.5 metres. Once into the bay, skirt around a large shoal area to bring up the best anchorage.

From the west, steer direct from the Flinders Group.

Anchorage can be found close to the beach between *Cape Melville* and *Bathurst Head*. During fresh trade winds, the most comfortable place is near the monument (which cannot be sighted from the sea). This remains comfortable even when the wind is slightly north of east. Any more northing and the anchorage becomes untenable. *The Flinders Group* offers the closest alternative anchorage as described next.

The bottom throughout Bathurst Bay is good-holding sandy mud, but a layer of seagrass can deny penetration. If the anchor drags, relaying usually remedies the situation and the bottom is often clear enough to visually choose a bare patch. This seagrass attracts dugong which are often sighted in this area.

Of Interest. *Mahina*, the great cyclone of 5 March 1899, swept this area drowning the owners and crew of the pearling mother ships, *Sagitta* and *Silvery Wake* plus the crew of the lighthouse ship then moored off Channel Rocks. As well, 50 open luggers and 300 native divers perished. It has been claimed that such was the height of sea at the cyclone's centre that dolphins became stranded in the small cliffs of Flinders and Denham Islands 12 metres above mean sea level and parts of wrecked boats were found many miles inland.

The monument to the event will be found a short distance in from the recommended anchorage.

In more recent years, up to the early 1960s, when trochus shell luggers still worked this far south from the Torres Strait, Bathurst Bay was a popular spot for capturing dugong which were then kept tethered and alive on deck until needed for the table. The dugong has since become a completely protected species and trochus shelling has long since been abandoned.

Climbing the rocks of Cape Melville and its neighbouring mountains looks much easier than it is. Many are so huge and smooth that instead of being easy stepping stones they prove to be stumbling blocks demanding a reappraisal of one's route. Those who accept the challenge are warned that snakes are very common amongst the rocks.

Also amongst the rocks will be found pools of excellent, clear, fresh water. One of the best was found and marked by the crew of the lighthouse service vessel, *Wallach*, in the early 1970s. The marking has long since faded but it will be found on the northern face of Cape Melville close to sea level. Considering the opportunity for total disorientation, under no circumstances should its discovery be depended upon.

SALTWATER INLET is a useful creek cutting into the mainland approximately half-way along *Bathurst Bay*. Shown in small scale only on the accompanying chart, there are depths of up to 5 metres within, but the sand bar dries at low water springs or, at best, carries just a few inches of water. Usually there are stakes indicating the deepest water through the bar. In an emergency and with a preliminary low tide survey, this creek could be used as cyclone hole.

Rounding Cape Melville, left. The Flinders Group is distant background.

H.M.S. Dart

Carved into a rock near the anchorage off Flinders Island is the inscription, H.M.S. *Dart* 1893. It was used as a survey bench mark by *Dart* which spent twenty years surveying from Tasmania to the Great Barrier Reef and from New Zealand to the Solomon Islands. A beautiful little vessel, H.M.S. *Dart* was built in 1882 as a yacht for the Colonial Office.

With Denham Island in the foreground, Pirie Head on Flinders Island is seen, right.

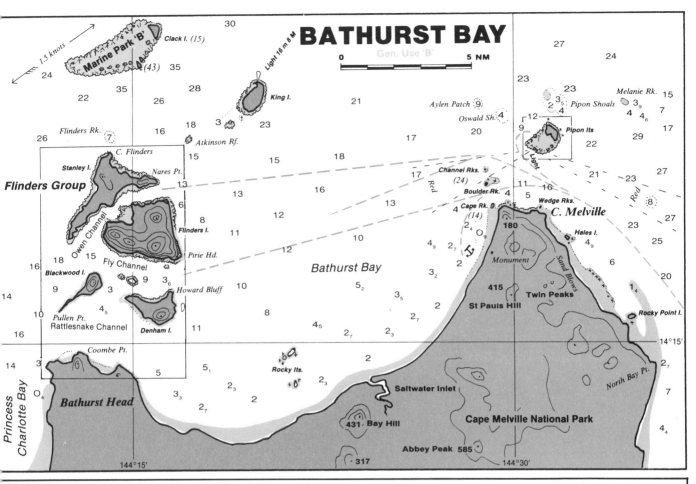

BATHURST BAY
Gen. Use 'B'

0   5 NM

1.5 knots

Marine Park 'B'   Clack I. (15)

(43)   35

30

Light 16 m 8 M

King I.

Flinders Rk. (7)

C. Flinders

Stanley I.   Nares Pt.

Flinders Group

Owen Channel

Flinders I.

Fly Channel

Pirie Hd.

Blackwood I.

Howard Bluff

Pullen Pt.

Rattlesnake Channel   Denham I.

Coombe Pt.

Bathurst Head

Princess Charlotte Bay

Atkinson Rf.

Aylen Patch

Oswald Sh.

Pipon Shoals   Melanie Rk.

Pipon Its

Light

Bathurst Bay

Channel Rks.

Boulder Rk.

Cape Rk. (14)

Wedge Rks.

C. Melville

Monument

180

Sand Blows

Hales I.

St Pauls Hill

415

Twin Peaks

Rocky Point I.

North Bay Pt.

Rocky Its.

Saltwater Inlet

Bay Hill   431

Abbey Peak   585

Cape Melville National Park

317

144°15'   144°30'   14°15'

Cape Melville on approach from the south-east. Boulder Rock is offshore.

Bathurst Head borders Rattlesnake Channel in the Flinders Group.

Entering Rattlesnake Channel from the east. Denham Island, right, Blackwood Island, background.

Stokes Bay, Stanley Island, provides good trade wind anchorage.

The north-west tip of Stanley Island, foreground with conspicuous Clack Island in the background.

259

FLINDERS GROUP. Comprising two major, two medium and two minor islands, this group lies off *Bathurst Head* and provides good shelter between Princess Charlotte Bay and Bathurst Bay. It lies 14 miles west from Cape Melville.

Approach from Cape Melville is direct, the logical landfall being *Fly Channel* between Denham Island and Flinders Island.

From the west, *Wharton Reef* is the last mark from where it is 12 miles to the same channel which, at that end, lies between Stanley Island and Blackwood Island.

Final approach to all anchorages in the group is relatively free of fringing reefs and isolated dangers.

Anchorage. The most popular anchorage is in *Owen Channel* in the area of a conspicuous sand spit and flat land. It is excellent in all winds but those from the south-west which are very rare except during wet-season thunderstorms.

Because this anchorage can be so packed with trawlers, the transient visitor might prefer the relative seclusion of the leeward sides of Blackwood or Stanley Islands as indicated on the accompanying plans.

Good northerly anchorage can be taken in *Rattle-snake Channel*, favouring the sand spit off the west tip of Denham when the wind slants north-east, or the bight of Blackwood Island when it slants north-west. Owen Channel also provides excellent shelter during northerlies.

Tides are based on Cairns data turning 15 minutes later and experiencing a similar range which, during springs, is typically around 1.9 metres.

Of Interest. Since the late 1960s, when prawns were found in abundance in the Gulf of Carpentaria, then along the Coral Coast, Princess Charlotte Bay and Bathurst Bay became major areas for this type of fishery, hundreds of trawlers working it over the years. Now it is common to see dozens of trawlers anchored in the Flinders Group during the day, the crews recovering from their night's toil.

Servicing this fleet and those further north are mother ships from Cairns. Primarily aimed at prawn

One of the best anchorages in the Flinders Group is off this sandspit on the western corner of Flinders Island. The plateau behind the spit was used as a base during World War 1.

trawlers, private vessels may occasionally avail themselves of their stocks of water, fuel and food. No dependence should be placed either on availability or timetable.

Warning. Cultured pearl rafts are anchored throughout the Flinders Group.

CORBETT REEF. Lying approximately 10 miles north-west of the *Flinders Group*, this reef cannot be recommended for anchorage owing to the deep water right to its edge.

For reference value, the boulders shown on the chart (*Aust. 833*) can be difficult to see and reliance on their sighting is dangerous, especially at high tide. In close they are obvious enough. Also obvious through binoculars, when within a couple of miles of the reef's southern edge, is a large tidal sand cay to the north-east and probably situated on the edge of the north-east bay.

The extraordinary hills of Cape Melville, east of the Flinders Group. They are comprised of countless piled-up boulders, many so huge as to be impossible to climb.

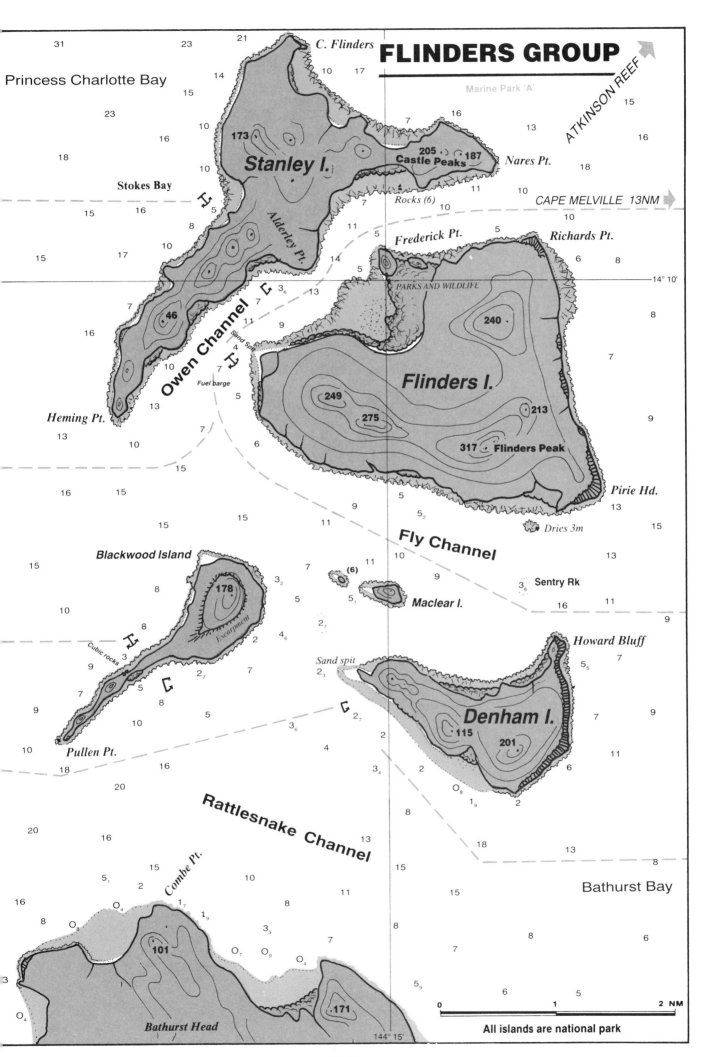

FLINDERS GROUP

Princess Charlotte Bay

C. Flinders

Marine Park 'A'

ATKINSON REEF

Stokes Bay

173

Stanley I.

Alderley Pt.

Castle Peaks
205 · **187**
Nares Pt.

Rocks (6)

CAPE MELVILLE 13NM

Frederick Pt. *Richards Pt.*

46

Owen Channel

PARKS AND WILDLIFE

240

Flinders I.

Sand spit

Fuel barge

Heming Pt.

249

275

213

317 · **Flinders Peak**

Pirie Hd.

Dries 3m

Fly Channel

Blackwood Island

(6)

Sentry Rk

178

Maclear I.

Escarpment

Howard Bluff

Cubic rocks

Sand spit

Denham I.

115

201

Pullen Pt.

Rattlesnake Channel

Bathurst Bay

Combe Pt.

101

171

Bathurst Head

144° 15'

0   1   2 NM

All islands are national park

261

PRINCESS CHARLOTTE BAY RIVERS.

With the more interesting anchorages of the Flinders Group close to its north, the indicated anchorage under *Bathurst Head* offers only seclusion. By tucking in as close as possible during onshore winds, good security and fair comfort is enjoyed.

Because the entire south-east coast of the bay offers similar protection, the visitor can pick and choose alternative anchorages whilst enjoying a fast, gusty, calm-water sail under the lee of the land. However, there is little to be gained by penetrating the bay too deeply unless intent on entering one of its five navigable rivers. These are briefly described here. All demand a low tide survey of their shoal or drying bars before entry at high tide.

Marrett River has good depths and its upper reaches are accessed by road from *Kalpower Cattle Station*. Like all the rivers, it penetrates a mangrove forest.

Normanby River. There is a drying rock shelf off the northern headland of this river and its western bank is the eastern border of *Lakefield National Park*. It also has good depths for much of its length.

Bizant River. The entrance can experience more swell invasion than the previous rivers, even during a true south-easterly wind. It is not excessive, but should be considered when matching draft to tide height. It penetrates the Lakefield National Park.

Kennedy River is the longest of these rivers, penetrating the Lakefield National Park for more than 20 miles. The western side of its entrance on each side of its first tributary, the *Annie River*, is not designated national park.

The Annie River is used as an offloading base by local fishermen, a freezer truck taking their load a few miles upstream on the south side. This is in the non-national park area of Marina Plains.

Until the advent of mother ships and fuel barges, the Kennedy-Annie Rivers were used extensively as an offloading base for prawn trawlers working the area. The channel into the Kennedy River is the deepest of all the rivers.

CLIFF ISLETS.

These two islets are 25 miles west of the Flinders Group in the western side of *Princess Charlotte Bay*. Neither afford good shelter, although the eastern islet is better than expected during developed winds from south-east to north-east, the latter demanding a shift around the islet from the indicated anchor.

The western islet has shallower ground under its lee and a larger drying bank to its south. If able to snug towards this bank, low tide protection is good. Generally speaking, Cliff Islets can only be recommended to those beating south against a trade wind and unwilling to throw a tack and beat across to Flinders before nightfall.

Port Stewart

Once serviced regularly from Cairns by a small cargo vessel, Port Stewart, on the north-west corner of Princess Charlotte Bay, is only navigable at high tide after which vessels must take the bottom if remaining in the Stewart River. This unlikely and now dormant port was the result of gold being found at inland Coen, February 1876. It was the most northerly goldfield in Australia.

In a bid to curb illegal drug and migrant activities, the north coast of Queensland is overflown regularly by surveillance planes.

The prawn trawler fleet at anchor in Owen Channel, Flinders group. The table top on Stanley Island is obvious, background.

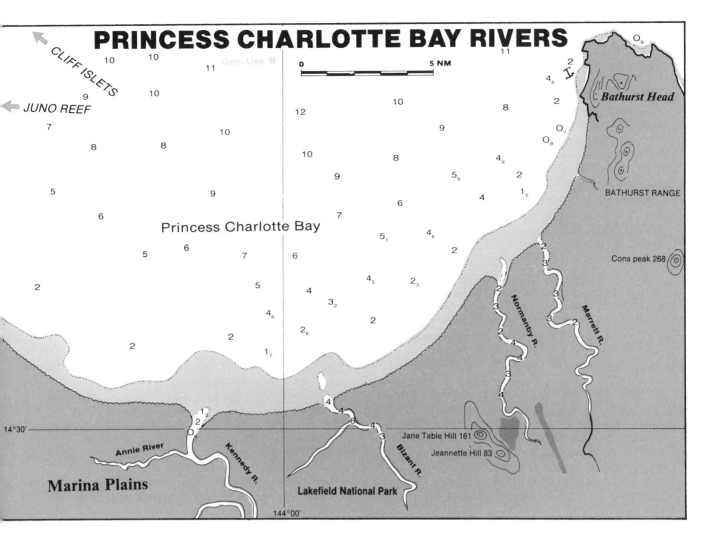

PRINCESS CHARLOTTE BAY RIVERS

Gen. Use 'B'

0   5 NM

CLIFF ISLETS

JUNO REEF

Princess Charlotte Bay

Bathurst Head

BATHURST RANGE

Cons peak 268

Normanby R.

Marrett R.

Jane Table Hill 161

Jeannette Hill 83

Bizant R.

Annie River

Kennedy R.

Marina Plains

Lakefield National Park

14°30'

144°00'

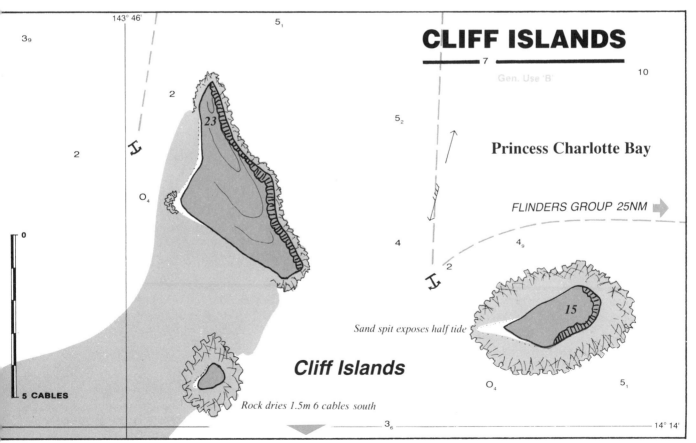

143° 46'

CLIFF ISLANDS

7

Gen. Use 'B'

Princess Charlotte Bay

FLINDERS GROUP 25NM ➡

23

O₄

Cliff Islands

Sand spit exposes half tide

15

O₄

Rock dries 1.5m 6 cables south

0

5 CABLES

14° 14'

WHARTON REEF is used as a daylight anchorage by trawlers working the bay area and is given a semblance of comfort only by their substantial flopper-stoppers. It cannot be recommended otherwise.

Lying 3 metres south of Corbett Reef, a red trellis light is situated on the north-eastern extreme of Wharton Reef and at the opposite end is a small sand cay supporting a few struggling bushes. *Not illustrated.*

EDEN REEF. Similarly useless as an anchorage, this reef also supports a light structure which is white cylindrical, similar to those in the Howick Group. There is a sand cay on the western edge of the reef and patchy scrub near the light.

GRUB REEF. A bush is marked on the chart of this reef, situated on its south-western extreme. It has degenerated into a single dead trunk on a part of the reef that dries at half tide exposing numerous boulders to its east and west. Along the reef's north-western edge is a line of tidal sand cays which appear almost unbroken at low tide with a few awash at high tide.

Anchorage cannot be recommended for the same reasons as given for Corbett Reef.

HEDGE REEF. Sprawling along a south-west/north-east line some 24 miles north-west of the Flinders Group, good anchorage can be enjoyed here subject to cautionary measures when making up to shallow water. It should also be stressed that anchorage is only suitable during developed south-east to easterly winds.

Approach. After rounding Grub Reef from the south-east, the south-western-most sand cay on Hedge Reef will be visible from a distance of 4 miles at low tide and 2–3 miles at high tide. Also, the grass-capped sand (Stainer Islet) on *Iris Reef* will rise along with *Pelican Islet* further north. But the best sighting will be of Hedge Reef itself to the north.

Contrary to the impression given by the chart (*Aust. 833*), the south-west edge of Hedge Reef is not clean cut. There are, in fact, numerous isolated coral heads lying at depths of less than 2 metres at low water springs. Eyeball your way around them and steer for the cay when it bears south-east. On this course the area under the lee of the sand cay and its trailing spits appear unencumbered by isolated coral heads, but proceed cautiously and presume otherwise to anchorage.

Anchorage. During the approach it will become obvious that the sand cay extends a considerable distance north and south and that another system of tidal cays exists to its north-east. Between the two systems the reef edge consists primarily of shoaling sand with a peppering of coral patches in shallow water. Anchorage can be chosen outside these patches in shoaling water over sand. Except at high tide when a small sea makes across the top of the reef, the anchorage is calm and the holding good.

The water along the north-western edge of Hedge Reef is somewhat opaque out to the 15 metre line. Coral patches at high tide may prove difficult to see, however, because none breaks the low tide surface, some insurance against grounding is provided. Nevertheless, approach and anchor with extreme caution and an excellent reef anchorage with a delightful sand cay for shore exercise will be enjoyed.

STAINER ISLET (*Iris Reef*) lies 1.6 miles west of Hedge Reef and is a grass-capped sand cay 2 metres high. The reef displays clusters of boulders to its south and north, most of which cover at high water and anchorage from south-easterly winds is very troubled by swell.

PELICAN ISLET is immediately north of Stainer Islet and also displays large clusters of boulders north and south. The northern boulders are on the leeward side of the reef and extend south nearly to the islet. The latter is mostly grass capped but has an area of scrub favouring its northern end. If passing close to the north of this reef beware an unmarked detached patch of coral close to the main body. There is no suitable anchorage here except in deep water.

BURKITT ISLAND is the first of the mangrove cays on this stretch of the coast. The type continues to Lloyd Bay and appears again in Temple Bay at the Piper Islands. Burkitt is different from most in that its beach-fronted cay is exposed to the north and north-east instead of the more common north-west and west. Mangroves extend south, covering the whole reef as is normal for this type of cay.

Anchorage is not comfortable in any strength of developed wind and excessive rolling is the order of the day during moderate to strong trade winds. The holding is good but the water rather deep at 12 metres on the north-west face towards the mangroves. Trawlers use this island during the season for daylight layovers.

HANNAH ISLAND lies 5 miles north-north west of *Burkitt Island* and less than 4 miles south-south-west of *Magpie Reef*. It carries an important main shipping channel light which is mounted on a tapering red trellis tower on the north-west corner of the cay. This cay is surrounded by mangrove forest and displays its beach only towards the north-west.

Anchorage is rather dismal during strong trade winds but the holding is excellent in mud at 12 metres. Shallower water will be found at the risk of fouling in the fringing reef's off-lying patches. Trawlers will often be seen here in their dozens during the day.

MAGPIE REEF carries a light beacon on its western tip which is a white cylinder with a maintenance landing half-way up. It has a white and red sector showing 7 and 5 miles respectively. The red sector covers *Ballerina Shoal* which has nearly 10 metres low water springs so is of little concern to the yachtsperson.

Along the northern edge of Magpie Reef is a string of tidal sand cays, some of which are awash at high water springs. Along the southern edge are numerous boulders, two of which are conspicuous for their excess proportions.

NODDY REEF lies midway between *Magpie Reef* and *Fife Islet* and has no special features beyond a remarkable, high, solitary boulder that stands proud at neap low tide. It is situated on the south-west tip and makes a good navigational mark when cutting corners in this area. Anchorage is possible in shoaling water along much of its western side and proves com-

THE COAST GRUB REEF TO FIFE ISLET

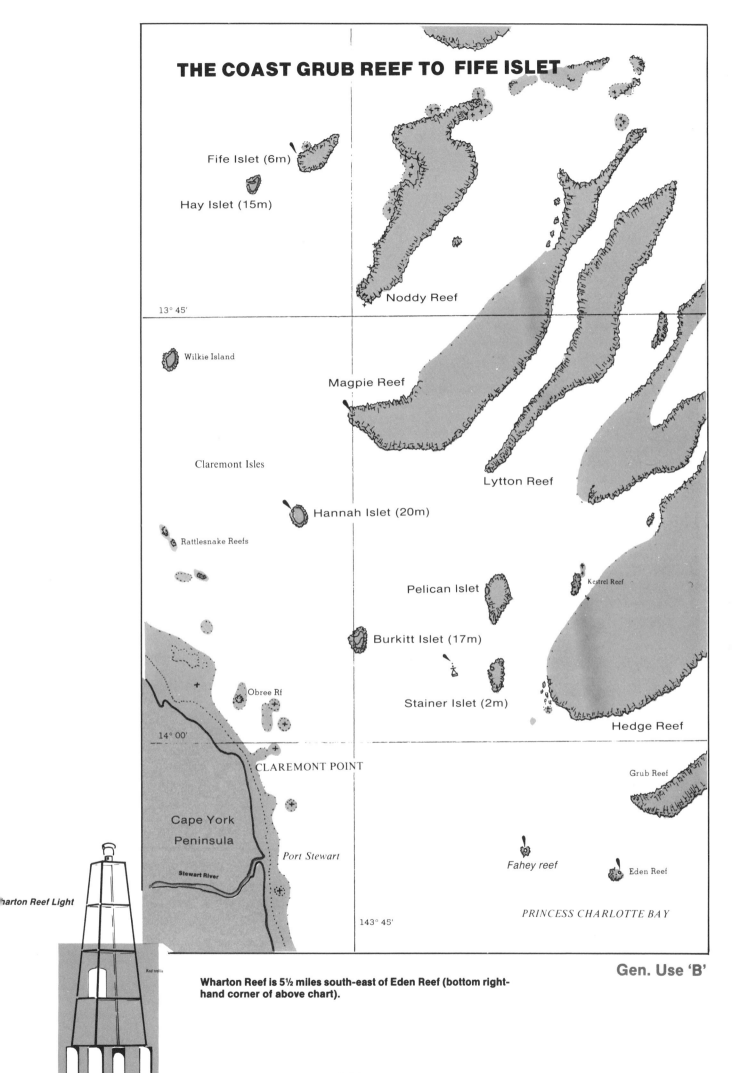

Fife Islet (6m)

Hay Islet (15m)

Noddy Reef

13° 45'

Wilkie Island

Magpie Reef

Claremont Isles

Lytton Reef

Hannah Islet (20m)

Rattlesnake Reefs

Kestrel Reef

Pelican Islet

Burkitt Islet (17m)

Stainer Islet (2m)

Hedge Reef

Obree Rf

14° 00'

CLAREMONT POINT

Grub Reef

Cape York

Peninsula

Port Stewart

Stewart River

Fahey reef

Eden Reef

Wharton Reef Light

143° 45'

PRINCESS CHARLOTTE BAY

Gen. Use 'B'

Red trellis

Wharton Reef is 5½ miles south-east of Eden Reef (bottom right-hand corner of above chart).

fortable in prevailing trade winds. However, numerous coral patches demand careful approach.

WILKIE ISLET

WILKIE ISLET lies to the west of the shipping channel 5½ miles offshore from the *Rocky River* entrance and nearly 7 miles north-west of *Hannah Islet*. Like most mangrove islets, it is a monumentally dull little speck, but does offer desperation anchorage in shallower ground than most. The bottom is excellent-holding mud at about 8 metres and the best south-east anchorage is with the small sandy beach bearing south-east. Northerly anchorage in a little deeper water can be found to the south trying to avoid a confluence of troubled water off the south-west tip. No comfort can be anticipated here except in light weather at which time rolling is replaced by sandfly attack, especially at dawn.

HAY ISLET

HAY ISLET. Separating the main shipping route into east and west factors and just a biscuit-toss from lighted *Fife Islet*, Hay is easily invaded by the wakes of passing ships which can be quite awesome at times. However, with a wind of any strength and from any direction, the difference will be difficult to detect, the anchorage being lively at the best of times. It is also rather deep at around 15 metres, but with good-holding mud. Anchor according to wind off the beach when the trade wind prevails as it should between April and November.

MORRIS ISLET

MORRIS ISLET. A coral cay roughly midway between Princess Charlotte Bay and Lloyd Bay, Morris offers the best anchorage on this part of the coast.

Approach. Now noted on *Australian Chart 834*, a solitary coconut palm is conspicuous and beacon-like from a distance of 7 miles. Beware of confusion when seeking *Heath Reef* light beacon, especially from the south.

On final approach from the south, Morris's reef can be brought up fairly close to starboard and held a constant distance to the anchorage. From the north, *Heath Reef Beacon* provides excellent reference. It is a white cylindrical upright supported on four similar base stumps with a second set of base stumps nearby.

Anchorage is over sand in reasonably clear water towards a mid-tide rock ledge skirting the beach and breaking where shown on the plan. This break provides ideal dinghy landing at low tide. Holding is excellent and a gale may be ridden here. There is no suitable northerly anchorage.

Of Interest. Ashore there is a diver's grave harking back to the not so distant days when pearling and trochus shell luggers ranged far and wide from their home port of Thursday Island. Away for months on end, deaths in the crew were dealt with on the spot, graves being dug wherever necessary.

Morris Island also reminds us of the British Admiralty policy of last century which was to provide many of the Great Barrier Reef islands with a means of support for shipwrecked crew. To this end, they put goats ashore and, in the case of Morris, planted coconut palms with sisal trees close by. The latter were intended as a means of knocking down ripe nuts, the sisal producing a long stick from amidst its needle-sharp leaves. They have proliferated here while, as stated, only one coconut palm remains.

ELLIS REEF

ELLIS REEF lies close to the main shipping route 6 miles north of *Morris Islet*. It sports a couple of sand cays on its north-west tip, the outermost one being sand only and awash at high water springs, the innermost having a stake in the centre and a high level ridge of rocks which are awash at high water springs. There is a solitary boulder to the south of these cays with numerous scattered boulders along the north-eastern edge. Anchorage cannot be suggested here owing to the poor shape for protection and deep water up to the edge. *Not illustrated.*

BOW REEF

BOW REEF. This tiny satellite, 3.25 miles north of Ellis Reef supports a light beacon which is visible for at least 5 miles in daylight and the same at night. It flashes white as do all lights down the coast. To the immediate north of the light there is a small tidal sand cay and to the south a section of reef dries prematurely at half tide. There are two stakes close to the light. The light is an offset white solid structure. *Not illustrated.*

LOWRIE ISLAND

LOWRIE ISLAND is a small version of the many mangrove cays along this part of the coral coast. Too small for anchorage, it identifies well when approaching *Night Island* thanks to a remarkable, separate sand cay that dries high on its reef edge to the north of the mangroves. *Not illustrated.*

Morris Islet is the best anchorage on the coast between the Flinders group and the Lockhart River.

Approaching Morris Islet from the south, the extent of its enormous reef must be considered. Its single palm tree shows from a good distance.

The palm tree on Morris Islet is a good reference point. The islet bears to the north here with the best anchorage being to its north.

Claremont Isles Area

MAGPIE REEF LIGHT
White column

Red sector shield

Buoy off STAINER ISLET

HANNAH ISLET LIGHT
Red trellis

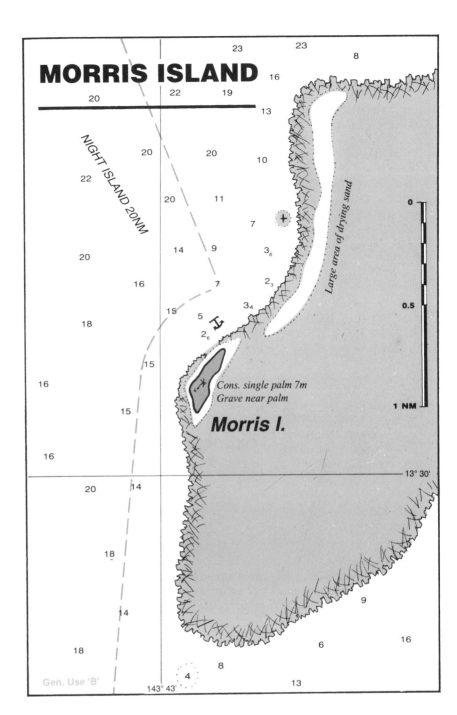

MORRIS ISLAND

23 · 23 · 8

16

20 · 22 · 19 · 13

NIGHT ISLAND 20NM

20 · 20 · 10

22

20 · 11

7

20 · 14 · 9 · 3·6

16 · 7 · 2·3

18 · 15 · 3·4

5

2·6

15

16 · 15

16

16 · 15

Large area of drying sand

0

0.5

1 NM

Cons. single palm 7m
Grave near palm

Morris I.

13° 30'

20 · 14

18

14

9

18 · 6 · 16

4 · 8

Gen. Use 'B' · 143° 43' · 13

Binstead Islet boasts a sand cay (arrowed). It is close south of Night island.

Night Island bears NNW. High Peak, above its southern end, is a good local landmark.

Night Island approach from the north.

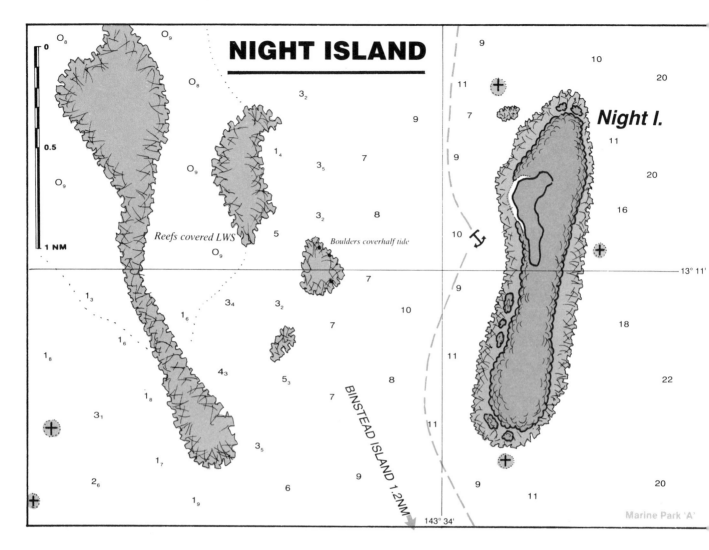

NIGHT ISLAND

Night I.

Reefs covered LWS

Boulders cover half tide

BINSTEAD ISLAND 1.2NM

Marine Park 'A'

13° 11'

143° 34'

NIGHT ISLAND is a peanut-shaped mangrove cay offering fair protection 21 miles north-west of Morris Islet. It rises from the horizon at a distance of approximately 7 miles and, from the south-east, *High Peak* (the highest hill on the mainland) held over the southern end of Night provides an easy lead in. From the north, if beating down against the trades, beware of setting in too close to *Stork* and *Sykes Reef*, and from either direction, hold Night close enough when bringing up anchorage that the foul ground to its west is avoided.

Anchorage in strong south-easterlies is most comfortable off the beach. If it favours north-east, the centre of the island is better. The bottom is a little deep but is good-holding blue mud apparently free of coral patches.

Of Interest. Torres Strait Pigeons will be seen and heard in their thousands here, especially at dusk when they fly in from the mainland, a scant 3 miles away. All white with black-tipped wings, they make a continual, haunted 'hooing' sound and were once considered a delicacy by the Torres Strait Islanders who regularly visited here in the pearl- and trochus-diving days. Their method of hunting was to go ashore at night, blind the birds with torches and knock them out of the trees with clubs. The birds are now fully protected.

Where dry land meets the mangrove swamp towards the former's south-east corner will be found a large, clear area of pumice that has obviously found its way from volcanic islands at least 1000 miles to windward of Queensland.

LLOYD BAY. Along a stretch of coast that is singularly devoid of useful indentations, Lloyd Bay comes as a welcome relief to those who enjoy a little inland exploration or just a calm-water anchorage. These attractions come at the expense of a fair dogleg off the main track and some concern regarding shoals and reefs.

Close to the mainland south of Lloyd Bay, Night Island is a mangrove forest on a reef extending from the sand-rimmed cay.

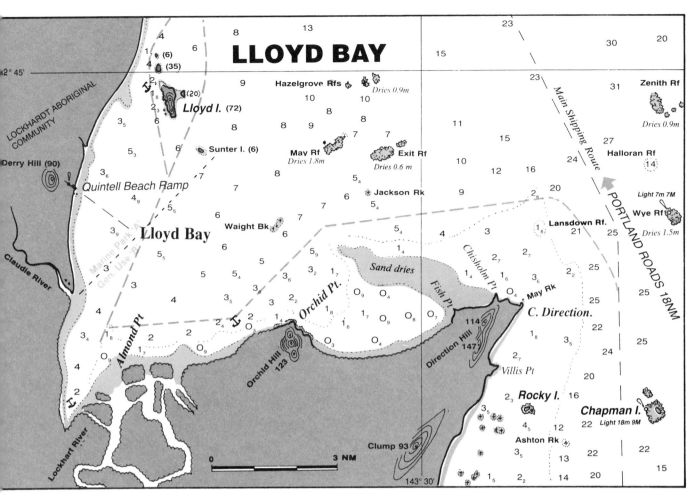

LLOYD BAY

(Chart labels:) Lloyd I. (72), Sunter I. (6), Derry Hill (90), Quintell Beach Ramp, Lloyd Bay, Hazelgrove Rfs — Dries 0.9m, May Rf — Dries 1.8m, Exit Rf — Dries 0.6 m, Jackson Rk, Waight Bk, Orchid Pt., Orchid Hill 123, Almond Pt, Sand dries, Chisholm Pt, Fish Pt, Direction Hill 114 147, C. Direction., May Rk, Villis Pt, Clump 93, Rocky I., Ashton Rk, Chapman I. — Light 18m 9M, Lansdown Rf. — Dries 1.5m, Wye Rf, Light 7m 7M, Halloran Rf, Zenith Rf — Dries 0.9m, Main Shipping Route, PORTLAND ROADS 18NM, Marine Park A, Gen. Use B, LOCKHARDT ABORIGINAL COMMUNITY, Lockhart River, Claudie River, 0 ... 3 NM, 143° 30', 2° 45'

Approach from the south is by the main shipping route, passing *Chapman Reef* to starboard and *Rocky Islet* well to port. *Cape Direction* starts showing 20 miles away as a single dot (Direction Hill) which rapidly becomes a fully developed headland. In the vicinity of Rocky Islet, a large sand blow is seen on the headland with other, less obvious, dunes to its north.

The sand-bottomed shoals of *Lansdown Reef* extend offshore from Cape Direction for nearly 2 miles and must be skirted in other than ideal conditions by the average deep keeler. Having cleared the shoals a short cut to Lloyd Bay's south-west corner (the Lockhart River) can be taken, with care, between drying sand extending west-north-west from Cape Direction, and *Jackson Rock*. Unfortunately, the water is never clear enough to sight either Jackson Rock or *Waight Bank*, however, the following assists in their avoidance; the sand shoals off Cape Direction show well enough to be sighted from aloft so that their edge may be safely favoured as long as the echo sounder is watched carefully. Jackson Rock lies immediately beyond a transit

of *Chapman Reef* light beacon and the tip of *Cape Direction*. These give a line, if not a pin-point, on which to stand special watch. At this stage, *Exit Reef* should also show from aloft and, soon after, *May Reef* which has an easily sighted tidal sand cay on its western end (covers high water springs.)

Holding the course that brought you between the shoals and Jackson Rock (around 260° true), turn for *Almond Point* when *Orchid Hill* bears 195° true. Almond Point comprises low mangroves but can be seen easily enough from this distance. This takes you south of *Waight Bank*, but a more extreme temporary dogleg might be advisable to ensure clearance.

Waight Bank is on a transit between the eastern tip of *Sunter Islet* and the southern tip of *Lloyd Island*, a fact that provides a line of reference for extra caution.

When Sunter Islet opens east of Lloyd Island, steer more west towards the *Claudie River* mouth which is not seen but lies at the southern end of a conspicuous line of sand dunes. When the eastern edge of a small unnamed islet off Lloyd's north end lies under *Red*

Cape Direction bears north-west.

Cape Direction abeam. Beware the extensive shoals offshore.

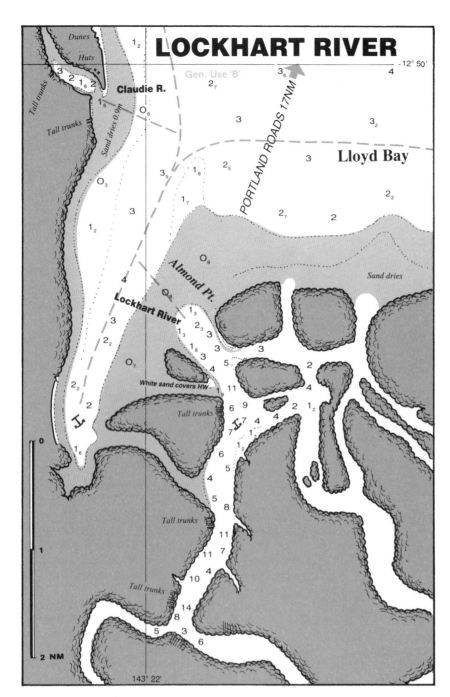

LOCKHART RIVER

Claudie R.

Gen. Use 'B'

Lloyd Bay

PORTLAND ROADS 17NM

Almond Pt.

Lockhart River

Sand dries

White sand covers HW

Tall trunks

Tall trunks

Tall trunks

Tall trunks

Tall trunks

Tall trunks

Dunes

Huts

Sand dries 0.9m

0   1   2 NM

12° 50'

143° 22'

Tall mangroves are a feature of the Lockhart River. Anchorage here is superb.

This deep, commodious river provides ideal cyclone protection. The bar carries about 0.8 metres LWS and is never invaded by swell.

Hill (on Cape Griffith), turn south and stay on this transit until shoaling in the inlet or over the river mouth demands its abandonment.

Approach from the north is an easier matter of rounding *Restoration Rock* or *Island* and steering for the south-west corner of the bay taking care to pass inside or outside *Edwards Shoals*. The water being deeper and clearer here, these shoals can sometimes be sighted from aloft. Sunter Islet provides good reference as the bay is entered but will not be seen much over 3 miles, being a low, unremarkable bunch of foliage.

Anchorage. The easiest anchorage is under the lee of *Orchid Point* in south-east weather or behind *Lloyd Island* in east to northerly winds (see individual descriptions later). Otherwise, in all but the most boisterous northerly wind, the inlet at the south-west extreme provides good shelter or, better still, the *Lockhart River* can be entered where total protection from all weather prevails, as described next.

Tides are based on Cairns being a little later and of similar height.

Nav Aids. The only beacons within Lloyd Bay are the small lit leading beacons on the barge ramp at *Quintell Beach* which is used to unload supplies for the *Lockhart Mission* a few miles inland.

LOCKHART RIVER. As the accompanying large-scale plan shows, this river is very navigable with good depths inside and many alternative channels.

Entering the River. A shoal mud bank wraps around the many mouths of the Lockhart, but is deepest off the one aimed at the Claudie River to the north-west. Here 0.8 metres covers the bank at low water springs and because the area experiences a spring rise of up to 2.7 metres, a vessel drawing 3.5 could conceivably enter. More sensibly, 2 metres draft should be considered maximum for average tides.

The great advantage of the Lockhart River is that

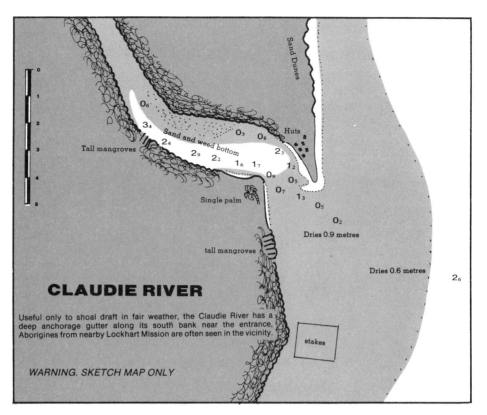

CLAUDIE RIVER

Useful only to shoal draft in fair weather, the Claudie River has a deep anchorage gutter along its south bank near the entrance, Aborigines from nearby Lockhart Mission are often seen in the vicinity.

WARNING. SKETCH MAP ONLY

The Lockhart River Aboriginal Community is based north of the Claudie River. Quintell Beach and Lloyd Island are part of its reserve.

its entrance is not a weather shore for most of the year. This means that a vessel enters against the wind in a calm sea and, as long as a flood tide is used, a grounding lasts only seconds. The best course is east-south-east using a white, partially scrub-covered beach on the left-hand bank as reference. On the opposite bank, extending south-east from the right-hand headland, will be seen a white sand spit which covers at two-thirds tide. If it cannot be seen then the bar carries at least 2.5 metres.

Anchorage outside the river, or in the inlet, is in excellent-holding mud. Inside the river the bottom is cleaner and the holding just as good. Anchorage within can be a matter of choice there being plenty of depth and swinging room. Except for the beach on entering, there are no landing places except well upstream beyond sensible navigation.

CLAUDIE RIVER. Penetrating the mainland immediately north of the *Lockhart River*, the Claudie can be entered by shoal-draft craft at high tide only.

Calm weather is preferable, but owing to the protection it enjoys from the prevailing south-easterly winds, entry can be effected in light to moderate winds.

As the accompanying plan shows, the bar has zero water on it at low water springs demanding a tide height matching your draft plus a little against wave lift and fall. Approach is exactly as outlined for the Lockhart River and anchorage is available near the mouth in water deep enough to remain afloat at low tide.

Huts belonging to Aborigines from the Lockhart Mission are on the north head of the Claudie. This is misnamed in the *Queensland Sailing Directions* where it is referred to as the 'Callide River' in relation to the Lockhart River approach.

LLOYD ISLAND lies close to the mainland north of the Claudie River in the western side of *Lloyd Bay*. Anchorage against east to north-easterly winds is good towards the beach in front of a coconut grove on the island's north-west tip. It is said that carpet snakes infest the island.

Orchid Point, Lloyd Bay, as it appears when safely past Cape Direction's west-tending sand spit.

Approaching the Lockhart River entrance. The bar carries about 0.8 metres LWS.

Cape Griffith is 5 miles north of Lloyd Island. Red Hill is on its tip.

271

Restoration Island lies close off Cape Weymouth (left). Old Man Rock is between the two.

Looking south towards Portland Roads. Restoration Rock is left, Rocky Island is left of centre.

Restoration Island bears SSE. Cape Weymouth is right with Red Hill on Cape Griffith between the two, background.

Rocky Island, off Portland Roads, is seen right.

Restoration Rock, Island and Cape Weymouth from the north.

PORTLAND ROADS. An outpost of civilisation 250 miles north of Cooktown and 150 miles south of Thursday Island, Portland Roads offers semi-protection from the trade wind under the lee of *Rocky Island* and *Cape Weymouth* further to windward.

Approach. From the south, *Restoration Island* at 116 metres high lifts from the horizon before rounding *Cape Direction* along with the land mass of Cape Weymouth further west. It makes an acceptable steering mark but, in fact, the safer track passes outside *Restoration Rock* which does not rise until 10 to 12 miles away. On final approach, the island and rock can be passed between, if preferred, from where Rocky Island is rounded to enter Portland Roads.

From the north, Portland Roads is recognisable as the westernmost and larger of two similar hills, the eastern one being Restoration Island. Between the two will be seen lower land and Rocky Island from about 12 miles. To the west of Portland Roads' hill, low land joins it to *Round Black Hills*, a well-wooded range without remarkable peaks. From as far away as 10 miles, a solitary house will be seen on the Portland Roads' hill close to the water. A bald patch will be seen above it.

Middle Reef, 4 miles north of Portland Roads, can be taken either side being aware of the presence of *Blue Bell Rocks*, with less than 2 metres low water springs, to its west. The light beacon on Middle Reef is a white cylinder with offset top similar to that illustrated for Howick Islands and can be seen in daylight from at least 6 miles. Its light at night shows for 9 miles.

Anchorage is in very good-holding mud wherever possible in the bay. A south-east wind of any strength sends a substantial easterly swell across the bay and rolling is the order of the day. This can be dampened by using a stern anchor if a long-term stay is intended.

During the late-October-through-December transitional calms and light north-easterlies, it can be very calm, albeit with the fundamental threat of being a lee shore if a northerly pipes up. The nearest good northerly anchorage is behind *Lloyd Island* as previously described.

Tides are based on Cairns using *Restoration Island* for reference. They are similar in range and turn nearly half an hour later.

Fuel and Water. The fuel barge once stationed at Portland Roads has been removed and is unlikely to return. In its place, offering similar services, are the mother ships which tend the needs of working trawlers. Water is available from a council tank near the root of the old wharf but it must not be relied upon.

Communications. It is possible to book flights out of Portland Roads from inland Iron Range Airfield from a local agent. A lift into the airport or collection of passengers and freight can also be organised. Mail can be taken and delivered through official mailman, Ross Pope.

Of Interest. With the invasion by trawlers of the Coral Coast over the past two decades, Portland Roads has become a favourite place to anchor after a night's work as well as a place to refuel and organise spare parts.

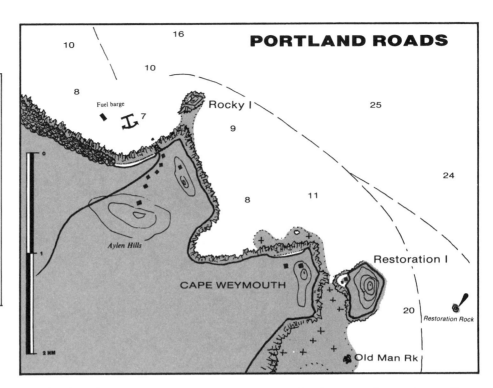

PORTLAND ROADS

The Kennedy connection

At Portland Roads there is a monument to the Kennedy Expedition which set out from Rockingham Bay (Cardwell area) in 1848 to trek to Cape York. Hardships of the terrain and slowed by a flock of sheep and excessive equipment, it became necessary to rest the main party whilst Kennedy continued north to make contact with a supply ship in Port Albany. Of the eight members left behind a few miles north-west of Portland Roads, only two survived whilst Kennedy perished near the Escape River as noted under that heading.

The fuel barge shown on the chart above had been removed as of 1993. Better prawning seasons may see its return but this is doubtful.

The wharf ruins comprise the rock rampart and one lonely dolphin immediately off the fringing reef. It was built in 1938 after a survey by Captain T.F. Roberts to supply the inland goldmines of the period. During World War II its 'T' head was extended and after the war it continued to be used for general cargo for the Lockhart Mission.

MIDDLE REEF *not illustrated* offers no sensible anchorage, but must be skirted 4 miles north of Portland Roads. It is in two parts, the southern part being the longest and they total 12 cables from south to north. The entire reef dries at low tide although the northern section appears to be slightly lower. A white offset column light beacon (similar to the Howick Group lights) stands on the south tip and displays its light for 9 miles. To the immediate north of the beacon will be seen an old stake and tripod.

Fourteen cables west of Middle Reef are *Blue Bell Rocks* which remain covered at low water springs. Passage between the rocks and the reef is perfectly safe but the rocks are often impossible to see regardless of conditions.

PASCOE RIVER. 10 miles north-west from Portland Roads and draining a very pretty section of the coast, this river is available to shallow-draft vessels in calm weather only. Under no circumstances can its entrance be negotiated during fresh onshore winds.

Approach from Portland Roads is by simple progression along the coast. *Pigeon Island*, standing 15 metres high, densely wooded on the north face and semi-bald on the south, is a good landmark although it can blend with the background easily. Otherwise, a stand of tall mangroves in its vicinity will be seen from where a short beach runs up to the Pascoe River mouth broken just once by a low, rocky headland. At the mouth itself, another stand of mangroves is clustered on the southern headland.

From the north it is best to hold the main shipping

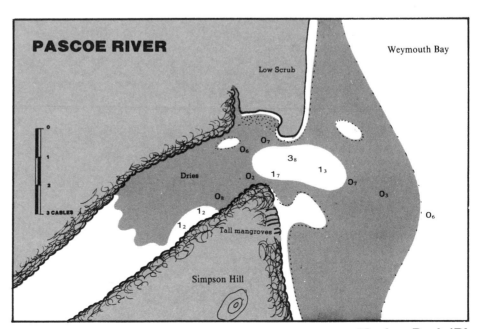

The Pascoe River penetrates beautiful countryside but is only available to shallow draft vessels using a high tide.

Stretching south from the Pascoe River is the Iron Range National Park.

Marine Park 'B'

channel until able to lay the mouth without any worries about *Kangaroo Shoals* or a foul-ground area to the north-east of *Stanley Hill*. At night, it is possible to take advantage of the red sector of the *Eel Reef light*, working the white-red (pink) zone up to anchorage off the river mouth. Trawlers commonly work in this red sector.

On final approach, bring the obvious narrow river mouth to bear approximately west-north-west and work only a flood tide of a height to suit your draft. Because calm weather only should be used, that height should match Cairns tide data with no extra necessary for wave lift.

Anchorage. Offshore, awaiting the tide, good holding in fine, light grey mud will be found at around the 9 metre level. Inside the river, depths greater than 1.5 metres are nearly impossible to find at low water. Only by snugging the vessel hard against the mangroves inside the south head will flotation at low tide be enjoyed. Maximum draft for this exercise is about 1.6 metres. Greater depths may be found well upstream, but a full-width bar soon after entering the river limits navigation to high tide leaving very little time to find better water.

The bottom is coarse sand and the water is often crystal clear. Two miles upstream it is often fresh.

EEL REEF *not illustrated* Stretching 13 miles from south-east to north-west off Portland Roads and forming the outside border to the main shipping channel, Eel Reef is only an average of 6 cables wide. There is no anchorage worth the trouble of finding except on fishing forays during calms. Its light stands on the north-west extreme and is on a trellis tower. Its red sector covers *Kemp Rocks* immediately outside the shipping channel and has no significance to the average small boat except as an aid to closing the coast at night as mentioned in the later section, 'Down the Peninsula' and the previous 'Pascoe River'.

FORBES ISLAND. 18 miles due north of *Portland Roads* and situated in semi-charted waters outside *Gallon Reef*, tolerable anchorage exists in the bay on the north-west side. The only safe approach is from the north after rounding Gallon Reef standing wide of a vast area of scattered coral patches. Do not navigate this region against the sun.

Forbes Island has the ruins of a building in the bay and a grave on a satellite island. Parts are under private leases which are not being used.

HUNTER AND GLENNIE INLETS penetrate the mainland in the south-west corner of *Temple Bay* nearly 25 miles north-west of Portland Roads. Both have barred entrances over mud which carry just a foot or two at low tide. To enter, use a tide of your ship's draft plus a safety margin if any swell is running. Although anchorage off these inlets is not recommended under normal circumstances, as a means of securing the vessel to do a land survey before entering it is quite suitable.

Inside the creeks will be found water enough to float at low tide and the fishing within can be extraordinarily good at times, colourful reef fish often being caught here. It is also a good crabbing area, albeit, at the cost of sandfly and mosquito bites. When approaching, beware of *Andrew, Daniell, Lion* and *Ada Reefs* scattered around the vicinity.

Five miles north of Glennie Inlet is Bolt Head from which it was proposed to build a breakwater and create a harbour. Its purpose was to service Australia's first space base, the story of which follows.

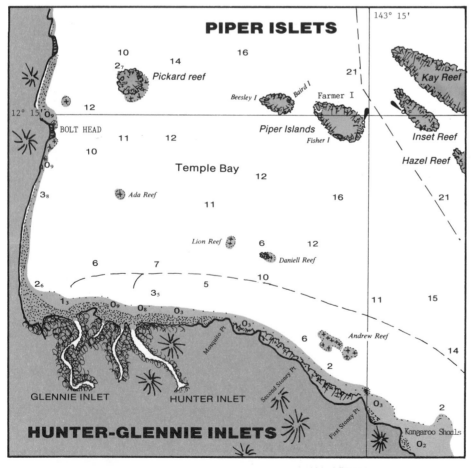

The key chart here shows the Temple Bay area in which Hunter and Glennie Inlets and the Piper Islands are situated. Both are described in detail and shown in large scale here and over the page. The reef anchorages in this bay are generally uncomfortable in developed weather and uncertain during calms whilst the inlets demand a high tide to enter.

GLENNIE AND HUNTER INLETS

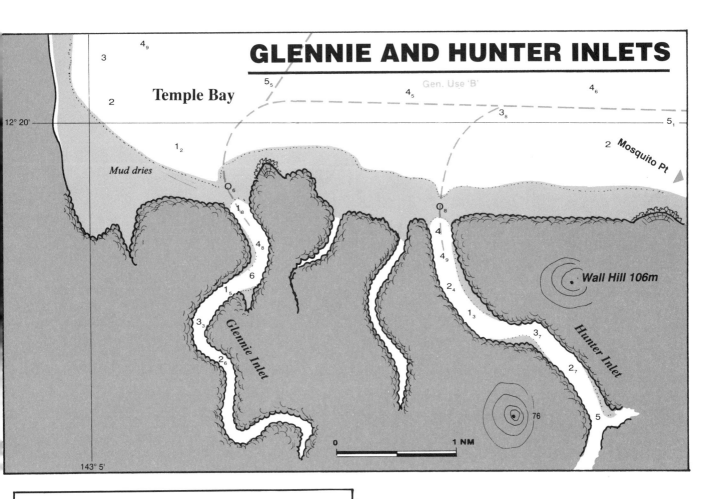

Temple Bay

Gen. Use 'B'

Mud dries

12° 20'

2 Mosquito Pt

Wall Hill 106m

Glennie Inlet

Hunter Inlet

76

5

143° 5'

0   1 NM

SPACE STATION. From Bolt Head, in Temple Bay, a breakwater was to be built to form a harbour for Australia's first space base. Situated four kilometres inland from the coast, it was to be developed by Space Transport Systems Ltd, headed by former Queensland Premier, Mr Mike Ahern.

Because of the backlash from environmentalists and Aboriginal activists, this site may be abandoned for the less delicate area closer to Weipa on the other side of the Cape York Peninsula. Certainly, it makes more sense to use an already developed, natural harbour with its infrastructure of access roads and airstrip.

Perhaps the most extraordinary aspect of this project is its potential for failure at enormous economic and environmental cost. Antagonists have pointed out that the disintegration of the USSR has presented the world with more launching pads than are needed and that even if Australia wins launching contracts, nearly all technology will be imported. It will, they say, be yet another step towards dependence on others.

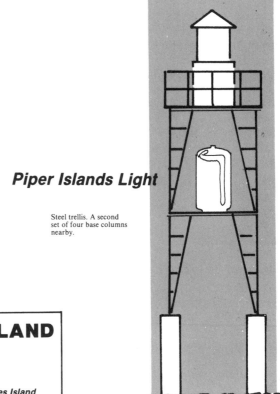

Piper Islands Light

Steel trellis. A second set of four base columns nearby.

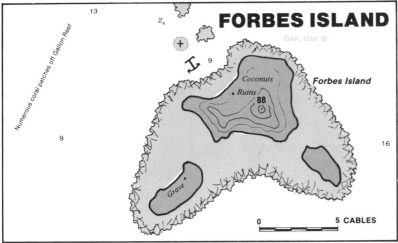

FORBES ISLAND

Gen. Use 'B'

Coconuts
Ruins
88

Forbes Island

Grave

0   5 CABLES

Forbes Island is off the beaten track and demands special care in its approach. The chart here is a sketch plan only, a proper survey never having been undertaken by the author. Under no circumstances should it be approached from the south.

275

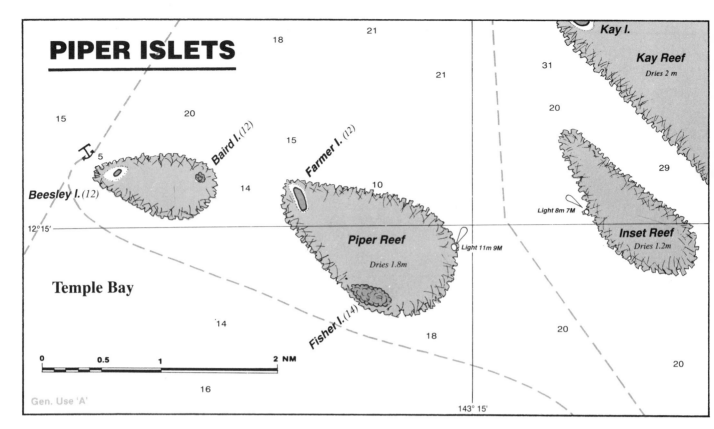

PIPER ISLETS

18   21   Kay I.

31   Kay Reef
Dries 2 m

15   20   20

5   Baird I. (12)   15   Farmer I. (12)   29

Beesley I. (12)   14   10   Light 8m 7M

12° 15′   Piper Reef   Inset Reef
Dries 1.8m   Light 11m 9M   Dries 1.2m

Temple Bay

14   Fisher I. (14)   18   20

0   0.5   1   2 NM

16   20

Gen. Use 'A'   143° 15′

PIPER REEFS comprise two reefs, the largest being east of the smaller and forming one side of the main shipping channel 22 miles north-west from *Portland Roads* and 16 miles south of *Cape Grenville*. On the other side of the channel are *Inset* and *Kay Reefs*, a light being on the western edge of Inset. A light is also placed on the eastern extreme of Piper Reefs and together they mark the boundaries of the narrowest part of the shipping channel along the entire Coral Coast. Here it is a mere 11 cables wide.

Piper Reefs support a number of small, low wooded cays, the only one having a beach being *Farmer Islet* on the western tip of the eastern reef. The other islets, *Fisher* and *Baird*, are mangrove cays. Anchorage can be taken under the lee of *Beesley Islet* on the western tip of the western reef during south-east winds where shoaling water and some scattered coral patches are found. It is not comfortable but better than nothing

when better anchorages are unobtainable before dark. There is no northerly anchorage without being obliged to drop into deep water.

Piper Reef Light is an open trellis type visible for 9 miles. Close alongside it is a second base of four columns.

Kay Reef, north-east from this light, sports a small grass-capped cay on its north-west tip.

HAGGERSTONE ISLAND is a dome-shaped continental island 5 miles south-east from *Cape Grenville*. Sporting a delightful beach backed by palms and a steep, heavily wooded mountainside behind, it is now under private lease and has a superb New Guinea style 'long house' which is not easily seen from seaward.

Anchorage is indifferent and often uncomfortable off the reef in 20 metres with the island bearing south-east in onshore weather. On the northern tip of the

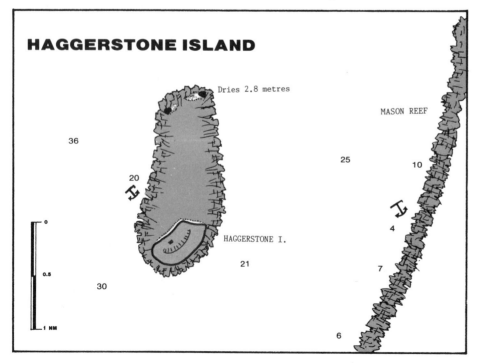

HAGGERSTONE ISLAND

Dries 2.8 metres

MASON REEF

36   25   10

20

4

HAGGERSTONE I.

21   7

30   6

A deep and comfortable anchorage, Haggerstone Island supports a small tourist resort.

276

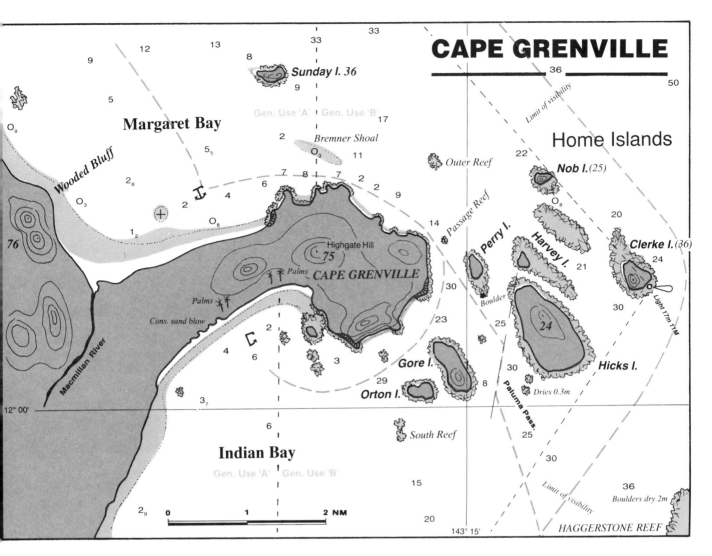

large reef will be seen tidal sand cays and boulders.

A resort is to be developed here.

Of Interest. Yet to be located is the wreck of the *Morning Star* lost somewhere near Temple Bay in 1814. This Indian-built brig was carrying a general cargo of colonial exports from Sydney to Batavia (now Jakarta, the capital of Indonesia). The colony of New South Wales then being only twenty six years old, the finding of this vessel will expand our knowledge of colonial trade with South East Asia.

CAPE GRENVILLE,
40 miles north of Portland Roads, promises security and comfort in the foulest weather; in *Margaret Bay* during south-easterly trades and in *Indian Bay* during northerlies. The *Home Islets*, scattered offshore, provide interesting, if slightly complex, approach.

Approach Indian Bay. From the south, steer direct from *Moody Reef*. When closing the coast a conspicuous line of sand dunes will be seen which make a fair steering mark to avoid the reefs in the north-east corner of the bay where will be seen a low barren islet. From the north, a reciprocal course through the islands to that described next for Margaret Bay can be steered or, with greater assurance of safety, outside the whole group.

Approach Margaret Bay. From the south, steer direct from Moody Reef to *Paluma Pass* which can be identified from abeam Moody Light Beacon despite the low nature of the Home islets. The western edges of *Hicks, Harvey* and *Nob Islet* in line make a good transit for entering the Pass, then, when Harvey and Hicks open up, steer across to miss the reef extending south from *Perry Islet*. On the south end of this reef there is high drying rock which provides good reference depending on tide.

From abeam Perry Islet, steer to hold the mainland close along the actual Cape to pass west of *Passage Reef* which is nearly always impossible to see. Beyond Passage Reef the hitherto good depths rapidly decrease until shoals are encountered where *Bremner Shoal* joins the mainland leaving a gutter deep enough for most yachts at low tide.

When the shoal is crossed, depths increase again as Margaret Bay proper is entered.

When navigating within the Home Islets, always take into account the tidal overfalls and spirals that can occur even during neaps. They are not dangerous, but readily alter the course and can catch a slack helmsman — or auto-pilot — off guard. Also, because the islets are low and somewhat featureless, do not place absolute faith in transits. Eyeball navigation remains the best form.

From the north, steer direct for Margaret Bay whose position is to the west of the obvious high ground of the Cape hills. Sunday Island offers good reference.

Margaret Bay Anchorage is in shoaling water over sandy mud that promises excellent holding in the hardest trade-wind gusts. The isthmus being low, wind

These two photographs show the type of headland which comprise Cape Grenville. They can be held close when working into anchorage, otherwise it pays to stand outside Clerke Island, the eastern-most of the Home Islands off the cape.

Looking south along Cape Grenville, Gore and Orton Island fuse to make three low peaks.

Approach the Home Island from the north, Nob Islet is centre with Clerke Island, distant left.

Clerke Island is now obvious with its sand cay, right.

The light on Clerke Island is separated from the main island.

bullets are not generated to any worrying degree here and very little swell invades the bay.

Indian Bay Anchorage is also in sandy mud. The bay is prettier than Margaret having sand dunes and palm trees and often cleaner water. However, both bays provide good beaches and bushwalking. Margaret Bay has a small creek in its south-west corner — grandly called *MacMillan River* — in which a dinghy can explore at high tide.

Home Islet Anchorage. At first glance of the chart the navigator might be forgiven for presuming the Home Islets to offer endless anchorage opportunities. In fact, the water is too deep and the reefs too steep-to for security leaving only daylight and calm weather situations grappled on to ledges or using light tackle into deep water. The mother ship is best secured in Margaret Bay from where an outboard-powered dinghy can be taken back to the offshore islets.

One of the islets — *Hicks* — has been privately leased for some time, changing owners recently and now earmarked for possible development.

Of Interest. Nearby *Sunday Islet* enjoys a unique place in Australian history being where Captain Bligh was threatened with another mutiny.

During his open boat voyage from the *Bounty* mut-

iny, Bligh and his fellows stopped on Sunday Island hoping to enjoy rest and recreation away from the potential of unfriendly natives. While ashore, one of the crew challenged Bligh, saying, 'I am as good a man as you are!' to which Bligh responded by throwing the man a sword and retorting, 'Let us see who is to be master here'. The threat died.

In August 1834 the 313 ton barque *Charles Eaton* struck a reef offshore from this area, the crew and passengers escaping on two rafts and a boat. One of the rafts drifted to within hailing distance of a large native canoe to which the shipwrecked folk transferred after friendly overtures. They were then taken to an island where they were all butchered except for two boys. These lads were well treated and were foster-mothered by tribal women on Murray Island.

Two years later, the *Isabella*, on a search and rescue mission, ransomed the lads with tomahawks, then proceeded to Aureed Island and found forty five skulls, seventeen of which were European. These were taken south and interred in Sydney's Botany Cemetery.

The incident prompted the dispatch of *HMS Fly* under Captain Blackwood to establish a site for a navigational beacon in the area. He chose Raine Island on the outer reef from where passage could be made into the mainland, landing it at Cape Grenville via the now-named Blackwood and Pollard Channels.

In 1844 the *Fly* returned in company with two other ships to commence work with twenty convict masons employed. They soon erected a superb 64-foot-high circular stone tower using locally quarried coral stone from the island and timber taken from the *Martha Ridgway*, wrecked 40 miles away on the reef bounding Wreck Bay. All convicts involved were given a six month remission from their sentences.

The Raine Island Beacon became Queensland's first navigational aid, providing a fine landmark for ships approaching the coast from the Coral Sea before the more logical route through the Torres Strait was surveyed. The beacon was never lit, nor intended as such, for night-time navigation in those days was never a consideration. The only lit beacon on the east coast at the time was on South Head, Sydney.

Having fallen into a sad state of disrepair, and despite occasional interest by the Department of Transport's Nav Aids division, a group of volunteers using a private grant rebuilt the beacon in the late 1980s.

Going ashore on Raine Island is prohibited.

HICKS ISLAND

HICKS ISLAND, in the *Home Group* scattered around Cape Grenville, is under private lease and offers poor anchorage in very deep water suggesting calm weather use only. It has a fringe of mangroves down its eastern side and a conspicuous spine of coconut palms along its low, plain ridge.

CLERKE ISLAND

CLERKE ISLAND, the easternmost of the *Home Islands* sports a red trellis light standing 17 metres high and visible for 11 miles. It has a fringe of mangroves around its north end and an isolated mangrove cay sitting on the north-west tip of its reef. There is no anchorage here but the fishing can be excellent in calm weather between Clerke and Hicks.

NOB ISLAND

NOB ISLAND, the northernmost of the *Home Islands*, is actually in two parts (not indicated on chart *Aus 835*), the highest at 25 metres being north west of the lower. The first is a vegetated rock and the other is a plain rock structure. Mangroves fringe the higher islet's south side.

SHELBURNE BAY

SHELBURNE BAY.   A large reef-bound bay starting 10 miles north-west of Cape Grenville, anchorage to a south-easterly can be taken under the lee of *Round Point*. It is every bit as secure as Margaret Bay.

Approach from Margaret Bay is safe taking a middle course between *Thorpe Point* and *Sunday Island* from where the coast can be closed in preparation for rounding *Rodney Islet* and *Round Point*. Thorpe Point is obvious for its red cliff and red earth patch on an unremarkable low, bald hill. Otherwise, the land both north and south of the headland is comprised of high, white sand dunes stretching beyond the horizon into Shelbourne Bay.

From the north, *Bird Islets* can be taken either side in safety from where a small twin-peaked hill with sand blows atop provides fair reference.

Anchorage is towards the south-east corner of the bay and immediately under *Round Point* in shoaling water. Move in carefully as the bay is poorly surveyed.

BIRD ISLETS *not illustrated* Comprised of two main islets on their own individual reefs, anchorage cannot be suggested here except in fair weather and with lightweight, deepwater gear. Both islets are a complex mixture of typical cay scrub (without palms) and fringing mangroves plus a scattering of beaches. While the birdlife does not seem any greater ashore than on many other islands, it is nevertheless common to sight thousands of small black birds attacking the surface of the sea in this area. They can be so thick, at times, that momentary conviction of the presence of an uncharted rock is possible.

For islets that do not smother the entire reef, the Bird Islets are unusual in that they occupy the weather

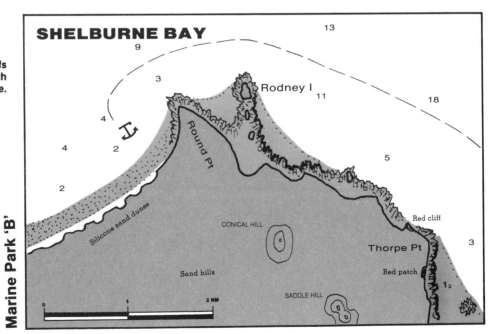

SHELBURNE BAY

Shelburne Bay has many reefs and must be navigated with care.

Marine Park 'B'

Rodney I

Round Pt

CONICAL HILL

Silicone sand dunes

Sand hills

SADDLE HILL

Red cliff

Thorpe Pt

Red patch

2 NM

13 miles north-west of Cape Grenville, Bird Islets are comprised of two mangrove cays.

279

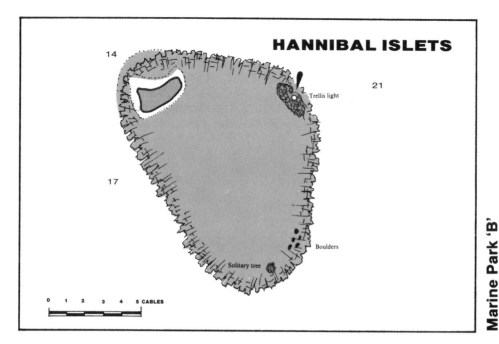

HANNIBAL ISLETS

14

21

Trellis light

17

Boulders

Solitary tree

0 1 2 3 4 5 CABLES

Marine Park 'B'

HARRINGTON REEF BEACON

side, as against the more common leeward edge of the host reef. This is a great help when navigating past them at night.

HANNIBAL ISLETS. 29 miles north-west of Cape Grenville and sharing a common large reef, are two islets, a tree and a few boulders, the latter being just awash at high water neaps.

The smaller islet of the two sits on the north-east edge of the reef and supports a light on a red trellis tower partly hidden by scrub. It has no beach or special redeeming features. The other islet sits on the north-western edge and has a delightful, almost wraparound beach which projects to the north-west as a large sand spit.

The light tower can be seen through binoculars at around 9 miles and the islets themselves rise from the sea to the naked eye at between 7 and 8 miles after which the tower melds into the background and loses its dominance.

Anchorage in fair weather to most winds can be found around the reef, and during trade winds the anchorage off the sand spit is good holding but most uncomfortable. It should be considered only where passage further north or south cannot be undertaken before dark.

The solitary tree stands leaning with the wind on the south-east corner of the reef.

CAIRNCROSS ISLETS. Claimed by some to be more comfortable than nearby Bushy Islet, the truth is, neither are pleasant during a fresh trade wind. In my opinion, Cairncross is worse because of the deeper water involved, but it must be admitted that the islets are more interesting for shore goers. The light, also, provides instant reference should dragging occur.

Cairncross was probably named after Captain Robert Cairncross who, during an investigation into navigation in the northern region of the Great Barrier Reef in 1865, was a strong proponent for developing the inner rather than the outer route. His views have long since been vindicated and enjoyed strong backing when the opening of the Suez Canal in 1869 encouraged the need for a shorter route over the top of Australia.

BUSHY ISLET offers secure but thoroughly miserable anchorage to those unable or unwilling to make the distance between Cape Grenville and the Escape River in daylight hours. During developed trade winds, the sea makes around the reef and collides in the area of the best holding ground promising gunwales-under rolling at times. If the wind favours east to north-east, conditions are acceptable where shown by the half anchor.

ESCAPE RIVER. Emptying into the sea between *Sharp Point* on the mainland and *Turtle Head Island*, the Escape River offers secure haven.

Approach from the south must take into account *Tern Islet* and a shoal lying 6 cables to its north-north-east. Tern Islet itself lies immediately off the mainland a little over 3 miles south-east of Escape River. Being low and featureless it is easily missed in hazy conditions, but *Tern Cliff*, to its south, will be recognisable for its smooth hill speckled with magnetic ant hills down the southern slope. The cliff itself is low and red. *Flat Hill*, further south, is relatively conspicuous for its moderate table top which is densely wooded. *Sadd Point*, off Flat Hill, has red cliffs with sand dunes north and south.

As Tern Islet is brought abeam, sand dunes are seen

Hannibal Islets' light (arrow) bears south-west.

280

BUSHY ISLET

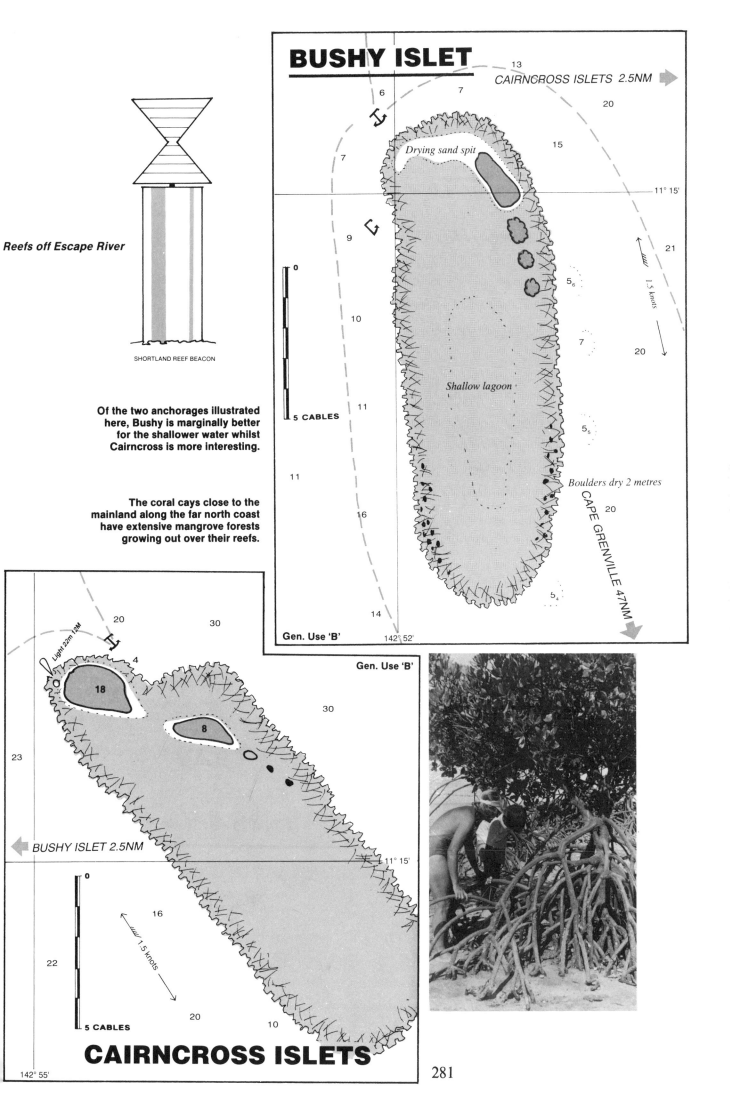

CAIRNCROSS ISLETS 2.5NM →

13

6   7

20

7   15

Drying sand spit

11° 15'

9

5₆

10   21

1.5 knots

7

11   20

Shallow lagoon

5₅

11

Boulders dry 2 metres

16   20

14   5₄

Gen. Use 'B'   142° 52'   CAPE GRENVILLE 47NM

Reefs off Escape River

SHORTLAND REEF BEACON

**Of the two anchorages illustrated
here, Bushy is marginally better
for the shallower water whilst
Cairncross is more interesting.**

**The coral cays close to the
mainland along the far north coast
have extensive mangrove forests
growing out over their reefs.**

0

5 CABLES

Gen. Use 'B'

Light 22m 12M

20   30

4

18

23   8   30

BUSHY ISLET 2.5NM   11° 15'

0

16

1.5 knots

22

20

5 CABLES   10

CAIRNCROSS ISLETS

142° 55'

281

The land south of the Escape River displays many fine sand dunes.

Albany Passage is described in full over the page.

Approaching the Escape River mouth from the south-east. Sharp Point is arrowed.

to run to *Sharp Point* which is a red bauxite cliff. *Turtle Head Island* continues red before sand dunes again prevail along most of its east coast.

When Sharp Point opens up on Turtle Head Island's south-western headland (where will be seen buildings) the course can lay direct for the river entrance, entering at midstream and continuing that way to anchor.

From the north, Turtle Islet makes fine reference as do the beacons on *Wyborn, Harrington* and *Shortland Reefs*. The tidal streams being very strong through Albany Passage and, to a lesser degree, through Adolphus Channel, the course should be watched against leeway and a decision made as to whether the current should be used, at the cost of stacking up south-east wind waves, or fought for the flatter sea enjoyed. If the wind is strong onshore consideration should be given to the state of tide at the river entrance by the time it is reached. Although there is at least 1.8 metres on the bar, low water springs, a flood tide used as late as possible guarantees a safe and comfortable entry into the river.

Turtle Head is seen from the southern exit of Albany Passage as low, flat land and Turtle Islet rises soon after. From about 8 miles north, the entrance to the Escape River is identified by the 45% angled headland to the left of which is a small pimple on the featureless background land. Soon after, the lower land of Turtle Head Island towards the true river headland is sighted and easily identified.

Anchorage is handiest off the cultured pearl company as indicated on the map. In fresh onshore weather a mild swell reaches here and can become unpleasant when the tide ebbs but is, on average, acceptable and often comfortable. Superior anchorage will be found upstream as far as, or immediately beyond, the upstream pearl rafts. A small red-earth patch will be seen in this area affording dinghy landing amidst an otherwise mangrove-fringed river.

When ascending the river, beware of small tidal rock patches on the edge of the river, not shown on the accompanying plan.

Of Interest. Visits to the cultured pearl farm ashore are sometimes possible with permission from the management. The management is Japanese who will enquire after your boat's name for their records whether you go ashore or not.

Embedded in the sand, forming whole cliffs and headlands and often dominating an area for miles around are the remarkable red rocks of this area. A walk to the weather side of Turtle Head Island is worth the effort to view these strata of bauxite. With the huge deposits at Weipa, on the other side of the Cape York Peninsula, and at Gove on the other side of the Gulf of Carpentaria, one cannot help but speculate that bauxite might extend from Escape River right across both the land and the gulf.

The Escape River was a natural boundary between two Aboriginal tribes, the Jadhaigana to the south and the Djadaraga to the north. The former were warlike and cruel, the latter friendly and kindly. The irony of Edmund Kennedy's death by spear, close to the upstream anchorage in this river, was that he was so nearly out of the clutches of one and into the welcoming arms of the other. He died here after heading one of Australia's most ambitious and disastrous explorations in 1848. Starting from Rockingham Bay near Cardwell he and his expedition walked up the Cape York Peninsula losing men, animals and equipment en route until only Kennedy and his faithful friend and guide, Jacky Jacky, remained capable of meeting up with a ship in Albany Passage. Only Jacky Jacky made it through finding his own way around the Escape River marshes to Albany after leaving Kennedy's body to the not-too-tender mercies of the Jadhaiganas.

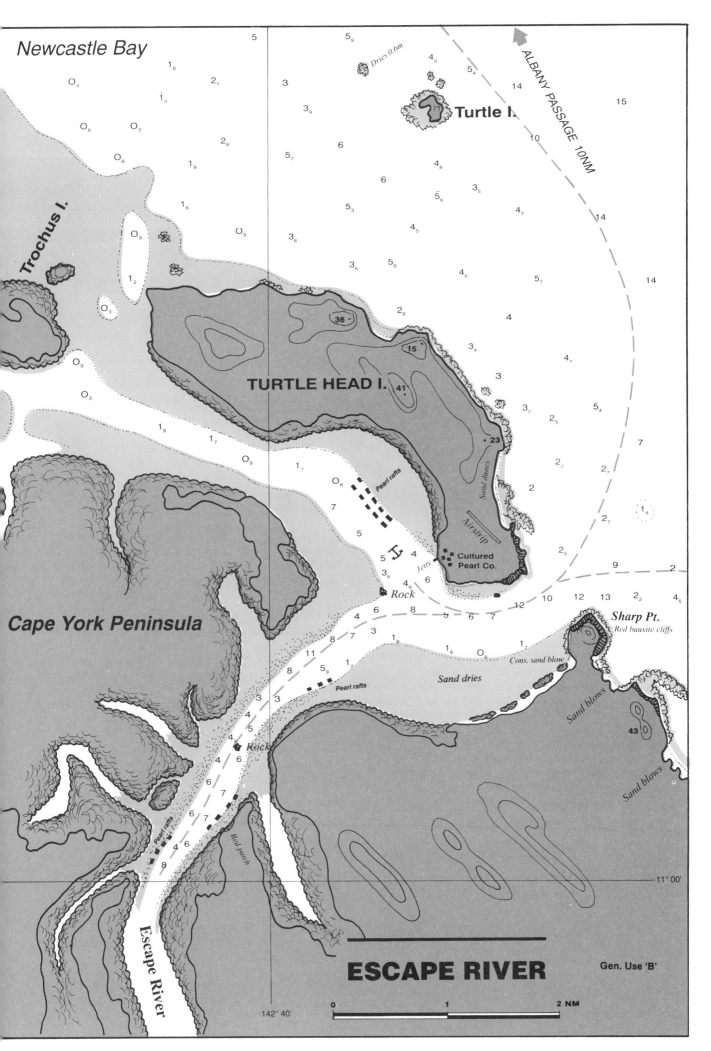

Newcastle Bay

ALBANY PASSAGE 10NM

Turtle I.

Trochus I.

TURTLE HEAD I.

Dries 0.6m

Pearl rafts

Sand dunes

Airstrip

Cultured
Pearl Co.

Jetty

Cape York Peninsula

Rock

Sharp Pt.
Red bauxite cliffs

Cons. sand blow

Pearl rafts

Sand dries

Sand blows

Rock

Red patch

Pearl rafts

Sand blows

11° 00'

Escape River

ESCAPE RIVER

Gen. Use 'B'

142° 40'

0   1   2 NM

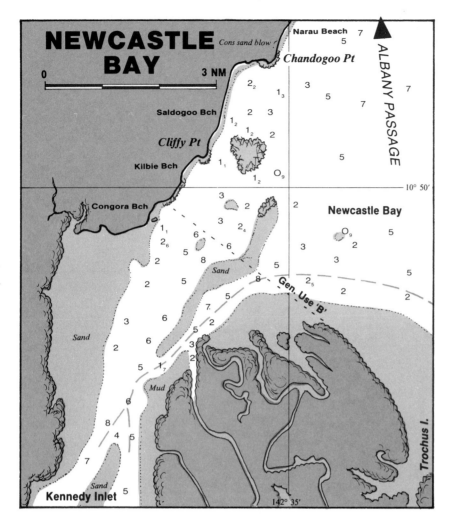

NEWCASTLE BAY

0   3 NM

Narau Beach   7
  5
Cons sand blow
Chandogoo Pt

ALBANY PASSAGE

Saldogoo Bch

Cliffy Pt

Kilbie Bch

Congora Bch

Sand

Sand

Gen. Use 'B'

Newcastle Bay

10° 50'

Mud

Sand

Kennedy Inlet   5

142° 35'

Trochus I.

Newcastle Bay is a *General Use 'B' Zone* west to the dotted line. West of the line it is known as Kennedy Inlet which becomes Jacky Jacky Creek. The Bamaga Aboriginal Reserve is to its west.

NEWCASTLE BAY

NEWCASTLE BAY. Slashing the north-east tip of the Cape York Peninsula, Newcastle Bay is the delta to the *Kennedy River*. This is also known as Jacky Jacky Creek and Kennedy Inlet, their namesakes having been discussed in the previous section (Escape River).

Newcastle Bay can be very rough during developed trade winds over an ebb tide, at which time it pays to stand off or seek an alternative destination. In suitable conditions and preferably with a flood tide, the best approach is close around the south headland which is low and mangrove forested. The water is seldom clear enough to visually judge depth so caution is prescribed; especially as to stand too wide is to risk fouling drying banks and reefs.

Once enclosed within the true river mouth, the main river trends south-west whilst a useful tributary will be seen to the south-east. Close to or within its mouth is the best anchorage without moving any further upstream.

Good depths prevail upstream and offer total security in the event of cyclonic weather.

ALBANY PASSAGE

ALBANY PASSAGE. Situated between the mainland and Albany Island, 14 miles north-west of the Escape River and less than 25 miles east of Thursday Island, Albany Passage offers a short-cut between the two. And when the tide is running in your favour, it can be a very fast short cut.

Approach from the south is usually from Escape River passing east of *Turtle Islet* then laying course for the passage direct. This course must allow for *Ariel Bank*, 1.6 miles south-east of the passage plus a non-drying shoal 0.7 miles further south-east. To safely pass outside these dangers, bring the sand cay on Ariel Bank in line with the left-hand sand patch obvious on the mainland at a distance of three miles offshore then open it as direct approach is made for the passage entrance. From there it is a conspicuous gap between steep headlands. The entrance headlands, *Fly Point* and *Ulrica Point* are low, fringed with black rock. Fly Point is a barren headland with poor grass, scattered cabbage palm and magnetic ant hills remarkable for their bright orange colour.

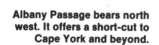

Albany Passage bears north west. It offers a short-cut to Cape York and beyond.

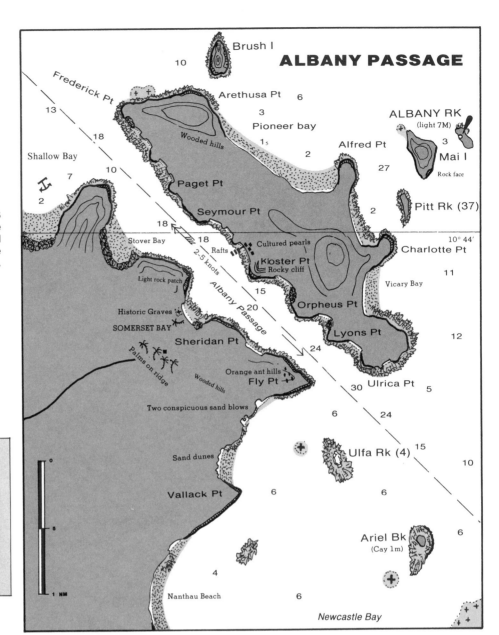

ALBANY PASSAGE

Brush I
10
Frederick Pt
13
18
Shallow Bay
10
7
2
Arethusa Pt   6
3
Pioneer bay
1₅
2
Alfred Pt
27

ALBANY RK
(light 7M)
3
Mai I
Rock face

Pitt Rk (37)

Wooded hills
Paget Pt
Seymour Pt
2

Stover Bay
18
18
2-5 knots
Rafts
Cultured pearls
Kloster Pt
Rocky cliff
15
Albany Passage
20
24

Light rock patch
Historic Graves
SOMERSET BAY
Palms on ridge
Sheridan Pt
Wooded hills
Orange ant hills
Fly Pt
Two conspicuous sand blows

Charlotte Pt
10° 44'
11
Vicary Bay
Orpheus Pt
Lyons Pt
12
30   Ulrica Pt   5
6   24
Ulfa Rk (4)   15
10

Sand dunes
Vallack Pt
6
6

Ariel Bk
(Cay 1m)
6

4
Nanthau Beach   6

Newcastle Bay

0
5
1 NM

Named in 1846 by Lieut. Yule of HMS *Rattlesnake*, Albany Island has the historic graves of Thomas Wall and Charles Niblett who perished in the famous Kennedy Expedition.

Sailing Ships Beware

Although the port of Somerset, in Albany Passage, proved itself as a port of refuge for shipwrecked crews, its tides were too strong for safe manoeuvring alongside for coal. It was also not recommended to sailing ships whose masters were warned in the sailing directions that a vessel 'could become unmanageable as she loses her wind and comes under the control of the tidal stream'.

From the north, Albany Passage is reached by steering direct for its entrance after rounding Cape York's *Eborac Island* and light. Be cautious of *Sextant Rock*, a 'fried egg' exposed 1 metre at high water springs to the right of the path.

Anchorage. Being a deep passage troubled greatly by strong tidal currents, anchorage within the passage cannot be recommended except during calms with light-weather, deep-water tackle. The most secure and comfortable anchorage during strong winds from all directions, except north, is in *Shallow Bay* between *Osnaburg Point* and *Bishop Point*. Between the two is a beach of sandy mud exposing at low tide and a fringe of mangroves. Anchorage is in shoaling water over good-holding mud and is troubled by a beam swell during strong trade-wind weather.

Tides. Being in the Torres Strait area, where Rafferty's Rules so often prevail regarding tide predictions, there is no guarantee that a current will run the way it should when it should. On more than one occasion I have planned departure from the Escape River to be in the channel when the north-running flood tide should be at its peak only to find it quite dormant. But, mostly, it behaves itself and a northerly current of up to 5 knots can be expected during flood and a southerly current at a similar rate can be expected during ebb.

Albany Passage predictions are based on Twin Island in the *Tide Tables* using Frederick Point as local reference. I personally find Cairncross Islet based on Cairns data closer to the truth although, as stated

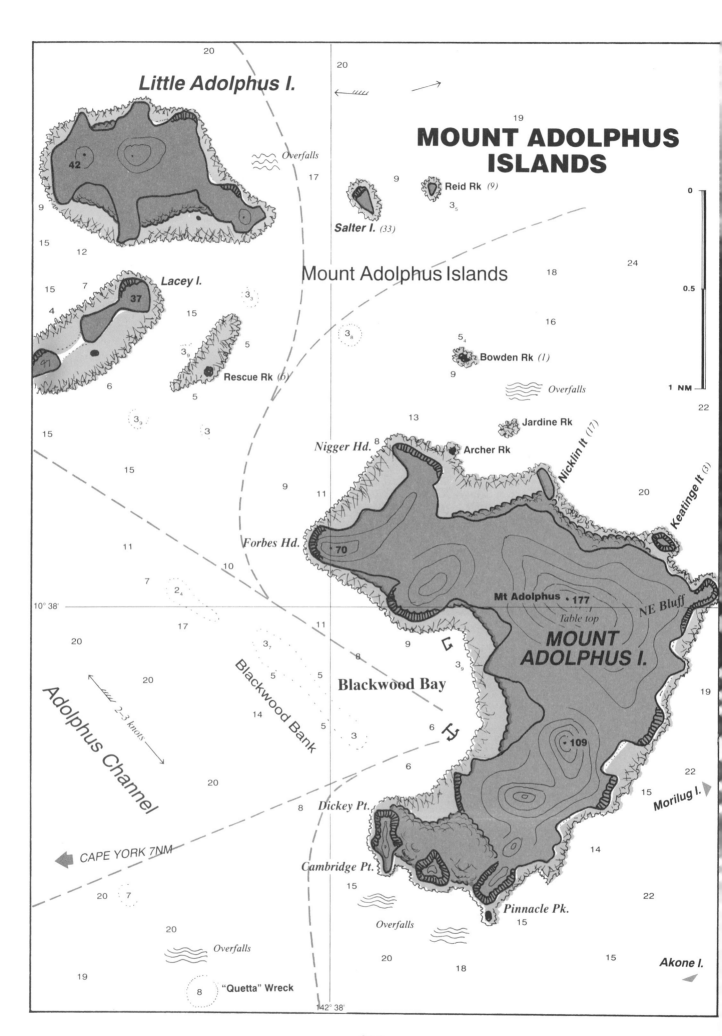

Little Adolphus I.

20

20

19

MOUNT ADOLPHUS ISLANDS

42

Overfalls

17

9

Reid Rk *(9)*

3₅

9

Salter I. (33)

Mount Adolphus Islands

18

24

0

0.5

9

15

12

16

15

7

Lacey I.

37

3₃

5₄

Bowden Rk *(1)*

4

15

3₉

5

9

Overfalls

1 NM

6

Rescue Rk (6)

5

3₉

22

3

13

Jardine Rk

Nicklin It (17)

15

15

Nigger Hd. 8

Archer Rk

Keatinge It (3)

20

11

9

11

Forbes Hd. 70

Mt Adolphus • 177

NE Bluff

Table top

10° 38'

10

MOUNT ADOLPHUS I.

17

11

3₉

19

20

3₇

9

Adolphus Channel

Blackwood Bank

8

Blackwood Bay

5

5

20

2–3 knots

14

5

6

• 109

20

3

6

22

6

20

8

Dickey Pt.

15

Morilug I.

◄ CAPE YORK 7NM

Cambridge Pt.

14

20 7

15

22

Pinnacle Pk.

20

Overfalls

15

360

Overfalls

15

19

18

20

15

Akone I.

8 "Quetta" Wreck

142° 38'

286

earlier, the truth can be very fickle in this area.

History. Extraordinary to anyone viewing Albany Passage today is the fact that it was once hailed as the future 'Singapore of Australia' and was, in fact, a major port, being proposed as such before the advent of either Townsville or Cairns and when Bowen was just one year old.

Queensland's first governor, Sir George Bowen, proposed the establishment of a far north port in Albany Passage after a cruise aboard *HMS Pioneer* in 1862. Although the site on Albany Island was suggested — and in fact used partially — the first Government Resident, John Jardine, chose the mainland site which to this day is known as Somerset.

After Jardine there followed many residents including George Elphinstone Dalrymple whose enthusiasm for the far north started a number of towns and earned him the nickname, 'father of North Queensland'. He died returning from his stint at Somerset.

The last resident was Frank Jardine, son of the first resident, who remained there long after the seat of power was moved to Thursday Island. He married a Samoan princess, a direct descendant of King Malietoa, and together they built an empire based on a coconut plantation, cattle and pearling and were responsible for making Somerset one of the most romantic ports in the world at the time.

MOUNT ADOLPHUS ISLAND is 7 miles east-north-east of Cape York where it provides ideal alternative anchorage between Escape River and Thursday Island. Its 177-metre main mountain is a conspicuous table top visible for 20 miles.

Blackwood Bay provides good anchorage in trade wind conditions and remains comfortable in north-easterly winds. Windward-tide conditions can prevail depending on the strength of currents which are not always related to height.

Of Interest. Eleven cables south-west of Cambridge Point lies the 3.2 metre shoal *Quetta Rock*. Despite the excellence of such diligent hydrographers as Phillip Parker King and Owen Stanley who spent years surveying the Australian coastline last century, this rock was continually missed until 21.30 hours February 28, 1890 when the British India steamer *Quetta* struck it and sank within three minutes. The 8.6 metre patch to the north-west of Quetta Rock are her remains.

Of the 169 passengers and 121 officers and crew, 133 persons were lost. Later, a memorial church was built on Thursday Island by the Church of England. It is interesting today for the Quetta relics preserved there.

Looking south at Cape York, the cape itself is peeking from between Eborac Island, left, and York Island, right. There is a major light on Eborac Island with arcs of green, white and red.

Albany Passage is General Use 'B' Zone.

Eborac Island, carrying the actual 'Cape York' light, is seen here from York Island. The road is a lighthouse service facility only, the service anchorage being towards the island's western tip.

Taken from York Island, this photograph shows Cape York with the passage between the two. This passage is navigable with care, there being a shoal patch north of mid-channel. Cape York anchorage is shown in large scale and described over the page. Its drying rock can be seen, right.

CAPE YORK. Almost exactly midway between the Escape River and Port Kennedy (Thursday Island Harbour) at 20 miles from each, Cape York provides tolerable anchorage and intense gratification that the top of Australia has been rounded.

Approach from the south is through Albany Passage, as previously described, or around Albany Island through Adolphus Channel. Conspicuous from either direction is the all-white, square-based lighthouse atop *Eborac Island* immediately to the north of Cape York. The land in the vicinity is mostly barren to seaward with rugged outcrops of rocks. Towards the tip of the cape, two man-made objects are seen; these are a directory similar to that mounted on Lizard Island at Cook's Lookout and a simple rock cairn. Neither are especially obvious from seaward until close aboard.

In calm weather the anchorage can be entered between the mainland and York Island by holding the former rather close where good depths will be found and a mid-channel gonker missed. But at all other times both Eborac and York Island should be rounded and then York Island held close aboard on final entry as shown in the accompanying plan.

From Thursday Island, approach is direct, the cape and its islands standing proud from the horizon immediately on leaving the harbour by either Flinders Passage or the Boat Channel.

From the west, close to the mainland and presumably approaching from Possession Island and the Simpson Bay region, the shallow banks extending from between *Cape York* and *Peaked Hill* can be safely crossed at low water springs by vessels drawing no more than 2 metres.

After rounding Peak Point close, steer straight for *Mona Rock* obvious for its low pyramid shape and, closer in, for the solitary tree on its peak.

Passing Mona Rock fairly close to starboard, steer direct for the obvious gap between Cape York and York Island, bending the course slightly to favour *Bay Point* rather than a drying bank half a mile offshore.

Anchorage is in excellent-holding, fine mud and sand, comfort being dictated by exact direction of wind and state of tide, but can be said to be acceptable in all winds of all strengths from the south to north-east with south-east being the most dominant direction throughout the year and especially April through October.

Northerly to westerly winds are best ridden in *Simpson Bay*, to the west, or *Newcastle Bay* to the south.

Cape York anchorage is dominated by a very deep 22-metre boil hole shelving steeply around its perimeter and especially towards the rock which is awash at high water springs. Being too deep to anchor in the hole, the surrounding shallows must be used and the exact spot will be a decision of the moment depending on wind direction, its strength and the number of other boats. The area least troubled by overfalls and strong currents is west of the rock.

Tides can be based on Frederick Point (Albany Island) which is based on *Twin Island* in the *Tide Tables*. Direction of flow is close to the information given for Hammond Rock Lighthouse although rates tend to be slower. Neither of the above are highly accurate but are nevertheless close enough.

Of Interest. Ashore at Cape York is the *Wilderness Lodge* offering the usual resort facilities to guests only. Transients may visit the kiosk which sells ice and confectionery. Arrangements to dine at the Lodge may be made with management.

Wilderness Lodge came under the control of the 500-strong Injinoo Aboriginal community in 1992. They bought it from the government-owned Australian Airlines for around $2.2 million. The deal included 1000 hectares of adjoining land including the camping reserve used by the thousands of annual 4WD visitors.

The deal ended a four year battle with Japanese and other overseas tourist groups to secure the historic area for the original inhabitants. Helping in negotiations was former Liberal Parliamentarian, David Byrne who lived aboard his yacht in Cowal Creek (west of Bamaga) and worked as their adviser.

On the waterfront there is a fresh water tap, but is not suitable for drinking. Where the dinghy is left ashore for long periods, a considerable drag distance is involved, the beach levelling off for some two cables at its mid-tide level. Near the low tide fringe mud is encountered that makes boarding difficult. Under such circumstances, the best boarding area is close to the south of the rock where sand covers the mud to some extent.

Approaching Cape York from the west holding the coast. Mona Rock, right, makes a good steering reference. York Island is distant left.

Bay Point is close to the west of Cape York and is conspicuous when approaching from that direction.

On final approach to the anchorage from the west, Cape York is centre with York Island off to its left.

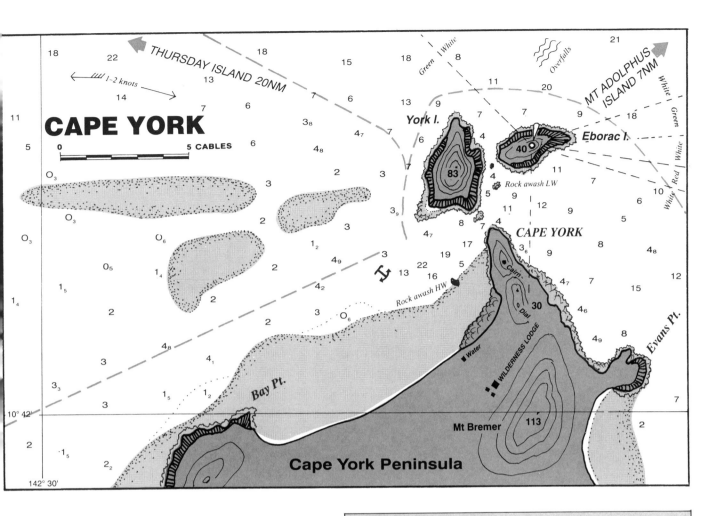

CAPE YORK

Cape York signals the end of Australia to those sailing over her top to points west. The anchorage is good in strong trades. The Wilderness Lodge is owned by the local Aboriginal community.

Wild white woman

Not really wild at all, but often classified that way historically, Barbara Thompson lived for four and a half years with Torres Strait Islanders after being declared the reincarnation of a leading islander's dead daughter. Her husband's ship, *America* struck Possession Island, the crew drowning and Mrs Thompson being taken ashore by the islanders. She was rescued in 1848 by H.M.S. *Rattlesnake*.

Peak Point, on the mainland immediately east of Possession Island, can be taken fairly close. It is nearly 6 miles west of Cape York.

Dayman Island, off the south-west tip of Possession Island. There is clear water between the two.

Approaching Possession Island from the south-west. Possession is left background with Dayman Island, right foreground.

289

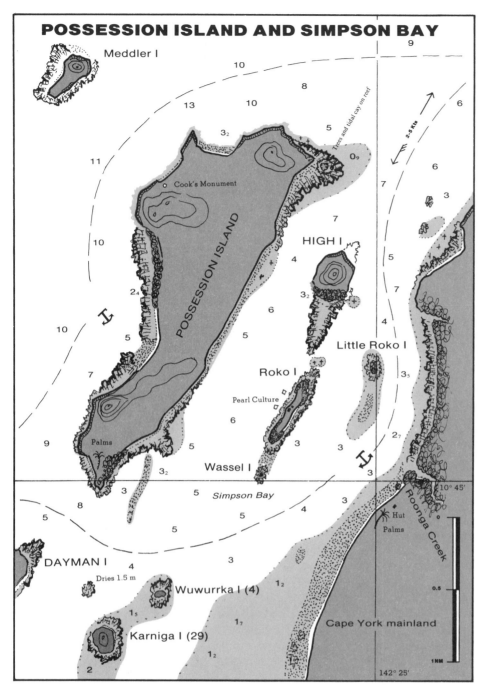

POSSESSION ISLAND AND SIMPSON BAY

Meddler I

10

8

13   10

3₂

5

11

0₉

Cook's Monument

Trees and tidal cay on reef

2.5 Kts

6

6

7

10

7

HIGH I

5

4

3

7

24

3₂

6

4

10

5

5

5

Little Roko I

7

Roko I

3₅

Palms

6

Pearl Culture

9

5

3

3

2₇

Wassel I

3

3

3₂

5   Simpson Bay

3

8

4

3

Roonga Creek

10° 45'

5

5

Hut
Palms

5

DAYMAN I   4

3

Dries 1.5 m

1₂

0.5

Wuwurrka I (4)

1₅

1₇

Karniga I (29)

Cape York mainland

1₂

1NM

2

142° 25'

Rounding the green buoy for Bamaga Anchorage. There is an Aboriginal settlement in from here.

Red Island protects Bamaga anchorage from the north.

POSSESSION ISLAND. Towards the north-west tip of this three-mile-long island is a monument to Captain Cook taking possession of the east coast of New South Wales from 38 degrees latitude to 'this place'. From here the *Endeavour* passed through the strait now bearing her name to make passage to Batavia for docking and proper repairs.

Approach. Being close to the mainland in the vicinity of *Peak Point*, Possession Island will be approached with landmarks always in evidence. From Bamaga, it pays to maintain a transit of Possession Island's east coast just open of Dayman Island's east coast to keep clear of the tongue of shoals extending south-west known as *Brady Bank*.

Anchorage is best off the beach in the long bay during easterly winds or between Possession Island and *Roko Island* during north to west winds. A beam swell is normal here, its severity depending on the strength of wind and current. Should it become unacceptable, superior anchorage can be enjoyed in *Simpsons Bay*.

SIMPSON BAY. Formed by a slight indentation in the mainland and offshore Possession Island and its satellites, Simpson Bay offers good, secure anchorage despite waters troubled by strong currents.

Approach from the north is by rounding *Peak Point* then steering to avoid two rock reefs which dry 1.5 and 1.8 metres close offshore in the vicinity of *High Island*. The current can reach speeds of over 5 knots here so beware of being carried further than presumed when running with it. Passage between High Island and the mainland is perfectly safe after which Little Roko Island can be passed to either side, to starboard offering better orientation.

From the south it is rather too nerve-racking taking a deep keel over the shoals between the mainland and *Brady Bank* although it is possible using the rocks on Brady Bank as reference and using the islands as transits. For example, the east tip of *Karniga Island* kissing the west tip of *High Island* shows the best water up to Markilug Island.

290

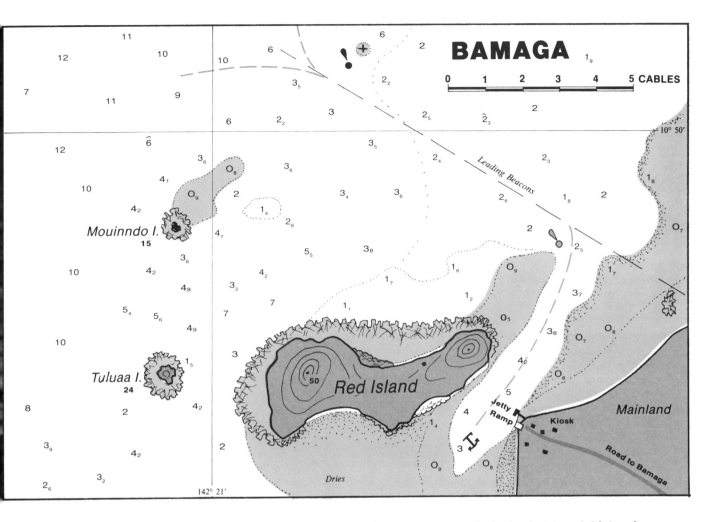

Anchorage is best as close to the land as possible towards *Ronga* (or *Roonga*) *Creek* where will be seen a small hut behind the beach.

Holding here can be indifferent owing to patches of small rock over sand and weed but once dug in it is secure in strong winds and currents. Very little swell reaches this part of the bay, however some discomfort must be expected during extreme windward-tide conditions.

Tides are best based on *Twin Island* and rates on *Hammond Rock*. The flood runs south-west and the ebb north-east with rates in no way related to range.

Of Interest. Towards the north-east corner of Simpson Bay, opposite High Island, will be noted the remains of an old jetty. This was built by Len Foxcroft in his cruising days for Thomas National Transport and Keith Holland Shipping in 1961. The purpose was to provide back-loading for ships plying from Cairns to Thursday Island in the form of tin ore. Regrettably ore was not found in economic quantities and the project was abandoned.

There is a small cultured pearl farm on nearby Roko Island.

BAMAGA is an Aboriginal settlement on the mainland some 15 miles from Thursday Island's Boat Channel. Fair shelter can be found in all winds but those strong from the north-east or west and south-west.

Approach. From the Boat Channel, *Barn Island* off Bamaga is easily recognised when Entrance Island is cleared. It appears as two dominant peaks, the right-hand one being a table top, the left-hand one com- prising twin peaks. *Red Island*, although higher, is not conspicuous, being a rounded bald hill well separated from Barn.

Steering a course that accounts for wind and tide, lay towards the east tip of Red Island being certain to clear the tail of *Brady Bank* from where a red buoy will be seen and, soon after, the white triangle leads should become apparent. Whether the leads are identified or not, pass the red buoy to port and steer to pass a green buoy to starboard. With the latter abeam, round up to aim for the now conspicuous jetty and anchorage beyond.

From the north, a flood tide will help make fast time and provide fair promise of safety against grounding should the route inside Brady Bank be chosen. Red Island and Barn Island are easily seen from the Simpson Bay area.

Anchorage. Watching the sounder against sudden shoaling beyond the jetty, drop anchor as far away from the jetty as possible to leave a swing basin for small coasters unloading here. The holding is excellent and comfort good depending on windward-tide activity.

Tides can be based either on Thursday Island or Twin Island in the *Tide Tables* with corrections for either being by guesswork.

Facilities. Under no circumstances may the jetty be used as a berth without permission from the Bamaga Manager who can be contacted by phone. There is an STD phone at the jetty.

Water is piped to the jetty and may be used with permission but must not be presumed to be available.

From the Jardine River, it is safe for drinking.

A small kiosk near the jetty has ice, cigarettes and confectionery while the settlement's supermarket has a good variety of victuals, but is three miles inland. A lift can sometimes be arranged but cannot be depended upon.

THURSDAY ISLAND

THURSDAY ISLAND. Australia's most northern port and administration centre for the Torres Strait, Thursday Island offers the rather unfortunate combination of staggering prices and lousy anchorages. However, for those wanting to spend more than a few days here, both these problems can be eased a little as shown later.

Approach. Being in the centre of the windiest trade wind area in the world, the islands surrounding Thursday Island are more often under haze than not during the April through October (and sometimes December) season. And in the wet season, January through March, they can be hidden under rain cloud. But mostly they will be identified from Cape York, when approaching from the east, and Booby Island, when approaching from the west. From the south, the mainland of Cape York is usually followed to Crab Island from where Prince of Wales Island is rarely out of sight.

Looking at the options in detail, the western approach will be examined first.

Under the heading, 'Torres Strait', on page 298, the western approaches to the Thursday Island region are described. Here the final approach into Port Kennedy (Thursday Island Harbour) will be reviewed.

Booby Island makes the logical landfall after crossing or emerging from the Gulf of Carpentaria. From here, a vessel passes through *Normanby Sound* between Goodes and Friday Islands and Hammond and Prince of Wales Islands where beacons and buoys show the way. Beware only of the rapidity of their appearance when working in with a strong current which, in this passage, can attain speeds of 7 knots, though more commonly 3 to 5 knots.

From the east, there are two choices of harbour entry: One through *Flinders Passage* and the other through *Boat Channel*. They are treated individually here.

Flinders Passage becomes Ellis Channel as it passes between Tuesday Islets and Wednesday Island to the north and Horn Island to the south. Even during severe haze the land lifts in time for course adjustment usually in the form of Tuesday Islets' *Strait Rock* and Horn Island's *Horned Hill*, the latter having two small peaks atop a common mountain.

Steer mid-channel for the red buoy on *Scott Reef*, passing it to either side, but preferably to port, then alter course for *Channel Rock*, a low dome-shaped islet which provides an ideal steering mark to pass safely between *Chapman Reef* and *Nereid Rocks*.

On this course, *Hovell Bar's* red buoy will be seen early enough to steer for it, passing it to port thence continuing into *Ellis Channel* passing a yellow buoy to port, if Thursday Island bound, or starboard if Horn Island bound. At all times allow for the effects of the strong currents of the area. Never underestimate them. This is especially so when closing on Horn Island from

Jardine Rock and beacon as they appear when passed to port. Prince of Wales Island — locally known as 'P.O.W.' — is behind.

Looking up-channel between P.O.W. Island, left, and Entrance Island, right.

The south-west tip of Prince of Wales Island opposite Entrance Island.

Looking up Boat Channel. Prince of Wales Island, left.

Looking up Boat Channel. P.O.W.Island, left, Thursday Island, right.

292

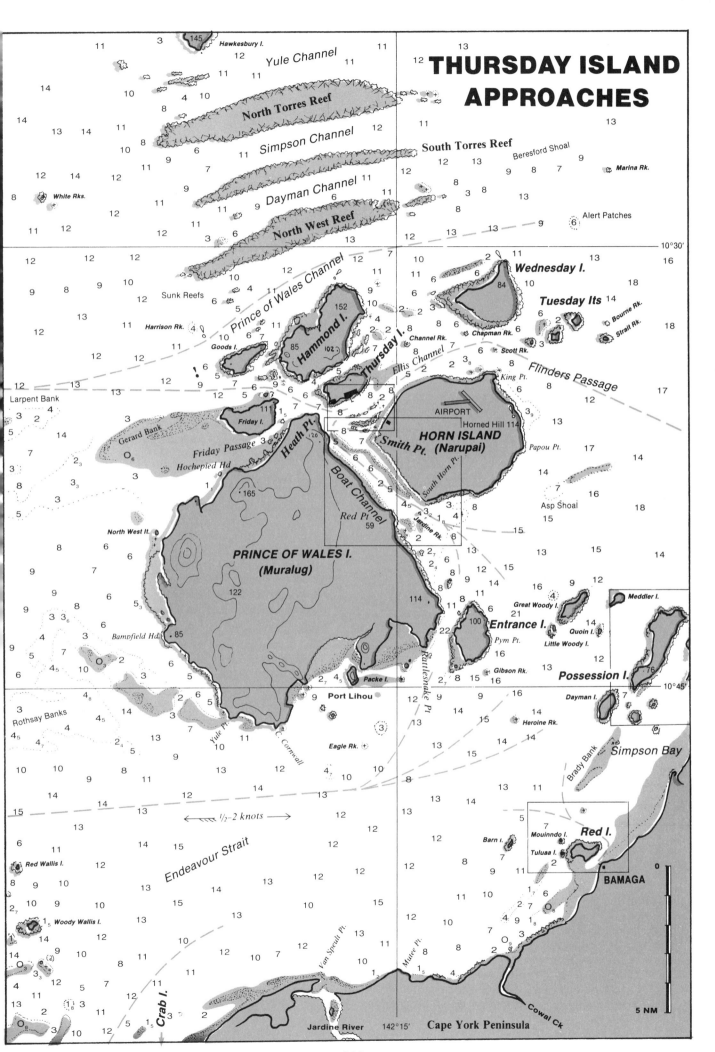

THURSDAY ISLAND APPROACHES

Yule Channel

North Torres Reef

Simpson Channel

South Torres Reef

Dayman Channel

Beresford Shoal

Marina Rk.

North West Reef

Alert Patches

10°30'

White Rks.

Sunk Reefs

Prince of Wales Channel

Wednesday I.

Tuesday Its

Bourne Rk.

Strait Rk.

Harrison Rk.

Goods I.

Hammond I.

Chapman Rk.

Scott Rk.

Flinders Passage

Larpent Bank

Friday I.

Thursday I.

Channel Rk.

Ellis Channel

King Pt.

AIRPORT

Horned Hill 114

Gerard Bank

Friday Passage

Heath Pt.

Smith Pt.

HORN ISLAND
(Narupai)

Papou Pt.

Hochepied Hd.

Boat Channel

Asp Shoal

North West It.

Red Pt.
59

Jardine Rk.

PRINCE OF WALES I.
(Muralug)

122

Meddler I.

114

Bampfield Hd.

85

Great Woody I.

Entrance I.
21

100

Quoin I.

Little Woody I.

Possession I.

10°45'

Packe I.

Pym Pt.

Port Lihou

Rattlesnake Pt

Gibson Rk.

Dayman I.

Rothsay Banks

Heroine Rk.

Brady Bank

Simpson Bay

Eagle Rk.

½–2 knots

Red I.

Endeavour Strait

Barn I.

Mouinndo I.

Red Wallis I.

Tuluaa I.

BAMAGA

Woody Wallis I.

0

Crab I.

Jardine River

142°15'

Van Speult Pt.

Mutee Pt.

Cape York Peninsula

Cowal Ck

5 NM

293

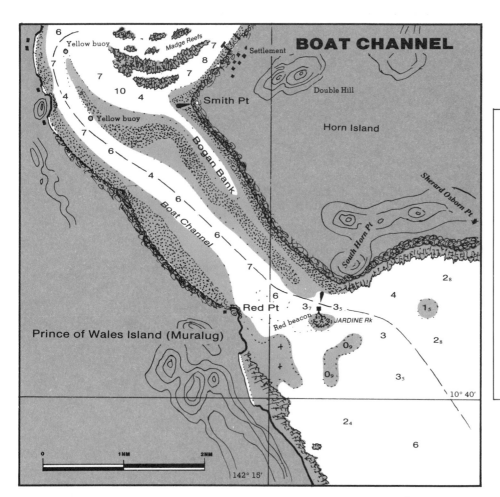

BOAT CHANNEL

Boat Channel is one of two
entrances to Thursday Island
Harbour from the east.

Heroine's find

Less than three miles south-east of Entrance Island, Endeavour Strait, Heroine Rock lies unseen beneath the surface. It was found by the schooner *Heroine* in the 1840's when she ran aground, but was quickly backed off. Whilst carrying Ludwig Leichhardt back to Sydney from Port Essington, Northern Territory, *Heroine* later fell into company with officers of the survey ship *Bramble* off Cooktown. They were not pleased to receive the information about the rock because it cast a doubt on their own abilities, having only recently completed a survey of Endeavour Strait. Despite their conviction that the rock was a flight of fancy on the part of the *Heroine's* captain, they nevertheless later found it exactly according to the captain's rough sketch and bearings.

eastward when a flood tide can flatten the course so that it goes dangerously close to *Asp Shoal* offshore from Horn's eastern extreme.

Boat Channel separates Horn Island from Prince of Wales Island and offers good alternative entry to Thursday Island Harbour from the east. It does, however, carry less water than Flinders Passage over its eastern entrance and therefore demands more guesswork on the part of the navigator.

Making up to the islands, *Horned Hill* again makes a good landmark and *Entrance Island* will also be identified easily enough. Before the shallow waters of Boat Channel's entrance are encountered, *Jardine Rock* beacon (red) will be seen and can be used as a steering mark as long as the approach course is sensible. This should favour the south coast of Horn Island which is held close from *Sherard Osborn Point* to *South Horn Point*, the latter being opposite Jardine Rock and carrying fringing reef.

Favouring Jardine Rock, pass it to port then steer for a conspicuous house behind a small beach on Prince of Wales Island and to the west-south-west of Horn Island's Smith Point. Before this house is reached, a yellow buoy is passed to starboard from where a second yellow buoy is steered for then also passed to starboard. This brings you into Thursday Island Harbour.

Tides. In the Thursday Island section of the Torres Strait, tides can be so fickle as to be beyond accurate prediction. It is a pivot point for a see-sawing effect between the Arafura Sea to the west and the Coral Sea to the east, the two experiencing different heights and times. As a result, a neap range can run faster than a spring range; a west-going current can suddenly become an east-going current before actual turn of tide,

and vice versa. Indeed, one channel can have opposing currents at the same time, a fact that has caught many a skipper of large vessels by surprise as he rounds up for the Main Jetty.

The *Tide Tables* do an admirable job of prediction both of height at Thursday Island and rate and direction of current based on Hammond Rock Lighthouse. Both sections are worth correlating before entering harbour.

Thursday Island Anchorage. In past editions of this book I have pursued a policy of recommending the use of an Admiralty Pattern anchor or Fisherman type for Thursday Island owing to its indifference towards mud types. However, visiting traffic having increased to a point where anchorage over the bad ground is unlikely, I can now suggest using your favourite mud anchor, the bottom in deeper water being fair holding for all types. But, because of the extreme windward-tide conditions possible here, stand by the anchor and be prepared to shift if necessary.

Because the Thursday Island anchorage is on a lee shore, it can be extremely uncomfortable in the thick of the trade-wind season. Only during the January-through-March wet season does the stern hang away from the land. A far more secure and comfortable trade-wind anchorage is at Horn Island.

Horn Island Anchorage. Less than one and a half miles to windward of Thursday Island anchorage, the lee of Horn Island offers minimal swell, no chop and only a slight increase in wind bullets during south-east trades. The bottom is also superior being good-holding mud. The inconvenience lies in the distance from facilities. These can be reached by regular ferry running between Horn Island's jetty and Thursday Island's Engineer's Jetty or by outboard dinghy on the basis

294

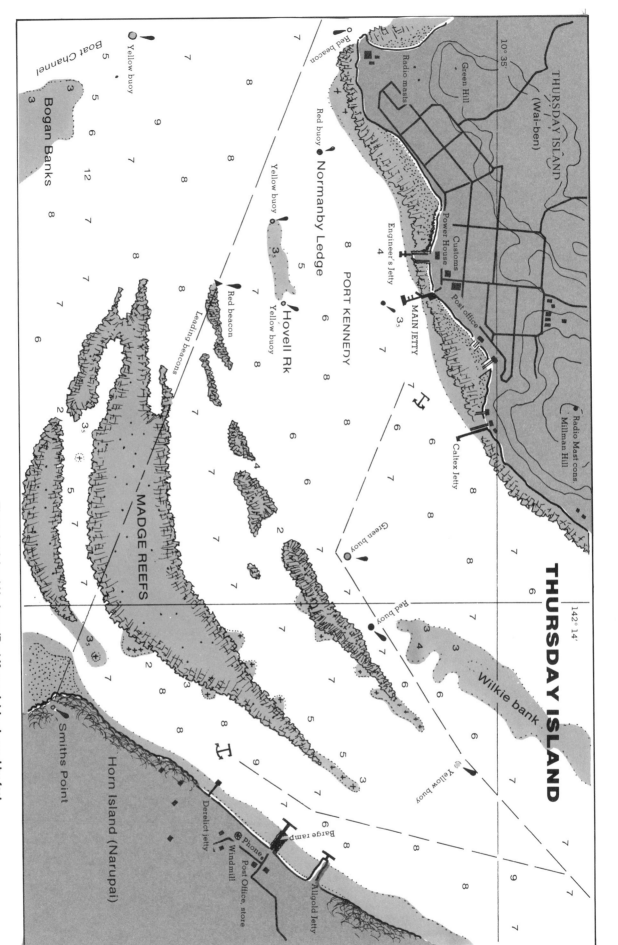

THURSDAY ISLAND

THURSDAY ISLAND (Wai-ben)

10° 35'

142° 14'

Radio Mast cons.
Millman Hill

Green Hill

Radio masts

PORT KENNEDY

Engineer's Jetty

Power House

Customs

MAIN JETTY

Post office

Caltex Jetty

Red beacon

Red buoy

Normanby Ledge

Yellow buoy

Hovell Rk
Yellow buoy

Red beacon

Leading beacons

MADGE REEFS

Green buoy

Red buoy

Wilkie bank

Yellow buoy

Yellow buoy

Bogan Banks

Boat Channel

Smiths Point

Horn Island (Narupai)

Derelict jetty

Post Office, store

Windmill

Phones

Barge ramp

Allgold Jetty

Thursday Island Harbour (Port Kennedy) is plagued by fast tidal streams and strong trade winds. The most secure and comfortable anchorage is under the lee of Horn Island where shown by an anchor. The Allgold Jetty now has a fuel and water barge alongside, and a hotel and restaurant are recent additions ashore.

295

King Point, Horn Island is seen here as Flinders Passage is approached from the south-east.

that precautions are taken during strong winds and currents. Carry oilskins, bailer, oars and anchor and plenty of fuel and the trip can be made successfully in all but the tiniest dink.

Dinghy Landing. At Horn Island there is a suitable beach between the two jetties allowing for the drying banks at low tide. Otherwise, it is sometimes possible to leave it on one of the wharves' embankments. Do not leave it on the face of either.

At Thursday Island, the least troubled area is under the lee of the Engineer's Jetty embankment or the beach to its west. Otherwise, with greater convenience at mid to high tide, and despite the slop, the beach immediately east of the Main Jetty provides more instant access to a greater selection of shops, post office, bank etc.

Dinghy thefts have occurred at Thursday Island but they mostly happen after pub closing hours when drunks roam the beach looking for a way to Horn Island. Daylight hours seem secure enough.

Facilities. Although an inconvenient and expensive place to victual and service a boat, everything of a basic nature will be found on Thursday Island and, to a lesser extent, on Horn Island.

Water is always a problem but can be taken aboard by arrangement with and payment to the Harbour Master's office and fuel is bowsered on the Caltex Jetty towards the eastern end of Thursday Island.

Daily jet flights landing at Horn Island and connected to Thursday Island by regular ferry maintain contact with Cairns. Small ships and barges also supply the area with fresh, frozen and processed food through the many stores on Thursday Island and one on Horn Island near the ferry wharf.

There are hotels and motels on Thursday Island and a hotel on Horn Island. Muggings have become a fact of life in the area with quite a few yachtspeople falling victim.

Hauling out on Thursday Island is no problem with slipways able to handle vessels of all shapes and sizes. Engineering and repair support services are available.

History. Thursday Island officially came into being in 1877 when the unsuitable anchorage in Albany Passage, off Somerset, obliged ship owners to seek a more accessible coaling station and the government needed to extend its boundaries to include the Torres Strait Islands which had previously been outside the law and consequently havens for prison escapees. Despite its lee shore anchorage, strong winds and tide and relative remoteness, it proved a winner and soon became a hive of boating activity. Dominant amongst the boats were the famous pearling luggers which started as open sailing tenders to mother ships and evolved into a decked, ketch-rigged craft of around 50 feet long with low topsides to facilitate diver access and a good plodding motion to windward as the divers walked the seabed behind them. It was especially interesting that their sails were named after the schooner-rigged mother ships rather than the ketch rig itself. As a result, the sails were called headsail, foresail and mainsail, not headsail, main and mizzen.

With the virtual death of pearl and trochus diving in the late 1950s-early 1960s as plastics replaced natural materials, a fleet of dozens of luggers rapidly reduced to a dozen or so which found work in the, then, foundling industry of cultured pearl. Now, two or three may be found, still working but suffering the ups and downs of an industry that enjoys little stability.

The traditional Torres Strait lugger is almost extinct, just a few being used commercially. Beside the foremast is a cooking enclosure with a gas stove where once naked flame dominated and up the mizzen (main in lugger language) mast are hinge-down swim ladders for diver access.

Looking Back

Back-loading

Up until the early 1960's when this photograph was taken from the Engineer's Jetty, Thursday Island saw only pearling luggers and their products. The prime back-loading to Cairns tended to be empty fuel drums. Since then, cultured pearling, prawning and crayfishing have improved exports although they have also increased imports. Above the head of this dinghyman, for example, is a butcher shop that has long since surrendered to imported frozen meat.

Japanese Graves

Thursday Island's cemetery is dominated by some 700 graves of Japanese divers who first came to the Torres Strait in 1878. Eager to make fast money in the pearl shell industry, they took greater risks than local natives and paid the ultimate price. They remained until World War II. During 1993, Japanese authorities pledged to restore and maintain these graves at no expense to the Thursday Island community.

In the late 19th century, three major European influences hit the Torres Strait almost simultaneously, these being missionaries, lighthouses and pearling ships. For this reason, many religious monuments symbolise all three as can be seen in this shrine on Darnley Island.

First Disaster

Queensland's first major oil spill disaster happened on 3 March 1970 when the tanker, *Oceanic Grandeur* ripped her hull open on a low, but critical rock on the bottom of the Torres Strait. 250,000 gallons of oil polluted the area, thick sludge being found on the shores of Cape York by the author a few months later. The rock was found to be 0.9 metres higher than charted and no blame was apportioned.

TORRES STRAIT separates Australia from New Guinea and provides good, navigable channels between the *Coral Sea* and the *Arafura Sea*. Because it is constantly used by ships of all sizes and speeds, its main channels are very well charted and numerous buoys and beacons allow passage at any time in any weather.

The whole strait is strewn with reefs and islands, the latter being a mixture of coral cays and continental types, many of which are inhabited by Torres Strait natives. These people are Melanesian, not mainland aborigines, and resemble Papua New Guineans. The latter often migrate illegally, creating a nightmare for Australian quarantine and immigration officials.

The main Australian port is *Thursday Island* as previously described whilst the main Papuan New Guinea port is *Daru Island*, described on page 300. Except for a few coastal islands along the Papua New Guinea mainland, the entire Torres Strait is part of Australia although the inhabited islands (other than Thursday Island area) have their own indigenous councils. Permission is necessary before landing on any inhabited island other than Thursday Island.

Customs, Immigration and Quarantine are represented at Thursday Island (for Australia) and *Daru Island* (for Papua New Guinea). Foreign vessels may pass through the Torres Strait without clearing, but without stopping. Those intending to clear into a country may anchor en route through the strait under duress only. Going ashore is strictly prohibited until legally cleared.

Approach from the west is out of the *Gulf of Carpentaria*, landfalling on the Carpentaria Lightship anchored over Carpentaria Shoal. This is 51 miles west-south-west of *Booby Island*, the next logical landfall if heading for Thursday Island (see its approach on page 292).

If passing through the strait without stopping or bound for points east such as Daru; Booby Island with its major light remains the logical landfall, being just 14 miles west-south-west of the main shipping channel: This is *Prince of Wales Channel* which passes north of Thursday Island between Hammond Island and North West Reef. Being used by all commercial shipping it is well beaconed for day or night navigation.

An alternative passage for small boats into the Torres Strait from the west is *Endeavour Strait*, between Prince of Wales Island and Cape York Peninsula. The hazards here are sand banks across the western entrance, depths being adequate in the channels, but these are separated by a number of shoal to drying sand banks. After crossing the Gulf of Carpentaria, these are encountered at approximately the longitude of Booby Island and 14 miles to its south.

The best channel to aim for is the one between *Rothsay Banks* and *Red Banks*, this taking you close south of Prince of Wales Island. It is best identified by bearings on *Red Wallis Island*.

Sailing north out of the Gulf of Carpentaria (from Weipa, for example), the most convenient channel into Endeavour Strait is the one 2 miles west of *Crab Island*, close to the north-west corner of Cape York Peninsula.

Approach from the east is out of the Coral Sea, commonly after passage from Port Moresby or the Solomon Islands. The landfall here is *Bramble Cay*, a tiny coral cay supporting a trellis light visible 11 miles.

In an age of GPS, there are no problems in locating this speck at the end of an ocean voyage, but should there be a failure in the equipment, or a continuing dependency on tables and sextant, extreme caution is needed. All too often Bramble Cay is missed altogether leaving the navigator in a cold sweat as to whether he or she is sailing into the Fly River mouth or about to crash onto reefs further south.

With the midday latitude sight so reliable and accurate, it pays to grab such a sight half a day's sail out from Bramble Cay so that its latitude can be found and steered along. This usually means that it will be brought up in the late evening, a probability that means the light itself will be seen instead of a very allusive tower.

This practise means that the *Great North East Channel* must be navigated at night, a perfectly safe situation as long as the crew is reasonably fresh, for although well beaconed, the hazards of reefs and tides must be handled.

Tides. The stream runs strongly throughout the Torres Strait, often diagonally across the course. This can set a vessel well off track without diligence. Generally, for every six hours of east set, there will be a compensatory six hours of west set, but strengths and durations may not necessarily be equal.

Tide heights and rates are shown in the *Queensland Tide Tables* with many observation points throughout the strait. Hammond Rock Light is used in the book as a tidal stream reference point, it being vital in that area to know times and directions of the tide as well as height. Because the Coral and Arafura Seas experience tides of different heights, a see-saw effect is created which can have a tide running longer in one direction than the other, or not changing direction at all for a full day, and so on.

Weather. It has been noted that the Torres Strait experiences the strongest and most prolonged trade wind in the world. This may be marginal compared to other great trade-wind zones, such as the Windward Islands in the West Indies and parts of the South Indian ocean, but is true enough overall. One of the reasons is undoubtedly the canalising effect of the two land masses to each side, especially the high mountains towards central and west New Guinea. It is also probable that the convection effect of warm air lifting off the shallow Strait waters brings air in off the colder Coral Sea faster. But the dominant reason is the simple fact that the Torres Strait lies at the end of an ever narrowing funnel that starts between the Solomon Islands and Queensland and concludes between Cape York and Papua New Guinea.

Whatever the cause, the south-east trade wind can blow for months on end, rising to above 30 knots in gusts for three days every two or three weeks and maintaining 15 to 25 knots at other times. Being influenced by the Strait, it sometimes slants east-south-east and even east, but mostly holds south-east regardless of strength. Slants to the east are more common towards the end of the season than the beginning.

The trade-wind season starts late March and goes through to early October often continuing right through to Christmas, albeit with progressively easier winds. Calms can occur during the height of the season,

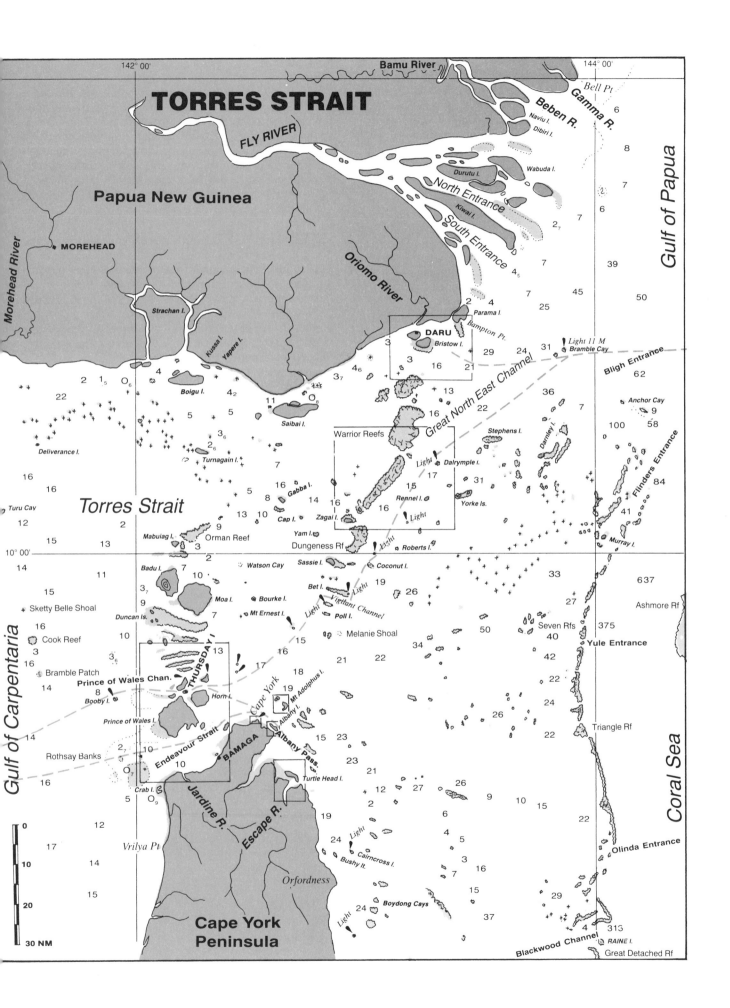

TORRES STRAIT

Bamu River

Fly River

Papua New Guinea

Bell Pt

Beben R.

Gamma R.

Gulf of Papua

Naviu I.

Dibiri I.

Durutu I.

Wabuda I.

North Entrance

Kiwai I.

MOREHEAD

Morehead River

Oriomo River

South Entrance

Strachan I.

Kussa I.

Yapere I.

Parama I.

Bampton Pt.

DARU

Bristow I.

Light 11 M

Bramble Cay

Bligh Entrance

Boigu I.

Great North East Channel

Anchor Cay

Saibai I.

Warrior Reefs

Stephens I.

Darnley I.

Flinders Entrance

Deliverance I.

Turnagain I.

Gabba I.

Dalrymple I.

Rennel I.

Zagai I.

Yorke Is.

Turu Cay

Torres Strait

Cap I.

Yam I.

Mabuiag I.

Orman Reef

Dungeness Rf

Roberts I.

Murray I.

Watson Cay

Sassie I.

Coconut I.

Badu I.

Bet I.

Vigilant Channel

Seven Rfs

Ashmore Rf

Sketty Belle Shoal

Moa I.

Bourke I.

Mt Ernest I.

Poll I.

Melanie Shoal

Duncan Is.

Yule Entrance

Gulf of Carpentaria

Cook Reef

THURSDAY

Bramble Patch

Prince of Wales Chan.

Booby I.

Horn I.

Cape York

Mt Adolphus I.

Albany I.

Triangle Rf

Prince of Wales I.

Endeavour Strait

BAMAGA

Albany Pass.

Rothsay Banks

Turtle Head I.

Crab I.

Jardine R.

Escape R.

Coral Sea

Vrilya Pt

Orfordness

Cairncross I.

Bushy It.

Olinda Entrance

Cape York Peninsula

Boydong Cays

Blackwood Channel

RAINE I.

Great Detached Rf

0

10

20

30 NM

but only for a day or two before business returns to normal.

The wet season starts in early January and continues through to late February during which time the wind can be constant from north-west but is sometimes fickle with storms from the south through to north. There are many calms during this period and especially during the transitional periods of December and early March.

Description. Except for Murray and Darnley Islands on the outer barrier reef to the south of Bramble Cay and the islands stretching north from Cape York (Thursday Island etc), all islands in the Torres Strait are coral cays standing about 3 to 6 metres above sea level with their trees rising another 20 to 30 metres. On average, they are not sighted until between 12 and 8 miles away, but because of their numbers, at least one island is always in sight during a passage through the Strait.

Of the inhabited islands, Darnley, Murray and Stephens are the furthest east while Badu and Moa are the most westerly. All islands have their own local indigenous council under the guidance of the relevant state government department. Turtle farming and crayfish diving are dominant industries, otherwise Australian welfare pays the bills. There is a strong move towards independence but, as yet the Federal Government rejects the idea.

Anchorages. During any developed wind, there are very few good anchorages within easy reach of the main channel through Torres Strait. Fortunately, the most common developed wind is the south-east trade wind whose reliability gives the sense of security that one will not wake up to a lee shore.

The following are offered as the best of a bad bunch, swell, wind and currents combining to deny a truly calm anchorage anywhere in the region. The list runs east to west.

BRAMBLE CAY

BRAMBLE CAY has shoaling water under its lee, but is too small to provide any worthwhile shelter during boisterous trade winds. It can, however, prove useful where a bad anchorage is preferred to navigating the strait after a tiring passage across the Papuan Gulf.

Bramble Cay was named after the survey ship of the mid 1800's, *Bramble* commanded by Lieut. C.B. Yule. Its light is unmanned and is the most easterly navigational aid of the *Great North East Channel* which is Torres Strait's main eastern entrance.

MURRAY ISLANDS

MURRAY ISLANDS comprise the main island of *Maer* and the two smaller islands of *Dowar* and *Wyer*, the latter two sharing their own separate reef. All of the group are continental types rising to 228 metres. Being on the outer edge of the Great Barrier Reef, their contrast to the more common coral cay makes them remarkable.

Maer Island is inhabited by, arguably, the most traditional of all groups in the Torres Strait. Its isolation has implanted a sense of local pride not found in many other communities. Indeed, during their numerous successful wars in times gone by, they believed they were the only worthwhile race.

On the island is the Drum of Maer, one of two remaining from the days of direct barter with Papua New Guinea. It was used in preparation for battle and to this day still has its own custodian. Its age is unknown.

The most easterly of the Torres Strait islands, Maer is rich in volcanic soil and tropical growth and may one day become a venue for tourism. Meanwhile it enjoys continued isolation thanks to a very deep and unpleasant anchorage and a difficult approach through miles of uncharted or semi-charted reef-strewn waters. From seaward, the best approach is via *Flinders Entrance* being conscious of the strong tidal streams at all times. Permission is needed to go ashore.

DARNLEY ISLAND

DARNLEY ISLAND is another continental type on the outer barrier reef, 27 miles south of *Bramble Cay* and 25 miles north-west of *Murray Islands*. Also inhabited, the settlement is in *Treacherous Bay* where anchorage is only available in depths to 30 metres. Shallower and more comfortable anchorage is possible under the lee of the crescent-shaped reef off the island's north-east end, but care must be exercised amongst numerous isolated coral patches.

Approach from the north-west is in well charted water between Brown Reef and Stephens Island.

DARU ISLAND

DARU ISLAND lies against the Papua New Guinea mainland 40 miles west of *Bramble Cay*. It is part of *Papua New Guinea* for which it is a full clearance port. Casual visiting is not possible. Australia's nearest clearance port is Thursday Island.

Referred to as simply 'Daru', the island is well known for its dugout canoes, a trade that stretches back to antiquity. It was a major trading post between mainlanders and Torres Strait Islanders, the latter trading human heads for New Guinea logs.

Since Papua New Guinea's independence from Australian mandate, Daru has suffered the common problem of the country; that of too many people seeking employment in the towns rather than staying in their villages. As a result, poverty is common and crime rampant. The visitor is warned against going ashore at night.

Approach from the south-east is in well surveyed water, the best channel being to the south of *Merrie England Shoals* thence direct to Daru passing the beacon off *Bristow Island* close to port. Whether approaching or departing, and regardless of direction, beware the strong east-west currents in this region.

Anchorage is tolerable off the settlement, preferably west of the jetty. All-round protection is available in the deep and easily navigated *Oriomo River* less than two miles north of Daru.

The drum of Maer, Darnley Island.

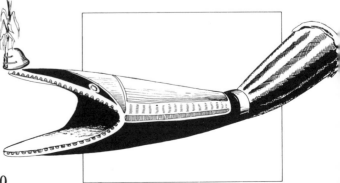

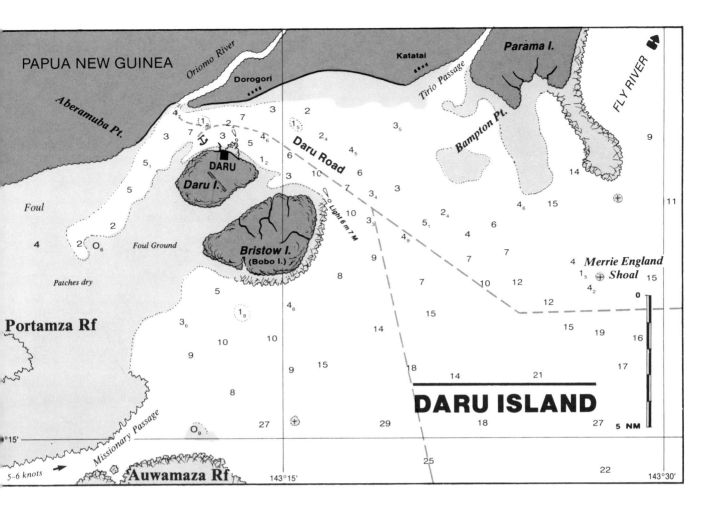

SAIBAI ISLAND

SAIBAI ISLAND is 77 miles north of Thursday Island and over 30 miles west of Daru Island. It is a low, swampy island built entirely from New Guinea silt and is the only place in Australia from where another country can be seen.

Being just two miles off Papua New Guinea, trading is allowed between the two regions without bureaucratic involvement. However, this leniency is not extended to visitors who must clear properly between the nearest customs ports of Thursday Island (Australia) and Daru (Papua New Guinea).

The people here are Torres Strait Islanders who have their own council. Their little church was built from stone brought across from the New Guinea mainland.

Saibai Island is in something of a no-man's land navigationally. The safest approach from the south is direct from *Gabba Island* to *Dauan Island*, the latter being easily sighted well offshore by its 295 metre high *Mount Cornwallis*. Dauan Island is close to the western tip of Saibai Island and passage between the two is safe.

Approach from the east crosses an unsurveyed section some 12 miles long (between Missionary Passage and the eastern tip of Saibai Island). A good lookout is essential.

STEPHENS ISLAND

STEPHENS ISLAND is passed close to port during any normal passage down the Great North East Channel. There being no navigational beacon established here, it poses a mild threat at night. However, domestic lights ashore are generally seen, the village showing from the north. Anchorage is unpleasant in deep water off the village or further west.

The remarkable trimaran canoes are still seen in the Daru district. There is no rudder, steering being effected by two in-line dagger boards whose lifting and lowering alters the centre of lateral resistance.

301

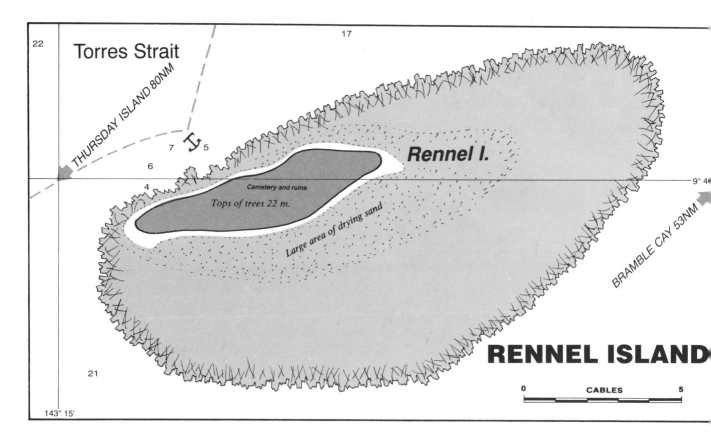

Map labels:
22 · 17
Torres Strait
THURSDAY ISLAND 80NM
7 · 5
6
Rennel I.
4
Cemetery and ruins
Tops of trees 22 m.
Large area of drying sand
9° 4(
BRAMBLE CAY 53NM
RENNEL ISLAND
21
143° 15'
0 CABLES 5

DALRYMPLE ISLAND provides a shelf on its north-western corner where the anchor can be dropped. It is more comfortable than Bramble, but nevertheless is subject to a heavy swell. The light is automatic and is visible 7 miles. It does not overlap Bramble light, there being a black spot between the two of some 26 miles.

RENNEL ISLAND. 9 miles south of Dalrymple Island and similar in that it is another coral cay, Rennel provides one of the better anchorages of the bad bunch. Shown in large scale here, the anchor can be dropped in relatively shallow water close to the reef from where a delightful beach is an easy row away.

Until the 1950s, Rennel was inhabited until scarcity of fresh water caused its abandonment. A graveyard and evidence of buildings can be seen.

WARRIOR REEFS. Comprising two major reef structures separated by navigable *Moon Passage*, Warrior Reefs run north-south for 30 miles and give guaranteed protection from the trade wind and calm conditions at low tide. The western side of both reefs are unsurveyed except for a couple of running soundings so great caution is necessary under their lee. Skippers with local knowledge have no trouble travelling under their lee.

If entering via Moon Passage, beware reef patches mid channel and if rounding for the southern reef, watch for numerous isolated heads extending from its north-west tip.

The better approach is around the southern tip, either through *Canal Mauvais* or around *Tudu Island*. Again, beware of isolated reefs, but this corner tends to be clearer than others.

Warrior Reefs are famous for the fact that pearl shell was first noticed here in the 1860s starting Australia's most romantic; albeit, at times brutal, industry.

COCONUT ISLAND is one of the least comfortable anchorages in the strait, the reef being too small and lying too much along a latitude to give protection. The inhabited cay is on the north-west end.

BET ISLAND is on the western tip of a seven mile long reef off which, in shoaling patches, fair anchorage can be found. The swell runs along the northern edge of the reef but, with the stream running west, it is tolerable. Windward-tide here can be miserable.

On the eastern end of the reef is a light showing 7 miles and the nearby wreck is that of the 400 ton *Wangalla*.

BADU ISLAND is about 25 miles north of Thursday Island and is the largest of the inhabited islands in the Torres Strait. A continental type rising to 197 metres, it lies close to the larger *Moa Island*, a narrow reef strewn passage separating the two.

THURSDAY ISLAND. For this and other anchorages within its vicinity, see page 292.

BOOBY ISLAND lies 18 miles west of *Thursday Island* and is the major Torres Strait western approach sentinel, having a manned light displaying 26 miles.

Anchorage is abyssimal during any developed wind, but is possible if the need is great enough. Landing can be difficult with a swell running.

The island was named by Captain Cook for the swarming boobies sighted in the area and twenty years later Captain Bligh gave it the same name without being aware of Cook's reference. Passing ships used it as a mail drop and it eventually became classified as an official post office just thirty-three years after Sydney's post office was opened. Legend suggests that the many caves around the foreshores may contain Spanish trea-

Darnley details

Approximately 375 hectares in area and called 'Erub' by the islanders, Darnley was named by Captain W. Bligh on 4 September 1792. During 1793, the ships *Shah Hormazier* and *Chesterfield* navigated the Torres Strait, some of the crew clashing with natives of Darnley which they called Tate Island. Several Englishmen were killed with the survivors sailing to Timor by open boat when they were unable to regain the ships.

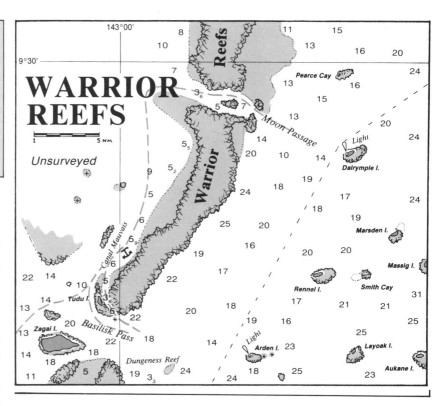

sure, as it is said that Asiatic pirates used it as a base from which to plunder passing galleons. In fact, Spanish coins have been found there.

The Torres Strait Pilot service, the light on Booby Island and Christian missionaries arrived in the area more or less at once in the latter half of last century. As a result, some memorials in community churches throughout the strait have on their altar a lighthouse in a boat supporting a cross.

Booby Island is more a barren rock than an island, but has neverthless been the home of lighthouse families for 100 years. The light was first exhibited on 24 June, 1890.

Repeated in simple detail, this chart of Torres Strait shows the potential cruising ground relative to the area just described. The south-east corner of the strait has great potential with dozens of reef anchorages on offer. However, it is largely uncharted and must be navigated with extreme caution.

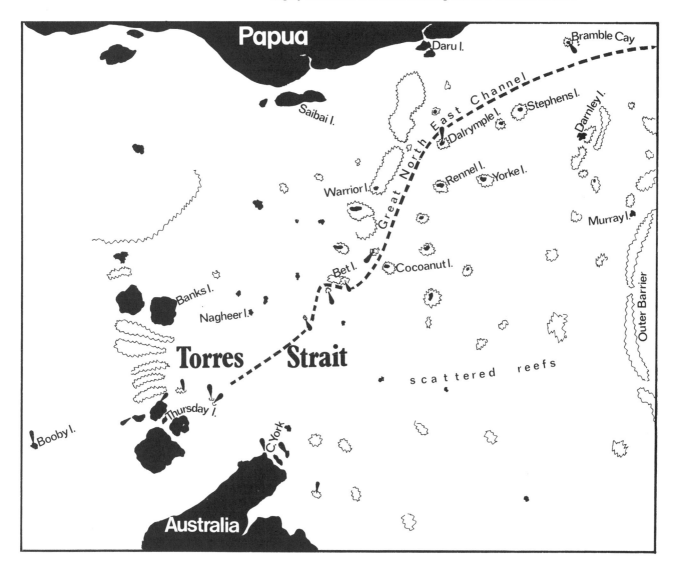

THE CORAL SEA

Queensland Approaches and Reefs in the Coral Sea.

The Coral Sea is the area of the South Pacific Ocean adjoining the north-east coast of Australia (Queensland). It was defined in 1953 by the International Hydrographic Bureau as bound by the Queensland coast on its western border; by 30° 00′ latitude in the south out as far as Elizabeth Reef (not shown in accompanying chart); by a line that wanders out to Vanuatu, around New Caledonia in the east, and from the south of the Solomon Islands across to the south coast of Papua New Guinea in the north. Although a deep and easily navigated sea, it is made hazardous by the numerous detached reefs scattered throughout.

Except for the *Chesterfield Reefs* in the south-east corner, which belong to New Caledonia, most reefs in the Coral Sea are controlled by Australia. They are classified as Coral Sea Islands Territory. Foreign vessels en route to Australia are free to take anchorage behind these reefs and islets without first clearing Australian Customs. This advice does *not* include those reefs, cays and islets belonging to the Great Barrier Reef.

QUEENSLAND APPROACHES. The most popular offshore approaches are indicated on the accompanying chart by green lines. There being countless navigable openings in the Great Barrier Reef, entry can be made at many other points. Those recommended are the easiest and safest and also happen to lead directly into a customs clearance port.

From north to south, these approaches are noted here.

Torres Strait. The most common approach from the east is from Papua New Guinea's capital city of Port Moresby. This is fully detailed on page 298.

From the west, out of the Arafura Sea and the Gulf of Carpentaria, the most common approach is directly into Thursday Island (Port Kennedy) after landfalling on Booby Island. This is fully described on page 298.

Thursday Island is a full Customs, Immigration and Quarantine station. Anchoring in the Torres Strait is not permitted except under duress and then only without going ashore.

Cairns. The bustling tourist city of Cairns with its large harbour is the east coast's most northerly mainland port of clearance. The most popular approach is from the charming Papua New Guinean port of Samarai, landfalling on *Bougainville Reef*. This small but well defined reef not only boasts a major, unmanned light, but also supports two large ships whose rusting remains stand proud enough to be seen from many miles off.

From Bougainville Reef, it is an easy 87 mile sail to the entrance of *Grafton Passage*, a major opening in the Great Barrier Reef. The entrance is lit on the southern side and the best water is held by directional lights on Fitzroy Island. Night entry is no problem.

The passage direct from Port Moresby to Cairns via one of the many excellent reef openings near Lizard Island is only useful to those willing to keep moving down the inner passage from Lizard Island to Cairns without stopping. It is illegal to stop and go ashore anywhere along this stretch of coast before clearing customs. This route is generally better in reverse; i.e, from Lizard Island to Port Moresby after clearing out of Australia from Cairns.

Bundaberg. One of the Coral Coast's favourite clearance ports, Bundaberg is easily found after landfalling on Sandy Cape or, more accurately, on *Breaksea Spit Lightship* anchored nearly 20 miles north of the cape.

Typically, Bundaberg is the destination for those who have crossed the Pacific Ocean and whose last foreign port was Vila in Vanuatu or Noumea in New Caledonia. In a direct line from the south tip of the latter, there are no reefs or islets. Too much leeway to the north, however, can press a vessel dangerously close to the Chesterfield Reefs and Cato Reef. The latter sports a conspicuous block building housing weather instruments and is fully described later.

Brisbane. As Queensland's capital city, customs clearance for small boats can be more trying here than elsewhere, a heavier hand sometimes being employed in the training of new officers. It is, nevertheless, a more logical destination from out of the South Pacific for those planning to sail south to such destinations as Sydney and Tasmania. It is also an excellent centre for boating in its own right and, of course, is at the south extreme of Queensland. This means that a northern cruise will take in the entire Coral Coast as against just parts of it.

Cape Moreton, on the north tip of sandy Moreton Island, is the best landfall from where entrance into Moreton Bay and thence Brisbane River can be made in a number of ways.

CRUISING THE CORAL SEA. This is not recommended to persons inexperienced in coral navigation. Because the isolated reefs strewn throughout the Coral Sea mostly demand longer than a day's sail between them, problems with safe landfall can easily arise. And those who feel their GPS will guarantee safety are warned that their instruments may prove more accurate than the chart and thus clip reefs that shouldn't be there.

And when the next reef is found and safely rounded into anchorage, there manifests the reality of reef cruising; namely, anchorages are mostly miserably uncomfortable and often insecure. The former is the result of poor windward protection, the latter from swell and excessive depths. Very few Coral Sea reefs have ideal shape, depth and bottom for serene, secure worry-free anchorage.

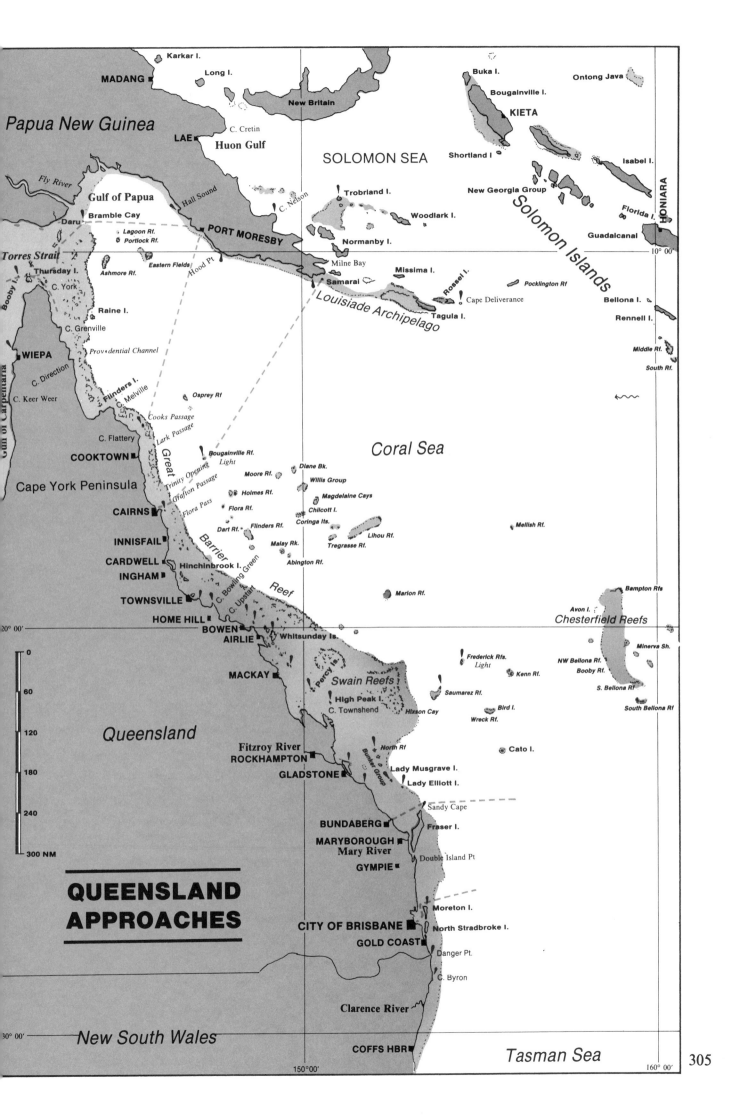

Papua New Guinea

Karkar I.

Long I.

MADANG

New Britain

Buka I.

Ontong Java

Bougainville I.

KIETA

C. Cretin

Huon Gulf

LAE

SOLOMON SEA

Shortland I.

Gulf of Papua

Hall Sound

C. Nelson

Trobriand I.

New Georgia Group

Solomon Islands

Isabel I.

Bramble Cay

Daru

PORT MORESBY

Woodlark I.

HONIARA

Lagoon Rf.

Portlock Rf.

Florida I.

Torres Strait

Eastern Fields

Hood Pt

Milne Bay

Missima I.

Rossel I.

Pocklington Rf

Guadalcanal

10° 00′

Thursday I.

Ashmore Rf.

Samarai

Louisiade Archipelago

Bellona I.

Booby I.

C. York

Raine I.

Cape Deliverance

Rennell I.

C. Grenville

Tagula I.

Middle Rf.

WIEPA

Prov·dential Channel

South Rf.

C. Direction

C. Keer Weer

Flinders I.

C. Melville

Osprey Rf

Coral Sea

Cooks Passage

Lark Passage

C. Flattery

Great

Bougainville Rf.

COOKTOWN

Light

Diane Bk.

Bampton Rfs

Cape York Peninsula

Trinity Opening

Moore Rf.

Willis Group

Grafton Passage

Holmes Rf.

Magdelaine Cays

CAIRNS

Flora Pass

Flora Rf.

Chilcott I.

Mellish Rf.

INNISFAIL

Dart Rf.·

Flinders Rf.

Coringa Its.

CARDWELL

Barrier

Malay Rk.

Lihou Rf.

INGHAM

Hinchinbrook I.

Tregrasse Rf.

Abington Rf.

TOWNSVILLE

C. Bowling Green

Reef

Marion Rf.

Avon I.

Chesterfield Reefs

HOME HILL

C. Upstart

20° 00′

BOWEN

Minerva Sh.

AIRLIE

Whitsunday Is

Frederick Rfs.

NW Bellona Rf.

MACKAY

Percy Is.

Swain Reefs

Light

Kenn Rf.

Booby Rf.

S. Bellona Rf

Queensland

High Peak I.

C. Townshend

Hixson Cay

Saumarez Rf.

Bird I.

South Bellona Rf

Wreck Rf.

Fitzroy River

North Rf

Cato I.

ROCKHAMPTON

GLADSTONE

Bunker Group

BUNDABERG

Lady Musgrave I.

Sandy Cape

Lady Elliott I.

MARYBOROUGH

Fraser I.

Mary River

GYMPIE

Double Island Pt

QUEENSLAND
APPROACHES

Moreton I.

CITY OF BRISBANE

North Stradbroke I.

GOLD COAST

Danger Pt.

C. Byron

Clarence River

New South Wales

30° 00′

COFFS HBR

Tasman Sea

150°00′

160° 00′

305

0

60

120

180

240

300 NM

A basic roundup of what to expect is offered here with a couple of large scale plans to assist. The descriptions run from south to north and are not comprehensive.

CATO ISLAND.
Lying 150 miles north-east of *Sandy Cape* (north end of Fraser Island) and 600 miles west of *Noumea*, Cato Island might be considered as an 'en route landfall' on passage to such customs ports as Bundaberg or Gladstone. Supporting an automatic weather station, the small but conspicuous blockhouse lifts above the horizon well in advance in the low cay and leaves no doubt as to its identity.

Anchorage is deep and uncomfortable and tide races are common. The large area of sand bottom around the cay can refract against the sky and be seen as a very light green patch above the horizon for a good distance off. This is not a dependable phenomenon.

WRECK REEF.
220 miles north-east of Bundaberg and offering useful depths of around 12 metres over sand and scattered coral, anchorage here is poorly protected from the prevailing south-east wind. The best of a bad bunch is behind the three reefs comprising *West Islet*.

It was here that hydrographer extraordinaire, Matthew Flinders was wrecked when travelling home to England as a passenger aboard *HMS Porpoise*. Also lost was the vessel *Cato* on 17th August 1803. Flinders took the best ship's boat and sailed back to Sydney to fetch assistance.

KENN REEF.
60 miles nor-nor-east of Wreck Reef, Kenn comprises four separate reefs, the south-easternmost one forming a useful crescent shape. Fair anchorage amongst numerous coral gonkers can be found in about 9 metres with the larger cay bearing around south magnetic. There is a tempting lagoon in the reef immediately north and a conspicuous boulder on the reef to the west.

SAUMAREZ REEFS.
Close to the southern tip of the Swain Reefs at the end of the Great Barrier Reef and 170 miles north-east of Gladstone, Saumarez Reefs are of the ribbon type of coral formation. Running across the south-east wind for a distance of around 20 miles, they are comprised of approximately ten reefs. The largest single reef is 10 miles long under the lee of which the best anchorage can be found. Finding usefully shallow depths is a problem here without tangling with coral heads.

FREDERICK REEF.
One of the best anchorages in the Coral Sea, Frederick Reef supports a light on its northern end and a cay on both north and south reefs. The passage between the two reefs, is navigable, but overfalls are common during an ebb tide. During developed trade winds, the reef is easily defined along its weather edge whilst its leeward edge shows well. Caution is necessary, however, when closing for anchorage owing to the countless isolated coral heads along the inner side of the crescent.

Frederick Reef lies 240 miles north-east of Gladstone and about 55 miles in the same direction from *Saumarez Reef*.

BOUGAINVILLE REEF.
About 115 miles north-east of Cairns and supporting a major unmanned light, Bougainville Reef is an important approach reference to *Grafton Passage* (Cairns' main reef entrance). The remains of two ships stand proud along the reef edge. Anchorage cannot be suggested here owing to the heavy swell pervading the perimeter and lack of useful depths.

OSPREY REEF
lies 80 miles north-east of Lizard Island and is often looked on as an ideal stopover en route to Port Moresby or Samarai. Enclosing a lagoon some 15 miles long by 5 miles at its widest, good anchorage seems assured. In reality, protection in the south-east corner of the lagoon is only good during low tide and the distance from the entrance is some 10 miles straight into the prevailing wind. The lagoon can be very rough. Caution is also necessary amidst the numerous scattered coral heads within the lagoon.

WILLIS ISLETS.
250 miles east of Cairns, well out into the Coral Sea, this group of islets and reefs is scattered north and south over a distance of 11 miles. The largest reef is to the north and lies along the wind offering no worthwhile shelter. Anchorage under the lee of South Islet is very uncomfortable in foul ground at excessive depths. It is a calm weather only anchorage.

South Islet is known as Willis Island and supports a weather station established in 1921. A three man station, it acts primarily as an early warning station for cyclones bearing down on the Queensland coast.

Louis Antoine de Bougainville

Born in Paris on 11 November 1729, the often overlooked navigator, Bougainville, was one of a number of Europeans who almost beat Captain Cook to Australia's east coast. Given the 26-gun frigate, *La Boudeuse* and the storeship *L'Etoile* he was ordered to the Frankland Islands, there to hand the French settlement over to Spain after which he was free to explore the Pacific.

In December 1767 he left Montevideo, passed through the Straits of Magellan, and crossed the Pacific by way of Tahiti, Samoa and the New Hebrides (now Vanuatu and called by him the Greater Cyclades). Intent on finding New Holland, he narrowly escaped shipwreck in the Coral Sea on Diane Bank soon after which he sighted the reef off Cairns now bearing his name, Bougainville Reef. For reasons somewhat obscure, he came to the erroneous conclusion that this constituted a sighting of 'New Holland' (Australia) after which he turned north.

Landfalling New Guinea in Hood Bay, he hoped to find a strait between New Holland and New Guinea (the one through which Torres sailed over 160 years earlier) and sailed west. Before travelling very far, a need for water and provisions changed the plan to that of rounding New Guinea to the east to which end he hauled sheets and beat against the trades for two weeks. On clearing New Guinea (around Rossel Island), he sailed to the Solomons thence on to Batavia and eventually back to St Malo to become France's first circumnavigator.

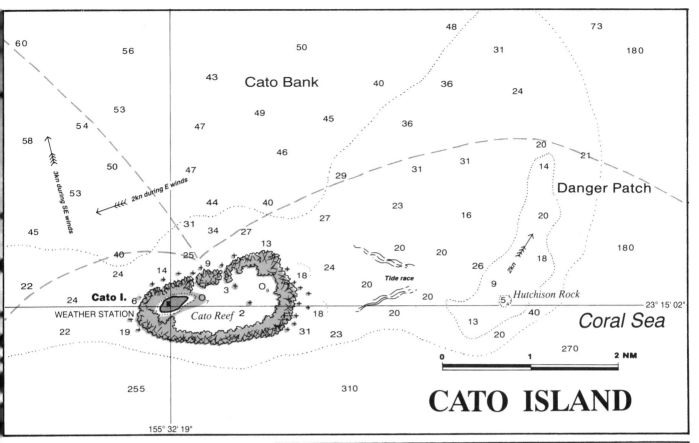

CATO ISLAND

Cato Bank

60　56　50　48　73　180

43　53　54　49　45　36　31

58　50　47　46　36　24　20　21

3kn during SE winds　2kn during E winds　29　31　23　14

Danger Patch

45　53　44　40　27　23　16　20　180

22　40　31　34　27　13　24　20　26　18

24　25　9　18　2kn

Cato I.　14　9　3　O9　20　9　Hutchison Rock

WEATHER STATION　6　O7　Cato Reef　2　Tide race　20　20　5₄　40　23° 15' 02"

22　19　18　13　Coral Sea

255　310　270　2 NM

155° 32' 19"

Frederick Reef Light

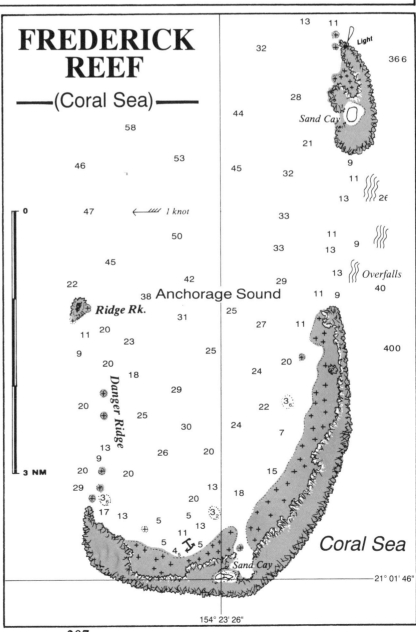

FREDERICK REEF
—(Coral Sea)—

13　11　Light

32　36 6

28　Sand Cay

44　21

46　53　45　32　11　13　2€

47　←┄ 1 knot　33　11　13　9

50　33

45　42　29　13　Overfalls　40

22　38 Anchorage Sound　11　9

Ridge Rk.　31　25　27　11　400

11　20　23　25　20

9　20　24

20　18　29　22　3₆　7

Danger Ridge　20　25　30　24

13　26　20　15

9　20　20　13　18

20　20　29　20　3₂

29　3₆　17　13　5　13　Coral Sea

5　11

5　4₅　5　Sand Cay

21° 01' 46"

154° 23' 26"

Lights and weather stations

Automatic lights in the Coral Sea are situated at Saumarez, Frederick and Bougainville Reefs. Weather stations are established on Cato Islet, Creal Reef, Flinders Reef, Frederick Reef, Gannet Cay, Lihou Reef, Marion Reef and Willis Islets. All are automatic except Willis Islet where three to four technicians live and work. Of the automatic stations, most meteorological equipment is housed in buildings of a bygone era with the result that they are of considerable size and thus easily sighted from a good distance. Under some circumstances they can be momentarily confused as being a ship's bridge.

307

GULF OF CARPENTARIA. More than half of this gulf's 1000 miles of coastline belongs to Queensland. The remainder belongs to the Northern Territory and, in particular, that part of the territory known as Arnhem Land.

Because there is no coral in the gulf, it is not part of the Coral Coast, nor does it rate as a very satisfying cruising ground. It does, however, attract a lot of trawlers (who base themselves in Weipa and Karumba), barramundi fishermen and a few of the more adventurous yachtspeople. Anchorages are poor to non-existent, although in the right weather the entire west coast of the Cape York Peninsula becomes an 'anchorage'.

The gulf had tantalised people with its possibilities for many decades and had always been a magnet to fishermen and crocodile hunters. But it was not until the 1950s that its most important contribution to Australia's economy was realised. This was the discovery of bauxite, the raw material for aluminium, by geologist H.J. Evans who first recognised the significance of its remarkable red cliffs.

The company of Comalco was formed expressly to exploit the Weipa deposits. In 1962 it shipped out the first load of bauxite from a natural harbour on the mouth of the Embley River. During the mid 1960s yet another fabulous deposit was found, this time directly opposite Weipa on the Gove Peninsula on the north-east corner of Arnhem Land.

Also in the 1960s, as a result of fisheries research, prawns were discovered in extraordinary numbers. Better still, they were banana prawns, a type that can be netted during daylight allowing trawler operators to work 'office' hours.

Weather. The gulf is a breeding area for cyclones during the wet season, December through March. The north-west winds of that period — especially late January through February — commonly extend further south than the same wind on the Coral Coast.

During winter, the south-east trade wind persists similar in principal to the Coral Coast, but with differences created by the land mass of the Cape York Peninsula to windward. In essence, a strong trade wind will lose little of its dominance and strength, especially in the northern half of the gulf, whilst a moderate trade wind commonly warps into an easterly or even north-easterly.

Because the Cape York Peninsula is to windward during these conditions, sailing under its lee is one of life's great experiences. Hundreds of miles can be covered at a good rate in swell-free seas. Once the coast is left well astern, however, seas rapidly build up and a gulf crossing can be similar in every respect to the Coral Coast regarding wave shape and form.

When the weather is calm to light on the Coral Coast during winter, the Gulf of Carpentaria can create its own weather patterns, the worst being a south-west gale. It is thus possible to have that dream sail turned into a nightmare of discomfort.

Anchorages. Ports are looked at separately later; here the opportunity for anchoring is reviewed.

When the wind is off the Cape York Peninsula, its beach-fronted coast can be closed on and used as a perfect lee for anchoring anywhere along its length. In some places underwater reefs of bauxite rock are encountered, but generally the bottom is good holding mud which shoals nicely towards the beach.

Some rivers have adequate depths within for all-tide anchoring, but are barred and demand a low tide survey by dinghy. Exceptions are the Embley River, into which a deep channel is maintained for ships loading at Weipa and, to a lesser degree, the Norman River which is used regularly by large trawlers.

The island groups, *Wellesley, Sir Edward Pellew* and *Groote Eylandt* are Aboriginal Land which cannot be visited without permission. Their anchorages can be disappointing depending on prevailing winds at the time.

Tides. Queensland's *Official Tide Tables* include most of the gulf; prediction areas being Weipa, Mornington Island, Wellesley Islands and Karumba. Tidal sequence is normal in the north whilst only two tides per day are common towards the head of the gulf. Here, four tides a day can also occur but only during neaps.

WEIPA is a company town dedicated to the strip mining of bauxite. Approximately 130 miles south of Thursday Island, the port is on the mouth of the *Embley River* which empties into the gulf through *Albatross Bay*. The northern headland of this bay, *Duyfken Point*, appears as a low hill at the end of a long beach. Its lighthouse is a steel trellis.

The harbour approach is through a 7 mile long dredged channel marked on each side by port and starboard beacons and held by directional lead beacons. Depths are suitable to ore carriers and thus present no difficulties for the private vessel. It is a customs clearance port.

Within the harbour are bauxite loading facilities, small boat wharf and slip and, upstream, is an Aboriginal settlement. Anchorage is where convenient according to the obvious demands of commercial shipping. Do not obstruct swing basins or channels.

The town of Weipa has a Woolworths supermarket, hotel, post office and the usual infrastructure of a small town.

KARUMBA. At the mouth of the *Norman River* in the south-east corner of the Gulf of Carpentaria, Karumba is dedicated almost entirely to the prawning industry. The river is entered over a bar using lead beacons and the private prawn processing companies and wharves are along the east bank as the river turns south.

The town of Normanton lies on the river banks many miles upstream. It can be reached by boat on a high tide but is better visited by road. Normanton has shops and hospital and is connected by sealed road to the Mount Isa-Townsville highway.

GOVE. Another bauxite strip mining operation with the best natural harbour in the Gulf of Carpentaria, the township here is known as *Nhulunbuy* where, again, there is a Woolworths supermarket and other support shops and facilities.

Gove Harbour is located on the north-east tip of Arnhem Land which, itself, occupies the north-east corner of the Northern Territory. The harbour is deep and commodious boasting a bauxite ore loading plant on its headland and small boat facilities within. These

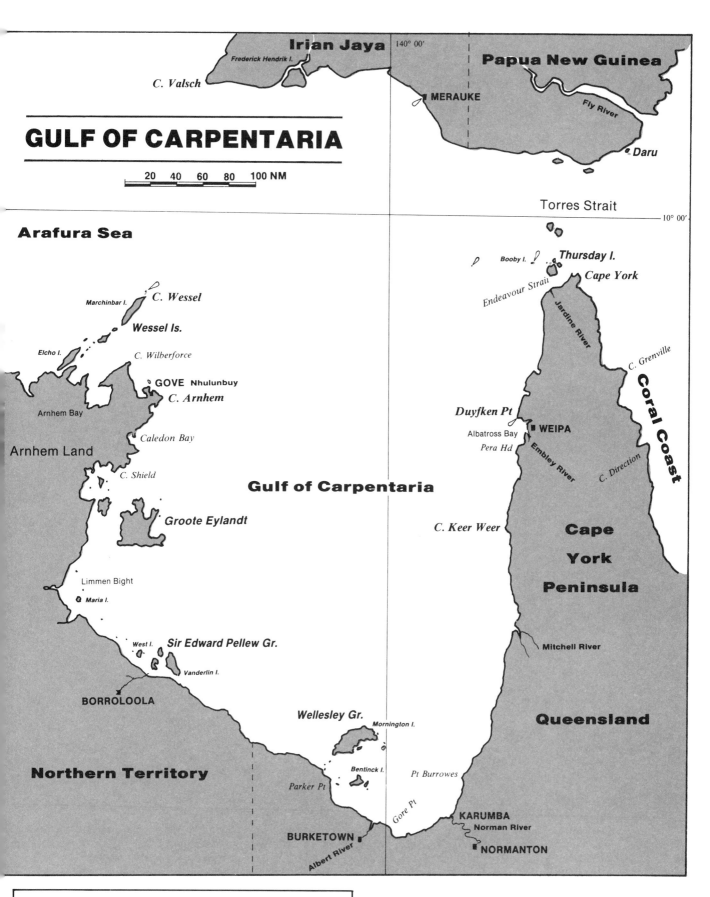

GULF OF CARPENTARIA

20 40 60 80 100 NM

Irian Jaya

Frederick Hendrik I.

C. Valsch

Papua New Guinea

MERAUKE

Fly River

Daru

Torres Strait

140° 00'

10° 00'

Arafura Sea

Booby I.

Thursday I.

Cape York

Endeavour Strait

Jardine River

C. Grenville

C. Wessel

Marchinbar I.

Wessel Is.

Elcho I.

C. Wilberforce

GOVE Nhulunbuy

C. Arnhem

Arnhem Bay

Caledon Bay

Arnhem Land

C. Shield

Groote Eylandt

Duyfken Pt

Albatross Bay

WEIPA

Pera Hd

Embley River

C. Direction

Coral Coast

Gulf of Carpentaria

C. Keer Weer

Cape

York

Peninsula

Limmen Bight

Maria I.

West I. **Sir Edward Pellew Gr.**

Vanderlin I.

BORROLOOLA

Mitchell River

Wellesley Gr.

Mornington I.

Queensland

Northern Territory

Bentinck I.

Pt Burrowes

Parker Pt

Gore Pt

KARUMBA

Norman River

BURKETOWN

Albert River

NORMANTON

include yacht club, careening grid, haul-out yard, public
jetty and fuel. There is excellent holding in calm water.
    Gove is a customs clearance port.

DOWN THE
PENINSULA

There was a time when the only cruising folk going north of Cairns were those departing Australia. Typically, they would anchor-hop up the Cape York Peninsula, pass through the Torres Strait after a short call at Thursday Island, then sail west to Darwin from where Australia would be officially cleared. The numbers sailing in the opposite direction were so small as to be insignificant.

Nowdays, with more and more folk cruising, there is a greater need to get away from those areas so rapidly becoming overcrowded; the Whitsundays being a fine example. As a result, traffic up the Peninsula has increased enormously and, because only a small percentage of that traffic departs Australia for points west, most of it must get south again. It is hoped the following will assist in planning the return down the Peninsula.

First and foremost, if you intend sailing south during the months April through September you *will* get south-easterly trade winds. These are often very strong. Also, they seldom let up, blowing night and day for weeks on end. To move south at this time of year is to be guaranteed a hard beat to windward. Many, many skippers have given up to await better times at Thursday Island and many of their boats have been fine windward machines, perfectly capable of the task in hand. The trouble is, the people fail, the truth about beating into short, steep seas against winds often rising twenty-five knots being more than they want to handle.

It is also folly to await fair winds. The presumption that the north-westerlies will take one down to Cairns during the January through March north-westerly wet season is a natural one, but it is also foolish. The fact is, the north-westerly winds rarely reach Princess Charlotte Bay, let alone carry right to Cairns. They are really only good for the passage from Thursday Island to Cape Grenville from where wet-season south-easterlies are likely to occur.

The best time to go is during the spring transition which takes place from October to December inclusive. Sometimes it is later, not starting until early November and continuing through January. A timetable cannot be predicted. The turn-around period in Thursday Island easily stretches into weeks waiting for the trade wind to die.

While waiting, watch the weather map on Thursday Island television every weeknight. As long as a high-pressure system prevails and maintains a ridge up the coast of Queensland, there will be no change in the south-east condition beyond, perhaps, a slant to the east and a promise (very rarely honoured) of a further slant to the north-east. But as soon as a low over New South Wales blocks the high and, better still, moves into the Tasman Sea to produce gales down south, that is the time to go. The resultant weather along the Peninsula is calm to light nor-nor-easterlies and these might prevail for as long as three weeks before a return to the south-east. In the name of expediency, think in terms of the calm lasting only one week and act accordingly.

As welcome as these calm periods are, the fact is they can be bad for anchoring en route in any secure sense. Never, for example, anchor behind a reef lest a night offshore wind or an evening thunderstorm puts you ashore or, more likely, gives you an unnecessarily worrying time. It is better to move into the coast on dusk as the northerly dies and drop anchor in shoaling water well away from rocks, islands and reefs so that a clear escape is available in the event of unpleasantries during the night. It will be joggled for a while if the afternoon wind has been at all fresh but it calms off quickly enough. Sometimes a light offshore wind wafts in but more commonly the night remains calm.

It can be fairly argued that any capable sailor can figure out the best piece of coast to anchor off at the end of a day's sail, but the following shows a few wrinkles that may not be automatically considered. It also looks at the logical choices down the coast between Thursday Island and Cairns. It does not include normal anchorages which have already been described separately in this book.

Cruising mode is usually switched off for this passage and is replaced by a simple desire to get south in great haste (before the calm is replaced by headwinds). On this basis, it can be presumed that the average vessel, whose owner is willing to use the engine mercilessly, will make around 65 miles a day. This figure is based on a 13 hour day at 5 knots. It will decrease or increase depending on mood of the time, stamina of the crew and power available in the engine room. There will be those times when, thanks to a clean section of coast and/or a moon lighting the way, much of the night will be sailed in which case it is entirely possible to put up 80 to 90 miles a day.

From Thursday Island, strong tides must be faced before being free to predict daily runs. It is difficult to leave the anchorage with a current that will remain favourable all the way across to Cape York and on down through the Albany Passage. Tides in both areas are fickle. Considering the possibility of being slowed down, it pays to make *Escape River* the first destination. Otherwise, carry on down to *Reid Point*, 8 miles further south, and snug against the mainland for the night. It is free of reef in that area except for a small fringe in close. Move in until 7 metres is sounded and drop anchor.

The next leg is best made to *Indian Bay*, on the south side of Cape Grenville, anchoring well off to allow freedom of movement in the event of a wind reversal. In fact, as long as the high-pressure system has not taken over the weather again, the most likely problem in this area is one of evening thunderstorms which tend to pull the wind from its afternoon nor-nor-easterly through north-west to west after which it usually calms right off by midnight.

If conditions are suitable for continuing into the night, a better mainland anchorage exists off the mouth of the *Pascoe River* in Weymouth Bay. The light on Moody Reef, plus the lights to each side of the narrow reef passage formed by Piper Islands and Inset Reef, make night-time navigation relatively easy on this stretch. Also, the light on Eel Reef provides a red sector in which safe water is found when closing the coast in the dark. By keeping the red-white sector pink, one can steer a perfect line towards Pigeon Islet then drop anchor as soon as soundings come to 9 metres.

By getting away at the crack of dawn, it is possible to get south of *Macdonald Reef* (4½ miles south of Heath Reef) then steer diagonally in towards the coast well south of the foul ground off the Nesbit River mouth. If there is any doubt about making Macdonald Reef before dark, stop opposite Ellis Reef or continue on the main track into the night and head for the mainland — just before Hay Islet prevents the move. Unless conditions are overcast, Hay will be seen in the darkest night and Fife Islet light provides a bearing.

The next hop is best made to the *Flinders Group* where all-round protection is available in Owen Channel and a night's sleep can be enjoyed without a thought or worry.

From Flinders, it is possible to reach the shoal water north west of *Pethebridge Islets*, there to drop anchor into 8 metres midway between Murdoch Islet and Pethebridge Islets and not west of a line between them. If this day's run is excessive, move into *Ninian Bay* or close to *Noble Island*.

The next suitable anchorage is in *Bedford Bay*, but not necessarily over shoal water well in the bay. In calm conditions it is possible to drop anchor in 8 metres between the cape and *Beor Reef* if time getting into and out of the bay is begrudged. Alternatively, and especially if the northerly persists at anchor time, the bay to the south of Cape Bedford provides good shelter and easy escape if the wind returns to the south-east overnight.

Cooktown, being a biscuit-toss away from this last anchorage, will probably be visited. But, if not, the next anchorage is best taken down near Cape Tribulation, or, if possible, against the mainland in the vicinity of *Snapper Island*. From here Cairns is well within reach and Port Douglas is just a few miles away.

It can be appreciated that the trip down from Thursday Island can be done in five to seven days depending, as I said earlier, on power plant and crew stamina. Certainly it could not be done in that time with a weak engine or by a person determined to get there without an engine. The useful winds rarely rise before midday and mostly die after dusk. Sometimes an offshore wind continues through the night but mostly it does not. This means that truly useful, favourable winds can only be expected for about 30 per cent of the trip.

The other aspect is, as mentioned, stamina. It may seem ridiculous to talk about stamina to keep a boat going over calm to slightly ruffled seas, but, the fact is, one does eventually scream for a rest. The trouble is a rest can cost a delaying south-easterly which may return for up to two weeks.

311

Under the circumstances, it pays to choose a place of rest where a delay will not be uncomfortable, such as the Flinders Group or the Lockhart River. Otherwise, if a south-easterly does head you off in an area of poor anchorages, there is no alternative to turning around and running back to the nearest suitable anchorage.

Night and day passage-making is perfectly feasible down the Peninsula, but it does presume the vessel to be well manned and the navigator quite accustomed to the special problems. The greatest single problem is that of distance judging at night. The passage is well lit all the way and commercial ships continue overnight without a problem, but without radar it is very easy to stand so far off a light that a reef two or three miles away is struck or, conversely, to hug it so close that the reef it is advertising is struck.

This question can only be answered by the individual. If the period is moonless then think hard and long about going all night. If there is plenty of moon, distance judging is not very difficult and, as long as the crew can stay awake, night navigation is relatively safe and easy. Just remember one simple fact about a coral reef: At high tide it cannot be seen at night with or without a moon and it does not show on radar.

Except in the off season, December through February, trawlers will be seen in their dozens working the coast at night during calm to light weather. The confusion that is possible from their lights when sailing after dark must be allowed for especially when closing the coast to anchor and obliged to pass through a working fleet. Always allow for the fact that the trawlermen are concentrating on their nets and not a small boat in their midst. Beware of sudden course changes and never assume they have seen you.

When stocking the ship in preparation for the passage south do not skimp on the assumption that a fast trip will be enjoyed and that the cheaper shopping of civilisation will be available soon. Allow for the possibility of a fortnight delay owing to a return of the south-easter and victual accordingly.

Weather Portents. For the time of year under review — October through December — on the east coast of the Cape York Peninsula in general and between Thursday Island and Cairns in particular, the following details are pertinent if not entirely dependable.

We have already presumed that Thursday Island was departed during a calm or, at least, towards the end of a south-east wind system that showed promise of easing to become a calm. Typically, a low-pressure cell over New South Wales moving into the Tasman Sea is the cause and the high-pressure systems in its wake are sluggish to regain control of Queensland weather. Usually, the more positive the low, the longer the high in regaining control. As a result we have probably a week and possibly two weeks of calms to look forward to. With a little luck, the calms will be complemented with afternoon north-easterlies.

If those north-easterlies tend to favour north-north-east, the probability is that the calms will continue, especially if they maintain the habit of dying around dusk. If, however, the wind favours north-east or east-north-east and shows a tendency to continue into the night, easing but not dying by midnight, the chances are a high pressure system of around 1022 hectopascals is asserting itself over the mid-Tasman Sea. This will not necessarily strengthen at this time of year, but will take control for at least a few days, pulling the wind into the east and maintaining a steady stream night and day but easing towards dawn. The seas associated with this wind are sometimes enough to kill easy progress under power and the wind can be slanted so that a fair course cannot be laid. Under the circumstances, it can pay to seek anchorage for a day or two until it either strengthens and establishes a solid south-east wind stream or eases back to calms. Either way there is sense in holding.

When this condition prevails, the weather forecasts typically advise of light to moderate east to south-east winds from Thursday Island to Cooktown and light to moderate east to north-east winds from Cooktown to Bowen. This is tantamount to saying an easterly flow on to the entire coast with probable easing down south before the north enjoys its next calm. There is, under the circumstances, sense in trying to get to Cooktown in the hope of finding those north-easterlies, but don't hold your breath. By the time you make it, the south-easterly may re-establish itself at strength enough to defy progress, or the 'north-easterly' may prove to be just more easterlies which, by the time the area is reached, have died.

At this time of year, the trade wind does not hang in for too long, so I repeat, it can pay to hold when the wind heads you, get some maintenance done, practise patience and get under way again when it all calms down. This will be indicated by a slowing down of scudding low cumulus, a possible return of thunderstorms trying to get off the coast and winds almost dead at dawn, freshening during the day and trying to move north of east in the afternoon.

The real question is: when deciding to hold station for the next calm, where do I go? The anchorages are not brilliant along this stretch of coast when the wind moves east of south-east and even though it may be dominantly light to moderate, discomfort can prevail.

This can only be answered by the individual according to position and true weather conditions. If a really good anchorage lies half a day's sail downwind, and the promise is for some hard headwinds, then it can certainly pay to run back. If such an anchorage is to windward and the wind is not too foul, then it pays to press on. Certainly one can no longer anchor against the coast as suggested for calm conditions, but the good news is that when a high re-establishes control, reef and island anchorages become safe and predictable again. There is no worry about a sudden backing or veering and rare indeed is a thunderhead that gets offshore against such a wind. Their lightning in the distance over the land should be watched but not feared.

In the interest of quick reference, the following might be useful.

At the time of year in question, useful daylight lasts from 05.15 to 18.45 with sunrise around 05.45 and sunset around 18.30. Being the tropics, the twilight period is very short, offering a mere half-hour maximum of useful pre- and post light.

Navigational lights are well maintained and are very rarely nonfunctioning, and, when they are, repairs are on their way. However, before departing Thursday Island, listen to any comprehensive weather forecast.

MARINA ROUNDUP

Most Queensland marinas accommodate transient vessels, maintaining a number of non-permanent berths for this purpose. Conditions and prices vary according to policies and these cannot be quoted here because of their changeable nature.

The purpose of the following marina list is to provide instant reference. Most on the list have already been described in the ports and anchorages section of this book. Unless otherwise noted it can be taken as stated that bookings can be made on VHF and that all berths have their own power and water outlets and that the premises are lock-up. It can also be assumed that the control dredged depth — where applicable — is adequate for all deep-keeled craft.

Southport Yacht Club Marina. In Southport Boat Harbour, Main Beach, Gold Coast. Fixed and floating sections. Check-in near fuel dock. Chandlery, yacht club, haul-out and hard stand. Public transport handy. Maximum sized vessel, 18 metres.

Mariners Cove Marina. In Southport Boat Harbour, Main Beach, Gold Coast. Floating. Check-in at fuel dock on south-west corner. Part of shopping and restaurant complex. Maximum size 30 metres.

Marina Mirage. Part of the Sheraton Hotel complex adjacent to Mariners Cove Marina, Gold Coast. Up-market restaurants and shops. Floating marina. Call VHF 73. Maximum size 60 metres.

Runaway Bay Marina. In dredged basin north of Labrador, Gold Coast. Floating berths, haul-out, hard-stand, dry storage, boat services, shops. Check in near fuel dock. Call VHF 74.

Hope Harbour Marina. In dredged basin off Coomera River's south branch, Gold Coast. Floating berths, all boat services offered, with shops to come. Check-in berth near office. Maximum size 30 metres.

Sanctuary Cove Marina. Opposite junction of North and South branches of the Coomera River, Hope Island, Gold Coast. Part of residential, tourist and shopping complex. Report to office on end of jetty. Maximum size 60 metres.

Horizon Shores Marina. Previously known as McLaren Marine Village, this floating marina is in a dredged basin off the channel near Steiglitz, north of Jacobs Well. All boat services are represented. Maximum size 24 metres.

Raby Bay, under the lee of Cleveland Point, south Moreton Bay, may have a public marina in its canal development in the future.

Manly Marina. In Manly Boat Harbour, Brisbane, owned by the port authority. Although public, berths are seldom available. Inquiries to office on public jetty. Maximum size 17 metres.

Royal Queensland Yacht Squadron. In Manly Boat Harbour, Brisbane. Report to marina office near Travelift. All boat services in yard or in area. Maximum size 20 metres.

East Coast Marina. Adjacent to above marina in Manly Boat Harbour. Report to jetty near office at southern end. All services including haul-out, hard-stand, chandlery etc. Maximum size 18 metres.

Moreton Bay Trailer Boat Club Marina. Also in Manly Boat Harbour close to main shopping centre. Floating berths, transients not always catered for.

Wynnum Manly Yacht Club. In Manly Boat Harbour. All services. Members only. Maximum size 17 metres.

Morris Marina. At the Brisbane suburb of Hemmant, in Aquarium Passage near Brisbane River entrance. Most services on site. Maximum size 17 metres.

Dockside Marina. Part of hotel complex on Shafston Reach, Brisbane River. Floating berths in and outside old Evans Deakin Shipyard drydock. Casual berths sometimes available.

Waterfront Place Marina. In Town Reach against City of Brisbane immediately north of the Botanical Gardens' pile berths. Floating berths, casuals welcome.

Olims Hotel Marina. Small appendage to Olims Hotel in Town Reach, opposite the Botanical Gardens, Brisbane. Casual berths rarely available.

Queensland Cruising Yacht Club Marina. In the Brisbane suburb of Shorncliffe, west of the Brisbane River entrance in Cabbage Tree Creek. For casual berths, contact the club secretary. Many services in area. Maximum size 15 metres.

Moreton Bay Boat Club. In Scarborough Harbour, on Brisbane's Redcliffe Peninsula. Floating berths, casuals welcome. Go to one of the pontoons close to the clubhouse. A few services on site, others in area.

Newport Waterways. Also on the Redcliffe Peninsula, west of Scarborough Boat Harbour, this marina is inside the mouth of a large canal development. Casuals should report to or near fuel dock. Maximum size 25 metres.

Mooloolaba Yacht Club. Seen to starboard soon after entering Mooloolaba Harbour (Mooloolah River), casuals are welcome to this large floating marina. All services in area. Call VHF 16 or 27MHz 88. Maximum size 30 metres.

The Wharf Marina. West of the Mooloolaba Yacht Club in the same stretch of river, this floating marina is part of a shopping complex. Visitors are welcome. Report to office near fuel dock. Maximum size 18 metres.

Lawries Marina. Queensland's first marina, this floating berth type is in Mooloolaba in the canal estate at Buddina. All services are on site with haul-out and large hard-stand yard. Report to berth near marina building. Maximum size 23 metres.

Tin Can Bay Marina. Located in dredged basin within Snapper Creek, close to the town of Tin Can Bay (south end of Great Sandy Strait). Floating berths, casuals welcome. Most services available on site or nearby. Maximum size about 30 metres.

Inskip Point. No development as of late 1993, but a marina is planned for this region, probably in Pelican Bay (at mouth of Tin Can Inlet).

Mary River Marina. Fixed and floating berths along river bank in Maryborough, Great Sandy Strait. Most services in area. Subject to flooding.

Great Sandy Strait Marina. In Urangan Boat Harbour where its growth will displace all public berths. Floating berths, transients catered for. Most services in harbour. Part of resort-residential complex. Call VHF 6.

Kingfisher Bay. This resort-residential development on Fraser Island will have a small marina at the end of its jetty in the near future.

Burnett Heads Marina. Situated in Burnett Heads Boat Harbour, at the entrance to Bundaberg's Burnett River, this small marina welcomes visitors when space permits. Good haul-out and hard-stand available plus most engineering services.

Midtown Marina. On Burnett River bank against the City of Bundaberg. Floating berths subject to flooding. Visitors catered for. Most services in area. Report to fuel berth. Maximum size approximately 30 metres.

Gladstone Marina. Located in Gladstone Boat Harbour at entrance to Auckland Creek, this is obligatory to visitors to the city. All services are offered on site or are handy and a new bridge connects the marina with the City of Gladstone.

Rosslyn Bay. This harbour has been developed to receive a floating marina in the future.

Mackay. A marina is planned by 1995 in a new extension of Mackay Outer Harbour.

Hamilton Island. In the Whitsundays, this resort-residential island offers all boating services. Berths are floating and casuals are welcome at a high daily rate. Maximum size 68 tons and a beam of 6.3 metres.

Laguna Quays Marina. Still under construction late 1993, this golf resort-residential development will offer floating berths to casuals. It is in Repulse Bay near Midge Point (Whitsunday region).

Shute Harbour. A marina is planned for here but had not started late 1993.

Port of Airlie. A marina is proposed for Muddy Bay to the immediate south of the township.

Abel Point Marina. Between Airlie Beach and Cannonvale, casual berths are available along with most services on or close to site. Floating berths protected by a breakwater.

North Queensland Cruising Club. Located in Bowen Boat Harbour and primarily for club members, casual berths at this floating marina are sometimes available.

Magazine Creek. Also in Bowen, this once natural waterway flowing into the boat harbour has been dredged in anticipation of private development as a marina.

Magnetic Quays. On the south side of Magnetic Island, off Townsville, this marina development has been abandoned for many years. It is expected to restart by the mid-1990's and will have 150 floating berths and a shopping infrastructure.

Ross Haven Marine. Located in the Ross River, Townsville, the existing pontoon here may be expanded into a small marina. Meanwhile, trawlers are favoured.

Townsville Motor Boat Club Marina. In Ross Creek near the city's heart, this floating marina accepts casuals who may use the club facilities. Go to fuel dock for allocation unless otherwise advised.

Breakwater Marina. Embraced by breakwaters outside the main Townsville Harbour, casuals are well catered for here with a complete marine services infrastructure.

Oyster Point Marina. At the southern end of the town of Cardwell, Hinchinbrook Channel, this development started in the late 1980's but after dredging lay dormant for many years. It is expected to be finished towards the mid 1990's.

Marlin Marina. Extending out from 'The Pier' shopping complex in Cairns, this public, floating marina provides easy access to the city. Casuals well catered for although the only associated infrastructure is comprised of shops.

Cairns Cruising Yacht Squadron Marina. In Smiths Creek, Cairns, this small floating marina accepts casuals subject to berth availability. All services on site or nearby including a heavy lift straddle lift further up the creek. Club facilities available.

Trinity Point Marina. Proposed for the future is a huge 'destination resort and marina development' to the north of the present Cairns Marina and The Pier.

Half Moon Bay Marina is enclosed by its own breakwater under the lee of Yorkeys Knob. Casuals are welcome and most services are available.

Marina Mirage Port Douglas. A part of the Mirage-Sheraton company which is also established on the Gold Coast, this floating marina offers casual berths, fuel and an associated shopping mall at Port Douglas. Call VHF 6 or 27 mg 88.

Closehaven Marina. Located in the same dredged basin as Marina Mirage, this Port Douglas marina offers floating berths to permanents and casuals. The nearby Port Douglas Yacht Club provides ablution facilities.

Cooktown Marina. A development that died in the late 1980's, it is possible that Cooktown will again be considered as a marina site. As of late 1993, nothing had been proposed.

INDEX

This index refers only to the Ports and Anchorages section.

A.

Abbot Point 175, 176
Acacia Island 143, 146
Acheron Island 187, **188**
Ada Reef 274
Admiralty Island 218
Adolphus Channel 282, 288
Agnes Island **200**
Airlie 159, 168, **169**, 170, 172
Albany Island 284, 288
Albany Passage 282, **284**, 285, 287, 288, 296, 311
Albatross Bay 308
Alexandra Bay 232
Alma Bay 182
Almond Point 269
Amity Point 54, 55
Anchorage Point Creeks **196**
Anchor Point 166
Andrew Reef 274
Annan River **240**
Annie River 262
Ann Street 58
Apostle Bay **164**
Aquatic Paradise Canal Estate 57
Aquila Island **128**
Arafura Sea 298, 304
Arcadia 182
Arch Cliffs 84
Archers Crossing Mark 108
Ariel Bank 284
Arlington Reef **223**, 224
Armit Island **170**
Arnhem Land 308
Arthur Point 125, 126
Asp Shoal 294
Auckland Creek 97
Aureed Island 282
Australia 62, 128, 287, 288, 298, 304
Avoid Island 128
Ayr 176

B.

Badger Creek 103
Badu Island 300, **302**
Bailay Creek **232**
Bailey Islet 136
Baird Islet 276
Balaclava Island 108
Balarrgan 67, **80**
Ball Bay **142**
Ballerina Shoal 264
Bamaga **291**
Banana Island 212
Bargara Beach 86
Barnett Rock 130
Barn Island 291
Barren Island 114
Barrow Islet 258
Barrow Point 253, 256, 257
Barubbra Island 87
Bathurst Bay **258**
Bathurst Head 258, 260, 262
Battle Bay 134
Bauer Bay 158
Bauer Inlet 236
Bay Point 288
Bay Village 48
Beanley Islets **256**
Beaver Rock Leads 76, 78
Bedarra Island **204**
Bedford Bay 311
Bedwell Group 128, 129, 130
Bee Reef **236**
Beesley Islet 276
Ben Lomond 172
Beor Reef 311
Berwick Island 130
Bet Island **302**
Beverley Group 134
Big Woody Island 67, 80, **81**, 83
Bingham 78
Bird Island 166
Bird Islets **279**
Bishop Island 58

Bishop Point 285
Bizant River **262**
Blackbird Patches 240
Black Rock 119
Black Swan Island 103
Blackwood Bay 287
Blackwood Channel 260, 278
Blackwood Shoals 142
Bloomfield River **236**, 238
Blue Bell Rocks 272, 273
Blue Pearl Bay **166**
Blue Water Club 88
Bluff Creek **195**
Bluff Island 137
Blunt Bay **133**
Boat Channel 288, 291, 292, **294**
Boat Creek 100, 103
Boat Passage, 58, **198**
Bolt Head 274, 275
Bongaree 52, **61**, 62
Booby Island 292, 298, **302**, 303, 304
Boomerang Shoal 128
Boonlye Point 67, 68
Border Island **165**
Botanical Gardens 52, 58
Bougainville Reef 304, **306**
Boulder Rock 258
Bowden Island **204**
Bowen **172**, 175, 176, 178, 287, 312
Bowling Green Bay 178
Bow Reef **266**
Brady Bank 290, 291
Bramble Cay 298, **300**, 302
Brammo Bay 204
Brampton Island 143, 147, **148**, 150
Breaksea Lightship 87
Breaksea Spit 82, **85**, 304
Breakwater Marina **184**
Bremner Shoal 277
Bribie Island 52, 60, 61, 62
Brisbane 37, 38, 44, 50, 52, 54, 56, **58**, 61, 62, 64, 97, 176, 184, 253, 304
Brisbane River 52, 54, 55, 56, 58, 60, 61, 62, 304
Brisk Island 191
Bristol 82
Bristow Island 300
Broad Sound **123**, 124, 126, 128, 137
Broadwater 37, 38, 39, 44, 52, 58
Brook Islands **203**
Brown Creek 230
Brown Island 44
Brown Reef 300
Brown Rock 120
Browns Crossing Mark 108
Browns Peak 253
Bundaberg 62, 67, 76, 78, 82, 85, 88, **89**, 93, 94, 95, 304, 306
Bundaberg Sailing Club 98
Bunker Group 94
Burdekin River 176
Burkitt Island **264**
Burnett Heads 82, 83
Burnett Heads Boat Harbour **86**, 88, 89
Burnett River 82, 87, 89, 90, 93, 94
Burrum Heads (River) **82**, 83
Burrum Point 82
Bushy Islet **280**
Bustard Bay 90
Bustard Head 92, 93, 94, 97
Butterfly Bay **166**

C.

Cabbage Tree Creek **58**
Cabbage Tree Point 46
Cairncross Islet **280**, 285
Cairns 215, 216, **218**, 222, 224, 243, 252, 254, 260, 270, 272, 274, 287, 296, 304, 306, 310, 311, 312
Cairns Reef **236**, 238
Calliope Island 129, 130
Caloundra 52, 61, **62**
Caloundra Head 52, 62
Cambridge Point 287
Canaipa Passage 44, 46, 48, **50**

Canaipa Point 44, 50
Canal Mauvais 302
Cannibal Group **124**, 125
Canoe Pass 124
Cape Bedford 240, **244**, 245, 246
Cape Bowling Green 176, **178**, 181, 187
Cape Capricorn 105, **110**, 111
Cape Cleveland 178, **181**, 184
Cape Conway 151, **154**, 155
Cape Creek 176, 178
Cape Direction 269, 272
Cape Edgecumbe 175, 176
Cape Ferguson 181
Cape Flattery 245, **246**
Cape Gloucester 172
Cape Grafton 215, 216, 218
Cape Grenville 276, **277**, 278, 279, 280, 310, 311
Cape Griffith 270
Cape Hills 277
Cape Hillsborough **142**, 143
Cape Keppel 105, 110
Cape Kimberley 228, **230**, 232
Cape Manifold 116
Cape Melville 254, 257, 258, 260
Cape Moreton 52, **56**, 62, 304
Cape Pallarenda 182, 184, **187**
Cape Richards 192, **200**
Cape Rock 154, 258
Cape Sandwich 200
Cape Townshend 123, **124**
Cape Tribulation **233**, 234, 311
Cape Weymouth 272
Cape York 240, 285, 287, **288**, 292, 300, 311
Cape York Peninsula 275, 282, 284, 298, 308, 310, 312
Capricornia Cruising Yacht Club 113
Captain Cook Bridge 58
Cardwell 192, 196, **198**, 213, 282
Cardwell Range 192
Cardigan Leads 108
Carlisle Island 148
Carpentaria Lightship 298
Carpentaria Shoal 298
Casement Bay **188**
Castle Hill 184, 187
Castlereagh Point 60
Cateran Bay 165
Cato Island 304, **306**
Cattle Crossing 100, 103
Central Island Mark 108
Channel Islet 128
Channel Rock 292
Chapman Reef 269, 292
Chase Point 132
Chesterfield Reefs 304
Cheviot Island 130
Cid Harbour **162**
Cid Island 162
Clara Group 120
Claudie River 269, 270, **271**
Clerke Island **279**
Cleveland Bay 182, 184
Cleveland Point **56**
Clews Point 92, 93
Coomera River, 39, 44
Cooper Point 213
Coquet Island **254**
Coquette Point 211, 212, 213
Coral Sea 44, 279, 298, 304, 306
Corbett Reef **260**, 264
Cordelia Rocks 187
Corio Bay **114**
Cowan Cowan 52, 54
Cowie Point 236
Cowlishaw Reef 240
Cliff Islets **262**
Cliff Point 116
Cobby Cobby Island 48
Coconut Island **302**
Coconut Point 211, 212
Coffs Harbour 52
Collins Island **125**
Collinsville 176
Combe Reef 256

Comboyuro Point 52, 54
Cooktown 166, 213, 222, 233, 236, 238, **240**, 244, 246, 250, 253, 272, 311, 312
Coolgaree Bay **188**
Coombabah Creek 39
Coombe Island **204**
Crab Island 39, 78, 292, 298
Crane Islet 124
Crescent Reef **253**
Crocodile Creek 230
Crocodile Rocks 212
Crusoe Island 46, 48
Cumberland Islands 147
Curacoa Island **191**
Curlew Island **137**
Curtis Island 98, 100, 104, 108, 110

D.
Daintree River **228**, 229, 230, 232, 236
Dalrymple Island **302**
Daniell Reef **274**
Darnley Island **300**
Daru Island 298, **300**, 301
Darwin 219, 310
Datum Point 80, 100
Dauan Island 301
Daydream Island **158**, 159
Dayman Island 290
Dayman Point 80
Dead Dog Islet 150
Deception Bay 52, 60
Delcomyn Island 116, 119, 120
Deluge Inlet 196
Denham Island 258, 260
Dent Island **162**
Derwent Island 136
Derwent Rocks 108
Devereux Rocks 148
Devils Elbow 108
Digby Island **134**, 137, 138, 140
Dinghy Bay 148
Dome Island 116
Donovan Point 236
Donovan Shoal 125
Don River 175
Double Bay **170**
Double Island **224**, 226
Double Island Point 64, **66**, 70
Double Sloping Hummock 87
Dowar Island **300**
Draper Patch 240
Duck Island 80
Duke Islands **125**, 130
Dundatha Reach 78
Dungeness **195**
Dunk Island 192, 199, **204**, 206, 216
Dunwich 50, **55**, 56
Duyfken Point 308

E.
Eagle Islet **249**, 250
Eagle Rock 108
Earlando Resort **170**
East Banks 97
East Channel 52, 97
East Coast Marina **57**
East Point 138
Eborac Island 285, 288
Eden Island 46
Eden Reef 269
Edgecumbe Bay 172
Edwards Shoal 270
Edward Street 58
Eel Reef **274**, 311
Egmont Reef 226
Egremont Pass 147
Elbow Point 67, 68
Elizabeth Reef 304
Elliot Heads 86
Ellis Channel 292
Ellis Reef **266**, 311
Embley River 308
Emily Patches 129
Endeavour Reef **236**
Endeavour River 240, 243
Endeavour Strait 298
England 89, 94
Enterprise Channel 195
Entrance Island 116, 119, 120, 291, 294
Eric Early Light 50
Escape Cay 128
Escape River **280**, 282, 285, 287, 288, 311

Eshelby Island **170**
Esk Island 164
Etty Bay 211
Eudlo Point 72
Euston Reef 218
Exit Reef 269
Eyrie Reef 249

F.
Facing Island 97, 98
Fairlight Rock 150
Falcon Island **191**
False Cape 218
False Nobbies Lookout 176
False Patch 56
Family Group 204
Family Islands 192, **204**
Fantome Channel **191**
Fantome Island **191**
Farmer Islet 276
Farmers Reef Leads 98
Farrier Island 150
Fife Islet 264, 266, 311
Fisher Islet 276
Fisherman Islands 58
Fish Reef 143
Fish Rocks 119
Fitzroy Island **215**, 218, 304
Fitzroy Motor Boat Club 109
Fitzroy Passage 304
Fitzroy Reef **96**
Fitzroy River 103, 104, **108**
Five Beaches Bay **182**
Flagstaff Hill 172
Flame Tree Creek 168
Flat Hill 280
Flat Island 116
Flat Isles 128
Flat Top Island 140
Flinders Entrance 300
Flinders Group 256, 258, **260**, 262, 264, 311, 312
Flinders Island 258, 260
Flinders Passage 288, 292, 294
Florence 89
Florence Bay **182**
Fly Channel 260
Flying Fish Point 211, 213, 214
Fly Point 284
Fly River 181, 298
Forbes Island **274**
Forgan Smith Point 140
Frankland Islands **214**
Fraser Island 67, 68, 74, 81, 82, 83, 84, 86, 93, 306
Frederick Point 285, 288
Frederick Reef **306**
Freeman Channel 56
Freshwater Bay **116**
Friday Island 292
Funnel Bay **168**

G.
Gabba Island 301
Gallon Reef 274
Garden Hill 108
Garden Island 48, 201
Garry's Anchorage 68, **74**
Gatcombe Channel Leads 100
Gatcombe Heads 97, 98
Gateway Bridge 58
Gavial Creek 108
Gayundah Creek 196
Geering Shoal 62
Genesta Bay **155**
George Island 129
George Point **170**
Georgie Hill 207
Geraldton 213
Gladstone 91, 92, 95, **97**, 98, 100, 103, 104, 108, 306
Gladys Inlet 213
Gladys River 213
Glasshouse Mountains 60
Glennie Inlet **274**
Gloucester Island 172, 176
Gloucester Passage 170, **172**
Gold Coast 37, 52, 62
Gold Coast Seaway 37, **38**, 39, 44
Golding Cutting 97
Goldsmith Island **150**
Goodes Island 292

Goold Island 193, **201**, 204
Gove **308**
Graf Rock 133
Grafton Passage 215, 218, 223, 304, 306
Graham Creek 103
Grange Rock 214
Grant Hill 215
Granville 78
Granville Bridge **78**
Grassy Hill 243, 244
Grassy Island **170**
Grave Point 240
Great Barrier Reef 82, 93, 218, 228, 266, 280, 304
Great Keppel Island **111**
Great North East Channel 298, 300, 301
Great Palm Island 184, **188**, 191
Great Sandy Strait 67, 68, 70, 74, 76, 80, 81, 82
Great Sandy Strait Marina 80
Green Island (Cairns) **223**, 236
Green Island (Mackay) 142
Greys Bay **176**
Grimstone Point 170
Groote Eylandt 308
Grub Reef **264**
Guardfish Cluster 137
Gubbins Reef 244
Gulf of Carpentaria 260, 282, 292, 298, 304, **308**
Gulnare Inlet **162**
Gympie 66, 76

H.
Haggerstone Island **276**
Half Moon Bay **224**
Half Tide Rocks 128
Halifax Bay Bombing Range 184, **187**, 188
Hall Point 208
Hall Rock 208
Halls Point 228, 229
Hamilton Island **162**
Hamilton West 162
Hammond Island 292, 298
Hammond Rock 288, 290, 298
Hannah Islet **264**, 266
Hannibal Islets **280**
Happy Bay **158**
Harrier Point 191
Harrington Reef **282**
Harvey Island 277
Haslewood Island **164**
Havannah Island **188**
Hawke Point Mark 108
Haycock Island **195**, 224
Hay Islet **266**, 311
Hayman Island **166**
Hay Point 138
Hazard Bay **191**
Health Island 56
Heath Reef 266, 311
Hecate Point 193, 198, **199**
Hedge Reef **264**
Helvellyn Rocks 148
Hemmant 58
Henderson Island 134
Henning Island **162**
Heralds Island **187**
Herbert River 195
Heron Island **96**
Hervey Bay 67, 68, 78, 79, 81, **82**, 83, 85, 86
Hervey Bay Boat Club 80
Hicks Island 277, 278, **279**
High Island **214**, 290
High Peak 268
High Peak Island **130**, 131
High Rock 247
Hilda Hill 207
Hill Inlet 164
Hinchinbrook Channel 184, **192**, 195, 196, 198, 204
Hinchinbrook Island 192, 196, 198, 200, 201, 204
Hinchinbrook Island Creeks **196**
Hodgkinson River 222
Holt Island 125
Home Hill 176
Home Islands 277, **278**, 279
Hook Island 166
Hook Point 70
Hope Harbour 38, **39**, 44
Hope Islands 232, **238**

Horizon Shores Marina 46
Horned Hill 292, 294
Horn Island 292, **294**, 296
Horseshoe Bay **182**
Hotspur Island **134**
Hovell Bar 292
Howick Group 253, **254**, 256, 264, 273
Howick Island 253, **254**, 257, 272
Hudson Island **204**
Hull Island 134
Humbug Mark 108
Hummocky Island 110
Humpy Point 158
Hunter Inlet **274**
Hunter Island 125, 130
Hynes Jetty **78**

I.

Ian Point 166
Indian Bay 277, **278**, 311
Indian Head 240
Ingram Island 256
Inner Freeman Channel 52, 54
Inner Rocks 92
Innisfail **211**, 212, 213
Inset Reef 276, 311
Inskip Point 67, **70**, 72, 74
Ireland 213
Iris Reef 264
Iron Range 272
Island Bluff 126
Island Head Creek **120**, 124, 125, 130, 131
Island Point 226

J.

Jabiru Island 39
Jackson Rock 269
Jacky Jacky Creek 284
Jacobs Well 46
Jansen Rock 93
Japanese 213
Jardine Rock 294
Jenny Lind Bank 97
Johnstone River 211, 212, 213
Julie Rock 129
Jumpinpin 46, 48, 52
Juno Bay 191

K.

Kalpower Cattle Station 262
Kangaroo Shoals 274
Karniga Island 290
Karumba **308**
Kauri Creek **74**
Kay Reef 276
Kedge Reef 247
Keelan Island 134
Kemp Rocks 274
Kennedy Inlet 284
Kennedy River **262**, 284
Kennedy Sound 154
Kenn Reef **306**
Kent Island 206
Keppel Bay 100, 108, 110, 111
Keppel Islands 113
Keppel Rocks 105
Keswick Island **147**
King Beach 216
Kingfisher Bay 81
King Island 57
King Reef 204, 206
Knight Island **138**
Krummell Passage 48
Kumboola Islet 204

L.

Lady Elliot Island 89, **93**, 94, 162
Lady Musgrave Island **94**, 95, 96
Lagoon Anchorage **84**
Lagoon Rock 164
Laguna Quays Resort **151**
Laird Point 103
Lakefield National Park 262
Lake Reef 236
Lakes Creek 108
Lake Shoal 128
Langford Island **166**
Lansdown Reef 269
Lark Reef 245
Laura 244
Lawries Marina **64**
Ledge Point 108

Leslie Rocks 78
Lindeman Island **154**
Lingham Island **125**
Linne Island **150**
Lion Reef 274
Little Pioneer Bay 188, 191
Little Sea Hill 105
Little Ships Club 56
Lizard Island 246, 248, **250**, 252, 254, 256,
    288, 304, 306
Lloyd Bay 264, 266, **268**
Lloyd Island 270, **271**, 272
Lloyd Roberts Jetty 160, 169
Lockhart Mission 270, 273
Lockhart River 269, **270**, 271, 312
Logan River 44
Long Beach 111
Long Island (Moreton Bay) 48
Long Island Sound **156**, 158
Long Island (St Lawrence) 125, 126, 128
Long Island (Whitsundays) 156, 158
Long Reach Leads 89
Long Shoal 154
Lookout Point 248, 252
Lower Quarry Reach Mark 108
Low Islets 226, **228**
Lowrie Island **266**
Low Wooded Isle **245**, 246
Lucinda 192, 193, **195**
Lucinda Point 192
Luggage Point 58
Lynchs Beach 178

M.

Maaroom 67
Mabel Island 214
Macdonald Reef 311
Mac Gillwray Reef 252
Mackay 114, 119, 122, 123, 129, 130, 131,
    134, 136, 138, 141, 142, 146, 147, 166
Mackay Cruising Yacht Club 141
Mackay Outer Harbour 138, **140**, 142, 147,
    148
Mackay Reef **234**
Macleay Island 48, 50
Mac Millan River 278
Macona Inlet **166**
Maer Island 300
Magazine Creek 175
Magnetic Island 178, **182**, 184, 187
Magnetic Quays 182
Magpie Reef **264**
Main Beach 38
Main Channel 44, **46**, 48, 52
Mandalay Point 168, 169
Manly Boat Harbour **56**, 58
Marble Island 125
Margaret Bay **277**, 278, 279
Marina Mirage 38, **39**
Mariners Cove Marina 38, **39**
Markilug Islet 290
Marrett River **262**
Martin Reef 246, 249
Maryborough 67, 68, 76, **78**, 79, 85
Maryport Bay 148
Mary River 67, **76**, 78, 79, 80, 81, 84
Mary River Marina **78**
Maud Bay 182
Mausoleum Island 143, 146
May Reef 269
Mc Kenzies Jetty 80
Mc Lean Bay 148
Meaburn Rock 207
Megaera Reef 254, **256**
Mendel Creek, 195, 196
Merrie England Shoal 300
Michaelmas Cay **224**
Middle Bank 70
Middle Island 111
Middle Reef 184, 272, **273**
Middle Pass 126
Middle Percy Island 130, 131, **133**, 134, 136
Middle Rocks 92
Midge Point 151
Mid Molle Island 159
Mid Reef 256
Millaquin Reach 89
Missionary Bay Creeks **200**
Missionary Passage 301
Mission Bay **216**, 218
Moa Island 300, 302

Molle Channel 169
Molongle Creek 176
Mona Rock 288
Mon Repos 89
Monte Christo Island 103
Monument Point 91
Mooan 84
Moody Reef 277
Mooloolaba 52, **62**, 64, 66
Mooloolaba Yacht Club Marina **64**
Moonboom Island 68
Moonlight Bay 158
Moon Passage 302
Moon Point 83, 84
Moore Park 87
Moresby Range 211
Moresby River 207, 208, **209**
Moreton Bay 44, 46, 48, **52**, 54, 58, 304
Moreton Bay Boat Club 61
Moreton Bay Trailer Boat Club **57**
Moreton Island 52, 54, 56, 304
Mornington Island 308
Morris Islet **266**, 268
Mount Adolphus Island **287**
Mount Bassett 140
Mount Cook 244
Mount Cornwallis 301
Mount Flinders 119
Mount Isa 186, 308
Mount Jukes 143
Mount Larcom 110
Mount Straloch 195
Mourilyan 206, **207**, 209, 211, 213, 244
Mud Island 58, 108
Mudjimba Island **64**
Mumford Island 125
Munro Reef 256
Murdering Point 206
Murdoch Islet 311
Murray Islands 278, **300**
Murray Prior Range 218

N.

Nara Inlet **166**
Narrows Rock 126
Neck Bay 154
Nelly Bay **182**
Nelly Bay Marina 182
Nerang River 44
Nereid Rocks 292
Nerimbera Slipway 109
Nesbit River 311
Never Fail Islands 44
New Caledonia 304
Newcastle Bay **284**, 288
New Guinea 209, 298
Newry Island 143, 146
New South Wales 37, 38, 52, 56, 78, 236, 277
Nhulunbuy 308
Night Island 253, 266, **268**
Ninian Bay 253, **256**, 257, 258, 311
Nobbies Inlet **176**
Nobbies Lookout 176
Nob Island 277, **279**
Noble Island **253**, 311
Noddy Reef **264**
Noosa Heads **64**, 66
Noosa River 64
Normanby Island **214**
Normanby Range 125
Normanby River **262**
Normanby Sound 292
Norman Point 72
Norman River 308
Normanton 308
North Banks 52
North Barnard Islands 204, **206**, 207
North Bay Point 258
North Channel 39
North Direction Island 248
North East Bay **188**
North East Channel 52, 54, 56
North East Island 131, 133
North Entrance 97, **98**, 175
Northern Rivers 236
Northern Territory 248, 308
North Head 172
North Island 203
North Keppel Island **113**
North Molle Island 159
North Point Islands 126, 128
North Queensland 236

North Queensland Cruising Club 176
North Rock 125
North Stradbroke Island 44, 48, 50, 52, 54, 55, 56
Northumberland Island 131
North West Bay **132**
North West Channel 52, 54, 61
North West Island **96**
North West Reef 298
North White Cliffs 80
Noumea 306
Nymph Island **250**

O.
Oak Island 48
Obree Point 236
Observation Point 98
O'Connell Wharf 97
Old Bar Cutting 58
One and a Half Mile Opening 248
One Mile 55
One Tree Mark 108
Orchid Hill 269
Orchid Point 270
Oriomo River 300
Orpheus Island 187, 188, **191**
Osnaburg Point 285
Osprey Reef **306**
Outer Banks 84
Outer Freeman Channel 52, 54
Outer Newry Island 143, 146
Outer Rock 92, 114
Owen Channel 260, 311
Oyster Point 198
Oyster Reef **224**

P.
Pacific Creek **104**
Pacific Ocean 304
Palfrey Island 249, 252
Pallion Point 164
Palm Bay 156, **158**
Palm Beach 224
Palmer Goldfields 213, 222
Palmer River 243
Palm Isles 187, **188**
Paluma Creek 196
Paluma Pass 277
Pancake Creek 90, 91, **92**
Pandora Reef 184
Pannikan Island 48, 70
Papua New Guinea 181, 250, 298, 300, 301, 304
Paradise Bay 156
Paradise Point 38, 39
Parramatta 78
Pascoe River **273**, 311
Passage Reef 277
Peaked Hill 288
Peaked Island 116
Peak Point 288, 290
Pearl Bay **120**
Pelican Bay 67, 70
Pelican Island 148
Pelican Islet **264**
Pelorus Island **191**
Penguin Channel 230
Peninsula Range 125
Penn Islet 134
Penrith Island **136**
Percy Isles 130, **131**, 133, 136, 140
Perry Islet 277
Pethebridge Islets **250**, 311
Philadelphia 236
Pialba 67, 81, 82
Pickersgill Reef **234**
Picnic Bay **182**, 187
Picnic Island 80
Pier Head 126, 128
Pigeon Island 273
Pilot Islet 104
Pine Islet 133
Pine Mountain 125
Pine Peak Island **134**
Pinkenba 58
Pinnacle Rock 142, 143
Pioneer Bay 170, **191**
Pioneer River **138**, 143
Pioneer Point 169
Pioneer Rocks 169
Piper Island 264, 311

PiperReefs **276**
Pipon Islets **257**
Pipon Reef 257
Pirate Point 108
Planton Island **158**
Platypus Bay 82, 83, **84**
Platypus Channel 184
Plum Tree 125
Point Cartwright 62
Point Danger 37
Point Lookout 250
Point Saunders 243
Point Vernon 67, 81, 82, 86
Pollard Channel 278
Port Alma 104, 105
Port Clinton 114, **116**, 119, 120, 122, 130
Port Curtis 97
Port Denison 176
Port Douglas **226**, 228, 230, 240, 311
Port Essington 248
Port Gladstone 97
Port Kennedy 288, 292, 304
Portland Roads **272**, 273, 274, 276, 277
Port Moresby 209, 219, 298, 304, 306
Port Newry **142**, 143, 146
Possession Island 288, **290**
Poynter Island **128**, 129, 130
Price Anchorage 50
Prince of Wales Channel 298
Prince of Wales Island 292, 294, 298
Princess Charlotte Bay 258, 260, **262**, 266, 310
Prudhoe Island **138**
Prudhoe Shoal 138
Pumicestone Passage 61, 62
Purdaboi Islet 204

Q.
Quail Island 125, 126
Quarry Reach Mark 108
Queens Beach 176
Queensland 37, 52, 54, 56, 58, 61, 72, 78, 82, 90, 93, 176, 186, 209, 215, 248, 268, 287, 298, 304
Queensland Cruising Yacht Club 58
Queens Park 79
Quetta Rock 287
Quintell Beach 270
Quoin Island 98, **100**, 116

R.
Rabbit Island 143, 146
Raby Bay Canal Estate 56
Rainbow Channel 54
Raine Island 279
Ramsay Crossing 103
Rat Island 39
Rattlesnake Channel 260
Rattlesnake Island 184, **187**
Rattlesnake Point 236
Red Banks 298
Redcliffe 52, 61
Redcliffe Island 103
Redcliffe Peninsula 58, 60
Red Hill 269
Red Island 291
Redland Bay 48
Red Point 253
Red Wallis Island 298
Reef Point 124
Refuge Bay 136, 166
Reid Point 311
Reis Point 195
Rennel Island **302**
Repulse Bay 136, 151, 154
Repulse Island **151**
Rescue Bay 133
Restoration Island 270, 272
Restoration Rock 270, 272
Rinkevich Point 212
Ripple Rocks 154, 155
River Heads 76
Rockhampton 103, 104, 105, 108, **109**
Rockingham Bay 204, 282
Rocky Island 272
Rocky Islet **246**, 269
Rocky Point 44, 98, 108
Rocky Reach 89
Rocky River 266
Rocky Shelf Bay 132
Rodds Peninsula 97

Rodney Islet 279
Roko Island 290
Rooney Point 84, **85**
Roonga Creek 291
Rooper Inlet 159
Ross Creek 184, 186
Rosslyn Bay **113**, 114, 116
Ross River 184, **186**
Rothbury Islet 130
Rothsay Banks 298
Round Black Hills 272
Round Head 155
Round Hill 90
Round Hill Creek 87, **90**, 91, 92, 93
Round Hill Head 91
Round Island 119, **214**
Round Point 279
Round Top Island 140
Rous Channel 54
Rowes Bay **187**
Runaway Bay 38, **39**
Runaway Bay to Tipplers Passage 44
Rundle Islet 110
Russel Island 46, 48, **50**, **214**
Royal Queensland Yacht Squadron 50, **56**

S.
Saddleback Island 170
Sadd Point 280
Saibai Island **301**
Salamander Reef 181
Saltwater Creek **79**
Saltwater Inlet **258**
Samarai 304, 306
Sanctuary Cove 38, **39**, 42, 44
Sandy Cape 82, **85**, 93, 304, 306
Sandy Strait 83
Satellite Island 108
Saumarez Reef **306**
Scarness 67, **81**
Scarborough 61
Scarborough Boat Harbour 52, **60**
Scawfell Island **136**, 148
Scott Reef 292
Scraggy Point **198**
Sea Channel 182
Seaforth 146
Sea Hill 100, 105, 108
Sea Hill Point 100, 103, 104, 105, 111
Seal Rocks 97
Seventeen Seventy (1770) 90
Sextant Rock 285
Shallow Bay 285
Sharp Point 280, 282
Shaw Island **154**
Shellburne Bay **279**
Shepherd Bay **200**
Sherard Osborn Point 294
Ship Channel 84
Shoalwater Bay 116, 120, **123**, 124, 128
Sholl Bank 56
Shorncliffe 58
Shortland Reef 282
Shute Bay 160
Shute Harbour **159**
Simpson Bay 288, **290**, 291
Sinclair Bay 172
Singapore 287
Sir Edward Pellew Group 308
Skirmish Point 52, 61
Slade Island 140
Slade Point 140, 142
Sloping Hummock 86, 87
Smith Point 294
Smiths Creek 218, 219
Smythe Shoals 129
Snake Reef **254**, 256
Snapper Creek 67, 68, 72
Snapper Island 226, 228, **230**, 311
Snare Peak Island 136
Snout Point 67
Solomon Islands 298, 304
Solway Pass 164
Somerset 287, 296
Southampton 89
South Arm 39, 42
South Barnard Islands 204, 206
South Channel 97
South Direction Island 246, **247**, 248
South East Islets 131
Southend 98

South Head 86, 279
South Horn Point 294
South Indian Ocean 298
South Islet 306
South Molle Island 66, 158
South Pacific Ocean 304
South Passage 52, **54**, 56
South Percy Island 131, **132**
South Point 81
Southport 37, 38, 39
Southport Boat Harbour 37, 38, 39, 44
Southport Hill 126
Southport Marina 38, **39**
Southport Yacht Club 39
South Sail Rock 128
South Stradbroke Island 44, 48
South Warden Reef 258
South White Cliffs **74**
Sovereign Islands 39
Space Station 275
Spitfire Channel 52
Stainer Islet **264**
Stanley Hill 274
Stanley Island 260
Stanley Point 166
Station Hill 84
St Bees Island 136, **147**
Steep Island 131
Steiglitz 46
Stephens Island 204, **206**, 300, **301**
Stewart Island 74
St Helena Island 55, 58
Still Islet 134
Stockyard Point 116
Stonehaven Anchorage 166
Stone Island 172
Stork Reef 268
Story Bridge 58
Stradbroke Island 48
Strong Tide Passage 123, **124**
Sunday Island 278, 279
Suez Canel 280
Sunshine Coast 62, 64
Sunter Island 269, 270
Surfers Paradise 37, 38, 39
Susan River **76**
Swain Reefs 306
Switzer Reef 256
Sykes Reef 268
Sydney 38, 56, 78, 94, 248, 277, 278, 279,
   302, 306

T.
Tangalooma Wrecks **56**
Tasmania 304
Tasman Sea 310, 312
Teebar Creek **72**
Temple Bay 264, 274, 275, 277
Ten Pin Rock 125
Tern Cliff 280
Tern Islet 280
The Aldershots 44
The Broadwater to Moreton Bay **44**
The Bun 176
The Island **158**
The Narrows 97, 98, **100**, 103, 104, 156, 166
The Peaks 116
The Spit 37
The Wharf Marina **64**
Thirsty Sound 124, **125**, 126, 128, 130
Thomas Island **150**
Thompson Point 211
Thompsons Point 108
Thorpe Point 279
Three Fathom Patch 156
Three Isles **245**
Three Rocks 136
Thursday Island 184, 219, 240, 266, 272, 284,
   287, 288, 291, **292**, 294, 296, 298, 300, 301,
   302, 304, 310, 311, 312
Ticklebelly Harbour **181**
Timana Island 204
Tinonee Bank 137
Tin Can Bay 67, **72**
Tin Can Bay Air Sea Rescue 70
Tin Can Inlet 68, 70, 72
Tinsmith Island **150**
Tipplers Passage **44**
Tipplers Passage to Russell Island **46**
Tongue Bay **164**
Toorbul Point Bridge 61

Torquay 67, 81
Torres Strait 258, 285, 292, 294, 296, **298**,
   300, 302, 304, 310
Town Reach (Brisbane) 58
Town Reach (Bundaberg) 89
Town Reach (Rockhampton) 109
Townshend Island 123, 124
Townsville 175, 178, 181, 182, **184**, 186, 187,
   188, 193, 287, 308
Townsville Motor Boat Club **184**
Trammel Bay 156
Treacherous Bay 300
Treble Islet 137
Triangle Cliffs 84
Triangular Islets 124
Trinity Bay 228
Trinity Inlet 218
Tuan 67
Tuan Creek **74**
Tudu Island 304
Tuesday Islet 292
Tulleen Island 44, 48
Turkey Island 68, 74, 84
Turn Island 128
Turtle Bay 148, **216**
Turtle Group **248**, 249, 250
Turtle Head Island 280, 282
Turtle Islet 284
Tweed Island 130
Twin Island 285, 288, 291
Two Isles **245**

U.
Ulrica Point 284
Undine Reef **234**
Ungowa 67, 68
Unsafe Pass **159**
Upolu Reef **223**
Upstart Bay **176**, 178
Urangan 67, 68, 76, **80**, 81, 82, 84

V.
Vanuatu 304
Victor Creek **146**
Vila 304

W.
Waight Bank 269
Walker Bay **240**
Walker Point 79
Walter Island 133
Walter Point 133
Warrier Reefs **302**
Waterfront Place Marina 58
Waterloo Bay **57**
Waterpark Creek 114
Wathumba Creek 84
Watson Island 254, **256**
Watsons Bay 250
Weary Bay 236
Webbs Channel 212
Wedge Island **142**
Wednesday Island 292
Weinam Creek 48
Weipa 275, 282, 298, **308**
Wellesley islands 308
Wellington Point 57
Wentworth Reef 226
West Bay 131, **133**
West Channel 182, 184
Western Bay 148
West Indies 298
West Island 306
West Molle Island 158
West Point 119, 182, 187
Weymouth Bay 311
Whalleys Gutter 46, 48
Wharf Marina (The) **64**
Wharf Street 58
Wharton Reef 260, **264**
Wheeler Island **204**
White Bay 164
Whitehaven Bay **164**
Whitehaven Beach 164
White Rock 125
Whites Bay **133**
White Shoal 125
Whitsunday Islands 131, 146, 147, 154, 162,
   164, 165, 168, 169, 310

Whitsunday Passage 162
Whitsunday Sailing Club 169
Whitsunday '100' 158
Whyte Island 58
Wide Bay 66
Wide Bay Bar 62, 66, 67, 68, **70**, 74
Wide Bay Harbour 70
Wide Bay Military Reserve 72, 74
Wide Bay River 78
Wild Cattle Leads 97
Wild Duck Island 128
Wilkie Islet **266**
Willis Island 48, 50
Willis Islets **306**
Winding Reach Mark 108
Windward Islands 298
Wistari Reef 96
Wolf Rock 66
Woodcutter Bay 156
Woodwark Bay **170**
Woogoompah Island 44
Wreck Bay 111
Wreck Reef 94, **306**
Wyborn Reef 282
Wyer Island 300
Wynnum Manly Yacht Club Marina **57**

Y.
Yanks Jetty 191
Yarrabah 216
Yellow Patch **110**
Yeppoon **114**
Yorkeys Knob **224**
York Island 288
Young Bay 182

Z.
Zoe Bay **200**

CRUISING THE NEW
SOUTH WALES COAST

Those sailing to or from New South Wales will find the author's other east coast guide, *Cruising the New South Wales Coast*, a useful adjunct to this book. They abut at Point Danger which is the eastern end of the New South Wales-Queensland border.